Hidden Champions in Dynamically Changing Societies

Alenka Braček Lalić • Danica Purg
Editors

Hidden Champions in Dynamically Changing Societies

Critical Success Factors for Market Leadership

Editors
Alenka Braček Lalić ⓘ
Postgraduate Studies
IEDC-Bled School of Management
Bled, Slovenia

Danica Purg ⓘ
Postgraduate Studies
IEDC-Bled School of Management
Bled, Slovenia

ISBN 978-3-030-65453-5   ISBN 978-3-030-65451-1 (eBook)
https://doi.org/10.1007/978-3-030-65451-1

© Springer Nature Switzerland AG 2021

This work is subject to copyright. All rights are reserved by the Publisher, whether the whole or part of the material is concerned, specifically the rights of translation, reprinting, reuse of illustrations, recitation, broadcasting, reproduction on microfilms or in any other physical way, and transmission or information storage and retrieval, electronic adaptation, computer software, or by similar or dissimilar methodology now known or hereafter developed.

The use of general descriptive names, registered names, trademarks, service marks, etc. in this publication does not imply, even in the absence of a specific statement, that such names are exempt from the relevant protective laws and regulations and therefore free for general use.

The publisher, the authors, and the editors are safe to assume that the advice and information in this book are believed to be true and accurate at the date of publication. Neither the publisher nor the authors or the editors give a warranty, expressed or implied, with respect to the material contained herein or for any errors or omissions that may have been made. The publisher remains neutral with regard to jurisdictional claims in published maps and institutional affiliations.

This Springer imprint is published by the registered company Springer Nature Switzerland AG.
The registered company address is: Gewerbestrasse 11, 6330 Cham, Switzerland

Foreword

In the foreword to the book *Hidden Champions in CEE and Turkey*, published in 2013, I wrote that I was surprised and impressed by the large number of Hidden Champions in Central and Eastern Europe and by the strength, passion, deep knowledge, and ambitions of the Hidden Champion founders and entrepreneurs. I expressed my optimism that many more new Hidden Champions would emerge in Central and Eastern Europe in the future. This new book proves that my optimism was justified.

IEDC-Bled School of Management, Postgraduate Studies and CEEMAN, the International Association for Management Development in Dynamic Societies, have taken my more or less "hidden" wish seriously. They started a new research project with a double aim: to report on the development of the Hidden Champions from the study of 2013 and detect new Hidden Champions that either were not discovered in 2013 or have been established after that time.

Although I have studied the Hidden Champions phenomenon intensively over 30 years and have many times spoken and written about the characteristics of those companies and their importance for their national economies, my curiosity about Hidden Champions is far from satisfied. Therefore, I appreciate that this book provides deep analyses of, and insights into, important features of Hidden Champions in Central and Eastern Europe and selected countries in Asia. It was an excellent decision to include Mongolia and China. We all know the names of Chinese Big Champions that have successfully achieved global market leadership. We could suppose that there are other companies in China with strong global market positions that are still unknown. This book reveals the names of the first group of Hidden Champions in China. I am certain that many others will emerge and be discovered in the future.

I would like to repeat what I expressed as my wish in 2013: that this book will encourage many young people, entrepreneurs, and midsized companies to use their knowledge and skills to go decisively for hidden championship. But the message of this book goes far beyond individual entrepreneurship and has great societal significance. The case studies show that the countries included in the study have a huge potential to develop world-class companies. I am convinced that these countries should not try to build their economic future on large Fortune-Global-500-type companies. It is much more effective to foster a strong *Mittelstand* and promote the emergence of numerous Hidden Champions. I see this as the most promising way to a prosperous future. The book makes an enormously important contribution to this endeavor.

Simon-Kucher & Partners, Bonn, Germany

Hermann Simon

Acknowledgement

We would like to acknowledge and thank all the researchers who contributed to this book, which is a follow-up project after the Hidden Champions study of 2013, edited by McKiernan and Purg. We would like to express our special gratitude to Prof. Hermann Simon, who inspired us to start this research and generously shared his methodology.

Our thanks go to the hidden champions and their presidents, owners, or top managers who made time for the interviews, opened their companies and minds, and let the researchers explore and learn. The researchers from management schools from 22 countries, members of CEEMAN, the International Association for Management Development in Dynamic Societies, made a fantastic job and we are proud of them! We also thank EBRD for its financial support, which was of great value for us. Artyom Ushnichkov had an important role from the beginning to the end of the research. We appreciate enormously his work. We thank Katja Babić, and Livija Marko, who collected the data and assisted in the research process.

We are very grateful to language editor Misho Minkov, and Kristina Soklič and Tanja Grilc, from the office of IEDC and CEEMAN president.

Thank you all!
The Editors
Bled, Slovenia, August 2020

Contents

Introduction 1
Danica Purg and Alenka Braček Lalić

Research Methodology 5
Alenka Braček Lalić and Denis Berberović

Hidden Champions: Leadership Success Factors 17
Danica Purg and Arnold Walravens

**Hidden Champions: Common Lessons Learned on the Path
to Success** 25
Denis Berberović, Amra Kožo, and Merima Činjarević

**Hidden Champions: Financing and Regulatory Environment
Development Needs—Context Matters** 41
Slavica Singer and Sunčica Oberman Peterka

**Hidden Champions: Management and Leadership Development
Needs** 57
Amra Kožo and Alenka Braček Lalić

Hidden Champions of Albania 67
Vasilika Kume, Elona Garo, and Anisa Kume

Hidden Champions of Belarus 85
Radzivon Marozau, Hanna Aginskaya, Pavel Daneyko,
and Natalia Makayeva

Hidden Champions of Bosnia and Herzegovina 107
Denis Berberović, Merima Činjarević, Amra Kožo, and Nenad Brkić

Hidden Champions of Bulgaria 123
Michael Minkov

Hidden Champions of China.............................. 133
Xiaobo Wu and Linan Lei

Hidden Champions of Croatia............................ 153
Slavica Singer and Sunčica Oberman Peterka

Hidden Champions of the Czech Republic................. 171
Jarolím Antal, Jana Vlčková, Ondřej Sankot, and Pavel Hnát

Hidden Champions of Hungary............................ 195
Miklós Stocker

Hidden Champions of the Republic of Kazakhstan......... 213
Christian Kahl, Aigerim Raimzhanova, Aigerim Serikbekova, and Sultanbek Kaiym

Hidden Champions of Kosovo............................. 229
Dafina Turkeshi Ballanca and Florentina Dushi

Hidden Champions of Lithuania.......................... 239
Erika Vaiginienė, Rasa Paulienė, and Laima Urbšienė

Potential Hidden Champions of Moldova.................. 263
Dumitru Slonovschi

Hidden Champions of Mongolia........................... 279
Eku Bold

Hidden Champions of Montenegro......................... 295
Milorad Jovović, Bojana Femić-Radosavović, and Nikola Mišnić

Hidden Champions of Poland............................. 313
Grażyna Leśniak-Łebkowska, Magdalena Popowska, Małgorzata Godlewska, and Mirosław Łukasiewicz

Hidden Champions of Romania............................ 341
Andrei Ştefan Neştian and Ana Iolanda Vodă

Hidden Champions of Russia............................. 359
Irina Skorobogatykh, Olga Saginova, Zhanna Musatova, Ekaterina Molchanova, and Sofia Sedenko

Hidden Champions of Serbia............................. 387
Goran Pitić, Nebojša Savić, Miloš Erić, Jelisaveta Lazarević, Zoja Kukić, and Ema Marinković

Hidden Champions in Dynamically Changing Societies: The Case of Slovakia.. 407
Janka Táborecká-Petrovičová, Jaroslav Ďaďo, and Michal Budinský

Hidden Champions of Slovenia 431
Katja Babič

Hidden Champions of Turkey 451
Dincer Atli and Nebiye Yasar

Hidden Champions of Ukraine 473
Iryna Tykhomyrova and Vadym Saveliev

Introduction

Danica Purg and Alenka Braček Lalić

1 The History of Hidden Champions Research

The majority of studies of corporate success relate to larger, well-known companies. The main reason is that historical data are easy to collect and the success of companies such as IBM, Hewlett-Packard, Dell, and Nokia appeal to young generations of students and entrepreneurs.

However, among economists, it is common knowledge that "the engine of economic growth and employment for many nations were the flourishing strata of small and medium-sized companies" (McKiernan and Purg 2013, p. 2).

In the mid-1980s, inspired by Harvard marketing expert Theodore Levin, Hermann Simon decided to analyze the success of small and medium-sized enterprises in Germany and the role that they played in Germany's export success. He named these companies "hidden champions" and defined three criteria for a company to be qualified as such:

(a) A hidden champion should occupy a number-one or number-two position in the world market and a number-one position in the European market as measured by market share.
(b) A hidden champion must be small or medium-sized. Its sales revenue should not exceed one billion US dollars (1996).
(c) A hidden champion must have a low visibility profile in the public domain.

D. Purg (✉)
Postgraduate Studies, IEDC-Bled School of Management, Bled, Slovenia

CEEMAN, The International Association for Management Development in Dynamic Societies, Bled, Slovenia
e-mail: danica.purg@iedc.si

A. Braček Lalić
Postgraduate Studies, IEDC-Bled School of Management, Bled, Slovenia

© Springer Nature Switzerland AG 2021
A. Braček Lalić, D. Purg (eds.), *Hidden Champions in Dynamically Changing Societies*, https://doi.org/10.1007/978-3-030-65451-1_1

Simon's research uncovered nearly 500 such companies in Germany alone.

The original hidden champions were mainly in mechanical engineering (37%), electronics (12%), and metallurgy (10%). The majority of their products (67%) were in the mature phase of the life cycle. Their average growth rate was around 6.5% and their employment size was around 735 people. The hidden champions earned over 51% of their sales revenues from direct exports. Their medium age was nearly 50 years, with some having a heritage of over 200 years. Hidden champions produce goods in niche markets, usually business to business, which are mainly family-run, single product entities. Their products stem from invention and innovation. According to McKiernan and Purg (2013), "Their passionate and persistent leaders enjoy ... skills and balance authoritarian strategic styles with cooperation on the operational level. They prefer controlled growth to exponential growth. Most important, they like to remain hidden" (p. 4).

Simon's (1996) original book *Hidden Champions: Lessons from 500 of the World's Best Unknown Companies* was published in 17 countries. New research identified hidden champions in many other countries, such as Brazil, Japan, South Africa, and New Zealand. As many big "star" companies, such as IBM, General Motors, and Nokia, lost their glitter, Simon showed that more sustainable lessons can be learned from hidden champions.

In 2009, Simon published a second book—*Hidden Champions for the 21st Century*—including Hidden Champions of Austria and Switzerland. He showed that these companies had grown impressively over a 20-year period in terms of revenues and employment. He drew eight lessons from this new research, referring to eight different needs:

1. A need for will power, ambitious goals, and decentralization to be a world leader
2. A need to maintain discipline and so inspire loyalty among employees
3. A need for depth in value chains and for restricted outsourcing
4. A need to decentralize the company's structure so as to encourage new hidden champions to emerge
5. A need to define markets precisely, focus on one thing, and do it right
6. A need to suspend national boundaries so as to capitalize on globalization
7. A need to pursue continuous innovation through creativity and quality, not through money
8. A need to prioritize customer orientation over competitor orientation

2 Hidden Champions in Central and Eastern Europe and Turkey: Carving Out a Global Niche

The financial and economic crisis of 2008–2009 forced governments to explore the vulnerability of their economies, particularly in the relatively new market-oriented economies of Central and Eastern Europe.

Introduction

These countries suffered from some disadvantages that slowed their recovery: a relatively small segment of small- and medium-sized companies, a strong dependency on bigger corporations, being an integral part of their supply chain consisting of Western, mainly German, companies, and absence of concentrated industry clusters throughout the region. The situation in Central and Eastern Europe seemed to become a remnant of the global recovery battle (McKiernan and Purg 2013, p. 6).

To analyze this issue, in 2011 CEEMAN and IEDC-Bled School of Management started a study of hidden champions in Central and Eastern Europe and Turkey. It was decided to include Turkey in the research as it was hypothesized that the role of hidden champions in this rising economy was of great importance.

The main goals of the research were to:

- Uncover examples of hidden champions
- Compare and contrast any examples with those in Simon's work
- Identify what support Central and Eastern European hidden champions might need to get stronger

The research was conducted by 32 researchers, who covered 18 countries. The results were surprising in terms of the number of hidden champions identified, their strength and potential, and the lessons learned about entrepreneurship, ownership, business leadership, innovation, and sustainability.

3 Hidden Champions in Central and Eastern Europe, Turkey, Mongolia, and China

Inspired by practical and scientific ambitions, CEEMAN decided to start a follow-up research with the aim to trace the development of hidden champions since the research published in 2013 and to identify new companies in this category. It was decided to include China in this research. That country had shown a specific interest in innovation and experienced impressive economic growth coupled with the rise of new industries and companies. And on the recommendation of Hermann Simon, we also included Mongolian hidden champions for the first time.

4 Structure of the Book

The introduction is followed by a chapter on research methodology. The latter relies on a combination of historical, quantitative, and qualitative methods, taking into account the companies' specific social, cultural, and economic environments. The next chapter offers a cross-country analysis of hidden champions. It contains sub-chapters on leadership success factors, management and development needs, and financing and regulatory environment development needs. The first part of the book ends with recommendations to different stakeholders.

The second part offers extensive information on hidden champions in the 22 countries of the research.

References

McKiernan P, Purg D (2013) Hidden champions in CEE and Turkey: carving out a global niche. Springer, Berlin, Heidelberg

Simon H (1996) Hidden champions: lessons from 500 of the world's best unknown companies. Harvard Business School Press, Boston, MA

Simon H (2009) HCs of the 21st century: success strategies of unknown world leaders. Springer, London

Research Methodology

Alenka Braček Lalić and Denis Berberović

1 Introduction

More than two decades ago, German management professor Hermann Simon coined the term "hidden champions" to describe the outstanding enterprises in his home country as he examined their role in Germany's economic development and innovation progress (1996). He developed his idea further and extended this research to global companies (2009). In 2011, CEEMAN and IEDC-Bled School of Management, Postgraduate Studies launched an elaborate project: 18 research teams worked with over 165 companies across Central and Eastern Europe (CEE) and Turkey to study the hidden champions of their respective countries. Published in 2013 and based on Simon's methodology, the book *Hidden Champions in CEE and Turkey: Carving out a Global Niche,* edited by Peter McKiernan and Danica Purg, sought to uncover examples of hidden champions, but also to compare the new findings with Simon's (Purg et al. 2019). An additional aim was to identify what support hidden champions needed in Central and Eastern Europe and in Turkey, as the business environment and historical background in which they were striving to succeed were (and still are) quite different from those of more mature market economies.

According to Purg et al. (2019) upon the initiative of the European Bank for Reconstruction and Development (EBRD) in November 2017, IEDC-Bled School of Management, Postgraduate Studies and CEEMAN decided to delve into the fascinating subject of hidden champions yet again to explore the characteristics of innovative companies operating in Central Europe and Southeastern Europe

---

A. Braček Lalić
Postgraduate Studies, IEDC-Bled School of Management, Bled, Slovenia
e-mail: alenka.bracek.lalic@iedc.si

D. Berberović (✉)
University of Sarajevo, Sarajevo, Bosnia and Herzegovina
e-mail: denis.berberovic@efsa.unsa.ba

(CESEE), that are leaders in their respective niche sectors and the international market. Furthermore, relaunching this ambitious research project would give the partners involved an opportunity to explore the growth and present-day status of the hidden champions identified in 2011, and extend the list with new hidden champions. The geographical scope of the second iteration of this research encompassed the following 22 countries: Albania, Belarus, Bosnia and Herzegovina, Bulgaria, Croatia, Estonia, Hungary, Kazakhstan, Kosovo,[1] Latvia, Lithuania, Moldova, Montenegro, North Macedonia, Poland, Romania, Russia, Serbia, Slovakia, Slovenia, Turkey, and Ukraine.

2 Methodology

In order to gain deeper insights into the development of the hidden champions identified in 2011 and a better understanding of the newly emerged hidden champions and their business practices, it was decided to apply a qualitative methodology (Gummesson 2000; Patton 2015). Once again, semi-structured interviews were chosen as the data collection method, since this is the most flexible form of data collection, suitable for investigating new business practices, and understanding operations and approaches to different business challenges. Furthermore, it leaves enough space for the interviewees to express themselves and share their own opinions and views in their own words. Interviews are particularly attractive in such research endeavors because they offer opportunities to the interviewees to address issues that they find most relevant and are not imposed by researchers (Brinkman and Kvale 2015).

IEDC-Bled School of Management, Postgraduate Studies also prepared a questionnaire for collecting quantitative data as supplementary inputs to interviews (Creswell 2014). Advice was given to complete the questionnaire preferably prior to the interviews for the interviewer to be able to conduct informed interviews. For the same purpose, the researchers collected secondary data, not only concerning the targeted companies but also concerning the persons to be interviewed. A detailed preparation of the data collection process guaranteed a thorough investigation of the issues relevant to this research.

Finally, all research results were reported through individual case studies of hidden champions. This form of presenting research result seemed to suit best the ultimate goal of the research—a deeper understanding of the hidden champions' complex success stories (Yin 2014).

---

[1] As defined in UN Security Council Resolution 1244

3 Research Protocol and Overall Coordination of the Research Project

In March 2018, IEDC-Bled School of Management, Postgraduate Studies and CEEMAN approached research partners in CESEE countries selected by the EBRD in order to gather insights into the business environment and companies in line with the hidden champions methodology. After selecting research partners, they prepared a detailed research protocol to help synchronize the research implementation among various research partners and countries.

The research protocol provided detailed instructions to researchers and country coordinators that were followed throughout the data collection. The document also included important and useful forms for the researchers, such as: a Letter of Initial Company Consent, a Research Interview Agreement, and Questions for the Companies. Besides ensuring the consistency of the applied methodology, timely implementation, uniform analysis, and reporting, the protocol also intended to give comprehensive explanations about the definitions, methods of analysis, intellectual property rights, and financial issues and provided contact details of the persons responsible for coordinating this research on behalf of CEEMAN members.

Research partners were instructed to approach the companies identified in 2011 but also to identify new or potential hidden champions in their countries and conduct the interviews with C-level executives. The research partners approached the companies of the 2011 study with the Letter of Consent and arranged meetings with C-level executives. The in-depth interviews were focused on the progress made since 2011 and their characteristics, main drivers of success, perspectives on the challenges that businesses face, current and future management and leadership development needs, as well as challenges and gaps in existing management and leadership development opportunities. All interviews were conducted following the principles of the Research Interview Agreement. Research partners were provided with suggestions concerning questions to be raised in the interviews and with some additional instructions connected to recoding, interview duration, and the competences of the interviewers.

IEDC-Bled School of Management, Postgraduate Studies and CEEMAN organized two face-to-face meetings in Bled and two online webinars in order to ensure the same quality standards across all 22 countries involved. The meetings were also intended to monitor the progress of the research done by research partners and to clarify any open questions. IEDC-Bled School of Management, Postgraduate Studies and CEEMAN reported to EBRD about the progress of the research from April 2018 to October 2019. The research project finished with an updated survey of hidden champions in Central, Eastern, and Southeastern Europe, which was presented at the international conference organized by the EBRD in October 2019 in London.

Table 1 indicates the number of hidden and potential hidden champions identified throughout the research project done for the EBRD. All companies identified in the

Table 1 Hidden and potential hidden champions, 2018–19, by country

	Hidden champions			Potential hidden champions		
Country	Old	New	Total	Old	New	Total
Albania	3	0	3	0	4	4
Belarus	5	5	10	0	2	2
Bosnia and Herzegovina	1	5	6	0	2	2
Croatia	1	2	3	0	1	1
Estonia	4	1	5	2	2	4
Hungary	2	3	5	0	2	2
Kazakhstan	0	0	0	0	0	0
Latvia	0	6	6	0	2	2
North Macedonia	2	3	5	0	0	0
Poland	5	6	11	0	3	3
Romania	0	0	0	2	1	3
Russia	2	4	6	1	2	3
Serbia	3	7	10	0	0	0
Slovak Republic	3	2	5	1	1	2
Slovenia	6	4	10	1	1	2
Turkey	6	0	6	0	0	0
Ukraine	2	1	3	0	0	0
New countries in 2018–19						
Bulgaria	0	1	1	0	2	2
Kosovo	0	1	1	0	2	2
Lithuania	0	7	7	0	2	2
Moldova	0	0	0	0	4	4
Montenegro	0	2	2	0	0	0
Total	45	60	105	7	33	40

Purg et al. (2019)

research project, gave their consent for their data to be published in the report for the EBRD.

According to Purg et al. (2019), Poland was the country with the greatest number of hidden champions (11), followed by Belarus (10), Serbia (10), and Slovenia (10). The biggest number of potential hidden champions was found in Albania (4), followed by Estonia (4) and Moldova (4).

Of the 105 hidden champions, 45 are old[2] and 60 are new. Of the 40 potential hidden champions: seven are old and 33 are new. Serbia and Lithuania boasted the largest number of new hidden champions (seven each), followed by Latvia and

---

[2]The analysis of the hidden champions initially identified in the 2011 study, which maintain their hidden champion status in 2018–19, allowed the team to observe upward trends in the companies' sales, number of employees, and public recognition. Several companies had received awards for innovation and significant growth since their foundation. Positive trends were also observed in relation to market leadership, with market shares increasing since 2011, or market positions strengthening (also with the internationalization of activities).

Table 2 Number of hidden champions by industry, 2018–19

Country	Number of hidden champions 2018–19, by industry NACE code								
	A	C	F	G	H	J	M	R	Total
Albania	2	1	0	0	0	0	0	0	3
Belarus	0	9	1	0	0	0	0	0	10
Bosnia and Herzegovina	0	3	0	1	0	2	0	0	6
Croatia	0	1	0	0	0	1	1	0	3
Estonia	1	2	0	0	2	0	0	0	5
Hungary	0	1	0	0	0	3	1	0	5
Kazakhstan	0	0	0	0	0	0	0	0	0
Latvia	0	3	1	0	0	2	0	0	6
North Macedonia	0	4	0	0	1	0	0	0	5
Poland	0	9	0	0	0	1	1	0	11
Romania	0	0	0	0	0	0	0	0	0
Russia	0	6	0	0	0	0	0	0	6
Serbia	0	7	0	0	0	2	1	0	10
Slovak Republic	0	2	0	0	0	3	0	0	5
Slovenia	0	7	0	0	0	2	1	0	10
Turkey	0	6	0	0	0	0	0	0	6
Ukraine	0	3	0	0	0	0	0	0	3
New countries in 2018–19									
Bulgaria	0	0	0	0	0	0	1	0	1
Kosovo	0	1	0	0	0	0	0	0	1
Lithuania	0	4	0	0	0	3	0	0	7
Moldova	0	0	0	0	0	0	0	0	0
Montenegro	0	0	0	0	0	1	0	1	2
Total	3	69	2	1	3	20	6	1	105

Purg et al. (2019)

Poland (six each). Albania and Moldova yielded the greatest number of new potential hidden champions (four each), followed by Poland (three) (Table 2).

Hidden champions were discovered in eight industries in Central, Eastern, and Southeastern Europe. These industries, as defined by the European industrial activity classification, NACE Rev. 2, are (in descending order by number of champions): C—manufacturing (69), J—information and communication (20), M—professional, scientific and technical activities (6), A—agriculture, forestry, and fishing (3), H—transportation and storage (3), F—construction (2), G—wholesale and retail trade, repair of motor vehicles and motorcycles (1) and R—arts, entertainment, and recreation (1).

Hidden champions are deemed likely to emerge in five industries. These are (as before, in descending order by number of champions): C—manufacturing (26), J—information and communication (9), M—professional, scientific and technical

Table 3 Number of potential hidden champions by industry, 2018–19

Country	Number of potential hidden champions, by industry NACE code					
	A	C	J	K	M	Total
Albania	0	2	1	1	0	4
Belarus	0	1	0	0	1	2
Bosnia and Herzegovina	1	0	1	0	0	2
Croatia	0	0	0	0	1	1
Estonia	0	4	0	0	0	4
Hungary	0	0	2	0	0	2
Kazakhstan	0	0	0	0	0	0
Latvia	0	2	0	0	0	2
North Macedonia	0	0	0	0	0	0
Poland	0	2	1	0	0	3
Romania	0	1	2	0	0	3
Russia	0	3	0	0	0	3
Serbia	0	0	0	0	0	0
Slovak Republic	0	2	0	0	0	2
Slovenia	0	2	0	0	0	2
Turkey	0	0	0	0	0	0
Ukraine	0	0	0	0	0	0
New countries in 2018–19						
Bulgaria	0	2	0	0	0	2
Kosovo[a]	0	1	1	0	0	2
Lithuania	0	2	0	0	0	2
Moldova	0	2	1	0	1	4
Montenegro	0	0	0	0	0	0
Total	1	26	9	1	3	40

Purg et al. (2019)
[a]As defined in UN Security Council Resolution 1244

activities (3), A—agriculture, forestry, and fishing (1) and K—financial and insurance activities (1) (see Table 3 for more details) (Purg et al. 2019).

For hidden champions in China, following the consideration of market leadership, firm size, and public awareness, we set the following selection rules: The main business or main product of hidden champions should be in a niche market, and their leadership should be deemed one of the top three in the world or number one in China. Then, with the rapid development of the world economy over the past two decades, Simon updated the sales requirement to control for the firm size from 1 billion dollars (Simon 1996) to 5 billion euros (Simon 2012). Given the fact that in 2016 the last firm in the top-500 private enterprises in China earned 10.18 billion RMB in sales, we set the upper limit of sales at 10 billion RMB in 2016 for our samples of hidden champions to control for their low public awareness.

Based on these selection rules, cases in the chapter on China include both process and discrete manufacturers, parts, and integrated system manufacturers.

Semi-structured interviews were conducted with founders, CEOs, or top managers in the case companies over an 11-month period from December, 2016. Each interview was attended by more than two researchers in order to achieve observer triangulation and to monitor or correct each other's interactions with the interviewee. We also gathered secondary data from company websites, news, and journal articles, which enabled the triangulation of data sources.

4 Research Challenges

Although in 1990 Hermann Simon updated several hidden champion criteria, IEDC-Bled School of Management, Postgraduate Studies and CEEMAN decided to use the same criteria, as in 2011 study as they are still relevant in CESEE.

The hidden champion identification criteria followed by the research partners were the following:

1. Companies that occupy a number-one or number-two market position globally and a number-one or number-two position in the European, Central and Eastern European, or regional market, as measured by market share. If the latter is unknown, a hidden champion company must lead its largest competitor (based on observations or perceptions by the companies in question).
2. A hidden champion company must be small or medium-sized and its revenue should normally not exceed one billion US dollars.
3. A hidden champion must have low visibility in the public domain.
4. The company must have been in operation for five years[3]. Otherwise, it is a potential hidden Champion (Purg et al. 2019).

Throughout the study, IEDC-Bled School of Management, Postgraduate Studies and CEEMAN and the research partners encountered many challenges related to the interpretation of the hidden champions criteria which CEEMAN used only as proxy measures for identifying hidden champions. The most undefined criteria are those related to market leadership and low visibility in the public domain.

In view of the numerous challenges, especially the high number of research partners and the need for synchronizing the study across them, the proxy criteria were one of the main challenges in this research. IEDC-Bled School of Management, Postgraduate Studies and CEEMAN wanted to get more clarifications from other publications and articles written by Hermann Simon, but unfortunately, it was realized that there are no concrete interpretations of the hidden champions criteria. As a result, IEDC-Bled School of Management, Postgraduate Studies and CEEMAN and the research partners had to rely on their own sound judgment of what companies could be considered hidden champions and on the statements about the nature of

---

[3]In case the company has been operating less than 5 years, but all other hidden champion criteria apply, the company has been labeled a "potential hidden champion."

market leadership and performance indicators provided by the approached companies.

For example, the first criterion is the nature of market leadership. A hidden champion should occupy the number-one or number-two position in the world market and the number-one or number-two position in the European or Central and Eastern European or regional market as measured by market share. In case the latter is unknown, a hidden champion must be a leader relative to its strongest competitor, based on observations and perceptions by the company in question. While conducting the interviews, the majority of the companies had many challenges in determining the market share that their companies hold in a specific geographic zone. The question that helped in identifying the market position was: "How many competitors do you have in a specific region?" Due to the fact that information from secondary sources about the market position of a company is often unreliable, to categorize the companies into hidden champions, potential hidden champions, and no-longer hidden champions, we relied mainly on the statements and performance criteria provided by the companies.

In this research, our aim was not only to identify new hidden champions, but also to find out whether there are any new companies that are potential hidden champions with prospects of becoming hidden champions in the following years. To determine if a company qualified as a potential hidden champion, we took into consideration whether it had operated longer than 5 years. It should also be a very successful small or medium-sized enterprise without holding a number-one or number-two position in terms of market share in any geographic region, while having a possibility to become a market leader in its niche in the following years. Besides hidden champions and potential hidden champions, we also identified a third category of no-longer hidden champions. The latter category includes companies identified in 2011 which, due to diverse reasons, did not satisfy the hidden- champion criteria in 2018.

The second criterion is better defined, but also needs additional clarifications. For example, according to the second criterion, a hidden champion company must be small or medium-sized and normally its sales revenues should not exceed one billion US dollars. Due to the fact that in the last 20–30 years Hermann Simon has also identified hidden champions that have more than 249 employees (which was also the case in the previous research), and after realizing that different countries have different definitions of what a small or medium-sized company is (for instance, in Kosovo the indicator is sales revenues, not the number of employees), we again encountered some challenges related to this criterion. After discussing this criterion in our first and second meeting, we decided to focus, if possible, on small and medium-sized enterprises, having in mind the number of employees, thereby keeping Simon's original criteria.

The third criterion was also a big challenge in this research as in our digital age it is not easy to define "hidden." At the same time, we also got some new insights into this criterion, which are different from those in the previous research. In the 2011 study, we discovered that some companies would like to stay hidden. They do not want to be exposed and known to the wider public. This is one of the major findings in this research. The majority of companies did not want to be exposed by sharing their competitive advantage and success factors. However, in this research, we realized that, due to the existence of numerous social media channels and the brand awareness trend, the majority of interviewed companies are active on social media channels (Twitter, LinkedIn, Facebook, Instagram), not necessary for sales purposes, but actually for recruiting the best talents. Due to the negative demographic trends in this region, all companies seek to get the best talents and keep them by raising their brand awareness and offering some personalized benefits. This has led us to the conclusion that this criterion in the digital era will probably need some modifications.

There are two sides to hiddenness. The first is related to brand awareness: some companies do not want to be hidden anymore. The second is related to the fact that some hidden champions are still reluctant to share their competitive advantage or success factors with external partners or the public. Therefore, some of the companies that were identified in 2011 did not want to participate in this research.

Besides these ways of dealing with challenges concerning the interpretation of the selection criteria in this research project, we employed some new methods to improve the quality of the study In his first book on hidden champions, Hermann Simon (1996) presented some hidden champions characteristics in addition to the presented criteria. As he observed that most hidden champions were *Mittelstand* companies, Simon realized that they had several traits in common: they were mostly both family-owned and family-run businesses and had developed through a family tradition, sometimes going back hundreds of years. They were usually located in small semi-urban or rural areas. They were strongly connected to their local communities and were also mainly situated in parts of the country with a strong entrepreneurial tradition and mindset. They conducted their business mostly in the business-to-business market. They were focused on market niches (often they even created market niches themselves with their products). It was particularly striking that, although they were small or medium-sized enterprises, they had strong research and development activities, which led most of the hidden champions to be strongly innovative. In fact, innovative solutions, either in the domain of business models, business operations, or business offerings, are the most important trigger that makes most companies become hidden champions. Therefore, in cases when researchers had doubts about whether an identified company could be regarded as a hidden champion, they were advised to assess these characteristics. This is how we ensured that the identified companies were true hidden champions.

5 Preparing the Second Book on Hidden Champions for CESEE

After finishing the research project for the EBRD, all research partners were invited to prepare a country chapter. They had to get the consent of all selected companies to be included in this book and an approval of their case study. Estonia, Latvia, and North Macedonia did not submit their chapters. However, we managed to get chapters also from China, the Czech Republic, and Mongolia, which extended the geographic scope of the study far beyond CESEE.

It should be noted that the authors of the country chapters are the only ones responsible for the accuracy of the case studies included in this book. Moreover, this book was finalized during the global corona virus outbreak (2020), which might have affected the companies presented in it. The case studies in this book are a result of the research project done in 2018–2019.

6 Recommendations

One of the main characteristics of hidden champions is indeed the fact that they are hidden. There is no list of such companies. They prefer to operate undetected by parties that might be interested in their business for whatever reason. This leads to the conclusion that there are probably more hidden champions to be detected. And as this book is being prepared, there is no doubt that new hidden champions are emerging.

Another recommendation concerns the scope of the sample. Our knowledge of hidden champions would increase if we studied companies of this type in other parts of the world. We have covered only a few Asian countries, but there are a lot more to be investigated. Such research could also go beyond Asia and include parts of the world that have not been yet investigated for hidden champions.

Finally, a longitudinal study would shed light on the development of hidden champions through time. How do hidden champions develop? What are the internal and external factors contributing to their rise or demise? It would be insightful to find out why some hidden champions have lost that status.

7 Conclusion

Our study of hidden champions encompasses 22 countries in two continents. The project has been carried out by more than 60 researchers. Interviews have been conducted with representatives of 145 companies, out of which 105 are true hidden champions and 40 have been labeled "potential hidden champions." But we must note that the label "potential" has been given mainly to those companies that do not fulfill the criterion of having conducted business operations longer than 5 years. In the digital business context, and considering the surge of born-global companies, this is a fairly restrictive criterion However, in order to ensure methodological rigor, the researchers have decided to respect that criterion.

Planning, implementing, and evaluating a research endeavor of such proportions always involves numerous challenges. Some of these cannot be foreseen during the planning process but are faced only during the implementation phase. And they have to be dealt with immediately. The coordinating team has been flexible and responsive to ideas and suggestions from national research teams, yet always bearing in mind the methodological settings and milestones. This research project has been a learning process with valuable lessons learned not only from successful companies but also from successful and devoted researchers. This is the reason that we are looking forward to repeating this project in due time.

References

Brinkman S, Kvale S (2015) Interviews: learning the craft of qualitative research interviewing, 3rd edn. Sage, Thousand Oaks

Creswell JW (2014) Research design: qualitative, quantitative, and mixed methods approach, 4th edn. Sage, Thousand Oaks

Gummesson E (2000) Qualitative methods in management research, 2nd edn. Sage, Thousand Oaks

McKiernan P, Purg D (eds) (2013) Hidden champions in CEE and Turkey: carving out a global niche. Springer, Basel

Patton MQ (2015) Qualitative research & evaluation methods, 4th edn. Sage, Thousand Oaks

Purg D et al (2019) Updated survey of "hidden champions" in central, eastern and south-eastern Europe. European Bank for Reconstruction and Development (EBRD)

Simon H (1996) Hidden champions: lessons from 500 of the world's best unknown companies. Harvard Business School Press, Boston

Simon H (2009) Hidden champions of the 21st century: success strategies of unknown market leaders. Springer, New York

Simon H (2012) Hidden champions Aufbruch nach Globalia: Die Erfolgsstrategien unbekannter Weltmarktführer. Campus, Frankfurt

Yin RK (2014) Case study research design and methods, 5th edn. Sage, Thousand Oaks

Hidden Champions: Leadership Success Factors

Danica Purg and Arnold Walravens

1 Introduction

In the study on hidden champions, Walravens and Filipović (2013) indicate that the overlap between three systems—company, family, and ownership—can be either a strength or a weakness. This is because they contain a number of bivalent elements that continually interact within any structure (Flören 2002), the company's strategy and culture, HRM, communication, ownership, finance, and the balance between company and family interests. For example, the spirit of ownership can be a binding element in a family or it could lead to reluctance to consider external financing and to blockage of the business's expansion.

In this chapter, we do not discuss the governance structure of hidden champions, but try to analyze deeper those leadership features that represent factors contributing to the success of hidden champions. The leadership of hidden champions has been analyzed before. Sutherland and Purg (2013) concluded: "Throughout the cases of these hidden champions, leadership was a central and important driver of organizational success" (p. 33). In their study, the focus was on leadership characteristics, such as vision and passion. Particularly, they identified the so-called "expert knowledge" as the basis of hidden champions' leadership. It is described as "part and parcel of passion" (p. 24) and thus, the main source of success.

The aim of this chapter is not only to confirm what has been said before about the leadership of hidden champions as a success factor, but also to provide a deeper

---

D. Purg (✉)
Postgraduate Studies, IEDC-Bled School of Management, Bled, Slovenia

CEEMAN, The International Association for Management Development in Dynamic Societies, Bled, Slovenia
e-mail: danica.purg@iedc.si

A. Walravens
Postgraduate Studies, IEDC-Bled School of Management, Bled, Slovenia

© Springer Nature Switzerland AG 2021
A. Braček Lalić, D. Purg (eds.), *Hidden Champions in Dynamically Changing Societies*, https://doi.org/10.1007/978-3-030-65451-1_3

insight into the complexity of hidden champions success, as it was clearly concluded before that no specific reasons for it can be identified (Flören 2002; Simon 2009).

Walravens and Filipović (2013) analyzed three factors—ownership, corporate culture, and organizational governance—that may explain hidden champions' success. They referred to publications suggesting that these factors and the decisions made in these fields can lead to success or failure (Breu 2001; Fredberg et al. 2008). However, Walravens and Filipović concluded that the literature on hidden champions provided evidence of different types of ownership and this appeared to be a particularly important factor behind the success of those companies.

Vaknin (2010) provided a good description of the two leadership cultures and the style of family ownership, which is the most frequent form of hidden champions ownership. He states that family-owned leadership tends to be nepotistic, characterized by an irrational decision-making process and conflicts of interests between family members and other stakeholders. On the other hand, family-oriented leadership is characterized by a high commitment to the business and a long-time horizon. Family management also involves a very strong identity and pride.

Walravens and Filipović (2013) concluded that hidden champions appear to benefit from this combination of ownership and governance structure—the interconnection of leadership style. Furthermore, they stated that in many cases this style is defined as charismatic. If so, it is interesting to know what this "charisma" is based on. Is it their expert knowledge, pioneership, the longevity of their leadership, or their contribution to the regional and local community? Or is charisma not the only and best description of the leadership culture and style of hidden champions?

2 Market Leadership: Success Factors

In this chapter, the leadership culture and style of hidden champions will be analyzed as an explanation of their success. It is necessary to define what "success" means in this respect. Of course, a company can be considered successful if it is not a "May fly," but has succeeded to build a sustainable basis. The meaning of success can be found by studying what it takes to become a "champion."

In this study, a company is described as a "champion," if it has succeeded to reach a leading market position. This is not an element that differentiates these companies from the rest, but a common feature. It is safe to conclude that many companies, particularly in the high-tech segment, reached their market position by what can be described as "technical leadership," and, as described by Sutherland and Purg (2013), "expert knowledge," bringing to the market the knowledge-based products that have unique characteristics and responding to the demand that has already existed or has been created.

A common characteristic of hidden champions is their strong base in science and technology. In publications on how to be or become a market leader, this element is not mentioned as a decisive factor, probably because it is hidden in the "quality" and "innovation" factors. Vision, the relevance of the product for the customer, quality,

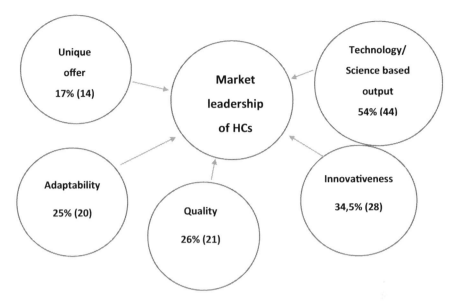

Fig. 1 Most important factors explaining the market leadership of hidden champions ($N = 81$).

innovation, customer service, and commitment are often mentioned as causes of market leadership (Tellis and Golder 2006; Mellina 2016; Rutsky 2019). Another factor is the choice of the right partners in order to fill the gap in the value-adding chain and vice-versa (Ryans et al. 2010).

In the five steps toward becoming a market leader, formulated by Zach Cutler (2015), the focus is on (1) finding a market niche, (2) becoming a leader by differentiation, (3) not waiting until perfection to launch a product, listening to customers' feedback, considering their wants, needs, and concerns, as well as striving to innovate, adapting to changes in the market, and staying two steps ahead of the competition, (4) satisfying customers, because they hold the power in today's social media and technology-driven world, and (5) looking for new and creative ways to market product and connect with customers.

An analysis of the success factors mentioned in this research on hidden champions produced the following picture (see Fig. 1).

Figures 1 and 2 show that the interviewees have often mentioned more than one success factor. As Mrs. Koprüner (GS-Tvornica Mašina Travnik, Bosnia and Herzegovina) said: "Success is a complexity of all factors, not a single one." As mentioned before, the majority of hidden champions delivers products and services from technological/science competences. More than half (54%) considered this an important element in reaching market leadership. Another 34% mentioned innovativeness as an important factor Good example are provided by MikroElektronika, Serbia, saying proudly that it produces "one new product per day," and Santino-Service, Moldova, owning "40 inventions and 11 patents." But, as the results show, there are many others. This factor has some general validity that is not restricted to

Fig. 2 All mentioned factors leading to the mindset leadership of hidden champions ($N = 81$)

1	Technology/science	44
2	Innovativeness	28
3	Quality	21
4	Adaptability	20
5	Unique offer	14
6	Human resources	8
7	Service	8
8	Globally/ Intern coverage	6
9	Environmentally friendly	5
10	Experience	5
11	Price	4
12	Complete solution	3
13	Location	2
14	Partnerships	2
15	Brand	1
16	Customer satisfaction	1

hidden champions. The same is true of the factors in Fig. 2 (Tellis and Golder 2006; Mellina 2016; Rutsky 2019).

Concerning "quality," we can mention two good examples: DOK-ING Ltd, Croatia, and Eko. Tekstil Tic. San. A.Ş, Turkey. Concerning "adaptability," almost all companies mention that continuous innovations are also examples of adaptability to market changes and costumer needs. VIGO Systems, Poland, and Polycom, Slovenia, are cases in point. Cyclolab Kft., Hungary, Deeper and Fidens (ViLim Ball), Lithuania, Carlex Design Poland, BTW Barrier, Russia, MikroElektronika, Serbia, and Akrapovič, Slovenia, are good examples of hidden champions that have a "unique offer."

As Fig. 2 demonstrates, a number of success factors identified in the literature, are not considered decisive by the hidden champions. Examples of these are choosing the right partners, differentiation, experience, human resource aspects, environmental aspects, location, and price. The fact that the price of products and services scores so low in the judgments of hidden champions can be understood as related to the generally large market share that they hold and the uniqueness of their offer. This probably explains also the fact that there are no examples of companies following Cutler's (2015) advice: "look for new and creative ways to market your product."

Also, the number of hidden champions that mention social responsibility and being environmentally friendly is rather low. This allows us to conclude that hidden champions operate differently from other companies. Examples of hidden champions that consider social responsibility as strategic are: AlbKalustyan, Albania; MOEA LLC, Kosovo; Soton, China; Ochir Daginas LLC, Mongolia.

A more detailed analysis of several of these topics could lead to different results. We may conclude that, concerning market leadership success factors, there is no difference between hidden champions and corporations in general. The only remarkable difference is the impact of technology-and-science-based output.

3 Leadership in Hidden Champions

Although this study of hidden champions leadership does not focus on culture and style, the collected material is rich enough for us to get at least some insight into the leadership "orientation" of the hidden champions. We define leadership here as the capacity to create, together with other people, a vision for the future, to organize cooperation, and to achieve strategic goals on the basis of this vision and cooperation.

Management can be defined as the way that cooperation is organized. As the material from this hidden champions study offers only a few indications about leadership styles, we try to analyze the companies' leadership and management orientation. Using the available material, collected from questionnaires and interviews, we arrive at a classification of four factors (see Fig. 3).

In order to discover dynamics in the development of hidden champions, we categorized them by the period of their establishment as in Fig. 4.

Connecting the period of establishment and leadership (and management) orientation resulted in the classifications shown in Figs. 5 and 6.

In our view, there is one unexpected result. This concerns "functional management items." The younger generation of companies mentioned these items less often,

Corporate cultural and organisational items	Vision and strategy	Functional orientation	Human resources
• Passion • Setting an example • Inspiration • Creativity • No-nonsense approach • Entrepreneurial spirit and atmosphere • Corporate governance • Leading by teams • Stakeholder relations	• Vision • Strategic approach • Strategy development • Setting goals • Partnerships • Internationalization	• Focus on quality management • Focus on R&D • Focus on cost control • Technical focus • Marketing and sales orientation	• People-oriented • Development of employees • Participation / empowerment of employees • Management development

Fig. 3 Focal factors of leadership (and management) in 81 hidden champions

Year of establishment of HC	N
Before 1992	25
1992-1995	15
1996-2005	20
After 2006	22

Fig. 4 The year of establishment of hidden champions

Categories Year of est.	Corporate culture and organisation	Various strategic items	HRM items	Functional management items	Total
Before 1992 N=24	8	9	6	13	36
1992-1995 N=15	3	3	4	4	14
1996-2005 N=20	11	8	8	8	35
After 2006 N=22	20	5	9	3	37
Total	42	25	27	28	

Fig. 5 Year of the establishment of hidden champions and leadership items

		N
1	Team orientation	22
2	Strategic approach	13
3	People oriented	12
4	Visionary	11
5	Marketing and sales oriented	10
6	Development of employees	8
7	Stakeholder policy	8
8	Participation, empowerment / co-ownership of employees	8
9	R&D focus	6
10	Quality management focused	6

Fig. 6 The most mentioned items of leadership and management orientation

which might be related to the smaller size of these companies. Older companies have experienced the importance of these items at a certain stage of their development.

Hidden champions that were established in earlier periods experienced the necessity to develop functional management during their existence. Marketing and sales often become fields of attention during the internationalization of a local or regional company. The oldest hidden champions have been very focused on R&D for necessary innovations and on the quality management so as to be able to compete internationally. An interesting and remarkable finding are the items on "corporate culture and organization" that are often mentioned by the younger generation of hidden champions. This is mainly related to team elements (teamwork, teambuilding). Was the older generation's leadership more characterized by single leaders, vision, and functional management? And is leadership in the younger generation of hidden champions a shared responsibility rather than individual? In the younger generation, everybody becomes a leader. Company success depends on team quality. According to Rutsky (2019), "the make-up of the team may be the number-one determinate of the success of a project." Good examples of these are Essent Optics, Belarus; Chocolife Holding, Kazakhstan; 8 devices, Lithuania; Romsoft, Romania; and Mikroelektornika, Serbia.

Older generation hidden champions—for instance, DOK-ING Ltd, Croatia; Capsys Informatikai Kft., Hungary; Grapefruit, Romania; BUCK, Serbia; Aisberg, Ukraine; and BIA Separations, Slovenia—also use teamwork, although not to the same extent as the younger generation.

4 Conclusions

Hidden champions are unknown or relatively unknown market leaders. . They are often described as symbols of a bright future for the economies of their countries. This study includes companies in the countries of Central, Eastern, and South-Eastern Europe, China, Kazakhstan, Mongolia, and Turkey. These companies are champions, because of the products or services that they offer, often based on the latest technological and scientific knowledge. As Mrs. Koprüner of GS-Tvornica Mašina Travnik, BiH, pointed out, complex factors have contributed to this success: a strong, technological or scientific basis, innovation, and quality drive, the uniqueness of their offer and the level of adaptability to market developments and costumer needs. They are certainly not champions in every respect, but they are good examples of what Cutler (2015) described as an important step toward success when he wrote: "Don't wait for perfection to launch a product. Instead, constantly execute and iterate; listen to customer feedback and consider their wants, needs and concerns. Strive to innovate, adapt to changes in the market, and stay two steps ahead of the competitor."

Although this research has produced only exploratory results concerning the leadership and management of hidden champions, there are certainly links between general leadership, management orientation, and market success. High levels of innovation capability, quality, and adaptability are achieved through strong functional management. Entrepreneurial initiatives in successful companies will certainly not be successful without the visionary minds of the founders-owners. Aspects of human resource management orientation have helped them build organizations with highly motivated employees.

The complexity of products and projects has called for new forms of leadership. This is not a completely new phenomenon, but in today's circumstances, characterized by global competition, strict quality norms, and fast-changing demands, the development of products and services is increasingly a team task and responsibility. This calls for dispersed leadership and for leadership qualities in all members of the team. It takes new qualities to perform in international, often remote teams. Employees will find inspiration and motivation in cooperating in top-performing teams, having different compositions, and being led by changing team coordinators that can be called team leaders.

To conclude: a strong basis, mostly in technology and science, a passion for continuous innovation, and working in teams of enthusiastic experts will help a company to become and stay a champion, known or unknown.

References

Breu K (2001) The role and relevance of management cultures in the organizational transformation process. Int Stud Manag Organ 31(2):28–47

Cutler Z (2015) 5 steps to become a market leader. Retrieved 2 June 2020 from https://www.entrepreneur.com/article/241517

Flören RH (2002) Crown princes in the clay. An empirical study on the tackling of succession challenges in Dutch family farms. Van Gorcum, Assen

Fredberg T, Beer M, Eisenstat R, Foote N, Norrgren F (2008) Embracing commitment and performance: CEOs and practices used to manage paradox. Working paper. Harvard Business School

Mellina E (2016) A customer-focused culture for market leadership and innovation. Retrieved 2 June 2020 from https://blog.hrps.org/blogpost/A-Customer-Focused-Culture-for-Market-Leadership-and-Innovation

Rutsky K (2019) Messaging, it's a team sport—part 1: three success factors to consider. Retrieved 2 June 2020 from https://kenrutsky.com/breakthrough-marketing/messaging-its-a-team-sport-part-1-three-success-factors-to-consider/

Ryans A, More R, Barclay D, Deutscher T (2010) Winning market leadership: strategic market planning for technology-driven businesses. Wiley, Toronto

Simon H (2009) HCs of the 21st century: Success strategies of unknown world leaders. Springer, London

Sutherland I, Purg D (2013) Leadership of hidden champions: from vision to communityship. In: McKiernan P, Purg D (eds) Hidden champions in CEE and Turkey. Springer, Berlin

Tellis G, Golder P (2006) First to market, first to fail? Real causes of enduring market leadership. Sloan Manag Rev 37

Vaknin O (2010) The family business risk profile. The Leonards N. Stern School of Business

Walravens A, Filipović N (2013) Three bivalent performance factors of hidden champions: ownership, organizational culture and organizational governance. In: McKiernan P, Purg D (eds) Hidden champions in CEE and Turkey. Springer, Berlin

Hidden Champions: Common Lessons Learned on the Path to Success

Denis Berberović, Amra Kožo, and Merima Činjarević

1 Introduction

When conducting a large-scale qualitative research project such as the one presented in this book, two major benefits for the business community arise. First, practitioners get the opportunity to peak into individual success stories and draw conclusions from separate case studies presented in country chapters (Yin 2014; Gummesson 2000). The second major benefit is general conclusions drawn from all the hidden champions involved in this research. These are the main lessons from the project: major findings offering invaluable insights into the formation of a hidden champion. Based on the methodology of meta-analysis of individual case studies, main conclusions were drawn and, according to their similarity, they were categorized into 13 themes (Patton 2015). These themes represent the general lessons of this research and sum up the project's major findings. It is important to note that these lessons are given by successful hidden champion managers and no reference is made to academic work within the lessons. This has been done on purpose, as the authors' intention is to let the voices of practitioners be heard. And they do have plenty to say.

2 Lesson 1: Model Your Business

> Business is not a sprint. It is a marathon.
> UniComs, Bulgaria

D. Berberović (✉) · A. Kožo · M. Činjarević
University of Sarajevo, Sarajevo, Bosnia and Herzegovina
e-mail: denis.berberovic@efsa.unsa.ba

One of the common grounds for developing a successful business model is business continuity. This implies permanent development, advancement, and customization of the portfolio as it is done in Elko Ep in the Czech Republic. From another Czech hidden champion, we have learned that it also means constant transition of the business model. NSoft, a hidden champion of Bosnia and Herzegovina, also claims that continuous improvement of both services and processes is the framework for continuous progress. And in order to achieve that, patience and consistency are needed, claims the managers of Bulgaria's UniComs. It is a learning process, he explains. Errors may be painful but they are valuable lessons. Hidden champion managers even consider errors to be more valuable in the long run than success, because success might sometimes come without clear reasons why it has occurred. Therefore, even after achieving success, one needs to understand why it has been achieved. Otherwise it is a temporary occurrence. Travod, a hidden champion in Moldova, suggests applying a stage-based continuity. It has been experienced that such an approach leads to sustainable growth. And the fact that most hidden champions are early entrants into emerging markets is beneficial to the learning process as a company grows with the market and its customers.

When modeling their business, some hidden champions rely strongly on lean management. For example, the Chinese company Soton has gradually developed its organizational structure and designed a sophisticated management system by reduction of non-value-adding activities in its operations. Another Chinese hidden champion, Shuanghuan, has also applied lean management for over 20 years and believes that was the crucial reason that it has conducted business operations with accelerating success.

Another important pillar of hidden champions involved in this research is the fact that a significant number of them have embraced servitization. Hidden champions have shifted their business models from a product-centric to service-centric approach. China's Noblelift believes this to be the key strategic move as it has grown to become a valuable integrated solution-provider in intelligent logistics. NSoft from Bosnia and Herzegovina aligns with this statement, as it believes that the main driver behind its long-term success and high-quality relations with customers across the globe is its integrated software solution accompanied by all-time available support. Belarus's Izovac Group has built a unique competitive advantage by offering complex turn-key solutions, which include unique equipment, coating technology, installation, maintenance, and staff training along the way.

3 Lesson 2: Know Your Markets—Everytime and Everywhere

Adapt to market changes and challenge new technologies to respond to customer needs rapidly and efficiently.
Travod, Moldova

One of the most striking revelations from interviews with hidden champions is their market-sensing capability. As China's Noblelift explains, subsidiaries and extensive network in the target market enable Noblelift to get the market dynamics on time and to capture the personalized needs of customers. Through information feedback, the company has gradually established a flexible production and service system.

Russian hidden champion Grishko adds to this the importance of understanding the difference between domestic and foreign markets, as well as adapting to it. This is also what Cyclolab of Hungary has realized. After analyzing the domestic and international markets, it has decided to seize global market opportunities as the company realized that margins are significantly higher on the global level.

Flexibility in terms of responding to trends and sudden changes in the market seems to be one of the major rules of thumb of the analyzed hidden champions. Poland's Growbots and Design are excellent examples of companies that customize their business operations to emerging market trends, such as complying with newly imposed data protection acts or changing consumer preferences in the segment of luxury products. Reactivity is the term that Lithuanian hidden champion Telesoftas uses when it comes to being responsive to market trends. This hidden champion says that companies must not stay in their comfort zones if they wish to accelerate their success. Romania's Romsoft has achieved steady growth as it has made the strategic decision to follow the development of digitalization, a market trend strongly shaping the biomedical industry in recent years.

Finding a specific market niche appears to be another market-related success factor, according to Capsys Informatikai of Hungary. This is also what Russia's NT-MTD Spectrum Instruments claims. Specifically, defining the target market along with its core competences, is of utmost importance. If companies manage to define these properly, then they can compete even with big global companies. Different approaches to niche markets can be taken. For instance, Polish hidden champion Telesto has observed the development of its niche market and its competitors for years before it decided to join the race. On the other hand, Marina Porto Montenegro decided to enter an underserved niche market, lacking strong competitors, with high quality offers. Hungary's Tresorit has taken a more radical approach. It not only decided to switch from the consumer market to business customers, but has also taken its operations to a more lucrative business niche market abroad.

4 Lesson 3: Your Consumers Are Your Partners

The customer-centric approach started to be implemented and brought results immediately.
Phonexia, Czech Republic

It has emerged through this research that hidden champions are living the marketing relationship approach. Building close relationships with their customers is at the center of their business models. Microstep from Slovakia seeks to build close relationships with its customers, trying to understand their processes and gain a deep insight into their needs. Here is how another Slovakian hidden champion, Inovatrcis, puts it: "We remain open to our customers, partners, and each other by sharing knowledge and information every step of the way. Having the freedom to choose our own direction, we always recommend what is best for our partners. We work with our partners, not just for them, with a positive approach and a dialogue-driven attitude to meet the respective goals of our partners as well as of our colleagues."

But many hidden champions have taken this one step further. They have developed not only relations, but also partnerships with their clients. According to Serbian hidden champion, Uniplast, this is the key to a leading market position. It has proven to be the successful recipe also for Yünsa. This Turkish textile industry hidden champion has established strong partnerships across the globe.

Partnerships imply common goals, perspectives, mutual respect, and, above all, values. Hungarian hidden champion Energotest argues that by focusing on innovative solutions, customers are being helped to capture more value. As a matter of fact, as Belarus's Aerodorstroy has experienced, many innovative solutions have actually been suggested by customers. And Kristal, a hidden champion of Bosnia and Herzegovina, emphasizes how important it is to understand that customer value creation covers many other aspects beyond traditional offering (i.e., meeting consumer's expectations about the product quality, delivery times, and product customization).

At the heart of high-quality partnerships is communication and all hidden champions seem to be fully aware of it. For example, Lithuania's Deeper, realized long ago that the most important connection is the one with people who use its products. And because the company has listened carefully, it has introduced a set of innovations suggested by its customers. This is something that Moldova's Noction has also realized—by listening to suggestions given by its customers, it has managed to keep a high pace with innovations. As for communication channels, anything from thematic workshops, via factory visits, to social media will do the job, as we have learned from Poland's Vigo System.

Social media are being increasingly used for communication purposes even with the most demanding clients. Lithuania's Parkis has experienced a surge in unexpected promotion via the Internet, due to excellent recommendations given by "right clients" which have attracted more "right clients," as explained by another Lithuanian hidden champion, 8devices.

Partnerships with consumers are also based on a positive consumer experience. However, this is often challenging to achieve as most hidden champion offerings include innovations that put the consumer experience at risk, since most consumers have not used such an offering previously. Being aware of the limited consumer experience, many hidden champions offer support to their customers. Growbots of Poland, for example, offers extensive support to its clients, which made its sales skyrocket. But user experience contains an additional benefit, as can be seen from the example of the Belarussian hidden champion, EssentOptics. This company uses customer support not only to elevate its consumer experience but also to receive feedback and use it for the purpose of incremental innovation, i.e., to improve the product further. Kosovo's hidden champion MOEA goes even further and uses its support to consumers not only to improve consumer experience but also to extend consumer knowledge in specific domains, such as sustainability, and achieve an eco-friendly approach to consumption.

Finally, all hidden champions have acknowledged that none of this would be possible without a thorough and continuous tracking of consumer trends and needs, as suggested by Mongolia's Leader Cashmere. Market research is at the core of developing high-quality partnerships with clients. Research is needed to provide a deeper understanding of consumer preference variety, as claimed by Romanian hidden champion Grapefruit.

5 Lesson 4: Suppliers Are Your Partners, Too

> You need to create intensive collaboration with all actors throughout the value chain.
> Kristal, Bosnia and Herzegovina

The need for high-quality relations within the supply chain appears to be one of the most important lessons that can be learned from the studied hidden champions. This is not all too surprising as most hidden champions are in fact members of global supply chains. It seems that they have applied locally the know-how gained from their global partners.

According to Hungary's hidden champion Capsys Informatikai, high-quality relations within the supply chain imply close relationships with all members of the supply chain. At Capsys Informatikai, they believe that the most important elements of success are team dynamics and the cooperative, creative team culture which guarantees close relationship with business partners. Lithuanian hidden champion Deeper adds to this the importance of close relations with like-minded suppliers. This indicates that everyone adheres to the same quality standards, bringing thereby value to everything that is done. Adding to this is also transparency and openness as it represents building blocks for a close a long-lasting cooperation. Even in the early development stages, it is important to build close relations with enthusiastic suppliers, as they need to be able to keep the pace of the hidden champions' development both inland and abroad. Poland's Telesto has learned this lesson the hard way, as it realized that some of its suppliers were not reliable.

Finally, what the hidden champion can take from its supply chain is not always the most essential thing. It is also important to give back value to the supply chain. Kosovo's MOEA has built its business model on the fair treatment of its suppliers. Interestingly, prices of raw materials are not negotiated but accepted as suppliers define them.

6 Lesson 5: Diversify, Diversify, Diversify!

> Diversify your activities. It is important to avoid the focus on one point.
> 8devices, Lithuania

What has become increasingly obvious after studying every hidden champion in each country involved in this research is their determination to diversify. In general terms, diversification implies increasing the scope of the business. Two types of diversification have been identified.

First, there is the option of *product diversification*—increasing the scope of the product portfolio. This can be achieved by widening the product assortment, implying a launch of new products, or by deepening the product assortment, which implies a launch of various versions of an already existing product. The latter is what the Chinese hidden champion Soton did when it only recently decided to launch degradable packaging options, responding thereby to the market trend of rising eco-awareness.

The second identified option is *market diversification*—a type of diversification that involves supplying the same or similar product or services across several markets. Now it must be noted that the term "markets" is understood differently by the hidden champions included in the research. Market diversification can imply simple yet frequently occurring geographic diversification. As Essent Optics of Belarus noted, geographic market diversification is a strategic tool for risk management. Being present in different geographical markets makes the company less vulnerable to crises in one of the markets. Another way to manage market risk is to target different market segments, also referred to simply as "markets." Lithuania's Telesoftas, for example, has a diversified portfolio of clients as a precautionary measure, which helps it decrease its dependence on one or few clients.

Finally, it must be noted that the studied hidden champions do diversify, but they also take different approaches. It has emerged that smaller hidden champions opt for one type of diversification, mainly the diversification of clients. Bigger hidden champions, due to their greater resource portfolio, apply a combination of diversification types, both product and market diversification. The latter one is implemented with all its nuances.

7 Lesson 6: Innovate, Innovate, Innovate...and Yes... Innovate!

> The key to success lies in the innovative approach and use of new technology in an effective way.
> Buck, Serbia

The ability to implement new or technologically improved products, processes, and systems, so as to take advantage of market opportunities, is a characteristic shared by all hidden champions. These companies seek to acquire knowledge from different sources (e.g., customers, suppliers, labs, universities, and public research organizations) aiming to generate successful innovations, i.e., to provide solutions that are better equipped to meet customer needs. The importance of the capacity to recognize new opportunities (sensing) and generate innovations based on these opportunities (seizing) is well recognized by the studied hidden champions. As noted by Kristal of Bosnia and Herzegovina, proactivity in seizing opportunities, innovativeness in developing new solutions, and readiness to take risks when a promising opportunity presents itself are the main pillars of business success in complex and uncertain environments. Hidden champions engage simultaneously or separately in different innovation types, such as *product innovation* (the commercialization of a new product or service to meet customer needs), *process innovation* (the introduction of new elements to a manufacturing or service production), and even *business model innovation* (the introduction of a business model that is new to the industry in which a company competes).

Some of the hidden champions have the capability to integrate and transform knowledge into radically new products and processes, thus acting as agents of transformation. As stated by Chinese hidden champion Shuanhuan, continuous improvement is a never-ending journey, and it accelerates smart manufacturing transformation across industries. In terms of open innovation, hidden champions engage more in inbound than in outbound open innovation. Inbound innovation takes different forms, such as technology purchases, inter-firm R&D collaborations, university-firm R&D collaboration, academic spinoffs, technological spinoffs, and customer-driven innovation. For example, Izovac Group, a hidden champion of Belarus, is a spin-out company that has been developed out of university research laboratories, and it is specialized in the production of vacuum coating equipment for optics, laser devices, and microelectronics. The university-firm R&D collaboration also leads to the development of new technologies and new products, as argued by Kordsa Teknik Tekstil, a hidden champion of Turkey.

8 Lesson 7: Be Kind Toward Nature and Society, and They Will Be Kind Toward Your Business

> Eliminate the harmful effects of our actions on the health of the environment.
> Eko Tekstil Tic. San., Turkey

Several hidden champions seem to pursue a triple-bottom-line approach to success, i.e., satisfying economic, social, and environmental goals. The commitment to the triple bottom line is reflected in the intention of hidden champions to find ways to address the requirements of shareholders (economic performance), regulatory authorities (environment performance), and community (social performance) simultaneously. Although financial sustainability concerns inherently drive hidden champions, they also aspire to solve environmental and social problems by providing sustainability-driven solutions. These solutions can be divided into two broad groups: environmentally-driven solutions and socially-driven solutions.

Environmentally-driven solutions are usually the result of modifications made in processes, technologies, systems, and products. A few hidden champions follow the eco-product pathway toward sustainability, i.e., using eco-friendly materials such as natural, recycled, and bio-degradable material. For instance, Russian hidden champion Grishko, uses natural materials to manufacture fashion products—dance shoes for professional ballet dancers. However, pursuing business sustainability goes beyond the use of natural materials and includes a range of environmental strategies and clean practices. For instance, Turkey's Eko Tekstil continuously evaluates the application of preventive environmental strategies to processes and products, aiming to increase efficiency and to minimize exposure to environmental risk factors. Also, the adoption of clean practices (e.g., waste reduction. noise pollution, energy saving, water saving) has become the backbone of the company's transition towards sustainability. Some hidden champions have embraced the role of change agents regarding sustainable production. Chinese hidden champion Noblelift accelerated the sustainability shift in the transport industry by developing innovative, environmentally friendly lithium batteries used in the production of light industrial trucks and electric storage vehicles.

Socially-driven solutions are results of the intention of hidden champions to nurture diversity and social inclusion by empowering socially excluded groups. Russian hidden champion Grishko shows how businesses can deliver a socially-driven solution by promoting and facilitating the employment of people with disabilities.

9 Lesson 8: Go Global—Internationalize!

> Dominate the home market first, then expand.
> Ukrainian Beer Company Group, Ukraine

The majority of the studied hidden champions are so-called traditional or gradual internationalizers. They are domestically focused companies that internationalize slowly and incrementally. However, a few hidden champions are focused only on foreign markets located far from the domestic market in terms of physic, cultural, and institutional distance. A good example of a born-global is Chinese hidden champion Noblelift, an entrepreneurial start-up that initiated its international business (exporting) soon after its inception. Moreover, a small number of hidden champions are born-again globals since they embraced rapid internationalization to capitalize on the full potential of foreign markets.

10 Lesson 9: Talented Employees Stand Behind Every Hidden Champion

> We consider our employees to be our main asset, which is the reason why we invest into best talent recruitment and talent development.
> NT-MTD Spectrum Instruments, Russia

All hidden champions studied in this research acknowledge the high importance of their employees. Leaders of hidden champions have a list of important human resource management practices: human resource planning, recruitment and selection, human resource development, systems of compensation and benefits, and managerial succession. Apart from this, these companies pay attention to the work climate and even generational distinctions among their employees. In hidden champions in the IT industry, many workers are millennials. Grapefruit of Romania recognizes the millennials' lifestyle as a meaningful predictor of job satisfaction. As a consequence, the company adapts the working environment, benefits, and work pace to the lifestyle of its workers.

Human resource planning is one of the crucial functions of the human resource department in every company. Since China's Soton operates in a specific niche where general talents are not applicable, this hidden champion puts a lot of effort in training and education to create excellent top-management and middle-management teams. Over 20 employees have been trained by the CEO who believes that dealing appropriately with succession issues could empower the employees of Soton, and provide at least 20 more years of sustainable development. This example confirms the importance of human resource planning, especially for high managerial positions, and positions that require a high level of responsibility. The companies plan their human resources and invest hard efforts in the recruitment and selection processes. To attract the best talents, some of the companies establish cooperation with the educational sector in their countries.

Companies are looking for valuable workers keen to learn and thrive. Some of the characteristics that companies search for job markets are agility, energy, a proactive approach to work, proper education, creativity, and enthusiasm. Still, in the modern business context, the employees' knowledge and skills at the beginning of their employment in a specific company are not enough for a lifetime. Companies cherish a lifelong learning approach since it provides a highly skilled and competitive workforce. Precisely, employees are considered a competitive advantage of hidden champions. To encourage employees to feel better and offer more at work, companies create a variety of benefits. Their focus is not solely on material benefits. They combine them with organizational climate and a plethora of non-material compensations and benefits. In hidden champions where employees are predominantly millennials, flexible working hours accompanied by positive organizational climate and competitive salaries are preferred over a combination of top salaries, a rigid organizational climate, and a stressful HR performance management system.

Results obtained through this research indicate that both motivation and work performance are enhanced with flexible work arrangements (i.e., schedule and space) and responsibility-based tasks. Different types of team-building and teamwork serve to establish an overall team dynamic. Some companies consider a dynamic, cooperative, and creative team culture the most critical success factor in the building of trust-based relationships with business partners and customers. Trust among team members is seen in their communication and business activities with business partners.

Partnership and close cooperation with co-workers result in high scores. Some of the hidden champions, such as Slovakia's Microstep, offer to their most skilled employees the option to become co-owners of the company. This hidden champion obviously goes far beyond passion, creativity, and flexible work schedules. It provides its best performers with options to create changes and stay actively involved in the company's most important decision making.

The success of a company depends mostly on its employees. The results of this study show that regardless of the industry, market, company size, geographical scope, or the region and culture where a company operates, skilled, educated, and talented employees are recognized by all top managers as the most valuable resource. Companies are ready to invest in human resource planning, recruitment, development, and succession. The organizational climates of hidden champions demonstrate boundless creativity, endless enthusiasm, flexible structures, schedules adapted to the lifestyle of the employees, open-mindedness, passion, and a propensity to learn and grow. Successful companies invest in the training and development of employees. Sharing responsibility with their co-workers, they create a high level of organizational trust.

11 Lesson 10: Entrepreneurship Is an Adventure

> Trust your instinct and create new opportunities.
> Mare Adriatik, Albania

Throughout this research, it has emerged that successful entrepreneurs share the same traits, such as persistence, open-mindedness, enthusiasm, high sensitivity, dedication, obsession, awareness, and the will to learn. For instance, the founder of Soton learned how to use a computer by himself, and tried around 20 different businesses before he entered the plastic straw industry. Also, as some of the respondents suggest, an entrepreneur should develop instinct and invent new opportunities. Entrepreneurship is adventure and obsession, and continuous improvement is critical for constant progress. Another conclusion with respect to entrepreneurship can be drawn from this research. There are two groups of reasons for starting up new businesses. The first is a desire to make something different and leave a mark. The second one is a necessity.

Even though they come from geographically different regions, all hidden champions that fit into the entrepreneurship category share the same spirit and business founder traits, as well as the reasons behind their business ventures. This implies that lessons learned from entrepreneurs should be explored and shared through more inspirational stories of ups and downs.

12 Lesson 11: Values Are Never Out of Fashion

Fast forward global leadership based on building value to stakeholders.
Selena, Poland

Values are timeless and universal principles that determine a general understanding of good and bad. Organizational values state what is essential for an organization, and they are the foundation of the corporate culture. Moreover, the personal values of employees should be aligned with organizational values in order to achieve higher levels of employee satisfaction, commitment, and motivation.

Most hidden champions clearly emphasized the role of organizational values. Depending on the industry, market, and managerial business philosophy, a plethora of corporate values can be noted. To name just a few, these are transparency, accountability, accuracy, consistency, trust, cooperation, creativity, support, and teamwork. Values are the foundation of corporate culture, and they define the behavior of managers and employees. Domen, a Montenegrin hidden champion, creates a positive and task-oriented organizational culture that enables the development of employee strength, vitality, and growth. Kosovo's, Moea, believes that transparency should be woven within the organizational culture, and it achieves this by sharing information. According to other hidden champions, transparency should be present in all business aspects, including financial ones. And most of them consider a high level of transparency one of the critical factors that helped them achieve a high level of trust with their investors.

However, hidden champions are driven by their values not only in their relationships with their employees but also in those outside the company. The values that they nourish motivate them in their dealings with partners, suppliers, customers, and other relevant stakeholders. Nowadays, companies should rethink their ideas about value systems. According to Energotest of Hungary, they should emphasize values related to society and the environment. Family values are the foundation of organizational culture in entrepreneurial organizations and some of the hidden champions indeed declare that they manage their businesses as big families, love them, and take care of them as if they were children.

13 Lesson 12: Adapt, Adopt, and Apply the Best Internal Organization

The growth of the company requires adaptations of the managerial and organizational systems.
Grapefruit, Romania

For the purpose of this study, "internal organization" refers to all processes and systems related to the everyday life of an organization. Thus, the internal organization describes the organizational structures, managerial methods, and techniques used during the working process. Hidden champions have dominantly flat and modern structures. They enable them to accelerate everyday processes related to decision making and communication and generally facilitate their adaptation to changes caused by the external environment. Carlex Design, a hidden champion of Poland, argues that the whole management process is crucial for the final solution. Other companies, such as 8devices, emphasizes the role of internal processes for good relations with clients. From the initial contact with the client to the delivery of the final product or service, all tasks should be accompanied by well-defined internal processes.

Polish hidden champion Growbots aims to improve internal processes and keeps its organization well defined yet flexible. It applies one of the popular management techniques—Management By Objectives (MBO). All studied companies rely on defined procedures and, at the same time, keep some open space for flexibility when needed. This is supported by organizational structures that avoid hierarchy, bureaucracy, and a lack of communication, as well as by managerial systems keen to change and adapt.

14 Lesson 13: Believe in Your Mission and You Will Keep Your Strategic Direction

> A strong vision, mission, and ambitious goals will definitely pay off.
> DOK-ING, Croatia

An organization can have an excellent strategy, but without competent leaders, a strategy might fail. Leadership is described as a process (not an act) between a leader and some team members that work together on the very same aim. It implies a two-way influence between leaders and team members as well as some form of hierarchy. The leaders' attitudes and behavior determine how well employees will perform their tasks. From the case of Marina Porto Montenegro, one can learn that a good leader should have specific traits (e.g., persistence, strong personality, good intuition, passion, etc.) and knowledge (e.g., knowledge on project management, global market, international business, etc.). Above all, a leader should maintain a positive reputation and build trust among employees and society.

It is remarkable that leadership and strategy are emphasized mostly by hidden champions in the Balkans. All study participants in this region point out the necessity of a clearly defined vision, mission, strategy, goals, and objectives. Also, hidden champions state that a strong belief in vision and mission can help the organization pursue a strategic direction. Regarding strategies, the observed hidden champions have chosen diversification and differentiation. For them, diversification provides the optimal balance in a business portfolio and enables the growth of the company. However, Albania's Venice Art diversified its business but did not lose its focus. This implies that diversification should be well planned. At the same time, differentiation is based on customer-oriented products or services and their customization.

Furthermore, most hidden champions see differentiation as the foundation of business success.

Strategic planning plays a vital role in overall business success. However, strategy execution also represents a significant step. In Kristal, the hidden champion of Bosnia and Herzegovina, clear vision and operational excellence are the company's strengths. These enable the company to respond quickly to changes in the hyper-competitive environment. Just as DOK-ING of Croatia noticed, a compelling vision and ambitious goals always pay off.

15 Conclusion

This chapter has summarized the main lessons learned from the hidden champion research project. There is one general finding that emerged from almost every interview: the importance of people. There seems to be agreement among interviewed managers that people—be they employees, customers, or suppliers—are the crucial ingredient of success. Employees, customers, and suppliers must not be treated as simple contributors of resources—labor, finance, or raw materials. They must be elevated to the level of partners, whose interests are as important as those of the company (Ellram and Ueltschy Murfield 2019).

Apart from knowing consumer needs and preferences, it is essential to be aware of broader market trends. Yet reading consumer trend reports would not be of much help here. What we have learned from hidden champions in terms of customer relations is how important it is to talk to customers, discuss products with them, use them together with them, and accept critiques, suggestions, and even innovative ideas (Najafi-Tavani et al. 2018). This is the best way to offer innovations that the world really needs. And what is needed will be bought. Price is not a decisive factor. Fortune smiles at innovation providers.

Hidden champions are global players. Some of them are born global, whereas others grow global. As we have learned, internationalization is the root as well as the consequence of success. Several hidden champions have achieved success by conquering the home market, only then to go abroad. But others have conquered specific markets because they first have faced the harsh terms of the global market and survived in those conditions. As many of the hidden champions have emerged and risen in unsupportive business environments (Berberović et al. 2019), they have grown into tough and resilient organizations. This has certainly made many of them appreciate the value of diversification, as one of the best risk-decreasing strategies.

We have also gained knowledge about the internal aspects of the hidden champions. Sometimes companies can rely on well-known business models (Cadden et al. 2020; Solaimani et al. 2019; Foss and Saebi 2018). But in other cases, they should not be deterred from adopting their own, customized business models (Lexutt 2020; Kowalkowski et al. 2017). Internal organization and its structure and processes should not be regarded as set in stone, but rather as something adaptable if circumstances require it. Most managers to whom we have spoken are true leaders who approach their businesses with compassion and take care not to lose sight of the strategic focus. This would not be possible if they did not have a clear system of values, which they impose on their organization and offerings. This comes undoubtedly at the risk of losing sight of other important values and opportunities and may be particularly delicate when it comes to the succession of the business, since most of them are family-owned companies. Then again, entrepreneurial spirits usually give their best when risk is around, do not they?

Last but not least is the lesson on the importance of environmental protection, understood in the broadest sense possible. This is not only a rich terrain for numerous innovations. It also ennobles the value system on which the company is built. This approach is usually accompanied by powerful business results.

What remains to be accentuated is that none of these lessons carry as much individual weight as when they are applied together. It is their synergetic effect, the combined application of them all, that paved the way for the interviewed companies to become what they are praised for—hidden champions.

The initial idea of this research project was to focus on hidden champions of Central and Eastern Europe. However, the project was broadened by the inclusion of hidden champions of Asia. At first, we were expecting to notice significant differences, but the data tell us otherwise. The data actually suggest that the Asian hidden champions are highly similar to those of Central and Eastern Europe. This can be seen throughout this chapter. If, however, we had to point out some nuanced differences, there would be two. While European hidden champions are more oriented toward the soft aspects of their businesses, such as consumer needs, employee issues, and value systems., Asian hidden champions tend to focus more on hard and technical aspects, such as the formal organizational structure, process efficiency, and technical innovations. This emerges not only from topics discussed during interviews, but also from the length of time dedicated to these topics during the interviews. Certainly, the time allocated to specific topics depends on the person conducting the interview. However, we need to keep in mind the fact that the interviews were conducted by local interviewers who have professional knowledge of business topics and are likely to have the same sense of the importance of specific issues as the interviewees. The second overall difference is that Asian hidden champions seem to be more sensitive to the environmental aspects of their businesses, as part of production management or market-related processes. Although an explanation of these observations is beyond the scope of this project, we do suspect that the strongly different cultural backgrounds could help explain these differences. Yet once again we need to emphasize that these are just nuances. The main conclusion is that hidden champions conduct their business in quite similar ways, be they stationed in Europe or Asia.

Successful business men and women have shared lessons that they have learned through years, and often decades, of individual experience. Behind these lessons are many successful undertakings, but even more erroneous moves. In the beginning, there is usually the process of trial and error. Yet, after a while, the right path starts to emerge. This means that lessons have been learned. In fact, as one of the managers pointed out during the interview, one learns much more from mistakes than from success. And in this chapter managers revealed to us the path that they followed to become the world's finest!

References

Berberović D, Činjarević M, Kožo A (2019) Success despite lack of support: lessons learned from hidden champions doing business in fragile business environments. Sarajevo Bus Econ Rev 37:192–204

Cadden T, Millar K, Treacy R, Humphreys P (2020) The mediating influence of organisational cultural practices in successful lean management implementation. Int J Prod Econ 229

Ellram LM, Ueltschy Murfield ML (2019) Supply chain management in industrial marketing- Relationships matter. Ind Market Manag 79:36–45

Foss NJ, Saebi T (2018) Business models and business model innovation: between wicked and paradigmatic problems. Long Range Plann 51:9–21

Gummesson E (2000) Qualitative methods in management research, 2nd edn. Sage, Thousand Oaks

Kowalkowski C, Gebauer H, Kamp B, Parry G (2017) Servitization and deservitization: overview, concepts and definitions. Ind Market Manag 60:4–10

Lexutt E (2020) Different roads to servitization success: a configurational analysis of financial and non-financial service performance. Ind Market Manag 84:105–125

Najafi-Tavani S, Najafi-Tavani Z, Naudé P, Oghazi P, Zeynaloo E (2018) How collaborative innovation networks affect new product performance: product innovation capability, process innovation capability, and absorptive capacity. Ind Market Manag 73:193–205

Patton MQ (2015) Qualitative research & evaluation methods, 4th edn. Sage, Thousand Oaks

Solaimani S, Haghighi A, van der Rhee B (2019) An integrative view on Lean innovation management. J Bus Res 105:109–120

Yin RK (2014) Case study research design and methods, 5th edn. Sage, Thousand Oaks

Hidden Champions: Financing and Regulatory Environment Development Needs—Context Matters

Slavica Singer and Sunčica Oberman Peterka

Hidden champions are characterized by the uniqueness of their products and services, which satisfy users' needs in a unique way, and the uniqueness of their business model, which combines organizational structure, organizational culture, and operations in a unique way. In this chapter, two elements (formal institutions and finance) of an entrepreneurial ecosystem will be discussed using information from the 2019 survey of hidden champions in 22 countries, mostly from Southeast Europe.

In business, everything is unique, from structure to culture, from resources to operations, from products to customers' needs. Uniqueness precludes imitability and provides a kind of protection of intellectual property, such as a developed business model. The development of this uniqueness does not happen in an isolated bubble, but in a complex system of interactions inside of an entrepreneurial ecosystem. This contextual approach is a part of Simon's (1996) original survey of internationalization patterns of small and medium-sized businesses, in which context was identified as a combination of components at the national and sub-national levels. Simon proved that hidden champions are more resilient to bad news than other companies. Immediately after the 2008 global financial crisis, Simon (2009) checked what had happened to the hidden champions of the 1996 survey. The survival rate of those companies was much higher than the average rate in their respective sectors. This means that the context matters, but the vulnerability of a company can be lowered with an innovative business model, difficult to imitate in the short run. In order to develop such uniqueness, a company has to observe what is happening in its entrepreneurial ecosystem, and, if possible, anticipate some changes. At the same

---

S. Singer (✉)
UNESCO Chair in Entrepreneurship Education, J.J. Strossmayer University, Osijek, Croatia
e-mail: slavica.singer@efos.hr

S. Oberman Peterka
J.J. Strossmayer University, Faculty of Economics in Osijek, Osijek, Croatia

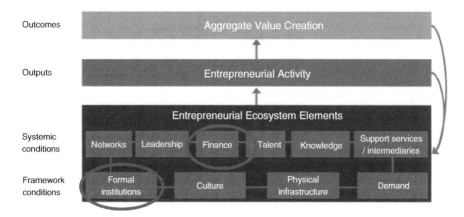

Fig. 1 Key elements, outputs, and outcomes of the entrepreneurial ecosystem. Source: Stam (2015)

time, entrepreneurial ecosystems should be supportive of such innovative initiatives. In other words, the designers of an entrepreneurial ecosystem have to be innovative as well.

Stam and Spigel (2016) define an entrepreneurial ecosystem as a *set* of *interdependent* actors and factors coordinated in such a way that they enable *productive* entrepreneurship within a *particular territory*. The concept is not entirely new. Feld (2012) discussed building an entrepreneurial ecosystem at the sub-national level, around cities, whereas Isenberg (2011) suggested four major characteristics of an entrepreneurship ecosystem. They share some similarity with clusters (Porter 1990), regional and national innovation systems, or the Triple/Quadruple Helix (Etzkowitz and Leydesdorff 1995). At the same time, the concept is not fully developed. Questions such as what components should be included, and at which level an entrepreneurial ecosystem is placed (national vs. sub-national) are still part of an ongoing discussion. Sternberg et al. (2019) developed a new framework to measure entrepreneurial ecosystems at the regional (sub-national) level, using Global Entrepreneurship Monitor data.

Stam (2015) describes the entrepreneurial ecosystem as a dynamic interconnectedness of different elements (framework and systemic conditions) enabling entrepreneurial activity (outputs) which leads to aggregate value creation (outcomes) (Fig. 1).

In this chapter, two elements (formal institutions and finance) of an entrepreneurial ecosystem will be discussed using information from the 2019 survey of hidden champions in 22 countries, mostly from Southeast Europe.

1 On the Regulatory Framework

Formal institutions have a regulatory framework in which companies are functioning. It is considered a part of fundamental framework conditions, including culture, physical infrastructure, and demand. In order to understand the flow of value creation, it is necessary to find out how systemic conditions, in interaction with framework conditions, lead to entrepreneurial activity, which creates aggregate value in the form of competitive products or services. Stam (2015) calls this 'the systemic conditions as the heart of the ecosystem', because all crucial resources are there: human resources, leadership, talent, knowledge, money, networks, and support services. Access to financing includes the availability of different financial instruments in timely manner.

This system approach enables the identification of the weakest link (bottleneck) that degrades the capacity of the whole entrepreneurial ecosystem to support entrepreneurial activities. At the same time, such information is important feedback to be used by creators of specific elements of the entrepreneurial ecosystem. It also reveals that entrepreneurs are not passive actors in designing and building an entrepreneurial ecosystem. It depends on them to be proactive and innovative in developing innovative products and innovative business models, as well as innovative, efficient, and effective entrepreneurial ecosystems.

Based on the collected information from hidden champions included in the 2019 survey, the focus of this analysis is on the regulatory framework and finance. The financing and regulatory context are part of an entrepreneurial ecosystem, which differs from country to country, as well as from region to region at the sub-national level.

The Global Entrepreneurship Monitor (GEM) is the biggest worldwide survey of entrepreneurship.[1] It has developed a composite index of the quality of the entrepreneurial environment at the national level[2] and has been publishing it since 2018. The composite National Entrepreneurship Context Index (NECI) index) is composed of the following components:

1. Access to entrepreneurial finance
2a. Government policy: support and relevance
2b. Government policy: taxes and bureaucracy
3. Government entrepreneurship programmes
4a. Entrepreneurship education at school
4b. Entrepreneurship education post-school
5. Research and development transfers
6. Commercial and professional infrastructure
7a. Ease of entry: market dynamics

---

[1] Global Entrepreneurship Monitor

[2] Since 2020, the portfolio of GEM's entrepreneurship indicators has included an Entrepreneurial Ecosystem Quality Composite Index (ESI), a new diagnostic tool that provides frameworks and data to analyze any sub-national ecosystem (city or region).

Table 1 National Entrepreneurship Context Index and three selected components (score on a 0–10 scale, country rank out of 54), 2019

	NECI		Entrepreneurial finance		Government policy: taxes and bureaucracy		Internal market burden	
	Score	Rank	Score	Rank	Score	Rank	Score	Rank
Belarus	4.24	34	3.24	49	4.35	22	4.28	31
Bulgaria	4.21	37	4.42	31	4.64	17	4.24	32
China	5.89	4	5.80	4	6.16	2	5.23	6
Croatia	3.57	50	4.15	35	2.46	50	3.37	47
Poland	4.24	36	4.94	20	2.88	45	4.07	36
Russia	4.04	41	3.71	42	3.05	43	3.35	49
Slovakia	4.03	42	4.5	28-29	2.71	45	4.38	28
Slovenia	4.49	30	4.49	31	3.43	36	4.65	21
The best-performing country								
Switzerland	6.05	1			6.21	1		
United States of America			6.04	1				
Netherlands							6.07	1

Source: Global Entrepreneurship Monitor 2019/2020, Global Report, 2020 (222–225) https://www.gemconsortium.org/file/open?fileId=50443 , 22.6.2020

7b. Ease of entry: market burdens and regulations
8. Physical infrastructure
9. Social and cultural norms

Not all countries involved in the hidden champion's survey are included in the GEM survey, but the results of the eight countries involved in 2019 are very indicative (Table 1).

Out of these eight Central and Eastern European countries and China, only China is ranked among the top 10. Four (Bulgaria, Russia, Slovakia, and Croatia) are in the last third with Belarus and Poland very close to them. Only Slovenia is close to the middle of the ranking. Scores on the three specific components of the entrepreneurship context (finance, taxes and bureaucracy, and market burden) yield almost the same pattern.

The high rank of China and the ranks of other countries in which the hidden champion's survey was done in 2019 indicate that the quality of the entrepreneurial ecosystem in Central and Eastern Europe needs to improve. Those indications are additionally confirmed by the World Economic Forum's surveys of global competitiveness, evaluating the quality of the different components of the context in which businesses function.

For analyzing the quality of the regulatory framework, three indicators are selected: the burden of government regulation, how effectively governments respond to change, and to what extent governments ensure policy stability (Table 2).

Table 2 Quality of the regulatory framework, 2019—rank out of 141 countries

Country	Burden of government regulation Value 1–7 (7 = best)	Score[a]	Rank	Government responsiveness to change Value 1–7 (7 = best)	Score	Rank	Government ensuring policy stability Value 1–7 (7 = best)	Score	Rank
Albania	4.4	56.5	18	3.6	42.8	79	3.3	39.0	107
Belarus[b]									
Bosnia and Herzegovina	2.1	18.4	137	2.0	17.2	139	2.3	21.0	137
Bulgaria	3.7	45.2	53	3.6	43.5	82	3.5	42.1	97
China	4.4	56.3	19	4.0	49.8	50	4.5	58.2	45
Croatia	1.9	15.8	139	2.2	19.9	136	2.6	27.1	132
Czech Republic	2.7	29.1	121	3.4	40.1	87	3.5	42.3	95
Hungary	3.0	33.0	106	3.5	42.2	82	3.3	38.0	109
Kazakhstan	4.0	49.4	34	4.2	53.0	39	4.5	58.1	46
Kosovo[b]									
Lithuania	3.3	38.0	85	3.3	38.5	94	3.7	45.7	83
Moldova	3.4	40.2	76	3.1	35.2	104	3.0	33.4	116
Mongolia	2.8	30.1	117	2.6	25.9	129	2.9	32.3	121
Montenegro	4.0	50.0	32	4.1	52.1	43	4.4	57.7	47
Poland	2.9	31.4	113	3.3	38.6	93	2.9	31.6	123
Romania	3.0	33.3	102	3.0	33.5	108	2.8	30.5	126
Russia	3.2	37.0	90	3.8	47.4	63	3.7	44.9	88
Serbia	3.1	34.9	95	3.7	44.3	75	3.6	44.2	92
Slovakia	2.4	23.1	135	2.9	31.7	117	3.0	32.6	119
Slovenia	2.6	26.5	126	3.3	38.0	97	3.7	45.6	84
Turkey	3.6	44.1	60	4.2	52.8	41	3.8	46.1	82
Ukraine	3.6	43.9	62	3.3	37.6	98	3.1	34.3	115
The best countries									
Singapore	5.5	74.4	1						
Singapore				6.1	85.2	1			
Switzerland							6.4	89.7	1

Source: Schwab (2019)
[a]The economy's progress score on a 0-100 scale following normalization, where 100 represents the optimal situation or 'frontier'
[b]No data

The distribution of countries across all three indicators (Table 3) show a prevalence of countries in the lowest 25% group, with the lowest rank.

The distribution of countries on Burden of Government Regulation indicates that some countries are successful in simplifying the regulatory framework: those in the first 25%. A good example is Belarus, which is not included in this survey on global

Table 3 Distribution of countries according to their ranks[a]

	Burden of government regulation		Government responsiveness to change		Government ensuring policy stability	
	Number of countries	Countries	Number of countries	Countries	Number of countries	Countries
Highest rank (highest 25%)	4	Albania China Kazakhstan Montenegro	0		0	
Lowest rank (lowest 25%)	8	Bosnia and Herzegovina Croatia Czech Republic Hungary Mongolia Poland Slovakia Slovenia	5	Bosnia and Herzegovina Croatia Mongolia Slovakia	10	Albania Bosnia and Herzegovina Croatia Hungary Moldova Mongolia Poland Romania Slovakia Ukraine

[a]Structure of 20 countries involved in Hidden Champions' survey, as Belarus and Kosovo were not included in the Global Competitiveness Report 2019

competitiveness. The World Bank reported that the regulatory reforms started by Belarus's government moved that country on the Doing Business list from 115th in the 2007 ranking to 37th in 2018.

The fact that no Central and Eastern European country neither Mongolia is in the highest rank group in terms of Government Responsiveness to Change and Government Ensuring Stability is an important message to governments, especially having in mind what the surveyed hidden champions identified as problems with the regulatory framework: slow responsiveness and instability.

1.1 What Hidden Champions Think About the Regulatory Frameworks in Their Countries?

The values of the three indicators of government regulation (burden, timeliness, stability) fully correspond to the opinions expressed by the hidden champions.

All interviewed hidden champions reported at least one example of complicated regulations (burden) and identified a need for tax reliefs (Table 4). They mentioned the regulatory burden as the most serious obstacle to their innovative companies, not only because of complicated and sometimes contradictory regulatory requests, but also because of delayed and slow reactions to changes, and even more because instability makes changes unpredictable and too frequent, without a real purpose.

Table 4 What is wrong with regulatory frameworks in the hidden champions' countries? Positions on the list reflect the frequency of complaints and suggestions

Government bureaucracy
– A stable and friendly regulatory framework is missing – Selective implementation of the legal framework and transparency (Ukraine) – Measures to eliminate monopoly are needed – Strong property rights protection is needed – Complicated administrative procedures to get government financial support – Contradictory legal requirements from different ministries (Moldova—IT park legislation and tax legislation) – Urgent simplification of the regulatory framework is needed (In Lithuania, only a group of five companies can get support for visiting international fairs!) – Difficult administrative requirements to enter the EU markets—customs, visas... – Complicated procedures to employ foreign workers from outside of the EU (visa, work permits) – Labour law recognizes only two professions in the IT sector (In Bosnia and Herzegovina, these are computer technician and IT engineer. This has implications for reward systems) – It is expensive to adjust the regulatory framework to EU requirements (An example from the Czech Republic, Poland, and Kosovo, is the issue of GDPR for companies in the IT and AI business) – There is a need for a faster tendering process – Certification of products is complicated
Legal framework for supporting innovations and collaboration between business and research sector
– Outdated regulation related to patenting
Tax burden
– Need for tax relief (Albania) for exporting above negotiated quotas—higher customs tariffs – Need for predictable tax regulations – Need for tax policies to stimulate research and development within small and medium-sized enterprises – Need for a lower parafiscal burden, especially in the development phase of a venture – Need for tax relief for free economic zones and hi-tech parks
General
– Political instability leads to an unstable regulatory framework – Need for a globally competitive environment

2 On Access to Finance

Access to finance is another component of the entrepreneurial ecosystem, which was specifically tested through interviews with hidden champions. For establishing a broader perspective, the World Economic Forum survey on global competitiveness was used for data on the financing of small and medium-sized enterprises, non-performing loans, and venture capital availability (Table 5).

The distribution of countries across all three indicators (Table 6) again shows a prevalence of Central and Eastern European countries in the lowest 25% group.

All three indicators suggest that access to finance is a more hindering than supporting component of the entrepreneurial ecosystem in many countries. The non-performing loans indicator reveals a huge illiquidity problem, which always

Table 5 Quality of access to finance, 2019—rank out of 141 countries

Country	Financing of SMEs			Non-performing loans (% of gross total loans)			Venture capital availability		
	Value 1–7 (best)	Score[a]	Rank	Value %	Score	Rank	Value 1–7 (best)	Score	Rank
Albania	3.9	47.6	76	13.2	74.3	120	3.0	33.6	81
Belarus[b]									
Bosnia and Herzegovina	3.5	40.9	106	10.0	80.7	108	2.3	22.3	117
Bulgaria	4.1	51.8	50	10.4	79.9	110	3.3	38.9	54
China	4.4	57.2	34	1.7	97.5	26	4.4	57.0	13
Croatia	3.5	41.1	104	11.2	78.4	113	2.6	27.1	106
Czech Republic	4.4	56.5	35	3.7	93.5	65	3.8	46.6	32
Hungary	4.0	50.2	56	4.2	92.6	68	3.5	42.1	47
Kazakhstan	3.7	45.1	87	9.3	82.2	103	2.9	32.0	89
Kosovo[b]									
Lithuania	3.8	46.0	84	3.2	94.6	58	3.3	37.6	63
Moldova	3.6	43.8	93	18.4	63.9	130	2.5	24.6	116
Mongolia	2.9	32.2	124	8.5	83.8	98	2.2	19.6	124
Montenegro	4.2	53.7	43	7.3	86.3	89	3.7	45.0	39
Poland	3.9	48.5	69	3.9	93.0	66	2.9	31.7	90
Romania	3.7	44.3	89	6.4	88.1	82	2.6	27.5	104
Russia	3.3	38.1	118	10.0	80.8	107	2.8	29.3	94
Serbia	3.9	49.1	65	9.8	81.2	105	3.2	35.9	69
Slovakia	4.2	52.9	45	3.7	93.5	64	3.6	43.6	42
Slovenia	4.2	54.0	42	3.2	94.5	59	3.3	37.9	60
Turkey	4.0	49.6	63	2.8	95.3	51	2.9	32.4	88
Ukraine	3.4	39.2	112	54.5	0.0	139	3.0	33.7	80
The best countries									
Finland	5.5	74.9	1						
Taiwan, China				0.3	100	1			
United States							5.2	70.6	1

Source: Schwab (2019)
[a]The economy's progress score on a 0–100 scale following normalization, where 100 represents the optimal situation or frontier
[b]No data

slows down or even depresses business activities. Again, this is fully consistent with the opinions of the hidden champions in these countries.

Table 6 Distribution of countries, according to the ranks[a]

	Financing of SMEs		Non-performing loans (% of gross total loans)		Venture capital availability	
	Number of countries	Countries	Number of countries	Countries	Number of countries	Countries
Highest rank (highest 25%)	2	China Czech Republic	1	China	2	China Czech Republic
Lowest rank (lowest 25%)	5	Bosnia and Herzegovina Croatia Mongolia Russia Ukraine	8	Albania Bosnia and Herzegovina Bulgaria Croatia Moldova Russia Serbia Ukraine	4	Bosnia and Herzegovina Croatia Moldova Mongolia

[a]Structure of 20 countries involved in Hidden Champions' survey, as Belarus and Kosovo were not included in the Global Competitiveness Report 2019

Table 7 What is wrong with access to finance in the hidden champions' countries? Positions on the list reflect the frequency of complaints or suggestions

Banks
– Overdependence on bank loans – Lengthy procedures for getting a loan – High interest rates – High costs of financing – Limited capacity of local banks (Kosovo)
Government support
– Need for government guarantees – Need for government funds – Need for special financial support for projects in selected industries (e.g., rural projects, social entrepreneurship) – Need for special financial support for ventures of young persons – Subsidized interest rates for banking loans would be helpful – Need for financial support for innovations, research and development, and export – An investment bank is needed (Kosovo)
Type of financial sources
– Overdependence on banking loans (Moldova) – Limited availability of venture capital – Lack of sufficient initial public offerings (Bulgaria, China) – Patient capital is missing – Lack of long-term financial arrangements
Low financial literacy
– Financial institutions need to invest in the clients' financial literacy (Bulgaria)
Regulatory interventions
– Legal framework for factoring, overdrafts…is needed
General
– Own funding is needed to avoid expensive loans. This restricts growth

2.1 What Do Hidden Champions Think About Access to Finance?

The opinions of the hidden champions in the 2019 survey are in line with the findings of the Global Competitiveness Report (Table 7).

3 Regulatory Framework and Access to Finance: The OECD's Perspective

Small and medium-sized enterprises and entrepreneurship are high on the policy agenda globally because they are essential drivers of economic and social well-being. They are the biggest employer, accounting for 66% of employment, and crucial value-adding contributors. Innovative ventures are a core driver of economic growth, and hidden champions are part of it.

The OECD monitors the changes in the vitality of small and medium-sized enterprises and entrepreneurship and has built a database related to recent and emerging trends, to be used in developing evidence-based policies at the country level. The main dimensions observed are institutional and regulatory framework, market conditions, infrastructure, and access to finance, access to skills, and access to innovation assets.

Therefore, the OECD's evaluation of the regulatory framework and access to finance will be used to verify the hidden champions' statements on those two components of the entrepreneurship ecosystem. This verification can respond to potential critiques of the subjectivity of these statements.

3.1 OECD (2019) on Regulatory Framework and Government

P. 93: 'Regulatory inefficiencies, complexities and high compliance costs are particularly detrimental to new firms and small and medium-sized enterprises, which are affected disproportionately by regulatory burdens or face greater constraints than large firms in seeking legal redress'. It was found out that there is 'cross-country progress in reducing regulatory barriers on entrepreneurship and administrative burdens on start-ups and small and medium-sized enterprises, such as through smart regulation, reforms in taxation and the strengthening of e-government functions, hinging on a comprehensive infrastructure for information exchange across government bodies, individuals, and businesses. It also highlights that the pace of structural reforms has slowed down in recent years'. Recent policy initiatives are aiming to implement a user-centric approach to regulation and policymaking, enhancing transparency and efficiency in public services and legal frameworks.

P. 94: 'In the majority of OECD countries, formal coordination mechanisms between levels of government exist, or the national government is required to consult sub-national governments prior to issuance of regulations that concern them'. 'Governments are increasingly institutionalizing the open government principles of transparency, accountability and participation'.

P. 100: 'As part of their smart regulation strategies, governments also increasingly consider flexible regulatory options that can reduce costs for small businesses'.

The hidden champions raised the same issues, or suggested the same solutions (Table 4).

3.2 OECD (2019: 183) on Access to Finance

'Access to finance, in the form and quantity needed at each stage of their life cycle, is critical for small and medium-sized enterprise creation and scale-up. Yet, small and medium-sized enterprises face difficulties in identifying and attracting appropriate sources of finance. Barriers such as information asymmetries, high transaction costs, and low levels of financial acumen of business owners explain why small businesses and entrepreneurs often face more difficulties in accessing finance than large enterprises'. While bank finance is still dominant, alternative finance instruments are emerging, especially through digitalization (crowdfunding, blockchain). More dynamic but concentrated venture capital markets and a rise in the uptake of asset-based funding solutions are playing stronger roles. This is reflected 'in the major policy trends to support small and medium-sized enterprise access to finance, e.g., a steady expansion of credit guarantees, new approaches to VC support, combining financial support with training and assistance and initiatives to reap the opportunities of Fintech and platforms'.

The hidden champions raised the same issues or suggested the same solutions (Table 7).

In its broader analysis of small and medium-sized enterprises and entrepreneurship, the OECD (2019) confirms this diagnosis of the institutional and regulatory framework as well as of access to finance for several countries which are also included in the hidden champion survey: Czech Republic, Hungary, Lithuania, Poland, Slovakia, Slovenia, and Turkey. See Annex.

4 Conclusion and Recommendations

Hidden champions are hidden assets of any country's economy and an innovative driving force. Their impact can be enforced by a well-designed entrepreneurship ecosystem in which all framework and systemic conditions are designed to fit each other, not to produce frictions or gaps. The 2019 hidden champions survey revealed frictions and gaps, which are reducing the capacity of the entrepreneurship ecosystem.

In order to have a vibrant and sustainable entrepreneurship ecosystem, it is necessary to check annual international surveys on entrepreneurship, competitiveness, ease of doing business, and transparency, identify one's country's patterns and trends and compare one's country with the best. This information should be used in the design and implementation of policies, and in interventions in bottlenecks (frictions or gaps) in order to rebuild the vitality of the entrepreneurship ecosystem. Therefore, it is important for governments, financial and educational institutions, and consultants to listen to the experiences of the hidden champions and do their best to support and innovate the entrepreneurial ecosystems. Listening to hidden champions is an additional diagnostic tool for policy makers.

This smart approach to intervention in strategies, policies, and the structural design of the entrepreneurship ecosystem will stimulate the initiatives of the existing hidden champions and nurture future ones.

Annex

OECD (2019) analysis of institutional and regulatory framework, and access to finance, for Czech Republic, Hungary, Lithuania, Poland, Slovakia, Slovenia, and Turkey.

A.1 Czech Republic OECD (2019: 292)

Institutional and Regulatory Framework 'Series of measures have been introduced since 2008 to reduce the administrative burden on SMEs. However, procedures remain complex, and the cost of enforcing contracts is one of the highest in the EU'.

Access to Finance 'The financing environment for Czech SMEs has continued to improve since the crisis. Loan rejections fell from 17.6% in 2013 to 3.2% in 2016, and SME interest rates have more than halved since 2008. However, equity funding and venture capital (VC) investments remain underdeveloped. In 2017, the first programmes supporting VC were introduced in co-operation with the European Investment Fund (EIF), along with the EXPANSION programme, which provides SMEs with guarantees and preferential loans. In 2018, the Czech-Moravian Guarantee and Development Bank launched VADIUM, which gives small entrepreneurs up to CZK 50 million guarantee for bids in public tenders'.

A.2 Hungary, OECD (2019: 313)

Institutional and Regulatory Framework 'The complexity of the Hungarian institutional and regulatory environment affects SMEs and has been a major target for reform. In addition, Hungary ranks poorly for digital public services. The Public Administration and Public Service Development Strategy (2014–20) aims to reform administrative procedures. Initiatives include the expansion of online cash registers connected to tax authorities for services and business activities mainly provided by SMEs. The government is planning to create an Enterprise Web Portal as a single entry point to all public support programmes to SMEs. In 2018, a digital post service for businesses was introduced to facilitate the dialog between government and businesses'.

Access to Finance 'Since the 2008 recession, the volume of SME loans dropped in Hungary from the peak of 24.3% of GDP (2009) to 19.5% (2016). Data on new SME lending point to strong volatility and weakened confidence in the credit market. About two-thirds of new SME loans are short-term which is high by international standards. The Central Bank has played a pivotal role in supporting SME access to finance, notably through the Funding for Growth Scheme (FGS, 2013–17) and the Market-based Lending Scheme (2016–19). The venture capital market is also improving, notably with the JEREMIE programme since 2008 and several new funds and the recapitalization of the Széchenyi Capital Fund since 2017'.

A.3 Lithuania, OECD (2019: 340)

Institutional and Regulatory Framework 'Since its independence in 1990, Lithuania has promoted market-friendly reforms; yet, stringent labour market regulations, complex licensing norms, and lengthy insolvency procedures weigh on business activity and contribute to informality. Reforms in licensing procedures are underway which should reduce the administrative burdens for firms.'

Access to Finance 'New business lending in Lithuania declined sharply after the crisis and recovered only slowly as of 2014, despite interest rates at historic lows. In 2018, more than a half of SMEs surveyed by the Bank of Lithuania stated that lending to them is fully or partially limited. To address these limitations, INVEGA, a state-established enterprise, provides individual and portfolio guarantees. Specific instruments, such as the EU Entrepreneurship Promotion Fund (2014–20), the Open Credit Fund 2 and Risk Shared Loans offer loans with favorable interest rates to new firms or SMEs that are developing a new business. To foster alternative financing sources, the government adopted a law on crowd-funding in 2016, and established 3 new venture capital instruments in 2017 and 5 new venture capital instruments in 2018'.

A.4 Poland, OECD (2019: 359)

Institutional and Regulatory Framework 'The government is streamlining business regulations. Key measures include an increase in the annual income threshold for the status of small taxpayer, from EUR 1.2 million to EUR 2 million. Micro firms with a turnover below 50% of the minimum wage will no longer be required to register, and start-ups might be exempted from social contributions in the first six months and can benefit from lower social contributions for the following two years. Ministries will be required to publish simple explanations of administrative rules and tax laws'.

Access to Finance 'SMEs' access to finance has improved in Poland in recent years, with more accommodative conditions. In 2017, the share of Polish SMEs citing access to finance as their most important concern stood at 7%, in line with the EU average. As in other OECD economies, government loan guarantees are the most common policy tool to facilitate SMEs' access to finance, amounting to about 0.8% of GDP in 2016. Poland has seen a sharp increase in available venture capital funding, feeding a nascent start-up scene'.

A.5 Slovakia, OECD (2019: 366)

Institutional and Regulatory Framework 'Burden on firms remain due to administrative requirements and the complexity of rules. In 2016, the government introduced the 'Act on the Promotion of Small and Medium Enterprises' which includes specifications on SME coverage in regulatory impact assessment. Furthermore, since the beginning of 2017, the 'simplified joint stock company', with minimum share capital of EUR 1 is particularly well suited for venture capital and private equity investments as it enables to issue various classes of shares and agree beforehand on the exit from the company'.

Access to Finance 'Total SME lending has been on an upward trend since 2012 and credit conditions for SMEs have been gradually improving. Government policies supported this trend by providing loans and guarantees for SMEs through specialised state banks. Other financing instruments targeted at SMEs are being backed by the EU structural and investment funds (ESIF). The closure of the funding support from JEREMIE was a major cause of the reduction by 83% of venture and growth capital in 2017, as SMEs being funded under the 2014–2020 programme have not yet received support'.

A.6 Slovenia, OECD (2019: 370)

Institutional and Regulatory Framework The costs associated with business start-up in Slovenia are among the lowest in the OECD area. The national online business portal e-VEM is the first level of the SPOT system, a system of one-stop shops on four levels, designed together by the Ministry of economic development and technology, and the public agency SPIRIT Slovenia. The second level is SPOT Information Points, the third level are 12 SPOT Advice Points and the national (fourth) level is SPOT Global (for investors and investments). Besides the SPOT system, the services of Institutions of innovative environment (technology parks, incubators, etc.) are being supported. Simplifications were also introduced in the tax system for the self-employed, with the creation in 2016 of pre-filled social-security contributions accounts in electronic format. At the same time, the Ministry of Economic Development monitors the implementation of mandatory SME tests in all new laws since 2016. The Action Plan Slovenia—the land of innovative start-ups (2018) highlights 36 obstacles to start-ups and measures for their elimination, of which only 20 are being implemented due to intragovernmental coordination requirements.'

Access to Finance 'SME lending has halved over 2011-16 while interest rates have declined. In 2017, a EUR 253 million Fund of Funds was created with EC Cohesion Funds to support SMEs, R&D and innovation, energy efficiency and urban development. First funds were allocated in 2018. The Slovene Enterprise Fund also supports MSMEs through multiple instruments (grants, microloans, seed capital, guarantees, etc.) and 'smart money' by combining instruments, especially seed capital and convertible loans, with mentoring, coaching and training. The SID bank implements, besides a Fund of Funds, different loan funds for SMEs, investments, internationalization, tourism and wood processing. The Patient loans (with lower interest rate and longer grace period) are still active. Public loan guarantees varied widely over recent years, amounting to EUR 520 million in 2016—up from 0 in 2015 but only half the 2013 level. In 2016, the government opened credit lines with long grace periods aimed at promising but over-indebted SMEs'.

A.7 Turkey, OECD (2019: 383)

Institutional and Regulatory Framework 'Improving the institutional and regulatory framework has been a key area of reform in Turkey, where administrative burdens are high relative to OECD levels. The review and simplification of legislations are part of the SME Strategy and are undertaken through various actions by the Prime Minister's Office. The Reduction of Bureaucracy and Simplification of Legislation Initiative (BAMS) was launched in 2014 followed by a number of legislative amendments, changes in application processes, new online services and digitalised documents. The introduction of paperless transactions as part of the

E-Government Strategy and Action Plan 2016–19 is also expected to streamline bureaucratic procedures for businesses and citizens'.

Access to Finance 'SMEs lending in Turkey grew steadily over 2007–17, also supported by a variety of government's programs. KOSGEB, the main body for executing SME policies in Turkey, runs a number of credit interest support programmes. In 2016, a bill was passed on movable collateral in commercial transactions, which allows SMEs' access to finance against receivables, machinery, inventory and stock. This reform led to the creation of security rights for an estimated EUR 9.3 billion. KOSGEB also introduced the SME Technological Product Investment Support and the Strategic Product Support Programmes in 2017 with a view to stimulating alternative sources of finance. The Turkish Growth and Innovation Fund, established in 2016, is a fund-of-funds targeting early stage and start-up businesses, technology transfer accelerators and investments involving business angels'.

References

Etzkowitz H, Leydesdorff L (1995) The triple helix—university-industry-government relations: a laboratory for knowledge based economic development. Rochester, NY. SSRN 2480085

Feld B (2012) Startup communities: building an entrepreneurial ecosystem in your city. Wiley, New York

Isenberg DJ (2011) Introducing the entrepreneurship ecosystem: four defining characteristics. Forbes http://www.forbes.com/sites/danisenberg/2011/05/25/introducing-the-entrepreneurshipecosystem-four-defining-characteristics/

OECD (2019) OECD SME and entrepreneurship outlook 2019. OECD, Paris. https://doi.org/10.1787/34907e9c-en

Porter ME (1990) The competitive advantage of nations. MacMillan, London

Schwab K (ed) (2019) The global competitiveness report 2019. World Economic Forum, 2019. http://www3.weforum.org/docs/WEF_TheGlobalCompetitivenessReport2019.pdf, 22.6.2020

Simon H (1996) Hidden champions: lessons from 500 of the world's best unknown companies. Harvard Business School Press, Boston, MA

Simon H (2009) Hidden champions of the 21st century: Success strategies of unknown (world market leaders). Springer, London

Stam E (2015) Entrepreneurial ecosystems and regional policy: a sympathetic critique. Eur Plann Stud 23(9):1759–1769. https://doi.org/10.1080/09654313.2015.1061484

Stam E, Spigel B (2016) Entrepreneurial ecosystems. In: Blackburn R, De Clercq D, Heinonen J, Wang Z (eds) Handbook for entrepreneurship and small business. SAGE, London

Sternberg R, Bloh J, Coduras A (2019) A new framework to measure entrepreneurial ecosystems at the regional level. Zeitschrift für Wirtschaftsgeographie 63. https://doi.org/10.1515/zfw-2018-0014

Hidden Champions: Management and Leadership Development Needs

Amra Kožo and Alenka Braček Lalić

1 Introduction

The main aim of this chapter is to introduce management and leadership development needs identified by the research conducted among Hidden Champions (HC) companies in Central Europe and South-Eastern Europe (CESEE) and the Asian market. Today's business environment is dynamic, turbulent, and hyper-competitive. It is characterized by rapid changes, and often, business literature describes it with the trendy managerial acronym VUCA (Bennett and Lemoine 2014). As a term, VUCA is first used in 1987 (Bennis and Nanus 1985) to reflect the volatility, uncertainty, complexity, and ambiguity of general conditions. By the time it got a deeper meaning, and each element of the VUCA acronym provide insights into the strategic movement and behavior of an organization.

Moreover, some of the observed hidden champions play in a more specific environment, so-called fragile business environment (FBE). The fragility of business environments describes difficult, post-conflict, transitional, or post-transitional contexts with high economic risks. In these environments, burdens for companies come from not wholly defined economic policies and limited supports of financial sectors due to the high risk of failure (Geda 2011; Berberović et al. 2019). However, some studies show that despite the lack of support (Berberović et al. 2019); or even in times of recession or financial turmoil (Balas Rant and Korenjak Černje (2017); and in mature and untransformed business environments (Muñoz et al. 2017) hidden champions do business successfully. What seems to be crucial for success is related to the way companies view the environmental conditions that influence their

---

A. Kožo (✉)
School of Economics and Business, University of Sarajevo, Sarajevo, Bosnia and Herzegovina
e-mail: amra.kozo@efsa.unsa.ba

A. Braček Lalić
Postgraduate Studies, IEDC-Bled School of Management, Bled, Slovenia

© Springer Nature Switzerland AG 2021
A. Braček Lalić, D. Purg (eds.), *Hidden Champions in Dynamically Changing Societies*, https://doi.org/10.1007/978-3-030-65451-1_6

business in terms of their anticipation and intervention. In addition to these factors that are certainly part of the environment, nowadays, it is critical to mention the impact of so-called Wild Cards factors, i.e., those factors that represent incidents with a low probability of occurrence but with an enormous consequence if they occur (e.g., pandemics).

Like many other countries around the globe, companies from CESEE and Asia, face a lot of challenges in dynamically changing societies. Most of these challenges are related, but not limited to the political and economic uncertainty, the transformed nature of the business, and increased competition as a result of globalization, changes in the workforce, and customer demands. To appropriately tackle the aforementioned issues, companies recognize particular developmental needs that should be met efficiently and effectively.

2 Rethinking Management and Leadership Development Needs

In a turbulent time, managers and leaders have a central role in ensuring business with continuity, thus providing competitive advantages for their companies. Many take as common sense that the economic and social wellbeing of society is primarily dependent on the success of organizations of all kinds. Organizational prosperity, in turn, depends on appropriate management and leadership capabilities that are enhanced by their development (Burgoyne et al. 2004).

Horney et al. (2010) argue that modern organizations should be agile, able to respond quickly to change, and keen to learn. The development of technology has made knowledge more swiftly and widely available. Transfer of learning is notably relevant for knowledge-intensive organizations where people and processes face the daily changes of a briskly changing business environments (Bennett and Lemoine 2014).

Business literature recognizes a distinction between management development, leader development, and leadership development. According to Day (2001), management development refers to prescribed learning programs. Leader development employs individualized methods with less defined learning outcomes (e.g., coaching and personal development plans), while leadership development involves collective learning activities (e.g., specific assignments, learning sets, etc.). Management and leadership development (MLD) activities might be view through the framework provided by Gold et al. (2003) where MLD activities within a company are observed through two dimensions - individual or collective and prescribed or emergent. In this context, management and leadership development is observed as a way of learning whose outcomes might be emergent, partly shaped, and delineated by the learning process itself. Furthermore, management and leadership development should be considered as a collective activity that includes the interaction of different groups of learners, combines prescriptive and emergent perspectives, and makes links (both qualitative and quantitative) between learners, HR, other stakeholders, and organizational outcomes (McGurk 2010).

Previous studies on HC have shown that developmental needs are mostly related to changes in organizational culture and mindset, strategic thinking, agility, soft skills (e.g., communication, negotiation), customer services, leadership, etc. (Purg et al. 2018). The last conducted research among CESEE and Asian countries shows a similar level regarding developmental needs as previous studies. Identified hidden champions from 22 countries look for better ties with educational systems, improved human resource management (HRM) practices, investments in R&D and new market entries, digital marketing, innovation, soft skills, etc. While some of the identified MLD needs are common for all HCs, others are related to regions or industries, even a particular country. The first coming part brings cross-cultural analysis for all identified MLD needs among countries and HCs. The second part depicts comparisons between regions and industries, where possible.

3 Cross-Country Analysis of Management and Leadership Development Needs

3.1 What Are the MLD Needs of HCs?

This research was conducted by 66 researchers from 22 countries, who examined 304 companies and identified 105 HCs among them. The study results denote that most of the recognized development needs are related to education and improved cooperation with educational institutions, all aspects of human resource management with a special focus on talent management. Educational and broad aspects of human resource development needs are among HCs from all countries. Apart from them, there is a wide range of development needs covering marketing and digital marketing, innovation processes, investments in research and development (R&D), entrance to a new market, infrastructure development, regulations regarding specific issues in particular countries. HCs also highlight strategic thinking, the role of vision, mission, and organizational values in shaping organizational culture. Organizational cultures are open to innovation, creativity, learning, and they celebrate agile leaders and employees. MLD needs common for most of the identified HCS are in detail described below.

– *Education and Cooperation with Educational Institutions.* Closer ties and collaboration with educational institutions are identified among many of the observed HCs. However, common for everyone is that this need is recognized as a foundation for all future improvement. HCs are looking for modernized and up-to-date educational programs, adjusted to the market requirements. Many HCs face problems when they need particular occupational profiles of workers. That is one of the reasons why HCs mostly do in-house training. The second reason for in-house educational programs is related to the cost of some highly specialized programs. As Russian HCs claim:

Formal education in business schools, such as MBA or executive programs, the company finds expensive.

However, HCs believe that educational institutions might do great work in this field and provide a workforce that will be well prepared for work requirements. Some of the companies ask from educational institutions to work on the development of competence and experience in international business. This is confirmed with one of the statements from Belarusian HC:

Export-oriented Belarusian companies are hindered in their development by the lack of employees and consultants with competence and experience in international business. In this regard, the state and educational organizations should promote the international exchange of students and professionals.

Determined to establish good relations with educational institutions and enhance students' practical experience, some of the HCs started working with universities and provide internships for students. HCs believe that educational institutions should create programs, curriculums, and courses that will prepare students to work in the era of the digital economy. The HCs expectations are connected with the belief that educational institutions should provide knowledge, skills, and competencies that are not one-size-fit-all oriented but are relevant for medium-sized businesses as well.

– *Human Resource Management.* Most of the identified and reported needs come from the field of HRM. HRM refers to the design and application of the formal systems in an organization that provides effective and efficient use of talents to accomplish organizational goals. Managers need to find the right people, place them on the position where there is the best fit between person and job and provide all activities related to the development of the talent (Daft and Marcic 2015). Core HRM tasks comprehend actions summed up at three main areas: attracting, developing, and maintaining talented people.

Companies find it challenging to select reliable and motivated experts (especially in times of low unemployment) who are flexible and have no fear of managing change. Some of the HCs that decided to expand their business on international markets are in lack of knowledgable, well-experienced workers with both experience from the sector and skills related to the internationalization of business. Thus, as one of the Bulgarian HC state:

...Now the company is in its international expansion and needs a lot of new people. Finding the most appropriate employees and training them is currently our biggest challenge.

Investments in talents should be considered seriously and observed as a part of the whole organizational picture. Management needs to find methods to engage employees in their tasks since, without their dedication and cooperation, success is impossible. Some evidence suggests that companies are strongly focused on human resource management. Moreover, the top management of the companies is convinced that they should provide immense attention to the development of the employees, and from them to choose and create future managers, especially for middle management levels. Companies from the information technology (IT) sector claims that their management and leadership needs are industry-specific and hardly based on the trends in this sector. In this area, some of the HCs claim to have difficulties in finding a particular IT specialist on the market, so they rely on a learning-by-doing approach within the company. Speaking about professional knowledge, they depend on the industry HCs belong to. However, study results indicate that HCs need to provide training and education on project management, customer relationship management, lean management, and global human resource management. Besides professional knowledge and skills, many interviewees mentioned a lack of soft skills, such as communication with customers, negotiation, collaboration, agility, global mindset, sense for employees of new generations, and intercultural business communication.

Investment in knowledge and education is recommended for both employees and their leaders. Continuous learning brings synergy to the organization and helps connect various essential parts. The story of HC from China shows that leaders keen to learn will create companies ready to succeed:

> ...Only practical experience is far from enough... In 1998 he (leader of the HC) chose a part-time program at Zhejing University for five years. He maintained the habit of studying for at least four hours every day to absorb the latest knowledge and information.

One of the challenges of HCs is related to their size, especially if a company belongs to family businesses. Since HC companies are small and medium enterprises (SME), by the time they face problems with succession. Thus, companies are putting a lot of effort into training members of top and middle management team. As a result, companies expect to avoid hidden problems regarding succession and provide ground for continuous growth in the long term. Lifelong learning should be a lifestyle for every employee, no matter the age, position, or industry.

- *Marketing and Digital Marketing.* Marketing techniques have changed, and there is a need to shift more significant marketing activities in the digital world. An active presence on social networks (e.g., Facebook, Instagram) is mandatory for almost all organizations. Additionally, HCs claim that the sales management skills of personnel are of high importance to present products to customers and stakeholders. However, nowadays, companies need employees with interdisciplinary knowledge, meaning that sales and marketing personnel should have functional expertise on products (characteristics, performances, etc.), which means that their educational background might come from technology and engineering. This implies that companies need a reliable marketing and sales team to inform and educate the market about product performances and terms of usage. As one of the Bulgarian HCs noted: "Marketing is critical for organizational success."
- *Innovation and Research and Development (R&D).* Doing business in the time of the Fourth Industrial Revolution means facing different challenges compared with those just a few decades ago. Moreover, changes caused by environmental

factors on a daily level bring new questions in front of many companies. To stay competitive, companies need to nurture an innovative organizational culture that will be carried by creative and highly skilled employees. Many HCS believe that future MLD needs mostly refer to the knowledge they need to obtain to become leaders in the implementation of new technologies in their products. Also, HCs strive to build innovative and knowledge-driven globally recognizable brands. Companies do their best to keep pace with first movers, and they do invest in R&D and building of innovative capabilities. Since this requires extensive investments, companies are besides their sources, also looking for additional funding from different EU sources. Above all, innovative activities ask for intensive learning and upgrading of knowledge among workers.

All previously identified MLD needs are mutually connected. Tailor-made educational programs that fulfill the requirements of companies create a skilled workforce that will deliver to companies professional knowledge and skills as well as workers with soft skills. Open-minded and prone to change employees will generate new ideas that might result in some new form of innovation.

Cooperation with educational institutions, HRM, digital marketing, and innovations are four identified groups of MLD needs that share the same pattern of understandings and application among almost all HCs and observed countries. However, there are other MLD requires that are not emphasized as the previous four, but are also of utmost importance for doing business successfully. Mostly, these MLD needs are predominantly related to some specific region or industry; thus, we will observe them in the subsequent section.

3.2 Comparison of Specific Needs Related to Industries and/or Regions

Mostly HCs come from the IT industry, and they carry specific challenges. Their management and development needs are industry-specific. In some countries, one of the major challenges is the deficit of particular IT specialists. HCs from the IT industry are in a strong need for narrowly specialized and experienced IT experts. Since HCs sometimes cannot find this type of professionals in the local labor market, HCs apply two approaches: (1) they do in-house training, or (2) they try to attract specialists from abroad. However, when taking the second approach, some of the HCs face barriers related to local laws and regulations. More precisely, this is the case in Bosnia and Herzegovina, where procedures related to obtaining the work permit for foreigners is often time consuming. Distance work would be an excellent solution, however, yet it is not defined by policy and lawmakers. More evidence from the IT sector discover soft skills needs, i.e., communication, teamwork, participation in decision making, presentation skills, and similar.

Bosnia and Herzegovina is not the only country with a lack of narrow profiles of particular expertise. According to the study results, engineering is a deficient vocation in Serbia. Study results show that companies face challenges with attracting skilled and talented young people and also, it is not so easy for companies to retain talents since many talented young employees get more attractive opportunities from abroad. The case of HC from Montenegro once more confirms that it is not an easy job for companies to find well-qualified and skillful employees. Precisely, in this case, it is not only hard to find employees for higher organizational positions but also blue-collar jobs. In Albania, one of the HC experience shows that it is not easy to find experts for two reasons. First, HC operates in an area far from big cities, and specialists are reluctant to relocate for a job. The second reason is related to already a well-elaborated general issue with HEI (lack of specialized courses for particular niche industries). Besides Balkan countries, some of the Slovakian HCs are in urgent need of skilled employees with technical knowledge. However, they hope that the government might support more practice-oriented education and make a better balance between the labor market and the need for companies.

In particular countries, HCs development needs are related to access to credits funds under favorable terms. Funds are usually planned for the maintenance of necessary infrastructure and investments in innovation, R&D, and entrance to new markets. Also, HCs need support in terms of open innovation, digital transformation, occupational health, safety, sustainable development, and environmental issues.

Yet, knowledge and skills identified within this research are in line with knowledge and skills predicted for the digital era from World Economic Forum (WEF) and The Organisation for Economic Co-operation and Development (OECD). World Economic Forum (2016) identified ten top skills to thrive in the IV Industrial revolution, as follows: complex problem solving, critical thinking, creativity, people management, coordinating with others, emotional intelligence, judgment and decision making, service orientation, negotiation, and cognitive flexibility. In addition, OECD provides indicators of skills involved in the performance of tasks (task-based skills) where one can again recognize skills identified with this research: ICT skills, readiness to learn, managing and communication, self-organization, accountancy and selling, and advanced numeracy (Grundke et al. 2017).

4 Recommendations and Conclusions

This study brings together insights about HC companies from CESEE and some Asian countries. Leaders and managers of these companies are aware of current trends, those coming from the global market, and influencing their business, as well as trends and requirements from regional and local markets. HCs adopt and preach ideas about necessary collaboration with higher education institutions (HEI). Moreover, they are aware that in today's hyper-competitive environment, human potential and innovations are crucial elements for creating and sustaining competitive advantages. Companies believe that a new era of marketing has come. Whenever one needs to do marketing for any form of products or services, one cannot do it without the involvement of digital channels (e.g., social media, web applications, search engines, websites, mobile applications, etc.) and electronic devices. Bearing these ideas in mind, this chapter intends to provide several recommendations for stakeholders and further development of HCs themselves.

- In order to "win-win," both higher education institutions (HEI) and HCs should develop ideas and suggest concrete steps for future collaboration. In general, HEI might revise curriculums and provide more educational programs oriented towards the new digital era. Besides, more values would be added if HEI could organize more practice-oriented hours from disciplines they teach. Modern business looks for highly specialized programs, lifelong learning programs, and new knowledge and skills needed for the digital age. Also, HEI should offer interdisciplinary programs (e.g., arts and business, biosciences and business, IT and business, etc.) and encourage students to gain international experience (study visits, paid internships abroad, etc.).
- Provide partnership between policymakers, HEI, and companies with the aim to stop brain drain in some countries from CESEE region. Experts from a particular field like IT and engineering are more attracted to work abroad.
- HRM programs should be improved and oriented to talent development. Therefore, companies can provide both in-house and external training programs for the development of professional knowledge and soft skills.
- Digital marketing is a new marketing. Its appliance may provide many benefits for companies and the environment.
- Create strategic bonds between policymakers, development agencies, HEI, and companies with the aim to induce funds for innovation and R&D.

This study indicates that one of the probably most essential characteristics of HCs is their propensity to learn and grow. They respect different needs among different generations, encourage talent development, fulfill the needs of customers and other stakeholders. HCs believe that those who learn today are leaders of the future.

References

Balas Rant M, Korenjak Černje S (2017) Becoming a hidden champion: from selective use of customer intimacy and product leadership to business attractiveness. South East Eur J Econ Bus 12(1):89–103

Bennett N, Lemoine GJ (2014) What VUCA really means for you. Harv Bus Rev, January – February 2014 Issue. Available at https://hbr.org/2014/01/what-vuca-really-means-for-you. Last accessed May and June 2020

Bennis W, Nanus B (1985) Leaders: strategies for taking charge. Harper & Row, New York

Berberović D, Činjarević M, Kožo A (2019) Success despite lack of support: lessons learned from hidden champions doing business in fragile business environments. Sarajevo Bus Econ Rev 37/2019

Burgoyne J, Hirsh W, Williams S (2004) The development of management and leadership capability and its contribution to performance: the evidence, the prospects and the research need. Lancaster Universit. ISBN 1 84478 286 7

Daft R, Marcic D (2015) Understanding management. Cengage Learning

Day D (2001) Leadership development: a review in context. Leaders Q 11(4):581–613

Geda A (2011) Capacity building in fragile and post-conflict states in Africa. World J Entrepren Manag Sustain Dev 7(2/3/4):217–266

Gold J, Rodgers H, Frearson M, Holden R (2003) Leadership development: a new typology. Working paper. Leeds Business School and Learning and Skills Research Centre, Leeds

Grundke R et al (2017) Skills and global value chains: A characterisation. https://doi.org/10.1787/cdb5de9b-en, based on OECD (2012) and OECD (2015), Survey of adult skills (PIAAC), www.oecd.org/skills/piaac/publicdataandanalysis

Horney N, Pasmore B, O'Shea T (2010) Leadership agility: A business imperative for a VUCA world. People Strat 33:4

McGurk P (2010) Outcomes of management and leadership development. J Manag Dev 29(5):457–470. https://doi.org/10.1108/02621711011039222

Muñoz EP, Ripoll-i-Alcon J, Berlanga Silvente V (2017) Hidden champions in Spain: the path to successful business decisions. Revista de Métodos Cuantitativos para la Economía y la Empresa 24:190–208

Purg D, Braček Lalić A, Pope JA (eds) (2018) Business and society making management education relevant for the 21st century. Springer, Cham

World Economic Forum (2016) Skills you need to thrive in the fourth industrial revolution. https://www.weforum.org/agenda/2016/01/the-10-skills-you-need-to-thrive-in-the-fourth-industrial-revolution. Last access June 2020

Hidden Champions of Albania

Vasilika Kume, Elona Garo, and Anisa Kume

Overview
Official name: Republic of Albania
Type of government: Parliamentary democratic republic
Population in 2017: 2873 million[1]
Land area: 28,748 km^2

History
1913 Treaty of London of May 1913 recognizes Albania as an independent state
1941 Albania is occupied by Nazi Germany and Italy during World War II
1944 At the end of the war, Albania becomes a socialist republic
1990 Demise of communism and first steps on the road to a market economy
1992 After the sweeping electoral victory of the Democratic Party, Sali Berisha becomes the first democratically elected president of Albania

---

[1]World Bank Report.

V. Kume (✉)
Faculty of Economics, Tirana University, Tirana, Albania
e-mail: vasilika.kume@unitir.edu.al

E. Garo
Strategic Management, Faculty of Economics, Tirana University, Tirana, Albania

A. Kume
The Ministry of Finance and Economy, Tirana, Albania

Management and Communication, Faculty of Economics, University of Tirana, Tirana, Albania
e-mail: Anisa.Kume@financa.gov.al

1997 The fall of pyramidal financial schemes causes a political and economic crisis
2006 The Stabilization and Association Agreement (SAA) signed with the EU in June
2006 Albania joins other countries in the region, signing the Central European Free Trade Agreement (CEFTA)
2009 Albania becomes a NATO member country and applies for EU membership[2]
2014 The EU grants Albania candidate status in recognition of recent reforms
2016 The governing Socialist Party and the opposition Democratic Party agree on sweeping judicial reforms seen as key to moving toward accession talks with the EU

1 Introduction: Context and History

Twenty years after the demise of communism, Albania is finally on a stable path to economic development and economic integration. Slowly but surely the country is beginning to emerge as a land of opportunities, opening its doors to foreign investment. The Albanian economy is now growing at an annual rate of over 3%. However, despite the full range of institutional reforms, Albanian export remains small and narrow and is not diversified. The country is rich in natural resources, and the economy relies mainly on agriculture, food processing, lumber, oil, cement, chemicals, mining, basic metals, hydropower, tourism, textile industry, and petroleum extraction. The Albanian economy still suffers from a trade deficit, albeit declining. The country's main trading partners are Italy, Greece, Turkey, China, and Russia.

1.1 Phases of Business Development

"The nature of entrepreneurial activity in Albania has gone through some very distinctive phases, also known elsewhere in the region.

Phase 1: 1990–1995 The first entrepreneurs profited from imbalances in existing resources, in goods and services. They found opportunities just across the border and brought in cheap goods from Turkey, Greece, Macedonia, Bulgaria, Russia, and other countries. This provided decent money-making opportunities and filled market gaps."[3] Sources of funds at this stage were limited, with cheap trade credits being hard to come by, and were only available to a select few. The alternative financing, known as "FFF" (friends, family, and fools) turned New Year's family dinner parties

---
[2] Albanian Business Angels (2012).
[3] Albania Economic Outlook (2018).

into shareholders' meetings. The entrepreneurs at this stage relied primarily on trust and friendship to counter information asymmetries.

"Phase 2: 1996–2001 Life went on, and so did the development of entrepreneurial business activities. The next big logical step was the importing of relatively high-quality, durable consumer goods. The consumer market was growing, and people paid more attention to the choices that they were making. This change went hand-in-hand with an improvement in the standard of living. Joint ventures came into being, and entrepreneurs realized that this was not the final stage in their growth spiral.

In most cases, Albanian entrepreneurs were managing a portfolio of activities at any time. Along with their management responsibilities that they had accumulated during the years of horizontal expansion, they acquired what they saw as a portfolio of businesses with varying risk profiles. A distinctive characteristic of the Albanian entrepreneurial model during this phase was the cutting out of the middlemen who beforehand would make large profits.

Phase 3: 2003 to the Present The evolution of entrepreneurial business continued with increasing numbers of home-grown local businesses, producing goods and services locally for home consumption, and some for export to world markets. At this stage, the Albanian entrepreneurs utilized a more solid resource map, as family and friends were no longer the primary money source for their ventures. Asset loans, trade credits, and venture capital were now used as instruments of injecting money, keeping business activities afloat and helping them grow."[4] There was more specialization and more focus on business activities. Entrepreneurs, also known as champions of change, depended on a robust set of competencies and business networks as the surest way to succeed. They showed maturity in protecting their achievements and were conscious that they needed to pass through numerous challenges to achieve success.

There is a qualitative change in how businesses operate now, easily identified in the profile of the hidden champions. Still, they remain small, young, and focused mostly on the region. The median age of the companies identified in this study is 13 years. They have successfully survived, grown, and expanded globally. For instance, Xherdo has formed a joint venture with Kalustyan, an American world leader in sage manufacturing and sales. Some companies are focused mainly on small customer groups (Venice Art Masks, Facilization), and are able to create more superior customer value (Mare Adriatik, Venice Art Masks) than their competitors. Some are also competing on lower costs (APM), or fast imitation (EasyPay, Facilization). Another important fact is that most of the hidden champions of Albania innovate successfully, but invest in both products and processes (APM, Pana, EasyPay). Strong entrepreneurial founders lead the majority of companies that were studied but, in a few cases (APM, Venice Art Masks), founders are sharing power with managers from the younger generation.

---

[4]Albania Economic Outlook (2018).

The nature of competitive advantage of Albania's hidden champions shows diversity in quality of products, partnerships, qualified staff, labor costs, market knowledge, customer orientation, expert knowledge, barriers to new entries, design, and more. "The companies clearly understand that entering the entrepreneurship game is about making money, but it is also about making a mark. The new generation is generally better educated and more informed than their predecessors and fiercely entrepreneurial. For many entrepreneurs, a dull corporate existence is not an option. They want more than just a cheque at the end of the month. Many want meaning and purpose as well. They want to change the world, to follow their star, taking the future in their own hands. They believe that they have an opportunity not just to make money but also to make history in their own way, in their clusters and communities.

Through the school of hard knocks, they have learned that freedom, the lifeblood of entrepreneurs, has a price to be paid, but it means more options as well. Along the journey of building and living their dreams, they display many characteristics,"[5] the most important of which are:

- Being very opportunity-oriented, looking for expanding into new businesses through a horizontal expansion of activities, very often losing focus.
- Embarking on a journey in a sea of troubles and uncertainties even if the odds of success are very slim.
- Delivering a superior performance even under stress.
- Taking charge of their destiny.
- Working hard under uncertainty.

"At the same time, they have a great need for control. This is a significant theme in the life and personality of many Albanian entrepreneurs. They often display a sense of distrust as they typically live in fear of being victimized, and they want to be ready should disaster strike. They have a desire for applause when success is knocking on their door. In their portfolio of skills, they have a good set of survival instincts."[6] As survival is critical for them. They tend to throw their life, family, and business partners into turmoil by getting into battles where they dodge bullets. This gives them the energy to start afresh.

1.2 Challenges

Entrepreneurs in Albania, as elsewhere, face many different challenges. They also display consistent operating weaknesses. The most profound one involves a lack of marketing and sales management skills. Entrepreneurs encounter difficulties with employees and management as managers are not willing to take on real

---

[5] Albania Economic Outlook (2018).
[6] Ibid.

responsibilities for their business activities. Many are still searching for short-term gains and do not focus on finding the right business partners. This means that they may deal with partners who are not entirely trusting and trustworthy.

Today, entrepreneurs want to be closer to the action. "They want to be entrepreneurial and remain that way. They want to challenge the business establishment while they see new wide horizons in maximizing future options, meeting new people, and having new experiences. To be successful in these challenging and turbulent times, Albanian entrepreneurs need to focus their business activities while diversifying their carefully selected portfolios.

As they have built up their ventures to the current status, they should be prepared to build barriers to competitors coming into the business, as success attracts success. They should be on the lookout for future challenges and erect higher bars that are challenging for competitors to overcome.

Growing with the customer is a must nowadays, as business, customers, distributors, and markets are becoming more sophisticated."[7] "Investment in people as the main asset in business should be considered seriously and incorporated in the larger picture. Continuously developing the skills and abilities of the staff should be a matter of high priority.

If entrepreneurs continue to measure themselves against their local competition, they will hurt their long-term success. The reference should be the broad international standard. By doing that, chances are that they will be unbeatable, readying themselves for greener pastures."[8]

Exhibit 1 Core economic indicators for Albania[a]

	2011	2012	2013	2014	2015	2016	2017	2018
GDP per capita (current US$)	4437.178	4247.614	4413.083	4578.668	3952.831	4124.109	4532.889	5253.63
GDP per capita growth (annual %)	2.822	1.585	1.187	1.981	2.528	3.515	3.932	4.261
Long-term unemployment (% of total unemployment)	74.9[b]	77.1	72.4	64.3	66.0	66.2	64.8	67.6[c]
Foreign direct investment, net inflows (% of GDP)	8.130	7.454	9.817	8.69	8.688	8.803	7.847	8.016
GDP (current US$, mio)	12,891	12.32	12,776	13,228	11,387	11,861	13,025	15,059

(continued)

---

[7]Albania Herbs and Spices & Essential Oils (2018).
[8]Albania Economic Outlook (2018).

Exhibit 1 (continued)

	2011	2012	2013	2014	2015	2016	2017	2018
Exports of goods and services (current US$, mio)	3769	3565	3.94	3732	3105	3437	4110	4.777
Exports of goods and services (% of GDP)	29,242	28,937	28,916	28,213	27,267	28,978	31,557	31.722
Merchandise exports (current US$, mio)	1951	1968	2332	2431	1.93	1962	2301	2.876
Merchandise exports to high-income economies (% of total merchandise exports)	75.397	78.343	74.587	74.105	73.136	78.05	77.053	No data
Merchandise exports to developing economies in Europe & Central Asia (% of total merchandise exports)[d]	21.137	16.741	19.443	20.649	22.507	17.496	18.758	No data
Ores and metals exports (% of merchandise exports)	11.903	10.913	9.784	4.582	7.546	8.809	4.834	2.028
Agricultural raw materials exports (% of merchandise exports)	2.569	2.398	2.303	1.269	2.276	2.401	0.44	0.314
Food exports (% of merchandise exports)	4.11	4.578	4.513	3.003	5.61	8.24	9.758	9.042
Fuel exports (% of merchandise exports)	21.192	26.591	31.003	1.568	8.807	11.179	0.835	1.663
Manufactures exports (% of merchandise exports)	60.076	55.249	52.294	31.364	52.694	66.313	51.372	41.568
High-technology exports (% of manufactured exports)	0.53	0.443	0.513	0.12	1.487	0.648	0.086	No data

Source: World Bank, September 2019
[a]https://www.seejobsgateway.net/sites/job_gateway/files/Western%20Balkans%20Labor%20Market%20Trends%202019; https://data.worldbank.org/indicator/TX.VAL.MRCH.R2.ZS?end=2017&locations=AL&start=1981
[b]These data are for 2010. No data for 2011
[c]Q1 Y.2018—65.3; Q2 Y.2018—67.6
[d]Merchandise exports to developing economies in Europe & Central Asia (% of total merchandise exports)

2 Case Studies of Selected Hidden Champions

2.1 Case Study 1

Alb Kalustyan

Overview
Address: Vlashaj Nr. 101, Maminas, Durres, Albania
Tel: +355 69 20 60 915
Fax: +355 575 80 645
Email: xhevit@albkalustyan.com
Web: www.albkalustyan.com

Company Information
Industry: Agriculture, forestry and fishing
Year of establishment: 1991; 1995 (registered as Xherdo shpk); 2014 (joint venture, renamed Alb Kalustyan shpk)
Sales revenues in 2017: 1.8 million euros
Sales revenues in 2007: 0.5 million euros
Average number of employees in 2017: 600
Brain(s) behind the company: Administrator and founder Xhevit Hysenaj

Nature of Market Leadership

Alb Kalustyan is a leader in the Southwestern Balkans in the niche of collecting and marketing medicinal herbs, meeting the quality standards of the prestigious USA and EU markets. The company exports mostly to the USA, but also to Canada, Germany, France, Italy, Spain, Austria, Belgium, Switzerland, the United Kingdom, Netherlands, Morocco, and Malaysia. It is the leading provider of essential oils and processed medicinal plants in Albania and the largest exporter of herbal essences in terms of experience, technology, and marketing. The company is mainly focused on bio-products. From 2011 to 2018, its market share increased from 60 to 75%.

Nature of the Competitive Advantage

The company's competitive advantages are built on:

- High quality
- Full production line
- Modern technology

- Keeping the tradition
- Exclusive focus on organic products
- Bio products

Core Lessons Learned on the Path to Success

- Challenging difficulties
- The struggle between new technology and old methods of work
- Companies should not change their direction but follow their vision
- Build relationships with your customers
- Adapt quickly

Management and Leadership Development Needs

Growing with the customer is a must nowadays, as the business, customers, distributors, and markets are becoming more sophisticated. Investment in people as the main asset in business should be considered seriously and incorporated into the larger picture. Continuously developing the skills and abilities of the staff should be a matter of high priority. Management needs to engage the company's staff in business matters fully. Without their cooperation, success is impossible.

Financing and Regulatory Environment Development Needs

The company cooperates successfully with banks. Still, the business community complains about lengthy procedures. International organizations have assisted with financial support (USAID) and training opportunities (DAAD). However more is expected from governmental institutions.

Alb Kalustyan Moving Ahead

The year 2014 was a special one for Xhevit Hysenaj, the owner of Xherdo Company. After more than 20 years in the market, he decided to begin a collaboration between Xherdo of Albania and Kalustyan of the USA. Xherdo merged forces with Kalustyan—a leader in the herb and spice industry to provide the marketplace with a reliable source of Albanian herbs and essential oils, using the latest technology to provide premium quality standards to global customers.

The mission of the company was and will always be supplying products worldwide to customers, providing the highest quality, latest technology, and excellent customer service. The company is a manufacturer and exporter of more than 26 bio organic medicinal aromatic plants and essential oils. The main product of the company is sage, which can be collected in the wild or cultivated on farms. It is an herb that is found in Albania and the other coastal Balkan areas, from Slovenia to the Albanian region of Himara. Xhevit and other Albania public institutions have worked hard and surpassed every obstacle in order to salvage this authentic herb.

A new factory has been established in Maminas, with business partners across Albania, Montenegro, and Bosnia and Hercegovina for the production of medicinal and aromatic plants (MAPs) and essential oils. Alb Kalustyan now has 26 different MAPs and essential oils certified by the Istituto per la Certificazione Etica ed Ambientale (ICEA) in Italy, the National Organic Program (NOP), the EU, and Canada, with products divided into semi-ready products (without stems, dust, or weeds); and essential oils.

Food safety is the company's top priority. Whatever is embarked upon, the safety of customers is always kept in mind. As part of the global Kalustyan family, the company is dedicated to exceeding the expectations of its global customers. The company brings together the knowledge and experience of food safety professionals from around the world by utilizing a center-of-excellence approach.

> As a company involved in food processing, it has a legal, commercial, and moral obligation to ensure that proper standards of food hygiene are maintained. All necessary steps are taken throughout the processing phase to ensure food safety and quality, and customer expectations are fulfilled and upheld. It is the responsibility of senior management to communicate the above requirements to all members of staff.[9]

Xhevit is determined to improve his business. He is present in every work process, from collection to processing, storing, and negotiating with government institutions and stakeholders involved in the industry. He has visited similar factories in many countries around the world, participating in global industry networks. He attributes his work ethic and perseverance to his family, who raised and cultivated him to be the leader that he is today. His primary support and business partner has been his wife, who has helped him to establish a healthy work-family balance.

The company strives to achieve the highest quality final product offered to consumers. In Albania, this is a constant challenge as some of the plants are wild and require a unique processing method.

The growth of the company has not been immediate but gradual, through continuous investment in infrastructure, warehousing, processing, and technology. The company's motto is "Catch the opportunity."

---

[9] Ahmadpour-Daryany. M. (2000).

2.2 Case Study 2

Mare Adriatik

Overview
Address: Shelqet – Vau i Dejës, Shkoder, 1000 Albania
Tel: +355 266 22146; +355 69 20 95644
Fax: +355 266 22146
Email: info@mareadriatik.com; mare.adriatik@yahoo.it
Web: www.mareadriatik.com

Company Information
Industry: Agriculture, Forestry and Fishing
Year of establishment: 1995
Sales revenues in 2017: 4.75 mio €
Sales revenues in 2007: 0.29 mio €
Average number of employees in 2017: 500
Brain(s) behind the company: CEO and founder Mark Babani

Nature of Market Leadership

Mare Adriatik is one of the largest Albanian processors and exporter to the European market of anchovies and sardines from the Adriatic Sea and is first in the Southwestern Balkan region, in terms of market share. The company operates in cooperation with Spain, Croatia, Greece, and Egypt. Mare Adriatic is the largest producer of salted anchovies in Eastern Europe. Adriatic anchovies are very rich in omega 6 oils. The company has a long experience in the industry and is known for the quality of its product. . It guarantees high-quality products, processed with craft methods, enabling clients to enjoy authentic bluefish. In the early years, Mare Adriatik worked for European companies, while today it prepares ready-made products for end-users. Due to its market expansion, along with Albanian fish, the company buys fresh fish from nearby markets and develops all processing activities for the market. From 2011 to 2018, the market share of the company in the Southwestern Balkans increased from 60 to 75%.

Nature of the Competitive Advantage

Mare Adriatik has the largest market share in Albania. The company processes about 4000 tons of fish per year. Mare Adriatik carries out the full chain of processing activities, preparing the product for the end consumer. The main competitors of anchovy fillets are companies in Italy, mainly in Sicily. Also, Morocco is a serious competitor in the European market.

Competitive Advantages:

- Very long experience
- Lower labor costs in Albania
- Potential international clients for salt anchovy fillets
- Adriatic sea fish is rich in omega3 and there is a high demand for it.

Core Lessons Learned on the Path to Success

- Continuously investing in new products, mainly focusing on introducing high-quality products in the market; improving technology, always aiming to add value to the product.
- Operating closely with suppliers and customers.
- Listen to your team, customers, and peers. The different perspective is valuable.
- Trust your instincts and invent new opportunities.
- Have a clear mission. Believe in what you are doing to achieve your goals.

Management and Leadership Development Needs

The company is continually growing and needs skilled employees to respond to its growth rates in the field of food technology, law, and management. The company has difficulty finding experts for two reasons. First, it operates in an area far from major cities, and competent specialists are reluctant to relocate. Second, Albanian universities cannot provide specialized classes for niche industry sectors and are far from market needs. As a result, the company needs to train its employees regularly.

Financing and Regulatory Environment Development Needs

Financial institutions are becoming more flexible, while the government needs to be closer to business needs.

Banking procedures are facilitated for established and credible companies. The expansion of the company was achieved by cooperating with the banking sector. The Strategy for Development and Integration of the Albanian Government should support the business. The company has been struggling due to government bureaucracy. Difficulties have also come from quotas not adequately negotiated with the

EU (regarding tax relief). Under these quotas, if companies exceed the limit of 1600 tons of exports, they pay higher customs tariffs. The customs tariffs hinder company growth, as they involve 25% extra tax.

Mare Adriatik, Believe in Your Mission

It was 1995 when Mark Babani set up a small family business in the fish industry. In the beginning, the business was working mostly for Italian and Spanish companies. Currently, 80% of the business is independent, and 20% works for other companies. Mark nostalgically remembers the days when his business was small, but he is proud of the incredible growth and maturity that the company has achieved. The success of his business is attributed to three key aspects: the quality of the products, the location of the company, and Mark's leadership personality.

There has been a strong emphasis and focus on the product quality since 2011. Consequently, the number of exports has doubled every year, and the number of employees has increased fivefold. The company buys raw material worldwide and processes about 4000 tons of fish annually. Mare Adriatik has invested in all aspects of the industry, from catching fish to distributing and selling it in supermarkets. All company processes are characterized by high quality. Mare has made many investments and has come up with new products over the years. New products, such as jars, marinated acetate fillets, vacuum cleaners, and aluminum vacuum (oil-free) bags, are all available to the consumer. The products are evaluated using two factors: price and quality. The fish that comes from the Adriatic Sea is some of the best, in terms of taste and value.

The geographic location of the company has been another key factor in Mare Adriatik's success. Its location has been paramount to the growth of the company. Albania's sea is one of the areas where fresh fish comes from three different directions: Croatia, Greece, and Italy. Its location gives it a substantial advantage for doing business in the fish industry.

Mark's leadership affects the way that the company is run. His determination to move forward and strive for achievement has created an environment that promotes hard work and positive energy. One of the most important assets of the company is the employees, who are chosen on merit and character. The employees are motivated and rewarded on a system basis. Everything produced is measurable and has a value, and all evaluations are work-based. The company maintains the quality of the products according to the European market's standards.

Mark is passionate about every aspect of his business and stays on top of all tasks, making sure that all operations are running smoothly. He ensures that his new projects are not disclosed publicly, as the success of the company can be easily derailed by the fact that Albania is a difficult place to work in due to corruption. For instance, someone can buy fish from a more expensive supplier and sell it at a lower price. This can lead to bankruptcy or create other problems for the company.

The support of Mark's family has been a source of strength. Without such support, it is difficult to find the willpower to strive for further achievement. On the other hand, his ability to engage and communicate with people is the key to success. Continued development, through growth and evolvement, is the motto of his business.

2.3 Case Study 3

Venice Art

Overview
Address: Rr. Pal Engjelli, Shkoder, Albania.
Tel: +355 68 2047 291; +355 68 2048 060
Email: edmondangoni@gmail.com
Web: www.veniceartmask.eu

Company Information
Industry: Art, Entertainment and Recreation
Year of establishment: 1998
Sales revenues in 2017: 0.5 million euros
Sales revenues in 2007: 1 million euros
Average number of employees in 2017: 200
Brain(s) behind the company: CEO and founder Edmond Angoni

Nature of Market Leadership

Venice Art's main market is Venice, from which it receives large orders for the day of carnivals. The company also exports carnival masks to Las Vegas and Australia. It is one of the biggest and finest mask-making workshops in the world. Some of the masks produced were featured in famous film productions, such as *Eyes Wide Shut* by Stanley Kubrick, and in theater, such as the Vienna Opera House, the Royal Opera House in London, and the Bolshoi Theater in Moscow. The company is known for one reason: its respect for tradition. However, the company has been able to interpret tradition in innovative ways, creating new and unique decorative styles and shapes. Venice Art crafts hand-made masks in the same way as Venetian artisans 800 years ago. The company never repeats a decoration, so each mask is unique. The products are hand-made, characterized by high-quality, and dedicated to a selected clientele. The advantages of Venice Art include expertise, a relatively long experience in the market, and a rich catalog of models. From 2011 to 2018, the company's market share increased from 70 to 80%.

Nature of the Competitive Advantage

Venice Art builds its reputation on quality products and efficient response to client needs. It has adopted the mission statement "Quality is our standard."

Since 2011, many improvements have been made in the process of mask production. As a result of experience and improvement of equipment, production times have been reduced.

The Advantages of Venice Art Are:

- The quality and originality of the products, the handling of every mask as if it were an artwork. This has resulted in the reputation of masks spreading almost at the same speed as globalization.
- The know-how was created throughout the years of experience. As a result, it is difficult for new entrants to be competitive in the market.
- Flexibility and continuous innovation. Eight hundred new models have been designed and crafted in the last 10 years.
- Timely production (maximum of 10 days).
- Special, differentiated, often unique products.
- A rich catalog of models that is very difficult to be created by a new entrant in the market.

Core Lessons Learned on the Path to Success

- Being present in the business. Love the job and treat it as a child.
- Close cooperation with co-workers.
- Consider your business a big family.
- Diversification of products, without losing focus. This enables growth and creates a balance in the business portfolio.
- Continuous investment and reinvestment of profits.
- Anticipate changes in the business and work in a proactive manner.
- Surround yourself with creative people who challenge, inspire, and propel forward the company vision.

Management and Leadership Development Needs

The company is known for one reason: its respect for tradition. However, the company has been able to interpret tradition in innovative ways, creating new and unique decorative styles and shapes. The current challenge is the completion of a showroom in Shkoder, which will be a museum, production area, and teaching center for future generations. Albania has a small population and operates in a mature market, which has forced the company to grow through diversification by entering the real estate market.

Finding a workforce with a working culture is a challenge for the company. New employees need time to learn the work culture and adjust to company values. They lack creativity and have few practical skills. For this reason, employees undergo periodic training. As a result, the company needs to develop joint training programs with schools in the field of art However, schools should develop a better relationship with businesses and be more responsive to their needs. Art disciplines need a more prominent place in school curricula.

Financing and Regulatory Environment Development Needs

Relationships with financial institutions are improving due to the strengthening of the business. However, the company emphasized the need for government presence in business problems. The company seeks state-sponsored business policies that provide incentives.

The Spirit Behind the Venitian Masks

As he sat in his workshop one afternoon, Edmond Angoni grabbed a brush from the nearest jar and began to add the finishing touches to his latest creation: a gorgeous Venetian mask. Over the years, Edmond has hand-crafted numerous masks, each one more unique than the previous. In his humble workshop, he and his employees have created a working environment that fosters creativity and collaboration. While painting the golden embroidery on the edges of a mask, he reminisces how he began his successful business and found the spirit behind the making of the Venetian masks.

The year was 1998. Edmond had just returned to Albania after working as an immigrant in Italy. After witnessing the production of hand-crafted masks in Venice, he was inspired to start a business producing and distributing Venetian masks but had no idea where to start.

At the time, Edmond was particularly drawn to the city of Shkoder. Historically, Shkoder has been a city filled with rich tradition and artisanry. During communism, all forms of creative expression were banned. However, Edmond felt the potential of the city. It was almost as though the city were alive, with a beating heart and passionate spirit waiting to be revived. The cobbled streets of the city had a striking similarity to those of Venice, convincing Edmond that this was the right city for his business. He set up his humble workshop and employed five employees. In doing so, he began the process of reviving the artistic identity of Shkoder.

With only five employees to assist him initially, the business started slowly, producing very few masks. These hand-made products were delivered to wholesalers in Venice. Overtime, Edmond built a larger workshop with more employees and materials to create unique masks. It was an immediate success. The streets of Venice were overflowing with masks produced in Shkoder.

To reduce cost, Edmond decided to relocate the shops from the more expensive main streets, to narrow, and more secretive, secondary streets. The demand was so high that people continued to find these shops, despite their location. In 2011, Edmond decided to take an essential step for the business since the masks were in high demand. He tried distributing the Venetian masks all over the world. From Venice to Las Vegas, from Dubai to Australia, Edmond created an empire based on his artistic creation. The global expansion was successful because the company was primarily focused on quality, originality, and client satisfaction, thus leading to the creation of the company's mission statement: "Quality is our standard."

Edmond brings uniqueness to every piece of artwork he creates. We are living in a world of mass-producing and replication, and handcrafts are becoming rare and precious. Handcrafts are his success!

Once done reminiscing, Edmond places the brush down and leaves the mask on the table to dry. He looks at his creation, marveling at its uniqueness. It is indeed one of a kind. He stands up and looks out the window of his workshop. He hopes that someday he can expand his workshop and turn it into a museum, where tourists from all over the world can visit, and young people can learn how to create a Venetian mask. He hopes that his legacy of bringing artisanry back to Shkoder continues to have a significant impact on the economy and society. Most importantly, he hopes that the spirit of the Venetian mask will never fade away.

3 Conclusions and Recommendations

Albania is a small country with limited business resources. Businesses in Albania are mainly located in major cities such as the capital city Tirana and the cities of Durres, Shkoder, Lezha, Fier, Vlora, and Saranda. The companies discussed in this chapter are located in the north of the country (Shkoder, Tropoja, Lezha), in the capital city (Tirana), and in the south west (Durres, Fier), covering central business locations in Albania.

It is was still challenging to identify hidden champions that meet the conditions of Simon's methodology in Albania in 2018. The data were collected through interviews. This helped the researchers to obtain highly personalized data and the viewpoint of business leaders. The companies became market leaders because they are more profitable than their smaller-share rivals in the region (southwestern Balkans). They dominate the market through customer loyalty, distribution, pricing, and other factors. Some of them enjoyed the first-mover advantage in new markets.

Venice Art was the first company to cover the Venice market fully and sell handmade crafts in the USA and Australia. Xherdo was the first to process wild medical plants, provide essential oils, and export them exclusively to the American market. Based on their perspective, market leadership does not come from sales and dominance but from products that are relevant to customers. Pana generates revenue by recycling materials, especially pallets, and transforming them into furniture. These innovative ideas will help the company to connect with marginalized people. Easy Pay was the first company to introduce e-wallet solutions in the Albanian market, which can add value to the customer. Mare Adriatik launched products that can redefine the customer experience in terms of product quality. AMLA has a "suspended status." During the interview, the company's administrator reported the difficult situation his business was facing, but he was optimistic that getting a loan would change the situation and he would continue to operate successfully.

Other successful companies may become hidden champions in the future. They are not high-profile publicly listed companies in Albania and the world. None of the companies in this study are politically affiliated.

The companies have cooperated successfully with banks, but the business community complains about lengthy procedures. In some cases, companies have encountered difficulties in getting loans. The government needs to be closer to business needs because companies are still struggling due to bureaucracy. They seek state-sponsored business policies that provide incentives. Funds for the development of rural businesses continue to be a challenge in Albania. The Albanian government can play an essential role in changing this situation by using incentive policies for the local government and communities. The Albanian state should be sensitive in supporting social businesses and create incentives for marginalized people working for these businesses.

The Albanian government and international organizations should support the development of vocational education in Albania. Companies are lacking professionals in the areas where they operate, such as engineering, management, and project management. The government needs to support companies that are exporting products and services. The pressure from the Customs and the Tax Department needs to be reduced as well. The legal framework is appropriate, but there is room for improvement. The government needs to revise its tax policy in the IT sector and be more supportive of start-up companies. At the outset, these businesses should be exempt from taxes. These initiatives should cover social businesses (supporters of marginalized groups) and newly created enterprises.

Higher education should serve to provide students with skills and knowledge in specific areas of business. Through internship programs and business incubators, students will gain experience in their specialization.

> In the short term, students are expected to be equipped with necessary skills that are considered important by employers; and in the long term skills need to be generated in the areas of creative thinking, workplace innovations, sustainable business practices, and balancing stakeholders' interests.[10]

---

[10]Ghosh (2014).

References

Ahmadpour-Daryany M (2000) Entrepreneurship: theories and models, 3rd edn. Tehran, Paris
Albania Economic Outlook (2018) Retrieved from https://www.focus-economics.com/countries/albania
Albania Herbs and Spices & Essential Oils (2018) Retrieved from http://www.albkalustyan.com
Albanian Business Angels (2012) J Entrepren Innovat. Retrieved from: http://www.dai.com/pdf/1211487618_Oils.pdf
Ghosh K (2014) Creativity in business schools: toward a need based developmental approach. Retrieved from https://www.researchgate.net/publication/271663106_Creativity_in_Business_Schools_Towards_a_Need_Based_Developmental_Approach
World Bank Report World development indicator. Retrieved from http://datatopics.worldbank.org/world-development-indicators/

Hidden Champions of Belarus

Radzivon Marozau, Hanna Aginskaya, Pavel Daneyko, and Natalia Makayeva

Overview
Official name: Republic of Belarus
Type of government: Presidential republic
Population in 2017: 9,475,200
Land area: 207,595 km^2

History

1915–1918	The present-day Belarusian territory is the scene of bloody battles between German and Russian forces
1918 (March 3rd)	The Treaty of Brest-Litovsk is signed, marking Russia's exit from World War I
1919	The Soviet Socialist Republic of Byelorussia is established
1921–1928	The Riga Peace Treaty results in the partitioning of Belarus between the Belarusian Soviet Socialist Republic and Poland. New Economic Policy (NEP) introduced across Belarus
1921–1930	The Polish part of Belarus is subjected to polonization
1922	The Belarusian SSR becomes a part of the Union of the Soviet Socialist Republics (USSR)
1936–1940	The Great Purge. More than 86,000 Belarusians suffer political oppression and over 28,000 are sentenced to death at the Kuropaty camp near Minsk

---

R. Marozau (✉) · H. Aginskaya · P. Daneyko
Belarusian Economic Research and Outreach Center (BEROC), Minsk, Belarus
e-mail: marozau@beroc.by

N. Makayeva
IPM Business School, Minsk, Belarus

© Springer Nature Switzerland AG 2021
A. Braček Lalić, D. Purg (eds.), *Hidden Champions in Dynamically Changing Societies*, https://doi.org/10.1007/978-3-030-65451-1_8

1939 (September)	The Red Army moves into West Belarus
1941	The start of the Great Patriotic War in Belarus. The German army occupies all of present-day Belarus
1945 (May)	The Great Patriotic War of the Soviet peoples against the Nazi aggressors ends. Belarus becomes one of the founding members of the United Nations
1954	Belarus joins UNESCO
1986 (April)	Chernobyl nuclear reactor disaster
1990	Belarus declares national sovereignty. The BSSR is formally renamed the Republic of Belarus
1991	The USSR collapses, Belarus is proclaimed an independent republic
1994	The first presidential elections are held and Alexander Lukashenko is elected president of Belarus
1996	A Belarusian referendum results in the amendment of the constitution that strips parliament of key powers
1997	Signing of the Union of Belarus and Russia
2001	President Alexander Lukashenko is re-elected in elections described as undemocratic by Western observers
2006, 2010, 2015	President Alexander Lukashenko is re-elected in the first rounds of elections
2014	The presidents of Russia, Belarus, and Kazakhstan sign an agreement on the establishment of the Euro-Asian Economic Union

Exhibit 1 Core economic indicators for Belarus

	2011	2012	2013	2014	2015	2016	2017	2018
GDP per capita (current US$)	17,166.696	17,807.418	18,298.847	18,949.882	18,389.744	18,098.423	18,915.94	19,959.543
GDP per capita growth (annual %)	5.572	1.78	0.987	1.635	−3.983	−2.649	2.567	3.19
Long-term unemployment (% of total unemployment)	N/A	N/A	N/A	N/A	N/A	N/A	N/A	N/A
Foreign direct investment, net inflows (% of GDP)	4.002	1.464	2.246	1.862	1.652	1.247	1.246	1.475
GDP (current US$, mio)	61,758	65,685	75,528	78,814	56,455	47,723	54,727	59,662
Exports of goods and services (current US$, mio)	48,458	51,745	44,058	43,301	32.75	29,831	36,552	41,883

(continued)

Exhibit 1 (continued)

	2011	2012	2013	2014	2015	2016	2017	2018
Exports of goods and services (% of GDP)	78.465	78.777	58.334	54.941	58.011	62.509	66.79	70.199
Merchandise exports (current US$, mio)	41,419	46,060	37,203	36,126	26,660	23,537	29,240	33,716
Merchandise exports to high-income economies (% of total merchandise exports)	38.946	39.054	29.387	30.911	33.509	25.685	28.812	32.00
Merchandise exports to developing economies in Europe & Central Asia (% of total merchandise exports)	50.183	52.348	63.101	59.869	54.675	63.597	61.657	56.80
Ores and metals exports (% of merchandise exports)	0.593	0.613	0.913	0.863	0.925	1.235	1.23	1.095
Agricultural raw materials exports (% of merchandise exports)	1.485	1.216	1.635	1.635	1.894	2.254	2.256	2.55
Food exports (% of merchandise exports)	9.154	9.810	14.378	14.781	15.638	17.06	16.375	14.974
Fuel exports (% of merchandise exports)	35.654	37.642	32.125	33.168	28.916	20.51	24.606	N/A
Manufactures exports (% of merchandise exports)	47.94	46.688	46.839	46.591	48.74	54.817	53.998	53.798
High-technology exports (% of manufactured exports)	2.572	2.883	4.400	3.929	4.315	4.694	3.814	3.543

Source: World Bank, September 2019

1 Introduction: Context and History

In 1991, Belarus entered a new stage of development as an independent country with a predominantly industrial economy, an export share of 50% of GDP, and a substantial R&D capacity.

The critical socioeconomic transformation accompanied by the substantial cuts in public expenditures on R&D and the precipitous fall in industry demand for R&D results placed researchers and engineers in "survival mode" (Marozau and Guerrero

2016) and made the most audacious of them start their own companies. The absence of large-scale privatization appeared conducive to the development of small, flexible, client-oriented start-ups in the field of technology. The relatively scarce entrepreneurial opportunities in Belarus, compared with those of Russia and Ukraine, made green-field investment the only way of launching a business (Daneyko and Golenchenko 2013). Moreover, the extremely high levels of inflation, currency devaluation, and interest rates in the 1990s, as well as the small stagnant domestic market for technological products and services, preconditioned the export orientation of many Belarusian enterprises. These circumstances have created a positive image of entrepreneurship in the manufacturing sector that was perceived as a "fair" business as opposed to trading or privatization-based business. In the late-1990s, the government started establishing free economic zones to create a preferential tax and customs regime for export-oriented manufacturing enterprises. After the transition period of the 1990s, these factors, among others, fueled the dynamic growth of the Belarusian economy during the 2000s, lasting until the global financial crisis of 2008 (Estes 2013).

In 2011, a domestic financial and economic crisis hit the economy. It was caused by administratively increased salaries, a substantial amount of policy-based lending, the over-valued fixed exchange rate of the currency, and the current account deficit (De la Rubia et al. 2012). The core inflation rate reached 118.1%, and the devaluation of the national currency was almost 300% (Pelipas 2012). This boosted exports and facilitated economic growth. The 59.4% increase of exports in 2011 created a golden financial year for hidden champions and other export-oriented enterprises in Belarus. But by 2013, the effects of the devaluation on export growth had disappeared. In 2014, the economic crisis in Russia—the country's main trade partner—led to continuing depreciation of the Belarusian ruble, and a decline in manufacturing output, as well as a further economic slowdown (Tarr 2014). In this situation, expansion to developed markets remained the only strategy for further development of Belarusian technological companies.

As a response, the government had to tighten monetary policy and start to take measures, such as market liberalization and introduction of legislation related to business liberalization, exclusion of redundant claims on businesses, licensing facilitation, tax consulting, decriminalization of economic risks, and more. The amount of subsidies to state-owned enterprises was scaled down. The National Bank carried out reforms that aimed to decrease inflation and establish a flexible exchange rate (Kruk 2019) that pushed exporters to improve their business efficiency, expand to new markets, and develop other competitive advantages.

In fact, Belarus has been undergoing moderate market reforms since 2006. In the *Doing Business 2019* survey, conducted by the World Bank in 2018, Belarus rose from the 115th position in 2007 to 37th.[1] Belarus is in the top-10 countries in terms of number of implemented reforms since 2005. Particularly, it is in third place in terms of reforms for easy tax payment.

---

[1] For further information consult https://www.doingbusiness.org/en/data/exploreeconomies/belarus

As opposed to the situation in most other post-socialist countries, these reforms were based not on the imitation of best practices or recommendations of international financial institutions but rather on the country's own experience and domestic institutional environment. Thus, the Belarusian High-Tech Park—a special tax regime established in 2005 for software companies—became a showcase of the Belarusian economy. In December 2017, the new Decree of the President of the Republic of Belarus №8 *On the Development of a Digital Economy* was introduced. It not only extended the special tax regime but also established a special legal regime with elements of English law and opened the door to the Belarusian Hi-Tech Park for many non-ICT technological companies. All these tendencies influenced the performance and strategy of Belarusian hidden champions in 2011–2018.

Based on secondary sources and interviews with hidden champions identified in 2011, 45 Belarusian companies that might meet the criteria of Hidden champions were selected for further analysis. At the next stage, a study of companies' web sites and sector and market research reports were conducted to check whether a company took a leading position in the niche at least in the Commonwealth of Independent States (CIS), was headquartered in Belarus, was not a part of an MNC, was not state controlled or affiliated, and had a low visibility profile in the public domain. In some cases, phone calls and meetings were needed. As a result, six new hidden champions were interviewed, while two relatively small Belarusian enterprises might be considered as potential hidden champions (see Table 1). In general, the Belarusian hidden champions identified in 2011 have mostly preserved and even strengthened their leading positions mainly due to internationalization and new market entries.

The list of new Belarusian hidden champions includes both companies tracing their roots to the 1990s and those established within the last 10 years. Belarusian hidden champions identified in 2011 (see Table 1) have mostly preserved and even strengthened their leading positions mainly due to internationalization and new market entries.

As in Western countries, the growth of Belarusian companies is predominantly driven by quality and innovation, especially in knowledge-intensive industries. This is consistent with the classical strategy of hidden champions. Constantly monitoring technological developments in their sectors and closely interacting with customers, Belarusian hidden champions are successful in achieving incremental innovations and increasing market share.

It is no wonder that we have not identified new hidden champions using the imitation strategy. This can be explained by the increasing competition from other developing countries in terms of labor costs, tax regimes, and production efficiency. Thus, the hidden champions from group one are still leaders in the CIS market but have been losing their positions for several reasons. Firstly, Belarusian companies cannot compete based on lower prices, producing easily replicable products, such as shutters and lids. Low levels of inflation and the devaluation of the national currency worked against these exporters. Secondly, the market size of the CIS countries contracted during the harsh economic crisis of 2014–2015 and jeopardized the companies' development. This crisis was driven, among other factors, by oil price

Table 1 Belarusian hidden champions

Hidden champions			
Company	Year	Business activity	Market Share
1. Adani	2018	Number one in the world in manufacturing of full-body personal X-ray inspection systems for prisons, airports, customs, etc.	About 50% in the USA, 20% in the CIS, and 30% in the world
2. Aerodorstroy	2018	Number one in the CIS region in reparation services for runway and airport road surfaces	100% in Belarus, more than 50% in Russia
3. EssentOptics	2018	Number one in the CIS region in the production of spectrophotometers for measurement of optical characteristics	90% in Russia and Belarus, 20% in some developed markets in Europe and Asia
4. Excavators[a]	2011	Number 1 in the CIS region in the production of excavators on automobile chassis and crawlers for inaccessible locations	70% in the CIS
5. Izovac Group	2018	Number one in the post-Soviet area in the production of vacuum coating equipment for displays, optics, laser devices and microelectronics	65% in the post-Soviet countries, 20% in the world in the niche of vacuum sputtering equipment for gadget touch screens.
6. Lids[a]	2011	Number one in the CIS region in the production of plastic and aluminum caps for alcoholic beverage containers	n/a
7. Photonics	2018	Number one or two in the world in the production of lasers for aerospace wire marking	50% of the global market for lasers for aerospace wire marking, 40% of the CIS market of spectral instruments
8. Polimaster (previously Radiation Meters[a])	2011	Number two or three in the world in the production of radiation detection equipment for security purposes, number one in the US and CIS markets in the production of personal radiation detectors.	n/a
9. Regula (ex. Document Scanners[a])	2018	Number one in the CIS region in the production of passport readers and criminal investigation equipment	Up to 95-100% in CIS and 30% worldwide
10. STIM	2011	Number one in the CIS region in the production of road marking machines and paints	50-80% in Russia, Belarus, Poland, Lithuania
11. Dorelectromash	2018	Manufacturing of road milling, snow melting and trenching machines	About 40% of the market in Russia, Ukraine, Kazakhstan, Azerbaijan, Uzbekistan
Potential hidden champions			
1. EnCata	2018	Number one in the world in providing innovative product	Up to 90% in the world (USA, EU, Russia, Arab World)

(continued)

Table 1 (continued)

Hidden champions			
Company	Year	Business activity	Market Share
		development services for start-up companies	
2. FOTEK	2018	Number two in the CIS region in the manufacturing of surgical technologies and laser instruments	n/a
No longer-hidden champions			
1. Shutters[a]		Number one in the CIS region in the production of aluminum blinds (shutters)	80% in the Russian, Ukrainian and Belarusian markets

[a]The name of the company is disguised

decrease, complicated relationships between Russia and Ukraine, sanctions, and countersanctions.

Thus, Shutters (group one) did not overcome the crises and needed to be sold. At the same time Excavators (group two) has managed to maintain revenues at the pre-crisis level by increasing its labor productivity and its market share from 50 to 70%, due to sanctions and counter-sanctions.

However, one can expect that Excavators and Shutters will increase their sales in the region due to economic recovery. On the other hand, the crises pushed the Belarusian hidden champions into more distant and unfamiliar markets. Hidden champions that adjusted their business models and products to more developed markets have achieved substantial growth. The geographical diversification of markets has become both a challenge and a cornerstone of sustainable development for the hidden champions in group one.

In general, since 2011 the Belarusian hidden champions have become more open and public. Importantly, in 2017 the Advanced Instrument Manufacturers Association was founded by some Belarusian hidden champions belonging to group three, identified in 2011,[2] in order to promote industry development and cooperation among high-tech companies. The hidden champions in this group have demonstrated considerable growth since 2011. They opened up new markets and continued their global expansion.

It is worth mentioning that these hidden champions have reached the stage when some teams start spinning off or set up independent ventures (spin-outs). Notwithstanding the capital intensity of the hardware business, one such spin-out appears on the list of new champions, while the development of others is still not sufficient for them to become local leaders (Table 2).

---

[2]According to the taxonomy developed in 2011, this group includes firms creating products based on R&D performed by Soviet research institutes and laboratories at universities and enterprises.

Table 2 Taxonomy of Belarusian hidden champions

Hidden champion group	Development path	Nature of leadership	What Has happened	Examples of products/services
1. Manufacturing of low-tech products that never existed in the former USSR	From importing to own manufacturing at lower costs	CIS	Loosing positions in the CIS but entering Western markets	1. Aluminum blinds 2. Plastic and aluminum lids
2. Employing the engineering potential of Soviet enterprises	From job-lot manufacturing to the leading position in the niches	CIS and neighboring EU countries	Dominating in the niches against the backdrop of the crisis in 2015–2016 in CIS, sanctions, and counter-sanctions	1. Excavators and cranes 2. Road-marking machines and paints 3. Road machinery and snow-melters
3. R&D-based high-tech companies from Soviet research laboratories	From the CIS as a test bed to global expansion with the OEM model	One of the leaders in the world with strong brands	Growing globally and diversifying product portfolios around core technologies	1. Document readers and validators 2. Radiation meters 3. Lasers for industry and surgery 4. Spectrometers 5. Vacuum-coating equipment for displays, optics, and laser devices 6. X-ray inspection systems

Source: Author's analysis based on Daneyko and Golenchenko (2013)

The recent boom in the Belarusian ICT sector has given rise to several startups, such as Masquerade (acquired by Facebook), Fabby (acquired by Google), Flo, and Target process (attracted investments from EBRD). However, these companies can hardly be identified as hidden champions for several reasons. Firstly, some of them were established to be sold to MNCs. Secondly, markets for IT-solutions and applications are extremely dynamic and in many cases, it is impossible to define a market or calculate a market share, as the latter may fall or grow exponentially over a single year. Thirdly, IT startups are flexible enough to quickly re-focus on other segments and niches. Lastly, they easily relocate to more advanced markets, leaving only R&D centers in Belarus.

Getting a glimpse of the future, we can expect that within the next few years IT product companies in the business-to-business sector (artificial intelligence, machine learning, and computer vision) will take dominant positions in some narrow niches, such as Scaled Agile in work and project management solutions. In addition, the steadily developing advanced instrument-building sector, represented by more than 100 innovative companies, may give rise to new Belarusian hidden champions.

Another potential hotbed of hidden champions may be the armament industry developed in the Soviet period. Recently, enterprises in that sector have started to diversify their product or service portfolios and export markets. Many enterprises became joint stock companies but are still controlled by the state. Development of corporate governance systems would be a key factor in future expansion.

In addition, other industries focused on the CIS market, such as manufacturing of different mining and extracting machines and equipment for gas, oil, and potash industries, as well as manufacturing of medical equipment, also have strong potential to give rise to new champions.

2 Case Studies of Selected Hidden Champions

2.1 Case Study 1

Izovac Group

Overview
Address: Bogdanovicha Str., 155-907, Minsk, 220040, Belarus
Tel: + 375 17 2931842
Fax: + 375 17 2931845
Email: info@izovac.com
Web: www.izovac.com

Company Information
Industry: Manufacture of special-purpose machinery, development, and manufacture of vacuum equipment and related technologies for the manufacture of displays, optical and microelectronic devices, as well as solar cells
Year of establishment: 1992
Sales revenues in 2017: 14.2 million euros
Sales revenues in 2007: 2.5 million euros
Average number of employees in 2017: 188
Brain(s) behind the company: Two founders, and three managing directors of companies within the group

Nature of Market Leadership

In the post-Soviet area, Izovac dominates the market of vacuum coating equipment for displays, optics, laser devices, and microelectronics without any considerable competitors, and controls 65% of the market. In the world market, the company holds about 20% in the niche of vacuum sputtering equipment for gadget touch screens. Initially, about a half of iPhone and iPad touch screens were made by Izovac. The company exports 95% of its products. Thus, the company is number one in the post-Soviet area in the production of vacuum coating equipment for optics, laser devices, and microelectronics. Its exports go mainly to Russia, Japan, China, South Korea, and Taiwan.

Nature of the Competitive Advantage

Izovac Group was started as a spin-out from one of the university research laboratories and had deep fundamental knowledge in the physics and chemistry of plasma and solid surfaces, as well as strong engineering potential. The entrepreneurial orientation and persistence of its leaders have allowed it to become a global company. Izovac manufactures only custom-made equipment for world-leading companies that face specific and complicated technical tasks in terms of productivity, quality, number, and structure of layers. Positioning itself as a scientific and technological company, Izovac reinvests about 60% of its profits in R&D to develop its innovative potential.

Core Lessons Learned on the Path to Success

1. An entrepreneur has to be resolute in starting up and developing a company.
2. Establishing personal relations and shared responsibility with employee's right after the foundation of a company is a necessary condition for its sustainable development.
3. Risk awareness and a risk-taking culture are drivers of innovative development for knowledge-intensive industries

Management and Leadership Development Needs

It is claimed that there is a common problem among many Belarusian manufacturing companies—a lack of capabilities and relevant experience in finding, attracting, and working with, investors who could be drivers of further development. Therefore, investment plans are not clear.

Export-oriented Belarusian companies are hindered in their development by the lack of both employees and consultants with competences and experience in international business. In this regard, the state and educational organizations should promote the international exchange of students and professionals.

Financing and Regulatory Environment Development Needs

Izovac's leaders consider the regulatory environment quite supportive of their activities. The company benefits from the legal and tax regimes of the free economic zone and hi-tech park.

Izovac Group: Equipment for the Manufacturing of iPhone's Touch Screens

To understand the role of the Izovac Group in the global display market, one figure would be enough: 20% of personal gadget touch screens are manufactured by Izovac's vacuum coating systems. Izovac Group is a typical representative of the third type of Belarusian hidden champions—R&D-based high-tech companies from Soviet research laboratories.

In 1992, a small scientific and technological firm was started up in the Radio Engineering Institute (currently Belarusian State University of Informatics and Radioelectronics) by four staff members—necessity-driven entrepreneurs from a research laboratory of the Ministry of Electronic Industry. Located in the university, the firm rented the university's equipment to fulfill small-scale orders, such as decorative coating on glasses and protective screens for cathode-ray monitors. Based on this experience, the firm switched to the development and manufacturing of industrial-scale equipment for thin-film coatings.

In the late 1990s, Izovac's leaders managed to establish relationships with the large Taiwanese cathode-ray tube manufacturer, Chunghwa Picture Tubes Ltd. That appeared to be an entry point to the global market. A "no-name manufacturer" from a "little known country" received the first order for more than 100 units of equipment and found a strategic partner in the region, where many manufacturers of displays and screens are located. Later on, this was one of the reasons to locate an assembly factory in Taiwan.

In the 2000s, a South Asian subcontractor needed a high-quality equipment to complete an order from Apple Corporation for touch screens of the first generation of iPhones and iPads. Being a well-known manufacturer of vacuum coating systems in the region, Izovac managed to convince Apple of its capability to develop high-quality equipment for thin-film coatings and its ability to deliver products on time. As a result, almost 70% of the first iPhones' and iPads' touch screens were manufactured with Izovac's equipment. After that, one can find among Izovac's clients' corporations such as Samsung, Sharp, Saint-Gobain, and others. Consequently, Izovac's share of the global market for vacuum sputtering equipment for gadgets' touch screens has reached 20%.

For a long time, Izovac has been positioning itself as a scientific and technological company, attracting staff with scientific degrees, participating in scientific conferences, and publishing in prestigious international journals. Throughout its history, Izovac has been closely cooperating with Belarusian universities, developing and attracting talents. These activities require investments in R&D that account for up to 20% of revenues. As a result, a combination of fundamental knowledge and engineering capabilities enabled the company to gain international prominence.

Since the late 1990s, two competitive and, at the same time, complementary business models evolved: manufacturing of equipment and thin-film coating services. Most of the R&D activities are concentrated in the coating service unit: Izovac TechnologiesIt is on the cutting edge of innovation, exploring and inventing new thin-film coating technologies.

Due to the general coordination within the group of companies, new technologies spill over to the equipment manufacturing unit. This unit does not produce a single type of equipment, but works on orders received by R&D. As a result, a client receives a unique equipment, coating technology, installation and maintenance services, as well as staff training services. Such complex turn-key solutions have become a peculiar and competitive advantage of the third group of Belarusian hidden champions that are trying to avoid price competition.

Continuity is provided by two founders who are still involved in the company's activities and focus on strategic visioning and personnel development. In the 1990s, the founders' entrepreneurial orientation and persistence enabled the company not only to survive but also to secure leading positions in its niche.

For its strategic development, Izovac pays special attention to the formation of spin-off companies. The company's leaders believe that they have created necessary prerequisites within the group: strong technological capabilities, modern equipment, a stock of knowledge from R&D activities, and organizational rules providing intrapreneurs with relevant stimuli.

Currently, the group consists of four enterprises, two of which were admitted to the Belarusian hi-tech park and benefit from the legal and tax regime. One of these—Izovac AR—has arisen from a small R&D project focused on the special coatings on augmented reality helmets. As a result, this spin-off explored a new niche and developed video modules for augmented reality glasses.

Another ongoing R&D project—a potential spin-off—focuses on coatings for flexible supercapacitors.

However, these spin-off formation practices were preceded by a spin-out that was formed by members of Izovac's team and evolved into a new, completely independent company. At that time, Izovac's leaders did not know how to retain departments and develop spin-offs and what to offer to teams. Therefore, this case was a good lesson for Izovac' founders.

2.2 Case Study 2

Essent Optics Ltd.

Overview
Address: 23a-81, 40 Let Pobedy street, Borovlyany, Minsk region, 223053, Belarus
Tel: +375 17 5112025
Fax: +375 17 5112026
Email: office@essentoptics.com
Web: www.essentoptics.com/eng/

Company Information
Industry: Manufacture of instruments and appliances for measuring, testing and navigation, watches, and clocks. Development and manufacturing of spectrophotometers
Year of establishment: 2009
Sales revenues in 2017: 1 million euros
Sales revenues in 2007: –
Average number of employees in 2017: 12
Brain(s) behind the company: Three founders with a background in optics

Nature of Market Leadership

The company is number one in the CIS region in the production of spectrophotometers for the measurement of optical characteristics. The company has recently started its expansion to Europe and other developed markets and controls about 20% of the market in this niche. It has tier-one corporations from around the world among its clients. Its exports go mainly to Russia, Germany, USA, Japan, and Israel.

Nature of the Competitive Advantage

Openness to customizations and introduction of additional features upon request along with high-quality solutions for the optical industry are key competitive advantages of Essent Optics.
  Some 60–70% of new product features were developed through communication with clients.

Core Lessons Learned on the Path to Success

1. Geographic market diversification makes a company invulnerable to crises in one

of the markets.
2. The development of a network of strong and reputable distributors in developed markets became a successful strategy for internationalization. Establishing personal relations with distributors helps in many business situations.
3. A strong focus on the niche allows the company to use resources in the most efficient way and become a leader.

Management and Leadership Development Needs

Like other hidden champions, EssentOptics lacks technical specialists for further development. For that reason, it started working with universities and accepts students for internships.

Financing and Regulatory Environment Development Needs

A more stable legal environment in Belarus would allow the company to focus on business development.

EssentOptics: A New Generation of Belarusian Hidden Champions

Arguably, the founders of EssentOptics chose the worst moment to establish a company when the world economy and CIS markets were hit by the financial crisis. To some extent, its market and business development strategy resembles that followed by old hidden champions. At the same time, EssentOptics was launched not by necessity-driven Soviet researchers and engineers, but by a new opportunity-driven generation of engineers and business managers employed at one of the successful private Belarusian companies who invested personal savings in the start-up.

In 2009, Taras Lisouski, CEO of the company, had 10 years of experience in business development, sales, and marketing, while the two other co-founders were outstanding engineers. This created a strong synergy of competences reinforced by goal-oriented teamwork. When the company was 1-year old, Taras Lisouski enrolled on an MBA program that equipped him with relevant knowledge and skills to perform market research and develop EssentOptics' strategic plan for entering new markets.

The seven-billion-dollar market of optical coatings worldwide has a 7–10% year-on-year growth rate. Almost each coating must be measured for transmittance and reflectance to ensure its conformance to specifications. From the supplier side, this measurement need is served by only four large corporations working for many decades without offering a tailored solution.

Until recently, most of the optics manufacturers have had to measure transmittance and reflectance of coatings using equipment initially developed for a bio-chemical analysis of liquids. Consequently, they used expensive equipment for just 20–30% of its functions, as well as different detachable and inconvenient accessories to measure optical characteristics. Although optics manufacturers suffered from this inconvenience and the upcharge for useless functions, rigid large corporation did not pay serious attention to this need in a market niche. Moreover, the measurement of optical characteristics was a complementary function and was not considered a strategic opportunity by all companies in the field. With its competencies, technologies, experience, and a very narrow focus, EssentOptics appeared in a small *blue ocean* with its need-driven solutions. The initial capital came from the founders' personal savings and was invested in R&D and prototypes.

The international expansion started with Belarus and Russia as test markets for several reasons. Firstly, these markets are accessible in terms of mentality, ease of communication, and cross-border trade. Secondly, EssentOptics decided to prove its technical consistency, estimate its effect on clients, and get feedback before entering developed markets.

After experiencing success in Russia and Belarus, the company's leaders clearly understood that they could not secure stable growth in the market since revolver sales of measurement equipment are rare. As a family does not need five refrigerators at home, clients may need only a couple of devices in the next 10 years. For that reason, the company considered two strategic options for entering developed markets. The first option was to establish small offices in a few countries. This approach required substantial investments, while the first sales might happen after several years. The second option was to find strong and reputable distributors in the countries with a developed optical industry, such as UK, Germany Switzerland, Italy, France, Israel, Japan, Korea, and the US, and to convince them to promote the equipment of a no-name company from a little known country. EssentOptics defined the profile of potential distributors: they had to be experienced experts in the field of optics and electronics serving similar market segments who did not work with the company's competitors. Exhibitions were chosen as the main channel to attract potential partners that were invited to test the equipment.

EssentOptics managed to attract the attention of potential distributors offering unique equipment with substantially better characteristics and more functions at a lower price in comparison to that of world-famous companies. As a result, distributors still play a substantial role in the company's business model, enabling EssentOptics to benefit from their reputation, client bases, and marketing activities. Moreover, establishing personal relations with all 13 distributors helped in many business situations.

The company focuses on the key processes—R&D, and design and assembling of devices—while the manufacturing of lenses, boards, and other parts are outsourced mainly to Belarusian companies. Some exclusive components come from leading world companies. Driven by the idea to expand on the EU market, the company leaders work on the establishment of a partially knocked-down assembly unit in Germany in order to manufacture assembled-in-Germany equipment.

Customers' and distributors' feedback enable EssentOptics to develop 60–70% of its improvements and innovations. Listening to users' experiences and quick reaction to their feedback are key factors of user-friendly incremental innovations and, consequently, the company's competitiveness in the niche. These circumstances require strong cross-cultural communication skills not only on the part of the company's leaders, but also on the part of engineers closely working with clients abroad.

Over the past years, EssentOptics has forced four leading international corporations out of the Russian and Belarusian markets of spectrophotometers for measuring optical characteristics. In these markets, the company's share reaches 90%. In the developed markets, EssentOptics grows by 20% annually and has leading Israel defense companies, Corning Inc., and the Lawrence Livermore National Laboratory, among its clients.

As a response, large corporations started investing in the *blue ocean* opened up by EssentOptics and adapting their existing equipment to the niche. However, their brands are still their only competitive advantage.

2.3 Case Study 3

Aerodorstroy CJSC

Overview
Address: Vaupshasova st. 42 A, Minsk, 220070, Belarus
Tel: +375 17 246 56 28
Fax: +375 17 246 56 28
Email: info@aerodorstroy.by
Web: www.aerodorstroy.by

Company Information
Industry: Construction of roads and railways, repairing runway and airport road surfaces
Year of establishment: 1996
Sales revenues in 2017: 5 million euros
Sales revenues in 2007: 2.5 million euros
Average number of employees in 2017: 120
Brain(s) behind the company: Two founders: director and chief engineer

Nature of Market Leadership

The company is number one in the CIS region in providing repair services for runway and airport road surfaces. Its exports go mainly to Russia and Kazakhstan. As a service company, Aerodorstroy focuses on nearby markets. Thus, it controls 100% of the Belarusian market, repairs more than 50% of runway and airport road surfaces in Russia, and receives the most tendered contracts. The company is starting its expansion to Kazakhstan, while Ukraine is the next in line.

Nature of the Competitive Advantage

Aerodorstroy is proud of its strong team of technical specialists. At the beginning of operations, the company's competitiveness was based on lower prices. Now the service quality and reputation are key competitive advantages. In addition, Aerodorstroy implemented several strategic approaches that have enabled it to secure its market positions:

1. The supply of exclusive surface materials with a low margin helps to attract additional clients and raise awareness about the company.
2. Its capacity to mobilize additional human and technical resources upon urgent requests in a short time has made the company the number one choice for urgent work in the region.

Also, the company steadily improves technologies in collaboration with material suppliers to satisfy clients' needs and implement technological advancements in future projects.

Core Lessons Learned on the Path to Success

In industries with frequent repeat sales, the emphasis should be on developing strategic relationships and reputation, sometimes at the expense of current profit. Therefore, even some loss-making projects bring new clients and revenues in the future.

Management and Leadership Development Needs

For organic development, the leadership team needs to adapt the organizational structure and processes. That requires new managerial capabilities. Another challenge, associated with the industry specificity, is to hire specialists or train employed engineers to develop marketing activities.

Financing and Regulatory Environment Development Needs

It is complicated to enter the EU market (Poland and the Baltic countries) because of customs, visas, and other regulatory issues.

Aerodorstroy: A FDI-Born Belarusian Hidden Champion

Aerodorstroy secures a safe landing in most of the airports in the CIS region because it specializes in repairing concrete runways and airport road surfaces. By the end of the 1990s, many runways in the CIS countries required repairs, while the passenger traffic flow and, consequently, the load on airports were steadily increasing. These circumstances triggered the establishment of Aerodorstroy in 1998.

The company was founded by several firms. OAT GmbH (Germany) provided high production machines. Intellectualnyye Sistemy (Russia) contributed technological solutions applicable in the CIS. A Belarusian state-owned enterprise, Belavtosrada, employed qualified specialists. In this regard, this hidden champion cannot be indisputably assigned to one of the three groups and takes an in-between position. Aerodorstroy relied on knowledge and technology transfer from the West, while locally based manufacturing allowed a significant price reduction because of the absence of customs duties and the availability of low-cost resources (Daneyko and Golenchenko 2013). On the other hand, the company benefitted a lot from existing construction and engineering competences and entered a capital-intensive market with large-scale projects where the service quality and reputation become more competitive advantages.

Over the last 2 years, Aerodorstroy has become a leader in the CIS market that is steadily developing. This geographic focus is explained by the nature of the business that requires the conveyance of people, equipment, and materials across borders. At the same time, strong Western competitors do not enter the market because of the higher costs and their inability to be as quick as Aerodorstroy in providing services in the region. Currently, Aerodorstroy's facilities and labor force are located in Belarus, while projects in distant regions, such as Siberia and Kazakhstan, are performed on a rotation basis.

In fact, the number of clients in the market—airports that need repairs on concrete runways—is very limited. Consequently, references, reputation, and a positive experience are key factors in the niche. In some repair projects, Aerodorstroy can afford losses in order to be regarded as a reliable and responsive contractor.

Apart from less than 2% of shares belonging to the state, the company is owned by its two leaders—CEO and chief engineer—who are responsible for the strategic development and operational activities. Arguably, the demand exceeds Aerodorstroy's capabilities to provide high-quality services. That creates a daunting challenge to develop an efficient organizational structure. Organizational and process innovations became part and parcel of the Aerodorstroy's culture. Thus, the company is capable of deploying workforce and machinery upon urgent request in a short time because it has a large base of unsalaried qualified workers having experience in Aerodorstroy's projects, and because it tends to buy up all special pre-owned equipment for concrete runway repairs in the region.

Having the highest level of technological expertise in the region, Aerodorstroy innovates due to close collaboration with material suppliers and one of the first founders, OAT GmbH (Germany). Many innovative solutions are customer-driven. Thus, one-runway Minsk International Airport cannot afford to close the runway for more than a few hours. Consequently, Aerodorstroy needed to develop a technological solution that would enable landing on a repaired surface after four hours. This solution is replicated for other airports having similar requirements.

The case of Aerodorstroy is a relevant example of how foreign direct investment brought new technologies and fueled the development of a regional niche leader. Securing a leading position in its traditional markets, the company is exploring new opportunities in the neighboring countries—Poland and Ukraine.

3 Conclusions and Recommendations

In general, several factors have determined the success of Belarusian hidden champions, allowing them to compete with global corporations in certain niches. First of all, small and medium enterprises appear quicker, more flexible, and ready to customize their products and services. This requires close and long-lasting collaboration with customers as well as participation in manufacturing chains that have contributed to the development of in-house engineering and innovative capabilities as well as an outstanding reputation.

In addition, establishing strong relationships with reputable and reliable distributors and partners is argued to be an appropriate internationalization strategy for no-name manufacturers from little known countries. In this case, a company benefits from networks, reputation, and the marketing activities of local partners, and ideally gathers feedback from end-users that in most cases are technological companies and even government bodies.

Alternatively, in some cases hidden champions from group three established subsidiaries or assembly units in the target regions and became a European or American company to benefit from tax and customs regimes and country image, as well as to participate in tenders and grant schemes.

However, becoming a real international company is still a challenge for Belarusian hidden champions. Since very few Belarusian companies have managed to do that, the Belarusian economy suffers from a shortage of qualified and experienced managers equipped with relevant knowledge and skills to work on the global market, as well as of consultants and instructors in this area. This seems to be a task for the government and business schools. They should bring in the necessary people, including diaspora representatives and expats, to contribute to the international expansion of Belarusian businesses. Acknowledging the lack of international marketing competences, Belarusian companies tend to expect that potential clients will find them at exhibitions and from referrals.

Belarusian hidden champions need to react quickly to rapidly changing global conditions and re-invent their business models. The price competition puts them in the disadvantageous position in comparison to South-Eastern Asian companies that have quick product development and an aggressive market strategy. On the other hand, Belarusian enterprises are not strong enough to compete with European and American companies in terms of R&D and innovation because of the availability of cheaper financial resources, R&D projects, and programs funded by governments or international institutions in Europe and the US.

One option to respond to these challenges is to sell not a product or service but rather a complex solution to customers' problems with post-sale maintenance and upgrading. For example, STIM ensures lower road death tolls by designing a new marking, making recommendations on the location of traffic signs and lights, and finally marking roads in a single region rather than selling road marking machines and paints.

Another option is to concentrate on R&D activities, become an engineering company, and outsource the manufacturing to subcontractors. However, this is contradictory to the strategy of classic hidden champions (McKiernan and Purg 2013). The vertical integration that is inherent in the business models of many hidden champions (Simon 2009) can be considered as both an advantage and a disadvantage of Belarusian hidden champions. It enables companies to control the quality of components and be independent of suppliers and logistic issues, as well as to customize products quickly and provide complex solutions. On the other hand, in some cases, a production cycle may appear longer and more expensive than is normally acceptable. In this regard, the existence of a sufficient number of reliable contract manufacturers in Belarus would allow hidden champions to concentrate on their core high-value-added activities.

One of the peculiarities of Belarusian hidden champions is that their product portfolios are quite diversified although they were developed around one core technology. Products may be targeted at unrelated niches and segments: business to business, business to government, and even business to clients. For example, Adani produces both X-ray security screening systems for prisons and X-ray chest screening systems. Obviously, Belarusian hidden champions cannot take leading positions in all their markets but can dominate in one of the niches. In fact, the diversification strategy is inherent in all the studied Belarusian hidden champions except EssentOptics. This is an important prerequisite for the formation of spin-off and spin-out firms with a narrow focus (Parhankangas and Arenius 2003). Consequently, the leaders of Belarusian hidden champions have faced a completely new challenge to make this process clear and manageable.

In general, the Belarusian business environment is relatively young—less than 30 years old—and many widely accepted international management practices have not been absorbed by companies, especially SMEs. In most companies, the founder is also the CEO and this approach to management creates certain barriers to the sustainable development of a company. The charismatic and often authoritative leaders of Belarusian hidden champions (Daneyko and Golenchenko 2013), who started their businesses in the 1990s and are about 60 years old, are not capable of performing most of the business functions in their companies and reasonably start thinking about a corporate governance system.

This is especially noticeable at technological companies, where leaders need to make decisions quickly, keep track of technology development, and realize how markets will change in the future. Being immersed in the operational management, founders do not have enough time to look ahead. In addition, most of the founders are scientists and engineers who studied management only from their own experience. They are sure that if they were able to create and sell high-tech products, they will be able to continue to develop their companies and grow them into large corporations. But this is far from the case. Growth problems are similar for many companies. And the probability of failure is very high in such industries. An important way out of this situation may be corporate governance and the creation of a board of directors with the involvement of independent non-executive directors.

Non-executive directors could bring fresh ideas to the business, giving the perspectives of customers, suppliers, or regulators. But this practice is not yet commonly applied by Belarusian companies because of a lack of information and understanding of the benefits of corporate governance and how company boards and independent non-executive directors are supposed to work. Moreover, there is a shortage of high-quality non-executive directors, especially in the high-tech sector.

Government and business schools could become drivers of corporate governance development for the enterprise sector. The government should popularize the benefits of corporate governance as well as support the creation of an association of independent non-executive directors. Based on their international experience, business schools should develop educational programs for training independent directors and corporate secretaries, as well as organize conferences, workshops, and round tables to promote the idea of corporate governance for SMEs.

A board of directors and the presence of non-executive directors on this board could be a criterion for financial institutions while making a decision on the terms of loans.

There is, however, a possible downside to the implementation of corporate governance at Belarusian hidden champions. It could jeopardize one of their competitive advantages as the decision-making process would not be as quick as it was when most of the decisions were made by a single leader.

As for financial resources, hidden champions are quite satisfied with the available credit opportunities in Belarus and in most cases do not need them. However, Belarusian enterprises still underexploit other forms of financing of business development, such as private equity investments and venture capital that are supposed to come from abroad. These financial sources may fuel an intensive growth of enterprises and spin-off formation.

Business founders fear that they could lose the total control that they have over their companies because of their lack of knowledge and experience in working with institutional and strategic investors. This seems to be a problem for the whole Belarusian economy. In this situation, the government, business schools, and institutional investors could pool efforts and resources to bridge this competence gap by raising awareness and providing training opportunities.

Domestic competition for qualified engineering and R&D specialists in the ICT sector has become an existential issue for Belarusian hidden champions of group two and group three. Although many of them offer similar employment conditions, most of the talented graduates in science, technology, engineering, and mathematics opt for a career in software development companies. In this context, the low public visibility of hidden champions plays against them as the wide public is not aware of successful high-tech private companies in the advanced instrument and machinery manufacturing sectors. This was one of the reasons for establishing the Advanced Instrument Manufactures Association. The state could contribute to the creation of a strong brand of sectors at least by popularizing engineering specialties and demonstrating the success stories of Belarusian innovation and export-oriented companies in order to generate an inflow of young people and fresh talent.

References

Daneyko P, Golenchenko P (2013) Hidden champions of Belarus. In: Hidden champions in CEE and Turkey. Springer, Berlin, pp 127–140. https://doi.org/10.1007/978-3-642-40504-4_10

De la Rubia C, Kirchner R, Zaretsky A (2012) The impact of the currency crisis on the Belarusian banking sector. Policy Paper Series [PP/02/2012]. German Economic Team Belarus & IPM Research Center

Estes KM (2013) Financial liberalization in Belarus and Estonia. Int J Bus Soc Sci 4(4)

Kruk D (2019) Крук, Д. Белорусская экономика в середине 2019 года: итоги периода восстановительного роста [Belarusian economy in the middle of 2019 year: the results of the period of recovery growth]. Working Paper No. 69. BEROC Working Paper Series [In Russian]

Marozau R, Guerrero M (2016) Conditioning factors of knowledge transfer and commercialisation in the context of post-socialist economies: the case of Belarusian higher education institutions. Int J Entrepren Small Bus 27(4):441–462

McKiernan P, Purg D (2013) Hidden champions in CEE and Turkey. Springer, Berlin. https://doi.org/10.1007/978-3-642-40504-4

Parhankangas A, Arenius P (2003) From a corporate venture to an independent company: a base for a taxonomy for corporate spin-off firms. Res Policy 32(3):463–481

Pelipas I (2012) Multiple structural breaks and inflation persistence in Belarus. Working Paper No. 21. BEROC Working Paper Series

Simon H (2009) Hidden champions of the twenty-first century: the success strategies of unknown world market leaders. Springer, New York

Tarr DG (2014) The Eurasian Customs Union among Russia, Belarus and Kazakhstan: can it succeed where its predecessor failed? In: Applied trade policy modeling in 16 countries: insights and impacts from World Bank CGE based projects, pp 509–516. https://doi.org/10.2139/ssrn.2185517

Hidden Champions of Bosnia and Herzegovina

Denis Berberović, Merima Činjarević, Amra Kožo, and Nenad Brkić

Overview
Official name: Bosnia and Herzegovina
Type of government: Parliamentary democracy
Population in 2017: 3.8 million
Land area: 51,209.2 square km

History

1189	First documented mentioning of Bosnia
1377	Bosnia becomes a kingdom after the coronation of its first king Tvrtko I Kotromanić
1463	Kingdom of Bosnia raided and annexed by the Ottoman Empire
1878	Bosnia and Herzegovina annexed by the Austro-Hungarian Empire
1918	Bosnia and Herzegovina joins the Kingdom of Serbs, Croats, and Slovenes
1929	The Kingdom of Serbs, Croats, and Slovenes becomes known as the Kingdom of Yugoslavia
1945	Bosnia and Herzegovina becomes one of the six constituent republics of the Socialist Federative Republic of Yugoslavia
1992	Bosnia and Herzegovina declares independence from Yugoslavia
1995	Aggression on Bosnia and Herzegovina ends by the Dayton Peace Agreement
2008	Bosnia and Herzegovina signs the Stability and Accession Agreement with the EU

D. Berberović (✉) · M. Činjarević · A. Kožo · N. Brkić
University of Sarajevo, Sarajevo, Bosnia and Herzegovina
e-mail: denis.berberovic@efsa.unsa.ba

1 Introduction: Context and History

The business environment of Bosnia and Herzegovina is considered fragile. According to Berberović et al. (2019), this is typical of transitional and post-conflict business environments, which bear considerable risks for business operations. Despite Geda's (2011) notion that the fragility of a business environment is not clearly defined, there is a growing body of work on business environments, which emphasizes that fragility implies mainly political and economic uncertainty, thereby posing a significant risk to businesses (Dimitrova and Triki 2018; Balas Rant and Korenjak Černje 2017). At the same time, evidence shows that despite the difficulties that they might face in dynamic business environments, hidden champions continuously review their performance and adapt to such circumstances (Voudouris et al. 2000; Din et al. 2013; Garaus et al. 2016; Grego-Planer and Glabiszewski 2016).

The hidden champions in Bosnia and Herzegovina operate in a highly turbulent political environment. The continuous tension between ethnically divided parties has a significant impact on the stability of government institutions as well as on law enforcement.

The legal environment is relatively stable, but the main challenge is the existence of different legal authorities and their sometimes unclear judiciaries. Another challenge in the legal environment is the weakness of law enforcement and implementation, although most aspects of the business are relatively well ordered. What poses a specific challenge in this respect is that it is difficult to start a business, as pointed out in the World Bank's *Doing Business Report 2020*.

The economic environment is considered to be an additional burden to business in Bosnia and Herzegovina. Although the national economy is experiencing continuous growth (see Exhibit 1 for macro-economic indicators), the country's fiscal and para-fiscal obligations present a serious obstacle that makes it hard to unleash the economic potential of Bosnian-Herzegovinian companies. Because of the small economy and the very limited market size, an increasing number of companies are shifting their focus on foreign markets, especially the EU. The volume of exports is rising significantly, especially in the IT industry, and in food and furniture production.

Bosnia and Herzegovina have a population of only 3.8 million. The social environment resembles that of other European countries. The complexity of the social environment is due to several factors. First, the Bosnian-Herzegovinian population is growing old. The effects of that trend are enhanced by a falling birth rate. At the same time, in the past 5 years, a growing number of young families have emigrated to the EU in search of a better life. In addition to this, the country is experiencing a brain drain: young, educated singles have been emigrating to the EU, seeking better work opportunities and living conditions.

Exhibit 1 Core economic indicators for Bosnia and Herzegovina

Indicator	2011	2012	2013	2014	2015	2016	2017	2018
GDP per capita (current US$)	5093	4779	5131	5330	4727	4995	5395	5951
GDP per capita growth (annual %)	2.2	0.7	4.2	2.9	4.7	4.5	4.2	3.9
Unemployment, total (% of total labor force) (modeled ILO estimate)	27.6	28.0	27.5	27.5	27.6	25.4	20.5	20.8
Foreign direct investment, net inflows (% of GDP)	2.5	2.3	1.7	2.9	2.4	1.7	2.6	2.5
GDP (current US$, mio)	18,645	17,227	18,179	18,558	16,212	16,913	18,080	19,782
Exports of goods and services (current US$, mio)	5973	5573	6134	6306	5653	6029	7246	8183
Exports of goods and services (% of GDP)	32.0	32.4	33.7	34.0	34.9	35.6	40.1	41.4
Merchandise exports (current US$)	5850	5162	5687	5891	5096	5327	6370	7500
Merchandise exports to high-income economies (% of total merchandise exports)	72.9	74.5	75.1	74.0	74.3	73.1	72.5	n/a
Merchandise exports to low- and middle-income economies in Europe & Central Asia (% of total merchandise exports)	23.3	21.3	20.9	21.9	22.1	22.7	23.9	n/a
Ores and metals exports (% of merchandise exports)	12.9	12.6	10.2	9.0	7.7	6.3	7.4	7.5
Agricultural raw materials exports (% of merchandise exports)	6.2	6.5	6.9	7.1	7.0	7.1	5.2	4.9
Food exports (% of merchandise exports)	6.8	7.4	7.5	7.0	8.5	9.3	8.7	6.9
Fuel exports (% of merchandise exports)	13.8	8.8	11.2	9.4	6.8	6.7	8.2	9.5
Manufactures exports (% of merchandise exports)	57.7	61.4	61.5	65.0	66.8	67.2	67.4	69.5
High-technology exports (% of manufactured exports)	3.2	2.6	2.4	2.4	2.9	2.7	5.5	5.2

Source: The World Bank https://data.worldbank.org/, December 5, 2019

1.1 General Lessons from Hidden Champions

Innovation The capacity to innovate—a company's ability to continuously transform knowledge and ideas into new products, processes, and systems for the benefit of the company and its stakeholders—is the one of main pillars of the success of the hidden champions in Bosnia and Herzegovina. Although their investment in research and development is lower than that of their counterparts in developed economies, Bosnia's hidden champions have critical capabilities (e.g., market-sensing capability, customer-linking capability, channel-bonding capability, network capability, absorptive capability) needed to stay ahead of their competitors at the global and regional markets.

Sensing and Seizing This is the ability to recognize new opportunities (sensing) and generate innovations based on these opportunities (seizing). For instance, Plastex, a producer of Klip-Klap (i.e., clapping sticks made of LDPE material and used for promotional purposes at various events) got the idea for the development of this product by recognizing market opportunities. The company developed the product by using its existing technological competencies. Similarly, NSoft has recognized the advantages of platform-based business models and strategies and, thereby, developed state-of-the-art software solutions for online gaming and the betting industry (e.g., platforms for virtual games, sportsbook, lotteries).

Creating Value Through Long-Term Customer and Supplier Relationships All hidden champions in Bosnia and Herzegovina stated that long-term relationships, including trust and mutual well-being with their customers and buyers, are one of the pillars of their business success. The CEO of Kristal, for example, claims that the quality of the product is an important business success factor. However, the company needs to create collaboration with all agents throughout the value chain, particularly with main buyers and suppliers.

Vision and Ambition The owners and managers of hidden champions are visionary leaders who tend to inspire followers with challenges that provide meaning and understanding. Moreover, hidden champions are nourishing a sense of belonging to a local community. The company is not an isolated entity that pursues only profit maximization. It is rather a member of a community that contributes to the well-being of all stakeholders.

Providing High-Quality Products and Services and an All-Around Offer Meeting consumers' expectations about product quality, delivery times, and product customization is another critical factor of business success.

When looking back at the hidden champion research from 2011, several conclusions may be drawn. First, there is now a much greater number of (potential) hidden champions than several years ago. This is unsurprising as there has been a strong surge of start-up businesses in the last two decades. Some of them have grown into powerful enterprises that conduct business operations on the international market. Second, the dispersion of (potential) hidden champions across different industries is much greater in the current research. This appears also to be the effect of two decades of nurturing and growing of potentially successful businesses in different industries. Third, the presence of (potential) hidden champions on international markets has also increased. As the national economy of Bosnia and Herzegovina keeps developing and intensifying its cooperation with international markets, hidden champions seem to be the front-runners. Finally, most of the currently identified hidden champions have increased their strategic focus in terms of product, and target markets, and the overall value they offer. After trials and errors and years-long learning processes, most of the hidden champions have arrived at the conclusion that customers value expertise and all-around solutions.

The hidden champions presented in this chapter were selected according to the official criteria defined by Herman Simon. Family-owned SMEs are geographically dispersed throughout the country. Their products and services are specialized for distinct purposes. These hidden champions operate on the international market, mainly as suppliers for leading brands. At the same time, they have introduced significant innovations in order to create a distinction between themselves and their competitors despite the fact that most of them have only indirect competitors.

2 Case Studies of Selected Hidden Champions

2.1 Case Study 1

GS Tvornica Mašina Travnik d.o.o.

Overview

Address: Slimena b.b., 72270 Travnik, Bosnia and Herzegovina
Tel: +387 30 519 300; +387 61 780 126
Fax: +387 30 515 479
Email: info@gs-tmt.com
Web: www.gs-tmt.com

Company Information

Industry: Metal industry
Year of establishment: 1952
Sales revenues in 2017: 12.6 million euros
Sales revenues in 2007: 0.4 million euros
Average number of employees in 2017: 247
Brain(s) behind the company: Snježana Köpruner

Nature of Market Leadership

GS Tvornica Mašina Travnik operates in the metal industry, offering solutions for different purposes. However, the product which nominates it for the hidden champion status is the uniquely handmade retro-designed electro-bicycles aimed at the high-end market niche. GS Tvornica Mašina Travnik is the global leader in that market niche. GS-TMT also produces electro-bicycle parts for other European brands—Ruff Cycles and Nicolai bicycles.

The company's main export market is Germany, but the final product is marketed in all parts of the world.

Nature of the Competitive Advantage

The competitive advantage of this company rests on innovation and human resources. The company continuously innovates its production processes as well as its final products. Human resources are seen as the most important resource which the company supports in terms of continuous education, financial support, social development, and more.

Core Lessons Learned on the Path to Success

1. Continuous investment in the development of human resources in terms of providing cutting-edge education. New trends shape not only the market and consumer needs, but also create a whole new set of employees' needs for additional knowledge, skills, and competencies.
2. Striving for a low employee turnover by enhancing their loyalty to the company. This can be done not only by creating satisfactory workplace conditions, but also by going beyond that. Being supportive of workers' needs beyond the workplace (private ambitions, social needs, etc.), exposes the organization's care and respect for its employees.
3. Innovation of production processes and launching innovative final products. Continuous growth and expansion are possible only in cases when the company has to offer something new to the market. Be it a complete innovation, which solves an existing problem, or simply a different, yet innovative, way of solving specific issues, the result is improved business operations and a leading position for the company in its field.

Management and Leadership Development Needs

Being strongly focused on human resource management, GS Tvornica Mašina Travnik Ltd. devoted immense attention to the development of management and leadership needs, particularly for its middle management. Therefore modern and up-to-date education programs are highly appreciated. There is a need for adjusted and flexible programs aimed at developing management and leadership needs. These are needed especially for forthcoming business trends.

Financing and Regulatory Environment Development Needs

As most businesses strive for cost efficiency, GS Tvornica Mašina Travnik Ltd believes that a strong overall cost efficiency can be increased further by lowering the costs of financing. Long-term finance solutions for companies in developing economies would strongly boost national economies and their companies. In addition to this, if emerging SMEs were freed of para-fiscal burdens, their growth would accelerate. A safe and stable regulatory environment would also contribute to company growth.

GS-TMT: The Arising Phoenix of Bosnia and Herzegovina

GS-TMT Ltd is a metal-processing company that dates back to 1952. After the Second World War, the company was part of the big and ambitious industrialization program of the socialist state of Yugoslavia. The company was situated near the city of Travnik, a small but historically significant city in central Bosnia and Herzegovina. Devastated after the war in the 1990s, the company went through a nation-wide privatization process and was partially acquired by Global Sourcing Ltd, a company where Snježana Köpruner and her late husband worked.

The trust that Mr. and Mrs. Köpruner had in this company with decades-long experience and success eventually paid off. Besides the necessary investments, the company has introduced modern processes and production facilities in order to keep up with international competition. GS-TMT Ltd soon started gaining ground on the international market, with a contract for the German company Messer Cuting & Wellding Ltd. That was one of the first and most important international contracts that the company concluded. Soon, other contracts followed and the company experienced a strong expansion. Unfortunately, the global financial crisis in 2009 interrupted the expansion, leading to an existential crisis, which hit even stronger and more resilient companies worldwide.

Despite being on the brink of a new disaster, GS-TMT Ltd managed to survive and entered another investment cycle. It discovered new business opportunities and initiated another growth period. After leading the company for almost 20 years, and despite her professional and private misfortunes, Mrs. Köpruner has managed to keep the business on course. She points out several success factors that have kept the company on the path to success.

One of the factors behind the success of GS-TMT Ltd is certainly Mrs. Köpruner's dedication to work. Being a true leader, she has given a good example to her co-workers of a successful approach to business operations and their improvement. Employees are highly valued at GS-TMT, which leads to high employee loyalty—another success factor. Respect for employees is also demonstrated by the fact that the company provides continuous education so that they improve their skills.

"In the beginning it was difficult. But nowadays, when I analyze the success of the firm, I think it happened mainly because we managed to handle the generation shift. I myself was extremely skeptical at times, and I thought it was impossible to succeed, but these young people, with their energy and knowledge, have managed to put the company back on its feet," says Mrs Köpruner.

Cooperation with world-known clients also contributed to the success story of GS-TMT. This company has gained significant know-how from its clients and applied it in all spheres of its processes. In addition to this, by successfully supplying global competitors, the company is being co-branded by global competitors, which attracts new clients as it signals insurance that GS-TMT is a reliable and high-quality supplier. By leading the industry, GS-TMT places itself at the top of the list of metal-processing companies.

Finally, Mrs. Köpruner emphasizes that there is no one single factor that has contributed to the company's success. It is rather the complexity of all the factors and their synergetic effect that have led to the strong and stable expansion of GS-TMT.

2.2 Case Study 2

Kristal Ltd.

Overview
Address: Business center 96, 72 250 Vitez, Bosnia and Herzegovina
Tel: + 387 (0) 30 717 733
Fax: + 387 (0) 30 713 111
Email: info@kristal.eu
Web: www.kristal.eu

Company Information
Industry: Glass processing
Year of establishment: 1994
Sales revenues in 2017: 10.20 million euros
Sales revenues in 2007: 6.67 million euros
Average number of employees in 2017: 177
Brain(s) behind the company: Nikola Franjić, founder and owner

Nature of Market Leadership

Kristal is the number-one company in the glass industry of the Western Balkans. It is in the business of glass procession, glass products, and glass accessories. For Kristal, product quality is a priority. The high product quality goes beyond satisfying standards and buyers' expectations. The company is continually looking for new ideas and ways to improve the quality of its products. Kristal has always made quality and security the focal point of its concerns. The company has proven the quality of its business and production processes, and its products, by obtaining relevant certificates and awards. The company exports mainly to Croatia, Montenegro, Albania, Austria, Germany, Switzerland, and Belgium.

Nature of the Competitive Advantage

The nature of the company's competitive advantage rests on continuous investment in product and process innovation, a capacity to manufacture special products (e.g., custom-made windows for ships, ferries, and cruise liners; fire-resistant glass, and custom-made vitrage), and the capability to create and sustain long-term relationships with all agents throughout the value chain, particularly with suppliers and customers.

Core Lessons Learned on the Path to Success

1. If doing business in a technology-intensive industry like glass processing, a propensity for innovation and market-led change is essential. The company has to be proactive in seizing opportunities, innovative in developing new solutions, and ready to take risks when a promising opportunity presents itself.
2. A clear vision and operational excellence provide the company with an inner power and an ability to respond quickly to changes in a turbulent environment.
3. It is crucial to understand that customer value creation covers many more aspects than a traditional offering, such as meeting consumers' expectations about product quality, delivery times, and product customization. Although the core offering—the quality of the product—is an essential business success factor, you need to collaborate with all agents throughout the value chain, particularly with your main buyers and suppliers.

Management and Leadership Development Needs

From the perspective of Kristal, the education system should be more adjusted to the market's needs. Specific job descriptions are difficult to find, which makes it complicated for Kristal to pursue business goals. Kristal offers highly sophisticated products on the business market. The quality of the company's products depends on the production process.

Financing and Regulatory Environment Development Needs

There is an urgent need for government policies and measures to improve the business climate and company competitiveness, encourage investments, and provide support for SMEs. It is advisable to pursue tax policies that would stimulate R&D at SMEs. Also, it would be useful to create a financial policy that provides an appropriate financial platform for financing innovation in the SME sector. It would also be a good idea to provide government funds for innovative and export-oriented companies. Finally, Kristal offers products that are outside of the regulated market. Hence, an updating of the regulations would unleash immense market potential.

Kristal: Embarking on an Innovation Journey with a Crystal-Clear Vision

Behind Kristal's success is the typical start-up story of a garage-business in the early days, which decades later becomes one of the leading companies in the market. A family-owned business established 25 years ago in a province that is well known for its business orientation, Kristal has become one of the leading glass producers in Bosnia and Herzegovina, as well as abroad. The company invests significantly in production facilities and the improvement of production processes. It is widely known for its creative and flexible product design as well as design solutions that appeal to customers around the world. Hence, quality and customer relations are the most important key competitive pillars that Kristal's business is based on.

Kristal's production is focused on producing glass lavabos, for which specified production facilities needed to be built. It is further entering the market niche of shipbuilding, with the production of high-quality round windows for ships and other vessels. Another important product is certified fire-resistant glass. Kristal is the only company in the Balkans that processes this glass.

At Kristal, they believe that the path to success is built by relations of trust between the company on one side and its employees and consumers on the other. Employees work especially hard and are dedicated to the company as the corporate culture includes a strong sense of belonging to the company. Employees' suggestions for innovations are highly appreciated and implemented in the industry.

"Stability, security, the emotions that people carry with them when they come to work or take with them when leaving this organization are very important to us. Besides, I have emphasized that this is also important to our clients. So, besides the relations that we build with the market, relations within the company are also extremely important. If that is achieved, success will surely come. Clients also want always a bit more. And that bit is the relationship built on trust," claims Ana Jerković, the commercial director of Kristal.

A market orientation is also present, particularly through market-sensing, an approach that helps the company to detect new trends in the market and react appropriately. As Kristal is engaged in business relations with successful global companies, it has used these relations to gain significant know-how and apply it either completely or with specific adjustments.

2.3 Case Study 3

NSoft, Ltd.

Overview
Address: Blajburških žrtava b.b., 88 000 Mostar, Bosnia and Herzegovina
Tel: +387 (0) 36 317 710
Fax: +387 (0) 36 32 00 37
Email: info@nsoft.com
Web: www.nsoft.com

Company Information
Industry: IT for the Betting industry
Year of establishment: 2008
Sales revenues in 2017: 10.99 million euros
Sales revenues in 2007: N/A
Average number of employees in 2017: 193
Brain(s) behind the company: Igor Krezić, founder

Nature of Market Leadership

NSoft operates on the global online betting market, but it is a leader in the CEE region. Besides the CEE region (e.g., Bosnia and Herzegovina, Montenegro, Romania, Serbia) it also operate in African countries: Lesotho, Nigeria, Zimbabwe, and Gana. At the very beginning, NSoft entered the regional market as a first-mover company. Now, after others have started to imitate its products, it has base its eir leadership position on constant changes, innovation, continuous improvement of products, and high-quality services for their software. It is essential to emphasize that services are provided online, using the so-called remote approach with extremely high quality, regardless of the customer's location.

Nature of Competitive Advantage

The company's competitive advantage is based on a combination of innovation, quality, post-sales services, efficiency, and effectiveness. The foundation of the competitive advantage is the company's approach to work that promotes some basic ideas: be the best on the market, create user-friendly products, and always have an excellent visual design. The main idea for every product is simplicity, so that everyone can use it.

Core Lessons Learned on the Path to Success

1. Continuous learning is a vital source of success.
2. Continuous improvement is a framework for continuous progress.
3. Always give more at work so that you can provide more to the client than your competition.

Management and Leadership Development Needs

NSoft's management and leadership needs are industry-specific. They are all related to the IT sector. One of the major challenges is the deficit of IT specialists. NSoft is in strong need of educated and experienced IT specialists since the company relies strongly on a learning-by-doing approach. Therefore, strong support from experienced experts would be highly valuable. Yet it is not only the lack of experts, but also the time-consuming procedures for securing cooperants from abroad that are a problem. Distance working would be one of the possible solutions, but it has still not been defined by law-makers. Finally, skilled IT personnel needs more soft-skills.

Financing and Regulatory Environment Development Needs

Unfair treatment of IT companies by the state is a problem for NSoft. There is a lot of bureaucracy in the provision of foreigner workers with work permits. Generally, there is a low level of knowledge of the IT industry in the environment. Regarding job systematization, labor law recognizes only two occupations—computer technician and IT engineer—although there are many variations of them in the IT industry that should be recognized. This negatively affects the payment and reward systems.

NSoft: The Routine-Free Zone

NSoft was established in 2008 as an IT start-up in the picturesque city of Mostar. After 11 years of existence and being driven by investment in people and innovation, it grew very quickly to become one of the leading IT companies in Bosnia and Herzegovina. Today, the company is proud to be the home of 210 highly motivated and qualified employees who work hard to meet the needs of more than 35 clients around the globe.

The vision of NSoftis to develops state-of-the-art software solutions. It is devoted to creating a business environment that will maximize sales opportunities for customers and empower those companies to reach new levels of growth. NSoft considers anything deemed "impossible" just another challenge and a new opportunity to prove the company's preeminence. Through innovation and constant education, the company embraces the perpetual change of this technology-driven business. Ideas that are born as a result of NSoft's quest for advancement are always shared with partners. It is precisely this additional value that helps NSoft cultivate long-term partnerships and allows p partners to achieve success in the gaming industry.

NSoft's mission is to provide bet shop owners with a powerful omni-channel platform, visually appealing and revenue-generating virtual games, and a data-packed sportsbook, in order to help them grow their business. NSoft's highly skilled, professional, knowledgeable, and friendly team will provide solutions, solve problems, and educate customers. NSoft believes that what really matters is an appealing design, secure and flexible software, and user-friendly installation and integration, along with constant support. Therefore, the company is always at its customers' disposal.

The process of value creation at NSoft begins with around 200 skilled individuals sharing their thoughts and insights. They are all equipped with cutting-edge software and hardware solutions, blended with sharp intellect, high creativity, and a set of different competencies. During its brief period of existence, the company has come to appreciate relationships with different stakeholders, whose insights are also taken into account when approaching a new challenge. The development process starts with research and analysis and planning, then moving on to development and designing, then testing and evaluating the final outcome. But the process does not end here. Maintenance and upgrades are highly important in the IT sector as they strongly influence overall customer satisfaction. The final outputs are a SEVEN platform, virtual games, a sports book, and lotteries for which an all-around-the-clock help desk is provided, including not only IT but legal advice, too.

"An innovative approach not only when it comes to products but also in our everyday work with our employees. The reward system is based on an individual approach, and we do not apply the same rewards for all employees. Our primary value lays in our people, and we are aware of it. We are trying to provide a pleasant atmosphere with stress-free zones, a family ambiance. For example, we provide an entertaining department that creates some specific forms of fun. Apart from this, we also do team-building and parties. We have a person in charge of this aspect of our work", says Ivana Perković.

Continuity in innovations, investment in human resources, and the striving for learning and developing beyond present horizons is what makes NSoft a true global company. With its software innovations, it has offered new solutions to existing challenges, thus offering new value to the industry that it operates in.

3 Conclusions and Recommendations

This study analyzed 35 potential hidden champions of Bosnia and Herzegovina. However, only few of the contacted companies agreed to take part in the research. The reasons for the refusal of the rest were different, but the majority desired to maintain a low profile. Although this is consistent with the hidden champion status of these companies, research ethics rules prevented us from testing this hypothesis empirically. Out of the companies that agreed to participate in the research, five were granted the status of hidden champions, and two were granted the status of potential hidden champions. The latter comply with all the criteria for such a status, but as they are still in the start-up phase of their existence, it will take some time to ascertain whether their potential will be properly exploited. Out of the five hidden champions, three have been selected for the purpose of this book.

There are several general conclusions that can be drawn from these case studies. The usual characteristics of hidden champions can be found in their Bosnian-Herzegovinian counterparts. These are family-owned and family-run businesses. They have not been family-owned for decades, or even centuries, as it is the case with some German hidden champions. This is understandable in view of the recent history of Bosnia and Herzegovina's national economy, which has rarely seen family-run business. Only state-owned big corporations existed as they conformed to the political and social system.

The Bosnian-Herzegovinian hidden champions also exhibit another hidden champions' characteristics: they are located mainly in the provincial parts of the country that are well known for their orientation to business. Being strongly customer-oriented and focused on offering all-around solutions has made these companies instant success stories. The hidden champions of Bosnia and Herzegovina are strongly export-oriented. They are present mainly on business-to-business markets. These successful companies have also experienced high growth rates. This applies to most of the hidden champions, even in times of economic and financial turbulence. This suggests another important characteristic—hidden champions are usually very resilient during turbulences from the business environment.

The business environment in Bosnia and Herzegovina is indeed highly dynamic. The chronically unstable political environment, with economic reforms leading to relatively stable economic growth, poses continuous difficulties for the hidden champions of Bosnia and Herzegovina. In addition to this, the social outlooks are not positive as the society is aging and emigration is a constant fact. Particularly hit are companies seeking young, relatively experienced, and well-educated employees.

The unstable business environment and the lack of well-educated employees are the main problems of all hidden champions of Bosnia and Herzegovina. Heavy fiscal and para-fiscal burdens are imposed on companies with which most of them struggle. And while hidden champions do experience growth in sales and market share, they believe that they manage to keep growing only due to their strong export orientation. The management challenge that they currently face because of the lack of well-educated employees is still kept under control. But the perspective is grim.

3.1 Comparison with the 2011 Research

A comparison with the research on hidden champions in 2011 allows several conclusions. First, most of the 2011 hidden champions have lost their hidden champion status. This has happened because most of them have expanded their businesses to consumer markets. In order to be successful, they have applied branding strategies, thus becoming widely popular. There has also been a shift in terms of industry between the 2011 research and the current one. While the majority of hidden champions in 2011 were in the manufacturing industries, the current research documents a sharp increase in hidden champions in the IT sector. Although only one IT hidden champion has been presented as a case study in this chapter, and another IT company is also a potential hidden champion, several more were detected in the first round of data gathering.

In terms of financial records and market data, the current hidden champions are doing far better. At the same time, they face much tougher trends in the environment, such as the slowing down of the world economy as opposed to the acceleration in 2011, the decreasing number of well-educated employees, and the fierce domestic and international competition, as opposed to the rather mediocre competition that hidden champions faced in 2011. And finally, the hidden champion pool—the companies that were considered for hidden champion status—is far greater now than in 2011. This can be explained by the overall expansion of the national economy. Despite various obstacles, it is constantly growing and companies become more focused and specialized. This makes them more successful.

3.2 Recommendations

1. Recommendations for Governments

   - Improve the country's image.
   - Promote Bosnian-Herzegovinian companies abroad.
   - Provide financial and organizational support for SME export strategies. Identify and monitor global industries of interest to Bosnian-Herzegovinian companies.
   - Create a platform for initiating the first contact between Bosnian-Herzegovinian companies and potential global clients.
   - Reform the fiscal and para-fiscal system in order to ease the burden on Bosnian-Herzegovinian companies.
   - Reform laws that regulate the labor market so as to improve flexibility.
   - Introduce distance working in the legal framework and engaging employees from abroad.
   - Adjust the education system to the dynamic needs of the labor market.

2. Recommendations for Financial Institutions

   - Decrease the price of financial resources.
   - Ease procedures for acquiring financial resources.
   - Diversify the offer of financial products.
   - Secure professional expertise as accompanying support for financial product users.

3. Recommendations for Business Schools and Higher Education Institutions

   - Adjust education program curricula to current labor market needs.
   - Adjust module curricula to current labor market needs.
   - Intensify practice-oriented learning in education institutions.
   - Continuously track the needs of companies.
   - Promote critical thinking in the curricula of education institutions.
   - Promote innovative approaches to problem-solving among students.

These recommendations have been derived from interviews with senior managers of hidden champions. Although some improvements could be detected in the period from the 2011 research to the current study, the results, however, suggest that significant action still needs to be taken in order to improve the business environment for hidden champions in Bosnia and Herzegovina, as well as the resources that they use as inputs.

References

Balas Rant M, Korenjak Černje S (2017) Becoming a hidden champion: from selective use of customer intimacy and product leadership to business attractiveness. South East Eur J Econ Bus 12(1):89–103

Berberović D, Činjarević M, Kožo A (2019) Success despite lack of support: lessons learned from hidden champions doing business in fragile business environments. Sarajevo Bus Econ Rev 37:192–204

Dimitrova A, Triki D (2018) Does state fragility matter for foreign direct investment? Evidence from Southern and Eastern Mediterranean countries. Manag Decis 56(8):1787–1803

Din F, Dolles H, Middel R (2013) Strategies for small and medium-sized enterprises to compete succesfully on the world market: cases of Swedish hidden champions. Asian Bus Manag 12 (5):591–612

Garaus C, Güttel WH, Konlechner S, Koprax I, Lackner H, Link K, Müller B (2016) Bridging knowledge in ambidextrous HRM systems: empirical evidence from hidden champions. Int J Human Resour Manag 27(3):355–381

Geda A (2011) Capacity building in fragile and post-conflict states in Africa. World J Entrepreneur Manag Sustain Dev 7(2–4):217–266

Grego-Planer D, Glabiszewski W (2016) The role of innovation in the business activity of hidden leaders of the Polish economy. Management 20(2):23–34

Voudouris I, Lioukas S, Makridakis S, Spanos Y (2000) Greek hidden champions: lessons from small, little-known firms in Greece. Eur Manag J 18(6):663–674

Hidden Champions of Bulgaria

Michael Minkov

Overview
Official name: Republic of Bulgaria
Type of government: Parliamentary democratic republic
Population: 7,000,000 (2019 estimate)
Land area: 110,994 km^2

History

681	Conventionally accepted by most Bulgarian historians as the year when the First Bulgarian Kingdom was founded, populated by Slavs, Thracians, Greeks, Romans, Goths, Celts, Proto-Bulgars, and other ethnic groups.
870	Khan Boris converts to Christianity and makes it Bulgaria's official religion. This stimulates the creation of two Slavic alphabets and a rich religious literature in the Bulgarian version of Old Slavic.
1018	Bulgaria loses its independence and becomes a Byzantine province.
1185	Bulgaria regains its independence. Foundation of the Second Bulgarian Kingdom.
1396	Bulgaria is conquered by the Ottoman Empire and loses its independence.
1878	Russia defeats the Ottoman Empire after a brief war and Bulgaria regains its independence.
1944	The Soviet Army enters Bulgaria and helps the establishment of a Soviet-style regime. Bulgaria becomes a Soviet satellite with a centrally planned Marxist economy.
1989	A coup within the Communist Party removes Todor Zhivkov from the helm of Politbureau (the supreme organ of power) and marks the beginning of political and economic liberalization.

M. Minkov (✉)
Varna University of Management, Sofia Campus, Bulgaria

1998   After almost 10 years of political and economic unrest and uncertainty, Ivan Kostov's new government launches a mass privatization process, resulting in accelerating economic growth.
2004   Bulgaria joins NATO.
2007   Bulgaria joins the European Union.

1 Introduction: Context

Bulgaria was an agrarian country until the Second World War. The first factory on the territory of present-day Bulgaria produced textile. It was built by Dobri Zhelyazkov in 1836 (Banker 2019) but industrialization remained slow till the end of the 1940s.

After the Second World War, Bulgaria started industrializing rapidly (Encyclopedia Britannica 2020) and several mega projects were launched, involving the construction of large power plants, metallurgy plants, a ship-building yard, a large oil refinery, and a plant for the production of calcined soda that has long been the largest in Europe. Nevertheless, Bulgaria remained one of the least developed nations in the European part of the former Soviet Bloc.

The fall of the Marxist regime in 1989 did not immediately result in fast economic growth. Although price controls were lifted and private enterprise was allowed, most of the economy remained state-owned and productivity was low. The 1990s and early 2000s were a lawless period, marked by several high-profile assassinations of business people, such as former prime-minister Andrey Lukanov in 1996, and billionaire Ilia Pavlov, head of one of the largest business conglomerates in the country, in 2003. (Wikipedia 2020a). In the same period, it was common knowledge that small businesses had a hard time surviving without paying protection money to extortionist groups or bribes to government employees in order to obtain and keep licenses. This situation started changing rapidly after Bulgaria's accession to the European Union. Despite the enormous progress in the fight against organized crime by 2020, Bulgaria is still being kept out of the Schengen zone as some West European politicians believe that corruption remains a significant problem.

The 1990s were characterized by serious economic problems. The lifting of price controls in the early 1990s resulted in high inflation. This unleashed mass protests and strikes. The heavy foreign debt had to be combatted by means of austerity, leading to extremely low pensions and poor social services. To stem inflation, the Bulgarian government pursued economic stability with the assistance of international financial institutions and introduced a so-called currency board in 1997 (Encyclopedia Britannica 2020). In practice, this meant that the Bulgarian national currency was pegged to the German mark at a 1-to-1 rate, and later to the euro at a rate of 1 euro = 1.96 levs. Runaway inflation stopped overnight, and the country gradually achieved financial stability. Unlike most developed economies, and many less developed ones, between 1997 and 2008 Bulgaria reduced its debt-to-GDP ratio almost miraculously from 97.3% to just 13.0% (Commodity.Com 2020). That rate currently stands at about 25%, still an enviable figure. Since 2016, Bulgaria has maintained a budget surplus, rather than a deficit, reaching 1.8% of GDP in 2018 (latest available data according to Natsionalen Statisticheski Institut 2020). This was the fourth highest budget surplus in the European Union in 2018, after those of Germany, Luxemburg, and Malta: an impressive feat, considering the fact that Bulgaria is the Union's poorest member (World Bank 2020).

In the past 20 years, economic growth has been strong by European standards. It was about 4-6% annually until 2008. Then, in the wake of the global economic crisis, it fell to −3% in 2009, but bounced back to 2% already in 2010 (World Bank 2020), and more than doubled after 2014.

Until 1990, Bulgaria's economy was almost completely state-owned, with the exception of agriculture, which was mostly owned by cooperatives, whereas a small percentage of the land was in private hands. By 2000, some 60% of the gross domestic product was supplied by the private sector (Encyclopedia Britannica 2020). The national budget continues to finance some capital investments, as well as enterprises under direct central management. Most social institutions, such as education and healthcare, receive most of their financial support from the state budget. Some 25% of all national budget expenses funds social services, such as pensions and unemployment benefits.

The strongest sectors of Bulgaria's economy are energy, mining, metallurgy, machine-building, and tourism (Wikipedia 2020b). Unemployment is low, currently about 5%. In Sofia, unemployment is negative as there is labor shortage in all spheres of the economy. Not only experts and managers, but also waiters, cleaners, and store clerks are in short supply, as one can see from job ads posted throughout the city. This has resulted in significant salary inflation in Sofia, where many jobs pay almost twice as much as in most other cities.

Bulgaria has a very business-friendly taxation policy. Corporate tax is set at 10% whereas value-added tax is 20%, except for some hotel services, where it is 9% (InvestBulgaria Agency 2020). The country has several mobile phone operators and numerous Internet providers, charging low fees. Broadband speeds in Bulgaria are among the fastest in Europe (Encyclopedia Britannica 2020). Exhibit 1 provides some core economic indicators for Bulgaria.

Although Bulgaria may have several hidden champions, due to various constraints only one was identified and included in this book.

Exhibit 1 Core economic indicators for Bulgaria

	2011	2012	2013	2014	2015	2016	2017	2018
GDP per capita (current US$)	7814	7378	7645	7865	6994	7469	8228	9272
GDP per capita growth (annual %)	2.6	0.6	1.1	2.4	4.1	4.7	4.6	3.8
Long-term unemployment (% of total unemployment)	56	55	57	60	61	60	55	58
Foreign direct investment, net inflows (% of GDP)	3.7	3.3	3.6	1.9	5.2	2.9	4.9	4.0
GDP (current US$, millions)	57,418	53,903	55,555	56,815	50,201	53,241	58,221	65,133
Exports of goods and services (current US$, millions)	33,917	32,773	36,043	36,876	32,399	34,461	39,676	43,600
Exports of goods and services (% of GDP)	59.1	60.8	64.9	64.9	64.5	64.7	68.1	67.0
Merchandise exports (current US$, millions)	28,208	26,686	29,579	29,246	25,371	26,572	33,437	33,151
Merchandise exports to high-income economies (% of total merchandise exports)	61.7	60.8	61.2	63.0	63.4	63.1	61.0	n.a.
Merchandise exports to developing economies in Europe & Central Asia (% of total merchandise exports)	29.5	28.4	27.0	26.5	24.8	23.7	24.9	n.a.
Ores and metals exports (% of merchandise exports)	18.8	17.2	16.0	14.1	14.1	11.5	14.2	14.1
Agricultural raw materials exports (% of merchandise exports)	1.0	1.0	1.0	1.0	1.0	1.0	1.0	1.0
Food exports (% of merchandise exports)	16.0	15.0	18.0	16.0	16.0	17.0	15.0	15.0
Fuel exports (% of merchandise exports)	13.0	16.0	15.0	11.0	9.0	8.0	9.0	8.0

(continued)

Exhibit 1 (continued)

	2011	2012	2013	2014	2015	2016	2017	2018
Manufactures exports (% of merchandise exports)	48.0	48.0	48.0	53.0	56.0	58.0	56.0	58.0
High-technology exports (% of manufactured exports)	8.0	8.0	8.0	8.0	8.0	9.0	10.0	10.0

Source: World Bank, January 2020

2 A Case Study

2.1 UniComs Switzerland GmbH—Sofia Branch[1]

Overview
Address: Boulevard Bulgaria 118, Albacus Business Center, fifth floor
Tel: +359 2 854 8525
Fax: NA
Email: office@unicoms.com
Web: https://unicoms.com

Company Information
Industry: Pharmaceutical
Year of establishment: 1998
Sales revenue in 2017: 7.22 million euros
Sales revenue in 2007: 3.11 million euros
Average number of employees in 2017: 90
Brains behind the company: Chief Executive Officer Damyan Damyanov

Nature of Market Leadership

Since 2010, UniComs has held a leading position in Bulgaria, Romania, and Northern Macedonia in the niche of blood pressure monitors. Its Sendo brand is a household name in Bulgaria and is considered one of the most reliable blood pressure monitors that have ever been manufactured. The Surecheck pregnancy test is also very well known and considered highly reliable.

UniComs achieved its market-leading position in Bulgaria in 2004 and has preserved it since then. Similar positions were achieved in Romania in 2008 and in Northern Macedonia in 2010. Currently, the company's blood pressure monitors account for 50% of all sales in Bulgaria in terms of pieces and 60% in terms of sales

---

[1]Although the company is registered in Switzerland, it is a purely Bulgarian company with key management decisions made in Bulgaria. Hence it is a Bulgarian hidden champion.

revenues. In Northern Macedonia, these figures are 30% and 40% respectively. UniComs holds 65% of Bulgaria's pregnancy test market in terms of pieces and 80% in terms of sales revenues. These figures are 40% and 50% for Romania, and 50% and 60% for Northern Macedonia.

Apart from these countries, the products of UniComs are available also in Albania, Egypt, Malta, Montenegro, Jordan, Latvia, Philippines, Bangladesh, Serbia, UAE, Oman, and Libya.

Nature of the Competitive Advantage

According to chief executive officer Damyanov Damyanov, the main factor behind the competitive advantage of UniComs is the democratic management system and the company's four values, serving as guidelines. They are known by the acronym "FEPS:"

F—Focus on clients. "We are a very focused company in every respect."
E—Enthusiasm. "We believe in passion at work."
P—Permanent growth.
S—Self-improvement.

In fact, there are also many other reasons that can explain the success of UniComs. According to Mr. Damyanov, the first one is the extremely well-organized sales force. UniComs has implemented a system called Effective Sales Behavior. The company trains its sales force staff and regularly evaluates the practical implementation of what has been learned during the training.

Another reason mentioned by Mr. Damyanov is the fact that UniComs has a very flexible and motivated workforce, capable of collecting market information instantly. This is made possible through the special system of management implemented by the company. They call it "democracy." In that system, people make decisions by voting. They elect their managers and share 50% of the profits. Employees in the company have complete access to information about the company's finances, including salary levels and salary formation. They also have the right to vote on day-to-day decisions, as well as strategic ones affecting the future of the company.

A third reason for the company's success is its strong investment in marketing communication.

Having provided in-company training seminars at UniComs on two occasions, I can share my own observation. First, I must point out that, as a rule, only large multinational companies in Bulgaria offer training in soft skills. Nearly all of the training that I have done in the past two decades was at companies like Nestle, Coca Cola, IBM, Lukoil, Italcementi, Mondi, and other giants. UniComs is a notable exception. Some 10 years ago, Mr. Damyanov called me after reading one of my books and asked for a seminar on cultural differences. To me, that was an indication of impressive broad-mindedness, yet I was not sure if his employees shared it. Much to my surprise, the seminar participants were the liveliest and most enthusiastic group of trainees that I had ever had. The reason that I was so surprised was that the company was making its first faltering steps on the road to globalization and it was not necessarily evident that the cross-cultural awareness skills that I was bringing in would be a strong asset. Nevertheless, Mr. Damyanov's employees were just as eager for new knowledge and skills as he was.

In 2019, I repeated my cross-cultural awareness seminar at UniComs. This time, the team was truly international. Apart from employees from nearly all Balkan countries and Russia, UniComs also employs a young Indian woman, who contributed greatly to the cross-cultural awareness session. Again, this is not typical of small or middle-sized Bulgarian companies. As cultural diversity makes for better innovation, it is not surprising that UniComs has been doing so well in that respect. During that seminar at UniComs, I learned that a similar training session had recently been given at UniComs by INSEAD lecturer Erin Meyer, author of a best-selling popular book on cultural differences in business. That strengthened my conviction that UniComs is really committed to upholding a competitive advantage by staying ahead of the competition in terms of knowledge.

Finally, the physical environment where the employees of UniComs work was a clear testimony to the company's desire to provide a pleasant and stimulating atmosphere. The offices have a modernistic appearance and provide a stunning view over the city and the nearby Vitosha mountain. The walls of the lavatory were painted by a Bulgarian artist and the premises are reminiscent of the entrance to a spa in a five-star hotel.

Core Lessons Learned on the Path to Success

To quote Mr. Damyanov, "The business is not a sprint. It is a marathon. You need patience and consistency. You need constant improvement and constant change. You may lose a battle. Then you need to learn the lessons. You may win the battle, then you need to understand why. Very often it is not clear why you win."

Management and Leadership Development Needs

Mr. Damyanov outlines several challenges that UniComs needs to address in order to maintain its leading position and grow further. First, he notes that marketing techniques have changed. It is becoming increasingly important to have an active presence on social networks, such as Facebook and Instagram. He indicates that the country is very good in the old marketing, but now needs to make a shift to the new world so as "to know, understand, feel, and use it much more efficiently."

Also, he points out that the chief executive officer, the marketing department, as well as everybody else, constantly need to be educated. Marketing is critical for the company's success. In order to do well, UniComs should be able to make use of the latest marketing techniques. "If the chief executive officer (that's me) does not understand that, he will never push his people in the right direction."

He adds that the company is in its international expansion phase now and needs a lot of new people. Finding the most appropriate employees and training them is the biggest current challenge.

Financing and Regulatory Environment Development Needs

According to Mr. Damyanov, bank loans have so far been sufficient for the company's growth. In order to have more options and to be ready for the future in case the company needs alternative funding sources, UniComs became part of the Elite Program of the London Stock Exchange. Most probably, in the near future, the company will use more financial instruments.

Regulatory Environment

The company has recommended to the Bulgarian government that it not allow a private monopoly. In Mr Damyanov's view, huge companies suppress variety. Also, he thinks that the education system should be changed in such a way that children get more knowledge about practical things, such as how to manage their own finances. They also need basic knowledge about the real world.

UniComs has recommended that the Bulgarian financial institutions invest in their clients' education. Most of those clients are very ignorant about finance and other business knowledge. "The financial institutions care only about the money they provide, but the money and the profit that they make will be much more secure if they educate their clients," Mr. Damyanov says.

Educational Institutions

Mr. Damyanov insists that education should be made more practical. Business people should participate in the education of students. The educational programs should be reformed in such a way that they allow students to work and study simultaneously. They should be prepared for tomorrow's real life.

Truly a Champion and Truly Hidden

According to the company's website (https://unicoms.com/company/), UniComs was established "with the core objective of developing and marketing the best and innovative diagnostics brands and food supplements with the aim to help improve lifestyles through better self-care." Its success testifies that it has achieved this goal.

UniComs is truly a business champion and a hidden one, too. Its rapid growth in terms of turnover and personnel is an impressive achievement. At the same time, despite the fact that some of its products are retailed throughout the country and have become household names in Bulgaria, the company is not as well known to the wide public as one might think. In this respect, it can be compared to Milka and Mondelez. There is hardly a Bulgarian who has not heard of the former and very few who know that the latter is the company that produces their favorite chocolate. However,

UniComs is also remarkable because of its almost complete absence on the Internet, outside its own website.

The fact that UniComs is not widely known may be due to the fact that the company is not making an effort to come into the spotlight. For instance, the website for its Japanese-technology blood pressure monitor Sendo (https://sendo.info/en/) does not mention UniComs anywhere. This seems due to the traditionally strong prejudice of the Bulgarian public against products and services delivered by Bulgarian, East European, or Chinese companies. Although this whole region by now produces many world-class technologies, the prejudice seems deeply embedded. In the view of a large section of the Bulgarian public, a medical product is fully reliable only if it is Swiss, German, American, Swedish, or Japanese. Another reason for the relative obscurity of UniComs may be the fact that worldwide and in Bulgaria, there are other companies, operating in different sectors, that have similar names, resulting in confusion.

Despite this potential handicap, UniComs has achieved something remarkable. In 20 years, it has become a true multinational in the very difficult niche of medical equipment and health products. It has achieved this by advertising its brands without focusing on the company. It is interesting to see how much longer this strategy will be successful.

Apart from the success factors identified in the interview with chief executive officer Damyan Damyanov, it is also worth mentioning the company's strong investment in research and development (https://unicoms.com/company/). From a cultural perspective, UniComs has correctly identified a world-wide shift toward an individualist culture where people value freedom and independence. Part of the company's official mission is to enable modern people "to stay informed, to be independent, and to be able to design their own life" (https://unicoms.com/company/).

3 Conclusions and Recommendations

Unlike most German hidden champions, which are positioned mostly in the business-to-business segment of manufacturing (Simon 2009), UniComs produces or distributes products primarily to individual customers. It also differs from German companies in terms of its market. After Bulgaria, the other Balkan countries seemed logical places for market expansion. The next logical choice was high birth-rate countries in Africa and Asia. Currently, UniComs is developing its Bangladesh market. If tackled properly, that market can have huge opportunities.

Just like the German hidden champions, UniComs relies strongly on product innovation. Another common aspect is that this is a high-tech company, where expert knowledge is a key competitive advantage. The organizational culture is also highly innovative by Bulgarian standards, as democracy is not a typical managerial tool in Bulgaria. Nevertheless, the role of the founder and chief executive officer remains essential. He is a visionary and ambitious leader, extremely passionate and dedicated to the development of his company and the societal role that it plays.

References

Banker (2019) Dobri Zhelyazkov stroi prvata textilna fabrika v Sliven. https://www.banker.bg/sudbi/read/dobri-jeliazkov-stroi-purvata-tekstilna-fabrika-v-sliven

Commodity.Com (2020) Bulgaria national debt clock: How one country drastically reduced its GDP-to-debt ratio. https://commodity.com/debt-clock/bulgaria/

Encyclopaedia Britannica (2020) Bulgaria: economy. https://www.britannica.com/place/Bulgaria/Economy

InvestBulgaria Agency (2020) Taxation. https://www.investbg.government.bg/en/pages/4-taxation-177.html

Natsionalen Statisticheski Institut (2020) Obsht drzhaven deficit (−) i izlizhyk (+). www.nsi.bg

Simon H (2009) Hidden champions of the twenty-first century. Springer, Berlin

Wikipedia (2020a) Bulgarian Mafia. https://en.wikipedia.org/wiki/Bulgarian_mafia

Wikipedia (2020b) Economy of Bulgaria. https://en.wikipedia.org/wiki/Economy_of_Bulgaria

World Bank (2020) World Bank open data. https://data.worldbank.org/

Hidden Champions of China

Xiaobo Wu and Linan Lei

Overview
Official name: People's Republic of China
Type of government: Socialist
Population in 2017: 1.386 billion
Land area: 9,634,057 km^2

History

2200–1700 BCE	The first non-mythical dynasty to rule China, the Xia (2200–1700 BCE), was founded by Emperor Yu. It was succeeded by the Shang Dynasty (1600–1046 BCE), and then the Zhou Dynasty (1122–256 BCE).
618 CE	Foundation of the Tang Dynasty. Chinese art and culture flourish. At the end of the Tang, China descends into chaos in the Five-Dynasties-and-Ten-Kingdoms period.
1912	Revolutionary Sun Yat-sen becomes the first president of the Republic of China
1927	The Ten-Year Civil War occurs between the Kuomintang nationalists, led by Chiang Kai-shek, and the communist party, led by Mao Zedong.
1945	World War II comes to an end and Japan is defeated. The Civil War between the communists and the nationalists resumes.

X. Wu
School of Management, Zhejiang University, Hangzhou, China

L. Lei (✉)
International Business School, Zhejiang University, Hangzhou, China
e-mail: leilinan@zju.edu.cn

© Springer Nature Switzerland AG 2021
A. Braček Lalić, D. Purg (eds.), *Hidden Champions in Dynamically Changing Societies*, https://doi.org/10.1007/978-3-030-65451-1_11

1949	The communists win the war and the People's Republic of China is formed by Mao Zedong.
1978	China's reform and opening-up policy, is launched under the leadership of Deng Xiaoping at the 1978 Third Plenum. This policy jump-starts China's transformation from a poor and underdeveloped centrally-planned economy into an economic powerhouse, increasingly driven by the market.
2001	China joins the World Trade Organization.
2008	The Olympic Games are held in Beijing.
2013	China's central government adopts a global development strategy—"The Belt and Road Initiative"—involving infrastructure development and investments in 152 countries and international organizations in Asia, Europe, Africa, the Middle East, and the Americas.
2015	China's central government issues a strategic plan "Made in China 2025" to totally upgrade Chinese manufacturing. With it, China aims to move away from being the "world's factory" and produce higher-value products and services. It is in essence a blueprint to upgrade the manufacturing capabilities of Chinese industries into a more technology-intensive powerhouse.

1 Introduction: Context

The development of China during the recent decades is a remarkable story. The economy of China embarked on the road of rapid development in 1978, when China began to implement a market-oriented reform and an opening-up policy. Its GDP grew from 367.9 billion yuan in 1978 to 90.03 trillion yuan in 2018, making it the second-largest economy in the world, accounting for 1/6 of the world economy, and second only to that of the United States. During the 40 years of reform and opening-up, the average annual growth rate of GDP reached 9.6%, while the average annual growth rate of the world economy in the same period was only 2.78%. China's average annual growth rate was more than three times that of the world. With a per capita GDP of US$9770 in 2018, China has entered the ranks of upper-middle-income countries. It took only 16 years for China to quadruple its GDP per capita from US$2000 to US$8000, compared with 81 for the United States, 20 for South Korea, 17 for Japan, and 54 for the world. According to the IMF, China's economic growth has contributed to nearly 30% of the world's growth. More information on China's core economic indicators is available in Exhibit 1.

Manufacturing is the backbone of national economic development. According to the National Statistics Bureau, the industrial added value in 2018 was 30,516 billion RMB, accounting for 33.9% of GDP. The added value of manufacturing was 26,482 billion RMB, which means that manufacturing is still the largest industry in China with a 29.4% contribution to the GDP. By the end of 2017, total employment in manufacturing in China was 102.97 million, or 19.9% of the figure across all sectors.

Exhibit 1 Core economic indicators for China

	2011	2012	2013	2014	2015	2016	2017	2018
GDP per capita (current US$)	5618.13	6316.91	7050.64	7651.36	8033.38	8078.79	8759.04	9770.84
GDP per capita growth (annual %)	9.02	7.33	7.237	6.75	6.36	6.16	6.16	6.08
Foreign direct investment, net inflows (% of GDP)	3.7088	2.8270	3.0398	2.5683	2.2013	1.5689	1.3676	1.4953
GDP (current US$, mio)	7,551,500.43	8,532,230.72	9,570,405.76	10,438,529.2	11,015,542.4	11,137,945.7	12,143,491.4	13,608,151.9
Exports of goods and services (current US$, mio)	2,006,296.85	2,175,080.63	2,354,248.58	2,462,839.44	2,362,092.88	2,199,967.57	2,424,199.91	2,655,609.1
Exports of goods and services (% of GDP)	26.568	25.492	24.599	23.593	21.443	19.752	19.962	19.514
Merchandise exports (current US$)	1.90E+12	2.05E+12	2.21E+12	2.34E+12	2.27E+12	2.10E+12	2.26E+12	2.49E+12
Merchandise exports to high-income economies (% of total merchandise exports)	74.351	73.478	72.495	71.178	71.503	70.857	70.292	N/A
Merchandise exports to developing economies in Europe & Central Asia (% of total merchandise exports)	4.64	4.68	4.80	4.72	3.59	3.98	4.25	N/A
Ores and metals exports (% of merchandise exports)	1.4966	1.2845	1.2231	1.2936	1.2057	1.1633	1.1601	1.2384
Agricultural raw materials exports (% of merchandise exports)	0.5335	0.4615	0.4402	0.4460	0.3970	0.4203	0.4129	0.4201
Food exports (% of merchandise exports)	2.8510	2.7463	2.7131	2.7077	2.7782	3.1545	3.0279	2.8820
Fuel exports (% of merchandise exports)	1.6934	1.5016	1.5213	1.4587	1.2273	1.2859	1.5668	1.8726
Manufactures exports (% of merchandise exports)	93.299	93.934	94.021	93.993	94.366	93.754	93.595	93.368
High-technology exports (% of manufactured exports)	30.499	30.859	31.584	29.699	30.426	30.249	30.887	N/A

Source: World Bank, December, 2019, https://databank.worldbank.org/home.aspx

The development of manufacturing in China started in 1978 when the household contract responsibility system began to be widely promoted throughout the country, and the private economy in rural areas began to appear in the form of self-employed households, which gave birth to the rise of a large number of urban enterprises.

In the 1980s, when China had just opened its doors, the world saw a transfer of labour, capital-intensive industries, and some low-value-added technology-intensive industries, from developed countries to developing ones. With its huge labour market, China seized this rare historical opportunity and successfully became the main agent in this industrial transfer. In the past 40 years, the number of Chinese small and medium-sized enterprises has been growing. By the end of 2018, there were 110 million market entities in China, of which 34,742 million were enterprises.

According to the classification criteria of SMEs and the data of the third economic census, SMEs account for 99.7% of the total number of enterprises. In the industrial sector, SMEs achieved revenues in the amount of 7.22 trillion yuan in 2016, accounting for 62.7% of the main business income of industrial enterprises. Figure 1 illustrates how the United States', China's, Japan's, and Germany's shares of global manufacturing value changed from 1982 to 2016, whereas Fig. 2 shows how numbers of small and medium-sized enterprises changed between 1999 and 2017 in the same countries.

However, rising wages and the appreciation of the RMB have reduced China's exports in recent years and focused global attention on its future viability as a low-cost manufacturing center. The trade liberalization has brought about a manufacturing transfer, but few technology transfers. China's ability to develop core technologies independently has stagnated in the long-term and fallen into a "low-end lock-in" situation. Specifically, the manufacturing capacity of key

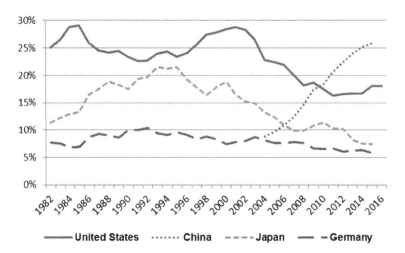

Fig. 1 Selected countries' shares of global manufacturing value added (calculated in current U.S. dollars) (Source: Congressional Research Service, Report 42135, 2018)

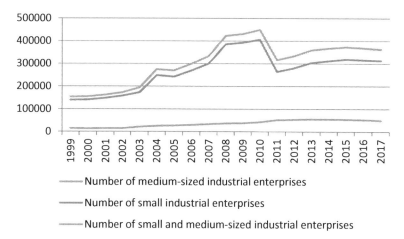

Fig. 2 Changes in the number of small and medium-sized industrial enterprises in China (1999–2017) (Data source: National Bureau of Statistics, China)

components and intellectual property rights in core technologies are relatively weak, especially in the fields of optics, engine, transportation, semiconductor, basic communication procedures, audio-visual technology, medical technology, and more. In a bid to move manufacturing up the value chain, the central government of China released the first 10-year action plan "Made in China 2025" designed to transform China from a manufacturing giant that relies on low-cost labour into a world manufacturing power. It articulated a goal of "develop[ing] a number of specialized medium-size enterprises that are prominent in niche markets," as a large number of world leaders in very specific markets called "hidden champions" (Simon 1996, 2012) are the backbone of the German economy.

China's Ministry of Industry and Information Technology initiated a program in 2016 to meet this goal through promoting more high-performing enterprises in manufacturing, as part of the reinforcement of the country's position as a global manufacturing power. Specifically, the Ministry of Industry and Information Technology of China put forward the "Implementation Plan of Special Action for Cultivating and Promoting Manufacturing Champion Enterprises" on March 21, 2016, aiming at identifying 200 manufacturing champion enterprises by 2025, and cultivating 600 potential enterprises to grow into champions. Guided by the central government, some provinces organized selection and cultivation programs for local champion firms in manufacturing (Fig. 3). For example, Zhejiang province initiated a hidden champions program on August, 9, 2016 and began identifying and promoting champion enterprises in manufacturing. More and more hidden champions are identified through the top-down champion-encouraging program.

By November 2018, the Ministry of Industry and Information Technology had released three lists of champion enterprises, including 193 manufacturers. The geographic distribution of the champion enterprises reveals development differences

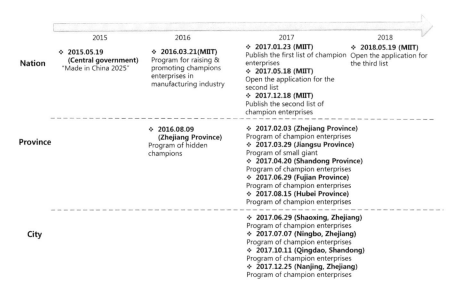

Fig. 3 Top-down champion-encouraging program (Source: The authors)

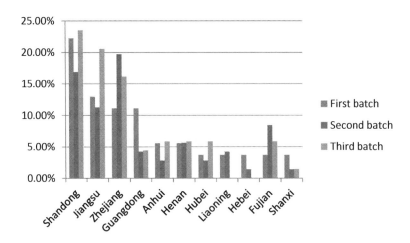

Fig. 4 Regional distribution of China's champion enterprises (Source: Sorted by authors)

between the East and the West of China (Fig. 4). At the same time, the provinces that have more champion enterprises, such as Shandong, Zhejiang, and Jiangsu, are also ahead of others in the development of institutions or policies for encouraging champion enterprises.

2 Case Study 1

2.1 Soton

Overview

Address: No. 378 Beiyuan Road, Beiyuan Industrial District, Yiwu, Zhejiang 322000, China
Tel: 86-579-8567 0515
Fax: 86-579-8567 9555
Email: st@china-straws.com
Web: http://www.china-straws.com

Company Information

Industry: Manufacture of plastic products
Year of Establishment: 1994
Sales revenues in 2017: 50 million RMB
Sales revenues in 2007: 130 million RMB
Average number of employees in 2017: 400
Brain(s) behind the company: Mr. Zhongping Lou

Nature of Market Leadership

Soton is an enterprise specializing in the development and production of plastic drinking straws and is the largest producer in its global niche market. Although the company has only about 400 employees, it has built a 40,000 square meter fully enclosed and clean workshop, nearly satisfying the good manufacturing practices standards of the US Food and Drug Administration. The company has more than 200 production lines for various drinking straws and produces nearly 10,000 tons (more than 20 billion units) of all kinds of drinking straws annually. It is a manufacturing enterprise producing the best-quality, highly innovative products, with the highest market coverage of plastic drinking straws in the world. The products are mainly supplied to shopping malls and supermarkets. Some are directly used by domestic and foreign catering chains.

Nature of the Competitive Advantage

In July 2016, the International Organization for Standardization in Geneva, Switzerland, formally issued an ISO International Standard for Polypropylene Drinking Straws to 162 member countries around the world. This standard was formulated mainly by Soton. Relevant organizational requirements, production process, rules for acceptance, and rules-based on international standards of the industry all come from the data and verification support provided by Soton, which has won the rule initiative and industry voice for the long-term development of China's straw industry. Additionally, Soton holds two-thirds of the patents of the global plastic straw industry (150 out of about 200 patents). This makes the Soton brand the best in the global straw industry.

Core Lessons Learned on the Path to Success

1. Focus on depth, but do not be restricted to a single business. Given the limited market size, hidden champions should also consider diversification for their long-term development, especially after industrial upgrading and transformation.
2. Emphasize on effective innovation. Continuous innovation has been identified as one of the key lessons for hidden champions, but effective innovation by considering market demand is important for firm growth.
3. Corporate social responsibility and environment-friendly production, caring employees, and corporate culture are crucial on the hidden champions' path to success.
4. Innovation in production equipment is also a key to achieving market leadership.

Management and Leadership Development Needs

Soton founder Mr. Lou thinks that practical experience is far from enough. As the leader, he needs to acquire a lot of new knowledge and constantly update it. Therefore, in 1998, he chose a 5-year part-time program at Zhejiang University. He still studies at least 4 hours a day to absorb the latest knowledge and information.

A Japanese businessman affected the management and leadership of Soton a lot. He came to visit Soton early in 1997 as a purchasing officer and established a deep friendship with Mr. Lou. They communicated a lot in the following years, and the thought of lean management, sustainable development, and a culture of caring employees in Soton were all his ideas.

However, Soton also had to deal with the issue of succession, like other small and medium-sized enterprises, especially in family businesses. Mr. Lou considered this issue around 2012 and tried to solve it by training successors. As Soton operates in a niche market in which general talents are not appropriate, Mr. Lou has spent a lot of efforts in training the members of the top management team, and the middle managers. Over 20 employees, in key positions at Soton, have been trained and deeply influenced by him. Mr. Lou believes that solving the succession issue well could guarantee Soton's sustainable development for at least another 20 years.

Financing and Regulatory Environment Development Needs

Soton has always focused on financial stability, even in its fast development stage. The company has gradually developed its organizational structure and formed a sophisticated management system. Following the concept of lean management,

Soton has formulated detailed operation instructions and related assessment documents even for its cleaning personnel.

Soton: Hidden Champion

The founder of Soton, Mr. Lou, is a base-of-the-pyramid entrepreneur, who tried some 20 kinds of business before entering the industry of plastic drinking straws. In 1994, Soton started from a small household workshop with one piece of semi-automatic equipment. Mr. Lou registered the trademark of Soton in 1996, when few people in China paid attention to intellectual property rights and entered the foreign trade business after learning by himself how to use a computer. Due to the disastrous Asian financial crisis in 1998, China's economy suffered an enormous shock and the drinking straws industry faced a reshuffle. As some companies collapsed during the financial crisis, Mr. Lou perceived an opportunity for internal growth through mergers and acquisitions. The number of employees at Soton increased from 3 in 1994 to around 200 in 2001. The company's production capacity continuously expanded during this period, and Soton had grown into China's largest producer by 2002, meeting around 1/4 of the global demand for drinking straws. Additionally, it also started producing related plastic products in order to expand more rapidly.

However, the development of Soton was by no means problem-free. In the process of expansion, when the demographic dividend kept disappearing but nothing improved in terms of technological capability or production efficiency, Soton reached a bottleneck in cost reduction. Competitors gradually forced prices down in an attempt to get big orders from international customers. Soton's largest customer at that time was a franchiser covering the whole European market in Austria. With all equipment in operation, it took Soton 3–4 months to deliver the ordered goods. Soton lost bargaining power and made little profit. What was worse, a large stock of products was detained overseas because of quality problems. At the same time, under the pressure of the company's continuous rapid expansion, Mr. Lou had a health issue and stayed at a hospital for 9 months. All this made Mr. Lou think about whether it makes sense to continue expanding and turn Sunton into a large enterprise. He made a key decision in 2003 that has entered the textbooks of many business schools in China. That is the rule of the "small customer."

Soton gave up its transactions with international large customers like Walmart and started exploring small domestic customers: cafes, bars, chain restaurants, and hotels. Mr. Lou even made the rule that a single customer's order could not surpass 3% of Soton's total output. The export ratio decreased from nearly 90% in 2000 to 50% in 2005. This helped the company survive in the global financial crisis in 2008. It also enabled Mr. Lou to rethink the position of Soton. Although Soton had been the largest producer of drinking straws in the world, it still catered to the low-end market and provided products of "relatively good" quality, before adopting the rule of the "small customer."

At that time, one drinking straw cost less than 0.01 yuan. During 2006–2007, Mr. Lou made a lot of effort exploring other functions of drinking straws, and finally developed dozens of innovative straws for different scenarios. In November 2009, 37 innovative products were patented, including the artistic drinking straws that could easily be produced in different shapes. They were mass-produced in the same year and still account for around 25% of Soton's total output.

The company also owns an industrial plastics laboratory. The ISO International Standard for Polypropylene Drinking Straws adopted by 162 member countries was formulated mainly by Soton. The increasing emphasis on innovation provides better protection from competitors. Since drinking straw production is a niche market with limited market size, there are no equipment manufacturers in this domain. Therefore, Soton continuously innovates its equipment and its production line achieves the efficiency and flexibility that is needed to meet the requirements of different customers.

Challenges come one after another. "We find that our growing rates slowed from 2015, so the current position will reach the ceiling in the next few years. Last year, we started to change our thinking, for breaking through the ceiling." To achieve a long-term competitiveness, Soton made a decision that does not seem to clash with the core lessons of hidden champions. The company deleted the phrase "specializing in making drinking straws for 50 years" from its mission, and diversified the business in 2018. As plastic products do not easily degrade in soil, in 2019 Soton started to explore degradable packaging products for sustainable development. The developing path of Soton evidences the rise of a late-comer and shows how a hidden champion can adapt strategically when dealing with industrial upgrading and transformation.

2.2 Shuanghuan

Overview

Address: Mechanical and electrical district ShengYuan Road No.1, Yuhuan County, Taizhou city, Zhejiang province, China
Tel: +86-0576-87204000
Fax: +86-0576-87239867
Email: server@gearsnet.com
Web: www.gearsnet.com

Company Information

Industry: Manufacture of general equipment
Year of establishment: 1980
Sales revenues in 2017: 2.64 billion RMB
Sales revenues in 2007: 430 million RMB
Average number of employees in 2017: 4511
Brain(s) behind the company: Mr. Changhong Wu

Nature of Market Leadership

Shuanghuan was founded in 1980, and listed on the Shenzhen Stock Exchange in September 2010. Over nearly 40 years, Shuanghuan focused on R&D, and design and production of gears. It has formed a multi-field and full-range product portfolio for conventional cars, electric cars, high-speed rail traffic, off-road machinery, motorcycles, ATV, electric tools, industrial robots, and more. This has made Shuanghuan one of the world's leading professional manufacturers of gear bulk products with considerable scale and strength.

In 2005, Shuanghuan began to follow a strategy of globalization. Its products were accepted by Demag and the company became the first Chinese gear enterprise to enter the European market. Since then, it has established cooperative relations with more than 30 key customers among the top 500 in the world, such as BorgWarner, Dana, Bosch, and John Deere, becoming the largest gear manufacturer in China with the strongest capability. Shuanghuan was listed as a hidden champion enterprise by China's Ministry of Industry and Information Technology at the end of 2017.

Nature of Competitive Advantage

Gears are one of the basic elements used to transmit power and position. The quality of gears depends mainly on their accuracy and strength, a result of continuous technology development. Identified by the National Development and Reform Commission of China, the engineering technology research center of Shuanghuan has been labeled a national enterprise research center, specializing in gear and driving system design, manufacture, testing, diagnosis; extension of working life, and other relevant fields of research. According to international standards, there are 13 grades of gear accuracy, grouped from 0 through 12, where 0 is the highest grade and 12 is the lowest. The development of Shuanghuan's technology is exactly a process of improvement in production accuracy and reliability. Now Shuanghuan is capable of mass-producing gears of 5–6 grades in all kinds of automobiles, motorcycles, engineering, and machinery, as well as electric tool gears. At the same time, it could also produce 3–4 grade high-precision gear products. Shuanghuan has been able to export high-precision gear products although most of them were monopolized by European and American gear manufacturers previously.

Core Lessons Learned on the Path to Success

1. Focus on drawing a group of concentric circles for hidden champions. For Shuanghuan, The center of the circles is transmission gears. The circles are different application scenarios according to the development of the market.
2. Learning by supplying. As a supplier of intermediate products, Shuanghuan has continuously improved the quality and precision of its products in accordance

with the requirements of world-class automobile enterprises. Apart from the detailed product requirements, leading customers from Fortune Global 500 companies send engineers and other experts to Shuanghuan for guidance. The emergence of supply chain quality management provides a new path for the cooperation between suppliers and customers.

Management and Leadership Development Needs

Based on the "specialized production" model and the business philosophy that "continuous improvement is a never-ending journey," Shuanghuan never stops making improvements and keeps forging ahead. Shuanghuan keeps investing and upgrading its production lines (hobbing, chamfering, shaving, etc.) for higher efficiency, including more than 95% numerical control production, advanced international equipment with full inspections, and proper measuring and testing. Shuanghuan has also been concentrating on the improvement of its software capabilities, TPS, and lean management during the past 20 years, which resulted in better implementation of the international standardization of quality management systems.

Financing and Regulatory Environment Development Needs

Shuanghuan applied for an initial public offering in August 2010 and got listed on the Shenzhen Stock Exchange in September, planning to sell 30 million shares of stocks. The funds were collected for investing in expansion projects. After the expansion, the production capacity and market power of Shuanghuan improved further, which helped Shuanghuan get better financing. And according to the requirements of enterprise governance, as a listed firm Shuanghuan continually improves its board of directors, top management team, and organizational structure, thus establishing a modern enterprise governance system.

Shuanghuan: Hidden Champion

In the spring of 1980, the founder of Shuanghuan, Mr. Shanqun Ye, founded the first business of Shuanhuan with only 3000 yuan in a county called Yuhuan in Zhejiang province. Yuhuan is an island county with limited resources, and the issue of freshwater there was not solved until 2008. Shuanghuan is one of the first groups of private enterprises in China. Its development is related to the national institutional and market environment.

The real development of Shuanghuan started in 1992 after the South Inspection Speech by Deng Xiaoping, the chief architect of China's reform and opening-up. That important speech outlined an unequivocal path for the country's further reform and opening-up and drove its political, economic, and social development. The first model of motorcycle gears was developed successfully in 1997. Then Shuanghuan's output doubled and reached 80 million yuan in 1998.

However, after Shuanghuan's output of motorcycle gears reached 100 million yuan, the company faced a serious challenge in 2000. Affected by the national macro-control policy, the market of motorcycles experienced a sharp downturn and the motorcycle-part market was in trouble. The price of gear declined from 180 yuan per piece to 60 yuan. Simultaneously, the Chinese market of auto motors and output grew ten times in 2001, especially after China joined the WTO. For gear producer like Shuanghuan, this was a challenge but also an opportunity.

In the first stage of Shuanghuan's development, the expansion of its market was mainly based on the domestic market. After taking the office of the new chairman Mr. Changhong Wu, the son-in-law of the founder, not only decided to expand the market from motorcycle gears to automobile gears but was also determined to globalize the company. The new chairman realized that with China's entry into the WTO, the automobile industry would become the mainstream and would certainly drive the huge market of automobile gears. Therefore, judging the development trend in this industry, he branched out the original motorcycle gear business to the field of automobile gears, then to industrial robots, rail transit, and other fields. The varieties of gears developed at Shuanghuan increased from a dozen to over 1000. Only in the field of automobile gears, the output of Shuanghuan grew to 200 million yuan in 2004, which was a nearly tenfold increase in 2 years.

In 2005, Shuanghuan began its journey toward globalization, benefiting a lot from the model of "learning by supplying." As a supplier of intermediate products, the quality and precision of products has been improved continuously to meet the requirements of the leading automobile enterprises in the world. In addition to the detailed product requirements, engineers, and experts from Shuanghuan's customers came to the company for guidance. Under this supply chain quality management system, Shuanghuan continuously improves production capacity. Its products were accepted firstly by Demag and became the first gear-producing enterprise in China to enter the European market. The development of the international market also boosted the domestic market business of Shuanghuan.

To achieve long-term success, Shuanghuan also pays a lot of attention to technology development. One of the company's innovative products, the 14 high-precision gear reducers, have been widely adopted in automatic control, aerospace, industrial robot, and other fields facilitating the technological development for achieving the goals of "Made in China 2025." As a leading firm in the industry, the technology center of Shuanghuan also offers services such as gear design consulting, testing, diagnosis, and technology service for reducing vibration and noise. It works with Saic Motor, Dongfeng Automobile, JAC, ZMPC, Dongfeng Cummins, etc.

It took Shuanghuan 23 years after its establishment to reach 100 million yuan in sales, 10 years from 100 million to 1 billion, and only 3 years from 1 billion to 2. Shuanhuan's motto in its nearly 40-year development has been "Continuous improvement is a never ending journey." It is on the way to constructing a demonstration model for a smart factory. Thus, after being a gear champion, it is becoming a manufacturing system champion.

2.3 Noblelift

Overview
Address: No. 528, Changzhou Road, Changxing County, Zhejiang province, China
Tel: +86-0572-6210906
Fax: +86-0572-6210905
Email: info@noblelift.com
Web: www.noblelift.cn

Company Information
Industry: Manufacture of general equipment
Year of establishment: 2000
Sales revenues in 2017: 2.55 billion RMB
Sales revenues in 2007: 1 billion RMB
Average number of employees in 2017: 1564
Brain(s) behind the company: Mr. Yi Ding

Nature of Market Leadership

Founded in 2000, Noblelift is one of the earliest enterprises in the field of industrial vehicle production in China. It is mainly engaged in research and development, as well as in the production and sales of light-small handling vehicles and electric storage vehicles. Since 2003, Noblelift has gradually started mass production of electric storage vehicles. Noblelift is a leading manufacturer and service provider of material-handling equipment and logistics solutions. It has been the world's largest manufacturer of hand pallet trucks for more than 13 years, and the leading manufacturer of Class 1–3 forklifts in China. Noblelift has always been committed to the research and development of key production technologies for industrial vehicles and has developed more than 70 innovative products with independent intellectual property rights. Meanwhile, it has actively participated in the formulation and revision of national and industrial standards, and its technologies have reached an advanced international level.

Noblelift has created history as the first Chinese enterprise that has turned the tables on its opponent in the EU anti-dumping investigation after China joined the WTO. Exports accounted for 47.28% of Noblelift's sales in 2017, and its light-small handling vehicles had 50% market share in the EU and 33% in the global market. Noblelift was listed as a hidden champion enterprise by China's Ministry of Industry and Information Technology at the end of 2019.

Nature of the Competitive Advantage

Noblelift has always been striving to be a technology leader. It invested a lot in R&D development for technology accumulation, and has lead, or participated in, the formulation and revision of 26 national standards, 3 industrial standards, and 2 group standards. It has more than 320 patents. Apart from collaborating with universities or research institutes, Noblelift also works with Germany's REMA in the research and development of control handle specialized for electronic use, for which Noblelift holds ownership rights.

Noblelift has continuously expanded its value network. It acquired Zhongding, a leading logistics system integrator in China in 2016. Noblelift provides its customers with planning and design, project management, and implementation of a variety of automated warehouse and logistics center customized solutions. Thus, the company has become an intelligent internal logistics system provider in all these fields. Then, the acquisition of Savoye in France in 2018 greatly enhanced Noblelift's capabilities in logistics system integration technology and software services, and also enabled it to compete with leading logistic system providers in the international market.

Core Lessons Learned on the Path to Success

1. High-end products and differentiation in product development. Noblelift was not the first company in the domestic market of industrial vehicles. Its high-end market helps it avoid intense market competition.
2. Servitization is an option to get long-term growth for a hidden champion in manufacturing, given the niche market size limitation.

Management and Leadership Development Needs

Management of costing control is the basis for Noblelift's competitiveness. The cost mainly includes raw materials, direct labor, manufacturing expenses, and investment in research and development. Raw materials account for about 90% of the total costs. In order to reduce the impact of raw material price fluctuations on Noblelift's profits, the company has set up a unique intensive procurement management system, based on the model of "basic inventory + forecast inventory," minimum safe stock, and order on production. Specifically, for basic raw materials, such as steel and steel castings, Noblelift has established a management platform for supplier information, continuously tracks the price of raw materials, and adopts the mode of "basic inventory + forecast inventory" to purchase raw materials.

Furthermore, for imported parts with large daily use and long procurement cycle, the mode of "minimum safety stock" has been adopted. Through its long-term strategic cooperation with high-quality suppliers, Noblelift keeps optimizing supply channel management, actively strives for preferential purchase prices, and ensures a reasonable daily stock volume. For raw materials of non-standard or small consumption, Noblelift adopts the "order by production" procurement, so as to reduce capital occupation. Thanks to the updating of processing equipment, the improvement of production technology, and the expansion of production capacity, Noblelift has gradually started to produce on its own some parts of industrial vehicles. This enables Noblelift to reduce production costs and increase profits while meeting customers' various needs for products. Noblelift is still exploring appropriate models in supply chain management for cost control.

Financing and Regulatory Environment Development Needs

The main challenge from the regulatory environment in the internalization of Noblelift is the anti-dumping investigation by the EU Commission. The EU had introduced the anti-dumping measure in 2004 to prevent exporters such as Noblelift and Ruyi from selling this type of machinery below the European market price. After 15 months, Noblelift finally won the lawsuit against the EU Commission for the dumping of hand pallet trucks, becoming the first domestic enterprise to reverse the anti-dumping ruling of EU court. However, this made the founder of Noblelift realize that products with low technology content can always be a subject of another lawsuit. In 2013, the anti-dumping investigation started again. Noblelift set up a Malaysian subsidiary to circumvent the 70% anti-dumping duty imposed by the EU Commission. It was also public-listed on the Shanghai Stock Exchange in 2015, in order to get financing support for its internationalization and further development of ecosystem building.

Noblelift: Hidden Champion

In recent years, the increasingly high logistics cost is restricting economic transformation and development in China. In 2017, the total social logistics cost in China was 12.1 trillion yuan, accounting for 14.6% of GDP, 6.5% higher than the global average. In this context, the improvement of operational quality and efficiency in the logistics industry is an urgent task, and the development of intelligent logistics is an irreversible trend.

Before the establishment of Noblelift, its founder Mr. Yi Ding was involved in the production of valves for hydraulic supports used in coal mines. Then in the early 1990s, he got interested in industrial vehicles. In the year of 2000, the company was transformed from a state-owned mining machinery manufacturer to a material-handling manufacturer under the name of Noblelift. When Noblelift entered the industry of industrial vehicles, there were three leading firms in the field in China with an annual output of 30,000–50,000 vehicles. As a late entrant, Mr. Ding decided to adopt a differentiated strategy to achieve a middle- and high-end market position through reverse engineering. Noblelift's first product was a manual hydraulic truck of the L60 model, introduced from the United States. Its first customer was the Boman company in Los Angeles. Therefore, the development of Noblelift, especially in its internationalization, follows the path of born-global firms

(Gerschewski et al. 2015; Knight and Cavusgil 2004; Purg et al. 2016), characterized as "young, entrepreneurial start-ups that initiate international business (typically exporting) soon after their inception."

As Noblelift was mainly an original equipment manufacturer and an original design manufacturer for the international market in its early stage, it was difficult to avoid the challenges of the institutional environment. In April 2004, the European Union announced the initiation of an anti-dumping investigation into China's logistics and handling equipment manufacturing industry, which was almost a disaster for a young enterprise like Noblelift. While other domestic competitors gave up, Noblelift actively defended itself against the EU Commission. It won the lawsuit against the EU Commission for the dumping of hand pallet trucks after a 15 month lawsuit and, in the same year, became the largest manufacturer of hand pallet trucks worldwide.

Because of the ever-increasing environmental pressure and ever-limited resources, environmentally friendly product development has become an urgent task for Chinese manufacturers. To consolidate its global leading position in the light-small transport vehicle industry, Noblelift seeks to take the full lead in the field of electric storage vehicles, as well as in the field of logistics integration scheme and intelligence. Noblelift got the first-mover advantage in the development of electric storage vehicles and achieved mass production in 2005. It actively expands to new markets and high-end fields, and the top-five industrial vehicle companies in the world, including KION of Germany and Toyota of Japan—are its customers.

In 2013, the anti-dumping investigation of China's hand pallet trucks and their accessories speeded up the internalization of Noblelift. It established a subsidiary in Malaysia for manufacturing hand pallet trucks. Then, subsidiaries in Europe and the United States were also established so as to counter the adverse effects of anti-dumping investigations. The subsidiaries and the extensive network in the target markets enable Noblelift to respond timely to market dynamics and to capture the personalized needs of customers. Through information feedback, the company has gradually established a flexible production and service system.

Servitization is also a key strategy in the development of Noblelift for growing into an integrated solution provider in intelligent logistics. In 2016, it acquired Wuxi Zhongding, a leading logistics system integrator in China. Zhongding mainly focuses on new energy lithium battery logistics automation, and its cooperative customers include CATL, BYD, LG Chem, Panasonic, and Murata. Additionally, it set up Shanghai Noblelift Intelligent for the R&D, manufacturing, and marketing of AGVs. Then the acquisition of Savoye in France in 2018, greatly enhanced Noblelift's capabilities in logistics system integration technology and software services, and also enabled Noblelift to compete with leading logistic system providers in the international market. Furthermore, it collaborates with China Unicom in the field of 5G, for building lighthouse projects in the field of smart logistics and smart manufacturing. All these efforts show the company's ambition to be a leading solution provider for material-handling business worldwide.

3 Conclusions and Recommendations

The Chinese hidden champions started out as late-comers, challenging the consensus that hidden champions are similar across countries. The changing market and institutional environment in China since the reform and opening-up policy 40 years ago engendered stricter requirements for their proactive organizational adaptation.

Consistent with Simon's summary of the core lessons of hidden champions (Simon 1996), most of China's hidden champions have long focused on a niche market. However, the choice of specialization or diversification has always been a difficult issue. Specialization could help enterprises concentrate limited resources to develop the advantage of depth. On the other hand, the limited market size of niche market challenges sustained growth. And enterprises with a single business layout may also face anti-monopoly measures. Through these case studies, we find that hidden champions in China adopt vertical or soft diversification (Din et al. 2013), servitization, or transformation from value chain construction to value network, to solve the dilemma.

The intra-product division has not only brought more benefits to developed countries, but has also provided new opportunities for developing countries like China to participate in emerging industries and cut into the global value chain by utilizing their comparative advantages in labor and other resources at an early stage. China has seized this historical opportunity to become the major recipient in the new round of industrial transfer, thus integrating into the global system of industrial division. It is now the only country in the world that has all the industries in the United Nations industrial classification. Therefore, the huge domestic market in China provides opportunities for the emergence of hidden champions. This makes them different from the globally-oriented European hidden champions.

The development of hidden champions in China shows that product and process innovation require a lot of effort. Although most of the hidden champion enterprises in Germany and other developed countries are leading in technology, in the context of China we must not ignore the development path of SMEs, especially those born as late-comers in process innovation. Leading the process can improve the product quality and reduce costs, thereby providing value for the customers. At the same time, it can also promote research and development of equipment for production and production methods, so as to help enterprises gain unique competitive advantages.

Nowadays, the rising digital economy creates new requirements for the development of hidden champions. The digital economy makes digital knowledge and information the key production factor. It has a supporting and leading effect on the real economy, especially the manufacturing industry. The integration of the digital economy and the manufacturing industry is reflected not only in the improvement of R&D, production, logistics, and management and other areas in the new generation of information technology, but also in new business models, and the new relations between suppliers and customers, or between competitors. Therefore, apart from deeply utilizing the new generation of information technology or big data in digitalized manufacturing and management, hidden champions, being market leaders, are encouraged to generate whole life-cycle manufacturing with big data resources. They also must initiate a new model and a new ecosystem in the digital economy. More and more hidden champions are expected to rise in the new era of the digital economy.

What is unique about Chinese hidden champions in comparison to hidden champions in Central and East Europe? Most of them are first-generation entrepreneurs rising from the market economy reform and opening the door of China since the end of the 1970s. They have worked very hard and humbly, firmly devoted to a specific niche market, relying mostly on their cost advantage. However, recently rising Chinese hidden champions are quite different. Their competitive advantage is much more based on network complementarity. The new generation of hidden champions is mostly attached to leading Internet platforms like Alibaba, Tensent, etc. The biggest advantage of Chinese hidden champions is that they are lucky to have the biggest uniform market in the world. As the world is connected more closely than ever, we see a huge potential when hidden champions in Central and East Europe approach the Chinese market. Moreover, we are optimistic concerning the amazing innovations that could be achieved when hidden champions from both places work together. The complementarity-based competence is rooted not just in market and technology, but also in culture and creativity.

References

Din FU, Dolles H, Middel R (2013) Strategies for small and medium-sized enterprises to compete successfully on the world market: cases of Swedish hidden champions. Asian Bus Manag 12(5):591–612

Gerschewski S, Rose EL, Lindsay VJ (2015) Understanding the drivers of international performance for born global firms: an integrated perspective. J World Bus 50(3):558–575

Knight GA, Cavusgil ST (2004) Innovation, organizational capabilities, and the born-global firm. J Int Bus Stud 35(2):124–141

Purg D, Saginova O, Skorobogatykh I, Musatova Z (2016) Family owned hidden champions in Russia: innovations, human capital and internationalization. Indian J Sci Technol 9(12):1–10

Simon H (1996) You don't have to be German to be a "hidden champion". Bus Strat Rev 7(2):1–13

Simon H (2012) Hidden Champions-Aufbruch nach Globalia: Die Erfolgsstrategien unbekannter Weltmarktführer. Campus Verlag, New York

Hidden Champions of Croatia

Slavica Singer and Sunčica Oberman Peterka

Overview
Official name: Republic of Croatia
Type of government: Parliamentary democratic republic
Population in 2017: 4,089,400
Land area: 56,594 km^2

History

1918	Shortly before the end of the First World War in 1918, the Croatian parliament severs relations with Austria-Hungary and declares the Kingdom of Croatia, Slavonia, and Dalmatia a free and independent state. On December, 1, 1918, the Kingdom of Serbs, Croats, and Slovenes is established.
1929	After a decade of unrest and political tensions, the country is renamed the Kingdom of Yugoslavia, and the system of government is further centralized under a royal dictatorship.
1941	Nazi Germany invades Yugoslavia. After the military collapse of the Kingdom of Yugoslavia, following the takeover by the Axis powers in April 1941, Croatia finds itself, along with Bosnia and Herzegovina, within the newly-established Independent State of Croatia (Nezavisna Država Hrvatska),

---

S. Singer (✉)
J.J. Strossmayer University in Osijek, Osijek, Croatia
e-mail: slavica.singer@efos.hr

S. Oberman Peterka
Faculty of Economics in Osijek, J.J. Strossmayer University in Osijek, Osijek, Croatia

	with a Quisling regime, under German and Italian protection (Yugoslavia and World War II 1918–1990).
1943 (June)	The National Anti-Fascist Council of the People's Liberation of Croatia is founded at sessions of representatives of the Croatian partisans.
1943 (November)	The Anti-Fascist Council of the People's Liberation of Yugoslavia is established. The rulings of that session are considered the foundation act of post-war Yugoslavia.
1945	Croatia becomes one of the six constituent republics within the Federal People's Republic of Yugoslavia (renamed the Socialist Federal Republic of Yugoslavia in 1963), and Croatia's present-day borders are set.
1971	The early 1970s mark the beginning of a protest movement known as the "Croatian Spring," during which many students and activists demand greater civil liberties and greater autonomy for Croatia. The movement is denounced as nationalism.
1974	A new Yugoslav constitution emphasized federalism, meeting some of the demands for Croatian autonomy.
1980	After the death of President Tito, the slow process of disintegration of Yugoslavia begins as federal units (republics) assert their desire for more autonomy.
1991	Croatia declares its independence, provoking military interventions by the Yugoslav army and an armed insurgency by Serb separatists. They proclaim the "Autonomous Region of Krajina" over a quarter of the Croatian territory, which they intend to unite with Serbia. The Croatian War for Independence starts.
1992	The EU recognizes Croatia as an independent state. Croatia joins the United Nations.
1995	Croatian forces retake three out of four occupied areas and the war ends with the signing of the Dayton Agreement.
1996	UN administration of eastern Croatia starts, ending in January 1998, when the occupied territory is re-integrated with the rest of Croatia.
1996	Croatia joins the Council of Europe.
2003	Croatia submits a formal application for EU membership.
2009	Croatia joins NATO.
2013	Croatia becomes the 28th member state of the European Union.

1 Introduction: Context and History

Croatia is a small country with an open market economy. As a member of the European Union, three principles of mobility—of people, money, and goods—define the broader context in which socio-demographic and economic activities take place. Additionally, the Croatian context is heavily influenced by two significant changes that started in 1991.

The first great change was the disintegration of the former Yugoslavia and the establishment of independent Croatia. It was accompanied by radical changes in the political and economic system. Croatia became a democratic state with a market economy. This required building a new institutional infrastructure, which was more difficult than expected. In the beginning, this aspect of transformation was marginalized, or even fully neglected. The result of this was a very corrupt privatization of previously socially owned (not state owned) companies and strongly negative feelings among the population.

The second important change was the war in 1991–1995. It upset the lives of all, not only during those years but for a long time after that. The war caused huge devastation. People died, the land was mined, and business facilities, houses, and schools were destroyed. There were active minefields even in 2019.

The 2008 world financial crisis additionally ruined Croatia's economic performance. In the European Union, Croatia experienced the slowest recovery: it took more than 6 years for the economy to return to growth. A positive GDP-per-capita annual growth rate was achieved only in 2014 (see Exhibit 1). Since 2015, the GDP-per-capita-growth rate has been above 3%. The low economic performance resulted in low productivity and low competitiveness, low export capacity, and low investment in research and development, as well as a lack of institutional reforms.

This led to degraded investment rankings: 2008 was the year when the first negative outlook was given by S&P (BBB), followed by negative/stable outlooks by S&P, Fitch, or Moody's in the years till 2016. After 2017, some of these institutions provided positive outlooks, and in 2019 all three institutions agreed on that. The main reason for regaining investment grade status was the improved fiscal and economic outlook: the fiscal imbalances had been reduced. The European Commission Country Report for 2019 confirmed that the stock of macroeconomic imbalances in Croatia continued to be reduced. This was largely driven by a positive economic environment and prudent management of government finances. This is boosting private sector activity, and, as a result, unemployment is falling and demand for labor is increasing.

As Croatia is a country with a small domestic market, export is essential. After joining the European Union in mid-2013, Croatia increased its export activities, achieving 51.2% of GDP in 2018, from 40.3% in 2011. This is a good trend, but the level of productivity and the lack of innovative products limit the competitive capacity of Croatian products in international markets.

Croatia scores at the bottom of Europe's ranking in terms of indicators of innovation and business expenditure on R&D (BERD) as a share of GDP. Although Croatia planned to achieve a R&D expenditure level of 2% of GDP in 2020 (the EU goal being 3%), in 2018 it was only 0.86%. This is much lower than the EU-27 average, and at the same level as in 2009. Underlying institutional factors that contribute to this low performance include a low level of R&D-driven innovation, limited access to internal and external resources including highly qualified personnel, barriers to science industry collaboration, as well as pervasive weaknesses in the

Exhibit 1 Core economic indicators for Croatia

	2011	2012	2013	2014	2015	2016	2017	2018
GDP per capita (current US$)	14,577	13,250	13,665	13,609	11,780	12,366	13,383	14,869
GDP per capita growth (annual %)	0.004	−2.002	−0.214	0.32	3.248	4.262	4.164	3.511
Long-term unemployment (% of total unemployment)	n/a							
Foreign direct investment, net inflows (% of GDP)	2.272	2.591	1.612	6.865	0.321	3.611	3.696	2.112
GDP (current US $, mio)	62,399	56,548	58,158	57,682	49,519	51,623	55,201	60,806
Exports of goods and services (current US$, mio)	25,147	23,483	24,858	26,113	23,836	25,161	27,674	31,149
Exports of goods and services (% of GDP)	40.3	41.528	42.743	45.27	48.136	48,739	51.086	51.228
Merchandise exports (current US$, mio)	13,338	12,371	12,659	13,835	12,925	13,813	16,069	17,372
Merchandise exports to high-income economies (% of total merchandise exports)	67.85	64.133	67.565	68.511	71.152	73.937	71.978	n/a
Merchandise exports to developing economies in Europe & Central Asia (% of total merchandise exports)	25.241	28.006	26.05	26.325	23.18	27.171	22.296	n/a
Ores and metals exports (% of merchandise exports)	5.195	5.294	4.479	3.733	2.836	2.807	3.816	3.886
Agricultural raw materials exports (% of merchandise exports)	3.885	4.033	4.872	5.355	5.213	5.072	4.338	4.335
Food exports (% of merchandise exports)	11.505	12.906	12.218	12.45	13.285	13.986	13.377	13.854

(continued)

Exhibit 1 (continued)

	2011	2012	2013	2014	2015	2016	2017	2018
Fuel exports (% of merchandise exports)	12.004	13.703	13.906	13.458	10.888	9.448	10.654	10.399
Manufactures exports (% of merchandise exports)	66.94	63.312	62.81	63.349	66.609	66.834	66.89	66.281
High-technology exports (% of manufactured exports)	8.719	11.885	12.633	10.548	10.792	14.703	8.796	8.894

Source: World Bank (2019)

governance of Croatia's innovation ecosystem. Focusing on closing the innovativeness gap and using technology to improve productivity and diversify the composition of its economy, Croatia will increase its competitiveness and economic stability.

Access to finance is another component of the Croatian business environment seen by the Croatian firms as a more binding constraint than it is usual in the European Union. Enhancing the responsiveness and relevance of the financial sector to the needs of enterprises, entrepreneurs, and society remains a key challenge for policy makers. Specifically, access to financing is limited, due to a lack of financial resources for the riskier stages of development, such as the growth phase, and the general risk-aversion of the banking sector with respect to SMEs, which rely mostly on their own resources.

This uneven development pattern is a long-term problem of the Croatian economy. It is visible in the structure of sources of economic growth—a heavy dependence on tourism, which might be exposed to the external environment—as well as in the differences in regional development. Unemployment in some counties in eastern Croatia is three times higher than in the western part, whereas GDP differences exhibit the opposite pattern. The long crisis that started in 2008, widened the gap between the more prosperous cities and the less developed regions. The stark differences in GDP per capita range from 60% of the national average in Slavonia (in the east) to 125% in Istria (in the west) and 175% in the City of Zagreb. The ageing population and growing emigration of young people additionally hurt the economic and social structure of rural areas.

The World Bank warns Croatia that a prospective growth rate of 2.5% over the medium term "is not enough to reignite, much less accelerate, the pace of convergence with other countries in the EU" (World Bank in Croatia, country review, updated October 2019).

The low level of total factor productivity (TFP) results from the excessive allocation of resources toward less productive sectors, a low level of R&D spending by both public and private sectors, a relatively low quality of human capital, a complicated and non-transparent business environment, a relatively large and inefficient SOE sector, as well as institutional and regulatory weaknesses. The performance of the Croatian business environment is deteriorating due to a lack of determined action. This has been confirmed for years by different surveys (*Doing Business*, the *Global Competitiveness Report*, the *Global Entrepreneurship Monitor*). In the 2019 *Doing Business* rankings, Croatia is ranked 58th of 191 countries and is among the lowest-ranked in the EU.

The degree of regulatory uncertainty and issues of regulatory neutrality relate to the lack of public sector transparency, resulting in a low level of predictability of the business environment.

Therefore, Croatia is planning the accession to the Eurozone as part of its medium-term agenda, accompanied by the implementation of ambitious and sophisticated reforms to boost growth, the building of economic resilience, and maximization of the benefits of euro-area membership. Critical reforms are planned in the business environment to achieve efficacy and efficiency of public institutions and human capital. The success of these reforms will ultimately rely on the strengths of Croatia's institutions.

The search for hidden champions in Croatia went through two phases. In the first phase, a pool of growing businesses was identified by using the OECD definition and data from annual reports (indicators on the growth intensity of sales, revenue, assets, and employment).[1] In the second phase, a group of businesses with products based on highly specialized knowledge was identified, and then several of them were approached for getting deeper insights through interviews.

Of the three Croatian hidden champions presented in the 2013 publication (McKiernan and Purg 2013), only one had maintained its growth path in 2019 (DOK-ING). Two others had lost this status due to a lack of innovative capacity and financial strength to keep and broaden their market base.

In this chapter, the following three hidden champions will be presented:

1. DOK-ING	Number one in the US, Russian, Croatian, Saudi Arabian, and South African markets in the field of remote-controlled demining machines
2. Genos	Global number one in the field of high throughput glycomics for clinical and epidemiological studies
3. MONO	Number two in the world in the production of electronic common technical document (eCTD) pharmaceutical software

One potential hidden champion is identified, with knowledge-based products that are just entering international markets:

---

[1] "All enterprises with average annualized growth greater than 20 percent per annum, over a three-year period, and with 10 or more employees at the beginning of the observation period. Growth is thus measured by the number of employees and by turnover." (OECD 2007). The analysis showed that high-growth businessess have more employees with highly specialized knowledge than non-growing businesses (based on 2012–2015 data, as part of the research project *Development and Application of Growth Potential Prediction Models for Small and Medium Enterprises in Croatia* financed by the Croatian Science Foundation, Singer et al. 2018, p. 93).

1. Alius Group—Pharmalogger	Market leader in a specialized product for monitoring the temperature and humidity of drugs from producer to consumer

2 Case Studies of Selected Hidden Champions

2.1 Case Study 1

DOK-ING, Ltd.

Overview
Address: Kanalski put 1, 10000 Zagreb 10000, Croatia
Tel: +38512481300
Fax: +38512481303
Email: info@dok-ing.hr
Web: www.dok-ing.hr

Company Information
Industry: Manufacture of special-purpose machinery
Year of establishment: 1991
Sales revenues in 2016: 26.3 million euros
Sales revenues in 2006: 7.2 million euros
Average number of employees in 2017: 100
Brain(s) behind the company: Vjekoslav Majetić, 100% owner and main visionary of the company

Nature of Market Leadership

DOK-ING is still a leading company on the market of remote-controlled demining machines, as it was reported also in McKiernan and Purg (2013), with a market share of 60% in its markets: US, Russia, Croatia, Saudi Arabia, and South Africa). The company's market structure and needs are quite stable. The nature of market leadership is the same as it was in 2011: high product quality, expertise (knowledge of the market, strong R&D team and continuous innovation, extensive experience in development and production of unmanned machines for special purposes, flexibility to adapt to clients' needs and requirements) and strong customer support. Two relevant competitors are Global Clearing Solutions, AG, Freienbach, Switzerland, and Way Industries a.s., Krupina, Slovakia.

Nature of the Competitive Advantage

The competitive advantage of DOK-ING is based on the same factors as in 2011: strong references, built-on-purpose machines (customized products), and strong and extensive experience in the industry.

Core Lessons Learned on the Path to Success

- A strong vision and ambitious company goals pay off.
- It is not a good idea to invest too much time in projects that are new on the market without a clear strategy, and neglect the development of activities related to customers' requests.

Management and Leadership Development Needs

The main business challenge for DOK-ING is the strong geopolitical influence on the market and the potential clients, as well as potential technological gaps. Therefore, for the company, it is important to keep a strong R&D and innovative capability so as not to lag behind competitors in terms of technology. This requires extensive investment in R&D activities for which additional funding from different EU sources would be needed. Additionally, it requires continuous and intensive refreshment of the engineers' knowledge so that they keep up with new technologies, as well as employing engineers with new technological knowledge. Parallel to this, it is of utmost importance to develop the soft skills of those in charge of HR and communication with customers. Strong networking, participation at specialized conferences and exhibitions, and a good agent network is needed to strengthen the company's marketing capacity.

DOK-ING plans to invest in in-house trainings for its employees.

Financing and Regulatory Environment Development Needs

Due to the strong dependence on innovative products, DOK-ING's development needs are mostly in the sphere of collaboration with research institutions, for which a supporting regulatory environment and financial resources are needed. A supporting regulatory framework is needed for all partners in such collaborative efforts. A public research institution should be stimulated to do this, and DOK-ING should have tax allowances because of such activities.

DOK-ING's Motto: "Don't have a human being do a machine's job"

DOK-ING is a 100% privately owned Croatian company, established in late 1991 and registered for the production of robotized and special-purpose systems and equipment. The production activities are organized in Croatia, in two locations: Zagreb and Slunj. Along with the branch office in the USA, there is a company in South Africa, DOK-ING Africa, which supports South Africa's demining program. In 2019, DOK-ING had 220 employees, almost 170 in Zagreb, another 30 in Slunj, and up to 20 in South Africa.

By integrating its own innovations and new technologies, DOK-ING develops and manufactures special-purpose systems to protect human lives in most dangerous environments, primarily in demining, mining, and firefighting.

DOK-ING was actively engaged in demining activities and has gathered vast experience in different types of landmine clearance on all types of terrain in the Republic of Croatia after the 1991–1995 war, as well as in the surrounding countries. This experience was the basis for designing and manufacturing the first remotely controlled demining systems, constructed exclusively for humanitarian demining. As those were upgraded, improved, and enlarged, the company has been doing R&D projects with various international and domestic organizations, including the Croatian Ministry of Science and Maritime Institute (Brodarski Institut), the Faculty of Electrical Engineering and Computing of the University of Zagreb, and the Geneva International Centre for Humanitarian Demining (GICHD).[2] The demining systems were sold to more than 20 countries worldwide, to a number of government agencies and humanitarian organizations, as well as to commercial companies. Altogether, more than 250 light and medium-size demining systems have been produced so far.

Trying to protect people working in the extremely dangerous domain of firefighting, DOK-ING designed a multifunctional robotic system, which helps them do the job and be safe at the same time.

Being dedicated to the delivery of innovative products and services contributing to the safety and security of people in the most dangerous situations throughout the world, DOK-ING believes that high standards in manufacturing and doing business are at the core of its corporate and individual goals.

DOK-ING's mission, vision, and values statements are consistent and provide a good framework for curiosity and commitments:

MISSION—What makes us go to work every day?
Through innovation in robotics, we strive to save human lives.

VISION—What is our direction?
Lead the way in the design and application of robotic solutions for hazardous, dangerous, and harmful environments.

VALUES—How do we do it?

---

[2]https://www.dok-ing.hr/company/about_us

D uty—do the right thing unconditionally.
O penness—promote agility, flexibility, and consistency.
K nowledge—create with curiosity, experience, and advanced tools.
I nnovation—do it our way!
N etwork—grow our family of clients and focus on their needs.
G roup—cultivate a team work culture[3]

2.2 Case Study 2

Genos, Ltd.

Overview
Address: Vatrogasna 112, Osijek 31000, Croatia
Tel: +38531210003
Fax: +38531251005
Email: info@genos-glyco.com
Web: www.genos-glyco.com

Company Information
Industry: Technical testing and analysis
Year of establishment: mid 2007
Sales revenues in 2017: 1,359,872 euros
Sales revenues in 2007: 10,000 euros
Average number of employees in 2017: 33
Brain(s) behind the company: Gordan Lauc

Nature of Market Leadership

High-throughput glycomics is an undeveloped service area, with multiple obstacles to market entry. However, a recent policy document endorsed by the US National Academies (National Research Council 2012) identifies it as one of the priorities for health research. More recently, the National Institutes of Health at the US Department of Health and Human Services, through its Office for Strategic Coordination, initiated a dedicated funding scheme for the establishment of this technology in the USA. Genos is a pioneer in this field. Its first service was performed in 2009. Currently, with close to 30,000 analyses a year, it provides over 50% of the global output in high-throughput glycomics for clinical and epidemiological studies. The market is increasing between 15 and 30% a year, and Genos's share of the market is increasing. The current estimate of just over 50% is probably conservative.

---

[3]https://www.dok-ing.hr/company/corporate_values

Major strengths that enable the company to hold a strong market position include strong strategic leadership, the long-term loyalty of key personnel, organizational culture and working atmosphere (ranked as the best place for researchers to work by the *Scientist* magazine), strong collaboration with leading research institutions across the world, and continuous development of leading-edge products. It is important to emphasize organizational culture as a main leadership success factor that has contributed to the company's success, which is based on a relatively soft hierarchical structure, delegating significant freedom and responsibility to each team leader. Combined with a rigorous selection of top professionals for each leadership position, this has created working conditions where individual achievements are recognized and appreciated.

Nature of Competitive Advantage

Glycomics is very complicated and requires extensive training of personnel. The number of laboratories that can perform a glycan analysis is less than 100 in the whole world. Translation from low-throughput glycomics is an additional challenge that requires advanced knowledge of biostatistics and experimental design, which is globally limited. Genos is building its team through multiple large European research projects: 6 FP7 and 6 Horizon 2020. This has enabled the company to acquire knowledge from multiple leading research institutions. Genos's main competitor in Europe is the Leiden University Medical School in the Netherlands, which performs less than 5000 analysis per year. Other commercial competitors are Ludger in Oxford, UK, GlyXera in Magdeburg, Germany, and Asparia Glycomics in San Sebastian, Spain, with 1000–2000 estimated analyses per year, based on research publications, pricing, and reported income.

The main drivers of Genos's success are the interdisciplinary team of highly competent, motivated, and well-trained individuals. Due to good working conditions and competitive salaries, the number of people that have left the company is negligible. This has enabled a significant accumulation of expertise and experience in the past 10 years. Together with research funding from various EU research and innovation programs, this has allowed Genos to maintain a very high level of investment in R&D, ensuring its global competitiveness. Genos maintains a sharp focus on the field of high-throughput glycomics. While still globally deficient, this field is progressing rapidly, due to support from both public and private institutions: NIH, big pharmaceuticals. R&D at Genos is performed mainly through large collaborative EU projects, linking Genos with dozens of leading research institutions in Europe, and enabling it regularly to exchange knowledge and experience with hundreds of researchers. This intensive R&D activity is the main source of sustained innovation that has contributed to the Genos's success.

Core Lessons Learned on the Path to Success

- Perform a better service for a lower price than your competitors.
- Treat customers as partners.

Management and Leadership Development Needs

The main business challenge, at present and in the near future, is the sustainability of R&D despite its high costs. This is important because R&D is the core activity behind Genos's business success. Additionally, threats from new technologies disturb the market, and the significant investments made by the US National Institutes of Health create strong competition. This requires more management attention than in the past.

In that context, human resources, including sales and marketing skills, at Genos can be seen as a major development bottleneck, because Genos has been growing quickly but this segment of the company has not followed the growth. In order to change this, the middle management, who was promoted from research staff and lack managerial experience, should be additionally trained in leadership and collaborative skills.

As a heavily R&D-based business, Genos is very effective in the discovery of novel glycan biomarkers but lacks the knowledge and funding to translate all these research discoveries into commercial products. Genos has already launched one globally innovative product, the GlycanAge test of biological age. It is currently selling in Croatia, UK, and China, but due to limited awareness of the existence of this product, its marketing outreach is limited, and Genos lacks both funding and knowledge to launch a global marketing campaign.

Financing and Regulatory Environment Development Needs

Genos's business is based on long-term research activities. It needs so-called patient financial resources whose expected rates of return are based on understanding of the research process behind the product development. Related to this nature of the business, tax policies should recognize the importance of research-based businesses for the national economy and its global competitiveness.

Balancing Science with Business at Genos: The Best Place to Work at

Established as an academic startup in 2007, Genos is the first private DNA laboratory in the region and one of the leading scientific institutions in Croatia in the field of DNA analysis, as well as the leading institution in the world in the field of the analysis of glycans.[4]

Scientific research in the field of glycobiology has resulted in significant international collaboration with a number of globally renowned institutions. Genos participates as an equal partner in large consortia. The company's DNA laboratory has

---

[4] https://www.tportal.hr/biznis/clanak/vlasnik-genosa-lansira-proizvode-koji-ce-donijeti-revoluciju-u-medicini-i-kaze-u-ovoj-zemlji-imamo-cudan-psiholoski-problem-foto-20180324

been involved in the development of high-quality products in the fields of human and animal genetics.[5]

The remarkable scientific and business results have also meant company growth in terms of people and activities. Therefore, the DNA laboratory is focused exclusively on the development of products and services for private clients and institutions, while the glycobiology laboratory is primarily focused on scientific research.

Following the latest trends in genetics, the task of this new knowledge-based company is a better market position for the existing tests and development of new tests that will help reduce the risk of illnesses and improve the quality of life. All this should be done through personalized medicine.

Genos is developing intriguing working settings and an organizational culture recognized by *The Scientist*, a life science journal, in its 2013 annual survey of *The Best Place to Work* series. The survey highlights companies where researchers love to work and where they feel valued. The award is even more important because Genos was topping the 2013 list, ahead of globally known large companies such as Genetech, Procter&Gamble, DuPonte, Monsanto, Wyatt, Promega, and others. Genos was also the only European company on this prestigious list. *The Scientist* based its list on a survey that included responses from 240 companies in the life-science industry around the globe. According to *The Scientist*, "Genos is a Croatian company of eager, young scientists, fresh out of—or even still in—school. Although it has just 25 employees, the company maintains strong ties to academia, allowing it to participate in large-scale projects, such as the first genome-wide association study of glycosylation in humans.

Founded in 2007 by University of Zagreb molecular biologist prof. dr. Gordan Lauc, top-ranked company Genos, located in Croatia, has stayed close to its academic roots, with many employees doing their PhD research at the company."

Employees describe the atmosphere as fun and creative, which is supported by Gordan Lauc, the company's founder, described by associates as open-minded and always willing to talk about his first and only love: science. At the same time, they are clear about the balance between business and science: "We are trying to survive on the market and earn the money, but we do not neglect the science."

When they are not developing products and doing analyses for clients, Genos's employees work on grant-funded collaborative projects. For instance, together with University of Edinburgh scientists, they are trying to identify biomarkers for inflammatory bowel disease—a project funded by the European Commission.

<small>And when it's time to relax, the Genos staff gather around one another's computers to watch science-related videos such as TED Talks, drink red wine, and munch on popcorn and chocolate (*The Scientist*, June 1, 2013).</small>

---

[5] https://genos-glyco.com/

2.3 Case Study 3

Mono, Ltd.

Overview
Address: Bihaćka 1d, 31000 Osijek, Croatia
Tel: +38531213 966
Fax: +38531213 967
Email: denis@mono-software.com
Web: www.mono.hr

Company Information
Industry: Computer programming activities
Year of establishment: 2003
Sales revenues in 2017: 2,873,700 euros
Sales revenues in 2007: 399,181 euros
Average number of employees in 2017: 42
Brain(s) behind the company: Founders Denis Sušac and Žarko Gajić

Nature of Market Leadership

Mono has several product categories, but with its pharmaceutical software products, it plays a very competitive role in the world market of such products. In the last 5 years, with 20% of the market share, Mono has been closing the gap between itself and its major competitor, holding a 30% market share. The main reasons for this success are recognition of customers' needs for a specific product at the right time, business domain knowledge in a specific industry, highly educated and competent engineers, and flexibility. It is of the utmost importance to maintain those strengths, because new competitors have arrived in the market and business rules have been constantly changing. In order to keep and increase its market leadership, Mono has successfully managed to attract the right talent, and develop an organizational culture based on continuous learning and leading by example, emphasizing the value of learning and innovation.

Nature of Competitive Advantage

Mono is number two in the world in electronic common technical document pharmaceutical software. Its competitive advantage is its agility and fast and flexible development cycle. This results in high-quality solutions that are less expensive than those of traditional companies. Mono has one competitor in Europe and five worldwide. The company's innovation culture and strategic orientation to specific fields contribute to Mono's competitive advantage in providing software solutions for pharmaceutical firms.

Core Lessons Learned on the Path to Success

- A strong need to have better and more agile project management
- The value of cooperation with the educational sector in obtaining the right talent

Management and Leadership Development Needs

A lack of qualified workforce and proper business infrastructure in the region are two major business challenges for Mono, currently, and in the near future.

The most underdeveloped skills at Mono are marketing and sales, due to the mostly technical background of key employees. Therefore, additional trainings are needed for project managers and young engineers joining the company. Both categories of employees lack certain key skills, due to insufficient development of such skills during their formal education. In order to avoid such situations, higher education institutions should be faster in embracing changes happening in the business sector, by introducing new programs that follow the requests of the business community. Mono intends to invest more effort in structured marketing plans.

Financing and Regulatory Environment Development Needs

Mono is very active in numerous public discussions related to the weak components of the entrepreneurship ecosystem. The company has three main concerns: (a) collaboration with educational institutions in order to provide young people with competences needed for the IT sector; (b) to increase the government funding for R&D and high-risk start-up projects; (c) competitive tax policies at the national level through successful use of experience from abroad, without constantly changing strategic directions and legislation.

Mono—One Stop Service, No-Nonsense, High Quality, and Honest Communication

Mono started its activities in 2003 and has been on a steady growth path ever since. It is achieving excellent business results that have been recognized internationally. Mono provides custom software design and development services to clients from around the world. Clients range from one-person startups to Fortune 500 companies and government organizations from more than 70 countries.

Three major groups of products are Baasic, eCTD Office, and Clokke. Baasic is a platform for rapid web and mobile app development, using pre-existing front-end modules and scalable back-end infrastructure, whereas eCTD Office is an off-the-shelf suite of integrated eCTD/NeeS/VneeS software products for the creation, validation, publishing, viewing, and manipulation of regulatory documentation for electronic submissions by pharmaceutical companies to regulatory authorities. Clokke is a tool for simple and straightforward time-tracking.

Mono's work is internationally recognized. Mono has held a Gold Microsoft Partner status with application development and independent software vendor competencies for more than 10 consecutive years. Gold partners are Microsoft's most highly accredited independent technical support providers. A prestigious annual survey in Central Europe—Deloitte's Technology Fast 50—included Mono on its 2013 list, appraising it as one of the fastest-growing Central European technology companies, based on the percentage of revenue growth over the 5-year period. Mono was identified as a national champion in the organic growth category for The European Business Awards 2014/2015.

Mono's growth is shaped by several values, whose combination and interrelatedness make Mono an attractive place to work at and a trustful working partner: one stop service, no-nonsense (Simplicity is important), honest communication, high quality, and cost-effectiveness.

3 Conclusions and Recommendations

The market leadership and competitive advantage of the three presented cases are strongly based on innovative products and highly specific knowledge.[6] The selection of such businesses was intentional in order to get better insights into the problems that Croatian businesses would be facing, if they wanted to achieve competitiveness by means of innovativeness. At the same time, the conducted analysis provides interesting evidence for Croatia's lagging behind the EU average in terms of product innovativeness.

In the three cases, the leading market position and sustainable competitiveness is heavily dependent on continuous and intensive investment in R&D. All companies identified a lack of support, either through direct funding of such activities or indirectly, through tax incentives, which they need to enhance their collaboration with research institutions. This confirms the findings of the GEM survey, that R&D transfer is one of the three weakest components of the entrepreneurship ecosystem in Croatia (Singer et al. 2018, p. 84). Another unfavorable component of Croatia's entrepreneurship ecosystem is access to finance for businesses with innovative products. The appropriate type of money sources with high-risk capacity, such as business angels and venture funds, is missing.

All analyzed businesses are based on R&D as well as on specific engineering or production knowledge. They all identified the lack of management knowledge and

---

[6]Although Croatia is struggling to identify its strategic priorities in terms of industries, there are several industries which show increasing capacity for innovation and competitiveness, and they are likely to be a source for future hidden champions: IT (software), food industry, tourism, wood industry, and the production of specialized boats.

skills as a major development obstacle, especially in dealing with human resources, marketing, and sales. This is especially true when a business is oriented to foreign markets right from the beginning. As Genos founder Gordan Lauc said, they do not have either money or skills for a global marketing campaign. All interviewed companies expressed their need for additional training of persons in management positions - project managers, and marketing and selling personnel- in fields such as communication skills, teamwork, and selling skills. Using the recent concept of entrepreneurial competences (Bacigalupo et al. 2016), which combines three groups of skills and knowledge—ideas and opportunities, resources, into action—it is clear that having only skills to innovate is not enough. This situation is an open call for higher education institutions to introduce education for entrepreneurial competences across campus, i.e., to provide all students regardless of their discipline, with access to educational programs that contribute to their ability to transform innovative capacity into commercial actions.

The success of all analyzed companies is based not only on the innovativeness of their products, but also on enthusiasm, commitment, vision, and perseverance. This was stressed by all interviewed founders or managers.

References

Bacigalupo M, Kampylis P, Punie Y, Van den Brande G (2016) EntreComp: the entrepreneurship competence framework. Publication Office of the European Union, Luxembourg; EUR 27939 EN; https://doi.org/10.2791/593884

McKiernan P, Purg D (eds) (2013) Hidden champions in CEE and Turkey. Springer, Berlin

National Research Council (2012) Transforming glycoscience: a roadmap for the future. The National Academies Press, Washington, DC. https://doi.org/10.17226/13446

OECD-Eurostat Manual on Business Demography Statistics (2007)

Singer S, Sarlija N, Pfeifer S, Oberman Peterka S (2018) What makes Croatia a (non)-entrepreneurial country? GEM Croatia 2017. CEPOR, Zagreb. http://www.cepor.hr/wp-content/uploads/2015/03/EN-GEM-2017-za-web.pdf

The World Bank in Croatia, country review, updated October 2019. https://www.worldbank.org/en/country/croatia/overview

World Bank Group Partnership Framework 2019–2024

Yugoslavia and World War II (1918–1990). https://croatia.eu/article.php?lang=2&id=23

Hidden Champions of the Czech Republic

Jarolím Antal, Jana Vlčková, Ondřej Sankot, and Pavel Hnát

Overview
Official name: The Czech Republic
Type of government: Parliamentary democratic republic
Population in 2020: 10,681,161
Land area: 78,867 km^2

History

1918	After the collapse of the Austro-Hungarian Empire, Czechoslovakia is created as an independent state.
1938	Most of today's Czech Republic is occupied by Nazi Germany, until the end of World War II.
1948	The Communist Party seizes power after a coup in Czechoslovakia.
1968	After the Prague Spring socialism reform process, Czechoslovakia is occupied by the armies of the Soviet Union and several Warsaw Pact countries.
1989	As a result of the Velvet Revolution, the Czechoslovak Republic is established as a democratic parliamentary republic.
1993	The independent Czech Republic is established after Czechoslovakia splits in the so-called Velvet Divorce.
1995	The Czech Republic is the first European post-communist country to join the Organization for Economic Cooperation and Development.
1999	The Czech Republic joins NATO.
2004	The Czech Republic joins the European Union.

J. Antal (✉) · J. Vlčková · O. Sankot · P. Hnát
Department of the World Economy, Faculty of International Relations, University of Economics, Prague, Czech Republic
e-mail: jarolim.antal@vse.cz

© Springer Nature Switzerland AG 2021
A. Braček Lalić, D. Purg (eds.), *Hidden Champions in Dynamically Changing Societies*, https://doi.org/10.1007/978-3-030-65451-1_13

1 Introduction: Context

The Czech Republic lies at the heart of Europe. It benefits from its favorable geographical location, relatively cheap and educated labor force, and a stable economy despite occasional political turmoil. Even though the Czech Republic is not part of the euro area, its close ties with other European countries, especially Germany, influenced the country during its transition and the latest economic and financial crisis.

To understand the main drivers behind the Czech Republic's economic development properly, it is necessary first to set out the initial conditions created by the process of economic transition started in 1989, which included liberalization of prices and foreign trade as well as the privatization of state-owned enterprises. During the country's transition process, foreign direct investment played an important role as "an important source of financing and a supplement to the inadequate resources needed to finance both ownership structure and capital formation. Compared to other financing options, Foreign Direct Investment (FDI) also facilitates the transfer of technology, know-how and skills, and helps local enterprises to expand into foreign markets" (EBRD 2001, p.1). On the other hand, the extensive inflow of FDIs created a dependency on transnational companies' (TNCs) decision-making, leaving most of the local companies without any significant control of the value chain that they were participating in. Even though the Czech Republic gained access to the global market, technologies, and know-how by those means, it got locked in a sub-contractor position, which currently seems to be difficult to overcome. TNCs brought contracts and jobs, and through those means also a certain social stability, but also had a demotivating effect on the creation of unique high-value-added products that would be competitive on the global market. The huge amounts of currently repatriated profits only underpin the weaknesses of the Czech transition strategy.

The main determinants of FDI in transition countries of the CEE region including domestic and potential export market size, gravity factors, resources and skills endowment, progress in transition reforms, and economic and political climate, were especially favorable in the case of the Czech Republic. As a result, together with its V4 peers, the Czech Republic attracted most of the FDI flowing into the region in the initial stages of economic transition. In terms of the share of gross capital formation or FDI inflow per capita, it was the Czech Republic that attracted the highest relative amount of FDI, even in comparison with the other V4 members. Both privatization and restructuring processes also markedly influenced the structure of FDI flows into the Czech Republic (De Castro and Hnát 2017). Even though the Czech Republic started with the highest share of state-owned enterprises among its V4 peers, the speed of its transition in terms of small-scale privatization soon outperformed that of other countries. Gravity factors and skilled labor eased the country's restructuring toward a more modern service-based economic structure, which was soon reflected also in the structure of FDI inflows (De Castro and Hnát 2017, p.52).

The Czech Republic had to face the challenges of building an adequate institutional infrastructure to support its further growth, while having to deal with privatization, the banking crisis in the middle of the 1990s, and the currency crisis in 1997, with speculative attacks against the Czech currency in the meantime. The Czech National Bank (CNB) had to raise interest rates considerably in an effort to protect the fixed exchange rate at that time. However, the speculative pressures were too strong, and the CNB was forced to change the exchange rate regime to a floating one. At the same time, a new concept of monetary policy, called "inflation targeting," was adopted and has been applied ever since.

As in the majority of CEE countries, rapid FDI inflows were soon accompanied by major profit repatriations that drove current accounts in CEE to negative numbers. The Czech Republic had been running positive balances of services during its transition process and a positive trade balance since the early 2000s. Therefore, the income part of the current account plays an even more significant role in the overall current account balance than in the other V4 countries (Office of the Government of the Czech Republic 2016, p.17). The negative current account balance has been mostly driven by profit repatriation. Reinvested earnings played only a limited role in the Czech balance of payments. Investors' reluctance to reinvest earnings in the Czech Republic is mostly explained by the institutional weaknesses of the Czech economy. For instance, the World Economic Forum's Global Competitiveness Reports (WEF 2014, 2019) repeatedly mentions institutions and a lack of innovativeness as the most evident barriers to innovation-driven competitiveness in the Czech Republic. The Czech Republic needs to explore ways to transition to a knowledge-based economy in view of its stage of development: compared with other economies at the same stage, business dynamism (32nd) and innovation capacity (29th place) remains low and the Czech businesses—although doing comparatively well in a regional context—are less sophisticated and innovative than those of other economies in the European Union. The country's competitiveness would be further enhanced by improvements to its education system. The skills of the Czech workforce are ranked as 29th in the world (WEF 2019).

As it is evident from the Global Competitiveness Report 2014, TNC managers mostly state inefficient government bureaucracy, corruption, policy instability, and restrictive labor regulations as the most problematic factors for doing business in the Czech Republic (WEF 2014, p.166). According to OECD "Czech firms are well integrated into the international supply chains, with 90% of the large firms active in the export market, a proportion falling to half for the mid-sized enterprises and to a quarter for the small firms. A relatively high proportion of all firms use material inputs/supplies of foreign origin. In terms of FDI restrictiveness, the Czech Republic is slightly less liberal than the top 10% of the OECD economies, and remaining restrictions are concentrated in agriculture, transport and real estate. On the other hand, the World Bank's Ease of doing business indicators show considerable room for facilitating trading across borders, particularly in terms of improving the documentation requirements, administrative delays and costs, which would support the export sector and facilitate the entry of SMEs into export markets" (OECD 2014, p.54).

In the early years of the Czech Republic's economic transition, the key factors driving the development of trade were the successful reform of the economic system and the transition to a market economy. Without a systemic reform, the development of international trade in the Czech Republic would have been impossible. The neighboring countries went through a similar transition, which was another driver for Czech businesses, starting their international expansion to the closest markets. A principal factor behind the rapid technology catch-up has been the rapid and deep integration of the Czech economy into German led supply chains. Bilateral trade with Germany alone amounts to nearly half of the Czech GDP. Germany, and other core European countries with favorable tax conditions for international holdings, such as the Netherlands, represent the majority of the Czech Republic's FDI inflow.

"Relatively few firms export to countries outside the EU. The rapid integration reflects an initial large differential in unit labor costs, a relevant labor skill endowment and bilateral advantages, such as geographical proximity, similarities in traditions and industrial sectoral structure, which attracted large inflows of foreign direct investment, particularly in the form of modern assembly technology in the electrical and transport equipment producing sectors" (OECD 2014, p.26). Machinery and equipment played the most important role in the industrial structure of the FDI inflows (42.9% in 2012). "As a result, Czech export-oriented manufacturing is focused on final products with a relatively large amount of imported intermediate inputs, while the Czech production of intermediate goods is relatively little used in Czech exports and as intermediate input in the international production. Likewise, the domestic service sector is poorly integrated as its content in exports is among the lowest in the OECD countries" (OECD 2014, p.26). Financial intermediation accounts for the highest share of FDI inflows into the Czech Republic: 31.2% in 2018. It is also well known that profit repatriations are extraordinarily high in the Czech banking sector.

In 2004, the Czech Republic joined the European Union and subsequently gained access to the single market. This meant trade liberalization with the Czech Republic's key trading partners and an improved international profile for the Czech Republic. Given the strong economic links between the Czech market and the countries of the European Union, it was a milestone event that resulted in a surge in trade and higher FDI flows with other EU countries. The EU membership has further strengthened Czech trade because the "made in the EU" label is globally associated with a lower risk and a higher quality of goods and services.

The global crisis in 2008–2009 undermined the upward trend in international trade. To be specific, a sharp decline in terms of international trade was observed in 2009. In that year, Czech exports declined by about 14%, imports fell by roughly 17%, and total trade turnover was lower by approximately 17% as well, all compared to the figures of the previous year. The following years brought a swift recovery. In 2010, trade figures already surpassed the pre-crisis levels (Czech Statistical Office 2017b). In fact, the economy experienced two small recessions: 2008–2011 and

2011–2013. The pre-crisis GDP figure was reached again in 2014 (Czech Statistical Office 2017a).

At the moment, Czech trade is set to continue growing. However, it is clear that it will not be possible to reach historical growth rates of the time when the economy was still transforming. Czech trade is currently over-relying on developed and aging European economies, which may indicate a danger of a slowdown in the future. More diversification is needed to tap into the opportunities in today's emerging economies, mainly in Asia. In addition, further significant progress could be made by boosting Czech education which, unfortunately, has been underfinanced for many years.

The Czech Republic has a skilled workforce. However, changes in the economic structure require individuals possessing an adequate skillset. The government should pursue thoughtful trade and foreign policy to protect the country's economic interests but, at the same time, a small and open economy should promote free trade initiatives, such as the Trade in Services Agreement, and oppose restrictions to free markets. It is evident that Czech businesses are in a difficult situation when it comes to expansion and growing internationally as they come from a relatively small country where no significant local economies of scale and scope are available. However, as the process of digitalization proceeds, small and medium enterprises have an equal opportunity to compete on global markets. There is also a lot of evidence that global service exports are gaining strong momentum and are catching up with exports of goods in many countries.

Another significant trend is product differentiation and customization. Consumers have become increasingly demanding when it comes to sophistication and quality of products and services. Businesses need to be flexible and should expect a further shortening of the life cycles of their products. We can see a rise of some Czech hidden champions already, and the trend should continue. Czech entrepreneurs are innovative in many industries, notably in IT, chemistry, and nanotechnology. However, with some support from the government, there is no reason why this should not get even better in the future (VSE 2019) (Exhibit 1).

2 Case Studies of Czech Hidden Champions

2.1 Case Study 1

Bioveta a.s.

Overview
Address: Komenského 212/12, 683 23 Ivanovice na Hané
Tel: +420 517 318 604
Email: prodejna@bioveta.cz
Web: https://www.bioveta.cz/

Exhibit 1 Core economic indicators for the Czech Republic

	2011	2012	2013	2014	2015	2016	2017	2018
GDP per capita (current US$)	21,717.458	19,729.871	19,916.019	19,744.559	17,715.617	18,463.387	20,379.896	23,078.573
GDP per capita growth (annual %)	1.568	−0.939	−0.517	2.07	5.02	2.254	4.076	2.655
Foreign direct investment, net inflows (% of GDP)	1.838	4.549	3.514	3.892	0.910	5.562	5.203	3.464
GDP (current US$, millions)	227.948	207.376	209.402	207.818	186.830	195.090	215.914	245.226
Exports of goods and services (current US$, millions)	162.543	157.959	160.970	171.545	151.424	155.205	172.139	192.233
Exports of goods and services (% of GDP)	71.307	76.17	76.871	82.546	81.049	79.556	79.726	78.386
Merchandise exports (current US$, millions)	162,939	157,041	162,274	175,022	157,877	162,692	182,143	202,197
Merchandise exports to high-income economies (% of total merchandise exports)	88.74	87.267	86.872	87.963	89.423	89.327	89.147	–
Merchandise exports to developing economies in Europe & Central Asia (% of total merchandise exports)[a]	7.544	8.846	9.070	7.920	6.438	6.552	6.713	–
Ores and metals exports (% of merchandise exports)	2.167	2.327	2.193	2.046	1.603	1.351	1.467	1.360
Agricultural raw materials exports (% of merchandise exports)	1.415	1.45	1.503	1.38	1.314	1.298	1.343	1.328
Food exports (% of merchandise exports)	4.73	4.723	4.929	4.841	5.061	4.948	4.492	4.120
Fuel exports (% of merchandise exports)	3.764	3.786	2.955	2.644	2.949	1.881	1.775	1.928
Manufactures exports (% of merchandise exports)	88.457	87.579	88.247	88.916	88.871	90.309	90.691	91.014
High-technology exports (% of manufactured exports)	18.707	18.593	17.349	17.397	17.788	16.993	17.903	19.561

Source: World Bank, January 2020
[a]Merchandise exports to low- and middle-income economies in Europe & Central Asia (% of total merchandise exports)

Company Information
Industry: Manufacture of pharmaceutical preparations
Year of establishment: 1918 (1995)
Sales revenues in the latest year (2017): 59 mil. euro
Sales revenues 10 years before (2008): 17.4 mil. euro
Average ROA [using P/L before tax (%)] in the latest year (2017): 14.09
Average ROA 10 years before (2008): 14.01
Average ROA in the past 10 years: 15.58
Latest debt to equity ratio: 13.3%
Average number of employees in the latest year (2017): 687
Brain(s) behind the company): Libor Bittner

Nature of Market Leadership

The main market for the products of Bioveta is the Czech Republic, Slovakia, and the countries of Central and Eastern Europe, although the company exports to over 100 countries. West Asian, South East European (Georgia, Armenia), and Southeast Asian countries (Vietnam, Indochina, Thailand, Korea) are particularly interesting in terms of sales growth potential.

The main reason for the company's market leadership is its lower price compared to that of Western brands, combined with high quality and constant innovation. The market share in the CEE region is between 10% and 50% in each market. The biggest competitors are foreign companies with the same business focus as Bioveta.

Since the foundation of the joint-stock company in 1995, Bioveta has been a leader in the markets of the Czech Republic and Slovakia. With the growing development of the company, research and development has significantly strengthened and the sales in individual countries of Central and Eastern Europe have increased. In 2018, the total turnover was approximately 67 million, whereas in 2008 it was around 19 million euros. Over the past 10 years, the company has strengthened its position in the segment of anti-parasitic agents, especially multi-components that are effective against external and internal parasites in the pharmaceutical field. Bioveta is involved in this market, but focuses only on generic production and does not have its own original molecule. In the biological area, sales of vaccines for basic livestock and domestic animals, including the production of complementary vaccines, have increased. Bioveta has an important position in this area and it produces all the necessary vaccine types for all animal species, including complementary vaccines, such as the Borrelia vaccine. Bioveta exports almost 85–90% of its production to its customers abroad. The most important export destinations are Russia, Poland, Ukraine, Thailand, Romania, Denmark, Hungary, Slovakia, and Turkey. Bioveta also exports to other countries, practically all over the world.

Nature of the Competitive Advantage

Bioveta produces high-quality products at an affordable price. The company is fully Czech-owned. The four owners decide on the company strategy, direction of the company, research and development, and production strategy. Thus, the company is very responsive and effective. In the Czech Republic and Slovakia, Bioveta is practically the only producer of veterinary bio-preparations and pharmaceuticals. In the 1990s, the markets in the CEE region opened up and there are several competing companies, such as Ingelheim, Zoetis, Pfizer, CEVA, Intervet, Virbac, and others.

Core Lessons Learned on the Path to Business Success

The core lessons learned over the past 25 years involve the necessity to follow market needs constantly and respond to them flexibly, personally interact with customers, meet their needs, share and solve their problems, and enjoy their success together with them. The major drivers have evolved over time. In the 1990s, it was necessary to keep the company running. Then the company had to make a profit so as to modernize, which was crucial in order to fulfill all legislative conditions. Last but not least, it is necessary to create a good working environment for the employees.

Main Drivers of the Company's Success

The overall strengths of Bioveta are based on several factors. These include the high quality of its products at affordable prices for the customer, a good marketing strategy, providing services to customers, the possibility of personal visits and consultations with customers, the possibility of taking biological samples to determine the cause of a disease or to determine the level of efficacy after immunization, the possibility of production of autogenous vaccines to order, and the benefits program and events that the company offers to customers.

Main Leadership Success Factors That Have Contributed to the Company's Success

The main factor is a clear definition of the company's long-term strategy. It includes the investment outlook for the modernization of the company, a research and development plan, a production plan, a business plan, a marketing plan, a company development plan, and more. This long-term plan of the company's strategy is subject to a thorough review every year and is regularly amended and supplemented.

Main Innovation Success Factors That Have Contributed to the Company's Success

The research and development plan is part of the company's long-term strategy. It is regularly supplemented with the current requirements of customers so that their needs are covered by the company's research and development plan. The main goal in this area is maximum readiness. That is, if a new disease occurs, then the company should be prepared. This, of course, requires monitoring the literature, evaluation of the epidemiological situation, and much more. This is also part of the activities of the R&D personnel. The company needs to be prepared for what is coming up and always be a step ahead of the competition.

Main Business Challenges for the Company

Currently, Bioveta plans to expand the number of its foreign branches in various, commercially interesting destinations. Bioveta already has foreign branches in Slovakia, Poland, Ukraine, Russia, and Turkey. These dealers do an extremely professional job and help the company increase sales. In the future, Bioveta wants to focus on further modernization of the company to meet all legislative requirements for the production of veterinary products. This includes strengthening all core sections of the company, from production, trade, and registration to quality control. Bioveta also plans to strengthen its R&D and transition to modern subunit and recombinant vaccines.

The Company's Developmental Needs in Terms of Management and Leadership, Knowledge, Skills, and Competences of the Employees

Bioveta has a highly professional workforce. Nobody at any school teaches research and development of veterinary preparations, their production, or control. Therefore, Bioveta must provide a special educational environment for these employees by itself. This level of expertise must be controlled and, in particular, maintained at the required level through training courses. There is still a lot of catching up to do in this area. Further, all employees must be continuously educated. Even the smallest mistake of any employee can cause a big problem, with enormous consequences. That is why all employees are continuously trained and the level of education and skills of each employee is regularly monitored. In terms of educational institutions, Bioveta needs people educated in basic biological sciences. The company's graduates and young professionals lack practical experiences. Bioveta would be glad if students selected their careers early on in their studies and if school systems allowed more internships and other practical experiences for students rather than focusing on theory only. This would enormously help Bioveta integrate young professionals into the company's environment and processes.

The Company's Developmental Needs in Terms of Financing or the Regulatory Environment in Order to Keep or Advance Business Results

Bioveta has historical experience with bond issues and bank loans. For operational financing and medium-term investment horizons, the company prefers to use its own financing. For medium and long-term goals, it increasingly uses foreign sources, most often in the form of bank loans because of their speed and standardization. Bond issues are more suited to specific projects or long-term goals, where they allow the optimization of the cost of such financing. They are also suitable for engaging and increasing employee engagement.

In terms of recommendations for financial institutions, governments, and international organizations, Bioveta suggests simplifying rules and laws. Furthermore, the state should behave economically and take care of individual components. Much greater investment in infrastructure, mainly roads and railways, is needed, and the state investment policy should reflect the phases of the economic cycle: it should invest more in times of recession, less in times of expansion, as well as use countercyclical tools.

The Company's Developmental Needs in Terms of Marketing

Bioveta plans to set up sales offices in other countries, which, apart from other tasks, collect and hand over information on the needs of the specific territory. They also provide contacts between breeders and veterinarians with the parent company, carry out sampling, and ensure the examination of biological samples, control and evaluate the effect of vaccinations, deliver educational activities in the area, inform in advance about news coming soon on the market, and are simply confidential intermediaries between the country and Bioveta in the field of agriculture and veterinary medicine. The expansion of sales offices to other countries will be accompanied by the strengthening of the marketing activities of Bioveta. This means that the business and sales strategies of the company, as well as product promotional materials for each country, will be based on the collection and evaluation of information gathered from individual dealerships.

"Fight Rabies All Around the World"

Bioveta is a Czech company focused mainly on the production of veterinary medicaments, with several pharmaceuticals, which are also intended for human use. It produces more than 200 products in 15 product categories and exports to over 100 countries. Bioveta was founded in 1918, the year when Czechoslovakia was established, as the State Institute for the Diagnosis of Animal Infections and the Production of Vaccines. Since its beginning, it has been located in Ivanovice na Hané. The name of the Institute was changed to Bioveta in 1951. In 1995, the state-owned Bioveta was privatized through a public tender and was transformed into

Bioveta, s. r. o. (limited company), which was again transformed into a joint-stock company in 1996.

The company's most important product groups are vaccines and hormonal preparations. Bioveta is a European leader in the production of rabies vaccines. Between 1992 and 2017, more than 350 million doses of Lysvulpen, a vaccine against rabies, were produced and shipped to 19 countries, including Belarus, Bosnia and Herzegovina, Bulgaria, Montenegro, Georgia, Croatia, Kazakhstan, Kosovo, Lithuania, Latvia, Hungary, Moldova, Poland, Romania, Russia, Slovakia, Slovenia, and Serbia. This vaccine contributed significantly to the eradication of rabies in these countries. The Czech Republic has not reported a single case of rabies for over 10 years and in 2004 the country c was proclaimed the first rabies-free Eastern European country by the World Organization for Animal Health. Lysvulpen is the most successful product of Bioveta. Currently, a newly improved vaccine against rabies Rabadrop is being sold. Apart from other improvements, it can be transported and stored within a higher temperature range from: +2 to +8 °C as opposed to −20 °C before. The company has its own e-shop.

2.2 Case Study 2

ELKO EP

Overview
Address: Palackého 493, 769 01 Holešov, Všetuly
Tel: +420 800 100 671
Email: elko@elkoep.cz
Web: https://www.elkoep.cz/

Company Information
Industry: Manufacture of electricity distribution and control apparatus
Year of establishment: 1997
Sales revenues in the latest year (2019): 20 million euros
Sales revenues 10 years before (2009): 6.5 million euros
Average ROA [using P/L before tax (%)] in the latest year (2018): 11.85
Average ROA 10 years before (2009): 10.96
Average ROA in the past 10 years: 14.67
Latest debt to equity ratio: 329%
Average number of employees in the latest year (2019): 340
Brain(s) behind the company: Jiří Konečný

Nature of Market Leadership

The electronic equipment industry has gone through a huge transition since the early 1990s when ELKO-EP was established. The connectivity of electro-components has become a crucial and greatly demanded feature. The ELKO EP company managed to address this and other challenges through permanent R&D and innovations. Despite the current pressure on prices and the growing position of low-cost producers, ELKO EP manages to maintain its position and convince customers with the quality and reliability of its products.

Another strength of the company is the drive and permanent ambition to develop its products and services further in order to meet the expectations of consumers. The INELS system shows that the company is able to deliver a complex smart solution globally.

ELKO EP CEO Jiří Konečný also highlights the importance of targeting the customers' needs. According to him, there are plenty of different products on the market whose quality is similar to that of the ELKO EP products. These products often offer too many functions, which bothers users, as they struggle to use the device in the way that they wish. The key to success is therefore to target not only functions but also connectivity in more complex situations, where the consumer fully enjoys the product.

Nature of the Competitive Advantage

What distinguishes ELKO EP from its competitors is its flexibility, operative approach, customization, and the desire to offer something more to the customer. The company focuses on a very personal approach to customers, where basically every detail of a product or solution can be customized according to the wish of the client.

Despite the fact that the company's production is strongly focused on relays, which ELKO EP also produces for the world's major OEM companies, in order to keep pace with competitors and the main trends in electro installations ELKO EP invests a considerable part of the profit in further advancing intelligent electrical installation systems.

Main Drivers of the Company's Success

The company permanently develops, advances, and customizes its portfolio. It is very open to ideas and the entire team and staff are convinced of the strategy and the need for innovations.

Management and Leadership Developmental Needs

The company started from scratch and managed to grow to become a leader in the segment of relays on the European market. This required a lot of effort which later became a systematic ambition. The success would not have been possible without investment in knowledge, innovations, and R&D. The company cares about its employees and offers opportunities for further career growth. In times of low unemployment, it is quite a challenge to find reliable and motivated experts who are flexible and do not fear change and the new challenges that come every day.

Financing and Regulatory Environment Developmental Needs

Since its establishment, the company has grown generically, without a need for external funding. It first opened a branch in Slovakia, which is perceived as the first market of entry when testing the competitiveness and quality of products. Since then, ELKO EP has opened other branches in Central Europe, Ukraine, and Russia. Nowadays it has offices worldwide, in countries such as Saudi Arabia, Vietnam, India, and the USA.

The company sees a huge challenge in the digitalization and further introduction of smart solutions in the public sector. For ELKO EP this is a field that has a huge untapped potential.

From a Garage to the Second Biggest Producer of Relays in Europe

ELKO EP was established in 1997 in a garage, when its owner and brain Jiří Konečný found a gap in the electronic parts market. He started to assemble electronic relays, first on a board, later on modular housing, and then on the DIN rail. As his products became well received by the market, he had to involve his whole family and the neighborhood in the production and development. Since its establishment, ELKO EP has produced more than 12 million relays and other products. It is the biggest producer in the Czech Republic, with an 80% share of the market, and is the second largest producer of relays in Europe, supplying eight out of ten OEM companies. The production portfolio of ELKO EP includes relays, lighting control for smart homes, buildings, offices, and cities, energy management, iNELS systems, and IoT components for indoor and outdoor usage.

ELKO EP remains a purely Czech manufacturer of electronic devices. Thanks to many years of experience, ELKO became a leader in electronic modular devices—relays—of which it produces more than 200 types. Having its own production, modern instruments, and a research and development center enables the company to meet the requirements of today's fast-evolving technologies. ELKO EP therefore developed its own smart iNELS electrical installation system. INELS allows different devices to communicate and manage IoT in commercial buildings, residences, and other environments, such as smart cities.

The company grew generically, with its own funds and the vision of the owner. Currently, it has 12 branches and employs around 340 people globally. ELKO EP products are exported to more than 70 countries worldwide. Despite the strong competition, the pace of shipping, and the customization requirements, the company keeps its R&D and production exclusively in the Czech Republic, in the town of Holešov.

The company sees several new challenges ahead. After launching and advancing its iNELS system, Jiří Konečný wants to expand to new segments, such as outdoor activities. He also wants to make a popular platform for IoT in homes. Another challenge is to access new markets, such as Australia, and expand further in the Middle East.

2.3 Case Study 3

MICRORISC s.r.o.

Overview
Address: Prumyslova 1275, Valdicke Predmesti, 506 01, Jicin
Tel: +420 493 538 125
Email: pr@microrisc.com
Web: https://www.microrisc.com/en

Company Information
Industry: Manufacture of loaded electronic boards
Year of establishment: 1991
Sales revenues in the latest year (2018): 4.6 million euros
Sales revenues 10 years before (2008):1.5 million euros
Average ROA [using P/L before tax (%)] in the latest year (2018): 2.6%
Average ROA 10 years before (2008): -2.8%
Average ROA in the past 10 years: 10.8%
Latest debt to equity ratio: 7.2%
Average number of employees in the latest year (2018): 20
Brain(s) behind the company): Vladimír Šulc, Ph.D.

Nature of Market Leadership

Over the past few years, MICRORISC, as a key driver of the IQRF Alliance, has been driving the IQRF interoperability standardization process, resulting in new end devices that communicate in a predictable and consistent way. The whole solution is opened for interconnection toward other technologies that can be deployed if necessary. With unified communications, the solution can be extended to new devices and functionality, without requiring a major redrawing of the original concept, such as monitoring the status of pneumatic tools and making recommendations regarding efficiency and cost savings, completion line torque wrenches are being used to ensure the accurate tightening of screws on all cars produced in automotive, a reliable and cost-effective remote lighting solution for a city neighborhood in Israel, and monitoring street occupancy in the Prague historical center. The technology is now widely used in Industry 4.0, smart-building, and smart-city projects worldwide. With the strategic financial investment, it has the potential to be transformed into a global open standard protected by several dozen international patents—a milestone rarely reached by technology companies in the region.

Nature of the Competitive Advantage

MICRORISC is a fully Czech-owned technological company that has shown a remarkable ability to transform continuously and always find the best course for its technological development. Using its founders' technical expertise, market specificities, and opportunities after the Velvet Revolution, the company entered a niche market with its innovative patented technology without the potential to compete with market leaders at that time. With a significant amount of market foresight, the company abandoned the production of final goods and moved into the fast-growing chip technology industry as a logistics and supply chain partner of a global leader. The company proved its high quality and endurance. It soon reached a leading position and achieved market growth awards in the European region.

In this position, the company transformed again into a hidden technology provider within value chains in the same industry, using chips to develop components and language for the internet of things. The company's IQRF technology is a mature wireless mesh technology, proven, reliable, robust, low-power, and secure, which can be easily integrated into any electronic product. Devices using the same simple language are fully interoperable. As such, the IQRF enables full local autonomy and control. It is complementary to existing standards, such as cellular wi-fi or Ethernet, and provides a strong base for vertical IoT solutions. IQRF offers a technological solution for manufacturers to make any device wireless. It is able to work in mesh networks and is connectable to the Internet. IQRF solves one of the biggest technical challenges and meets customers' needs—it wirelessly connects products to the IoT through mesh networks.

Core Lessons Learned on the Path to Business Success

The company's path to continued business success lies in technology and constant transition of a business model. At every stage of its existence, the company has focused on new technology with a significant potential to grow not only in the local market but with a global potential. At every stage, the company was able to assess its potential and has been able to transform its business model timely: from patent-based end-product provider in a niche market for the automotive industry, it transformed into a logistics partner and a direct representative of a global leader in an underling technology. The company left the logistics industry to become a research-based component-provider in a growing industry of the internet of things.

MICRORISC's components and standards create new possibilities for tools and med-tech products and provide new possibilities for street lighting in Israel, control supermarket lights in Mexico, monitor nuclear power plants and hotel heating systems, and monitor transportation and smart cities. The transition continues further, as in 2017 the company started a technological spin-off to attract investors. The new ambition is to decrease the share of component manufacturing sales in revenues and transform into a license-provider of what should become the number-one wireless mesh technology for IoT, while remaining responsible for the further development of the IQRF core infrastructure.

Main Drivers of the Company's Success

MICRORISC has been able to find solutions to customers' problems, sometimes even to those that the customers have not yet discovered. The company's partners are manufacturers of electronics. The main objectives of MICRORISC include the constant delivery of the best products and solutions in the field. The solutions are based on technology and innovation, continuous development, and improvement. The company builds upon reliability and high quality and approaches each partnership as a long-term commitment.

Main Innovation Success Factors That Have Contributed to the Company's Success

For MICRORISC, both good results and continuous improvement of all business processes and corporate management system are commonplace, as well as continuous improvement of labor conditions and promoting regional social events. IQRF wireless technology that has now been taken over by the IQRF Tech spin-off is protected by several dozen patents, industrial designs, and trademarks in the Czech Republic, the European Union, and the USA.

Main Business Challenges for the Company

A frequent obstacle to the rapid deployment of a suitable solution in internet-of-things projects is the large fragmentation of sub-components, such as differently communicating end devices and various transmission technologies, or the need to customize IoT gateways and applications to a given requirement. This results in long development times, high costs, and a closed, specialized project that has problems with scalability or adaptation to new requirements. At the IQRF Summit 2019, the IQRF Alliance members demonstrated that they were able to deliver solutions through cooperation and the development of interoperable solutions within a few weeks, and this solution could be scaled to new customer requirements. The projects were various, ranging from water and air quality monitoring in South African poultry houses, through people and cars counting, temperature monitoring in refrigerators and freezers at the VFN Hospital in Prague, and demonstrations of specific products that can be used for projects.

IQRF technology has come a long way since its beginning in 2004 and is now in a transition to an open standard. Every manufacturer will be able to use reliable mesh technology to connect his devices to IoT and use any processor and any radio.

The Company's Developmental Needs in Terms of Management and Leadership (Knowledge, Skills, and Competences of Your Employees)

Thanks to years of good experience, the company selectively engages in custom development and optimization of electronic and electromechanical applications. A significant part of the production consists of visual control panels and touch displays. Both specialized custom development and high focus on innovations result in the fact that over half of the employees are working in the company's R&D department. To develop the company's global impact further, innovation and a focus on creativity should be supplemented by perfect project management and a strong focus on marketing.

The Company's Developmental Needs in Terms of Financing or the Regulatory Environment in Order to keep or Advance Business Results

Preparing a global open standard is an ambitious plan and a big challenge, both technically and financially. Thus, MICRORISC founded the technological spin-off, IQRF Tech s.r.o., to allow IQRF technology to develop with the help of investors in the near future.

The Company's Developmental Needs in Terms of Marketing

Due to the limited financial resources of SMEs and the global impact of big manufacturers that can deploy IQRF transceivers as communication components in their products, it is somewhat challenging to compete with them. Thus, MICRORISC started to develop a few vertical solutions and products based on the IQRF technology as a horizontal platform in 2020. Besides faster monetization, there are also other reasons behind this activity: the availability of more interoperable products allows the easier building of IoT solutions and systems by integrators. This is expected to result in higher market awareness and technology acceptance by both end customers and integrators. Core marketing focus is expected to be achieved in cooperation with partners, especially global ones, associated with the IQRF Alliance.

Enabling Future Innovation

MICRORISC is a Czech company that has been focusing on research and development, delivering technologies and components to electronics manufacturers since 1991. At the moment, it is one of the world's leading companies in the field of wireless technologies for slow mesh networks. The company's mission to help customers innovate their products is expressed in the motto "Enabling future innovation." Its history dates back to 1991 when it was founded as the first Czech manufacturer of car alarms with dynamic codes based on the company's own patent. The present company was established in 1999 through capital restructuring, which created the current holding, selling the manufacturing part. In the fast-growing segment of microchips, the company first served as a valued part of the supply chain and turned into a direct sales representative in 2007. In 2003, the company received an award for being the fastest-growing European distributor of Fujitsu and was ranked as a TOP five Fujitsu partner in the EU in 2008.

In the meantime, the company introduced its first IQRF wireless transceiver in 2004, and in 2013, MICRORISC launched an international IQRF Alliance, an association of developers, manufacturers, system integrators, universities, development centers, and business professionals using wireless technology IQRF. In 2017, the company founded a technological spin-off, IQRF Tech s.r.o., to attract strategic investors and to enable global expansion with an open standard for wireless mesh networks. Despite the fact, that the MICRORISC component is a tiny electronic component behind a more complex final product, it accounts for a substantial part of its price. In market segments with the most suitable application fit, such as street lightning and the internet of things, the company has already obtained a remarkable market share. With the financial expansion, it is planning to transform from a hardware and chip-manufacturing company to a global open-standard license-provider by 2030. At the moment, the company holds over 40 patents in the USA, the European Union, Japan, and China.

2.4 Case Study 4

Phonexia

Overview
Address: Chaloupkova 3002/1a, 612 00, Brno
Tel: +420 511 205 265
Email: info@phonexia.com
Web: https://www.phonexia.com/en/

Company Information
Industry: Computer consultancy activities
Year of establishment: 2006
Sales revenues in the latest year (2018): 2 million euros

Sales revenues 10 years before (2009): 500,000 euros
Average ROA [using P/L before tax (%)] (2019): 3%
Average ROA 10 years before (2009): N/A
Average ROA in the past 10 years: N/A, 25% in the past 5 years
Latest debt to equity ratio: 0, no debt
Average number of employees in the latest year (2019): 50
Brain(s) behind the company: Petr Schwarz, PhD—co-founder and CTO, Pavel Matějka, PhD—co-founder, Michal Hrabí—CEO

Nature of Market Leadership

Phonexia has been one of the pioneers that started developing unique approaches in the field of voice recognition. The company has been working together with a team of university experts from the Technical University of Brno on setting new standards for speaker and language recognition, revealing them to the general public. The innovations that Phonexia developed have also been internationally recognized. Since 2008, the team of Phonexia and Brno University of Technology has always ranked in the top six in speaker recognition evaluations organized by the US National Institute of Standards and Technology, which in the field of speaker recognition is similar to the Olympic Games.

The company's leadership is based on innovations. Phonexia applies new algorithms to its speech engine based on a REST API, which provides stability and robustness to developed technologies. Also, in March 2018 Phonexia was the first company on the market with a speaker identification system exclusively based on deep neural networks. The system, called Phonexia Deep Embeddings, had greater accuracy, higher speed, and reduced server memory use at the same time. The technology achieved the highest accuracy when compared to the products of industry leaders in tests performed by independent forensic laboratories. This demonstrates Phonexia's ambition to be a market leader in this area.

The company is one of the leaders due to its unique portfolio, which includes products such as Phonexia Voice Verify, offering clients the ability to verify their customers by voice within 3 seconds. This type of authentication does not require the remembering of passwords and is safe, fast, and reliable.

Phonexia also developed its own Voicebot-building solution which helps to automate call centers. The Voicebot Suite has AI-powered speech-to-text, text-to-speech, and voice authentication features, combined with seamless support for the integration of natural language processing layers. This enables the building of almost any type of Voicebot.

Phonexia has also designed software for law enforcement, public safety, and investigation and forensic experts. The Phonexia Speech Platform software can handle almost any speech-processing challenge, whether it is the analysis of massive amounts of audio recordings for investigation purposes or just a few audio tracks for forensic experts.

In the field of voice recognition and supporting evidence of criminal behavior, Phonexia developed a special tool—Voice Inspector for Forensic Experts—which enables analysis by using a speaker recognition solution explicitly designed for forensic experts, powered by state-of-the-art deep neural networks. It is often used by police or forensic experts.

Phonexia is a leader in the business-to-business market with voice recognition solutions for governments in Europe.

In the *Intelligent Authentication and Voice Biometrics Intelliview* report released in June 2019 by Opus Research—a technology analysis and marketing firm that specializes in conversational technologies—Phonexia was recognized as an innovator in the sector.

Nature of the Competitive Advantage

The solutions of Phonexia are mainly for other businesses. Therefore, Phonexia is not well-known to the public. Phonexia develops specific solutions that are saved on local servers. These also allow companies to have better control over the sensitive data of consumers. The company has managed to build exceptional expertise and knowledge, which allows them to address and solve clients' specific needs and issues in a very precise and accurate way.

The team of Phonexia is lean and flexible. Therefore, it is able to respond and deliver solutions much more quickly than most of the competitors. Overall, it is the expertise, flexibility, and focus on the specific needs of the clients that make the company successful.

Core Lessons Learned on the Path to Business Success

The main challenge for the company was the transition from an academic-based to a profit-oriented company. This was particularly difficult as the whole model had to change completely, focus on goals, and deliver value to the client. The company had huge value added but had to learn how to satisfy the customer. A customer-centric approach started to be implemented and brought results immediately.

Management and Leadership Development Needs

Leadership is crucial to the company. Its CEO comes from a consulting firm. This allowed him to reshape and change the company's focus from technologies to customers' needs and from the governmental segment to the commercial segment.

A challenge that the company perceives is to develop a business focus attitude and orientation for talent management. The gradual growth of the company pushed some specialists who are highly professional in the technical field into management roles, although they did not have much previous experience with leadership.

To grow further, the company would greatly benefit from focusing on developing people management skills. Phonexia plans to extend its current approach, which is individual coaching and a follow-up discussion of profile and developmental needs with a specialist in the area of development.

Financing and Regulatory Environmental Development Needs

The company understands that the protection of personal data is a key element of personal protection. However, given the fast-evolving artificial intelligence sector, the European regulations and restrictions are becoming an obstacle to Phonexia's growth. Companies must comply with the new regulations, whereas information, and data needed for their activities are more expensive and less accessible. This negatively affects the companies' competitiveness globally, as other countries do not have such strict rules. Training of AI models is a good example. Companies in other countries can make more significant progress as for them the training process is cheaper in comparison with the process at companies based in the EU. Phonexia would benefit if the EU's regulations supported AI companies, allowing more freedom in the acquisition of data for training AI models.

Another issue that Phonexia perceives as a challenge for the government is the recruitment of non-EU experts. The company's narrow profile demands highly talented and motivated professionals who can contribute to the company's growth.

As the number of experts in the region and in Europe with competence in voice technologies is very limited, Phonexia needs to seek suitable specialists globally. However, hiring an expert from another country is anything but easy. The experience with the hiring of high-skilled experts from abroad shows that rigidity, slow visa procedures, and the work permit process negatively affect the company's plans.

Therefore, Phonexia would be glad if the government improved the e-access to experts from non-EU countries through the easing and digitalizing of the visa and work permit application, and the entire process.

From Academia to Business

In recent years, voice technologies have become one of the fastest expanding segments of the tech business. Due to the reliability of the information that voice provides, it can be compared to a fingerprint. Therefore, it has started to be widely used in various areas, such as the verification of a person in day-to-day activities when used as an assistant at home. Particularly the AI home solutions based on voice recognition are a well-known part of the internet of things.

On the market, various companies offer complex solutions, particularly Google and Amazon, which are some of the leaders. It is less known that the Czech company Phonexia develops unique instruments and voice technologies, characterized by some of the highest reliability and quality in the world.

Phonexia was established in 2006, when a few researchers from an award-winning group at Brno's University of Technology seized an opportunity to satisfy a customer's request that was beyond the capacities of the research team. Nowadays, the Phonexia founders and owners remain integral parts of the University, teaching new students and cooperating with research groups to deliver high-quality speech technology solutions. They are ambitious innovators who endlessly tinker and analyze, share a commitment to excellence, and inspire and share new discoveries, keeping the company's best interests at heart.

Phonexia exists to ensure that people and businesses wisely utilize the knowledge in their voice technology. This company offers a complex portfolio of cutting-edge speech recognition and voice biometrics technologies for both companies and governments and their specific needs.

All products are permanently developed and advanced in artificial intelligence, acoustics, phonetics, and voice biometrics science. Therefore, Phonexia's products are extremely accurate, fast, and scalable.

Phonexia's clients include the German police, leading global banks, and telecommunication companies from more than 60 countries. In the future, Phonexia would like to expand and focus on the business-to-customer sector in addition to the business-to-business sector.

3 Conclusions and Recommendations

The Czech Republic, together with other CEE countries, went through a major structural change after the fall of the centrally planned economic system in 1989. The Czechoslovak and Czech companies were facing severe problems related to the fact that after 40 years of central planning, companies were lacking capital and advanced know-how, as well as established sales channels to a diversified set of countries in the world economy. The Czech Republic adopted a successful set of transition reforms, transforming its economy to a free market. The lack of domestic capital was solved predominantly by opening the economy to foreign capital, which also markedly influenced the privatization process. Foreign investors brought both the know-how and the distributional channels and helped to maintain jobs in the economy. At the same time, most of the Czech participation in international trade was based either on sub-contractual cooperation with a transnational company, or on exports with rather low value added in the Czech Republic. As a result, the Czech economy was for quite some time dependent on its cost efficiency, including lower wages.

Three decades after the transition process began, numerous Czech companies progressively succeeded in the global market with unique high-value-added products. Some Czech companies became so successful that they currently dominate the local market or play a significant role in the world market. Four examples of those success stories are provided in this chapter. The four companies have some things in common: they control the value chain of their key product, they maintain the innovative edge in their industry, they are flexible in adapting to changes, and, despite the ongoing cost-advantage compared to counterparts in Western Europe and North America, and they do not have to rely on a cheap labor force. On the contrary, specialized know-how together with high ambitions, a to-do approach, and managerial and marketing skills, are crucial for their success. All of those companies managed to find their own market niche, which they currently dominate.

All four case studies of successful hidden champions lead to the same policy recommendations, which have been highlighted by international organizations for quite some time (see WEF 2014, 2019). The case studies clearly show that these recommendations are followed very slowly or not at all. Straightforward rules and regulations, level playing fields, and a pro-business approach of the state are necessary. The government should actively build an environment with a developed physical and social infrastructure, while also mitigating the market fluctuations by using appropriate economic policies, such as adjusting spending in accordance with the business cycle and less with the political cycle. Regulation should adjust more flexibly to the latest trends, so that the Czech innovators, and European innovators in general, can do business in an environment, comparable to that of their American and Asian competitors. The responsibility for the creation of this enabling environment therefore lies partially also with the EU institutions, which should take into account the high level of the Czech Republic's integration into European and global markets.

Access to a highly qualified labor force is also an issue, which highlights the underfunded and less practically oriented education system as well as the limited access to professionals from outside the EU. Any government support should take into account the long-term objectives of the state. This, nevertheless, requires the state to have a long-term strategic vision, shared across various political actors, and created in line with entrepreneurs' needs and foresight.

References

Czech Statistical Office (2017a) Databáze národních účtů [Hrubý domácí product]. http://apl.czso.cz/pll/rocenka/rocenka.indexnu

Czech Statistical Office (2017b) Databáze zahraničního obchodu v přeshraničním pojetí. https://apl.czso.cz/pll/stazo/STAZO.STAZO

De Castro T, Hnát P (2017) Czech FDI performance: between global value chains and domestic reforms. In: Foreign direct investment in central and eastern Europe. Palgrave Macmillan, Birmingham, pp 51–75

EBRD (2001) Foreign direct investment financing of capital formation in central and eastern Europe. European Bank for Reconstruction and Development, London

IQRF (2019) Cooperation in IoT as the key for a quick solution. https://www.iqrfalliance.org/press-releases/cooperation-in-iot-as-the-key-for-a-quick-solution

OECD (2014) OECD economic survey. Czech Republic. Paris, OECD

Office of the Government of the Czech Republic (2016) Analýza odlivu zisků: Důsledky pročeskou ekonomiku a návrhy opatření

UNCTAD (2011) Investment country profiles. Czech Republic. UNCTAD, New York, NY

VSE (2019) 20 years of internationalization of the Czech Republic's economy. Research study for HSBC Czech Republic
WEF (2014) Global Competitivenegss Report 2014-2015. WEF, Geneva
WEF (2019) Global Competitiveness Report 2019. WEF, Geneva

Hidden Champions of Hungary

Miklós Stocker

Overview
Official name: Hungary
Type of government: Parliamentary democratic republic
Population in 2017: 9,797,561
Land area: 90,530 km^2

History

1920	After the collapse of the Austro-Hungarian monarchy and the signing of the Treaty of Trianon, Hungary loses two thirds of its territory and more than half of its population.
1940	Hungary joins World War II.
1945	At the end of the war, Hungary loses its regained territory.
1949	Hungary becomes a People's Republic under the influence of the Soviet Union.
1989	Hungary becomes a republic.
1999	Hungary is admitted to NATO.
2004 (May)	Hungary is one of ten new states to join the EU.
2011 (January)	Hungary takes over the EU presidency for the first time in its history.
2018	Viktor Orbán is elected prime minister for the fourth time and FIDESZ-KDNP to govern the country, gaining a two-third majority for the third consecutive time.

M. Stocker (✉)
Department of Business Studies, Corvinus University of Budapest, Budapest, Hungary
e-mail: miklos.stocker@uni-corvinus.hu

1 Introduction: Context and History

After the Second World War, Hungary's economic system was a planned economy under the influence of the Soviet Union and the country was one of the founding members of the Council of Mutual Economic Assistance (COMECON), an economic organization led by the Soviet Union. One of the crucial policies of this organization was the specialization of its members, which meant that in the member countries some selected industries were developed, while others withered. Hungary had a special focus on pharmaceuticals, the chemical industry, food processing, agricultural machinery, bus production, and electronics, while other industries were developed in other member countries (Stocker and Szlávik 2013).

Hungary started its economic and political transition is 1989 to change the planned economy into a market economy and to shake off the Soviet influence. Foreign investors were invited to the country and leading industrial companies were sold to international corporations. Hungary had the most intensive foreign direct investment of all transition economies of Central and Eastern Europe. As a result, the number of foreign-owned companies increased substantially in the transition period and the traditional openness of the Hungarian economy increased further as foreign companies drove exports and imports (Chikán and Czakó 2002).

After the privatization, some of the world's leading companies invested significantly in their Hungarian subsidiaries: e.g., General Electric, General Motors, Nokia, Samsung, TEVA, and Audi. They were attracted by the well-educated and inexpensive workforce, industrial tradition and experience, good infrastructure, and investment incentives (Stocker and Szlávik 2013).

Because of these processes, economic growth was relatively stable in Hungary from 1997 to 2006. Annual GDP growth was around 3–4%, and a relatively small number of large companies created almost 50% of the added value in the country. According to Román (2009), 49.7% of the added value was created in 2009 by 870 large companies, which was significantly higher than the EU average of 42.1%. The economic development pattern differed not only in terms of company size but in ownership as well, as foreign companies operated much more efficiently than Hungarian ones. According to Reszegi and Juhász (2014), in 2011 the added value per capita of foreign companies was 11.3 million HUF, compared to 4.5 million HUF of companies with only Hungarian ownership.

The Hungarian economy stumbled in 2007. This situation was worsened by the financial and economic crisis and resulted in −6.7% GDP growth in HUF in 2009 and −1.5% in 2012. GDP growth rates were even worse in US dollar terms as the Hungarian forint was significantly weakening (Központi Statisztikai Hivatal 2019).

Because of the negative trends, high unemployment rate, and even worse expectations, tens of thousands of Hungarians left the country to work in Austria, Germany, the United Kingdom, or other countries. According to Hárs and Simon (2017), in the period from 2006 to 2016 the Hungarian labor market lost 260,000 people who were employed in other countries and the return rate was significantly lower than the emigration rate.

In 2012, the Hungarian government started to create strategic partnerships with significant large companies—mostly multinational enterprises—to facilitate investment and growth. Coca-Cola HBC Hungary Ltd. was the first company that signed the strategic partnership treaty on July 20, 2012, followed by 81 other companies up until the end of 2019 (Stratégiai partnerségi megállapodások n.d.).

The Hungarian government also reinvigorated the Hungarian EXIM Bank in 2012 to facilitate internationalization-based growth with relatively inexpensive financial solutions. The Hungarian National Bank initiated the Funding for Growth Scheme, with which it supplied interest-free credit to retail banks, offered at a fixed 2.5% interest rate to companies financing their growth.

Because of all these initiatives, the Hungarian economy returned to growth in 2013 and another stable growth period started. Hungary even over performed almost all EU countries in 2018 according to the World Bank (2019), with its 5.1% annual GDP growth.

The financial crisis put a significant burden on Hungarian companies. Credit amounts were cut back, and interest rates increased significantly, which led to severe consequences for small and medium enterprises. Several Hungarian entrepreneurs started to think of credit as a risk and started to deleverage their companies. The initiatives of the Hungarian government and the Hungarian National Bank eased the financial constraints and offered inexpensive financial solutions to entrepreneurs, but the psychological damage caused by the financial crisis was already done and most of the entrepreneurs were less eager to resort to debt-financing than before.

The economic growth in Hungary decreased the unemployment rate significantly, from 11% in 2011 to 3.6% in 2018 (Exhibit 1). As a consequence, wages started to increase steadily. The government eased the labor cost increase by decreasing the tax wedge annually after 2016, but it is not known yet whether companies can offset the labor cost increase with efficiency increase or economic growth will decrease in the next few years.

There is also some venture capital activity in Hungary, but the number of venture capital and private equity investments was very low from 2009 to 2017 and it only started to take off in 2018 (see Fig. 1).

The economic environment, combined with the Prussian-based educational culture, does not truly motivate entrepreneurship. It is far easier and less difficult for a Hungarian to be employed or to go abroad to get a job than start his own enterprise even if he has the knowledge to do it. The educational system does not really support entrepreneurship.

Despite the unfriendly environment, there is a significant number of international new ventures (INV) in Hungary: around 1000 new INVs are set up in the country annually. Around one-third of the INVs are terminated in the first five years of their existence and another one-third withdraw to their domestic markets. The remaining one-third achieve steady growth (Stocker 2019).

Hidden champions can emerge from successful INVs. Former hidden champions are following different paths. Some of them remain successful, some are acquired by big multinationals, and some withdraw to the domestic markets due to changes in technology and consumer behavior.

Exhibit 1 Core economic indicators for Hungary

	2011	2012	2013	2014	2015	2016	2017	2018
GDP per capita (current US$)	14,150.97	12,918.25	13,687.25	14,246.11	12,651.57	12,992.38	14,457.61	16,161.98
GDP per capita growth (annual %)	2.11	−0.96	2.24	4.48	4.09	2.50	4.60	5.30
Long-term unemployment (% of total unemployment)								
Unemployment, total (% of total labor force) (modeled ILO estimate)	11.02	11.00	10.17	7.72	6.81	5.11	4.16	3.66
Foreign direct investment, net inflows (% of GDP)	7.44	8.29	−2.79	9.17	−4.43	54.22	−9.5	−46.12
GDP (current US$, mio)	141,109.58	128,153.69	135,409.05	140,558.79	124,529.74	127,507.47	141,510.58	157,882.91
Exports of goods and services (current US$, mio)	122,180.63	110,624.93	115,889.09	122,873.57	109,560.51	111,124.98	123,316.70	134,104.03
Exports of goods and services (% of GDP)	86.59	86.32	85.58	87.42	87.98	87.15	87.14	84.94
Merchandise exports (current US$, mio)	112,312	103,570	107,503	110,622	98,524	101,919	113,806	125,864
Merchandise exports to high-income economies (% of total merchandise exports)	78.72	78.12	78.35	79.98	81.62	82.02	80.74	n/a
Merchandise exports to low- and middle-income economies in Europe & Central Asia (% of total merchandise exports)	16.55	16.75	16.91	15.56	14.21	13.77	14.89	n/a
Ores and metals exports (% of merchandise exports)	1.89	1.80	1.67	1.47	n/a	1.19	1.34	1.45
Agricultural raw materials exports (% of merchandise exports)	0.75	0.77	0.77	0.70	n/a	0.63	0.64	0.65
Food exports (% of merchandise exports)	8.03	9.13	8.91	8.31	n/a	8.00	8.3	7.61
Fuel exports (% of merchandise exports)	3.47	4.01	3.57	3.32	n/a	1.83	2.48	2.76

Manufactures exports (% of merchandise exports)	81.76	80.79	82.08	83.59	n/a	87.84	86.71	86.57
High-technology exports (% of manufactured exports)	25.15	21.20	19.36	16.68	n/a	17.47	17.30	16.91

Source: World Bank, December 2019

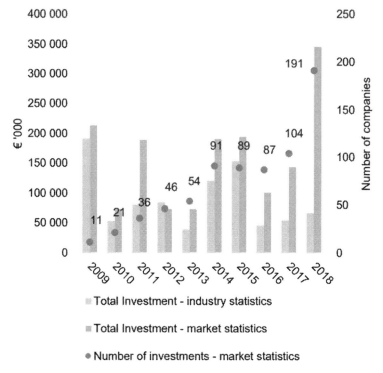

Fig. 1 Number and deal size of venture capital and private equity investments in Hungary. Source: Hungarian Private Equity and Venture Capital Association (2019)

In the 2018–2019 hidden champions research program, 11 potential champions were identified with the help of research organizations, industry organizations, and personal relationships. Six of these were interviewed in the present study, whereas the remaining ones either refused to participate or did not even respond. It turned out that two companies are only potential hidden champions and two of those identified in the 2011–2012 research are not hidden champions anymore. Therefore five valid hidden champions will be discussed in this country chapter. Interestingly, the Hungarian hidden champions are well-capitalized, usually deleveraged companies, which are in need of management capacity and internationalization-minded employees.

Although the number of hidden champions seems to be less than what would be required for healthy economic growth and faster catching up with well-developed western economies, the Hungarian hidden champions are successful companies. Hopefully, in the long run several INVs will become potential hidden champions or even real hidden champions.

2 Case Studies of Selected Hidden Champions

2.1 Case Study 1

Capsys Informatikai Kft.

Overview
Address: Montevideo u. 7, 1037 Budapest, Hungary
Tel: +36 1 436 7230
Fax:
Email: capsys@capsys.hu
Web: www.capsys-europe.com

Company Information
Industry: Banking software
Year of establishment: 1998
Sales revenues in 2017: 5.56 million euros
Sales revenues in 2007: 3.78 million euros
Average number of employees in 2017: 28 full-time employees and 130 contracted experts
Brain(s) behind the company: Founder & CEO Szeles Zoltán, co-CEO Miklós Erdélyi, Chief Architect Tamás Domonkos, Director of Services Róbert Kiszely

Nature of Market Leadership

Capsys is a technical, cost, and market share leader in the CEE in the field of payment and treasury solutions. As a business expert company and a software developer, Capsys has a long tradition of developing business applications for banking services, with vertically specialized front-to-back, front-office, and back-office solutions for treasuries or retail banks in the CEE region. Most of the company's exports go to Poland, Russia, and Saudi Arabia, as well as other CEE, CIS, and GCC countries.

Nature of the Competitive Advantage

Very deep expertise in some niches of banking activities, such as immediate payment and open banking, combined with strategic business consultancy, to create and implement software solutions with a complex value-creation-based approach. Quality comes first.

Core Lessons Learned on the Path to Success

1. As a competitive market, balanced against international vendors, CEE is a dream. The market is only determined by relationships (capital).
2. To find a CEE-specific niche market is the key success factor for companies like Capsys.
3. To become a successful entrepreneur is an adventure and obsession.
4. The most important elements of success are the team dynamics and the cooperative, creative team culture with a trust-based close relationship with business partners and customers.

Management and Leadership Development Needs

The development needs are to solve the human resource scarcity, to bridge cultural differences, and to revive the motivation of the employees for solving client problems abroad.

Financing and Regulatory Environment Development Needs

There is no direct development need in terms of financing or the regulatory environment. What is needed to make these companies competitive abroad is the globally competitive business environment driven by the regulators in CEE.

Capsys Leads Digital Transformation in Financial Service Software Solutions

Capsys Ltd. is a financial services software company that provides services in the CEE, CIS, and MENA regions. Capsys delivers payment and treasury solutions to its clients and offers vertically integrated, customized software solutions with price and technology leadership.

Capsys was able to create a culture where three different generations work together to create and nurture client relationships, leading to significant sales. The company's success is based on strategic thinking, collaboration, creativity, quality delivery, tenacity, and luck. There is an interesting cultural difference between the sales team, the development team, and the delivery team in the company, as sales and development have a cooperative culture, but the delivery team needs authoritarian management for efficient delivery. To solve this cultural difference, extensive team dynamics and collaboration are needed.

With these capabilities, Capsys was able to identify the right niche in the market and create a successful action plan to seize the niche. Capsys created a clientele with which their recurring revenues are around 50–60%. This has stabilized the company and created new growth opportunities. Capsys developed several business applications to serve non-standard business needs with state-of-the-art practice and know-how. Zeus, ZeusGPI, ZeusNXT, and Europé are solutions developed by the company, but they also deliver solutions with strategic partners ACI Worldwide and Calypso.

In innovative financial solutions, there is usually a discrepancy between the regulatory environment and the needed solution. Capsys's innovations can create solutions but the regulatory body has to be persuaded to let the developments take place.

2.2 Case Study 2

Cyclolab Kft.

Overview
Address: H-1097 Budapest, Illatos út 7, Hungary
Tel: +36 1 347 6070
Fax:
Email: cyclolab@cyclolab.hu
Web: https://cyclolab.hu/

Company Information
Industry: Researcher and manufacturer of basic pharmaceutical products (Research and experimental development on biotechnology)
Year of establishment: 1989
Sales revenues in 2017: 2.33 million euros
Sales revenues in 2007: 1.57 million euros
Average number of employees in 2017: 35 full-time employees
Brain(s) behind the company: Lajos Szente, Erzsébet Szilágyi, Gabriella Szejtli, and Tamás Sohajda

Nature of Market Leadership

Cyclolab remains the only company in the world in the business of R&D and small-scale manufacturing of all-round cyclodextrin. Cyclolab exports to a wide range of countries: 70% of exports go to the EU, 15% to the USA, and 15% to China and India.

Nature of the Competitive Advantage

Cyclolab's research and development capabilities, as well as the world-wide recognition of its cyclodextrin solutions, helps Cyclolab to avoid direct competition. Cyclolab's control of the whole value system remains also a key competitive advantage. Cyclolab is a world market leader in cyclodextrin solutions.

Core Lessons Learned on the Path to Success

1. Seize the whole value system and use state-of-the art scientific research to improve it.
2. Focus research and development activities on different stages of product and solution development to create a sustainable pipeline.
3. Seize global market opportunities as margins in foreign markets are significantly higher than in Hungary.

Management and Leadership Development Needs

The development needs are to solve the scarcity of research-oriented, specialized, well-educated human resources. This could help develop cyclodextrin solutions.

Financing and Regulatory Environment Development Needs

There is no direct development need in terms of financing. The financing structure of the company is stable and is based mostly on equity (about 95%).

Cyclolab: Research Excellence with Manufacturing Capabilities

Cyclolab was identified as a hidden champion in the 2011 research as well. The company's success was based on the research of the founder, Professor József Szejtli (PhD, DSc), and his capability to organize talented scientists in the research process. The company is already going through a generation change and a change in ownership and is climbing to new heights.

Cyclolab is in the business of R&D and small-scale manufacturing of all-round cyclodextrin and leads the world market in its niche. The company serves customers in the global value chain for whom it can create significant added value and thus achieve better margins. Cyclolab avoids price competitions. Instead of competing on price, the company offers research capabilities. Although Cyclolab is an expert in small-scale manufacturing, it can provide the highest added value in research and development and analytics. The company serves several recurring clients but also sells through agents in different continents. Cyclolab exports more than 97% of its sales. As a research-oriented company, Cyclolab always faces some degree of uncertainty but its scientists try to solve research tasks. Cyclolab's research-and-development capabilities connect with the world-wide recognition of their cyclodextrin solutions. This helps Cyclolab to avoid direct competition. Cyclolab's control of the whole value system remains a key competitive advantage.

The company is well recognized in their scientific field. Cyclolab's team has more than 500 publications. It has filed over 100 patents and has been awarded several scientific or business awards, such as the Pegasus Award in 2016, Professor Lajos Szente's Gábor Dénes Award in 2017, and the Derek Horton Award in 2018.

Another management succession happened in 2018 as Professor Lajos Szente finished his managerial duties and became scientific advisor. The new management team will have to guide the company through the digitalization challenge as it will need new marketing and management capabilities to be competitive in the increasingly digitalized world.

2.3 Case Study 3

Energotest Kft.

Overview
Address: H-2330 Dunaharaszti, Gomba u. 4
Tel: +36 24 501 150
Fax:
Email: kereskedelem@energotest.hu
Web: http://www.energotest.hu/energotest

Company Information
Industry: Modular, network-integrated technical testing stations. Manufacture of instruments and appliances for measuring, testing, and navigation.
Year of establishment: 1990
Sales revenues in 2017: 4.6 million euros
Sales revenues in 2007: 6.4 million eurosIO
Average number of employees in 2017: 87 full-time employees
Brain(s) behind the company: Tamás Zentai

Nature of Market Leadership

Energotest is a regional market leader, operating in and around Hungary, in modular, network-integrated technical testing stations. Most of the company's exports go to Germany, Austria, Romania, Slovakia, and the UK. New markets, such as India, are also being explored.

Nature of the Competitive Advantage

Energotest created a niche market in the garage industry by redefining its technical testing stations segment with its modular, network-integrated solution. The company also collaborates with universities in high-class development projects and tries to integrate its results into core businesses. Energotest is able to customize networking-based solutions, connect knowledge bases, and govern automation.

Core Lessons Learned on the Path to Success

1. Financial constraints create a push for innovative solutions.
2. Redefining the value stream creates a possibility to capture more value or exclude competitors from the market.
3. Focus on solutions that give clients more value.
4. Focus on social and environmental value in addition to profit.

Management and Leadership Development Needs

A lack of management capabilities can compromise further growth.

Financing and Regulatory Environment Development Needs

The company decreased significantly its debt in the previous years and the financing of the company is stable and mostly based on equity (about 79%), which is enough for gradual, organic growth, but more capital accumulation is needed for faster international expansion.

Modular, Network Integrated Solutions Offered by Energotest

Energotest was identified as a hidden champion in the 2011 research as well. The company has remained successful ever since and has created new business opportunities with which it can compete in new industries.

In 2013, the company invested into a new plant, with which it increased its production capability by some 160%, deployed new container-sized technology, and introduced renewable energy solutions. Although Energotest became a hidden champion based on its modular, network-integrated technical testing stations, the company is consciously creating new solutions. The company partners with universities in high-class research and development projects for the production of complex brake-audit systems, and a photoacoustic emission examination system for exhausts. Energotest even ventured into energetics solutions where automation solutions can decrease environmental exertion and decrease operation costs. Energotest proves that thinking and creativity can overcome a lack of financial resources. The company's modular solutions can be integrated into several network-based solutions, with which it can compete on a broader scale.

2.4 Case Study 4

Tran-SYS Kft.

Overview
Address: Lajos u. 48-66. B lépcsőház, V. emelet, 1036 Budapest, Hungary
Tel: +36 1 336-2071
Fax: +36 1 336-2061
Email: transys@transys.hu
Web: www.transys.hu

Company Information
Industry: Simulation systems for interlocking and railway operations. Computer programming activities.
Year of establishment: 1994
Sales revenues in 2017: 2.42 million euros
Sales revenues in 2007: 1.2 million euros
Average number of employees in 2017: 30 full-time employees
Brain(s) behind the company: CEO and founder Dr. István Hrivnák, Dr. Ferenc Parádi, Zoltán Bozsóki

Nature of Market Leadership

Technology leadership in lifelike, complex simulation systems for interlocking and railway operations. Tran-SYS together with its strong co-operation partner Scheidt & Bachmann System Technik GmbH have been market leaders in the European Union for 25 years, with 80–90% market share. Their most important markets are Germany, Austria, Switzerland, Sweden, and France.

Nature of the Competitive Advantage

The company's main competitive advantage is innovations integrated into IT architecture to provide real-life based complex simulations. Integrated solutions—such as offerings from training, planning, energy optimization, validation, verification and testing—and consulting are combined. Tran-SYS customizes its solutions for railway companies.

Core Lessons Learned on the Path to Success

1. Dynamic, agile, young, well-educated engineers form the development team are the key pillar of continuous innovativeness.
2. Strategic partnerships, reliability, trust, exemplary leadership, knowledge, expertise, and luck are needed to succeed in the long run.

3. Flexible working hours and responsibility-based flexibility enhance motivation and performance.

Management and Leadership Development Needs

The company faces development needs in the fields of employee communication skills, foreign language skills, and project management capabilities. These have to be enhanced by fostering a positive attitude toward working abroad in implementation projects.

Financing and Regulatory Environment Development Needs

The company does not have financing needs, but needs a stable regulatory environment. Simplified, predictable tax regulations would be welcomed, and a faster tendering system is needed.

Simulation Software for a Safer Railway Operation

Tran-SYS Ltd. started its business as an international new venture. Right after the company was set up in 1994, it had its first international client, the city railways of Cologne. The company creates complex simulation systems for interlocking and railway operations. These complex simulations systems offer training solutions from regular training to emergency simulations, planning solutions for validation and verification of plans, energy consumption, and power simulations, testing solutions for the before real life geographic installation, and even consulting solutions.

The company's first innovations came from the scientific research of the founders who were researchers in the Budapest University of Technology and Economics. They met German co-operation partners through the university connections, of the company founder, Dr. Ferenc Parádi.

Tran-SYS's competitive advantage is the customized solutions for railways created through a bottom-up approach that ensures life-like simulations. The founders were passionate about their solution and were driven by new challenges. Reliability, tenacity, knowledge, expertise, trust, strategic partners, and luck were the main ingredients of Tran-SYS's success.

Succession is the main challenge of the company as one of the founders passed away. Therefore, the management realized that succession plans need to be created in the long run and that the strategic partners' succession plan could be a challenge as well.

2.5 Case Study 5

Tresorit Kft.

Overview
Address: Köztelek utca 6, 1092 Budapest, Hungary
Tel: N/A
Fax: N/A
Email: info@tresorit.com
Web: www.tresorit.com

Company Information
Industry: Encrypted enterprise file sync and share (Computer programming activities)
Year of establishment: 2011
Sales revenues in 2017: 3.18 million euros
Sales revenues in 2012: 40,000 euros
Average number of employees in 2017: 58 full time employees
Brain(s) behind the company: Founders István Lám, Szilveszter Szebeni, and György Szilágyi

Nature of Market Leadership

Tresorit is a technology leader. It is an enterprise cloud encryption and collaboration company, which provides end-to-end encrypted file sync and sharing for businesses. Its solutions are used worldwide. Its main markets are the DACH, USA, and UK. Tresorit has led its market by market share since 2017.

Nature of Competitive Advantage

Tresorit is a global challenger in the rapidly expanding enterprise file sync and sharing market. It provides zero-knowledge, patented encryption technology, and unique encryption key management, and guarantees on-premise equivalent security for businesses while offering consumer-grade simplicity. Tresorit's competitive advantage lies on the pillars of its founders' vision and the high-quality, skilled Hungarian labor that the company nurtures.

Core Lessons Learned on the Path to Success

1. It is not enough to have a sound business idea. The implementation has to be based on high-quality human resources to be able to unleash the potential of the solution. The business had to be transformed from engineer-driven to market-driven.

2. Moving from the consumer market to businesses, where security and compliance is much more appreciated, and a presence in Switzerland, increases the company's credibility.
3. A solution can be good enough to get financing, but the financed innovations have to win the customers as well. A series of fundraising events allowed the company to grow.

Management and Leadership Development Needs

Efficiency increase will be needed in the medium term as the company has to turn profitable. Acquisition of new businesses has to be scaled up significantly at the current ROI level.

Financing and Regulatory Environment Development Needs

The next level of capital infusion is happening right now, as 11.5 million euros were secured in September 2018.

Tresorit Encrypts Everything to Know Nothing

Tresorit creates secure, zero-knowledge apps that empower people to take control of their data. With its end-to-end encryption, the company protects information in the cloud from everyone, even from itself.

Founders István Lám, Szilveszter Szebeni, and György Szilágyi started Tresorit while still at university in 2011. They did not trust mainstream file sync apps and decided to create a service with end-to-end encryption at its heart. With its technological solution, Tresorit and vision obtained US$1.7 million Series A funding in January 2012 and the company won its first award in May 2012: the European Prize at the Global Security Challenge. In the meantime, Tresorit also experienced rapid growth as its user base increased more than 200 times by June 2013. In 2013, the company founded its Swiss-based subsidiary Tresorit AG, which boosts its credibility even more. A second round of investment was closed in May 2014, with a capital infusion of US$3-million. Tresorit used crowd-sourcing solutions as it dealt with hackers' attempts to crack its encryption, with which it could test and prove its solution. In September 2018 Tresorit obtained US$11.5 million in Series B funding.

In the beginning, the founders fulfilled all kinds of senior executive roles, but they realized that they could fulfil all senior executive roles. Hence they had to hire experienced business managers. The actual CFO had more than 10 years of experience at KPMG as head of finance and controlling. The new sales and marketing leaders are seasoned professionals, as well.

As Tresorit is a young IT start-up, its employees are generally young and therefore lack experience. The top management realized that the lack of leadership experience will be an obstacle to future growth. Therefore, the company started a leadership development program for team leaders in the fall of 2017. In 2018, it started the next series for future potential leaders.

Tresorit became a global challenger in the rapidly expanding enterprise file sync and sharing market. The company provides zero-knowledge, patented encryption technology, and unique encryption key management, with which they can guarantee on-premise equivalent security for businesses while offering consumer-grade simplicity.

3 Conclusions and Recommendations

The Hungarian hidden champions continue to be small, highly innovative companies with strong, centralized leadership, just as in the previous round of research. Although some still rely on traditional Hungarian industries, newly emerging hidden champions come from the field of applied software solutions, where they could find their competitive advantage in customized state-of-the-art solutions or technologies. Hungarian hidden champions excel in knowledge-based niches of big industries.

The financial crisis and after-crisis years affected the Hungarian hidden champions. Typically, they no longer use debt to finance growth and usually deleveraged themselves in the past few years, although their return on equity decreased because of this. Some hidden champions identified in the 2011 research have retained or even improved their innovation capabilities, creating new innovative solutions or even new markets, and have remained hidden champions. Other hidden champions of the past were acquired or had to withdraw to the domestic market, and although these companies are very successful, they do not qualify as hidden champions anymore.

Governments could support hidden champions with knowledge, expertise, and relationship assistance in market-entry strategies in the short term, facilitating company-university research cooperation in the medium term, and fostering a more entrepreneur-oriented culture in the long run.

Financial institutions can support hidden champions with easy-to-obtain, low-interest credit. Where these solutions already exist, they could be developed to become reliable long-term financial solutions, whose conditions do not change radically if the macro environment changes.

Business schools and universities could support hidden champions with executive education and company-university research cooperation, and by educating open-minded, internationalization-oriented fresh graduates with excellent language proficiencies to supply employees who could generate growth.

Although the number of hidden champions seems to be lower than what would be required for healthy economic growth and faster catching up with developed Western economies, the Hungarian hidden champions are successful companies. Hopefully, in the long run several INVs will become potential or real hidden champions.

References

Chikán A, Czakó E (2002) Competitiveness of small economies in the global economy – the case of Hungary. In: Chikán A, Czakó E, Zoltay-Paprika Z (eds) National competitiveness in global economy – the case of Hungary. Akadémiai Kiadó, Budapest, pp 23–33

Hárs Á, Simon D (2017) A külföldi munkavállalás és a munkaerőhiány. In: Fazekas K, Köllő J (eds) Munkaerőpiaci Tükör 2016. MTA Közgazdaság- és Regionális Tudományi Kutatóközpont Közgazdaság-tudományi Intézet, Budapest, pp 94–109

Hungarian Private Equity and Venture Capital Association (2019) Venture Capital and Private Equity update Hungary – 2018. https://www.hvca.hu/documents/Investment_monitoring_report_2018_Final.pdf

Központi Statisztikai Hivatal (2019) 3.1.1. A bruttó hazai termék (GDP) értéke, volumenindexe és implicit árindexe (1995–). Retrieved from Központi Statisztikai Hivatal website: https://www.ksh.hu/docs/hun/xstadat/xstadat_eves/i_qpt001.html

Reszegi L, Juhász P (2014) A vállalati teljesítmény nyomában. Alinea Kiadó, Budapest

Román Z (2009) Statisztikai Tükör 2009/109. KSH

Stocker M (2019) Survival, growth, and performance of Hungarian international new ventures. Society and Economy 41:47–64. https://doi.org/10.1556/204.2019.41.1.4

Stocker M, Szlávik P (2013) Hidden champions of Hungary. In: McKiernan P, Purg D (eds) Hidden champions in CEE and Turkey. Springer, Berlin, pp 201–217

Stratégiai partnerségi megállapodások (n.d.). https://www.kormany.hu/hu/kulgazdasagi-es-kulugyminiszterium/strategiai-partnersegi-megallapodasok

World Bank (2019) Data; countries and economies. https://data.worldbank.org/country/hungary

Hidden Champions of the Republic of Kazakhstan

Christian Kahl, Aigerim Raimzhanova, Aigerim Serikbekova, and Sultanbek Kaiym

Overview[1]

Official name: Republic of Kazakhstan
Type of government: Consolidated central government
Population in 2017: 18.28 million
Land area: 2724.9 m^2

History

1936	The territory becomes a Soviet republic, the Kazakh SSR
1953–1965	Under Nikita S. Khrushchev, the Kazakh territory continues to cultivate wheat and other cereal grains. The decimation of the nomadic Kazakh population and the immigration of non-Kazakhs continues, turning Kazakhs into a minority
1989–1990	December protests against the removal of D. Kunaev, leader of the Kazakh SSR. Eventually, G. Kolbin is replaced by a Kazakh, Nursultan Nazarbayev. Moscow declares formally the sovereignty of the Kazakh central government, forcing Kazakhstan to elaborate its own statement of sovereignty

---

[1] https://data.worldbank.org/country/kazakhstan?view=chart

C. Kahl (✉)
Beijing Jiaotong University, Beijing, China

A. Raimzhanova
Narxoz University, Almaty, Kazakhstan
e-mail: aigerim.raimzhanova@narxoz.kz

A. Serikbekova
Almaty Management University, Almaty, Kazakhstan

S. Kaiym
Atyrau Oil and Gas University named after Safi Utebayev, Atyrau, Kazakhstan

1991	Formation of the Republic of Kazakhstan, Nursultan Nazarbayev is elected president
1991–2019	Under Nazarbayev's governance, significant social and economic reforms are implemented, leading the country to significant economic progress. Economic development is mainly driven by the export of large oil, gas, and mineral reserves
1992	Kazakhstan is admitted to the United Nations and the Conference on Security and Cooperation in Europe, the predecessor of the Organisation for Security and Cooperation in Europe (OSCE)
1993	A new constitution increasing the president's powers is adopted and a major privatization program is launched. Kazakhstan ratifies the first Strategic Arms Reduction Treaty and the Treaty on the Non-Proliferation of Nuclear Weapons
1995	Kazakhstan signs an economic and military cooperation pact with Russia. Nuclear-free status is obtained. President Nazarbayev's term in office is extended until December 2000 and a new constitution is adopted by national referendum
1997	Major oil agreements secured with China. In later years, cooperation with China expands. Kazakhstan's capital is moved from Almaty in the south to Akmola (formerly Tselinograd) in the north
1998	The new capital is renamed Astana. The constitution is amended, extending the president's term in office from 5 to 7 years and removing the upper age limit for the president
1999	Nursultan Nazarbayev is re-elected president. Subsequent parliamentary elections criticized by OSCE for irregularities
2000	A 10-year economic security strategy is adopted. The World Bank praises the country's economic reforms. Kazakhstan strengthens security on all borders, following incursions by Islamist militants from Kyrgyzstan and Uzbekistan
2001	First major pipeline for transporting oil from the Caspian Sea to world markets opens in March, running from the huge Tengiz oil field in western Kazakhstan to the Russian Black Sea port of Novorossiysk
2001(June)	Kazakhstan joins China, Russia, Kyrgyzstan, Uzbekistan, and Tajikistan in the launching of the Shanghai Cooperation Organisation (SCO), which aims to fight ethnic and religious militancy and promote trade
2001 (December)	President Nazarbayev and US President George W. Bush meet and declare commitment to a long-term, strategic partnership
2004	A deal is signed with China on the construction of an oil pipeline to the Chinese border

2005	Nursultan Nazarbayev returns for yet another term as president with more than 90% of the vote. He inaugurates a 1000-km (620 mile) pipeline to carry oil to western China
2009 (April)	President Nazarbayev announces his readiness to build a nuclear fuel bank to ensure other countries do not need to develop their own fuel sources. Idea first proposed by the International Atomic Energy Agency in 2005, and supported by both the USA and Russia
2009 (October)	France and Kazakhstan sign energy and business deals worth 6 billion US dollars during a visit by President Nicolas Sarkozy. Kazakhstan also agrees to allow French military supplies to pass through on their way to Afghanistan
2009 (December)	Chinese President Hu Jintao and President Nazarbayev unveil the Kazakh section of a natural gas pipeline connecting Central Asia and China
2010 (January)	Kazakhstan becomes the first former Soviet state to chair the Organisation of Security and Co-operation in Europe (OSCE) security and rights group, despite criticism of its own democratic credentials. President Nazarbayev signals a change in emphasis from rights to security
2010 (July)	A customs union between Russia, Belarus, and Kazakhstan comes into force after Belarus ratifies a key customs code
2011 (April)	President Nazarbayev wins re-election in a poll boycotted by the opposition
2011 (December)	Clashes between striking workers and police in the western oil town of Zhanaozen leave 16 people dead. The government declares a state of emergency
2013	David Cameron becomes the first serving British Prime Minister to pay an official visit to Kazakhstan. The UK is the third-largest investor in the oil-rich central Asian nation
2014	Russia, Kazakhstan, and Belarus sign an agreement creating an economic union. The Eurasian Economic Union aims to create a shared market and integrated economic policy across the former Soviet countries
2015 (January)	The Eurasian Economic Union between Russia, Kazakhstan, Belarus, Kyrgyzstan, and Armenia comes into force
2015 (April)	President Nazarbayev is re-elected with 97.7% of the votes
2015 (November)	Kazakhstan becomes the 162nd member of the World Trade Organization (WTO)
2015 (August)	Kazakhstan's currency, the tenge, plunges by more than a third in 1 day. An agreement is signed to create the world's first bank of low-enriched uranium in the northeast of Kazakhstan. The bank is to be managed by the International Atomic Energy Agency (IAEA)

2017	Parliament approves a constitutional reforms that will reduce the president's powers in favor of lawmakers and the cabinet
2019 March	President Nazarbayev announces his resignation. The nation's capital is renamed Nur-sultan
2019 (April)	President Kassym-Jomart Tokayev, the former Senate chairman, announces snap presidential elections for 9 June
2019 (June)	Tokayev wins the presidential elections with 71% of the votes

Source: BBC (2019)
https://www.bbc.com/news/world-asia-pacific-15483497

1 Introduction: Country Context

The Republic of Kazakhstan is a Central Asian country that gained independence and sovereignty in 1991, following the dissolution of the Soviet Union. Kazakhstan is the largest landlocked country and the ninth's largest country in the world, with a territory of 2,724,900 km^2 (CIA World Factbook 2016). While Kazakhstan is the largest country in Central Asia, it is one of the world's most sparsely populated countries, with only 18 million people. The nation is endowed with considerable mineral resources, including significant oil and natural gas reserves, as well as vast areas of arable land (Coleman 2015). The geographical location and natural resources represent the economic and political might of the country.

The economic development of the country has been steady but complex. After the dissolution of the Soviet Union, the centrally planned economic system collapsed and the sharp decline of demand for Kazakhstan's traditional heavy industry products led to a steep drop in output. Nevertheless, with the implementation of economic reforms, the country's economic performance has been growing steadily since the late 1990s (Coleman 2015). In 2018, Kazakhstan's GDP was 172.94 billion US dollars (Plecher 2019). Since achieving its independence, Kazakhstan has become the leading state in former Soviet Central Asia in terms of GDP, GDP per capita, privatization of the economy, volume of exports, rate of economic development, volume of energy production, effectiveness of the banking system, development of transportation, growth of technical education, and more (Qamar and Sumera 2014). The discovery of the Kashagan oil field in Kazakhstan's sector of the Caspian Sea in July 2000 marked a new chapter in the country's oil explorations (Bertelsmann Stiftung 2018: 5).

At the same time, Kazakhstan suffers from being landlocked and paying large overheads for the transport of imported goods. Heavy industry and machinery, for instance, are still imported and are not widely developed in Kazakhstan (World Bank 2019). One of the most critical issues for the country is finding solutions for the geographic location by opening exit routes, such as rail, roads, and pipelines, in all directions (Diyarbakırlıoğlu and Yiğit 2014). At the same time, Kazakhstan's vast area in the Eurasian center makes the country an area of strategic interest for economic, political, and security purposes, regionally and internationally. Kazakhstan aims to have positive relations with various partners, especially Russia and China, but also the European Union and the USA. The interests of these countries can be viewed from the perspective of a New Great Game, whereby the great world powers compete over influence in the region. In the framework of the New Great Game, Kazakhstan follows a pragmatic foreign policy titled multivectorism. This foreign policy is primarily motivated by the country's need to secure alternative oil pipeline routes, but it is somewhat complicated by the country's growing integration into the Eurasian Economic Union (Bertelsmann Stiftung 2018: 39). Multivectorism's goals include preserving the country's territorial integrity and independence through the prevention of the influence of one external country on the territory and enabling the development and modernization of the country.

Multivectorism translates into multiple political and economic partnerships. Kazakhstan is a member of numerous international organizations, including the United Nations, and many of its specialized and regional agencies. Kazakhstan was a non-permanent member of the United Nations Security Council in 2017–2018. In addition, Kazakhstan is a member of the World Trade Organization, the Organization for Security and Cooperation in Europe, the Eurasian Economic Community, the North Atlantic Cooperation Council (Euro-Atlantic Partnership Council), the European Bank for Reconstruction and Development, the Asian Development Bank, and the Organization of the Islamic Conference. Importantly, the state is a founding member of the Shanghai Cooperation Organization and the Conference for Interaction and Confidence in Asia. The fact that Kazakhstan is one of the founding members of the Eurasian Economic Union provides opportunities for the expansion of its businesses in various sectors. For instance, the Astana International Financial Center (AIFC), launched in July 2018, aims to become the financial hub for the Eurasian Economic Union and Central Asia. Kazakhstan is also an active participant in the North Atlantic Treaty Organization's Partnership for Peace program (Coleman 2015). Kazakhstan emerged as a fourth nuclear power in the world following the dissolution of the Soviet Union. Yet, the state voluntarily gave up its nuclear weapons, not least to build a cooperation with Western countries.

Overall, Kazakhstan's resources play a significant role for both the political and economic priorities of the state. However, scholars and practitioners have often highlighted the country's resource dependency as a one-sided path, as it can result in a dangerous reliance on many external factors, such as the price of oil, access to export routes, and so forth. In fact, the reliance on an oil-dependent economic model led to the recent economic recession and devaluation crisis in the country. The 2015 economic crisis served as a clear indication of risks and vulnerabilities arising from inadequate economic diversification, stressing the need for further structural reform (IHS 2015) The World Bank (2019) confirms that the economic growth has slowed down mainly because of the devaluation of the local currency (World Bank 2019). This, of course, had an effect on the consumers' purchasing power and investment climate in Kazakhstan. The country's economy has been recovering steadily since 2009, growing at an 8–9% rate, again, largely because of increased oil and gas production (BTI Report 2018: 26).

Kazakhstan aims to diversify its production structure to reduce the economy's dependence on world market commodity prices, decrease external vulnerability, and support long-term growth. This includes providing a sustainable economic environment for the growth of businesses. Kazakhstan is investing massively in the infrastructure of the country to enhance its business environment (World Bank 2019), not least owing to the hosting of recent EXPO on Green Energy. The latter represents another important strategic goal for the country. Kazakhstan has committed to national and international actions to achieve sustainable growth and has already taken steps to address the use of renewable resources, to achieve energy efficiency, and cut greenhouse gas emissions (OECD 2018: 96). Overall, the Kazakh market offers many attractive niches for business development and economic growth.

The entrepreneurial culture in Kazakhstan is on the rise and the country has seen the growth and development of diverse companies. MNEs and SMEs of various forms are developing in Kazakhstan. Apart from homegrown companies, there are many franchises and joint ventures. Globalization and open trade relationships have intensified the product offering and service industry in Kazakhstan. The business environment in Kazakhstan is actively developing, with several chambers of commerce opening up in Nur-sultan and Almaty, aimed at supporting international business cooperation. The largest are the American, French and German chambers of commerce, with more than 100 members. The Chinese Chamber of Commerce has also opened recently in Kazakhstan and is actively growing, not least due to extensive cooperation between the two countries and the "One Belt One Road" initiative. In fact, Kazakhstan has an opportunity to become a logistics hub for trade between China and the European Union.

The overarching government policy is to support business growth and promote the emergence of non-profit organizations dedicated to supporting the private sector. Atameken, the National Chamber of Entrepreneurs of the Republic of Kazakhstan, is one such example. The goals of Atameken include the protection of business rights and interests, the involvement of entrepreneurs in the formation of the legislative and regulatory policies connected to business activities, and support for domestic and foreign investors (Atameken 2019). Nevertheless, to a certain degree, the government continues to interfere in business processes, which reduces the potential of the private sector to play a role in strengthening the domestic economy. Moreover, the private sector continues to be largely dependent on the state for funds. In order to ensure a holistic development of the private sector, the country needs to provide an easier access to SME financing and an increased private participation in larger projects, for instance in infrastructure. The implementation of deeper institutional reforms, effective property rights protection, and anti-corruption measures are imperative to enable long-term development (Bertelsmann Stiftung 2018: 21–23).

In terms of human capital, the government draws on the largely well-educated workforce from the Soviet era and on a pool of young, Western-trained political and economic leaders (Bertelsmann Stiftung 2018: 3). It is important to note the change of business culture in the Kazakh market and the emergence of a new generation of entrepreneurs and leaders. The new generation (namely, Generation X and Y) is becoming an important agent in the business sector, changing the rules of the game in the spheres of business innovation, transparency, and management style. Indeed, as in many other countries, Gen Y and Z representatives are breaking out of all cultural models and represent a new type of workforce (Black 2010; Fok and Yeung 2016; McEwan 2009; Snaebjornsson et al. 2015).

While the entrepreneurial spirit in the country is growing, it is not fully developed. The development of entrepreneurship is an important pillar for the government (KazkMinistry of Information and Social Development of the Republic of Kazakhstan, JSC 2019), reflected accordingly in *Strategy 2050*, as well as in numerous other policy documents. According to the *Global Entrepreneurship Monitor*, almost 75% of the population sees entrepreneurship as a desired choice of work, but 82% still see it as a high-status sphere (OECD 2018: 77). The OECD advises the country to include entrepreneurial education in a broader set of curricula. Generally, the country needs to build upon its educational reforms to enable market growth and entrepreneurship activities (Exhibit 1).

2 Challenges in the Search for Hidden Champions

Companies across the world, including those of Kazakhstan, strive for transparency, development, and innovation. Yet, the market share, internationalization aspect, and market visibility may not always mean hidden champion status. We often met with a paradox when a company was innovative, successful, and rapidly developing, and yet, due to a certain factor (i.e., being a national company or not hidden), it could not be included in the research. In other words, if it was innovative and international, but a small company, it had to be dropped from the hidden champion list. Also, a hidden champion must be a regional leader, but not too well-known to the market. Meanwhile, in Kazakhstan and the Central Asian region, big companies are mostly well-known.

Hence, for the purpose of this research, we were primarily interested in large companies with regional leadership in a certain niche. Yet, these companies often received some form of state subsidy or government support. As highlighted in Michael Porter's Five Forces Model (Visual Paradigm 2019), political influence continues to remain a strong success factor in many countries. For large companies, a connection with the government (for both political and economic reasons) remains one of the key success factors in Kazakhstan. We will not reveal the names of these companies for confidentiality reasons.

The two companies that were identified as hidden champions in 2011 (Alsi and Tulpar-intech) chose not to participate in the survey and interview this year. Based on secondary data, both companies are still doing well. Yet, due to the new hidden champion methodology and the lack of an interview, we cannot comment with certainty on their hidden champion status. From the list of potential companies who could have satisfied the hidden champion criteria, not a single company decided to disclose information, follow-up on the initial communication, and participate in the research. This may not necessarily mean that they wanted to hide something, although a certain political pressure and the complex business framework may have contributed to that. More likely, because of the tough market conditions, the

Exhibit 1 Core economic indicators for Kazakhstan

	2011	2012	2013	2014	2015	2016	2017	2018
GDP per capita (current US$)	7165.223	11,634	12,386.7	13,890.63	12,807.26	10,510.77	7714.842	9030.319
GDP per capita growth (annual %)	7.4	4.8	6	4.2	1.2	1.1	4.1	4.1
Long-term unemployment (% of total unemployment)	–	–	–	–	–	–	–	–
Foreign direct investment, net inflows (% of GDP)	7.14	6.56	4.23	3.30	3.57	12.54	2.83	0.12
GDP (current US$, billions)	192,626.5	207,998.5	236,634.5	221,415.57	184,388.4	137,278.3	166,805.8	179,339.99
Exports of goods and services (current US $, mio)	41.83842	46.46466	44.10966	38.61704	39.34176	28.51671	31.84389	34.35781
Exports of goods and services (% of GDP)	46.46466	44.10966	38.61704	39.34176	28.51671	31.84389	34.35781	–
Merchandise exports (current US$)	62.94149	63.84996	56.41864	54.53817	41.50152	45.24677	47.94923	54.82035
Merchandise exports to high-income economies (% of total merchandise exports)	61.01071	58.41663	59.41094	61.68304	63.60146	61.85622	61.3228	61.59961
Merchandise exports to developing economies in Europe & Central Asia (% of total merchandise exports)	–	–	–	–	–	–	–	–

Ores and metals exports (% of merchandise exports)	11.20635	12.92027	13.00696	9.94253	8.644619	12.05714	14.7729	15.18542
Agricultural raw materials exports (% of merchandise exports)	0.23876	0.111544	0.131268	0.24781	0.152992	0.180914	0.297546	0.310123
Food exports (% of merchandise exports)	3.819399	3.819399	3.377596	3.175376	3.288588	4.627998	5.725797	4.878645
Fuel exports (% of merchandise exports)	70.58698	72.8257	70.55868	76.70113	76.62713	68.01826	60.73527	63.44043
Manufactures exports (% of merchandise exports)	14.13338	12.03786	12.92243	9.927731	11.28098	15.09617	18.41853	16.14536
High-technology exports (% of manufactured exports)	24.78307	30.24285	37.21629	38.01209	41.36245	30.66906	22.8972	22.23531

Source: World Bank, October 2019
https://databank.worldbank.org/reports.aspx?source=2&country=KAZ#

devaluation of the tenge, and the general political uncertainty, the companies did not see involvement in the study and information sharing as their priority. To reiterate, in those instances where companies were willing to share such information, they did not satisfy the hidden champion criteria and, hence, could not be included in the analysis.

Generally, companies in Kazakhstan do not have a culture of openness (Dudovskiy 2019; Hofstede 2019; Hofstede et al. 2002). They are not obliged to have an open public profile online. Hence, gathering information, especially financial, on a company or a particular product is a challenge without a personal interview and consent. This is changing, and global norms and standards are emerging in the business culture of Kazakhstan. Still, companies do not always wish to share information so that it does not reach their competitors. To some extent, businesses also worry about transparency and security. If they become too big, they may generate too much interest in some circles. The political and economic prospects are not always certain and clear business regulations are still in the process of formation in the country.

In the end, our team was able to select two companies as potential hidden champions that satisfied all the criteria and provided personal interviews. Both companies are on their way to becoming national leaders with aspirations to grow regionally. Taking into account the efforts of the country to bring the business regulations to international standards and the development of markets, it is believed that in the future there will be more hidden champions, i.e., regional market leaders with no government ties. The next section presents the potential hidden champions of Kazakhstan.

3 Potential Hidden Champions*

3.1 Chocolife Holding

Company Information
Address: 280, Bayzakova St. (corner of Satpayev Street), Almaty Towers Business Center, Almaty
Tel: +7 (727) 346-85-88
Email: hr@chocolife.me
Web: www.chocolife.me

Industry: IT, internet—retail, E-commerce
Year of establishment: 2011
Sales revenues in 2017: 50 million US dollars
Revenues in 2007: n/a
Average number employees in 2017: 250
Brain(s) behind the company: Founder Ramil Mukhoryapov

Nature of Market Leadership

Chocolife Holding is currently one of the largest e-commerce companies in Kazakhstan. Currently, the holding consists of the following companies: Chocolife.me, Chocotravel.com, Chocofood.kz, iDoctor, Chocomart.kz, and Lensmark.kz. Chocolife.me operates in Almaty, Astana, and Shymkent. Chocotravel operates across Kazakhstan. Chocofood operates in Almaty and Astana. The company aims to enter international markets with their Rahmet and Chocotravel services (Forbes Kazakhstan 2016).

Nature of Competitive Advantage

- People-oriented approach
- Fast, high-quality customer service
- The only IT-company in Kazakhstan that was able to go through four rounds of investments. It has a trusting relationship with Kazakh investors. Focus on teamwork and teambuilding
- The majority of employees are young.
- Strong corporate culture where innovative ideas are welcomed
- Successful mergers and acquisitions: each business in Chocolife Holding is the leader in its respective markets—Chocotravel (after merging with Aviata) with 65% of the market, Chocofood (after buying out FoodPanda) with 87% of the market, and Chocolife (after merging with Be Smart) with 95%.
- Elimination of key competitors occurred via merging (e.g., Foodpanda and others). The company is currently looking to expand into other e-commerce sectors in the country and abroad.

Core Lessons Learned on the Path to Business Success

Chocolife has two key lessons to share in terms of developing an e-commerce company in Central Asia. The first lesson is the shift in mentality toward an online lifestyle through a smart and comprehensive market strategy. The company required time and effort to change gradually the existing culture toward online purchases, especially in the middle-age demographic sector. The younger generation had more experience with the Internet and became comfortable with e-commerce at a faster rate. In this respect, smart marketing and promotion are vital. Chocolife was able to harness to growing e-commerce sector in Kazakhstan and successfully push new and innovative services on the market.

The second lesson is that you have to know your market and adapt well. For instance, Kazakhstan is a small market, with only 18 million people. The reason that similar start-ups in the USA are 50 times more expensive, and yet more rewarding financially, is the larger population. In Kazakhstan's case, the approach to promoting and offering services has to be smart and flexible. Since the market is small, only a few companies can compete in the market. Moreover, when expanding to other regions, one has to re-evaluate one's strategy. Knowing your competitors—both obvious and hidden—is crucial. Eventually, Chocolife could expand its market focus on the entire Central Asian market to gain more customers. The hidden nature of the company is reflected in the fact that it targets different sectors under different names, creating the impression that these are different companies, when in fact they belong to a single holding.

Further Development Needs in Terms of Management, Financing, or the Regulatory Environment in Order to Keep or Advance Business Results

The company representative stated that advanced diverse IT-skills are in great demand, especially web-designers and web-analysts. In addition, there is a need for a greater marketing infrastructure and activities. Chocolife Holding aims to expand the IT knowledge of employees to ensure the competitive advantage of the company.

3.2 Chaplin Cinemas

Company Information
Address: Makatayev Str. 127, Almaty, Kazakhstan
Tel: +7 (727) 357 28 31
Email: assistant@chaplin.kz
Web: www.new.chaplin.kz

Industry: Film distribution
Year of establishment: 2009
Sales revenues in 2017: 5.9 million euros
Revenues in 2007: N/A
Average number employees in 2017: 200
Brain(s) behind the company: Founder Sabina Kuzenbayeva

Nature of Market Leadership

Market share: 12% and growing
Key competitor: Kinopark film distribution

Nature of Competitive Advantage

- Flexible management style
- First company in this field to become fully transparent financially
- Financial backing (e.g., EBRD investment) enabling the company to purchase high-end technology and equipment. Not every company can successfully apply for international grants as it is necessary to adhere to certain standards. Thus, the company sets a precedent in this respect
- Focus on content and setting your own trends, not following or shadowing other companies
- Loyal attitude toward the consumer
- Corporate culture: active, positive, and dynamic
- New business model: select new partners, international studios, for the first time in the industry
- Pioneers in the implementation of cinema technologies in Kazakhstan
- Technologically advanced, i.e., the first to introduce the Rentrak technology platform, Real-D, and concession bars
- Direct distribution of films from independent movie companies, which was unprecedented as well

Core Lessons Learned on the Path to Business Success

Two lessons can be highlighted. First, transparency. Second, a unique approach to the distribution processes.

The biggest initial challenge for the company was the market. It was controlled by a few film distribution companies that cooperated closely with partners from Russia. The rights to distribute movies were purchased via Russian film distributors and the business processes of the companies were not always transparent. The competitive advantage of Chaplin Cinemas is that they buy their movie rights directly from the US and local markets, allowing them to diversify the product offering and pioneer a new development business model in this industry. Chaplin Cinemas was able to mix the mass-market and independent (professional) movie showings, thus influencing the consumer as well. For instance, many films are shown in the original language. The challenge to further expansion, nationally and regionally, is a strong competition with companies that have already existing networks.

Further Development Needs in Terms of Management, Financing, or the Regulatory Environment in Order to Keep or Advance Business Results

Just like the previous company, Chaplin highlighted IT skills and, specifically, IT engineering skills, as the most-needed at this moment. Currently, the company outsources some of its work, which is costly and time consuming. The second challenge is marketing. The company plans to switch to more aggressive strategies in order to survive and grow. The competitors are employing similar strategies, so the company needs to prove that their products and services are more attractive. Clarifying the niche of consumers and marketing strategies is imperative.

4 Conclusion and Recommendations

This chapter has provided an overview of the political and socio-economic context of Kazakhstan in the context of hidden champion research. The country is developing rapidly. However, an important part of the modernization path is continued support for entrepreneurship and private sector on the national level. In terms of hidden champion research, there were issues in selecting the companies due to the strict methodology and nuances of the business framework in Kazakhstan. Finding a true hidden champion in Kazakhstan was a challenge as many potential companies had connections with the government, were too visible and known to the market, or were not willing to share information. Nevertheless, we were able to select two companies—Chocolife Holding and Chaplin Cinemas—as potential hidden champions due to their rapid growth, transparency, and innovative business practices. These two companies confirm that a new wave of entrepreneurs is emerging in Kazakhstan and the private sector is able to participate effectively in the country's market development and economic growth. Importantly, the observations made in this chapter can also be applied to other Central Asian states and emerging economies.

Acknowledgments Our team would like to express our deep gratitude to the organizing committee, and especially to Mr. Artyom Ushnichkov and Ms. Katja Babič, who supported us tirelessly throughout the project. Furthermore, we would like to thank the EBRD for the creation of the hidden champion research project, highlighting the importance of the private sector in economic development.

References

Atameken, the National Chamber of Entrepreneurs of the Republic of Kazakhstan (2019) Official website. https://atameken.kz/en/pages/39-missiya-palaty. Accessed 30 Nov 2019

BBC (2019) Kazakhstan profile timeline. Sept 18. https://www.bbc.com/news/world-asia-pacific-15483497

Bertelsmann Stiftung (2018) BTI 2018 country report—Kazakhstan. Bertelsmann Stiftung, Gütersloh

Black A (2010) Gen Y: who they are and how they learn. Educ Horiz 88(2):92–101. http://www.pilambda.org/horizons/publications%20index.htm

CIA World Factbook (2016). https://www.cia.gov/library/publications/the-world-factbook/geos/kz.html. Accessed 20 Aug 2015

Coleman DY (ed) (2015) Kazakhstan review 2015. Country Watch, p 1

Diyarbakırlıoğlu K, Yiğit S (2014) Kazakh multi vector foreign policy in action. Altern Turkish J Int Rel 13(4):70–82

Dudovskiy J (2019) Research methodology. Sept 18. https://research-methodology.net/trompenaars-and-hampden-turner-cultural-dimensions/

Fok RHM, Yeung RMW (2016) Work attitudes of Generation Y in Macau's hotel industry: management's perspective. J Worldwide Hosp Tour Themes 8(1):83–96. https://doi.org/10.1108/02656710210415703

Forbes Kazakhstan (2016) 50 largest IT-companies. September. https://forbes.kz/process/internet/5o_krupneyshih_internet-kompaniy/

Hofstede G (2019) Geert Hofstede. Sept 18. https://geerthofstede.com/culture-geert-hofstede-gert-jan-hofstede/6d-model-of-national-culture/

Hofstede GJ, Pederson PB, Hofstede G (2002) Exploring culture. Nicholas Brealey, London

IHS Economics and Country Risk (2015) Country reports—Kazakhstan. November. IHS Global

McEwan AM (2009) Generation Y: coming to a workplace near you. The Smart Work Company, pp 1–5

Ministry of Information and social development of the Republic of Kazakhstan, JSC (2019) Kazakhstan. Sept 30. http://government.kz/en

OECD Report (2018) Reforming Kazakhstan: progress, challenges and opportunities. Part Global Relations Eurasia program

Plecher H (2019) Kazakhstan's gross domestic product (GDP) in 2024. statista.com. October. https://www.statista.com/statistics/436143/gross-domestic-product-gdp-in-kazakhstan/. Accessed 24 Nov 2019

Qamar F, Sumera Z (2014) New great game: players, interests, strategies and Central Asia. Southeast Asian Stud 29(2):627–655

Snaebjornsson IM, Edvardsson IR, Zydziunaite V, Vaiman V (2015) Cross-cultural leadership: expectations on gendered leaders' behavior. SAGE Open 5(2). https://doi.org/10.1177/2158244015579727

The World Bank Group (2019) Kazakhstan. Sept 18. https://data.worldbank.org/country/kazakhstan?view=chart

Visual Paradigm (2019) What is five forces analysis? Sept 18. https://www.visual-paradigm.com/guide/strategic-analysis/what-is-five-forces-analysis/

Hidden Champions of Kosovo

Dafina Turkeshi Ballanca and Florentina Dushi

Overview[1]
Official name: Republic of Kosovo
Type of government: Parliamentary republic
Population in 2017: 1.8 million
Land area: 10,908 km^2

History

Fifteenth–twentieth century	Ottoman Empire
1912–1913	First Balkan War
1912–1913	Albanian Independency, including Kosovo's territory
1913	Treaty of London, recognizing Albania's independence, excluding Kosovo
1913	Second Balkan War and Treaty of Bucharest
1913–1941	Kingdom of Serbia and Kingdom of Montenegro (Dukagjini), resulting in an increase in Serb settlements and expulsion of the Albanian population
1946–1974	Kosovo becomes an autonomous province of SFRY
1974–1989	Self-governance under SFRY's constitution
1989–1998	Reversal of self-governance, repression, violence, self-declared independence
1998–1999	Kosovo war

---

[1]World Bank (2018, December).

D. T. Ballanca (✉) · F. Dushi
Business Development Group LLC, Pristina, Kosovo
e-mail: dafina@bdgroup-ks.com; florentina@bdgroup-ks.com

© Springer Nature Switzerland AG 2021
A. Braček Lalić, D. Purg (eds.), *Hidden Champions in Dynamically Changing Societies*, https://doi.org/10.1007/978-3-030-65451-1_16

1999–2008	Kosovo is administered by the United Nations Interim Administration Mission in Kosovo (UNMIK) under the United Nations Security Council Resolution 1244.
2008	Kosovo declares independence
2013	The EU opens negotiations with Kosovo
2017	Kosovo's economic growth rate is estimated at 4.4%, the highest rate in the Western Balkans

1 Introduction: Context and History

Kosovo's economy is in a transition. Being new and dynamic, its foundation has been transformed form a centrally-planned and controlled economy, to a free-market. Kosovo was the poorest province of former Yugoslavia, with a modern economy established only after a series of federal development subsidies in 1960s and 1970s (World Bank 2017). Economic growth in 2017 was estimated at 4.4%, the highest rate in the Western Balkans, due to investment and the export-driven recovery in external demand, which also improved external indicators (World Bank 2017). The relatively good growth performance was related to the international community and the diaspora of Kosovo. The country's population is the youngest in Europe, with an average age of 26 years. A well-educated workforce, enviable natural resources, such as mining and agriculture, low taxes, a transparent tax system, custom-free access to the markets of CEFTA, EU, and the USA, as well as the euro as the official currency, are believed to be a competitive advantage and a key resource for economic growth in Kosovo (World Bank 2017). Additionally, World Bank statistics of 2017 show that there is great potential for the IT sector, as well as the textile and wood processing industries in Kosovo.

A historic overview of Kosovo shows that during most of its history the country has been under foreign rule. Foreign powers and regional neighbors have ruled over the territory, which reinforced a mentality of, and created incentives for, parallel structures and economic informality, a reliance on extended family relationships, and a widespread skepticism toward government and the public sector (Malcolm 2001).

The Illyrian region of Dardania included the territory of modern Kosovo, which is the reason that most Kosovars see themselves as descendants of the Illyrians. After the Romans had conquered the Illyrian tribes in 168 BC, the region experienced a period of development as a transit point for most of the Balkan's trade. Ulpiana, located a few kilometers from where Prishtina stands today, became an important trade center and was promoted to the status of a Roman municipium (Dushi 2002). Since then, the main industries of Kosovo have been mining, due to the large reserves of lignite, lead, zinc, silver, nickel, cobalt, copper, and iron, and, agriculture. In addition, lead, silver, and gold were the most important export items during the medieval period (Dushi 2002). Archaeological explorations show that Trepça (*also Tripça, Trebza*) has been used since the Roman Empire period.

The Ottoman Empire ruled over the area for approximately 500 years and left the region economically ruined and in poverty. In Ottoman times, Kosovo's agriculture was a vital industry. The main products were cereals and meat. After the Ottoman Empire collapsed, Serbia regained control over the region and incorporated Kosovo into the Kingdom of Serbs, Croats, and Slovenians, later named Yugoslavia (Malcolm 2001). There is little information concerning the condition of the mining fields left behind by the Ottoman Empire. Nevertheless, research conducted since 1924 shows the extensive use of mining fields in Kosovo (Dushi 2002).

The present-day boundaries of Kosovo were established after World War II. Kosovo became an autonomous province in the Socialist Federal Republic of Yugoslavia. Under Yugoslavia, a significant degree of industrialization was achieved. Manufacturing played a significant part in the economy, driving the urbanization of Kosovo (Malcolm 2001). Small market towns, such as Peja and Gjakova, developed on Ottoman trade routes, expanded when local industry surfaced. Transport and telecommunications were very underdeveloped in Yugoslavia's Kosovo, mainly due to political reasons. This significantly slowed the economic development of Kosovo's rural areas. The impact is noticeable to date (Malcolm 2001).

According to Mustafa (2017), in 1974, Kosovo gained political and economic autonomy and direct representation in the federal government of Yugoslavia. Kosovo recorded the highest rate of economic growth in 1965–1975. Substantial and qualitative changes were made in the production structure, and moderate growth was achieved in 1976–1980. The economic and political system of that time was decentralized to some extent, while Kosovo's constitutional position in the economic and political system of former Yugoslavia was identical to that of other federal units (Mustafa 2018). After the political reforms of the 1970s, Kosovo reached the point when it became more independent in the field of self-government in politics, economics, and social development, and especially in the areas of budget, finance, and taxation. At that time, Kosovo had the right and power to plan and finance economic strategies and enter contractual relations with international financial institutions (Mustafa 2018).

After the end of the Cold War and the fall of Yugoslavia, the Serb communist leadership changed the Yugoslav constitution to revoke Kosovo's autonomy. This ignited Albanian nationalism in Kosovo, generating protests and calls for Kosovo's independence. In the early 1980s, as a result of political and economic crises, the situation in Kosovo deteriorated. Domestic production in the period 1981–1989 increased by 1–1.8% (Mustafa 2018). These political and economic events resulted in Kosovo's declaration of independence in September 1991, and the creation of a parallel political, legal, and economic structure, beginning in 1992. However, the declaration was not widely supported at the international level (Mustafa 2018).

The 1990s was a lost decade, followed by Yugoslavia's violent disintegration. Kosovo suffered a sharp drop in output and trade, large-scale destruction of infrastructure, a severe deterioration in entrepreneurship and in the financial and social sectors, worse social indicators, and increased poverty and inequality (World Bank 2017). It was a decade of accelerating economic neglect and destruction, increasing discrimination against citizens of Albanian-ethnic origin, including in education, and an intensifying conflict that led to greater violence. Following the failed negotiations of Rambouillet, this culminated in the Kosovo war of 1998–1999. The war ended on 12 June 1999 after a 78-day bombing campaign led by the North Atlantic Treaty Organization (NATO) over Serb military, paramilitary, and police forces (World Bank 2017).

The war formally came to an end through the adoption of UN Security Council Resolution 1244 of June 1999, Kosovo was placed under the administration of the UN Interim Administration Mission in Kosovo. The war caused a massive humanitarian crisis for such a small country (Perritt 2004). Kosovo declared independence from what was left of Yugoslavia, on February, 17, 2008, the year globally known as the economic recession year. It is recognized as an independent country by 114 of the 193 United Nations members and by 23 of the 28 European Union (EU) members. Kosovo is a potential candidate for EU membership, a process that was accelerated with the signing of the Stabilization Association Agreement in October 2015, in force since April 2016 (European Commission 2017).

With no formal economic ties to the global financial and trade market, the 2008 global economic crises had barely any impact on Kosovo's steadily growing economy. The structure of Kosovo's economy to date is linked to remittances from migrants in Europe and Switzerland and depends heavily on private consumption and investment. Hence, the net exports in 2008–2014 contributed negatively to economic growth, due to the larger expansion of imports than exports. This was partially a result of the absence of a government for 6 months in 2014. However, in 2015, private investment, fueled by the recovery in the inflow of foreign direct investment, was the key driver of growth recovery. Only in the last few years have net exports contributed positively to growth (World Bank 2017) (Exhibit 1).

2 Case Studies of Selected Hidden Champions

2.1 Case Study 1

MOEA LLC

Overview
Address: Str. Jonuz Zejnullahu, 10000, Prishtina, Kosovo
Tel: +377 (0) 44 327 256
Fax: N/A
Email: info@moea-ks.com
Web: www.moea-ks.com

Company Information
Industry: Fruit producer
Year of establishment: 2010

Exhibit 1 Core economic indicators for Kosovo

	2011	2012	2013	2014	2015	2016	2017	2018
GDP per capita (current US$)	3736	3601	3877	4055	3574	3697	3948	4281
GDP per capita growth (annual %)	3.9	2.1	2.3	1.3	5.4	3.2	3.4	3.3
Long-term unemployment (% of total unemployment)	–	–	–	–	–	–	–	–
Foreign direct investment, net inflows (% of GDP)	8.0	4.5	5.2	2.7	5.3	3.6	4.5	3.0
GDP (current US$, mio)	6.7	6.5	7.1	7.4	6.4	6.7	7.2	7.9
Exports of goods and services (current US$, mio)	1581	1512	1551	1662	1413	1591	1926	2203
Exports of goods and services (% of GDP)	23.63	23.25	21.93	22.50	21.93	22.69	26.65	27.88
Merchandise exports (current US$)	–	–	–	–	–	–	–	–
Merchandise exports to high-income economies (% of total merchandise exports)	31.03	28.31	28.47	29.29	29.09	25.78	30.30	–
Merchandise exports to developing economies in Europe & Central Asia (% of total merchandise exports)	–	–	–	–	–	–	–	–
Ores and metals exports (% of merchandise exports)	–	–	–	–	–	–	–	–
Agricultural raw materials exports (% of merchandise exports)	–	–	–	–	–	–	–	–
Food exports (% of merchandise exports)	–	–	–	–	–	–	–	–
Fuel exports (% of merchandise exports)	–	–	–	–	–	–	–	–
Manufactures exports (% of merchandise exports)	–	–	–	–	–	–	–	–
High-technology exports (% of manufactured exports)	–	–	–	–	–	–	–	–

Source: World Bank (2018, December)

The company is established in 2010 there are no sales revenues in 2007. The appendix 2 is explaining the missing data.[2]
Average number of employees in 2017: 100
Brain(s) behind the company: CEO and founder Armend Malazogu

---

[2]MOEA was established in 2010.

Nature of Market Leadership

MOEA is the number-one fruit grower and natural juice producer in Central and East Europe, using an advanced fruit-processing technology to produce unique and healthy fruit drinks. It started processing fruit with a modern line and advanced fruit-processing technology based on the principle of cold juice extraction and fruit ripening, including the juice content of the whole fruit, all the fiber, and all vitamins and antioxidants. All the fruits are selected and hand-picked, and only the healthiest and fresh fruits are selected for the Frutomania Brand. No preservatives, sugar, flavouring, colour, concentrate, or water are used, just squeezed fruits, packed in glass bottles. Frutomania is one of the most exceptional and healthiest brands that exist in the world today. Frutomania is now available in seven different countries, with a vision to become one of the world's best-quality brands.

Nature of the Competitive Advantage

Today's wide range of food and drink trends reflect changing attitudes toward the community, one's health, and the environment. This philosophy has been adopted by MOEA and its brand Frutomania. The region where the company is located has arable land and is suitable for the plantation of fruit trees. The region consists of several villages, which for decades have maintained their tradition of cultivating fruit trees. MOEA took this opportunity to start a plantation and build a factory in the region. A favorable climate, a cheap workforce, and new trends in the food industry contributed to the company's success.

Frutomania has over 400 contractors from different regions of Kosovo, making its production 100% "produce of Kosovo." Over time, the company has been certified with most international quality certification standards, such as Global Gap (fruit production), HACCP (fruit processing), and ISO (quality management of the company).

Core Lessons Learned on the Path to Success

The founder of the company believes that the fair treatment of farmers, with whom he has a very close cooperation, accounts for the success of his business model. He does not set a price on fruits or raw materials. This is up to local farmers. They are considered not only suppliers but also partners, transparently sharing key performance indicators in the business. The company has an innovative and transparent corporate culture, based on the sharing of information concerning its strategies, business model, partnerships, and key performance indicators. The marketing strategy was another innovation process during the establishment and functionality of this model. Product placement marketing is the right strategy for new food trends. Confident of the quality of the product and of their marketing strategy, buyers are educated to consider the social role of health and environment preservation. This sets a standard for others to follow. Customers want to be part of, or above, the standard.

Another reason for the company's success is the partnerships established with farmers in the neighborhood as well as the employees of the company. This special partnership contributed to the company's success in reaching quality and high production levels.

Management and Leadership Development Needs

During its development process, the company had a shortage of qualified staff, especially in the production department. Qualified staff members were identified and trained and thus contributed to the development of a partnership between the company and the employees. The majority of the employees were recruited from neighboring villages with decades of experience working in the field of agriculture.

Financing and Regulatory Environment Development Needs

While the company has a vision to increase production and export, the setbacks are linked to finances. Although the company received some financial assistance in the past, this has not been sufficient to cover expenses for advisory functions and consultancy.

The company is considering creating an investment bank enabling it to raise the needed capital.

Leadership Is the Key

Armend is an experienced entrepreneur who previously managed service-oriented businesses and specifically a business in the IT industry. During the privatization process that started in 2001, Armend decided to buy 200 hectares of land. This industry was new to him: he did not have any previous experience in agriculture or production. Armend had an innate drive to start working in agriculture and to use Kosovo's potential. He did not have experience in agriculture but he had extensive experience in establishing and leading other successful businesses. Hence, he brought his experience and leadership strengths to build up his business in agriculture and fruit production. Armend states, "I became aware of the size of the land after I have privatized it and after I have visited the land."

Armend's approach was to build partnerships with all families on the surrounding land who had extensive experience in agriculture. The partnerships with the families make the business and leadership model of MOEA unique. The leadership model includes the employment of different human resources and continuously acquisition of knowledge and skills for production. The leadership model has led to the development of unique tools to produce a highly qualitative product. The previous experience of MOEA's founder in other industries has helped him to identify the skills that can be transferred from one field to another. Hence, for him agriculture has been the industry where he could develop a unique model of leadership and apply special production tools.

3 Conclusions and Recommendations

Kosovo's economy is in transition. It is new and dynamic, and its foundation has been transformed from a centrally planned and controlled economy to a free-market. Throughout its history, the country has had natural resources and potential for agricultural development. This research has identified one hidden champion in Kosovo and two potential ones. They are in the IT sector and in the aftermarket automotive industry.

This study finds that MOEA has become a hidden champion due to its unique business model and leadership style. The latter has led to the development of unique tools for the production of high-quality products.

Nevertheless, hidden champions face daily challenges in the market, and lack financial support from the government as well as specialized personnel in the field of fruit production.

3.1 Recommendations

1. Government institutions need to establish standards and technical regulations that are compatible with European Union standards. This would help strengthen institutions and policies to ensure the implementation of technical standards and regulations.
2. As it is difficult to raise capital in Kosovo, it is recommended that an investment bank be created. It would help hidden champions raise the capital that they need.
3. The hidden champions in Kosovo find it hard to develop human capital. One of their biggest investments is in staff specialization. .The higher education institutions in Kosovo do not offer sufficient study programs that would provide hidden champions with specialized human capital.

It is, therefore, recommended that higher education institutions closely collaborate with hidden champions to provide specialized study programs.

References

Dushi M (2002) Trepça: an integrated technico-technological system. Dukagjini, Pejë
Malcolm N (2001) Kosova: Një histori e shkurtër. KOHA, Prishtinë
Mustafa M (2018) Ekonomia e Kosovës. Envinion, Prishtinë
Perritt H Jr (2004) Economic sustainability and final status for Kosovo. J Int Law 25(1):*259*
The World Bank Group (2017) Republic of Kosovo systematic country diagnostic. Report no. 114618-XK. https://openknowledge.worldbank.org/bitstream/handle/10986/26573/Kosovo-SCD-FINAL-May-5-C-05052017.pdf?sequence=1&isAllowed=y
The World Bank (2018, December). https://www.worldbank.org/en/country/kosovo/overview

Hidden Champions of Lithuania

Erika Vaiginienė, Rasa Paulienė, and Laima Urbšienė

Overview
Official name: Republic of Lithuania
Type of government: Unitary semi-presidential system
Population in 2017: 2,808,000
Land area: 65,300 km^2

History

1009	The name "Lithuania" is first mentioned in documents.
1815	Lithuania and Poland are occupied by Russia.
1918	Lithuania regains its independence.
1918	The first trade and industry banks established.
1921–1924	The first production companies, mainly in the food industry, are established.
1922	The Bank of Lithuania starts operating.
1944	Lithuania is occupied by the Soviet Union.
1990	Lithuania regains its independence. The Bank of Lithuania is re-established. Beginning of a transition to a market economy and privatization of state-owned companies.
1992	Lithuania joins the International Monetary Fund and the World Bank.
1994	Lithuania's economy survives the private banks' collapse.
1997	A battle against the black economy starts.
2004	Lithuania enters the European Union and NATO.
2008	Financial crisis
2015	Lithuania enters the Eurozone.

E. Vaiginienė (✉) · R. Paulienė · L. Urbšienė
Vilnius University, Vilnius, Lithuania
e-mail: erika.vaiginiene@cr.vu.lt; rasa.pauliene@evaf.vu.lt; laima.urbsiene@evaf.vu.lt

2018   The Law on Innovation and Technologies is passed.
2018   Lithuania joins the OECD.

1 Introduction: Context and History

Lithuania is located in Northern Europe, on the eastern shore of the Baltic Sea. The country has 2.8 million inhabitants, living in an area of 65,300 km^2. between Latvia, Belarus, Poland, and Russia.

1.1 Economic History of Lithuania

The first Lithuanian tribes maintained close trade contacts with the Roman Empire. Amber was the main good provided to the Roman Empire from the Baltic Sea coast, via a long route, called the Amber Road (Lithuania Country Study Guide). The consolidation of the Lithuanian lands began in the late twelfth century. The expansion of the Grand Duchy of Lithuania reached its peak in the fourteenth century under the Grand Duke Gediminas (reigned 1316–1341), who established a stable central government, expanded the Lithuanian territories from the Baltic Sea to the Black Sea, and opened the Grand Duchy for men of every profession. Immigrants improved the quality of handicrafts. During the reign of Duke Kęstutis (1297–1382), the first cash taxes were introduced, although most taxes were still paid in goods, such as wheat or livestock

In 1569, the economy of the Polish–Lithuanian Commonwealth was dominated by feudal agriculture and played a significant role in supplying sixteenth century Western Europe with exports of three sorts of goods: grain (rye), cattle (oxen), and fur. These three items amounted to nearly 90% of the country's exports to Western markets by land and sea (Davies 1996).

The Commonwealth declared a national constitution in 1791, after the 1788 ratification of the United States' Constitution. Economic and commercial reforms were introduced, and the development of industries was encouraged (Lithuania—Official Gateway to Lithuania, History).

During the occupation by the Russian Empire from 1772 to 1917, the emancipation reform of 1861 put an end to self-dependence, and thus boosted the development of capitalism in Lithuania.

In 1918, the Independent State of Lithuania was re-established. Soon, many economic reforms for sustainable economic growth were implemented, and in 1922 a national currency, litas, was introduced. It was one of the strongest and stable currencies in Europe during the inter-war period (Klimantas and Zirgulis 2019). Lithuania had a gold standard system: one litas was covered by 0.150462 grams of gold stored by the Bank of Lithuania in foreign countries. The litas remained stable even in the period of the Great Depression. During the time of its independence, 1918–1940, Lithuania made substantial progress: it was the third-largest flax producer and exporter in the world market. The country exported superior quality farm products, such as meat, dairy products, many kinds of grain, potatoes, and more. Lithuanian farmers were joining into cooperative companies, such as Lietūkis, Pienocentras, and Linas, which helped farmers sell their products more efficiently and profitably in the world market.

The Union of Soviet Socialist Republics (USSR) occupied Lithuania in 1940. Land and business were nationalized, and farms collectivized. Later, many inefficient factories and industry companies, highly dependent on other regions of the USSR, were established in Lithuania. The Soviet-era brought Lithuania intensive industrialization and economic integration into the USSR, although the level of technology and state concern for environmental, health, and labor issues lagged far behind Western standards. Production declined and did not reach pre-war levels until the early 1960s.

The overall damage, resulting from the Soviet occupation, including the loss of gross domestic product, estimated according to UN-recognized methodologies, amounted to approximately 800 billion US dollars. The direct damage, including genocide, deportations of citizens, and property looting, is estimated at 20 billion US dollars (Ziemele 2003).

Reforms since the mid-1990s led to an open and rapidly growing economy. Open to global trade and investment, Lithuania now enjoys a high degree of business, fiscal, and financial freedom. One of Lithuania's most important reforms was the privatization of state-owned assets, which was implemented during two stages.

During the first stage of privatization (1991–1995), citizens were given investment vouchers worth 3.1 billion euros in nominal value, which let them participate in assets selling (Vilkas 1997). More than 5700 enterprises, with 2.0 billion euros worth of state capital in book value, were sold using four initial privatization methods: share offerings, auctions, best business plans competitions, and hard currency sales (Vilkas 1997).

During the second privatization step (1995–1998), a new privatization law ensured a greater diversity of privatization methods and enabled participation in the selling process without vouchers. Between 1996 and 1998, 526 entities were sold for more than 0.7 billion euros, and the share of the private sector in the GDP increased to over 70% by 2000 (Vilkas 1997).

A monetary reform was undertaken in the early 1990s to improve the stability of the economy. In 1993, the Lithuanian litas was introduced, and in 1994 it was pegged to the United States dollar according to a currency board system, which enabled Lithuania to stabilize inflation rates to single digits. The stable currency rate helped to boost foreign trade (Statistics Lithuania). In 2002, the litas was pegged to the euro until Lithuania adopted the euro in 2015.

The Russian crisis in 1998 shocked the economy into negative growth and forced the reorientation of the trade from Russia to the West. The share of exports to the Commonwealth of Independent States dropped to 21% of the total in 2006, while exports to EU members increased to 63% of the total.

The Vilnius Stock Exchange, now renamed the NASDAQ OMX Vilnius, started its activity in 1993 and was the first stock exchange in the Baltic states. In 2003, the

VSE was acquired by OMX, and in 2008 the Vilnius Stock Exchange became a member of the NASDAQ OMX Group.

1.2 Economic Environment of Lithuania

The economy of Lithuania is the largest of the three Baltic states, and it has the second-highest GDP per capita of the Baltic states. With a GDP per capita of 16,112 euros in 2018, Lithuania belongs to the group of high income and very high human development countries (OECD).

Lithuania was the first country to declare independence from the Soviet Union in 1990 and rapidly moved from a centrally planned to a market economy, successfully implementing numerous liberal reforms in all sectors of the economy. Open to global trade and investment, Lithuania now enjoys high degrees of business, fiscal, and financial freedom and is considered one of the most open and business-friendly economies in the OECD, sometimes called a Baltic Tiger. Lithuania's economy (GDP) grew more than 500% since regaining independence in 1990 (Eurostat).

After a strong rebound in 2017, GDP growth, led by buoyant investment, exceeded 3% in 2018, and the same forecast was made for 2019 (OECD, Lithuanian Department of Statistics). Falling unemployment and rapidly increasing wages support consumption, although a shrinking labor force depresses on growth. Export growth remains substantial, and financial markets are stable.

Per-capita income growth is above that of most OECD countries and exceeds the growth of other economies in the region, facilitating convergence toward OECD average incomes (OECD). Since 2000, living standards have been increasing rapidly and were dented only by the global financial crisis of 2009, when foreign investment stopped abruptly, and unemployment reached almost 18%. The growth of living standards also suffered in 2014 when the recession in Russia hit exports and there was a slowdown in other major trading partners (OECD).

The wage growth in Lithuania is the result of strong long-term economic growth (Ministry of the Economy and Innovation of the Republic of Lithuania). The country's fiscal position is sound. After 10 years of deficits and rising debt, the budget achieved a small surplus in 2016 and has remained positive since then (Lithuanian Department of Statistics).

Business regulation is relatively transparent and efficient, with foreign and domestic capital subject to the same rules. The financial sector is advanced, regionally integrated, and subject to few intrusive regulations.

The structure of Lithuania's economy has changed significantly. The biggest changes occurred in the agricultural sector as the share of total employment there decreased from 19.2% in 1998 to just 7.8% in 2017, and the share of total employment in the financial sector in 2017 more than doubled compared with the 1998 figure (Lithuanian Department of Statistics).

Lithuania still faces important challenges in different economic areas.

Nevertheless, Lithuania has been one of the fastest-growing EU member states over two decades in terms of labor productivity growth, based on purchasing power parity. However, labor productivity was still 25% below the EU average and 30% below the OECD average in 2017 (Ministry of the Economy and Innovation of the Republic of Lithuania; Blöchliger and Koutsogeorgopoulou 2018). The main reason for the growth of productivity is EU investments that have enabled companies to update technologies with more efficient and more productive ones. This has improved the business environment and has helped attract high-value foreign capital companies to Lithuania, facilitating the establishment and development of innovative start-ups. But the difference between the most productive and other activities of manufacturing has also increased in Lithuania. When the economy is small and open, like Lithuania's, external demand is an essential driver of export and labor productivity growth.

Export indicators have improved, but exports are concentrated in low and medium value-added activities. Integration into global value chains is weak. Collaboration between firms and research institutions is weak, and skills often do not match the needs of the businesses.

Another huge challenge is the rapid aging and high emigration, mostly of the young. As a result, the labor force is shrinking by 1% every year and there are skills shortages. Nevertheless, Lithuania's emigration rate fell by 14.2% in 2018 compared with the rate in the previous year. Still, the number of emigrants exceeds that of immigrants.

1.3 Socio-political Environment of Lithuania

Lithuania is tightly integrated into the international community and is a member of the European Union, the Eurozone, the Schengen Agreement, NATO, the World Trade Organization, and the OECD. It is also a member of the Nordic Investment Bank, and part of the Nordic-Baltic cooperation of Northern European countries.

Formal democracy is well developed in Lithuania. Participation rights, electoral competition, and the rule of law are generally respected by the Lithuanian authorities. However, democracy suffers from several weaknesses. Anti-corruption legislation is well developed, but remains insufficient (Nakrošis et al. 2018). Lithuanian policy-makers have sought to establish and maintain social, economic, and environmental conditions that promote citizens' well-being. The political and economic environment is overall democratic and market-friendly.

1.4 Business Environment of Lithuania

Lithuania's economic policies have created a reliable economic environment, fostering the country's competitive capabilities and improving its attractiveness as an economic location. In its 2019 *Doing Business* report, the World Bank ranked Lithuania 11th out of 190 economies. The criteria assessed most positively included registering property (ranked 4th), enforcing contracts (ranked 7th), dealing with construction permits (ranked 10th), and the ease of starting business (ranked 34th) (WB).

Lithuania made starting a business easier by introducing online VAT registration in 2016, eliminating the need to have a company seal, introducing online registration for limited liability companies, and eliminating the notarization requirement for incorporation documents in 2013.

Lithuania made paying taxes easier by merging the filing and payment of two labor contributions, issuing pre-populated value-added tax returns, and introducing an electronic system for filing and paying VAT, CIT, and social security contributions. On the other hand, the environmental tax was increased.

Lithuania made dealing with construction permits easier by reducing the time needed for processing building permit applications and the time needed to obtain a building permit.

Lithuania made exporting easier by enhancing its automated customs data management system.

To make employing workers easier, Lithuania changed its legislation on working hours, paid annual leave, notice period, and severance payments in case of redundancy.

The country also strengthened minority investor protection by clarifying ownership and control structures, introducing stricter requirements for the disclosure of the compensation of directors, increasing corporate transparency, prohibiting subsidiaries to acquire shares issued by their parent company, and introducing strict requirements for corporate disclosure to the public and in annual reports.

Lithuania made getting credit easier by strengthening its secured transactions system by broadening the range of movable assets that can be used as collateral, allowing a general description in the security agreement of the assets pledged as collateral and permitting out-of-court enforcement.

Lithuania made resolving insolvency easier by establishing which cases against the company's property shall be taken to the bankruptcy court, tightening the time frame for decisions on appeals, abolishing the court's obligation to notify creditors and other stakeholders individually about restructuring proceedings, and set new time limits for creditors to file claims. Also, the law on company reorganization was amended to simplify and shorten reorganization proceedings, grant priority to secured creditors, and introduce professional requirements for insolvency administrators (The World Bank 2019).

As the review of the development of the Lithuanian economy shows, Lithuania is going through tremendous economic changes: from an agrarian country to an innovation-driven economy. World Bank data (see Exhibit 1) demonstrate the growth of high-technology exports, a small proportion of agricultural raw materials exports, and a quite high export percentage to high-income economies. Policy makers are also making efforts to improve the business environment in Lithuania

Exhibit 1 Core economic indicators for Lithuania

	2011	2012	2013	2014	2015	2016	2017	2018
GDP per capita (current US$)	14,357.7	14,341.2	15,693.8	16,545.1	14,291.9	14,982.5	16,809.6	19,089.7
GDP per capita growth (annual %)	8.47	5.23	4.55	4.432	2.99	3.66	5.61	5.94
Long-term unemployment (% of total unemployment)	15.39	13.36	11.77	10.70	9.12	7.86	7.07	6.01
Foreign direct investment, net inflows (% of GDP)	3.54	1.34	1.53	1.04	2.34	2.24	2.50	1.63
GDP (current US$, mio)	43.477	42.848	46.417	48.516	41.517	42.973	47.544	53.251
Exports of goods and services (current US$, mio)	32.64	34.959	39.046	39.259	31.393	31.817	38.623	43.998
Exports of goods and services (% of GDP)	74.99	81.62	84.06	81.10	75.82	74.10	80.90	82.29
Merchandise exports to high-income economies (% of total merchandise exports)	68.11	65.36	64.04	62.72	71.86	72.17	69.96	
Merchandise exports to developing economies in Europe & Central Asia (% of total merchandise exports)	28.99	31.01	32.79	33.85	25.55	24.13	26.57	
Ores and metals exports (% of merchandise exports)	1.77	1.51	1.36	1.36	1.3	1.27	1.72	1.87
Agricultural raw materials exports (% of merchandise exports)	2.43	2.15	2.49	2.64	2.89	3.01	2.72	2.98
Food exports (% of merchandise exports)	15.80	17.59	18.24	17.91	18.21	18.26	17.40	16.32
Fuel exports (% of merchandise exports)	25.40	24.61	23.16	17.68	16.45	13.96	14.78	14.61
Manufactures exports (% of merchandise exports)	53.03	52.19	52.91	57.89	59.01	61.70	62.87.	62.33
High-technology exports (% of manufactured exports)	10.64	11.06	11.05	11.16	12.81	12.72	12.57	12.11

Source: World Bank, October, 2019

(Business Reforms in Lithuania), which makes the Lithuanian economy attractive for the development of hidden champions.

In this chapter, we analyze hidden champions based on Simon's (2009) methodology. Hidden champions are highly successful innovative SMEs that command a top-two share of their respective niche markets globally or are market leaders on their continent. Their annual revenues do not exceed one billion US dollars and they tend to be unknown to the wider public. Hidden champions operate mostly in the business-to-business market. Those criteria were used for the identification of hidden champions in Lithuania.

The identified Lithuanian hidden champions are alphabetically listed in Exhibit 2. Two of the identified companies are start-ups with high potential to become hidden champions in the nearest future, as currently, they fulfill almost all hidden champions criteria.

All interviewed hidden champions demonstrated some uniqueness, either in terms of some product, or service, or business culture. They achieved market leadership because of their sensitivity to customer problems and the high appreciation of their employees.

2 Case Studies of Selected Hidden Champions

2.1 Case Study 1

Deeper

Overview
Address: Antakalnio st. 17, Vilnius, LT-10312, Lithuania
Tel: +370 659 89559
Email: info@deeper.eu
Web: https://deeper.eu

Company Information
Industry: Manufacture of instruments, appliances for measuring, testing, navigation, and control
Year of establishment: 2012
Sales revenues in 2017: 5–10 million euros
Average number of employees in 2017: 50
Brain(s) behind the company: Everyone in the company.

Nature of Market Leadership

Deeper's smart sonar is the world's first wireless echo sounder compatible with iOS and Android devices. Today, Deeper's range of smart sonar devices is sold in more than 50 countries, enabling avid anglers from Sydney to Singapore, and from

Exhibit 2 Lithuanian hidden champions in 2018

Name	Market leadership definition	Sales revenues in 2017	Average number of employees in 2017
Deeper ("Deeper, UAB", Rekvizitai.lt; "About us" Deeper)	Manufacturer of the world's first wireless echo sounder compatible with iOS and Android devices; Deeper App is the leading fish-finder app on Google Play and in App Store globally	5–10 mio euros	62
8devices	European leader in the development, manufacture, and sale of embedded wireless modules (electronic equipment of unique design and functionality)	Approx. 2.5 mio euros	50
CGTrader ("UAB "CGTrader"", Rekvizitai.lt; "CGTrader—3D content made easy", CGTrader)	The leading 3D content market place globally	Approx. 1 mio euros	59
Ekspla	Global leader in lasers, laser systems, and laser components for R&D and industrial applications	Approx. 17 mio euros	124
Game Insight ("Game Insight, UAB", Rekvizitai.lt; "About", Game Insight)	The world's leading innovator of mobile and social games	50–100 mio euros	More than 600
Light Conversion ("Light Conversion, UAB", Rekvizitai.lt; "News", Light Conversion; "About us", Light Conversion)	World-leading manufacturer of wave-length tunable femtosecond optical parametric amplifiers	30–50 mio euros	240
TeleSoftas	One of the biggest and fastest-growing mobile IT services development houses in CEE, creating mobile applications; among the Financial Times TOP 1000 EU companies (https://www.ft.com/content/238174d2-3139-11e9-8744-e7016697f225) (as of 1 March 2019); no direct competitors on this list	7 mio euros	126
Potential hidden champions			
Fidens (ViLim Ball)	Leader in therapeutic devices for the reduction of essential tremor, Parkinson's disease, and rheumatoid arthritis symptoms; has no direct competitors globally	Aprox. 0.01 mio euros	5
Parkis	Potential Global/European/CEE/Baltics HC in bike racks	Aprox. 300 k euros	3

Michigan to Manchester, to experience a completely new way of fishing. And the Deeper App is the leading fish finder app on Google Play and App Store in the World.

The company sells in Europe, North America, Russia, and Australia. It works with Apple, Amazon, Walmart, Best Buy, Rapala, and Virgin, and sports retailers such as Decathlon and Dick's Sporting Goods.

Nature of the Competitive Advantage

Right from the start, when Deeper launched its product, it was the only one on the market. The company managers believe that if a company is alone on the market that usually means that either the company will soon disappear because the product is not needed or the market is too small, so others are not interested in competing with new products. But the situation has been changing rapidly: competitors did appear. Deeper's managers state that currently there are similar American, Canadian, and French products. There are cheaper Chinese products on the market, too. However, Deeper remains the market leader in the product category. Competitors are active; eventually, they also copy and make similar products. This is natural because the market leader is often copied. Deeper also introduces new products and improves old ones as this is essential in a competitive environment.

Core Lessons Learned on the Path to Success

A company needs boundless creativity and endless enthusiasm. Real innovation comes from having both an open mind and a passionate heart.

The most important connection is with the people who use the company's products. The company always listens to the customers. And from them, Deeper has learned the need to design smart devices that are accessible and intuitive to use.

Connections with like-minded people are essential. These are for instance suppliers who share the same quality standards and business partners who bring value to everything that they do.

Transparency and openness in both partnership and collaboration with partners are also important.

Management and Leadership Development Needs

Deeper lists a number of its strengths: a strong team of employees at all managerial levels as well as excellent leaders, patience, entrepreneurial intuition, flexibility, a pleasant working atmosphere, employee motivation, and interest; employee qualification and competencies; organizational image, innovation, risk management, financial strength; knowledge of market needs, and long-term cooperation with clients and partners. Deeper's managers call these as the "ingredients" to make a cake, or a pancake, or a bun: the ingredients are the same, but the process is different, and the amount of each ingredient is different, too. The unique recipe and combination of these ingredients are what leads Deeper to success. The key is a timely market opportunity and product launch at the right time. However, the implementation of the initial business idea and the longevity on the market can be achieved only through a smart combination of the mentioned ingredients.

Deeper's managers believe that people are at the heart of all businesses, it is up to them whether they will deliver or sustain lasting success: "You can buy all the equipment as well as raw materials. You can do market research, but there are many companies that had all the resources and slipped somewhere, and they disappeared." Deeper's managers believe that if they have people who can notice the market opportunities and make decisions, they can achieve any results.

Financing and Regulatory Environment Development Needs

Deeper's managers claim that the world's current patenting system is entirely outdated. In Europe, it is better, but in the USA it is particularly bad. In the USA, almost anything can be patented, even generic things. Patenting problems in Asia are different. Patents can be duplicated there, i.e., what is already patented is patented again. Deeper's managers describe this as a significant problem for businesses.

Deeper: The Hidden Champion

The business idea started with an in-time perceived opportunity—noticing that while fishing from the coast it is impossible to use the same technology that can be used for fishing from a boat.

Sonar technology has been adjusted so that it can be used without a boat. Instead of a big heavy sonar, which usually weighs two, three, or four kilograms, the company made a small ball that a fisherman can tie to the fishing line and throw from the coast. In this way, the fisherman can explore the depth of the water, whether there are fish, and whether there are any objects or underwater vegetation.

Deeper's managers tend to think that all of these factors were the most important: to notice the opportunity, to come up with a solution, and then to turn that idea into a real product.

Deeper participates in international fairs together with its partners. According to Deeper's managers, in the early years, many people did not even understand the product, what it is used for, and how it works. However, "the number of such people has been decreasing over time, so a certain stage of the product introduction to the market was completed because people also know how fishing can change, what kind of technologies can be used."

Deeper has partners in every country that it works with. The company works with both distributors and retail partners to conduct its marketing campaigns in a particular country. Deeper does not make products and dispatch to partners. Deeper's managers are always interested in results: how much merchandise has been sold to final buyers within a month or a quarter. The marketing activity is not about finding and selling to partners but reaching the final customers.

When it comes to the formula for success, Deeper's managers believe that employees' personality traits and the right set of competencies are vital to the organization's success. It is better when a strategy, though wrong, is implemented than when people have an excellent strategic plan but do not implement it. Instead, Deeper's founders think that they have had a perfect set of competencies since the very beginning. There were three business partners at the start, who had different competencies. However, they have always been sharing the same values and core attitudes that are expected from their staff. They believe that this is what delivers a result: "If we make a decision, we must implement it." Deeper's managers notice, that "if we slip somewhere, if we allow ourselves not to do something, then there is no result." Naturally, sometimes implementation requires adjustments or changes to the plan. In this case, they change the plan but still take this approach: if a decision is made, it must be implemented.

Deeper survived the period when products were returned as they were defective. Deeper does not produce the products itself. They are manufactured by trained partners according to the technological schemes developed by Deeper. Deeper's managers realized that the defects had occurred during the manufacturing process, but decided to stop the whole process: to remove the products from all points of sales, from warehouses, and overall logistics. In doing so, Deeper's managers risked losing some partners but decided that in such a critical case, openness and transparency were the best choices for a reliable long-term partnership. Instead of hiding or ignoring the problems, Deeper chose an openness policy, which not only helped the company retain its partners, but also strengthened its relationship with them.

Describing the meaning of innovation, Deeper's managers state that innovation always means new ways to achieve a result related to a product or a process. Deeper has produced a lot of innovation. Certain things may have already been well established in the organization, and in some areas, the company has applied the best practices available on the market. Still, it is constantly thinking about innovation in marketing because of the limited resources. Deeper tries to find new ways to reach customers. In product development and production, Deeper is always looking for new ways to solve problems better or assist its customers. Deeper thinks about this every time a problem occurs or when something is not going well. The company then looks for new technological solutions or makes adjustments to make the company processes more efficient.

What Specific Lessons Does Deeper Teach Us?

Deeper's success story demonstrates that the hardest times can be survived by means of transparent behavior with respect to customers and partners. A shared business development vision among top managers, their disciplined behavior, and responding employees, as well as continuous care about the problems of the customers, are the vital success factors of the company.

2.2 Case Study 2

8devices

Overview
Address: Antakalnio st. 17-7, 10312 Vilnius, Lithuania
Tel: +370 5 2001014
Email: jonas.jr@8devices.com
Web: www.8devices.com

Company Information
Industry: Manufacture of electrical equipment. Manufacture of communication equipment. Development and sales of electronic equipment. Embedded software development.
Year of establishment: 2011
Sales Revenues in 2017: Approximatley2.5 million euros
Average number of employees in 2017: 50
Brain(s) behind the company: Everyone in the company

Nature of Market Leadership

8devices is an authorized design center and producer of embedded wireless modules based on the chipsets of Qualcomm, which is one of the biggest chipset producers in the world. 8devices is in close partnerships with the biggest chipset producers in the world in the wireless networking industry. The company's production is used for the products of the Internet of Things (IoT) market, which is growing at a very high speed due to the need for connectivity. The main competitors are from China and America. However, the latter does not have the flexibility to produce smaller quantities for niche markets, while 8devices has such capabilities and offers industrial grade modules for enterprise customers. Globally, Europe, the USA, and Israel are the main markets of their exports.

Nature of the Competitive Advantage

In order to survive in the high-speed growing electronics market, you need to "run with the rapidly developing" very quickly and build new products based on the latest 802.11 standards. The new standards appear every 2–3 years. 8devices launched one embedded wireless module in 2011 and now has 15. Every electronics manufacturer every year has to show a new product that differentiates it from its competitors.

The close relationships with Qualcomm and other chipset producers provide 8devices with information about the forthcoming products and technologies. This allows the company to be among the first in the market.

There are a number of manufacturers in Europe who can develop similar products. However, customers choose 8devices because of its high-quality. In summary, the main competitive advantages of 8devices are high quality, competitive price, and the company's flexibility to work with niche vertical markets.

Core Lessons Learned on the Path to Success

1. You need strict order when you work with clients from Germany. The right clients require well defined internal processes, starting from order acceptance and finalizing the delivery to the client.
2. Diversify your activities. It is important to avoid a focusing on a single client. There was a situation when the main client canceled an order, and 8devices had to reorient its activities.
3. The right clients attract more right clients.

Management and Leadership Development Needs

Moving production is one of the biggest challenges facing 8devices currently. This creates a need for professional management. There is also a need for process optimization in the company. Thus, it has been decided to implement the ISO standard for quality assurance. This decision was strengthened by the clients' requirements that the company proves the quality of its products.

Financing and Regulatory Environment Development Needs

The building of the new production line requires additional financing. Thus, it was partly financed via a bank loan. Now, due to its quick growth and expansion, the company is also using additional financial instruments from banks, such as overdrafts and factoring, and will likely use additional ones, since the production of electronics requires financial resources to grow.

Time Machines

8devices is a privately owned company with a shared vision to innovate and deliver products that minimize time to market and absorb the complexity of RF development. Lowering new market entry barriers for the company's customers is a way to success. Besides the embedded wi-fi modules, the company also engages in various wireless networking related projects, requiring both software and hardware development. Due to the company's flexible structure, 8devices can carry out multiple projects at the same time and has enough experience to use multiple types of business engagement models, from fixed price to dedicated development center.

A new production line allows the company to offer a full scope of development services, from initial idea generation to prototyping and even mass production. A recently introduced fast-track development program additionally boosts 8devices' customer development process since this allows the company to get involved in any stage of product development and provide help.

The business of 8devices grew organically from a single embedded wi-fi module, called Carambola, to a company with a lot of expertise and full-design house capabilities. "Our modules can be called 'time machines' because by adding them to the product, our clients speed up product launch and reduce their development costs", says Jonas Sabaliauskas, general manager of 8devices.

The "right clients" are one of the most crucial success factors, as they are the distributors who must be well aware of customer needs and know the market. The right clients attract other right clients and make it easier to grow the customer base, and build trust and awareness of this new brand name in the electronics world.

Of course, the key to the company's success is not only the clients but also the "young and vigorous" team. The average age of the employees is about 25 years. The majority of new employees start their career at 8devices while they are still students. The company is successfully running summer internship programs to attract new engineers and find the most suitable positions for them in the company. Of course, from time to time 8devices also hires experienced professionals, especially for senior positions, but young students are a priority segment for the company's growth.

Another advantage of 8devices is the quick launching of the new products as they are manufactured locally and in-house. For example, it would take at least 6 weeks to start the manufacturing of new product in China, while it takes only 2 weeks to prepare for production locally.

What specific lessons does 8devices teach us? A unified vision of the future is vital for the successful development of the company, as well as the right customers who know the market and its needs, plus a team that is not afraid to experiment and pursue tasks that sometimes seem unworkable.

2.3 Case Study 3

Parkis

Overview
Address: Piliakalnio g. 7, LT-06229 Vilnius, Lithuania
Tel: +370 687 49555
Email: parkis@parkis.eu
Web: https://parkis.eu

Company Information
Industry: Manufacture of lifting and handling equipment (bicycle lifts)
Year of establishment: 2015
Sales revenues in 2017: Approximately 300,000 euros
Average number of employees in 2017: 3
Brain(s) behind the company: Bronius Rauba

Nature of Market Leadership

The idea of Parkis was born out of a desire to find a bike lift that saves space and is easy to use. All available space saving solutions for bikes had one flaw in common—they all required physical effort to lift a bike. So, the company decided to create a bike-parking solution, which could be easily used by any bike-rider despite his age or how physically strong the person is. The company's export markets are Belgium, France, Germany, Sweden, Canada, USA, and Australia (Where To Buy). The company is expected to grow into a regional hidden champion in the medium term, due to a unique and patented product, and the current sales trends.

Nature of the Competitive Advantage

The company provides a unique and patented vertical bicycle parking solution: the bicycle lift. It is a very eco friendly facility because it uses no electricity or fuel. It is made entirely of metal, which is fully recyclable. Its packaging is made of plain unpainted cardboard. This means that the bicycle lift becomes a secondary raw material immediately after its life cycle.

Core Lessons Learned on the Path to Success

At the start, Parkis made videos and photos of the product because the company targeted a broad international market. Parkis wanted to test the usability and popularity of the product. The campaign exceeded its expectations as about 60 million people viewed the videos in a month. According to Parkis's managers, the product itself has attracted the customer. The product was very visually appealing and the online videos attracted customers who shared that information virtually. Thus, Parkis got unplanned dissemination. And the reliability of the power of virtual advertising, as well as online customers' word-of-mouth, was proved by the fact that Parkis sold about 80,000 euros worth of products in 1 month.

Soon, the Parkis bicycle lift occurred on popular sites, such as businessinsider.com and, kickstarter.com. Therefore, another lesson learned was high online popularity. However, Parkis did not have enough products at the time, and it was not able to satisfy the suddenly increased customers' demand. Fortunately, this led to further product development as Parkis's managers made sure that the product was really interesting and sought after on the international market. Parkis's achievements in marketing are impressive. The company is striving for business success and impressive financial results.

Management and Leadership Development Needs

Parkis's managers emphasize the lack of employees capable of adapting to new challenges on the market. Therefore, there is a need for employees who can quickly adapt to the organization and to market changes, re-profile, and learn on their own. Life-long learning must be a lifestyle for all employees, no matter how old they are.

Financing and Regulatory Environment Development Needs

Small businesses often do not have access to financial support due to bureaucratic issues in Lithuania. The procedures are very complicated and it is confusing to submit applications for business support. For example, at least five companies of a similar area should apply for an opportunity to get funding to go to international fairs. It takes a lot of time to find a similar business, especially when a company is unique in the market. So the Lithuanian government both helps and creates additional obstacles at the same time.

Parkis: The Hidden Champion

Parkis's managers associate the company's initial idea with the balcony of an apartment building. There are too many bikes on the balcony, and too little room to park them all vertically, since hanging one bicycle on a hook makes it impossible to hang another. So the idea was that something should lift that bike so that three bikes could be accommodated very sparingly on one square meter. In practice, the idea came from a household.

According to Parkis's managers, it is difficult to define what the bike parking market is. Much has been written about the need for bikes and the demand for them, but there is no information on how many hooks will be needed to hang those bikes.

Parkis produces bicycle hooks that are not standard. They are convenient to use by older people and children. Those who are physically unable to lift their bike can park it with the bicycle lift. It is a unique product, so it is difficult to identify direct competitors. Parkis is currently attracting and training customers, and disseminating information about the product and its functionality. The product name—bicycle lift—has been created by Parkis's managers.

Ideas for improvement of Parkis's product often come in the form of feedback from customers. Parkis also cooperates with architects and gets special orders for the adaptation and installation of bike-parking equipment in new buildings and offices under construction.

Parkis sells products in 50 countries, but geographic expansion is not its objective currently. Parkis's managers focus on the depth of the markets. They seek opportunities to sell as many products as possible in these 50 countries and cover the broadest potential segment of consumers in those countries.

Currently, Parkis's managers are considering attracting new financial investment, as well as a new strategic partner. Parkis's product, the bicycle lift, is unique in the international market. It is still a technical innovation that needs to be developed. Currently, Parkis is selling a second-generation model, and athird-generation one is being developed and tested. Parkis believes that it has extensive knowledge of product design and development. So, the company is looking for a strategic partner who knows how to work with the media, expanding the company's public relations, and developing other appropriate sales activities.

What Specific Lessons Does Parkis Teach Us?
Parkis's managers demonstrate that it is not enough to penetrate the markets. A much more significant challenge is to remain competitive and grow successfully in those markets. This case also shows the importance of complementary competences in the company.

2.4 Case Study 4

Telesoftas

Overview
Address: Savanoriu ave. 178, 44150 Kaunas, Lithuania
Tel: +370 694 20374
Email: info@telesoftas.com
Web: www.telesoftas.com

Company Information
Industry: Computer programming activities. Information and telecommunication technologies
Year of establishment: 2004
Sales revenues in 2017: 7 million euros
Sales revenues in 2007: 2.5 million euros
Average number of employees in 2017: 126
Brain(s) behind the company: Everyone in the company, but inspiration comes from CEO Algirdas Stonys

Nature of Market Leadership

TeleSoftas is the first company that started to produce mobile applications in Lithuania. It is one of the largest and most significant mobile IT service development houses in Lithuania. The company's main clients reside in America, the United Kingdom, Germany, and the Scandinavian countries. However, in general, the company is operating worldwide. Since the company is headquartered in Lithuania, the main competition comes from similar companies in Central and Eastern Europe, India, Ukraine, and Russia. It is difficult to evaluate the company's market share, due to the broad portfolio of services and the very nature of programming services being a borderless service. In 2019, the *Financial Times* featured TeleSoftas among Europe's 1000 fastest growing companies in CEE during the previous 5 years, based on the company's revenue growth of 333% (Žuolytė 2019).

Nature of the Competitive Advantage

The company's competitive advantage is its long-term experience and the professionalism of the staff. This creates a base for a high level of involvement with the project's business results, and a rapid access to a diverse set of skills.

Core Lessons Learned on the Path to Success

1. Be reactive, do not stay in the comfort zone for a long time. Be in constant change depending on what is going on around and inside the organization.
2. Have a diversified portfolio of clients.

Management and Leadership Development Needs

There is a desire to implement management methodologies that are appropriate for a non-hierarchical organization where people are empowered to make decisions and management does not take place through the hierarchy, but through teams united through knowledge sharing.

Financing and Regulatory Environment Development Needs

Lithuanian labor taxes are not competitive anymore. Western clients work with TeleSoftas because of other advantages, not because of cheap labor costs. For TeleSoftas's clients in Denmark or Germany, it is cheaper to hire a person in their own country than one from TeleSoftas. So, Lithuania has to rethink its labor tax system.

Telesoftas: Hidden Champion

In 2004, Algirdas Stonys formed a team of friends and founded TeleSoftas. The company started when iPod and Android did not exist. TeleSoftas was the first company in Lithuania to launch mobile applications. When Android came, TeleSoftas was already working with the systems. Today, TeleSoftas has grown into an international smart and innovative IT service company, providing software and product engineering solutions to clients worldwide. TeleSoftas consistently invests in R&D, allocating some 2–2.5% of its annual turnover, which allows it to expand its technological know-how. For example, one of the latest successful projects to showcase the company's technological potential is VR Inner Child, a unique virtual reality demonstration based on elements of transactional theory in psychotherapy for altitude fear.[1]

Since its establishment, the company has consistently invested in an ecosystem of excellence and creativity. TeleSoftas's main goals are based not on financial performance, but above all on people. And this gives excellent results. For example, all TeleSoftas employees generate new ideas, and continuously monitor the market. As soon as they see something new, they immediately analyze the need for it and build a team to develop the idea. Of course, most ideas come from those involved in strategic decisions, such as the CEO, CFO, or CPO. But as a whole, everyone in the organization is conscious and empowered to propose new activities. Probably all employees have generated some ideas in their fields of activity. In 2018, TeleSoftas established an in-house unit to develop new and proprietary products using the Stage-Gate methodology.

Šarūnas Putrius—chief production officer—says that the company is a market leader with years of experience and high employee loyalty. TeleSoftas retains all the know-how because all those who started this business are still working today. The organization invests heavily in recruiting, both hiring and growing. There are summer camps where people come for retraining, or right after university. The company takes a lot of interns and retains them. This ensures employee loyalty because such people tend to stay in the company and are grateful.

Agility, employee retention and loyalty, and company values are critical factors in the success of the company. Pleasing customers is important but being an attractive employer is also essential because it is people who generate income. Recently, a lot of attention has been paid to marketing the company as an attractive employer, which is also essential in recruiting employees.

Success is also determined by the ability to deal with uncertainty when employees are empowered to take the initiative and make decisions. In essence, this means freedom, trust, and empowerment. Freedom is incompatible with orders such as "we must make five million," and disregarding everything else. Freedom means letting employees do what they do well. This generates millions of euros. This company

---

[1] http://kaunasin.lt/telesoftas-kaune-isaugusio-verslo-pamatas-tvirta-profesionalu-bendruomene/?lang=lt

operates by focusing on employee happiness, not on employee efficacy or efficiency, because the former leads to the latter anyway. This leadership principle stems from the views of TeleSoftas CEO Algirdas Stonys.

What Specific Lessons Does TeleSoftas Teach Us?
The foundation of the success of all company goals is not financial performance but, above all, people. It is people who grow businesses.

3 Conclusions and Recommendations

During this research, seven hidden champions and two potential hidden champions were identified in Lithuania. Four hidden champions and two potential hidden champions work in the manufacturing industry, three hidden champions work in the information and communication industry. So, in general, six companies produce innovative products, while the rest three companies are service providers internationally. All companies are located in the biggest Lithuanian cities, such as the capital Vilnius and Kaunas. This fact reflects the underdeveloped business structure in the regions of Lithuania. All companies are export-oriented globally. None works just for Europe.

As the main success factor, all companies mentioned the importance of addressing the needs and solving the problems of their client.

This research demonstrates that hidden champions arise from companies that address the immediate and painful problem facing their clients through the development of must-have, rather than just nice-to-have, products or services. For the success of business development, it is essential to have a shared business development vision among owners or top managers, as well as patented products and diversified clients' portfolios. Also, companies emphasize the importance of transparency, trust, and respect in the relationships with the clients and business partners, connections with like-minded people, suppliers, who share the same quality standards, and business partners who bring value to everything that they do.

As real innovation comes from having an open mind and a passionate heart, it is vital to develop an ecosystem of excellence and creativity in the company. Representatives of the hidden champions noticed that it is easier to develop one's own organizational culture when one employs students who are still not damaged by experience in other organizational cultures.

The following characteristics describe the organizational culture of hidden champions: a flat structure, qualified, loyal, happy, and empowered employees, proactivity, agility, and constant change, strong organization values, trust, respect, transparency, and the highest level of quality.

The following are recommendations for the Lithuanian government, describing how it could support the emergence and growth of hidden champions.

Small businesses often do not have access to financial support due to bureaucratic issues in Lithuania. The procedures are very complicated, and it is not easy to submit applications for business support. It takes a lot of time to fulfill all the requirements and fill out the required forms, as well as to administer the financial support afterward. These issues can be avoided through the development of more open application requirements and more comfortable project administration procedures. Also, there is no opportunity for start-ups to get financial support while the company is not legally established. That raises additional administrative problems while it is not clear if a product is required in the market, and a prototype has not been tested.

Although there was a review of the labor tax system recently, it is still not competitive internationally. Hidden champions feel the need for more competitive labor taxes.

The success and viability of hidden champions depend strongly on the patented product. Thus, there is a need to help companies with patenting processes not only in Lithuania but also in Asian countries or even in the USA. In general, there is a lack of consultants who can provide consulting services to innovative companies in Lithuania.

Lithuanian financial institutions should review the process of loan-giving. Currently, it is too slow.

Higher education institution can support the growth of hidden champions in the country by teaching their graduates to address societal needs and by demonstrating such behavior on their own. Empathy, adaptability, and proactivity are the most sought-after graduate competences in the job market of hidden champions. Graduates should be ready for work in non-hierarchical institutions, which are flexible and agile. Speaking about instrumental competences, representatives of hidden champions highlighted intellectual property management, process management, quality management, and new market penetration.

References

Blöchliger H, Koutsogeorgopoulou V (2018) Lithuania: a fast-growing economy needs to boost inclusiveness. Lithuania Desk, OECD Economics Department. Posted on July 5, 2018 by oecdecoscope. https://oecdecoscope.blog/2018/07/05/lithuania-a-fast-growing-economy-needs-to-boost-inclusiveness/. Accessed 7 Oct 2019
CGTrader. CGTrader—3D content made easy. https://www.cgtrader.com/pages/about-us. Accessed 16 Mar 2019
Davies N (1996) Europe: a history. Pimlico
Deeper. About us. https://deeper.eu/about-us/. Accessed 16 Mar 2019
Deeper, UAB. Rekvizitai.lt. https://rekvizitai.vz.lt/imone/deeper/. Accessed 16 Mar 2019
Eurostat. https://ec.europa.eu/eurostat/data/database. Accessed 6 Oct 2019
Game Insight. About. https://www.game-insight.com/en/about. Accessed 16 Mar 2019
Game Insight, UAB. Rekvizitai.lt. https://rekvizitai.vz.lt/imone/game_insight_uab/. Accessed 16 Mar 2019
Klimantas A, Zirgulis A (2019) A new estimate of Lithuanian GDP for 1937: How does interwar Lithuania compare. ISM University. https://www.lb.lt/en/events/a-new-estimate-of-lithuanian-gdp-for-1937-how-does-interwar-lithuania-compare-by-adomas-klimantas-ism-university. Accessed 7 Oct 2019
Light Conversion. About us. http://www.lightcon.com/about-us.html. Accessed 16 Mar 2019

Light Conversion. News. http://www.lightcon.com/news.html. Accessed 16 Mar 2019

Light Conversion, UAB. Rekvizitai.lt. https://rekvizitai.vz.lt/imone/sviesos_konversija_moksline_gamybine_firma/. Accessed 16 Mar 2019

Lithuania Country Study Guide Volume 1 (2015) World country study guide library by Ibp. https://www.amazon.com/Lithuania-Strategic-Information-Developments-2015-01-31/dp/B01A64SCE0. Accessed 7 Oct 2019

Lithuanian Department of Statistics. https://osp.stat.gov.lt/statistiniu-rodikliu-analize#/. Accessed 5 Oct 2019

Lithuania—Official Gateway to Lithuania. History. Lietuva.lt

Ministry of the Economy and Innovation of the Republic of Lithuania. http://eimin.lrv.lt/en/. Accessed 5 Oct 2019

Nakrošis V, Vilpišauskas R, Jahn D (2018) Sustainable governance indicators 2018. https://www.researchgate.net/publication/328281105_Lithuania_Report_Sustainable_Governance_Indicators_2018. Accessed 7 Oct 2019

OECD (2018) Economic surveys. Lithuania, June. http://www.oecd.org/economy/surveys/Lithuania-2018-OECD-economic-survey-overview.pdf. Retrieved 7 Oct 2019

Parkis. Bicycle lift Parkis—innovative bike rack. https://parkis.eu/. Accessed 16 Mar 2019

Parkis, UAB. Rekvizitai.lt. https://rekvizitai.vz.lt/imone/parkis/. Accessed 16 Mar 2019

Simon H (2009) Hidden champions of the twenty-first century. Springer-Verlag, New York. https://doi.org/10.1007/978-0-387-98147-5

The World Bank (2019) Doing business. https://www.doingbusiness.org/en/reforms/overview/economy/lithuania. Accessed 6 Nov 2019

UAB "CGTrader". Rekvizitai.lt. https://rekvizitai.vz.lt/imone/cgtrader/. Accessed 16 Mar 2019

Vilkas E (1997) Experience and challanges of privatisation in Lithuania. Warsaw School of Economics, Warsaw

Where To Buy. Parkis. https://parkis.eu/where-to-buy/. Accessed 16 Mar 2019

Ziemele I (ed) (2003) Baltic yearbook of international law, vol 3. Brill, Nijhoff, Leiden. https://brill.com/view/title/11025. Accessed 6 Nov 2019

Žuolytė J (2019) Trys lietuviškos kompanijos pateko į "Financial Times" reitingą. 5 March. Delfi: https://www.delfi.lt/m360/naujausi-straipsniai/trys-lietuviskos-kompanijos-pateko-i-financial-times-reitinga.d?id=80531937. Accessed 16 Mar 2019

Potential Hidden Champions of Moldova

Dumitru Slonovschi

Overview
Official name: Republic of Moldova
Type of government: Parliamentary republic
Population in 2017: 3,549,196
Land area: 33,850 km^2

History

1991	Moldova becomes an independent and sovereign state.
1992	Transnistrian conflict.
1992	Moldova joins the United Nations and the Organization for Security and Co-operation in Europe.
1994	Constitution is adopted, granting substantial autonomy to Transnistria and the Autonomous Territorial Unit of Gagauzia.
1995	Moldova becomes a full member of the Council of Europe.
1998	The Partnership and Cooperation Agreement with the European Union (EU) comes into force in July.
2001	The Communist Party wins the elections and Moldova becomes the first former Soviet republic to return unreformed communists to power.
2005	The European Union Border Assistance Mission to Moldova is launched.
2009	The Alliance for European Integration (AEI) formed by four pro-West parties comes to power.
2009	Moldova joins five other countries in the Eastern Partnership initiative.
2014	The EU-Moldova Association Agreement is signed in June.

D. Slonovschi (✉)
Magenta Consulting, Chisinau, Moldova
e-mail: d.slonovschi@consulting.md

2014   The Schengen area visa waiver for short stays is applied to citizens of the Republic of Moldova holding a biometric passport.

1 Introduction: Context and History

Moldova is a small country with an area of 33,850 km^2 situated between Romania and Ukraine, and a population of 3.5 million.

In 1991 Moldova gained independence as a result of the Soviet Union's collapse and embarked on ambitious structural reforms aimed to implement a market-driven economy. Notwithstanding the continuous economic hardship, with a few exceptions Moldova has been committed to the economic reform program, supported by international institutions such as the EU, the European Bank for Reconstruction and Development, the World Bank, and the International Monetary Fund. Reform policies have been aimed essentially at macro-economic stabilization, liberalization, and privatization (Council of Europe 2003, para. 19).

Shortly after independence, Moldova was involved in a conflict with the separatist region of Transnistria, which proclaimed its independence in 1992. Economic ties between Transnistria and the rest of the country have been disrupted, investor confidence has been undermined, and tensions have occurred in trade links with certain neighboring countries due to extensive, and clandestine economic activities in the region, including smuggling (Council of Europe 2003, para. 20).

The foreign trade regime in Moldova is fairly liberal. Since its accession to the World Trade Organization in 2001, the Republic of Moldova has been strongly committed to the multilateral trading system (Bertelsmann Stiftung 2018, p. 19).

In June 2014, Moldova signed an association agreement, along with the Deep and Comprehensive Free Trade Area Agreement (DCFTA) with the European Union. The provisional implementation of the association agreement regulations started on 1 September 2014. In July 2016, the agreement fully entered into force. Additionally, in December 2015, the EU decided to extend the application of the DCFTA, however on a slightly different basis to Transnistria.

In 2015–2017, Moldova's exports to the EU increased by 22% compared with those in 2012–2014, and imports decreased by 14% over the same period, despite fears of an overabundance of imported products from the EU. This allowed some mitigation of the imbalance in the trade between Moldova and the EU, reducing the trade balance deficit by 45% during that period. Therefore, during the implementation of DCFTA, domestic products became more competitive on the EU market, contributing to the growth and diversification of exports, which contributes to sustainable economic growth (Lupusor and Gumene 2018, p. 30).

In addition to the increase in exports, the DCFTA also had deeper macroeconomic implications, boosting economic growth, budget revenues, imports, investment, and employment. The business climate for private entrepreneurs in Moldova is improving, among other things due to the implementation of the DCFTA (Bertelsmann Stiftung 2018, p. 22).

Moldova is a small lower-middle-income economy. The economy has recently expanded by an average of 5% annually, driven by consumption and fueled by remittances. The latter account for a quarter of GDP, among the highest share in the world (Exhibit 1). The continued economic stabilization, the advancement of key economic reforms, and the creation of a rule-based environment for businesses are the country's key goals (World Bank 2019a, b).

In 2018, the Republic of Moldova registered a 4% economic growth. The most dynamic sectors have been information and communications technology (ICT), manufacturing, automotive industry, and agriculture. Historically, the largest industries in Moldova have been manufacturing, agriculture and food processing, textile, apparel, and footwear. The ICT sector is a rather new and fast-growing sector in Moldova, with many foreign companies entering the market. The industry reached 15.2% of GDP in 2018, followed by agriculture with 10.2% of GDP. The increase of 1.3% of the industrial production was mainly driven by the 1.8% growth of the manufacturing industry (The Moldovan Investment Agency 2019).

In the World Bank's *Doing Business Report 2019*, Moldova ranked 14 out of 190 countries in the *Starting a Business* category, with a score of 95.55 out of the maximum of 100 and ranked 47th out of 190 countries on ease of doing business (Doing Business 2019).

In 2018, the combined IT services market had an estimated value of 154.40 million US dollars, with 33.50 million US dollars from the domestic market and 120.90 million from exported services.

In order to create the necessary premises for stimulating the IT industry development, the first virtual information technology park—"Moldova IT Park"—was established on January, 1, 2018 for a period of 10 years. One of the incentives, granted by the state to the residents of IT parks, is the application of a single 7% tax on sales revenues, but not less than a minimum monthly amount per employee (Moldova IT Park 2019).

As the Moldovan IT services market has gradually evolved in the past 10 years, an entire ecosystem of companies drawing from the available talent pool has appeared. These companies have filled numerous service niches and span a wide range of markets and business sizes. From the usual outsourcing centers to independent software vendors, global vendors, system integrators, start-ups, and companies in technology or industry niches, they run the gamut from small IT companies to huge centers with staff in the hundreds. One outstanding characteristic of Moldovan IT companies is their worldwide customer base. In addition to customers in Europe, the United States, and CIS, Moldovan IT firms have references for on-premises implementations in Canada, South America, Africa, and Asia. Some of the companies now provide modern solutions to various industries across the globe, with a high concentration of clients in finance (including the development of fintech solutions), automotive, telecommunications, and government (International Data Corporation 2019, p. 8).

We contacted 21 companies suggested by the EBRD as potential hidden champions, and six other companies that we considered innovative and successful businesses.

Exhibit 1 Core economic indicators for Moldova

	2011	2012	2013	2014	2015	2016	2017	2018
GDP per capita (current US$)	2363.59	2446.73	2668.68	2674.12	2179.23	2272.41	2724.49	3189.36
GDP per capita growth (annual %)	5.88	−0.58	9.07	5.06	−0.27	4.47	4.77	4.10
Long-term unemployment (% of total unemployment)	–	–	–	–	–	–	–	–
Foreign direct investment, net inflows (% of GDP)	4.13	2.88	2.55	3.59	2.79	1.17	1.66	2.05
GDP (current US$, mio)	8414.4	8709.2	9496.7	9510.2	7745.2	8071.5	9669.8	11,309.1
Exports of goods and services (current US$, mio)	2738.07	2711.41	3047.73	2964.40	2470.38	2607.82	3007.18	3440.58
Exports of goods and services (% of GDP)	32.54	31.13	32.09	31.17	31.90	32.31	31.10	30.42
Merchandise exports (current US$, mio)	2217.00	2162.00	2428.00	2340.00	1967.00	2045.00	2425.00	2707.00
Merchandise exports to high-income economies (% of total merchandise exports)	32.85	32.32	34.14	38.74	40.94	39.95	41.76	n/a
Merchandise exports to developing economies in Europe & Central Asia (% of total merchandise exports)	64.12	64.91	63.88	57.97	53.21	53.13	52.70	n/a
Ores and metals exports (% of merchandise exports)	5.99	3.35	4.11	2.32	1.74	1.30	1.45	1.37
Agricultural raw materials exports (% of merchandise exports)	1.04	0.76	0.68	0.81	0.95	0.84	0.64	0.64
Food exports (% of merchandise exports)	70.13	58.35	57.60	64.10	62.69	64.94	63.86	57.53
Fuel exports (% of merchandise exports)	0.69	0.31	0.19	0.25	0.13	0.06	0.06	0.05
Manufactures exports (% of merchandise exports)	22.09	37.22	37.40	32.51	34.48	32.91	33.96	40.41
High-technology exports (% of manufactured exports)	6.31	4.78	2.36	4.81	3.99	3.10	5.15	n/a

Source: World Bank, September, 2019b

The companies that were nominated as potential hidden champions have a low visibility on the local market, have registered high growth in recent years, and have expanded to other markets. All three companies identified as potential hidden champions are present on the global market, having customers in Europe, North America, Asia, Africa, and South America. This feature is considered important for the companies' development and growth.

Two representatives do not consider their companies leaders on the market. In one case, the market is fragmented and the company is not a recognized unique leader. In the second case, the product has a different logic compared to other products on the market. It was mentioned that these companies are different from their competitors as they provide an improved product or service. Their products and services were characterized as advanced as and better than anything else on the market.

A common characteristic of the interviewed companies is that their service or product development is a result of identified problems. Before the companies' inception, their services or products were unavailable or underdeveloped on the market.

The potential hidden champions operate on a large market, positioning themselves as worldwide companies and being able to provide services or products to any client on the global market.

The customers appreciate the companies for their competency, expertise, and ability to offer solutions to the most challenging problems. The respondents underlined the fact that their positions are built on ambitious and diligent teams, their visions, and their ability to deliver preeminent services or products.

The respondents mentioned the following core lessons learned on the path to business success:

- The team behind the services or products is very important. The ability to recruit professional, passionate, and persevering persons, and to invest permanently in their training and development is one of the success factors.
- Invent something unusual and revolutionary, and focus on the established priorities to ensure company evolution and fast growth.
- The company should not stop innovating once it has reached some good results. It should always try something new, adapt to market changes, and implement new technologies to respond rapidly and efficiently to customers' needs.
- Optimize and reduce the production costs at the beginning by hiring a financial director.

At present, the main challenges that the companies face are:

- Finding and recruiting qualified human resources.
- Technological—the emergence and implementation of new technologies based on artificial intelligence can make current business models irrelevant.
- Legal—the respondents do not have a clear understanding of how the new laws (the Moldova IT Park Law and the Tax Law) and regional markets (GDPR) could be implemented.

The representatives of the interviewed companies listed the following characteristics of the environment that they operate in:

- The companies do not receive any concessions from the government and the existing financing environment is rather demotivational, because companies are constrained to take credits in critical situations.
- There are contradictions between certain laws on company operation. The law is implemented selectively and unequally, which creates unfair competition.

Following the above-mentioned circumstances, the companies highlighted their desire to operate in a fair business environment and be supported by the government through uniform law enforcement and financing programs.

In terms of marketing needs, the companies mentioned that they were still learning how to do global marketing and that they did not have a good understanding of cultural differences in the way that they could reach customers in various national markets.

2 Three Case Studies of Potential Hidden Champions

2.1 Noction

Overview
Address: 63 Lev Tolstoi Street, Chisinau, Moldova
Tel: +37322921920
Fax: –
Email: info@noction.com
Web: www.noction.com

Company Information
Industry: Information and communication
Year of establishment: 2011
Sales revenues in 2017: Confidential
Sales revenues in 2007: Confidential
Average number of employees in 2017: 60 in Moldova (80 including employees from abroad)
Brain(s) behind the company: CEO John Strong and director Victor Bordian

Nature of Market Leadership

Noction is an industry-leading technology company whose main area of expertise is network traffic analysis and border gateway protocol (BGP) network performance automation. The company's leadership position is ensured by the quality and innovation of its products, internal ISO-certified processes, international brand recognition, a large and loyal customer base, as well as specific technological know-how backed by several secured United States Patent and Trademark Office patents.

The company became a leader in the area of BGP network optimization as soon as its main product—the Noction Intelligent Routing Platform (IRP)—became available to the general public. Maintaining this leadership position is an ongoing effort. The IRP offers unique innovative ways to overcome the legacy of BGP routing limitations and is a product of much better quality than anything else available on the niche market today.

Nature of the Competitive Advantage

The competitive advantages that put the company in a favorable business position are:

- Unconstrained approach to research and innovation. The company develops new products on an ongoing basis and adds unique features to the existing ones.
- The company's size and structure allow it to pivot its offerings and overall strategy so as to take advantage of new market opportunities with ease.
- Product customization to end-user particular requirements, accompanied by a fast-track development and testing procedures, allows the company to respond to requests for modification or new features in a shorter time than the industry standard.
- Extensive knowledge and networking industry expertise accumulated over the years.

Core Lessons Learned on the Path to Success

1. Human resources are scarce. While it is delusional to expect every employee to be extraordinary and differentiate the company from the rest, it is possible to create and maintain a people management and motivation system that gets noticed by employees and makes them devoted to the company, performing their best at all times.
2. Innovation is exciting and necessary. To stay relevant, the company should never stop at what has been already achieved. Constant communication with customers and market understanding are to be reflected in innovation, which in turn fuels business agility.

Financing and Regulatory Environment Development Needs

The company representative indicated that there are currently contradictions between certain laws concerning the company activity.

Noction: Network Intelligence

Noction is a privately funded technology company with offices in the USA, Europe, and Asia. Founded in 2011, it is providing cutting-edge network intelligence technologies, enabling companies of all sizes to take full advantage of maximum network performance for their business-critical applications such as e-commerce, VoIP, and media streaming across IP networks.

Noction's products help network professionals keep a close eye on their networks, proactively find, diagnose, and fix network related issues, overcome the shortcomings of the underlying Internet routing protocol, BGP, by minimizing network latency and packet loss, avoiding congestions, intelligently managing bandwidth, balancing traffic, and a lot more.

The company maintains an extensive portfolio of clients with a very wide range of business activities. These include hosting providers, data centers, enterprises, telecoms, media, healthcare providers, content delivery networks, call centers, network service providers, VOIP, research and educational institutions, etc.

A large number of customers, both big and small, have been greatly satisfied with the company's products and services. The detailed feedback collected over the recent years from clients such as Thomson Reuters, Rutube, Hivelocity, 365 Data Centers, Steadfast, and others, is reflected in a multitude of case studies. Most companies highlight the following benefits of using Noction products:

- Reduction of downtime and improved network stability, leading to decreased customer churn and a reduced cost of troubleshooting and service restoration.
- Reduction of service-level agreement penalties due to network uptime increase.
- Labor savings and reduced risk of human errors due to the automation process.
- Improved operational efficiency, including faster incident and problem resolution.
- Overall competitiveness increases due to improved network performance and overall customer satisfaction.

With a large number of reported success stories, Noction's products have enjoyed a favorable image of being phenomenal tools enhancing the routing and manageability of multi-homed networks.

The company is heavily investing in research and development and plans to introduce new products to the market in the near future.

2.2 Travod

Overview
Address: 90 Bucuresti street, Chisinau, Moldova.
Tel: +373 68728755; +44 207 193 0080
Fax: –

Email: welcome@travod.com
Web: www.travod.com

Company Information

Industry: Information and communication
Year of establishment: 2010
Sales revenues in 2017: undisclosed
Sales revenues in 2007: undisclosed
Average number of employees in 2017: about 100 in Moldova and about 25 in Romania, a few in the UK, about 5000 subcontractors around the world.
Brain(s) behind the company: Founders: Andrei Spinu, Sergiu Matei, Mihail Stipanov and CEO-Managing Partner Elena Grigoras.

Nature of Market Leadership

Travod is a fast-growing leader in translation and localization. The company was recognized as one of the 50 most promising start-ups in the world at the 2015 Web Summit Conference in Dublin. Published in June 2018 by independent market research firm Common Sense Advisory (CSA Research), *The Language Services Market: 2018* ranked Travod as a top-grossing translation agency in the 46.52 billion US dollar global market for outsourced language services and technology. Travod was the 93rd largest translation agency in the world and the 22nd largest in Northern Europe (Travod.com 2018, para. 2).

With 70% annual growth last year, Travod outperformed more than 18,000 other translation companies to achieve this rank. The company's success is attributed to its expansion into new Scandinavian, North American, and Western European markets. A big role in Travod's growth was played by the diversification of the service portfolio offered to end clients, incorporating services such as website localization, software localization, desktop publishing, and automated translation solutions. The agility and customer-centric workforce at Travod helped it get ahead of the other companies in the industry (Travod.com 2018, para. 3).

The trusted network of translators and partners that the company has built over the years sustain its business model and help translate content into over 100 European, Asian, and African languages for over 6000 brands.

Nature of the Competitive Advantage

Travod's goal is to help global brands connect with new markets faster and support them in their interaction with their global audience easily and consistently. The company developed smart project management and a home-grown proprietary business system that blends well with international companies, big and small. Travod's business process system helps companies manage the way that their content is written, localized, controlled, and distributed across business units.

Travod's competitive advantage includes:

- Agile technology—deployment of the latest translation technology that seamlessly blends with the clients' organizational ecosystem.
- A trusted network of language professionals—Travod employs professional translators and linguists with a strong background and subject-matter expertise.
- Continuous delivery—Travod ensures regular operational availability to clients across the globe, delivering on the spot, while most of the projects are delivered before the deadline, speeding up delivery time to clients' global markets
- Smart project management—production resources that allow the company to optimize processes without wasting time and money.
- Cost-optimization strategy—high-volume projects are strategically cost-optimized thanks to an advanced translation technology and human expertise. Being technology-savvy means the company never translates the same thing twice, saving money, and guaranteeing consistency.
- Customer centric support—Outstanding pre- and post-delivery customer care for every project and request.

Core Lessons Learned on the Path to Success

1. Focus on stage-based business priorities to ensure sustainable evolution and growth of the company. Each development stage comes with its own priorities and challenges. It is paramount to identify a company's priorities based on its development stage.
2. Adapt to market changes and challenge new technologies to respond to customer needs rapidly and efficiently.
3. Recruit valuable people and invest in their development and motivation. Retain the know-how and share business success and profits with them.

Management and Leadership Development Needs

The company is in a transition phase from a startup to a medium-size organization and needs to solidify its knowledge about a process-based approach to business development. External mentorship and coaching are indispensable at this stage.

Financing and Regulatory Environment Development Needs

Companies in Moldova are not supported financially, and the financing environment is rather demotivating, because companies have difficulty obtaining credit in critical situations.

The application of the regulatory framework and the selective implementation of laws creates unfair competition. The General Data Protection Regulation implementation is unclear as well.

The company is still learning how to gear marketing activities for global markets.

Travod: Connecting Experts and Technology to Deliver Stories Globally on Time, in Any Language

Travod was born in Moldova, founded by three students who were friends. The company achieved its operational excellence over the years by refining what the customers need in order to present their brand identity to an international audience.

Today, Travod is a leading provider of cost-effective, professional translation services, delivering culturally appropriate language solutions. The clients receive exceptional value and turn-key solutions to ensure that their brand communicates directly with each and every customer, no matter where they are in the world. Now and fast.

Over the years, Travod has built an extensive expertise in translating content in all European and major Asian languages, covering exotic languages, too. The worldwide network of trusted professional linguists delivers translated content around the clock, into more than 100 languages.

Through an inspiring leadership and people-oriented culture, Travod builds on the principles of service excellence, customization, and perfect timing. With a team of over 120 employees, the company works in unison, passionately caring about the quality and the value that it delivers. Travod serves its clients devotedly with a swift, meaningful response and agility, from the first contact right through to the final delivery. The core services include translation, editing, proofreading, transcription, media localization, desktop publishing, software localization, and platform integration solutions. To date, the company has served over 6000 brands worldwide from various industries including technology, marketing, law, finance, government, automotive industry, life sciences, travel, games, manufacturing, and media. The year 2018 marked a milestone in Travod's success as it became the number 22 translation agency in Northern Europe.

Driven by passion, Travod connects people and empowers organizations to drive their international business to continuous success.

2.3 Santino Service

Overview
Address: 12, Feredelului street, Chisinau, Moldova
Tel: +373 22 548 986
Fax: –
Email: info@santino.md
Web: www.santino.md

Company Information
Industry: Manufacturing
Year of establishment: 2003
Sales revenues in 2017: Undisclosed

Sales revenues in 2007: Undisclosed
Average number of employees in 2017: 92 in Moldova and about 100 around the world
Brain(s) behind the company: Serghei Odobescu, Vladimir Imbirovski

Nature of Market Leadership

Santino Service is a potential regional leader in Central and Eastern Europe and the USA in the niche of manufacture and trade of household plastic (polypropylene) products. Santino is currently one of the leaders in Moldova in this field.

The company was founded in Moldova in 2003 and currently has its head office in Moldova. It also has subsidiaries in Russia, Germany, and the USA. The company has over 40 inventions and 11 patents. One of its leading products is flowerpots with a self-watering system. The company exports its products to Russia, Ukraine, Belorussia, Romania, Bulgaria, the Czech Republic, Poland, Germany, USA, and Australia. Santino reportedly has a share of approximately 90% of the Moldovan market, with shares of 3–10% in other regions.

The company is a potential hidden champion because of the innovative product and the market share information provided by the CEO.

Nature of the Competitive Advantage

Santino Service has creative and innovative internal capabilities to create products that are adapted to the customers' changing demands.

Core Lessons Learned on the Path to Success

To focus on creating products of superior quality and offering them at a reasonable price.

Management and Leadership Development Needs

At present, the company focuses on improving business processes by implementing a quality management system (ISO 9001:2015).

Santino Service: A Company that Simplifies Gardening

Santino Service is a company based in the Republic of Moldova, whose goal is to reduce significantly the cost of self-watering systems and make them available and affordable to everyone. The company offers products for all types of flowers, from the simplest to the most demanding.

The company's mission is to combine convenience, aesthetics, and efficiency. Its priority is to match clients' interests and the company's products. Santino Service has a wide range of colors to match any setting, from the cheerful colors of a children's playground to the subtle discreet colors of a business office.

The company has continuously increased the quality of its products during the 10 years of its existence. The design of the flowerpots is patented and is the company's intellectual property.

Keeping indoor plants in a pot is not the only thing that the pot can be used for. It has an aesthetic function as well. The company's pots have a self-watering system, so the user can devote less time to the flowers. Usually, indoor plants are watered once in 2–3 days. With the company's products, flowers are watered manually only once in 2–6 weeks. Therefore, the flowerpots made by Santino have attracted international customers from the USA. The company has a branch in the USA and its products can be bought directly from their deposits or through various online resources: Amazon, Sears, Houzz, and others.

Elements of high quality are incorporated in the matrix itself, represented by the mold where the pots and other household products—buckets, scoops, and watering cans—take shape. Santino created its own molds. Initially the company bought them from the adjacent Armet factory. But Santino soon bought its own machines and equipment and started producing molds for the workshop.

The mold's quality determines the quality of the final product. The pots made by Santino last longer than the regular Chinese goods. The plastic surface of the products—buckets, basins—is mirror-smooth. Usually, they are polished 4–6 times, but Santino repeats the procedure 14–16 times. All this became possible thanks to the company's designers, the qualitative matrix, the well-trained masters, and the skilled workers. Therefore, the products sell fast as there are few manufacturers able to assure such high quality (Madein.md 2016).

3 Conclusions and Recommendations

The potential hidden champions of Moldova are fast-growing companies that provide services and products to global brands worldwide. The challenges of the local economic environment force the potential hidden champions to develop businesses without borders and promote services and products on the international market. Being in a small country with few natural resources, the potential hidden champions have focused their attention on strengths and opportunities rather than weaknesses. Two of them are positioned in the business-to-business segment in the information and communication field—a promising and fast-growing sector in Moldova. The third potential hidden champion is specialized in manufacturing, which historically has been one of the largest industries in Moldova.

At present, the companies have offices in Europe, North America, and Asia. Their ability to adapt to market changes and to respond rapidly and efficiently to clients' needs has helped them gain international recognition of their services and products. The high standards set in their work and in the cooperation with customers have remained unchanged over the past years.

The potential hidden champions share some values—innovation and investment in employees' development. Innovation is what drives them in terms of product development. In a continuously changing world, companies make constant efforts to improve the services and products that they deliver. They strive to provide the best, cost-effective, and quick solutions to their worldwide partners.

Given the emigration of Moldova's human capital, having a stable and professional team has been one of the companies' main challenges. There is a great emphasis on people development and motivation among potential hidden champions in Moldova. Companies offer education and training opportunities for their employees. Some of the representatives mentioned that there is a significant gap between education institutions' curricula and market realities. That is why companies provide strong training programs aimed at aligning their needs and students' skills. By investing in human capital development, potential hidden champions improve the quality of the solutions that they deliver and keep their teams motivated and productive.

Another characteristic of Moldova's potential hidden champions are the ambitious brains behind the companies. The top management of the companies are individuals with a vision and values. They have created a healthy corporate culture.

On the basis of this study, a list of recommendations is presented in order to emphasize the need to improve certain spheres for the development of Moldovan companies.

The government has a direct influence on Moldovan companies. Both the legislation and political instability can influence businesses. Therefore companies would benefit from different programs that encourage business development. Also, the different partnerships concluded with international companies provided by the government can lead to the growth and development of local companies. In order to increase the number of local companies, the government should organize more grant contests to encourage citizens to invest and set up their own businesses. As regards the political instability, there should be laws that do not change permanently so as not to create difficulties for the existing local companies.

The financial institutions play an important role for the companies. Many companies that are in the first years of activity encounter difficulties caused by the lack of financial resources. Hence, aid from financial institutions would be welcome. With advantageous credit options, more companies could apply and maintain a stable economic situation. Some of the barriers that companies encounter when taking a loan is the high interest rate and the economic instability. For this reason, the emergence of better offers from financial institutions will encourage more entrepreneurs to set up companies. Also, the financial institutions should create programs for young people so that they can easily invest in their ideas and plans. This would give them the confidence to set up a business.

Education is an important factor in business development in Moldova. Education is the basis for creating a new workforce. Unfortunately, companies are lacking employees. As a result, to increase this resource, schools, colleges, and universities should provide programs to encourage young people to get involved in business and gain experience. Young people should be encouraged to participate in activities and events that will help them find out in what area they would like to work in the future. The curricula should be aligned with the market realities, so that the graduates have a professional background. The mutually advantageous cooperation between companies and education institutions, combining theory and practice, can be a promising opportunity for the professional development of young people.

At present, there are some initiatives aimed at helping the youth to pursue their dream career.

The brain drain is an obvious phenomenon in the Republic of Moldova, and measures should be taken to create good conditions and opportunities for young people to study and work in the country.

References

Bertelsmann Stiftung (2018) BTI 2018 country report—Moldova, pp 19–22. https://www.bti-project.org/en/reports/country-reports/detail/itc/MDA/. Accessed 13 Aug 2019

Committee on Economic Affairs and Development of the Council of Europe (2003) Report on Economic development of Moldova: challenges and prospects, para 19–21. http://www.assembly.coe.int/nw/xml/XRef/X2H-Xref-ViewHTML.asp?FileID=10151&lang=EN. Accessed 3 Sept 2019

International Data Corporation (2019) Moldovan IT players priming for worldwide presence, pp 8–14. http://ict.md/files/documents/IDC_Report_Moldova_2019.pdf. Accessed 9 Sept 2019

Lupusor A, Gumene V (2018) The economic impact after 4 years of implementation of the Association Agreement RM-EU, pp 30–31. https://dcfta.md/impactul-economic-dupa-4-ani-de-implementare-a-acordului-de-asociere-rm-ue-1. Accessed 6 Aug 2019

Madein.md (2016) Moldova flowerpots exported even to USA and Russia. https://madein.md/en/news/national-production/moldovan-flowerpots-exported-to-usa-and-russia#. Accessed 9 Sept 2019

Moldova IT Park (2019) Presentation of information technology park. Moldova IT Park. https://moldovaitpark.md/en/home-english/. Accessed 10 Sept 2019

The Moldovan Investment Agency (2019) Economic overview. http://www.invest.gov.md/about-moldova. Accessed 4 Sept 2019

Travod.com (2018) Travod recognised among largest translation companies in the world. https://travod.com/blog/travod-recognised-among-largest-translation-companies-world. Accessed 5 Sept 2019

World Bank (2019a) The World Bank in Moldova. Overview. https://www.worldbank.org/en/country/moldova/overview#1. Accessed 4 Sept 2019

World Bank (2019b) Data; countries and economies. https://data.worldbank.org/country/moldova

World Bank Group (2019) Doing business. Economy profile of Moldova. https://www.doingbusiness.org/en/data/exploreeconomies/moldova#. Accessed 12 August 2019

Hidden Champions of Mongolia

Eku Bold

Overview
Official name: Mongolia
Type of government: Parliamentary democratic republic
Population in 2017: 3,177,899
Land area (in km^2): 1,566,000

History

1911   After more than 200 years under Qing Dynasty rule, Mongolia declares its independence.
1921   The Mongolian People's Revolution concluded after pushing out Chinese military forces.
1924   The Mongolian People's Republic is established, replacing the monarchy system.
1961   Mongolia becomes a member of the UN.
1990   A democratic revolution is ignited and the country's first free and multi-party elections for a bicameral parliament are held. This marks the beginning of a shift to a free market economy.
1991   Mongolia becomes a member of the IMF and the World Bank.
1992   A new democratic constitution is introduced. Privatization of state properties begins.
1997   Mongolia becomes a member of the World Trade Organization.

E. Bold (✉)
iConsulting, Ulaanbaatar, Mongolia

© Springer Nature Switzerland AG 2021
A. Braček Lalić, D. Purg (eds.), *Hidden Champions in Dynamically Changing Societies*, https://doi.org/10.1007/978-3-030-65451-1_19

1 Introduction: Context and History

Mongolia is a landlocked country between Russia and China in Central Asia. It has an area of 1.56 million km^2 and is the 18th largest country in the world. In 2019, the population was approximately 3.25 million. This makes Mongolia the least densely populated country in the world, with a density of 1.9/km^2. Lacking access to the sea and sharing borders with two large economies, Mongolia's economy is mainly based on exports of minerals and agricultural products to its neighbors. The country is rich in mineral deposits and attracted many foreign investors during the early 2010s which made Mongolia the fastest-growing economy in the world during that time. It was known as the "mining boom of Mongolia." Investors flocked to the country to tap into its resources of copper, gold, coal, molybdenum, fluoride, uranium, tin, and tungsten. The global decline in commodity prices caused the Mongolian economy to slow down significantly during 2014–2016, but it picked up again in 2017. Mongolia currently has a steadily increasing economic growth rate—7.2% in 2018, and 7.3% in the first half of 2019—but it is dependent on one country as more than 90% of its exports go to China, and the mining sector (ores, metals, fuel products) accounted for 48% of the GDP in 2018.

In addition to its vast mineral deposits, Mongolia has a rich history in the agricultural economy. Although modern agriculture became widespread only in the 1950s, it used to be the largest GDP driver until the mining sector overtook it. However, in addition to crop cultivation, the Mongolian people are traditionally nomadic. They were very skilled in animal husbandry and remnants of this culture can still be seen today. The Mongol people processed milk from livestock into different kinds of dairy products, and even into alcohol. Recent industrialization of these processes has allowed SMEs to promote more traditional and obscure products in the local market, such as milk curds, Mongolian butter, and milk vodka. In the past decades, the cashmere industry has become the largest agricultural activity. Privatization of the state-owned factories allowed the cashmere and wool industry to flourish and Mongolia currently supplies about one-third of the global cashmere output, with 5413 tons of clean cashmere produced in 2018.

Mongolia is well known mostly due to its affiliation with Genghis Khan, the first great khan who united all the nomadic tribes into a unified Mongolia. This led to the establishment of the largest empire in the world. Despite being seen as a fierce warlord, Genghis Khan introduced many forward-thinking technologies during his time in the thirteenth century. One such example is the Paiza or Gerege, which was one of the first passport systems, using engraved gold, silver, or bronze tablets that showed the status of the bearer and could grant diplomatic immunity in the empire. Paper currency was also introduced during his reign and was backed by silk and precious metals. It was one of the earliest paper currency systems in the world, later standardized in China. The Mongols are also credited with the establishment of the first postal system, with its "yam" arrangement, based on e postal relay stations throughout the empire. Couriers would either transfer the message to the next courier or stock up on food and continue riding on a fresh horse. This system was necessary to send vital information quickly in the expanding empire.

Though once the largest empire in history, disunity weakened the Mongols and the empire eventually collapsed. By the seventeenth century, the land of the Mongols was split into Outer and Inner Mongolia and came under the rule of the Qing dynasty for almost three centuries. The Qing dynasty fell in 1911 and Mongolia declared its independence but the Chinese army occupied Outer Mongolia in 1919. During this time, Mongolian revolutionaries founded the Mongolian People's Party and established relationship with the Russian Bolsheviks. In 1921, with the support of the Red Army, the Chinese were driven out and the Mongolian People's Republic was established. Mongolia became a Soviet satellite, heavily influenced by socialist philosophy. The Soviet Union however supported the Mongolian economy by building factories and industrializing production. The primary market for the industrial output was the Soviet Union, buying about 80% of Mongolian exports. The rest went to other countries in the Council for Mutual Economic Assistance This improved production in various industries.

One of the most important developments was the establishment in 1974 of Erdenet, a Soviet-Mongolian mining company at the site of a copper deposit considered the largest in Asia and fourth largest in the world. The Erdenet mining company is still in operation today. It is an important factor in the economic development of Mongolia, accounting for most of Mongolia's hard currency income.

The country shifted to a multi-party democratic and free market system in 1990 when a youth movement called the "New Generation" took part in peaceful protests and hunger strikes that eventually induced the Politbureau to resign. A new parliamentary system was introduced, called the People's Great Khural, and eventually adopted multiple constitutional amendments, legalizing new political parties, allowing multi-party elections, setting a second legislative body, and establishing the presidency. The existing Mongolian People's Revolutionary Party (MPRP) won the majority of the seats in the new parliament. The MPRP eventually split into two parties. One kept the original name, whereas the other was called the Mongolian People's Party. That party and the Democratic Party are now the largest in the country.

Before the revolution, Mongolia relied heavily on the Soviet Union for economic support. After the shift to a market economy, the lack of economic support and hard currency caused an economic crisis in the 1990s. Furthermore, Russia claims that Mongolia owes it a significant sum of money for its economic support in the past decades but has since written off part of it.

Mongolia became a full member of the UN in 1961. It joined the IMF and the World Bank in 1991 and is still strengthening its international presence. As a country that strongly advocates democracy, it hopes to become an economic hub in Central Asia and pave the way for developing the region through its ambitions of becoming the "Switzerland of Asia." Mongolia has a very young median age: 55% of the population are under 30 years old. The country aims to equip this new generation of young people with the necessary education to be more competent in today's quickly evolving world, especially in the STEM field. By doing so, the country aims to deconcentrate its economic dependency on natural resources and build a solid economy based on technological advancement and IT services.

The business environment of Mongolia is considered to be relatively competitive, with numerous companies striving to increase their market share, while almost half of the population is centralized in the capital city. Market penetration into other towns and the countryside is a costly endeavor due to the limited infrastructure in the countryside, and only market leaders are able to provide services in these areas. In addition, each year increasingly large numbers of people are moving into the capital city, continuously expanding the largest market while smaller towns see limited growth. This competition is made possible due to the relatively low barrier to entry, without a lot of red tape. However, certain industries, such as mining and financial services, are more heavily regulated.

Because of the small market, it is crucial for local businesses to establish overseas operations or export their output. Mongolia has seen gradual growth in its exports, with 4.9 billion US dollars in 2016, 6.2 billion in 2017, and 7.0 billion in 2018. The mining sector contributes a large portion of total exports. Many smaller companies are also striving to introduce Mongolian products in the international market. Some of the successful companies produce cosmetics, cashmere, and food and beverage. Although they are not ready to be classified as hidden champions, they will soon reach their full potential in the domestic and international markets (Exhibit 1).

2 Case Studies of Selected (Potential) Hidden Champions

2.1 Ochir Daginas LLC

Overview
Address: 25-1, 8th khoroo, Bayanzurkh district, Ulaanbaatar, Mongolia
Tel: 976 76007530
Email: od@ochirdaginas.mn
Web: www.ochirdaginas.mn

Company Information
Industry: Production of meat and poultry products
Year of establishment: 2005
Sales revenue in 2018: 3.3 million euros[1]
Sales revenue in 2013: About 2.2 million euros[2]
Average number employees: 80
Brain(s) behind the company: CEO Khanginakh

---

[1] As of 2018, 1€ = 3023.61MNT.
[2] As of 2013, 1€ = 2288.81MNT.

Exhibit 1 Core economic indicators for Mongolia

	2011	2012	2013	2014	2015	2016	2017	2018
GDP per capita (current US $)	3757.5	4351.8	4366.1	4158.5	3918.5	3660.1	3671.9	4103.7
GDP per capita growth (annual %)	15.15	10.15	9.43	5.74	0.38	−0.74	3.36	5.04
Long-term unemployment (% of total unemployment)	7.70	8.20	7.90	7.90	7.50	10	8.80	7.80
Foreign direct investment, net inflows (% of GDP)	43.9	34.7	16.4	2.8	0.8	−37.1	13.1	15.0
GDP (current US$, mio)	10,410	12,293	12,582	12,227	11,750	11,187	11,434	13,010
Exports of goods and services (current US$, mio)	5471	5356	4893	6388	5363	5616	6832	7843
Exports of goods and services (% of GDP)	52.5	43.6	38.9	52.2	45.6	50.2	59.8	60.3
Merchandise exports (current US$, thousand)	4,817,496.30	4,384,669.20	4,269,055.80	5,774,330.90	4,669,280.50	4,916,335.40	6,200,593.00	7,011,765.00
Merchandise exports to high-income economies (% of total merchandise exports)	10.7	9.9	11.3	10.8	14.5	19.3	13.5	–
Merchandise exports to developing economies in Europe & Central Asia (% of total merchandise exports)	2.0	1.7	1.6	1.2	1.7	1.2	1.2	–
Ores and metals exports (% of merchandise exports)	37.9	40.6	47.0	62.2	67.2	54.2	42.7	42.9
Agricultural raw materials exports (% of merchandise exports)	3.7	4.0	6.8	5.9	6.8	6.9	5.4	5.4

(continued)

Exhibit 1 (continued)

	2011	2012	2013	2014	2015	2016	2017	2018
Food exports (% of merchandise exports)	0.4	0.3	0.8	0.7	1.3	1.9	2.5	2.9
Fuel exports (% of merchandise exports)	52.4	51.0	41.6	27.8	22.7	31.7	47.4	46.7
Manufactures exports (% of merchandise exports)	–	–	3.5	3.2	1.8	5.2	1.9	1.9
High-technology exports (% of manufactured exports)	–	–	16.2	19.6	4.1	16.5	3.4	4.9

Source: World Bank (2019)

Nature of Market Leadership

The company is one of the leading domestic producers of meat products in the country. It exports its products to China, Korea, and Buryatia. The meat of pasture animals is more flavorful. This makes it more suitable to some markets. Investing in advanced production technologies and innovations allowed the company to introduce new products into the market.

Nature of the Competitive Advantage

The company's factories use solar energy which reduces production costs. This provides more investment possibilities in product development. The company has implemented ISO 22000 and HCCP standards, which allows its products to meet international standards. This has also allowed Ochir Daginas to launch its products in international markets.

Core Lessons Learned on the Path to Business Success

The company faced many difficulties when introducing new products. For example, customers were not used to white sausages and this product did not sell well for 3 years after its launching. However, the company continuously strived to find a position for this product in the market through improvements and marketing. The workers quickly embraced the new technology and learned that the products will find a place in the market if given enough care. Some of the major lessons learned over the years are outlined below.

- If you are in the business of continuous product customization, you are in fact in the business of innovation. Your innovations are the core of success. You should never stop improving your production process.
- You need a continuous desire for improvement and innovation.
- Do not underestimate the importance of motivation for your staff.
- Focus on the quality of the product and invest in a process that will allow you to certify your product.
- The production process is the most important part. Pay maximum attention to production conditions and methods.
- The personality of the leader is very important, especially for employee morale.

Ochir Daginas: A Potential Hidden Champion

Ochir Daginas has produced sausages, ham, and preserved meat products for the past 13 years, encompassing 25–30% of the domestic market. The company invested in a new meat-processing factory in 2009. Some 80% of the new plant equipment was automated, whereas the remaining 20% was hand-operated. The new facilities were three times larger than the previous factory. After its humble beginnings as a producer of boiled packaged meats, the company now offers over a dozen different types of products and aims to continue to introduce new products in the market. Ochir Daginas has cooperation agreements with Germany's Moguntia and Kuhlmann brands to bring European standards to Mongolia. The product line today includes smoked hams, liver pates, various sausages, and ready-to-eat boiled meat products, to name a few.

"The Chinese market, especially the mass market, is too big a market to be supplied by Mongolian producers," the directors say, but the company already has buyers in China, and aims to increase exports. The company is currently employing a strategy to make Mongolian meat products the most eco-friendly and healthy in the world and supply them to high-end markets. For this reason, the Song of the Steppe brand was established in China and its unit price increased.

Ochir Daginas has adopted numerous cost-cutting production methods. Solar energy is increasingly employed as the main source of power. German and Korean technologies are utilized in factory processes. The company strives to introduce advanced technical and technological solutions, engage in socially responsible production, and become a leading company in the industry.

2.2 Leader Cashmere LLC

Overview
Address: 95/2, Tovchoo road, 18134 Sonsgolon, 20th khoroo, Songinokhairkhan district, PO Box 401, Central Post Office, 15160 Ulaanbaatar, Mongolia
Tel: 976 91910004
Email: contact@leadercashmere.mn
Web: www.leadercashmere.mn

Company Information
Industry: Manufacture of cashmere products
Year of establishment: 2000
Sales revenue in 2018: 9,260,000 euros[3]
Sales revenue in 2011: About 5,735,000 euros[4]
Average number of employees: 80
Brain(s) behind the company: CEO Chinbold L.

---

[3] As of 2018, 1€ = 3023.61MNT.
[4] As of 2011, 1€ = 1935.05MNT.

Nature of Market Leadership

The company has three large factories producing wool and cashmere. Cashmere, sheep, camel wool, and yak wool are processed through six stages in three plants and provide consumers with high quality. Some 86% of the company's products are exported to Japan, India, and China.

Nature of the Competitive Advantage

The nature of the competitive advantage is the production of final goods from Mongolian goat cashmere—the world's highest-quality cashmere with a wide variety of choices. The company utilizes much more sophisticated production methods in its factories than its competitors and is one of the few cashmere fashion producers that export overseas.

Core Lessons Learned on Path to Business Success

Although the products are manufactured from the best raw materials, the quality and design of the product still remain one of the crucial issues.

- Endorse innovations, invest in new technologies, and do not be afraid to combine the non-combinable so as to stay one step ahead of your competitors.
- Study your market segment constantly and tirelessly.
- Employees are the main assets. Invest in training, trust, and respect.
- Design all-around offers.

Leader Cashmere: A Potential Hidden Champion

The cashmere industry is an ever-growing industry in Mongolia and new competitors are constantly emerging. This is the natural course of things, given that Mongolia produces a third of the global supply of cashmere. Goats are some of the fastest reproducing livestock, and this expands the supply of cashmere available for producers. In the 1980s, goats accounted for 19% of the total livestock in Mongolia, whereas now they account for over 60%. Despite this availability of raw materials and increasing competition, only a handful of cashmere clothing producers rise above the rest.

One of the main obstacles for cashmere producers is that despite having the best materials and production methods, they are essentially fashion and clothing companies. Without fashionable designs and market demand for those items, cashmere would be a wasted resource. In that sense, a few of these cashmere producers in Mongolia either employ fashion designers or work in cooperation with fashion houses. Leader Cashmere has an in-house designer combining the contemporary fashion trends with the natural properties of cashmere. The designs of the products offer both conservative and trendier options, allowing greater coverage of different customer segments. The clothes are also offered in both vibrant and neutral colors, tailored for different tastes. This gives the company an advantage as smaller cashmere producers offer fewer designs and color choices. Moreover, thanks to its three large processing factories, the company can produce semi-finished wool and cashmere for export. Most of these semi-finished textiles are exported to Japanese garment producers and are further processed into Japanese clothing. The company's ability to produce its own textile allows better pricing of both semi-finished and finished products.

Leader Cashmere exports its products to China and India as well, and is currently aiming to target more Western markets, such as Canada, Russia, Italy, USA, and UK. For that purpose, the company is in the process of introducing ISO and OHSAS standards in its production. The company aims to finalize this before the end of 2020. Once this has been completed, Leader Cashmere will have a vast amount of planning and market analyses to conduct before entering these Western markets. The head of the company is strongly convinced that its products can be a strong contender, and if the company successfully penetrates the Western markets, it will easily become Mongolia's leading cashmere exporter.

2.3 Bodi Insurance LLC

Overview
Address: Jigjidjav street 3, Sukhbaatar square, Ulaanbaatar 15160, Mongolia
Tel: 976 70004800
Email: info@bodi-insurance.com
Web: www.bodi-insurance.com

Company Information
Industry: Financial services
Year of establishment: 1995
Sales revenue in 2018: 11.7 million euros[5]
Sales revenue in 2012: 3.1 million euros[6]
Average number employees: 135
Brainr(s) behind the company: Chairman and founder Boldkhuyag L.

---

[5] As of 2018, 1€ = 3023.61MNT.
[6] As of 2012, 1€ = 1807MNT.

Nature of Market Leadership

The company is Mongolia's first private insurance company and market leader in the non-life insurance market. As a regional partner of AXA Healthcare and AXA Corporate solutions, Bodi Insurance provides international insurance products in the local market. The company provides most multinational companies that operate in Mongolia with commercial, healthcare, and travel insurances.

Nature of the Competitive Advantage

The nature of the company's competitive advantage rests on strong management with modern knowledge and experience, and international cooperation. Innovative use of information technology also makes a significant contribution. At the international arena, Bodi Insurance provides management of high-yield assets due to Mongolia's high-interest rate.

Core Lessons Learned on the Path to Business Success

As a financial services company, Bodi Insurance knew that it had to introduce and offer services that are consistent with international standards. Right at the start, the management realized that services cannot be differentiated like physical products and the company has been striving to provide great customer service. Some key lessons learned are:

- The first-mover advantage is extremely important in the insurance industry as insurance policies are annual purchases.
- Customer service and customer-oriented insurance policies are the most important competition factors.
- A proper allocation of assets can greatly determine profitability.
- The digitalization of the insurance sector is just as important as that of other industries.

Bodi Insurance: A Potential Hidden Champion

With 24 years of experience, Bodi Insurance is one of the longest-operating private insurance companies in Mongolia. The company started with only about a dozen of employees in 1995, and a limited number of insurance products, whereas now it employs over 135 people and offers more than 70 different insurance products.

The insurance sector in Mongolia is overshadowed by the banking sector and accounts for less than 10% of the financial services. However, the company has been continually striving to improve the insurance industry by spearheading the introduction of innovative services. A decade ago, insurance claims were settled after almost a month. The insurance industry itself requires a lot of paperwork and assessments in order to process an insurance claim. Bodi Insurance realized that the speed of settlement is a major factor in customer satisfaction and streamlined its internal operations toward the end of the 2000s. They promised clients that insurance payouts can be settled within 2 weeks and gradually implemented this into their operations. Soon after that, competing insurance companies naturally followed suit. Bodi Insurance continued to shorten the period required to settle an insurance claim. It eventually settled claims in 1 week, in 3 days, and in 8 h. The company's latest achievement is that it does the insurance payout at the scene of a car accident.

Other areas of progress include the company's cooperation with the French insurance company AXA, and the global health insurance product of that partnership, which caters to multinational organizations and middle-to-upper-class clients. Body Insurance also offers multiple levels of car insurances that cater to the needs of each client segment. This was possible due to the company's broad knowledge of the market and segmentation. The company is now migrating onto a digital platform for retail clients. The solutions include purchasing insurance policies online, submitting an insurance claim, sending photos from an accident scene through a mobile app, and immediate insurance payout through a connected account. The company is currently testing drones in video and photo capturing of car accidents, instead of sending an insurance appraiser to the scene.

From its experience in the insurance industry in the past two decades, the company has established working relationships with other international insurance and reinsurance companies around the world. This has enabled Bodi Insurance to undertake insurance policies for large businesses in Mongolia, such as mining companies and airlines, through proper allocation of risk. The company also works with multiple insurance brokers, both domestic and international. Unlike the laws of some other countries, those of Mongolia do not require individuals and businesses to acquire insurance through a broker. Therefore, Bodi Insurance is working to increase their reach to clients through direct contacts and effective channel management. The company's medium-term goal is to acquire over 30% of the Mongolian insurance market, and the operations indicate that this is a very reachable goal.

2.4 *Tod Oims LLC*

Overview
Address: Rashaan 4-23, 13th khoroo, Sukhbaatar square, Mongolia
Tel: 976 96090888
Email: todsocks@gmail.com
Web: www.todsocks.mn

Company Information

Industry: Manufacture of knitted and crocheted hosiery
Year of establishment: 2011
Sales revenue in 2017: 5,205,000 euros[7]
Sales revenue in 2013: About 21,000 euros[8]
Average number employees: 90
Brain(s) behind the company: CEO B. Bayarjargal

Nature of Market Leadership

Tod Oims produces a variety of different types of socks made from cotton, yak wool, camel wool, and cashmere. The company caters to multiple segments, offering products for both men and women, sports socks, and winter socks. Tod Oims covers 25% of the domestic market and has export businesses as well. Using South Korean technology and raw materials from South Korea allows easy access to the South Korean market.

Nature of the Competitive Advantage

The first success was the introducing of the Quality Cotton Socks brand in Mongolia. This was a great achievement as most socks are imported. The company's competitive advantages are built on:

- Control—the raw material and product quality is controlled at every stage of the production process.
- Quality—today the demand for quality products is growing.
- Domestic brand entices customers to prefer locally made products instead of imported ones.

Core Lessons Learned on the Path to Business Success

- Establishing and maintaining close relations with customers is essential.
- Building a strong network of distributors is crucial for entering global markets more quickly and economically.
- Importing industrial raw materials creates price risks and increases the cost of production. The way forward is to focus on the Quality Cotton Socks brand and reduce production costs.

---

[7]As of 2017, 1€ = 2882.39.
[8]As of 2013, 1€ = 1659.3.

Tod Oims: A Potential Hidden Champion

While most clothing manufacturers create fashion apparel, few businesses are producing accessories such as socks. Tod Oims has found this gap in the market and decided to establish a sock factory in 2011. Since then, the company has captured about 25% of the hosiery market. It was a very opportune time for the company as most hosiery was imported and local producers did not have the facilities to produce quality socks. Especially in winter, when temperatures can reach −40 °C, there is a high demand for warm winter socks in Mongolia. Thus, the founders of the company were at the right place at the right time. But it was not luck that led the company to where it is today. Quality raw materials, an excellent production process, and the brains of the directors, all contributed to its success.

Establishing a domestic processing plant for raw materials has created a comparative advantage in reducing production costs. As a result, quality products could be sold at very competitive prices, both domestically and abroad. In the past 6 years, the company's revenues have risen 500 times. The company has business partners in South Korea, supplying them with raw materials for their sport socks line. Through this partnership, Tod Oims established a strong presence there. In addition, the company's production processes are deemed to be fully compliant with European standards, which gives them an edge over other producers. Therefore, it is fully possible for Tod Oims to enter the European market in the next few years.

3 Conclusions

Mongolia accounts for a small percentage of the global economy. However, it is not the absolute economic figures that define a country. What matters most is whether the country is growing in real value and whether the local companies are improving the lives of the country's citizens. After all, that is what a business should do: provide value to its customers. Mongolia is largely an importer country and that poses a great threat to the economy. Without factories producing essential items, all of the earned foreign currency is leaving the country. This can significantly affect currency rates. Fortunately, the mining industry provides the bulk of currency inflows. But a country should not depend on a single industry.

It is a good sign, however, to see that there are multiple businesses and value creators rising in almost every industry. Small as they are, they are undoubtedly there. As can be seen from the study of the potential hidden champions of Mongolia in this chapter, there are real people and real businesses that are aiming to provide the best quality products and services to their customers without relying on imports. However, as the largest producer of goods is Mongolia's neighbor, most businesses will have difficulties competing on price. This gives incentives to businesses to produce cheaper higher-quality goods. This would be beneficial for both producers and customers because over the past decade, Mongolian consumers have shown an increasing preference for domestic products.

One of the greatest obstacles to growth for these businesses is the market size of Mongolia. Even if a business has a sizeable market share, if the size of the whole pie is relatively small then the business's real reach is also small. This is why it is important for local companies to t export their products. That is also good for the growth of the company and the national economy. Unlike Germany however, Mongolia is not seen as a country of production and export. While Germany has its *Mittelstand*, where highly-specialized products are manufactured by small companies that are mostly family-owned and have been operating for generations, Mongolia has only recently begun to industrialize. Mongolian companies are not well known globally as quality producers. However, local companies are very optimistic. Each year there is an increasing number of international partnerships with Mongolian companies. This suggests that Mongolia is establishing its presence abroad. And since China relies on quantity, it is important for Mongolian producers to understand the quality-over-quantity issue and gain this qualitative advantage over China in the region.

Reference

World Bank (2019) Mongolia | Data, World Bank Group. https://data.worldbank.org/country/mongolia

Hidden Champions of Montenegro

Milorad Jovović, Bojana Femić-Radosavović, and Nikola Mišnić

Overview
Official name: Montenegro
Type of government: Parliamentary democracy
Population in 2017: 622,387
Land area: 13,812 km^2

History

1878	Montenegro is recognized as an independent and sovereign state at the Congress of Berlin.
1910	Montenegro becomes a kingdom during the rule of King Nikola Petrović I.
1918	Shortly after the end of World War I, Montenegro becomes part of the newly formed Kingdom of Serbs, Croats, and Slovenes, a parliamentary monarchy whose capital was Belgrade, Serbia.
1945	After the great human losses and economic devastation of World War II, Montenegro becomes one of the six constituent republics of the Socialist Federative Republic of Yugoslavia ruled by the communist party.
1980	The death of post-war Yugoslavia leader Tito marks the starting point of Yugoslavia's slow disintegration, culminating in a war and its dissolution during the 1990s.
1992	After Slovenia's, Croatia's, Macedonia's, and Bosnia and Herzegovina's declarations of independence, the Federal Republic of Yugoslavia is formed, consisting of Serbia and Montenegro.
1999	

M. Jovović (✉) · N. Mišnić
Faculty of Economics Podgorica, University of Montenegro, Podgorica, Montenegro

B. Femić-Radosavović
United Minds Academy CEO, Podgorica, Montenegro

	Still being part of FR Yugoslavia, Montenegro officially introduces a dual currency system, consisting of the German mark and the dinar. After 1999, Montenegro starts introducing its own laws on main political and economic issues (e.g., the law on taxes and customs), different from those of Serbia. This paves the way to independence.
2001–2002	The German mark becomes the only legal tender in Montenegro from 2001 to 2002 when Euro replaces the German mark. The adoption of the German mark and the euro bring greater stability, predictability, and lower inflation (Fabris 2015).
2003	The Federal Republic of Yugoslavia disintegrates and a new state is established under the name of State Union of Serbia and Montenegro.
2006	An independence referendum is held in Montenegro. After the clear victory of the people voting in favor, Montenegro officially declares its independence.
2007	Montenegro signs the Stabilization and Association Agreement with the European Union (EU).
2011	After fulfilling the required conditions, Montenegro becomes a candidate country for EU membership.
2016	Montenegro becomes a member of NATO. This offers a good prospect of becoming a member state of the EU in the near future.

1 Introduction: Context and History

Montenegro has a small open economy characterized by a small domestic market with significant import dependence, which results in a negative trade balance of 1859.6 million euros (Central Bank of Montenegro—CBCG 2018). This is somewhat mitigated by the positive balance in the service sector: 836.4 million euros (CBCG 2018). The 2017 current account deficit amounted to 799.3 million euros (CBCG 2018).

Montenegro is a predominantly mountainous country, but flat in a significant part of the central region, with a total coastline length of 293 km. Montenegro is divided into three regions: northern, central, and southern. In the last two decades, the northern part of Montenegro has experienced economic stagnation and depopulation, while the central and southern parts have been growing at a significant pace.

The current social, political, and economic tendencies are shaped by the country's turbulent history. Before World War II, Montenegro had suffered a lot from political and social instability as a consequence of the country's relatively small territory and strategically important location. The period after World War II was a period of stability and economic development, interrupted by the disintegration of Yugoslavia in the 1990s. By the beginning of the twenty-first century, another period of relatively general stability occurred, which enabled the acceleration of economic growth in Montenegro, especially after it gained independence in 2006. The economic growth was partially slowed down by the world economic crisis of 2008. Since 2006, Montenegro's annual GDP has almost doubled, from 2170 million euros to 4299 million in 2018, or 6908 euros per capita (Monstat 2019).

Exhibit 1 Core economic indicators for Montenegro

	2011	2012	2013	2014	2015	2016	2017	2018
GDP per capita (current US$)	7318.74	6586.72	7186.43	7378.35	6514.27	7028.94	7784.07	8760.69
GDP per capita growth (annual %)	3.12	−2.81	3.45	1.68	3.33	2.93	4.70	4.86
Long-term unemployment (% of total unemployment)	n/a	n/a	n/a	n/a	n/a	n/a	n/a	n/a
Foreign direct investment, net inflows (% of GDP)	12.26	15.13	10.00	10.83	17.27	5.18	11.57	8.91
GDP (current US$, mio)	4538.20	4087.73	4464.26	4587.93	4052.91	4374.13	4844.59	5452.17
Exports of goods and services (current US$, mio)	1921.88	1785.21	1845.63	1841.76	1707.01	1769.81	1988.96	2356.26
Exports of goods and services (% of GDP)	42.35	43.67	41.34	40.14	42.12	40.46	41.06	43.22
Merchandise exports (current US$, mio)	628.00	469.00	498.00	438.00	352.00	361.00	421.00	472.00
Merchandise exports to high-income economies (% of total merchandise exports)	64.11	53.18	43.05	36.67	38.60	41.42	44.62	n/a
Merchandise exports to low- and middle-income economies in Europe & Central Asia (% of total merchandise exports)	33.38	44.97	53.83	59.66	50.56	46.33	49.04	n/a
Ores and metals exports (% of merchandise exports)	52.92	44.35	31.15	32.01	31.37	31.90	37.75	31.21
Agricultural raw materials exports (% of merchandise exports)	5.68	6.47	6.42	8.25	10.14	9.81	8.02	7.30
Food exports (% of merchandise exports)	9.58	15.55	15.08	27.43	16.97	15.75	12.88	11.78
Fuel exports (% of merchandise exports)	14.98	13.90	29.25	14.56	14.82	16.11	12.38	20.81
Manufactures exports (% of merchandise exports)	16.30	19.65	17.89	17.07	25.30	25.92	28.69	28.76
High-technology exports (% of manufactured exports)	4.30	9.50	5.44	10.28	7.27	3.03	2.54	n/a

Source: World Bank, September 2019

The structure of the country's economy has changed dramatically since the socialist period. After World War II, Yugoslavia's economic growth was based primarily on industry and the country's economy was centrally planned and organized, rather than being liberal and free-market oriented. Nowadays, many factories and production facilities from that period are closed and bankrupt as a consequence of a difficult transition period toward an open market economy and those companies' inability to face the open market without state support. The current Montenegrin economy is largely dependent on tourism, the small and medium-sized enterprise (SME) sector, energy production, the financial sector, and trade. With the support of investments in infrastructure, these sectors, have contributed to GDP growth since 2006.

Tourism remains the strongest driver of the Montenegrin economy, accounting for 988.2 million euros, or 23.7% of the national GDP in 2017 (World Tourism & Travel Council—WTTC 2018). Since Montenegro gained independence in 2006, the total number of tourists has more than doubled, reaching over two million in 2018 (Monstat 2019). We hope that several important investment projects—new resorts, hotels, and significant infrastructural projects in the southern and northern parts of Montenegro—will reshape tourism in Montenegro, increasing the number of first-time visitors, extending the tourism season, and reducing seasonal inequality. It is expected that in 2028, the travel and tourism industries will contribute 1582 million euros or 27.9% of the national GDP in Montenegro (WTTC 2018).

Besides tourism, SMEs are very important for the economic development of Montenegro. Over 99% of the companies in Montenegro are in the SME category, employing around 75% of the total workforce (Government of Montenegro 2018). Further steps are needed in order to encourage an entrepreneurial spirit and support the development of entrepreneurship in Montenegro. The primary fields that must be developed are finance (through credit lines, the establishment of a guarantee fund, which is of extreme importance for the internationalization of SMEs), entrepreneurial infrastructure (business centers, incubators, etc.); and entrepreneurial knowledge (organization of training and education, promotion of lifelong entrepreneurial learning, etc.).

Foreign direct investments (FDIs) are also a very important source of economic growth in Montenegro, reducing the deficit in the current account. With 474.3 million euros in 2017 (CBCG 2018) creating 11.2% of GDP, they are especially important for tourism (investments in marinas and luxury resorts) and energy (renewable sources and distribution), which are two very important sectors of the Montenegrin economy. A significant part of FDIs is achieved through the formation of new foreign-owned entities. Those companies are reshaping, improving, and additionally expanding the economy by bringing in international business standards, know-how, technology, and new business cultures to Montenegro.

Because of the small domestic market, successful companies from Montenegro have identified foreign markets as a source of growth and development. Thus, for most Montenegrin enterprises internationalization is a prerequisite for long-term success.

Taking into account the size of the Montenegrin market and the structure of its economy, it was not realistic to expect that there would be a large number of companies in Montenegro that have achieved a leading position in the international market. As a consequence, our initial list of companies worth interviewing in search of hidden champions consisted of six enterprises that have been focused on foreign markets. At the end of our field research, three companies were identified as meeting the hidden champion criteria (Simon 2009). Each of them occupies the number-one position in their regional market measured by market share. Since one of them might be regarded as part of a foreign entity, that company was excluded from the list. In the end, just two out of six initially interviewed companies met all criteria. We are sure that all of them have had an important role in helping Montenegro improve its competitiveness index in 2018 in comparison to 2008 (World Economic Forum—WEF 2018). It is important to note that almost all of them might be regarded as young companies. Five out of six were founded after Montenegro declared its independence in 2006.

We strongly believe that the two companies that we present here are true Montenegrin hidden champions. One—Marina Porto Montenegro, which is part of the Adriatic Marinas Ltd.—is in the tourism sector. The other one—Domen—is in the information and communication technologies sector.

Marina Porto Montenegro is a luxury marina for yachts, superyachts, and megayachts, located in Tivat, in the Bay of Kotor, with a capacity of 450 berths. In order to provide a premium service to Marina's clients, a luxurious settlement was built around the Marina, including deluxe residential facilities, hotels, restaurants, and more, providing services that satisfy the needs of a very demanding high-income target group, whose price sensitivity is relatively low. Today, Marina Porto Montenegro is the market leader in the Adriatic Sea in its market segment of superyachts and megayachts.

Domen Ltd. is a joint venture founded in 2008 by Afilias Ltd., GoDaddy.com (foreign partners), and ME-net (a domestic partner), that does business as a ".me" registry. After a formal public request for proposals was issued by the government of Montenegro to find a registration agent who could provide a world-class registry platform, run operations for an international registry, and deliver marketing expertise to make .me a globally successful CCLTD, the contract was awarded to Domen. Now, this company is a market leader in the region in terms of numbers of registered CCTLDs and is third in Europe in terms of numbers of CCLTDs registered outside one's home country.

Both companies were founded after the Montenegrin declaration of independence in 2006. In a relatively short time, they have achieved a leading position in competition with companies from other countries in the region. For obtaining a leading position in the market, identifying a business idea with high market potential based on a full understanding of the needs of potential customers in a timely manner was of extreme importance. The clear visions of the founders, operationalized through well-chosen and implemented strategies, and based on a differential focus, led these companies to success. They demonstrate that, in a fast-changing environment, the readiness of companies to adapt and their adaptation speed are crucial for business success. The companies' employees also had a special role in this process. Aware of their employees' importance, these companies constantly invest in the development of skills of managers and other employees.

2 Case Study 1

2.1 Marina Porto Montenegro (Part of Adriatic Marinas Ltd)

Overview
Address: Obala bb, 85320 Tivat, Montenegro
Telephone: +38232660700
Fax: +38232674656
Email: marinaoffice@portomontenegro.com
Web: www.portomontenegro.com

Company Information
Industry: Amusement and recreation activities (yacht homeport with berths)
Year of establishment: 2006
Sales revenue in 2017: 9.6 million euros
Sale revenue in 2012: 3.4 million euros
Number of employees in 2017: 351 in Adriatic Marinas Ltd
Brain(s) behind the company: Founder and visionary Mr. Peter Munk (1927–2018)

Nature of Market Leadership

Marina Porto Montenegro (part of Adriatic Marinas Ltd) occupies the number-one position in the Adriatic Sea in the market segment of super-yacht and mega-yacht accommodation measured by market share. Porto Montenegro, a homeport for the largest berths of up to 250 m, is the only marina with this kind of facility in the Adriatic Sea.

Nature of the Competitive Advantage

The competitive advantage of Marina Porto Montenegro is its well selected and consistently implemented focus strategy (Porter 1998), focusing on a particular buyer group, and serving them very well. Consequently, each functional policy is developed with this focus in mind. The founders focused on a significant, yet underserved market segment of super-yacht and mega-yacht owners who are looking for a homeport for their yachts in the Adriatic Sea. Marina Porto Montenegro identified this segment as a great opportunity and made a clear choice to focus on the needs of super-yacht and mega-yacht owners already in the process of project design and marina planning. By doing so, Adriatic Marinas built a new marina that is completely adapted and equipped to serve its narrow strategic target more effectively and efficiently than their competitors do.

This good competitive strategy is additionally supported by the fact that, according to the Montenegrin legal framework, Marina's clients' yachts may remain in the waters of Montenegro without time constraint or import taxes. That gives Marina a significant competitive advantage in comparison to marinas in EU countries, Montenegro's key competitors.

Core Lessons Learned on the Path to Success

The company's first years of experience highlights the importance of the following factors in their path to success:

- A clear vision and strategy that led the company to success.
- Carefully selecting an underserved target market.
- Adapting offers to the demands of the selected target market.
- Financial strength of the founders and investors due to the high investments that marina construction and the accompanying real estate business necessitate.
- A leader with a strong personality, intuition, vision, passion for the project, great international recognition, positive reputation, and trust in the business world.
- Good cooperation with the government and public authorities, and in particular with the local community.
- Continuity in leadership.
- Investing in human resources and employee satisfaction as these are prerequisites to the premium service that the clients of Porto Montenegro Marina expect.

Management and Leadership Development Needs

When Marina Porto Montenegro started doing business in Montenegro, it faced a problem: insufficient management and leadership skills and a lack of expertise across most employees. This was obviously a consequence of an outdated educational system. At that time, it was almost impossible to find companies in Montenegro that provided education services for managers, leaders, and other employees. Therefore, the company has decided to put in place an in-house training program in general skills, such as project management, time management, leadership effectiveness, and more. The company also identified a need for additional training for employees who are in direct contact with customers. For those employees, specific customer relationship management trainings have been provided. Additionally, for certain employees from the legal and accounting department, the company covered the costs of certified trainings and courses organized by other institutions.

A significant gap still exists between the educational system and the real demands of the market in terms of employees' skills. Although the official statistics are showing significant numbers of unemployed people, the experience of Porto Montenegro management has been that it is not easy to find well-qualified and skillful workers. This human resource management problem has been identified not only in higher level positions, but also at lower levels, such as carpenters, builders, and painters. Porto Montenegro has realized that blue-collar jobs, which have been neglected for a long time, also warrant attention. This phenomenon seems to be very pronounced in Montenegro. As a consequence, competition, which usually revolves around customers, is shifting more and more towards human resources, complicating management's job. As a result, investing in human resources and employee satisfaction are the prerequisites of the premium service that the clients of Porto Montenegro Marina expect.

Financing and Regulatory Environment Development Needs

The financial sector in Montenegro represents a challenge for the company because the market is relatively small, meaning that local banks are limited in their lending capacity. This could be solved if banks had a better understanding of this issue and were willing to cooperate and supply syndicated loans. As this is not a common practice of Montenegrin banks, the company tried to find a solution by approaching foreign banks. However, banks that are not represented in Montenegro, are rarely motivated to lend to companies that do business in the country, which is financially unfavorable for Porto Montenegro Marina.

Porto Montenegro: From an Abandoned Military Boatyard to a Unique and Exquisite High-Class Marina

The Porto Montenegro project has started with the clear idea and vision of Canadian entrepreneur Peter Munk who made use of the exquisite natural environment and central Mediterranean location in the Bay of Kotor, one of the most beautiful bays of the Adriatic Sea. He purchased the former Yugoslav military boatyard in Tivat, in the Bay of Kotor, in 2006. He built a unique marina with state-of-the-art facilities that could accommodate superyachts and megayachts, with a length of up to 250 m. With backing from some of the world's most respected business figures, such as Bernard Arnault of LVMH and Lord Jacob Rothschild, the largest private-sector investment in Montenegro, the ex-military base was transformed into a beautiful marina. Today, Marina Porto Montenegro is a super attractive and financially advantageous destination and the only marina in the Adriatic Sea with berths that can accommodate superyachts and megayachts while satisfying the needs of this kind of high-income market segment. Since 2016, Porto Montenegro has been owned by the Investment Corporation of Dubai, which continues developing this project. Right now, the company is investing in facilities for maintenance, repair, and ship-building in Bijela (a former state-owned shipyard close to Tivat).

In the case of Marina Porto Montenegro, the founder, innovator, and leader Mr. Peter Munk's crucial role can clearly be seen. His intuition, vision, strong personality, passion for the project, great international recognition, positive reputation, and trust in the business world, attracted not only new investors, but also many of Marina's clients. The financial strength and reputation of the company and its founders and investors were important prerequisites for the business's success, especially because of the huge investments that marina construction and the accompanying real estate business require.

A key factor of Marina Porto Montenegro business's success is the exceptionally competitive strategy, which was based on a differential focus on a clearly defined underserved market segment. Starting the marina project almost as a greenfield investment allowed the company to adapt its market offer—facilities and services—perfectly to the needs of the selected target market. The fact that the company both designed and constructed the Marina enabled the introduction of state-of-the-art technology compatible with the market segment needs and the characteristics of contemporary superyachts and megayachts.

It is clear that leadership plays a crucial role and represents an important basis for the market success of Porto Montenegro. For that reason, it has been of extreme importance to maintain continuity and consistency in leadership, even after changes in company ownership. New investments in Porto Montenegro—new hotels and buildings—and connected businesses—a shipyard—which occurred after the change in ownership structure, are proof that Porto Montenegro Project has sustained the same pace in development.

Furthermore, relationships of mutual trust and respect have been built between owners, managers, and employees, leading to the development of a positive organizational culture. Porto Montenegro has developed a specific task-based and customer-oriented organizational culture, which is different from that of most other companies in Montenegro. In this company, they regard that culture as a very important element of their success. Investments in the development of employee knowledge, skills, and growth, resulted in high levels of employee satisfaction and enthusiasm.

Besides already mentioned competitive advantages, Marina Porto Montenegro has a good understanding and cooperation with the government, public authorities, and in particular with the local community. For the company and the local and public authorities, the benefits are mutual: increased public revenues, increased volume of exports, growth in the employment rate, development of supporting companies and suppliers, development of entrepreneurship, and growth of the real estate prices in the wider area of the Municipality of Tivat.

Porto Montenegro opened its doors in 2009. The changes that have occurred between 2008 and 2018 clearly show the impact that Porto Montenegro has had on the development of tourism in the Municipality of Tivat and the Bay of Kotor. We found that the number of foreign tourist arrivals in Montenegro grew by 101.4% during that period (Monstat 2019). In the same period, the number of foreign tourist arrivals in the Municipality of Tivat grew by 278.1% (Monstat 2019). This difference suggests that the number of tourist arrivals in Tivat grew 2.74 times faster than general tourism in Montenegro as a whole. Additionally, after the opening of Porto Montenegro, two more modern internationally competitive marinas—Porto Novi and Luštica Bay—were open recently in the Bay of Kotor, with more than 400 berths in total. These marinas will further increase the quality of tourist offers and the international positioning of Montenegro as an important yachting tourism destination. Investments in new marinas were clearly spurred by the example that Marina Porto Montenegro had set.

3 Case Study 2

3.1 Domen Ltd.

Overview
Address: Vojvode Maša Đurovića, Lamela 3/1, Podgorica, Montenegro
Tel: +382 77 300 070
Fax: +382 77 300 079
Email: info@domain.me
Web: www.domain.me

Company Information
Industry: Data processing, hosting and related activities (Internet domain registration)
Year of establishment: 2008
Sales revenue in 2017: 6.5 million euros
Sale revenue in 2012: 5.4 million euros
Number of employees in 2017: Five
Brain(s) behind the company: CEO Predrag Lešić

Nature of Market Leadership

With is 918,097 registered CCTLDs, Domen Ltd. is the market leader in the region, which consists of ex-Yugoslav countries plus Albania, Bulgaria, and Greece. Domen is also highly ranked in Europe, placing third, behind only Germany's .de and the United Kingdom's .uk, in terms of numbers of CCTLDs registered outside their home country.

Nature of the Competitive Advantage

The main competitive advantages of Domen are:

- The attractiveness of the .me domain because of multiple meanings and limitless wording possibilities in multiple languages, allowing personalization (e.g., text.me, travel.me, pay.me, about.me, etc.).
- A competitive strategy based on differentiation through marketing and promoting domains directly to customers.
- The creation of a safe environment for customers who are developing their own businesses in the digital world, using domains and platforms provided by Domen. Since new digital customers need a secure and trusted registry for their domains, the company has positioned itself as a reliable and trusted partner, and has successfully created strong relationships with customers.

Core Lessons Learned on the Path to Success

Probably the most important lesson that the company learned on the path to success is that, in the digital era, it is of extreme importance to identify and operationalize business ideas with a high market potential in a timely manner. This process must also be based on a deep understanding of the needs, behavior, and expectations of potential customers. Domen believes that this is also true of companies that are not directly involved in the ICT sector.

For the company, differentiation is the foundation of business success. Since the need for personalization is one of the most important characteristics of a new digital customer, opening the space for differentiation through personalization lies at the core of Domen's business strategy.

Domen has developed a positive organizational culture that emphasizes employee strengths, individual vitality, and growth. The organizational culture is task oriented and is accompanied by a flat organizational structure. As a consequence, the employees show a high level of satisfaction and enthusiasm, which are important success factors.

Management and Leadership Development Needs

Knowing that the nature of the market and the environment are changing very fast, Domen realized that it is very important to have up-to date-skills. Therefore, it provides a lot of training opportunities for employees. The company asserts that it is necessary constantly to invest in the development of managerial and employee skills. Domen relies on a lot of online courses to stay up-to date because the necessary trainings are very hard to acquire locally.

The company strongly believes that Montenegro's educational system should put an emphasis on preparing students for work in the digital economy era, with an emphasis on programming.

University students as well as employees in Montenegro need more leadership courses dealing with developing, inspiring, guiding employees and teams, and effectively influencing stakeholders across an organization.

Financing and Regulatory Environment Development Needs

In terms of the regulatory environment, very soon the Montenegrin government will be obliged to implement some new EU regulations. The one that may have an impact on Domen is the General Data Protection Regulation on data protection and privacy for all individuals.

Domen: Limitless Opportunities Behind the Limitless Wording Possibilities

Understanding that "me" has multiple meanings and has mass appeal as a word in numerous languages, the government of Montenegro embarked on generalizing the .me name space so that anyone could obtain a .me. As a result, in November of 2007, a formal public request for proposals was issued to find a registration agent who could provide a world-class registry platform, run operations for an international registry, and deliver marketing expertise to make .me a successful CCTLD worldwide. The contract was eventually awarded to Domen. Due to its deep inherent meaning in multiple languages (English, French, Spanish, Dutch, Italian, Portuguese, Bulgarian, and languages spoken in former Yugoslavia) and limitless wording possibilities, just 3 days after its official launch, .me recorded its 100,000th registration. Me has continued its success throughout the years with a continuous and stable rise in registrations and more and more big brands connecting to .me and its development program. Despite being a CCTLD, .me is very similar to generic TLDs in terms of policies, domain cycle, and search engine optimization benefits. Most importantly, according to the company's CMO, Google treats it like any other generic TLD.

Since the company sees differentiation as the foundation of business success, Domen started the business with a huge awareness-raising campaign. The company wanted to be seen and recognized by its customers as different. It is trying to satisfy the need for personalization, which is one of the most important characteristics of a new digital customer. An understanding of customer needs and opening of space for both company and individual personalization on the Internet lies at the core of Domen's business strategy.

Domen also differentiates itself by diverging from the usual marketing approach that the competition was using and by starting to market and promote domains directly to customers. That approach was the innovation that gave the company a special strength and a competitive advantage. Due to a lack of internationally competitive local marketing agencies, the company has mostly outsourced and acquired these services outside of Montenegro. However, it would be much easier for Domen to outsource its marketing to the domestic market, which highlights a potential business opportunity for the marketing industry in Montenegro.

The company has also created a safe environment for its customers who are developing their own business in the digital world on platforms provided by Domen Ltd. New digital customers need a secure and trusted registry for their domains, and Domen has positioned itself as a reliable and trusted partner, successfully creating strong relationships with customers.

Like many successful companies, Domen believes that the most important factor behind its success is the motivated employees. This company has developed a positive organizational culture that emphasizes employee strengths, individual vitality, and growth. The organizational culture is task oriented and accompanied by a flat organizational structure. As a consequence, the employees are showing high levels of satisfaction and enthusiasm. This creates a great atmosphere in the company and reflects the leadership continuity.

Another important factor is that the company leaders have a great vision, a lot of knowledge of the market and marketing, and a good intuition. They have used appropriate tools for targeting customers, creating brand awareness and image, and maintaining strong relations with customers and partners.

4 Conclusions and Recommendations

The clear visions of the founders of Montenegrin hidden champions were the starting points of the companies' successes. Those visions were the basis for well-chosen and consistently implemented strategies and were developed on a good understanding of their target market customers. The Montenegrin hidden champions' leaders, characterized by strong personality, intuition and vision, as well as passion for the project, led the companies toward the leading market position that they hold in the region. These companies' histories emphasize leadership as a crucial element for market success.

They also see differentiation as the foundation of business success. Because of that, differentiating themselves from their competitors is at the core of the strategies that they have applied.

In both companies, managers understand and implement elements of personalization and an individual approach in the service that they provide, knowing that this personalization is an almost mandatory customer request nowadays. This necessity is highlighted by the fact that all the basic instruments utilized for the marketing mix were well suited to the needs of every single customer. Their new and different approach to customers and promotion as well as their consistent adaptation of their services to meet their customers' demands were especially poignant.

They both regard organizational culture as a very important element of their success. Their task and customer-oriented organizational culture that emphasizes employee strengths and growth resulted in high levels of employee satisfaction and enthusiasm. Both Marina Porto Montenegro and Domen perceive investing in human resources and employee satisfaction as prerequisites to the service that clients expect. This understanding is very important since they think that the competition, which usually revolves around customers, is shifting outward to the area of human resources. This problem was initially typical of higher level positions only, but now exists at lower-level positions as well.

The companies also have a good understanding of the local political and legal frameworks and their easy cooperation with the government and public authorities strengthens their market position. The benefits for companies and public and political authorities are mutual due to the increase in public revenues, volume of exports, decrease in import dependence, growth in the employment rate, development of supporting companies and suppliers, development of entrepreneurship, and promotion of Montenegro. The benefits have led both Marina Porto Montenegro and Domen to be recognized as socially responsible companies. Their corporate social responsibility programs are mainly implemented in the sphere of education, contributing to the development of a new digital generation of customer-oriented employees.

Although they regard the business environment in Montenegro as favorable in general, the financial sector in Montenegro represents a challenge because local banks are limited in their lending capacity, which forces companies to work with foreign banks in case they need to make bigger investments.

Because of the differences in the sectors that they belong to (tourism vs. ICT), these companies have a different understanding of the key business challenges that they face and expect. As Montenegro is one of the fastest-growing tourist destinations and tourism is one of the most important industries in Montenegro, we find it very important to mention some challenges that companies like Marina Porto Montenegro face. They pointed out that infrastructure problems, especially roads and airports, as well as long lines at border crossings, have a negative impact on the tourism industry in Montenegro.

In the beginning, both companies faced the same challenge, related to the fact that Montenegro was insufficiently recognized in the international market. We are sure that Marina Porto Montenegro and Domen have both helped to elevate the image of Montenegro internationally.

Moreover, both companies find that formal education should be more focused on developing the skills needed for jobs that are essential today, especially when it comes to the service industry and ICT: programming and other skills that are important in the era of the digital economy. Thus, we found that a stronger link should exist between educational institutions and the labor market.

Montenegro's hidden champions are aware of the abovementioned shortcomings of the educational system and they dedicate a lot of effort to the development of their human resources. The development of human resources is not only limited to employees, but also applies to managers. Aside from that, they continuously invest in different educational programs in their local communities through various CSR activities.

We identified their pioneer role in promoting the concept of education as a lifelong process as particularly important. It is to be expected that this kind of approach, deeply embedded in their organizational cultures, will motivate other companies in Montenegro to follow in their footsteps.

This study of the hidden champions of Montenegro has resulted in recommendations for key stakeholders, based on key conclusions summarized below.

Based on interviews with the top management of the hidden champions, it is possible to provide several very important recommendations to the government. Most of these recommendations relate to the need to solve infrastructure problems that have direct consequences for the quality of Montenegro's business offers, primarily in tourism. In that sense, it is suggested that the government continue its investments in road infrastructure, airports, and especially border crossings, so as to do away with the bottlenecks that have a negative impact on tourist satisfaction. The hidden champion in the tourism sector also emphasized the intensification of investment in the electrical energy system, water supply, and waste and wastewater treatment systems, especially given the government's tendency of positioning Montenegro as an ecological state. In addition, it was recommended that the rate of the reinvested income tax be reduced, as this would certainly greatly stimulate investment, and bring benefits for all.

The hidden champion companies of Montenegro also mentioned that the educational system does not reflect the needs of companies. Education should be aimed more toward developing skills necessary for professions that are in high demand in the labor market, especially in the service industries. There should be a stronger connection between educational institutions and the labor market. Educational systems should put an emphasis on preparing students for work in the era of the digital and service economy. This particularly refers to the development of usable knowledge and skills in the field of management, leadership, and establishing quality relationships with customers. Although certain business schools have made some progress in this area, the hidden champions estimate that it is not enough to meet the needs of successful companies, especially in terms of offering programs for improving the specific knowledge and skills of employees. A special role in this respect belongs to the government, which should pursue a modernization of the educational system at all levels, so that it meets the needs of the labor market. In this regard, it would be important to influence, through the education system, the development of an entrepreneurial spirit, as well as information, economic and financial literacy, and more strongly support the concept of lifelong learning.

The recommendation of these companies is that the government continue to promote Montenegro, aiming to increase recognition in the international market. Although in the post-independence period major advancements have been made in this respect, and the hidden champions have played an important role, these activities should be continued.

A key recommendation to banks concerns the problem of their limited credit potential, identified in this study as a significantly limiting factor in the banking system. It could be solved by increasing the degree of openness to cooperation with other banks by offering syndicated loans. Therefore, we believe that, whenever it is deemed necessary and mutually beneficial, banks should include elements of cooperation in their competitive struggle, combining competition and cooperation in the way suggested by Brandenburger and Nalebuff (1996) in their book *Co-opetition*.

Business schools should intensify their cooperation with companies, especially the most successful ones, because the benefits of such cooperation are multiple. Through cooperation, problems in companies would be easier to solve, business schools would improve their knowledge, experience, and programs, and graduates would be better prepared to face every day professional problems.

The lack of local consulting agencies in different fields (marketing, programming, human resource management, etc.) can pose an additional challenge for business schools to expand the range of their own consulting services. Some of them already use this market niche, but if we take into account the estimate that the demand for this type of service will only increase, a significant market space will continue to exist.

References

Brandenburger AM, Nalebuff B (1996) Co-opetition. HarperCollins Business, London
Central Bank of Montenegro (2018) Macroeconomic report I-XII 2017. www.cbcg.me/en/publications/regular-publications/cbcg-macroeconomic-report/annual-report. Accessed 1 Sept 2019
Department of Public Revenues Montenegro. Official web site. https://eprijava.tax.gov.me/TaxisPortal?app=FI. Accessed 1 Sept 2019
Domen Ltd. Official web-site (www.domain.me) Accessed 1 Sept 2019
Fabris N (2015) The history of money in Montenegro. J Centr Bank Theory Pract 4(1):5–18
Government of Montenegro (2018) Strategy of SME Development in Montenegro 2018–2022. file:///C:/Users/Korisnik/Desktop/22_87_26_07_2018.pdf. Accessed 1 Sept 2019
Monstat—Statistical office of Montenegro (2019) Dolasci i noćenja u kolektivnom smještaju 2018. http://www.monstat.org/userfiles/file/turizam/din2018/12/SAOPSTENJE%20decembar%202018.pdf. Accessed 1 Sept 2019
Porter ME (1998) Competitive strategy: techniques for analysing industries and competitors. The Free Press, New York

Porto Montenegro. Official web-site www.portomoontenegro.me. Accessed 1 Sept 2019
Schwab K (2018) Global *competitiveness* report. World Economic Forum. www.weforum.org/reports/the-global-competitveness-report-2018. Accessed 1 Sept 2019.
Simon H (2009) Hidden champions of twenty first century. Springer, Berlin
World Travel & Tourism Council (2018) Economic Impact 2018 Montenegro. www.wttc.org/economic-impact/country-analysis/country-reports/. Accessed 1 Sept 2019

Hidden Champions of Poland

Grażyna Leśniak-Łebkowska, Magdalena Popowska, Małgorzata Godlewska, and Mirosław Łukasiewicz

Overview

Official name: Republic of Poland (POL)
Type of government: Democratic, with a prime minister heading the government, and a president who is head of the state.
Population in 2017: 37.98 million
Land area: 312.7 thousand sq. km

History

1989   Collapse of the communist government in Poland and beginning of the social, political, and economic transformation from a centrally planned economy to a market economy
1999   Access to the North Atlantic Treaty Organization
2004   Access to the European Union

G. Leśniak-Łebkowska (✉) · M. Godlewska · M. Łukasiewicz
Warsaw School of Economics (SGH), Warszawa, Poland
e-mail: lebkowska@sgh.waw.pl

M. Popowska
Faculty of Management and Economics, Gdańsk University of Technology, Gdańsk, Poland

1 Introduction: Context and History

Since the fall of the communist government in 1989, Poland has come a long way in terms of its political, economic, and social transformation from a centrally planned economy to a market economy. According to the *Index of Economic Freedom* Poland has moved from the group of countries with limited economic freedom in 1993 (world rank 60) to the group of countries with average economic freedom in 2018 (see Gwartney et al. 1996; Miller et al. 2019). On May, 1, 2004, Poland joined the European Union and became a full member. As a result of Poland's accession to the European Union, the Polish government had to adapt Polish laws to those of the European Union.

Moreover, the quality and power of formal institutions determine the quality of entrepreneurship (Estrin and Mickiewicz 2010; Levie et al. 2014; Williams et al. 2017), whereas institutional support has a crucial influence on entrepreneurship (Baumol 1990; Williams et al. 2017; Godlewska and Morawska 2019). For that reason, Poland participates in active regulatory competition between its own legal system and the legal systems of other Central and Eastern European countries. The aim of this rivalry is to create an increasingly competitive regulatory environment that will allow Poland to strengthen the competitiveness of its business entities and attract economic entities from other countries to Poland. To achieve this, on 1 January 2017, in addition to the 19% basic rate of the corporate income tax (CIT), Poland introduced a reduced rate of 15% for small taxpayers. As of January, 1, 2019, the reduced rate of CIT for small taxpayer is 9% instead of 15%. Relatively small changes of the CIT rate in 2011–2018 may be associated with a very large tax reduction of the CIT rate that took place in 1995–2005, when Poland reduced the CIT rate from 40% to 19% (Polski Instytut Ekonomiczny (2020).

Furthermore, in 2011–2018, Poland used a number of tax incentives in accordance with the European Union law, in the form of various tax reliefs and exemptions, in order to increase its tax attractiveness. For example, the government provided CIT rate reductions from 25% to 50% depending on the region in which the business is located, and an R&D tax relief in 2018 by allowing certain expenses to be qualified as a tax-deductible cost by including them in the costs and by additional deduction of 100% of eligible costs from the tax base (EY 2018; Delloite 2019). It is also worth stressing that Poland is one of the friendliest states of the region for start-ups as embryonic forms of future businesses. Start-ups benefit from tax incentives for SMEs in the form of reduced social security contributions for new entrepreneurs, accelerated depreciation on innovative investments, and the exemption from the tax on the intellectual property when it is in the form of contribution in kind (Gałagus et al. 2018).

From the entrepreneurs' point of view, the predictability and the effectiveness of the national legal system is particularly important (Perry 2000: 1628–1631). Before making a new investment decision, entrepreneurs pay a lot of attention to the protection of property rights. As Demsetz (1967) noted, they are not interested in investing in countries where the fruits of their investments may be taken over by others. Poland guarantees the protection of property rights and inheritance rights in its constitution. However, in 2011–2018, according to the *International Property Rights Index*, Poland's position on the protection of property rights indicator, fell from 43rd place in the world in 2011 to 47th in 2018 (Jackson and De Soto Fellow 2011; Levy-Carciente and De Soto Fellow 2018).

From an entrepreneurs' point of view, the effectiveness of contract enforcement is also crucial. Among other factors, this depends, on the degree of respect for the rule of law in a given country. Effective contract enforcement improves the business climate, accelerates innovation, attracts foreign direct investment, and provides tax revenues (Esposito et al. 2014). According to the *Doing Business Report,* in terms of enforcing contracts, Poland improved its position from 77th in the world in 2011 to 53rd in 2018 (The World Bank 2010, 2019). Furthermore, according to Article 107, sections 2 and 3 of the Treaty of the functioning of the European Union and Commission Regulation (EU) No 651/2014 and Consolidated version (2012), in 2011–2018 Poland used horizontal, regional, and sectoral public aid directed at overcoming business barriers, stimulating the growth of competitiveness and investment attractiveness. In 2011–2017, Poland granted entrepreneurs 11,439,900 euros for employment (state aid of 5065.5 million euros), research and development including innovation (state aid of 2200.1 million euros), SME including risk capital (state aid of 128 million euros) and sectoral development (state aid of EUR 4045.3 million euros) (European Commission 2018). In 2011–2017, Poland used two aid instruments. The most popular one was granted for entrepreneurs (80.85%) with total state aid spending of 21,332,000 euros. The second most popular aid instrument were tax exemptions for entrepreneurs (17.57%) with total state aid spending of 4,636,600 euros.

The global economic situation in 2011–2018 was profoundly marked by the crisis provoked by the collapse of the Lehman Brothers investment bank in 2008. The devastating impact of the crisis varied across European countries, therefore it is important to emphasize that until 2012, the Polish economy suffered little from the effects of the global crisis. It was one of the fastest-growing economies worldwide before the crisis and the fastest-growing economy in post-crisis Europe (McKinsey & Co. 2015). This crisis resistance resulted from the skillful ongoing response of enterprises, households, and public authorities to the very negative changes in their international environment. All economic actors used their capabilities and resources in a way that in the long run supported domestic demand and economic growth. After 2012, the dynamics of economic development were falling, and Poland entered a phase of the economic slowdown. In the following years, Poland lost its position of economic growth leader among Central and Eastern European countries. Moreover, the pace of catching up with the more economically developed EU-15 countries fell. While in the first 6 years of EU membership (2004–2010) Poland progressed by 14 development gap points in relation to the EU-15 countries, in the next 7 years this development gap decreased only by 9% points. Poland's growth has been based primarily on dynamic exports, strong internal demand, productivity improvements, foreign direct investment, and the inflow of EU funds. Without the latter, the accumulated GDP during Poland's EU membership would have been 2% lower. (Rapacki and Próchniak 2018).

Accession to the European Union opened the way to foreign capital inflow. In 2004–2018, Poland reported a net inflow of 110,350 billion euros of direct investments. It was slightly more than the net inflow of EU funds. The inflow of foreign capital was accompanied by the inflow of modern technologies, and—equally important—the integration of Polish enterprises with foreign ones, including international corporations. This resulted in very fast growth of exports and imports. The Polish economy has become increasingly open, and today Poland is one of the world's leaders in the business services sector, with a total of 1236 Polish and foreign BPO, SSC, IT, and R&D service centers operating in Poland, employing a total of 279,000 people. Of the 831 companies with their own service centers, 10% (83 investors) were Fortune Global 500 companies in 2017. This is reflected in the strengthening of Poland's position in the Global Competitiveness Index, from 57th in 2011 to 37th in 2018 (ABSL 2018).[1]

Nowadays, modern industries are increasing their share of the Polish economy. They develop faster than traditional sectors. Manufacturing and trade, which together generated about 39% of value added in 2017, remain the two largest sectors. In 2010–2017, their value added increased at the fastest pace in information and communication, business services, finance and insurance activities, manufacturing and transportation, logistics, and storage. Because of its higher growth since 2010 (44.4%), the manufacturing industry is currently dominant over trade, which has grown by 15.6%. Manufacturing now accounts for 21%of the total value added.

As far as politics is concerned, the midpoint of the analyzed period (2015) was marked by parliamentary elections, which brought a substantial change in the subsequent political and economic strategic choices. The liberal political power was replaced by the right-wing conservative party, despite the good economic performance of the country in the years preceding the elections, when human development indices were documenting the extraordinarily encouraging social developments in Poland, such as increased life expectancy for both sexes, significantly lower infant mortality, a boom in educational attainment, and rise of happiness (Czapinski and Panek 2015; Eurostat 2016; Markowski and Kwiatkowska 2018).

Hitherto, the heaviest reforms carried out by the current government have been related to the education, legal, and social systems. The change of the education system at the universal level consisted of the liquidation of junior high schools, and thus a return to the educational situation before Poland's accession to the EU. At the higher education level, according to the government's declarations, the introduced changes were focusing on excellence in teaching and research activities, therefore pursuing a more elite education. In turn, legal adjustments were supposed to improve the quality of the judicial system. However, so far the relevant EU institutions have been questioning the legitimacy of some of them. This discussion on Poland's compliance with the EU legal regulations is still ongoing. A large share of society

---

[1]Association of Business Service Leaders (ABSL) in cooperation with EY, Randstad Polska and Randstad Sourceright.2018

took advantage of the reforms in the social system and the direct subsidies for families with children, supposed to improve fertility in the country. The declared goal was not achieved. However, in the short term this money, contributed to the improvement of the financial situation of many Polish families by reducing child poverty and promoting well-being and inclusiveness (OECD 2018). Unfortunately, it also contributed to price increases and, consequently, to the rise of inflation in the last 2 years.[2] Together with the recent lowering of the retirement age back to only 60 for women, this will heighten the risk of old-age poverty. The current government is also famous for being distrustful of the idea of opening borders to immigrants. Given the current demographic situation, this may cause even greater shortages in the labor market.

In consequence, Poland is facing many challenges. First of all, its economy is not particularly innovative. The export production in Poland is focused on medium and low technology products, while the share of high-technology goods does not exceed 10.6% of total exports (World Bank 2019). Poland, in contrast to Western countries, has no national champions, i.e., widely recognized brands. Poland is considered a supplier of cheap accessories and semi-finished products or is seen as a place where assembly facilities are located because of the relatively cheap and competent labor.

Additionally, Poland is in a very unfavorable demographic situation. This is a common problem for EU countries. However, Poland has one of the lowest fertility rates in the world, and at the same time, it has no budget reserves that could alleviate the raising costs of the retirement system. According to the studies conducted by the European Commission and the European Central Bank, the availability of qualified staff or winning and retaining customers are currently the main problems for the majority of Polish enterprises.

Moreover, the Polish economy remains heavily regulated. This increases the transaction costs for entrepreneurs and in the long run may inhibit their development ambitions, including their investment effort. Although at an aggregate level the size and structure of enterprises' investment are significantly closer to those of mature, richer economies than to those of emerging economies, Polish entrepreneurs are aware that their level of investment is insufficient and that they relatively rarely use the best equipment and machinery available in their industry. The percentage of companies using state-of-the-art solutions available in their sector is one of the lowest in the EU. Also, entrepreneurs are increasingly often encountering barriers to financing. Poland is one of the countries with the highest percentage of companies with unmet financing needs (EIB 2018).

Despite these challenges, referring to the latest international analysis by the International Monetary Fund, GDP in Poland will continue to grow in the next 5 years. This increase will fluctuate around 3% year, which is a slowdown in comparison with the last 2 years, when it was growing around 5% annually. According to experts, this will make Poland the world's 22nd largest economy in

---

[2]According to GUS, (Main Statistical Office of Poland) it was 2.0% in 2017, 1.6% in 2018 and 2.9% in July 2019.

2024. In nominal GDP, it will get close to the top 20. In this very optimistic scenario, Poland would enter the G20 as early as in 2029.

Polish hidden champions build their position using strong partnerships with suppliers or potential customers so as to get to know their needs better. They realize that they have a weaker competitive position compared to their Western competitors because of the underdeveloped business culture and the complexity of regulations, increasing the transaction cost and business risk. They learned how to use the internationalization paths not only for exporting their products and services but also for securing their access to scarce resources. They offer strongly innovative products, very often developed by their own R&D units in cooperation with other market stakeholders. They are looking for ways to strengthen their brands, also through new distribution channels, such as e-commerce and digital marketing.

The search for hidden champions in Poland started in 1999 with Marek Dietl's cooperation with Simon-Kucher & Partners and his activities within the Polish Capital Fund Jsc providing knowledge and financial support for small and medium-sized companies in Poland.[3] He identified 40 hidden champions but only 12 agreed to give an interview. In his main conclusions, the author pointed out the hidden champion's high productivity per employee, resulting from the high skills of the companies' teams and their strong leadership, as main similarities to Western peers. However, the Polish companies were lagging behind those in the West in profiting from the globalization opportunities and building a stronger presence in the international arena despite the relevant potential of their products and services. The limited scale had a negative impact on sales growth. The next investigation took place in 2011 when 41 hidden champions agreed to give interviews.

In 2011–2018, Poland underwent accelerated growth within the European Union framework, benefiting from the EU funds for restructuring, innovation, technology, and regional development. This had a strong impact on the investment climate and new opportunities for business companies. Even if a company was not a direct beneficiary of these funds, it could take advantage of the infrastructure development and openness of the economy for internationalization and globalization as well as of the relatively large size of the internal market and the growing demand. This period was an intensive learning of market economy rules as a new type of environment for doing business, corrected by state administrative, legal, social, and fiscal policies.

In the 2011 research on hidden champions, 41 companies were identified in Poland as meeting the criteria of Hermann Simon. Poland, with its liberal economic policy, created a favorable climate for entrepreneurship. Numerous unprecedented opportunities have been perceived and exploited mainly by small and medium-sized companies attempting to catch up with the European Union's level of development and profit from this unique situation. Larger Polish companies, previously state-

---

[3]H. Simon, M. Dietl, *Tajemniczy Mistrzowie XXI wieku. Strategie sukcesu nieznanych liderów na światowych rynkach*, Polish edition, Simon-Kucher@Partners, Difin 2009. M. Dietl is the author of the Chapter 12: *Hidden Champions in Poland*, pp. 409–431).

owned or cooperatives, were heavily restructuring, especially in view of the economic crisis in 2009.

The level of competition was low, but the capital needed for investments was insufficient. Therefore, the initial offerings were relatively low in capital intensity and not of the highest quality. Still, the companies managed to raise more capital and gain experience for further growth. They represented the whole variety of industries, both traditional and modern ones, such as furniture, software, transportation, equipment and components for heavy and light industries, food, medical devices, and hygiene products. Many of them delivered highly specialized components to large Polish and foreign companies.

As the information on the 41 hidden champions identified in Poland in 2011 was updated in 2018, it was found that some companies no longer existed. Some had grown and become visible in the public space. Thus, they were no longer hidden. Numerous companies had become part of larger international groups while sustaining operations in Poland. Another group no longer met all hidden champion criteria, but should still be considered potential hidden champions in view of the market conditions in Poland. These companies have the potential to become global or regional leaders in some industries. The 2011 hidden champions could be classified into six categories: foreign M&A (14), full champions (8), still hidden champions (5), restructuring (6), in bankruptcy (5), unknown status (3).

In the 2018 research, nine new hidden champion candidates were analyzed. Only seven met Simon's criteria. The major selection criteria were related to major global market trends and challenges. The criteria were as follows:

1. The highest pace of growth in a particular industry. On average, the annual pace of growth of the ICT sector was 17%cent (Central Statistical Office data). Being early entrants with innovative technologies, Cloud Technologies SA and Growbots established strong leadership positions as global companies. They entered the market at the early stage of the industry life cycle and were able to set up new trends in information acquisition, processing, and sales. Their high pace of growth attracts new firms. Because of the global wave of digitalization, demand for their products keeps growing, although the first consolidations are already taking place.
2. Unique quality with high value added due to creative customized solutions. An example is Carlex Design with its limited customized car design editions. A distinguishing feature of this company is its close partnerships with the world's best automotive companies based on trust and the conviction of the latter that they are getting high added value from this relatively small company.
3. World-class technology in a niche market represented by Vigo System S.A with its technology excellence in manufacturing high operating temperature HgCdTe detectors, and Telesto S.A., with its patented technology to atomize liquids into super fine mists for firefighting, dust control, object decontamination, and a growing number of other applications.
4. A leading global position in the mass tangible products category. For example, Selena FM S.A. manufactures and distributes chemical products for construction

and accessories for the DIY segment. There are a growing number of companies working for the construction industry sectors, producing windows and doors.[4]

Exhibit 1 Core economic indicators for Poland

	2011	2012	2013	2014	2015	2016	2017	2018
GDP per capita (current US$)	13,893	13,145	13,781	14,347	12,572	12,431	13,861	15,424
GDP per capita growth (annual %)	4.96	1.61	1.45	3.40	3.91	3.11	4.80	5.14
Long-term unemployment (% of total unemployment)	nd	nd	nd	nd	nd	nd	nd	nd
Foreign direct investment, net inflows (% of GDP)	3.495	1.471	0.152	3.626	3.154	3.881	2.028	2.054
GDP (current US$, mio)	528.83	500.36	524.23	545.39	477.58	472.03	526.37	585.78
Exports of goods and services (current US$, mio)	225.09	222.38	242.82	259.44	236.39	246.37	286.02	323.99
Exports of goods and services (% of GDP)	42.56	44.44	46.32	47.57	49.50	52.19	54.34	55.31
Merchandise exports (current US$)	188.70	185.37	204.98	220.05	199.12	203.82	234.36	260.61
Merchandise exports to high-income economies (% of total merchandise exports)	83.89	81.94	81.70	83.99	85.61	85.58	85.49	nd
Merchandise exports to developing economies in Europe & Central Asia (% of total merchandise exports)	12.48	13.97	13.99	11.77	9.93	10.26	10.65	nd
Ores and metals exports (% of merchandise exports)	5.04	4.85	4.19	4.02	3.61	3.04	3.18	3.04
Agricultural raw materials exports (% of merchandise exports)	1.24	1.26	1.36	1.35	1.29	1.27	1.16	1.26
Food exports (% of merchandise exports)	10.75	12.02	12.85	12.76	12.86	12.66	13.02	12.89
Fuel exports (% of merchandise exports)	4.85	4.92	4.59	4.05	3.25	2.52	2.48	2.50
Manufactures exports (% of merchandise exports)	78.04	76.84	76.85	77.75	78.86	80.30	79.97	80.16
High-technology exports (% of manufactured exports)	6.62	7.89	8.85	10.25	11.02	11.04	10.89	10.60

Source: World Bank 2019 https://data.worldbank.org/

2 Case Studies of Selected Hidden Champions

2.1 Vigo System S.A.

Overview
Address: ul. Poznańska 129/133, 05-850 Ożarów Mazowiecki
Tel: +48 22 733 54 10

---

[4]Some of them already became market Champions, other refused to participate in the research.

Fax: +48 22 733 54 10
Email: info@vigo.com.pl
Web: https://vigo.com.pl/

Company Information

Industry: Manufacture of instruments and appliances for measuring, testing, and navigation (high operating temperature HgCdTe detectors)
Year of establishment: 1987 (initially VIGO ltd.)
Sales revenues in 2017: 6.8 millon euros
Sales revenues in 2007[4]: 1.8 million euros
Average number of employees in 2017: 91
Brain(s) behind the company: Józef Piotrowski, Adam Piotrowski,

Nature of Market Leadership

The market for high operating temperature HgCdTe detectors is very concentrated. There are only a few competitors with equal shares and power. The success factor is the innovative technology of detectors production due to constant innovation and an ability to increase the production power in order to gain higher operational effectiveness.

Nature of Competitive Advantage

The nature of the Vigo System competitive advantage is the ability to implement innovative technology in business and its ability to modify it in accordance with clients' needs. Moreover, Vigo System is one of the leaders in research projects funded by the European Union. Due to these research projects, the Vigo System constantly increases its yearly production of detectors.

Core Lessons Learned on the Path to Success

The core lesson is the need for constant innovation, strong R&D, and improving the cost effectiveness of detectors production. For Vigo System, continuous interaction with clients is very important. The company meets them at thematic workshops or visits them in laboratories and their factories. In the field of marketing, Vigo System works on the development of the distributor system and improvement of clients' relationship management. Vigo System wants to enhance the demand for its detectors through rebranding, marketing campaigns, and dedicated sales activities.

Management and Leadership Development Needs

The period of dynamic growth began in 2010. Since 2014, the management board of the company has experienced generational change. Initially, there were impediments to the dynamic growth of the Vigo System: language barriers, a lack of delegation skills, and project management skills among the research and development staff. There has also been a transformation of the leading research and development staff from engineers to managers who manage several projects at the same time. Recently, Vigo System introduced programs such as the Leader Academy and the Talent Academy, designed to motivate, reward, and support the further development of the company's leaders and create their successors.

Financing and Regulatory Environment Development Needs

Vigo System needs to participate more frequently in the photonic industry fairs, particularly on the USA and Asian markets, establish stronger relationships with existing clients, prepare a strategy for expansion into new markets, make organizational changes, including the introduction of a new bonus system for sellers of their equipment, and review the efficiency of the existing sales network. In order to increase its production power, Vigo System is building a new production plant in Ożarów Mazowiecki, which will enable cost-effective mass production of up to 100,000 detectors annually. In order to develop, Vigo System needs a stable law environment, strong property rights protection, tax incentives for more R&D, and easier access to European Union funds or external funds for financing R&D, as well as for financing the building of a new production plant.

Competitors, Market Situation in the Sector, and the Company's Competition Position on the Market

Vigo System does not have direct competitors in the European market. Two companies from the USA and one from Japan compete with Vigo System globally. The quality and strength of the Vigo brand is demonstrated by the selection of its products by NASA for Mars missions, where the Vigo System detectors detect methane on the Curiosity rover board.

Plans for the future include increasing the scale of detectors production from 5000 pieces to 100,000 pieces annually. This will allow the achievement of economies of scale and, consequently, increased operational efficiency. The increase of the Vigo System's production capacity will be related to the increase in the intensity and scope of sales activities to create appropriate demand for the increased supply of detectors. This increase is related to investments in the Machine Park and new technologies, but first of all in the skills and abilities of technical staff and the team's attitude toward mass production of components adjusted to the needs of Vigo System's clients.

Since 2002, Vigo System has been actively cooperating with the Polish Military University of Technology in conducting joint research and development projects. However, when it comes to implementing the technology in business, this cooperation is only one of the few examples of effective scientific cooperation in Poland.

2.2 Carlex Design

Overview
Address: ul. Świerkowicka 41, 43-502 Czechowice-Dziedzice
Phone: +48 322101022
Email: www.carlexdesign.com/en/contact
Web: www.carlexdesign.com

Company Information
Industry: Manufacture of parts and accessories for motor vehicles
Year of establishment: 2007
Sales revenues in 2017: N/A
Sales revenues in 2007: N/A
Average number of employees: 75
Brain(s) behind the company: Damian Skotnicki, Roksana Skotnicka

Nature of Market Leadership

Carlex Design holds a leading position on the world market in the design and production of limited car editions (up to 1000 per model) for renowned global automotive companies. Carlex Design focuses on complex design and production of car interiors, body kits, external car elements, and modifications of standard solutions. The company is the global number-one producer of limited series of Mercedes X-Class—based vehicles, such as EXY. Carlex Design is a second-level modificator for Daimler and Ford, and a converter for Nissan. Altogether, it offers modified editions for six highly recognized brands. Carlex Design designs both car interiors and exteriors. It has broad global customer service structures, dedicated to different segments. It produces limited series of vehicles—own editions as well as in partnerships with large manufacturers. Limited editions are created directly for, and under, the brands of importers and modificators. Carlex design also produces parts for the first line of car manufacturers.

Nature of the Competitive Advantage

The major source of Carlex Design's competitive advantage is the creativity and uniqueness of the solutions offered to clients in shaping car interiors and exteriors in accordance with their preferences and dreams. Costs are less important than customized differentiation. The company's offers appeal to rich clients who care about their image of prestige and originality. The prerequisite for the successful delivery of such solutions is a profound knowledge of standard models construction and technology of luxury automobiles, such as Rolls Royce Ghost, Lamborghini, Mercedes 300S, or Dodge Challenger Hellcat. This requires reliability and close cooperation and trust with large original car manufacturers. The company also offers total refurbishing of the standard models. Carlex Design exports amount to 75% of its total sales. The majority of the clients come from Germany, South Korea, Australia, New Zealand, Canada, Russia, the Netherlands, France, Spain, Portugal, Belgium, Denmark, Austria, Lichtenstein, Luxembourg, Monaco, and Andorra.

Core Lessons Learned on the Path to Success

The segment of luxury-seeking clients requires a specific approach to every detail. The first part of it is the understanding of the customer needs, preferences, and dreams, as well as the latest fashions, trends, and technology innovations. The second part relies on the creativity of designers and their knowledge of all available materials to make an impression, while the third one is the disciplined production of the final version of every vehicle. Without a mastery of the whole process management and delivery, the final solution may appear disappointing.

Also, the company environment should make a strong impression of elegance, pleasure, comfort, and confidence on potential clients visiting the company site or any of the showrooms in Wales, Germany, Finland, and South Korea. The company demonstrates the collaborative culture of a family company.

In designing the limited editions of cars for any of the top leading automotive companies, a close cooperation is essential to take into account all important contingencies and likely market changes. The competitive advantage of Carlex Design is the fast delivery of a limited series. From design to finished product, it does not exceed 30 weeks.

Management and Leadership Development Needs

In view of growing competitive pressures and rising customer expectations, the company needs to provide regular training to the whole staff so as to sustain and develop their skills up to top performance levels.

Financing and Regulatory Development Needs

The major concern related to the Polish government and the European Union regulatory environment is the pace of changing law and tax obligations of companies. Business expects more stability to be provided at least in the mid-term so that healthy adjustments and full compliance can be achieved.

Competitors, Market Situation in the Sector, and the Company's Competition Position on the Market

Carlex Design systematically participates in business missions and industry-related trade fairs and exhibitions. It provides the best opportunities to analyze progress and update information on the state of the automotive industry, and detect early signals of change. The company attempts to delineate its own development paths, taking into consideration innovations in the area of technology, changes in legal standards, and regulation related to environmental protection. Each of them has, or will have in the near future, a strong impact on the company's growth and the modeling of its offer and performance management.

2.3 Cloud Technologies S.A.

Overview
Address: ul. Marszałkowska 8900-693 Warszawa
Tel: +48 225353050
Fax: N/A
Email: biuro@cloudtechnologies.pl
Web: www.cloudtechnologies.pl

Company Information
Industry: Information service activities
Year of establishment: 2011
Sales revenues in 2017: 16.8 million euros Sales revenues
Average number of employees in 2017: 55
Brain(s) behind the company: Piotr Prajsnar, Łukasz Kapuśniak, Maciej Sawa

Nature of Market Leadership

Cloud Technologies is number one in Europe in the niche market of big data profiling services for Internet advertising companies. As a capital group that works in the datatech area, the company operates on the global data market and delivers high-quality data, innovative products, and big data services based on artificial intelligence. Cloud Technologies collects and analyzes data from 200 markets worldwide with a proprietary data management platform technology. Cloud Technologies specializes in big data marketing and data monetization.

The company competes and cooperates in data exchange with other global companies from the same industry sector. Its leading position in the European market resulted from the early entry into this emerging industry and constantly following the market growth trends. Cloud Technologies has been continuously upgrading its products and service portfolios with technologies and algorithm modeling, based on machine learning and artificial intelligence, designed for mobile devices and using elements of the Internet of Things. Cloud Technologies focuses on companies having high-growth potential to create value for shareholders. It does not compete with the world's global leaders in the broad cloud computing industry, such as Amazon Web Services, Google Cloud, and Microsoft Azure.

Nature of the Competitive Advantage

Since its origin, the company has pursued a global strategy of growth based on unique competences in big data cloud computing, using anonymous information from the Internet and the most advanced tools of the digital economy. The sustainable competitive advantage can be attributed to the integration of two aspects of competitive leadership: economies of scale typical of the broad ICT platform solutions, and uniqueness of the offering, due to high digital and business competences of the company's leadership and staff. It is demonstrated in intelligent data acquisition and processing. Early entry into the market enabled the long and deep learning of customer needs, attracting skilled staff, and building relationships with the financial community on the New Connect market of the Warsaw Stock Exchange. It is one of the bases of competitive advantages over new start-ups. Cloud Technologies has been well prepared to play the role of a consolidation center, which in turn enabled a further systematic expansion of the company's operations based on scale and synergy.

The strengths of Cloud Technologies can be attributed to technology development, a strong team, good leadership, and unique know-how in data acquisition. What differentiates the company in this increasingly competitive market is, first of all, the high quantity and quality of data, scale and scope of operations, relative costs, and good market reputation. The company is attracting the attention of leading global firms searching for transformation paths of their business models and new partners to prosper in the disruptive era of digitalization.

Core Lessons Learned on the Path to Success

Being an early entrant in the emerging industry allowed the company to set up an asystematic learning process, which never stops in view of the dynamic global data market growth and its constant evolution with new market players and business models.[5] From the very beginning, technology has been the heart and soul of the company's value creation model. To receive funding from the stock exchange, the company has to demonstrate solid business foundations and perspectives for further growth. The energy and education of the young company's cadres allowed it to build a culture of entrepreneurship and responsibility for the company's growth by delivering satisfaction and value to customers. However, the company has to face the impact of legal business environment change, such as the general regulation on private data protection. Although this does not affect the company's model of doing business directly, in practice it creates new resistance to data-sharing, restricts direct contacts, and reduces trust. Cloud Technologies has worked out a solution to solve these problems.

Management and Leadership Development Needs

Networking, flexibility, and efficient decision-making are the key success factors in the ICT industry, where the company operates. The market is relatively small and young but fast-growing. Sustaining good working relationships with key market stakeholders requires utmost attention. The company should be prepared to make flexible, agile adjustments to changing needs so as to design its own R&D activities adequately and successfully implement new solutions for the market.

Financing and Regulatory Development Needs

Personal data protection is one of the most important legal regulations in the ICT business. They should be crystal clear. The company's processing of Internet users' data and its leading global positioning among suppliers of such data requires respect for privacy. Therefore, consistent with the new regulations, in the wholesale database only anonymous data are offered. The company carefully monitors the behavior of its business partners and competitors. Although the General Data Protection Regulation (GDPR) introduced in May 2018 does not directly affect the company's business, it has a strong impact on the Internet advertising market, where the company operates. The current legal environment is very dynamic. There are new regulations, such as the e-Privacy and the California Consumer Privacy Act (CCPA). Although these radical changes are valuable initiatives aimed at the standardization and harmonization of private data protection, they create chaos. The whole market needs clearer guidelines on their implementation.

---

[5]In Poland only about 1000 new companies are established every day. (https://www.coig.com.pl/nowe-firmy-w-polsce_2016_2015_2014_2013.php. Accessed 31 Oct 2019).

Competitors, Market Situation in the Sector and the Company's Position on the Market

Market Environment

Everyday Internet users generate 2.5 quintillion bytes of data and their pace of growth will accelerate alongside the development of the market of connected devices with the Internet, i.e., IoT (Internet of Things). Every minute Internet users from all over the world open millions of pages and undertake millions of micro actions, e.g., placing 55,000 photos on Instagram, streaming 644 h of movies on Netflix, and running 231,000 conversations on Skype. This is only a small part of the daily generated digital information.

Only in 2019, the value of the global digital data market will reach 26 billion USD. (Report: Global Data Market Size 2017–2019, On.Audience.com.)

Information on the interests and intents of Internet users is the driving forces of online advertising.

Magna Global predicts that advertising revenues will grow in 2019 for the 10th consecutive year to reach 600 billion USD. The fastest growing are digital ad sales. They will grow by 14%, having reached a 52% market share at the end of 2018.

The behavioral data are first of all used in digital advertising in the programmatic model, which has been constantly growing. In Europe, 70% is already realized in the display advertisements, versus 85% in the USA (US Programmatic Ad Spending Forecast 2019, eMarketer). In Europe, the value of the programmatic market in 2018 amounted to 16.7 billion EUR.[6] This means that it has grown up by 33%.

Data Management Platforms (DMP) are used to run the campaigns in the programmatic ecosystem. They enable data collection from all resources to complete the picture of a client. It is forecast that the DMP platforms market will grow annually at 20% in 2018–2023. (Forrester Analytics: Adtech Forecast, 2018 To 2023 (Global), Forrester.com).

The Cloud Technologies market is growing and developing at a high speed. Research results show that 68% of marketers use data from external suppliers to understand their clients better. Market observations show the growth of investments in data and in programmatic models, followed by the skills of marketers in their use of digital data. This is an optimistic forecast for more effective data-based advertising campaigns.

Competitive Environment

In view of its unique business model, Cloud Technologies does not have direct competitors. It can be distinguished in terms of specific activity areas, products, and services. The specificity of the online advertising market is competition, which means that the majority of competitors are at the same time contractors. Taking into account

---

[6]EU Programmatic Ad Spending Forecast 2019, eMarketer.

the way of data acquisition, analysis, processing, and sales, the direct competitors for the DMP services and data exchange are BlueKai, Inc., now a part of Oracle Corporation, Eyeota Pte Ltd., Lotame Solutions, Inc., and Salesforce.com, Inc.

Market Position

The leading position of Cloud Technologies is based on its unique business model, unique strategic assets developed in the company from its start, i.e., a global base of anonymous data of Internet users, as well as proprietary technologies of data integration, management, and optimization of Internet advertising campaigns (data management platform). The unique staff competences, relationships, contracts, and technology integration with important partners and editors in the global advertising ecosystem constitute the solid base for the positioning of Cloud Technologies in this modern, attractive, and highly competitive market.

2.4 Growbots

Overview
Address: ul. Hoża 51; 00-681 Warszawa, Poland
Tel: (925) 237-0222
Fax: N/A
Email: greg@growbots.com
Web: www.growbots.com

Company Information
Industry: Advertising and advisory services (based on the ICT platform)
Year of establishment: 2014
Sales revenues in 2017: 2.7 million euros
Average number of employees in 2017: 73
Brain(s) behind the company: Grzegorz Pietruszyński, Adam Mazan, Łukasz Deko

Nature of Market Leadership

The company was established at the beginning of 2014 and started to qualify as a hidden champion at the beginning of 2016, when it gained the number-one position in the world in software development and services for sales optimization based on the software as a service (SaaS) solution). The company's market share is larger than the one of its two major competitors in the USA (Apollo, Growlabs). Ninety percent of the exports of Growbots go to the USA market. Although the company started its business in 2014, after only 2 years it employed 50 persons and achieved a 25%

monthly sales growth. Within this period, the company became independent of venture capital and was attractive to innovative investors in the technology sphere. A 1200% growth rate of sales in 2016 helped the company build new functionalities in the system and set up three offices: in Warsaw, San Francisco, and Cleveland.

Nature of the Competitive Advantage

The major sources of Growbots' competitive advantage are the market development trends and expectations of businesses interested in increasing their sales fast through automated selling software. This enables companies to reach sales leads from the whole world in real time and at a relatively low cost. Growbots created this possibility through its unique technology of big data mining and original artificial intelligenvce, which allows it to profile a search and thus save time for the sales force thanks to a higher response rate. The data are of excellent quality. Importantly, the company is well protected against leakage and pays high attention to the instant updating of databases and software.

Core Lessons Learned on the Path to Success

The company founders adopted realistic assumptions concerning business development starting with short-term tactics, based on the Internet and emails as the most universal way of communication. The next assumption was the limited experience of customers in the use of digital platforms and SaaS solutions in their marketing strategies to elevate the sales level faster and at a competitive cost. Creating a positive experience of ease of use of the company's services and high effectiveness of investments, Growbots was able to grow very fast. Through continuous upgrading of technology and expertise based on early and fast learning, the company outperformed the emerging competition from new start-ups of the fourth digital revolution. Growbots keeps working on sustaining its competitive advantage through investing in human capital and tacit knowledge of people, a Google-type organizational culture, and a flexible structure beloved by young employees. Processes in the organization are well defined and flexible. The company has adopted management by objectives. Products result from intellectual property rights. This type of company is less capital intensive than traditional (tangible) businesses.

Management and Leadership Development Needs

The company has a well-established management and leadership team and is not planning to hire new executives.

Financing and Regulatory Development Needs

The company is profitable and does not need financing from external sources.

Competitors, the Market Situation in the Sector, and the Company's Position on the Market

Growbots operates on the sales automation market for the business-to-business sector. Its customers' portfolio contains 500 clients from 43 countries, but 90% of them come from the USA. On the USA market, there are around 1.2 million business-to-business companies, employing over 10 persons each, and the value of the whole market is estimated at about 30 billion USD.

On the SalesTech market, there are 950 registered companies (Sales Tech Landscape 2019). Growbots competes with other companies in two categories: databases and communication tools. Discover.org became the leader of the database market after taking over its largest competitor Zoominfo. In the category of communication tools, the leadership belongs to Outreach and Salesoft. They offer sophisticated and expensive tools directed to enterprise clients: medium and large companies. At the other end of the market, there is a number of companies, such as Reply.io, Woodpecker, Seamless.ai, and others, offering simple tools for non-advanced users at a monthly cost of 100 USD. At present, Apollo is the only direct competitor of Growbots, offering an all-in-one solution, while Growlabs has been sold.

2.5 Selena FM S.A.

Overview
Address: Strzegomska Str. 2-4, 53-611 Wrocław, Poland
Tel: +48 71 78 38 290
Fax: +48 71 78 38 291
Email: office@selena.com
Web: http://www.selena.com/en/

Company Information
Industry: Construction chemicals
Year of establishment: 1992
Sales revenues in 2017: 119.90 million euros
Sales revenues in 2007 1.69 million euros
Average number of employees in 2017: 1770
Brain(s) behind the company: Krzysztof Domarecki

Nature of Market Leadership

Selena is one of the world's leading producers and distributors of chemical products for construction and accessories for the DIY segment, and one of three leading producers of polyurethane foam in the world. Other products include adhesives, sealants, and building insulation systems.

Nature of the Competitive Advantage

Selena is developing and improving thanks to its excellent managers. It has operations in 70 countries in Europe, North America, Asia, and the Middle East. It works closely with developers and builders to achieve best practices through experience sharing. Selena has four large competitors in the European market and 40 small local competitors.

Core Lessons Learned on the Path to Success

Fast forward global leadership based on professionalism in building value to stakeholders.
   Importance of continuous innovation in products and processes.
   Product innovations that have always been in Selena's DNA.
   Internationalization (i.e., international expansion to other European and non-European markets), thanks to which Selena has become an interesting place to work for leading specialists and for diversification of geographical risk.
   Excellent managers, thanks to whom Selena is constantly developing and improving.

Management and Leadership Development Needs

Needs in the field of new construction technologies, in terms of performance as well as innovative solutions for new products:

– E-commerce department in the scope of changing distribution channels.
– Knowledge management field regarding the possibilities of using new technologies, commercialization of innovative products, or new distribution channels.
– Information management field in connection with the increase of information and the need to manage their weight in a skillful manner.

Financing and Regulatory Environment Development Needs

Selena has no development needs in terms of financing, because it is characterized by high financial liquidity, which exceeds its current needs. Selena would like to see changes in the regulatory environment, which has recently deteriorated significantly. The poor business culture in Poland, and the significant number of low-quality regulations, imposing standards on entrepreneurs or post-communist clerical practices, means that Selena has a worse competitive position than its competitors from other EU countries.

Competitors, Market Situation in the Sector and the Company's Competition Position on the Market

The development needs of Selena in the field of marketing are related to the implementation of digital marketing on a wider scale. Selena wants to take advantage of the opportunities offered by digital marketing in order to reach with its offer the saviors of construction works, i.e., small and medium-sized enterprises. Selena has four large competitors in the European market and 40 small local competitors.

2.6 Telesto S.A.

Overview
Address: Ludwinowska 17, 02-856 Warszawa, Poland
Tel: +48 (0) 22648 84 46
Fax: +48 (0) 22648 87 64
Email: telesto@telesto.pl
Web: www.telesto.pl

Company Information
Industry: Manufacturing
Year of establishment: 1994 (The water mist operation in 2003)
Sales revenues in 2017: 580,000 euros
Sales revenues in 2007: 170,000 euros
Average number of employees in 2017: 25
Brain(s) behind the company: Zygmunt Łada and Anna Łada

Nature of Market Leadership

Telesto designs, develops, and markets devices and systems that utilize its patented technology to atomize liquids into super fine mists for firefighting, dust control, object decontamination, and a growing number of other applications. Telesto offers off-the-shelf devices as well as custom solutions specifically designed to customer requirements. Outside of Poland, Telesto relies on partners, who are trained and encouraged to create their own demo-centers where customers are invited for presentations. Partners' engineers are trained to supply local customers with designs. In Poland and in some foreign locations, company experts oversee each project from conception and design through installation, testing, handover, and service. Telesto is committed to rigorous internal quality assurance and has been certified to internationally recognized standards ISO 9001:2000 as well as ISO 14001:2004. Telesto products and solutions undergo international certifications by LPCB, BSI, and IBS, as well as local certifications that are country-specific. The company is number one in Europe in these solutions: atomizing liquids into super fine mists. Telesto's main exports go to Germany and South Africa (coal mines).

Nature of the Competitive Advantage

The distinguishing feature of Telesto's award-winning dual-fluid, low-pressure technology is its ability to atomize liquids into extremely small droplets and carry the droplets on an air stream. By adjusting the nozzle design, water volume, and air pressure parameters, Telesto is able to control the qualities of the mists it generates. Droplets can range in size from 10 to 150 µm while mist streams may range from cm to 12 m. This unique flexibility allows Telesto to create optimal mist solutions for a broad range of applications.

Core Lessons Learned on the Path to Success

Introducing a new product takes time and effort. Choosing the right partner for development is crucial. Telesto has relied on partners for international development. It started out as an innovative company in a pretty conservative market. Telesto partnered with people who seemed enthusiastic about handling something new and difficult. With time, the company learned that some of those partners were not equipped for business success. The reliable partners are key factors in the development of the company.

Management and Leadership Development Needs

In response to this demand, the company has launched subsidiaries in Germany and South Africa and is presently expanding its presence in a number of additional countries via local partners. Right now, Telesto is working with partners and is not creating subsidiaries as Germany and South Africa are now operated through partners. Telesto used to offer exclusivity in each market, but now it is opening the distribution to various companies and the product range is broad enough to offer partners specialized solutions, for example only for fire brigades or only for transformer protection. The challenge right now is to increase profitability through greater share in the realized projects abroad. Telesto seeks key salespeople that have a strong desire to develop sales outside of Poland and Europe and are willing to travel. Those are independent individuals who can create a strategy for a particular country or customer without supervision. Telesto appears on customers' own products as a "Telesto Technology inside" logo or statement. In the future, the company might attempt to create a unified product that will carry Telesto branding and partners' branding as an additional item. In this case, a brand strategy combined with a unique product design would be required. Regarding other challenges, Telesto has struggled with the lack of regulations regarding water mist in many industry applications. This is still a limiting factor in the implementation of the water mist solutions more broadly.

Financing and Regulatory Environment Development Needs

At the current stage of its development Telesto seeks financing to take its products through certification processes for specific products. So far, the funds for that purpose have been either offered by the owners or obtained for partners who co-fund certification processes. There are still no regulations requiring the use of water mist in residential and commercial buildings. Currently, this type of protection is used only under special conditions.

Competitors, Market Situation in the Sector, and the Company's Position on the Market

Water mist has been gaining popularity in the market over the past 15 years and its growth is expected to continue. Some experts claim that the water mist market itself would be growing at approximately 25% a year. Seeing this opportunity, many companies have emerged in the market to offer water mist solutions, either for a specific need in a particular industry or more generally. There are well-established companies with a worldwide presence, such as Marioff (UTC Company) or Johnson Fire Controls (formerly Tyco). Telesto currently can be seen as a niche producer of water mist fire protection systems with dominance in some of the niches, for instance, fire extinguishers and engine protection systems.

3 Conclusions and Recommendations

Hidden champions are a category of companies, striving to achieve and sustain championship positions while staying hidden from the broad public. They make a lot of efforts to have close and strong relationships within their business ecosystems:

customers, business partners, staff, competitors, regulators, and media. Depending on the scale of operations and market reach—home, European, CEE, or global—the external environment, creates different expectations, opportunities, and threats, each of them requiring different adjustments. Especially in highly attractive sectors with a fast-growing competition, innovation is a key success factor, as is always being at least one step ahead of the competitors. For that reason, hidden champions carefully observe the market changes in growth potential, innovation rate, profitability, and market structure with major competitors, mergers and acquisitions, and their own positioning.

Having become leaders, they impose the pace and direction of innovation. Thus, they delineate the new competitive landscape and new demand streams. For large global manufacturers, despite mass scale and value-to-quality ratio, it is important to perceive the role of customization of their products, services, and responses to the needs of major clients. This requires flexible and efficient manufacturing systems. To anticipate the changes, companies have to screen the early signals of technology advancements, new materials, machinery, components, distribution channels, promotion means, transaction costs, and fashion trends shaping demand and clients' preferences. These could be detected in specific ways: through direct close contacts based on trust with present clients, screening for new clients, and meetings at industry fairs, exhibitions, and conferences. Commissioning scientific research and analyses are not popular. It is rather the companies' role to initiate research and pave the way for innovative products. They care about their staff's education—not only professional but also in the field of foreign languages needed for expansion and communication aimed at close and long-lasting relationships with selected partners.

Polish hidden champions most often hide in narrow, highly specialized market niches and constantly update their offers. Their size depends on the industry or niche specificity. If they mass-produce materials for the global market, they usually employ much more people than companies with a narrow specialization. They strive to keep costs at a competitive level and to use the most efficient production lines. Design and perfect finishing by means of modern technology and skillful staff, still available in many locations in Poland, make it possible to beat the competition and expand operations.

New ICT platform companies stay small but are able to operate on the global scale. The major requirement of their growth is the pace of digitalization. They process and profile big data from the global cloud with the use of machine learning, artificial intelligence, augmented and virtual reality, and the Internet of Things and Services.

The hidden champions stay small. They develop and rely on their creative skills and potential to deliver added value to large industry leaders. To become reliable partners for them, they have to exceed standards and sustain their reputation of reliable and preferred partners.

In view of the fast-changing global environment in politics, economy, society, technology, and natural environment, the hidden champions expect from their home countries friendly, relatively stable regulations at least in the mid-term period, so as to avoid painful adaptation. This includes regulations on tax policy, R&D, an economic policy related to intelligent specialization, and an educational policy reflecting their needs for highly skilled and specialized staff. Compliance with political decisions to raise the minimum wage and immediate implementation of broad social programs does not leave much space for rational adjustments and sustenance of a high-performance level.

Polish hidden champions participate in diverse educational post-diploma programs. They do not suffer from a shortage of skilled labor but usually need experts. Hidden champions are viewed as attractive employers, offering international career opportunities. The major sources of financing their operations and growth are their own profits and low-cost European funds. They do not declare an interest in bank loans. They go beyond existing regulations in the area of environmental protection, thus meeting the demands of their clients and other stakeholders. They also implement good CSR policies and frequently sponsor a lot of sport, culture, or charity activities.

There is an inherent logic in the three stages of the development of hidden champions in Poland. The early ones, functioning in a highly constrained environment, aspired to become full champions, but their chances were limited before Poland's access to the EU. Even after the accession, the shortage of available resources for investments and innovation limited the real possibility of such change. Numerous projects funded by the European Union contributed to better education and the growth of the economy. Since 2011, Polish hidden champions have profited from the opening of the economy. This resulted in numerous international mergers and acquisitions, which the Polish companies were attractive targets for international and global corporations. The acquired companies gained unprecedented opportunities for further growth within broader structures. There was also a situation when the Polish hidden champions had the best product but limited marketing and distribution. After joining a global leader, their growth was blocked as the acquiring company had a competitive product. Finally, this company decided to buy back its shares and restart its business. The recently identified hidden champions take full advantage of the openness of the economy and are active in the international arena with their tangible products or digital solutions. Still, there are no global leaders in Poland that are as big as Google or Amazon, but past experiences show that the potential for agile adjustment to a turbulent environment is high.

A new wave of hidden champions may emerge from the very fast-growing start-up community with already outstanding achievements and further prospects for fast growth.[7] The country provides special financial and institutional schemes for their innovation development and commercialization as well as for international expansion.[8] Moreover, a new legal form has been introduced: simple joint stock company, specially designed for investments in innovative ventures. Thus, Poland is seventh in

---

[7] About 1000 new companies are established in Poland every day. See: https://www.coig.com.pl/nowe-firmy-w-polsce_2016_2015_2014_2013.php. Accessed 31 Oct 2019.

[8] https://www.coig.com.pl/nowe-firmy-w-polsce_2016_2015_2014_2013.php. Accessed 31 Oct 2019.

the world in terms of support for start-ups.[9] Some of them are already advanced and generate interest in their business success.[10]

References

ABSL (2018) Business Services Sector in Poland. Association of Business Service Leaders (ABSL)

Baumol WJ (1990) Entrepreneurship: productive, unproductive, and destructive. J Polit Econ 98 (5):893–921

Commission Regulation (EU) (2014) No 651/2014 of 17 June 2014 declaring certain categories of aid compatible with the internal market in application of Articles 107 and 108 of the Treaty. Off J Eur Union 187:1–78

Czapinski J, Panek T (2015) Diagnoza społeczna 2015. Warunki i jakość życia Polaków. Rada Monitoringu Społecznego, Warszawa

Deloitte (2019) International Tax Poland Highlights 2019

Demsetz H (1967) Toward a theory of property rights. Am Econ Rev 57(2):347–359

Esposito G, Lanau S, Pompe S (2014) Judical system reform in Italy –a key to growth, *IMF Working Papers*, International Monetary Fund. https://doi.org/10.5089/9781475573022.001

Estrin S, Mickiewicz T (2010) Entrepreneurship in transition economies: the role of institutions and generational change, Discussion Paper No. 4805, Germany. IZA, Bonn

European Commission (2018) State Aid Scoreboard 2018, Poland. https://ec.europa.eu/competition/state_aid/scoreboard/index_en.html

European Investment Bank (2018) Investment Report 2018/2019: retooling Europe's economy. https://www.eib.org/en/publications/investment-report-2018.htm

Eurostat (2016) Gini coefficient of equivalized disposable income—EU-SILC survey

EY (2018) Worldwide corporate tax guide 2018

Gałagus M, Kamiński A, Michalak A (2018) Start-up supporting systems in central and eastern Europe. SGH Report, Gazeta SGH, Krynica Forum, pp 14–15

Godlewska M, Morawska S (2019) Development of local and regional entrepreneurship—which institutions matter? Evidence from Poland. Econ Res Ekonoms Istraživ. https://doi.org/10.1080/1331677X.2018.1553680

Gwartney J, Lawson R, Block W (1996) Economic freedom of the world 1975–1995. The Fraser Institute. https://www.fraserinstitute.org/sites/default/files/EconomicFreedomoftheWorld1975-1995.pdf

Jackson KA, De Soto Fellow H (2011) International property rights index, report 2011, property rights alliance. https://www.internationalpropertyrightsindex.org/previous-reports

Levie J, Autio E, Acs Z, Hart M (2014) Global entrepreneurship and institutions: an introduction. Small Bus Econ 42:437

Levy-Carciente S, De Soto Fellow H (2018) International property rights index, report 2018, property rights alliance. https://www.internationalpropertyrightsindex.org/countries

Markowski R, Kwiatkowska A (2018) The political impact of the global crisis in Poland: delayed and indirect effects. Hist Soc Res *43*(4):250–273. Historische Sozialforschung Challenged Elites—Elites as Challengers. The Impact of Civil Activism, Populism and the Economic Crisis on Elite Structures, Orientations and Agendas

McKinsey & Company (2015) Poland 2025: Europe's new growth engine

---

[9]https://ceoworld.biz/2019/01/02/most-startup-friendly-countries-in-the-world-2019/. Accessed 31 Oct 2019.

[10]E.g., Biotts, Quotiss, challengerocket.com. See: https://ceoworld.biz/2019/01/02/most-startup-friendly-countries-in-the-world-2019/. Accessed 31 Oct 2019.

Miller T, Kim AB, Roberts JM (2019) 2019 index of economic freedom. The Heritage Foundation, Washington. https://www.heritage.org/index/pdf/2019/book/index_2019.pdf

OECD Economic Surveys (2018) Poland. Overview. https://www.oecd.org/eco/surveys/Poland-2018-OECD-economic-survey-overview.pdf

Official Journal of the European Union (2012) Consolidated version of the treaty on the functioning of the European Union. Official Journal C 326, 26/10/2012, pp 0001–0390

Perry A (2000) An ideal legal system for attracting foreign direct investment? Some theory and reality. Am Univ Int Law Rev 15(6):1627–1657

Polski Instytut Ekonomiczny (2020) The CIT gap in Poland in 2014-2018.

Rapacki R, Próchniak M (2018) Porównawcza ocena tendencji rozwojowych w polskiej gospodarce w latach 2010–2017: Polska na tle UE, w "Polska. Raport o konkurencyjności 2018. Rola miast w kształtowaniu przewag konkurencyjnych Polski". SGH, Instytut Gospodarki Światowej

The World Bank (2010) Doing business 2011, making a difference for entrepreneurs. https://www.doingbusiness.org/content/dam/doingBusiness/media/Annual-Reports/English/DB11-FullReport.pdf

The World Bank (2019) Doing business 2019, training for reform. https://www.doingbusiness.org/content/dam/doingBusiness/media/Annual-Reports/English/DB2019-report_web-version.pdf

Williams N, Vorley T, Williams CC (2017) Entrepreneurship and Institutions. The Causes and Consequences of Institutional Asymmetry. Rowman & Littlefield International, London

World Bank (2019). https://data.worldbank.org/indicator/TX.VAL.TECH.MF.ZS?locations=PL. Accessed 26 Sept 2019

World Happiness Ranking (2013–2018). https://worldhappiness.report/

World Trade Statistical Review (2017). https://www.wto.org/english/res_e/statis_e/wts2017_e/wts2017_e.pdf

Hidden Champions of Romania

Andrei Ștefan Neștian and Ana Iolanda Vodă

Overview
Official name: Romania
Type of government: Semi-presidential republic
Population in 2017: 19.6 million
Land area: 238,397 km^2 (92,046 miles^2)

History
1859 Modern Romania is formed through the union of the Danubian principalities of Moldavia and Wallachia.
1877 Romania gains independence from the Ottoman Empire.
1918 Bukovina, Bessarabia, Transylvania, as well as parts of Banat, Crișana, and Maramureș become part of the sovereign Kingdom of Romania.
1941 Romania enters the Second World War, in June 1941, fighting against the Soviet Union until August 1944.
1949 Romania joins the Allies and recovered Northern Transylvania.
1948 A communist regime is installed in Romania for the following 42 years, after King Mihai is forced to abdicate on December 31, 1947.
1989 Romanian revolution and a transition from a planned economy to a market economy.
2007 Romania becomes a European Union Member state.

A. Ș. Neștian (✉)
Management, Marketing and Business Administration Department, Alexandru Ioan Cuza University, Iași, Romania
e-mail: nestian@uaic.ro

A. I. Vodă
Institute for Interdisciplinary Research, Social Science and Humanities Research Department, Alexandru Ioan Cuza University, Iași, Romania

© Springer Nature Switzerland AG 2021
A. Braček Lalić, D. Purg (eds.), *Hidden Champions in Dynamically Changing Societies*, https://doi.org/10.1007/978-3-030-65451-1_22

1 Introduction: Context and History

Romania is one of Europe's *former Soviet* bloc *countries* ruled by a *communist* government for almost 42 years, starting in 1948. The transition from a centralized economy to a free market was initiated in December 1989. Romania started its transition without any external debt and with many motivated individuals who desired change. However, these advantages were not sufficiently exploited, and Romania faced a drastic fall in GDP at the beginning of 1990s. The reconstruction of the economy was difficult to achieve due to structural imbalances and the dysfunction of the system as a result of an over weighted and outdated industry sector, an inefficient agricultural sector, and poor management (Daianu and Murgescu 2013). The communist regime impeded technological progress and made it increasingly difficult for firms to be competitive in foreign markets. Given the high level of path dependency and behavior inertia inherited from more than 40 years of Soviet-style socialism, Romania started its post-socialist transition with one of the biggest dysfunctions: a lack of a class of private entrepreneurs (Daianu and Murgescu 2013). As a result, during the transition stage, Romania had one of the lowest business density rates among the Central and Eastern European Countries (Fuentelsaz et al. 2019).

Starting in 1990, Romania implemented several gradual reforms in order to reduce the existing imbalances: foreign trade and price liberalization, taxation reform and introduction of VAT, and closure of inefficient enterprises, among others. The economic recovery started in 2000, when the accession negotiations with the European Union (EU) were opened and Romania had fostered institutional progress and stimulated foreign direct investment, which lead to a period of high economic growth. As a result, Romania entered the EU, on January, 1, 2007.

However, the recent economic crisis brought a major setback for Romania. Given the fragile growth model, characterized by high external deficits, inadequate resource allocation, and a high increase in private-sector foreign-currency debt, the economic crisis deeply affected the living standards of the population. The consequence was a fall of GDP, starting in the fourth quarter of 2008. During the first quarter of 2009, the GDP declined sharply by 2.6% compared to that of the fourth quarter of 2008, and 6.4% compared to the figure in the first quarter of 2008 (Zaman and Georgescu 2009). Therefore, expenditure on consumption decreased, leading to a decline in production and investment. Also, there was a significant reduction in the volume of exports and the external balance of payments was maintained by a greater reduction in imports, which negatively affected economic growth (Duguleană and Duguleană 2014).

Since its accession to the European Union, Romania has been catching up with the rest of the member states in terms of GDP per capita and productivity. However, although significant progress has been made, with GDP per capita rising from 30% of the EU average in 1995 to 59% in 2016, Romania still remains the country with the largest share of poor people and the second lowest GDP per capita of all European Union member states. Also, the country is characterized by uneven distribution of economic opportunity and poverty across regions and between urban and rural areas. Romania is also one of the least urbanized countries in the EU (De Rosa et al. 2018). Nevertheless, the Romanian capital—Bucharest—has exceeded the EU average income per capita, widening the already large gap between regions.

The main indicators of the Romanian economy are presented in Exhibit 1.

Exhibit 1 Core economic indicators for Romania

	2011	2012	2013	2014	2015	2016	2017	2018
GDP per capita (current US$)	9105	8535	9555	10,027	8977	9567	10,793	12,301
GDP per capita growth (annual %)	2.51	2.53	3.90	3.80	4.36	5.40	7.62	4.70
Long-term unemployment (% of total unemployment)	41.0	44.2	45.2	41.1	43.9	50.0	41.4	44.1
Foreign direct investment, net inflows (% of GDP)	1.29	1.78	2.02	1.94	2.43	3.32	2.82	2.87
GDP (current US$, mio)	183,443	171,196	190,949	199,627	177,893	188,494	211,407	239,553
Exports of goods and services (current US$, mio)	67,932	64,043	76,137	82,175	72,968	77,632	87,790	99,754
Exports of goods and services (% of GDP)	37.03	37.41	39.87	41.16	41.02	41.19	41.53	41.64
Merchandise exports (current US$)	63,035	57,841	65,835	69,725	60,595	63,534	70,761	79,671
Merchandise exports to high-income economies (% of total merchandise exports)	74.90	73.98	73.71	74.94	77.77	78.16	78.57	–
Merchandise exports to developing economies in Europe & Central Asia (% of total merchandise exports)	18.25	17.96	17.20	15.97	13.44	12.44	13.10	–
Ores and metals exports (% of merchandise exports)	4.14	3.80	3.24	2.68	2.36	2.02	2.09	2.18
Agricultural raw materials exports (% of merchandise exports)	2.14	2.27	2.23	1.98	1.72	1.30	1.33	1.26

(continued)

Exhibit 1 (continued)

	2011	2012	2013	2014	2015	2016	2017	2018
Food exports (% of merchandise exports)	8.55	8.50	10.15	10.16	10.41	10.28	10.10	9.46
Fuel exports (% of merchandise exports)	5.48	5.09	4.85	5.76	4.43	3.58	3.74	4.02
Manufactures exports (% of merchandise exports)	77.79	77.49	75.84	76.33	77.78	79.52	80.13	82.21
High-technology exports (% of manufactured exports)	11.63	8.13	7.36	8.39	9.41	10.39	9.82	10.08

Source: World Bank (2019)

Romania performs well in terms of macroeconomic environment, health and primary education, and to some degree also higher education and training. The main weaknesses are the institutional framework, business sophistication, and innovation (WEF 2018). The latest data show that growth accelerated further from 2011 until 2017 and was fueled by domestic demand. GDP growth increased from 2.51% in 2011, to 7.62% in 2017, followed by a decline in 2018 to 4.70%. Private consumption was the main contributor to growth, alongside indirect tax cuts and wage increases in the private and public sectors (Eurostat 2018).

Foreign direct investment has been the main source of external funding for Romania's economy. Foreign direct investment (net inflows) increased from 1.29% of GDP in 2011, to 2.82% GDP in 2017 and 2.87% in 2018, according to the World Bank's collection of development indicators. But although the total investment ratio has improved, its quality is hampered by legal uncertainty and management deficiencies (Eurostat 2018).

Unemployment rates have improved gradually since 2015, reaching the lowest level in 2018: 4.29%. Although unemployment rates have been decreasing, the emigration of high-skilled workers, the aging population, and the low birth rates represent real challenges that may hamper Romanian's competitiveness. However, Romania has a very high human development index (HDI) and a skilled labor force. The HDI consists of three basic measures of human development: healthy life, access to knowledge, and decent standard of living. In Romania, between 1990 and 2015, life expectancy at birth increased by 5.3 years. Mean number of years of schooling increased by 1.8 years, and the number of expected years of schooling rose by 2.8 years. Also, GNI-per-capita growth rose by about 74% in the same period. Overall, the HDI value increased from 1990 to 2017 by 11.56%, from 0.701 to 0.811, ranking Romania 52nd out of 188 countries and territories (UNDP 2018).

According to the lasted data, in 2018 the most important sectors in Romania were industry (26.1%), followed by wholesale and retail trade, transport, accommodation and food services (20.2%) and public administration, defense, education, human health, and social work activities (14.5%). Intra-EU trade accounts for 77% of Romania's exports. These go mainly to Germany (23%), Italy (11%), and France (7%). Outside the EU, the exports go mainly to Turkey (3%) and the United States (2%). As regards imports, 75% come from EU member states (Germany 20%, Italy 9%, and Hungary 7%), while 5% come from China and 4% from Turkey (Eurostat 2018; World Bank 2019).

In terms of the business environment, Romania ranks 37th worldwide out of 189 countries. The country's main strength, according to the World Bank's Doing Business Index is the simplicity of trading across borders (rank 1). The main drawbacks related to the business environment are dealing with construction permits (rank 146) and obtaining access to electricity (rank 154) (World Bank Group 2019).

Since 2010, the number of Romanian businesses has grown, especially as a consequence of the increasing number of individual entrepreneurs. In 2008, almost 14% of the nearly 700,000 Romanian companies consisted of individual entrepreneurs. This percentage increased to more than 49 in 2014, reaching a total of 341,817 individual firms. The number of companies that had between one and four employees decreased from 298,070 in 2008 to 251,810 in 2014. In 2014, only 7.4% of the Romanian companies had ten or more employees (Radauer and Roman 2017).

Among the prospering companies, those that have specialized in industries with fast technological change are the strongest. They are focused mainly on the production of electronic devices with communication technologies, as well as the production of software and provision of digital services for the marketing of companies. In the following section, we look in depth at examples of hidden champions mainly from these sectors.

2 Three Case Studies of Selected Hidden Champions

2.1 Case Study 1

Electra Group

Overview
Address: Bd. Chimiei nr. 8 Iasi, 700291, Romania
Tel: +40 232 214.370
Fax: +40 232 232.830
Email: office@ELECTRA.ro
Web: www.ELECTRA.ro, www.ELECTRA-grup.ro

Company Information

Industry: Manufacture of loaded electronic boards (loaded printed circuit boards), manufacture of communication equipment (door phones)
Year of establishment: 1991
Sales revenues in 2017: 7.31 million euros
Sales revenues in 2007: 2.36 million euros
Average number of employees in 2017: 166
Brain(s) behind the company: Marian Berdan, CEO

Nature of Market Leadership

Electra is a Romanian company, specialized in the design, development, and production of door phone systems, access control systems, and electronic equipment, operating since 1991 in Romania and on the international market.

Electra is number one in Romania in manufacturing high-quality door phones (entrance telephones) and other related security system solutions for a wide range of buildings, from single villas to large residential compounds. The company enjoys the same leadership in Romania as in 2011, with a market share of 70–80%, and has increased its international presence. However, because of the nature of the business, Electra has a low visibility profile in Romania.

The company maintains its national market share due to the reliability of its products, its constant presence, and the customer care for the maintenance of the installed systems.

Since the domestic market could not provide enough growth opportunities, the company has grown internationally. In Romania, as in Europe, the competitors are much older companies. There are dozens of them in Europe. .

The company is steadily growing, with about 30% of sales from exports to countries in Europe, Latin America, and North Africa. The current challenge is to develop the new market in Latin America and to become a significant competitor in Central and Eastern Europe. The future challenges are perceived as linked to the potential financial instability in the Central and Eastern European region, which could affect the commercial operations of the Austrian branch of the company, established in Vienna. The company is expected to grow by expanding its operations in the Central and Eastern European area, using the bridgehead in Austria, in the next 10 years.

Nature of the Competitive Advantage

The two main drivers of the competitive advantage of Electra are technological. The first competitive advantage source is product innovation, focused on introducing new features and new functions for the products. Electra keeps up with technological innovations and with the needs of its customers, launching products with modern and practical functions. In order to handle this multitude of technologies better, the original company, Electra, turned into Electra Group, incorporating the following Romanian companies:

- Electra—Producer of video door phones and access control systems.
- PCB Electra—Producer of printed circuit boards.
- EMS-Electra—Supplier of SMD and THT electronic assembly services.

The second source of the company's advantage is innovative technologies, focused on introducing new, more efficient, and more advanced manufacturing methods. The simple and cutting-edge design, as well as the user-friendly interfaces of their products, transforms the Electra door phones into genuine gadgets for living spaces and offices.

A third competitive advantage used by the company is the establishment of a commercial branch in Austria to coordinate the marketing and sales efforts in Europe. The company is steadily growing. About 30% of sales are now from exports to countries in Europe, Latin America, and North Africa.

Since its establishment, the company has had stable and powerful leadership in the person of the CEO. Competitive technologies and patents registered in Europe are equally important. Another strength of the company is the focus on learning and understanding the characteristics of each market before entering them with adapted products.

The leadership success factors are the vision of the CEO, the competency of the managers, the wellbeing of the employees, and the acquisition of valuable information about the technological and commercial evolution of this industrial sector. The two main innovation success factors are the highly skilled professionals and the realistic anticipation of the market evolution in terms of the expected features of the products.

Core Lessons Learned on the Path to Success

Today, the company believes that innovation is the most important driver of competitiveness. Qualification in the technologies closely linked with the expectation of customers is the path leading to the most valuable innovations. For example, in 2012 Electra was the first company to present a product with a front surface made of chemically toughened glass.

Another lesson is that an international launch allowed the company to test its real competitiveness, determining the elaboration and implementation of relevant improvements at the level of processes and products.

The main lessons of the first internationalization attempts showed that market leadership in Romania was not an important asset. Hence, the company actually became international by launching a branch in Austria—Electra Building Communications GmbH—and by creating Bellcome, its international brand of products.

Management and Leadership Development Needs

The company is mature and does not have underdeveloped competencies but admits its heavy reliance on highly skilled engineers. Wage competition is not considered a real issue. The company is mature in terms of its marketing approach, using relational business-to-business strategies to penetrate new markets and grow its business where it is established.

Financing and Regulatory Environment Development Needs

The company is reluctant to accept major investments through non-refundable European funding, due to the national institutional instability and lack of precise commitments by Romanian institutions. Both represent a risk of failure or delay of any new business project.

The International Expansion of the Romanian Door Phone Leader

Electra was founded in 1991 by Marian Berdan, the current general manager of the company, with a clear vision: to produce electronic equipment in Iasi. Thus, in 1993 the first Electra brand intercom was designed, a customized access control solution, 100% produced in Romania. The product was designed entirely within Electra. Orders increased and the company expanded with country-wide sales. This product became the star of the company.

In 1997, the company consolidated its unique character in Romania by obtaining two patents for access card door phones and ten industrial model certificates registered at OSIM Bucharest. Since 1998, Electra's has been developing its national distribution network in Romania. Due to high demand, technological development was necessary. Therefore, in 2000 new equipment for the production of printed circuit boards and the assembly of electronic components was acquired, which gave the company an advantage: in-house production of a high number of components for the Electra door phones.

In 2002, the company's quality management system was certified in accordance with ISO 9001:2000 by Tüv Thuringen, Germany. In 2005, it obtained certification for its environmental management system, in accordance with ISO 14001:2005. The year 2005 represented a turning point in the expansion of the business. Two years before Romania joined the EU, the company began exporting printed circuit boards and electronic assembly services to EU countries and expanded its production facilities to 4000 m^2.

In 2006, the implementation of the RoHS technology for printed circuit boards and electronic assemblies began, and in 2007, Electra started producing color video door phone systems. The new products feature a digital data transmission system and multiple interconnection possibilities.

In 2008, Electra took an important step toward becoming more technologically flexible, and transformed into Electra Group. The company was divided into three specialized companies, each with its own area of activity. Electra produces intercoms and access control solutions for the end user, while EMS-Electra and PCB-Electra produce components for the industrial sector. In 2009, an innovation that would prove to be a highly successful competitive advantage was implemented in the products. Electra integrated glass technology and touch keyboards in its products, laying the foundation of a range of products with a modern and attractive design, in tune with the trends of the time.

Another important competitive step forward was taken in 2010, when the company launched a project for the development and production of its own RFID technology, determining another necessary expansion of its production facilities. The year 2012 was dedicated to increasing Electra's visibility internationally, by participating as an exhibitor at a specialized fair in Germany. On this occasion, the most innovative range of video and audio door phones at that time—touch line—was launched. In 2014 the company launched a new generation of video and audio door phones—Touch Line Smart—and continues to participate in specialized fairs with this new range of products. In 2015, the company took new steps toward its international expansion in Latin America, by participating in a specialized fair in Mexico.

In 2016, the company consolidated its presence in Central Europe by creating a subsidiary in Vienna. Electra keeps investing in developing its Latin American market by participating as an exhibitor at the Expo Seguridad Mexico City fair. In 2018, Electra further expanded its business in Germany by participating in the Light and Building Frankfurt fair, where the marketing strategy was built around the Bellcome brand, sold since 2014 on the German market. In terms of products, 2018 saw the launch of the company's latest range of products—Electra Touch Line—4 wires/Residential. In the autumn of 2018, Electra took an important step in the development of the company and began the construction of a factory with an area of approximately 10,000 m^2 in the Miroslava Industrial Park, near Iasi, Romania.

To consolidate its leading position in Romania, Electra also participates in the Romanian Security Fair in Bucharest. In 2019, the company will make an important leap into becoming an even better and bigger competitor. The completion of the new factory, which will be known as the Electronic Industry Center of the Electra Group of Companies, is expected at the end of the year. The relocation of Electra's operations to the new facility marks the beginning of a new chapter in Electra's history. Furthermore, in 2019, during the participation in the Power Days Salzburg fair, the company launched a new range of access control devices—the Access Line.

3 Case Study 2

3.1 Grapefruit

Overview
Address: Bd. Poitiers nr.16, Iasi, Romania
Tel: +40.332.882.993
Email: office@grapefruit.ro
Web: www.grapefruit.ro

Company Information
Industry: Computer programming activities
Year of establishment: 1999
Sales revenues in 2017: 850,000 euros
Sales revenues in 2007: 670,000 euros
Average number of employees in 2017: 24
Brain(s) behind the company: Georgiana DragomirR (CEO), Marius Ursache (founder and main shareholder)

Nature of Market Leadership

Grapefruit is the number-one agency in Romania in the niche of user experience and digital consulting, delivering software for a digital strategy, user experience design, content strategy, and other related needs. The clients are usually big domestic and foreign companies doing business in Romania. After being a leader in branding 5 years ago, Grapefruit has become a leader in this newly-emerged competitive domain.

The company is expected to grow by expanding its operations in the European countries and using its contracts with multinational companies as well as other major companies with operations in Romania and other Central and Eastern European countries. In 2018, the company passed an important milestone, when its revenues reached one million euros. This signaled that the recent growth strategy of going fully digital had been fully justified.

Nature of the Competitive Advantage

The competitive advantage of the company is the uniqueness of the offer on the Romanian market, as the company has no major competition because of its exclusive focus on user experience and digital consulting. The company competes with other companies, but all of them are diversified, with a minor interest in this business field, such as software producers, general or specialized advertising agencies, or website solution providers.

This focus strategy allows Grapefruit to provide more valuable integrated solutions than other competitors and to enhance its knowledge base in order to provide better services.

This strategy creates a superior multidisciplinary accumulated experience compared with other competitors, which involves business consulting, design, marketing communications, user experience, and digital aspects.

The adaptable leadership of the company, understanding the digital shift of the market in 2012, is an important factor behind its success. Another core competitive advantage resides in the long presence on the market and the brand image among major potential clients in Romania. Grapefruit has contracts with Dacia, Philip Morris, Heidi, OTP Bank, Pepsi Americas, and Renault.

Core Lessons Learned on the Path to Success

1. Find what is relevant to the end users through research that provides a deep understanding of their behaviors, needs, and desires, as the only way to design the right features for the product.
2. Focus on passionate and loyal customers in designing product features, and not those that only use the product occasionally.
3. Master the perspective of your business provided by three hats: designer and strategist—the one who gets his hands dirty well above the elbow; manager—the one who must organize and keep people happy, budgets under control, and the whole organization running; and the entrepreneur—the one who must move away from the previous two in order to find a vision and gather appropriate resources in order to generate value (Purg and Rant 2011: 70).

The last 6 years added some new insights:

4. It is paramount to understand the company, the competitors, and the core business needs of your clients, not just what they are able to express.
5. Provide millennials with the right work context and the right personnel benefits.
6. The growth of the company requires adaptations of the managerial and organizational system, hence the creation of new roles for some team members.

Management and Leadership Development Needs

The company has been constantly growing in the last years. Now it has passed the threshold of one million euros in annual revenues and is preparing to expand the workforce to more than 50 employees in the next years by extending contracts with multinationals companies and other major companies with operations in Romania and other European countries. This will create a need for an upgrade of the financial and operational system.

Financing and Regulatory Environment Development Needs

With annual revenues above a million euros, the financial management of the company has a new dimension. The company is paying attention to all changes in work taxation and the regulatory environment for the information technology and communication industry.

The 2.0 Digital Agency: The Speed to Keep Up

The success story of Grapefruit is a story of reinventing the business several times, a story of seeking to find new ways to evolve in order to be able to anticipate the market and grow alongside the business partners.

This requires a focus on flexibility and versatility, practically achieved through the creation of a dynamic team model. The internal model of flexible fitness to the needs of the clients is based on a weekly analysis and potential change of components of the internal teams, responding to the needs of each customer. It is a model designed to react faster and better to changes in the market and in the weekly workload. In the digital industry, fast adaptation is a key advantage.

Grapefruit was founded in 1999 by three ambitious medical school graduates—Marius Ursache, Laurian Gridinoc, and Ștefan Liute. Grapefruit is known as a pioneer of branding and digital products in Romania. Although today the company is focused only on building digital products, it is still the most awarded Romanian agency, having received 23 international awards for branding and digital projects.

The company declares that it creates digital experiences, finding the best solutions for the business of its clients, by mixing together digital strategy, marketing, design, user experience, and business knowledge. The company is focused on large clients, and bringing profit to them, endeavoring to maintain a long-term relationship.

In 2019, the company had 28 full-time employees in two offices—Bucharest and Iași—and a reliable network of external resources, including former employees, business and marketing consultants, front-end and back-end software engineers, copywriters, audio and video production, SEO and social media, and legal, financial, and administrative support.

The 20 years journey to this success was marked by important transformations. In 2011, the company was listed as a hidden champion working in branding. It was Romania' leader in consulting in marketing, advertising, and design of client image. In 2011, the core competitive advantage was designing solutions that do not only enhance the image "as packaging" but provides an extended user experience.

One radical change occurred when the company decided to remove the branding services from its offer and keep only digital services. It was a decision based on the conviction that digital products were the future, whereas branding would be covered by an increasing number of agencies and do-it-yourself tools.

Another radical change was the decision to make Grapefruit a user experience agency, which came along with creating new competencies and roles inside the agency, helping create and deliver new services to business partners.

The company takes pride in its open corporate culture and positive working environment, fully integrating agile and lean start-up work philosophies in order to create value and meaning for clients. Grapefruit declares that it uses the following defining principles at work:

- Proactive communication. "We are accessible and open. We discuss any idea, suggestion, issue or problem."
- Getting out of the comfort zone. "Make smart and fast decisions so that you can progress in the right direction."
- More than expected. "We focus on a few things that we do the best, and we always try to improve them."
- A team of A-players. "We expect everyone on our team to aim to be number-one in his field."
- Accepting failure if one can learn from mistakes. "Our mistakes are used as a learning tool, and are not viewed as wrongdoing. We are always headed towards evolution."
- People, not positions. "You are assigned to a project as an expert but you work as a team member on it."

Grapefruit CEO Georgiana Dragomir points out that the company will face two main challenges in 2020. The tremendous growth of the last years has brought many changes and the company is looking for stabilizing and efficiently exploiting the changes that it has already made. The second challenge is to consolidate the services offered to international clients. Grapefruit wants to provide the same high-quality products and services that it has accustomed the Romanian clients to, and this requires some internal changes. In the following years, the company's technological evolution and strategic focus will build on the current broad, yet specialized technological portfolio: user experience agency, user experience consulting, web design, digital marketing, responsive design, web development, user experience design, information architecture, content strategy, digital strategy, visual design, front-end development, and web app development.

4 Case Study 3

4.1 Romsoft

Overview
Address: Chimiei 2 bis, Excel Business Center, 700391 Iasi, Romania
Tel: +40 232 266831
Fax: +40 232 266831
Email: office@rms.ro
Web: http://www.rms.ro

Company Information
Industry: Computer programming activities
Year of establishment: 2001
Sales revenues in 2017: 2.63 million euros
Sales revenues in 2007: 0.46 millon euros
Average number of employees in 2017: 76
Brain(s) behind the company: Dorin Cristea, CEO and founder

Nature of Market Leadership

Romsoft is a strong world competitor and potential hidden champion in the niche of software development with a unique presence in creating software for the medical industry (labs, automated labs, and medical devices) and for business process outsourcing and business intelligence, with commercial partners only from other countries: Japan, Norway, and the USA. Due to the non-transparent nature of the market, it is impossible to estimate the market share or the relative competitive position on the Romanian market or internationally. On the same perspective, the products in which the software is embedded are distributed worldwide.

The company is expected to grow by extending its contracts with prominent producers of labs and medical devices. We consider this company a potential hidden champion due to its presence in the supply chain of major world producers of labs and computerized medical devices. The company might grow into a fully fledged hidden champion in the long term.

Nature of Competitive Advantage

With 18 years of experience on the market, the company enjoys a perception of seriousness and prestige among the customers in this field. One of the key advantages resides in the fact that the company provides software solutions certified for compliance with the latest international quality standards for software in the medical industry. The company enjoys an exceptional position due to the combination of this advantage with lower prices, as Romsoft's prices are two times lower than those of certified competitors.

Other success factors are the reliability of the software solutions, the availability of maintenance for the installed products, and the highly skilled workforce. The stable and visionary leadership of the founder is an important factor behind the success of the company.

Core Lessons Learned on the Path to Success

The company's constant growth was achieved through the strategic choice to follow the digitization of the medical industry, providing constant opportunities for growth.

The company learned that a flexible and positive work climate with competitive salaries is better than a combination of top salaries with stressful human resource performance management systems and a rigid internal climate.

The company is constantly investing in acquiring the latest software development technologies by sending the staff to formation programs and by involving the company in scientific research programs.

Management and Leadership Development Needs

With moderate growth, the company remains competitive and strives to develop its network of international partners and stay ahead by using new technologies that allow better personal data protection, better internet security, and better product traceability.

Financing and Regulatory Environment Development Needs

The company is affected by the change in the taxation of wages in the information and communication technology sector in Romania, as the government significantly increased the level of taxation in 2018.

An Outstanding Team Delivering Outstanding Quality Software

Romsoft was founded in 2001 by Dorin Cristea and Nicu Popescu. Each of them had extensive experience in an Austrian-Romanian joint venture software development company.

The company builds software applications to be used in medicine, in various industries, or in culture. It always seeks to engage in challenging projects and partnerships and have a true potential to contribute to a lasting, sustainable future.

The business model of Romsoft relies on delivering software solutions certified for compliance with the latest international quality standards, created by outstanding teams, connected to the world of science of computers and software. All development team members are computer science graduates and some are PhD students or PhD graduates in computer science. The company is developing a strong collaboration with local universities—the Faculty of Automatic Control and Computer Engineering at Gheorge Asachi Technical University in Iasi, and the Faculty of Computer Science at Alexandru Ioan Cuza University in Iasi—recruiting graduated students with special software development skills, with an internship program for dedicated students pursuing software development degrees.

The company's journey to success is marked by milestones represented by continuous involvement in scientific research and development projects, international certifications, and important customer projects. The company got ISO 9001 certification in 2004 from TÜV Austria CERT GMBH. It was certified for scientific development and research by the National Authority for Scientific Research in 2008. It became a Microsoft certified partner in 2010 and was recognized at "Gold Partner" competency level in May 2016. Also, the quality management system of Romsoft was checked and audited against ISO 13485 and IEC 62304 (software for medical devices) as part of the Sysmex Integrated Quality Model.

The company embraces a very flexible approach to satisfy client requirements by promoting a cooperation model based on "out-tasking," meaning that Romsoft project teams are becoming part of customer project teams. This is better than outsourcing, where the task is externally realized by a subcontractor, leading to a more limited transition of the deeper meanings of the customer needs. In out-tasking, depending on the expertise of the customer, the development teams can be grafted under the control of customer product management, project management, or technical management. This also creates total transparency, giving customers full access and control to the artifacts produced during the development process.

The company's technical expertise is shown by the array of software that they produce: for medical laboratories and hospitals, for automatic medical laboratories, for medical equipment and devices, as well as the Internet of Things for smart houses, measuring air quality. The company also produces, software for business processing, document management, and sales force, solutions for data security (privacy as a service) and blockchain technology, and solutions for tracking systems using blockchain technologies for the pharmaceutical industry.

Currently the company is active in four areas:

1. Custom application development for non-IT companies, based on a well-defined development process, covering requirements definition, software architecture, detailed design, and coding and testing.
2. Outsource and co-source for software development companies, especially in the programming phase.
3. IT consultancy for software development start-ups, as well as for other companies looking to improve their development process.
4. Research and development activities, as a partner in some EU-funded projects, in e-health, telemedicine, and medical devices.

As key strengths, the company considers its cross-functional teams, organized with people with varied levels of skills and experience, brought together by common goals, the "get-things-done" attitude in solving daily problems, the flexibility in assuming different roles on different project teams and, not least, the engaged employees, some with more than 10 years' experience in software development, skills in project management, and software architecture.

5 Conclusions and Recommendations

The Romanian hidden champions were born in an economy that is catching up with the rest of the EU member states in terms of GDP per capita and productivity. The three hidden champions presented in this chapter are operating in industries with high dynamics of technological changes, and a defining role in the interconnected society that we all live in production of electronic devices with communication technologies, production of software, and provision of digital services for the marketing of companies.

Their competitiveness in Romania represents a solid foundation for international expansion. All of them have proved their competitiveness on a global scale. Electra is selling electronic devices in Germany, Grapefruit is selling digital services to major global companies like Renault, Philip Morris, or Pepsi, and Romsoft is selling software to one of the world's leading companies of lab medical devices. Although they have advantages in terms of labor costs, these are not their current drivers of competitiveness, as they rely more on the technical know-how of employees and the internal dynamics that rapidly generate new products or services, allowing continuous expansion and growth of the business. All three hidden champions are direct beneficiaries of the simplicity of trading across borders in the EU and stand apart in the Romanian economic landscape from the point of view of human capital, business sophistication, and innovation.

In order to enhance the companies' competitiveness and strengthen the Romanian entrepreneurship ecosystems, this chapter makes some specific recommendations:

1. Establish a connection hub platform in order to promote successful ventures and exchange of good practices.
2. Reform the institutional system to reduce corruption, and enhance transparency and accountability.
3. Monitor and adjust the tax system in order to encourage equity and stimulate entrepreneurial activities.
4. Invite university faculty members, students, and business representatives to an open discussion on how the educational system can be improved in order to provide better support to entrepreneurship.

References

Berdan M (2019) Personal Interview. https://www.electronica-azi.ro/print.php?id=3075
Biz Team (2019) Cum arată agenția digitală 2.0? [How does digital agency 2.0 looks like?]. https://www.revistabiz.ro/cum-arata-agentia-digitala-2-0/?fbclid=IwAR2hhDRjbHZerSrdFoIlzkmm2mJ-8DRFighPmis4VHfajbXtKEHSmzAbvOU
Blanaru C (2016) Grapefruit—20 years of digital on the Romanian market. http://www.adhugger.net/2019/10/21/grapefruit-20-years-of-digital-on-the-romanian-market/?utm_campaign=coschedule&utm_source=facebook_page&utm_medium=Grapefruit&fbclid=IwAR36gpiSbuo1cnavs3-r643Sug0D3gLT0oJGv7lF3IoYoqSGlYwCxmnhK9g

Cristea F (2019) Digital Agency 2.0. https://www.grapefruit.ro/ideas/digital-agency-2-0/?fbclid=IwAR2FgpadJ1zP63WJ032e-FbuT01K96lKJjsFUPdXqMLPPNIdLOW7AhpNFJ4

Daianu D, Murgescu B (2013) Which way goes romanian capitalism-making a case for reforms, inclusive institutions and a better functioning European Union. Roman J Eur Affairs *13*(4):5–34

De Rosa D, Kim YS, Chatzinikolaou A, Bulman DJ, Hopkins J, Dospinescu AS, Karver JG, Meisner CM, Murisic M, Pauna C, Tsoungui Belinga VP (2018) From uneven growth to inclusive development: Romania's path to shared prosperity—systematic country diagnostic. World Bank Group, Washington, DC

Duguleană L, Duguleană C (2014) Analyzing the economic potential of romanian administrative regions. Int J Econ Pract Theor 4(2):262–272

Electra (2019a) About electra company. http://www.ELECTRA-grup.ro/about.php

Electra (2019b) Electra company short history. https://www.electra.ro/en/about-us#short-history

European Comission (2018) Country Report Romania 2018. https://ec.europa.eu/info/sites/info/files/2018-european-semester-country-report-romania-en.pdf

Eurostat (2018) Eurostat indicators for Romania. European Commisssion. https://ec.europa.eu/eurostat/web/sdi/indicators

Fuentelsaz L, González C, Maicas JP (2019) Formal institutions and opportunity entrepreneurship. The contingent role of informal institutions. BRQ Business Res Q 22(1):5–24

Grapefruit (2019) Grapefruit company briefing. https://www.grapefruit.ro/about/

Iqads (2016) Două schimbări majore la început de 2016 pentru Grapefruit [Two major changes in the beginning of 2016 for Grapefruit]. https://www.iqads.ro/articol/34021/doua-schimbari-majore-la-inceput-de-2016-pentru-grapefruit

Purg D, Rant M (eds) (2011) Hidden champions in CEE and dynamically changing environments. Research report. CEEMAN, Slovenia. http://www.ceeman.org/Publications

Radauer A, Roman L (2017) The Romanian entrepreneurial ecosystem background report. European Commission. https://rio.jrc.ec.europa.eu/sites/default/files/report/KI%20AX%2017%20002%20EN%20N%20Romania_Background.pdf

RomSoft (2015) RomSoft company presentation. https://slideplayer.com/slide/2913191/

RomSoft (2017) RomSoft company presentation. https://www.marketplaceromania.ro/wp-content/uploads/2017/06/Presentation2_RomSoft.pdf

RomSoft (2019) RomSoft company presentation. http://oi.nttdata.com/program/forum/history/20180507/pdf/12_RomSoft.pdf

UNDP (2018) Human development for everyone. Briefing note for countries on the 2016 Human Development Report—Romania. http://hdr.undp.org/sites/all/themes/hdr_theme/country-notes/ROU.pdf

World Bank (2019) World Bank Indicators. https://data.worldbank.org

World Bank Group (2019) World Bank doing business 2019. Training for reform. https://www.worldbank.org/content/dam/doingBusiness/media/Annual-Reports/English/DB2019-report_web-version.pdf

World Economic Forum (2018) Global competitiveness report 2018. http://reports.weforum.org/global-competitiveness-report-2018/downloads/

Zaman G, Georgescu G (2009) The impact of global crisis on Romania's economic development. Ann Univ Apulens Ser Oeconom 11(2):611–624

Hidden Champions of Russia

Irina Skorobogatykh, Olga Saginova, Zhanna Musatova,
Ekaterina Molchanova, and Sofia Sedenko

Overview
Official name: Russian Federation
Type of government: Semi-presidential republic[1]
Population in 2017: 144,496,740
Land area (sq.km): 17,125,191

History

1917–1922	The Great October Socialist Revolution. Civil war. Nationalization of land, industry, and small business.
1922	Formation of the Union of the Soviet Socialist Republics (USSR).
1929–1939	Establishment of a command economy. Collectivization and industrialization. Rise of Joseph Stalin.
1941–1945	World War II, in which the Soviet Union loses around 27 million people.
The 1950s	The golden period of the Soviet economy with high growth and high productivity rates (Popov 2010). The period is also characterized by the development of nuclear technologies and active space exploration.
1960–1980	Slowdown of economic growth with ensuing stagnation.

---

[1]State power is exercised by the President, the Federal Assembly, the Government and the courts.

I. Skorobogatykh (✉) · O. Saginova · Z. Musatova
Plekhanov Russian University of Economics, Moscow, Russia
e-mail: Skorobogatykh.II@rea.ru; Saginova.OV@rea.ru; Musatova.ZHB@rea.ru

E. Molchanova · S. Sedenko
Global Strategy Studies, Moscow School of Management Skolkovo, Moscow, Russia
e-mail: Ekaterina_Molchanova@skolkovo.ru; Sofia_Sedenko@skolkovo.ru

1985–1991	The period spans from Perestroika to the dissolution of the Soviet Union. The most significant economic reform is the Law on Cooperatives, enacted in 1988, that permitted private ownership of businesses. The timeline of the collapse of the Soviet Union can be traced back to 1985 when oil prices fell significantly (Gaidar 2007). Several republics began resisting central control and started their journey to independence.
1991	Declaration of USSR's disintegration. The Russian Federation becomes an independent state on 31 December.
1992	Price liberalization. Privatization of state assets.
1992–1997	Slump in the Russian economy. Contracted production, high inflation, and consumer market deficit.
1998	Default of the Russian currency. Collapse of bond and currency markets. Severe devaluation of the ruble.
1999	Beginning of industrial growth. Rise of oil prices.
2000	Start of Putin's presidency period. Introduction of institutional reforms aimed at strengthening federal power. Flat income tax reform.
2001–2007	Growth of private business, including in non-commodity sectors. IPOs in Russia and world financial markets.
2008–2009	Economic slowdown. Establishment of state corporations in strategic sectors (Rostech, Rosnano, Rosatom, Roskosmos).
2010	Formation of a Customs Union with member states of the Eurasian Economic Union (Russia, Kazakhstan, Belarus, in 2015—Armenia and Kyrgyzstan).
2014	Tension with the West. Sanctions and counter-sanctions. Plunge of the ruble's exchange rate. Sharp decrease of FDI inflow.
2016–2018	Increasing state ownership in some key industries.

1 Introduction: Context and History

During the Soviet period, the state was the major owner of all organizations, both manufacturing and servicing. Five-year plans and annual plans were the main tools of the centrally-planned economy. The Soviet government set the goals, distributed resources centrally, and controlled the fulfillment of 5-year plans. The State Planning Committee elaborated output targets for all the industries and all the enterprises. The prices of all goods and services were established by the government. In order to allocate resources among individual customers and enterprises, some prices were lower than costs. Without competition and with a limited number of markets (only domestic and Soviet bloc countries), companies were very restricted in their development and innovation initiatives.

Since 1990, Russia has abandoned the centrally-planned isolated economic structure and adopted a market-oriented economy. These changes were quite dramatic for the country, the economic system, and the population.

As of 1 January 2019, Russia had a population of over 146 million,[2] including different nationalities and cultures. Most citizens live in cities. Of these, 15 have a metropolitan population of more than one million.[3] The biggest cities are Moscow with a population of about 12,615 million and Saint-Petersburg—about 5389 million. The most developed economic regions are located in the center (Moscow and the Moscow region), Saint-Petersburg, and in the territory of the Ural mountains (Yekaterinburg, Perm, Cheliabinsk). The main oil and gas producing areas are located in the Khanty-Mansi Autonomous District, the Republic of Tatarstan, Sakhalin Island, and the Pacific Ocean. Other economically developed regions are located in the Volga river region (Samara, Saratov), and in the South of Russia (Rostov-on-Don, Krasnodar) (McKiernan and Purg 2013).

The unique geographic location and large territory of Russia have provided the national economy with significant reserves of natural resources: gas, oil, ores, wood, and more. Mineral reserves have given Russia's economy an important competitive advantages in the world market but have shifted the development of the economy to commodity industries.

However, Russia is attempting to diversify the national economy by developing different industry sectors, such as mechanical engineering, automotive industry, aerospace industry, aircraft and helicopter engineering, pharmaceutical industry, and production of construction materials. Still, the nation's welfare strongly depends on industries based on natural resources. In 2018, the share of fuel, ore, and metal exports reached 57.5% of total exports (see Exhibit 1). The share of oil and gas revenues in the total revenues of the consolidated budget in 2018 was 24.16%.[4]

When the first wave of hidden champion research was undertaken in 2011, the Russian economy was recovering from the recession of 2009. The 50% fall in the oil prices and the international economic sanctions have kept Russia from returning to its previous strong economic growth. One of the most negative factors for Russia's business development is the sharp growth of the key rate of the Bank of Russia. Starting at 5.5% at the beginning of 2014, it reached 17% in December. Afterward, the key rate slowly declined, and on September 9, 2019, it was 7%.[5] The high cost of money is still one of the main barriers to business development.

From 2014 through 2016, the economy contracted by an average of 2% per year, and the share of the population living below the poverty line rose by 23%. The ruble has been devalued twice since 2014 against major world currencies, making foreign goods and services more expensive. Inflation has risen nearly twice as fast as incomes, reflecting negatively on household purchasing power. Only in 2017 did the Russian economy return to modest growth: 1.7%. Consequently, Russian consumers have grown more cautious, pragmatic, and value-conscious. They prefer to

---

[2]According to data of the Federal State Statistics Service of the Russian Federation.
[3]Ibid.
[4]According to data of the Ministry of Finance of the Russian Federation.
[5]Ibid.

save money. As the statistics show, the total savings of the Russian population grew by approximately 10% in 2018 (Kotov et al. 2018).

As a way to boost manufacturing development, including high-tech industries, ship-building, transport infrastructure, and tourism, the government has been active in establishing and promoting special economic zones (SEZs) (Golubkin et al. 2018). The formation of SEZs started in the mid-2000s, but has accelerated in recent years. SEZ residents are entitled to federal and regional tax privileges, concerning mostly profit tax, property and land tax, and some social payments. They enjoy national guarantees, advanced infrastructure, and preferences in rental costs and purchase of the land (Golubkin et al. 2018). As of January, 1, 2018, there were 25 SEZs in Russia: nine industrial production zones, six technology innovative zones, nine tourism and recreational zones, and one port zone. They attracted many residents and 4591.9 million US dollars of private capital investment. Also, 28,421 jobs were created (Golubkin et al. 2019). None of the current national hidden champions is a SEZ resident, although there were some in 2011.

Since the first hidden champions study, Russian business, especially small-and-medium-sized companies (SMEs), have undergone many changes. Higher trade barriers and protectionism, geopolitical risks, lower core business revenue, rising barriers to entry into new markets, and lower consumer interest in new products have had a direct impact on the hidden champions in the previous research. Because of the high cost of capital and difficulties in borrowing funds, many companies started looking for strategic partnerships, joining bigger holdings, or merging with well-known corporations. Some SMEs, developing innovative products and services in their specialized market niches, have now become part of diversified corporations. Formerly independent and autonomous parts of large entities that could be considered hidden champions, as they operated in their own specific markets, are now completely integrated into corporate structures and have lost control of the decision-making process. As a result, the overall situation of Russia's hidden champions identified in 2011 has changed. Some have grown too big to be considered SMEs. Some have become public, due to their new orientation to mass-market segments. Others have joined state-owned holdings. Some potential hidden champions have not managed to grow into regional leaders due to geopolitical factors hindering their international expansion.

In this research, we have decided to go for depth rather than breadth of observations. Instead of trying to identify all hidden champions in Russia, we have chosen to concentrate on a few compelling case studies, which, in our opinion, provide a more thorough understanding of the nature of Russia's hidden champions, their strategies, and their success factors. According to the methodology of the project, we have looked for SMEs that hold top positions in their markets and have a fairly low visibility profile in the public domain.

The hidden champions that we observed are predominantly in the manufacturing sector. There are also many extremely successful companies in the Russian IT industry. Unfortunately, many of them do not meet the hidden champions' criterion because their headquarters are located outside Russia. While most hidden champions on the current list operate in business-to-business markets, some of them cater to the business-to-customer sector, too. Due to their narrow specialization, these companies are rarely a subject of wide media coverage. Therefore, in order to identify hidden champions, we have scanned industry news, business ratings, professional contests, and awards. We have looked for companies with a proven track record, which explains why there are no start-ups on our list.

Most of the companies are on average over 20 years old, with their history dating to the 1990s. Back then, the turbulent times in the aftermath of the collapse of the Soviet Union and subsequent economic liberalization gave way to a new breed of businessmen whose legacy echoes today. Either established professionals or recent university graduates, those novice entrepreneurs were pushed out of their comfort zone to look for new means of subsistence and explore what the new reality had to offer. So, it is those years that seem to have born not only big Russian businesses but also most hidden champions.

Innovation, exemplified by innovative products and original production systems, is the core characteristic of Russia's hidden champions. In fact, some of the studied companies operate in sectors that border highly advanced science. It is not surprising that many hidden champions on the new list and the previous have been chosen to participate in the National Champions priority project of the Ministry of Economic Development of Russia. Started in 2016, the project is aimed at promoting the growth of domestic private high-tech export-oriented companies by granting them access to government support mechanisms.[6]

Below, we tell stories of hidden champions in different industries. What unites them is their niche strategy, focus on innovation, and global presence.

Exhibit 1 Core economic indicators of the Russian Federation

	2011	2012	2013	2014	2015	2016	2017	2018
GDP per capita (current US$)	14,351	15,434	16,007	14,100	9313	8745	10,750	11,288
GDP per capita growth (annual %)	4.219	3.526	1.583	−1.081	−2.518	0.146	1.515	2.262
Unemployment, total (% of total labor force) (national estimate) Russian Federation	6.536	5.436	5.458	5.16	5.571	5.559	5.212	4.846
Foreign direct investment, net inflows (% of GDP)	2.685	2.289	3.013	1.069	0.503	2.537	1.809	0.53
GDP (current US $, mio)	2052	2210	2297	2060	1364	1283	1579	1658

(continued)

---

[6]According to the RVC webpage.

Exhibit 1 (continued)

	2011	2012	2013	2014	2015	2016	2017	2018
Exports of goods and services (current US$, mio)	573.448	589.774	591.958	562.551	393.035	332.353	410.734	507.756
Exports of goods and services (% of GDP)	28	26.9	25.8	27.1	28.7	25.7	26.1	30.7
Merchandise exports (current US$, bln)	522,011	529,256	521,836	496,807	341,419	281,710	353,548	444,008
Merchandise exports to high-income economies (% of total merchandise exports)	57.531	64.321	66.83	65.895	62.658	59.428	58.267	n/a
Merchandise exports to low- and middle-income economies in Europe and Central Asia (% of total merchandise exports)	12.876	21.891	20.044	18.964	20.287	19.96	20.245	n/a
Ores and metals exports (% of merchandise exports)	4.872	5.291	4.722	4.746	6.054	6.648	6.381	5.54
Agricultural raw materials exports (% of merchandise exports)	1.927	1.783	1.805	1.821	2.15	2.576	2.528	2.219
Food exports (% of merchandise exports)	2.174	3.195	3.074	3.797	4.67	5.916	5.746	5.466
Fuel exports (% of merchandise exports)	66.982	70.934	71.248	69.784	62.996	47.186	59.054	52.017
Manufactures exports (% of merchandise exports)	13.207	16.302	16.582	17.374	20.54	21.765	22.313	20.605
High-technology exports (% of manufactured exports)	8.51	9.205	10.762	12.196	16.413	11.324	12.472	10.963

Source: World Bank (2019)

2 Case Studies of Selected Hidden Champions

2.1 Atlantis-Pak

Overview
Address: 72 Onuchkina str., village of Lenin, Aksay district, Rostov region, Russia
Tel: +7863 255 8585
Email: info@atlantis-pak.top
Web: www.atlantis-pak.top

Company Information
Industry: Manufacturing
Year of establishment: 1993
Sales revenues in 2017: 100 million euros
Sales revenues in 2007: 65 million euros
Average number of employees in 2017: 2700
Brain(s) behind the company: CEO Igor Perepletchikov

Nature of Market Leadership

Atlantis-Pak is a major producer of plastic casings for the meat and dairy industries. Home-based in Russia, the company has clients in over 90 countries, with nine representative offices internationally. In the Commonwealth of Independent States (CIS), the company is a leader, holding over 35% of the market. On a global scale, Atlantis-Pak's market share in the segment of plastic casings is around 20%. Its position is particularly strong in barrier casings for boiled sausage and mortadella, small caliber casings, and permeable casings for smoked sausage.

Nature of the Competitive Advantage

The company stands out from the competition thanks to its flexibility and speed. Being narrowly focused on the category of plastic casings helps Atlantis-Pak to know its customers. The company not only quickly responds to its clients' requests but also anticipates their evolving needs. This is made possible by flexible production lines and continuous innovation. Atlantis-Pak is an acknowledged pioneer in several categories of plastic casings. It is particularly known for its permeable casings and small caliber plastic casings that it was the first in the world to introduce.

Core Lessons Learned on the Path to Success

1. One should not try to embrace what cannot be embraced. The company must be focused and identify its key competence to develop and build on.
2. The company should not seek quick gains at the expense of long-term relationships with its clients.

Management and Leadership Development Needs

Atlantis-Pak grows its management talents mainly from within. Being part of Agrocom Group, the company trains its executives at the Group's corporate university. The company finds formal education in business schools, such as MBA or executive programs, too expensive.

Financing and Regulatory Environment Development Needs

Since 2011, Atlantis-Pak has been part of the Agrocom Group of companies.[7] The acquisition provided financing to the company, albeit leaving Atlantis-Pak's management largely independent in terms of decision-making. Other sources of financing include re-investment of the company's revenue, borrowing from banks, and, recently, allocated loans from the Industrial Development Fund. This is a Russian federal agency established in 2014 to support the development of new high-tech products, modernization, and creation of competitive production processes.

Concerning the regulatory environment, the company's main challenges are the high custom duties imposed on its products due to their Russian origin. Unlike competitors from other countries, especially from the EU, which have much more preferential rates, Atlantis-Pak faces a higher import tax burden in many foreign markets. For this reason, the company opened a production and logistical center in the Czech Republic, which allows it to minimize import duties when selling to European and other global markets.

A Bespoke Atelier with International Vision

Atlantis-Pak was established in the Russian city of Rostov-on-Don in 1993 by six associates who had tried their hand at different businesses before finally settling on the production of casings. It was the difficult time of the economic turmoil in the wake of the collapse of the Soviet Union, so the young companions were exploring different business possibilities. The idea of the casings production arose when one of the founders visited a collagen casings plant near Saint Petersburg and learned that

---

[7]Agrocom Group is a large private company in Russia with assets in the food industry, the agricultural sector, the package industry, and retail trading.

demand for casings in Russia significantly exceeded supply. Unfamiliar with the casings industry, the team consulted scientists at the National Russian Meat Research Institute and studied the market. Eventually, the entrepreneurs decided to focus on the fledgling segment of plastic casings, which was deemed to have the greatest potential.

In the words of Igor Perepletchikov, the CEO of Atlantis-Pak, "from the very beginning, the company was centered on two guiding principles: firstly, we wanted to create value through innovative products and cutting-edge manufacturing, and secondly, we aimed to expand internationally." Mr. Perepletchikov, now the brain behind the company, joined Atlantis-Pak in 1994 as the head of sales and marketing and has since been an integral part of the company's growth.

Today Atlantis-Pak is an established medium-sized company. Its annual sales are over 100 million euros, having grown more than 1.5 times from 2007 to 2017. Almost half of Atlantis-Pak's revenues come from outside of Russia and the CIS. The company is appreciated for its ability to adapt quickly to clients' needs, which greatly vary by country depending on technical specifications, climatic conditions, and cultural preferences. This is an admirable accomplishment as the company sells to over 90 countries across the globe. In this sense, Atlantis-Pak is "the world's largest bespoke atelier" as Mr. Perepretchikov puts it.

Although innovation has played a vital role in the company's development, the route to success has been strenuous, particularly in the beginning, as plastic casings were new to Russia, so the company had to develop the technology itself. Failures happened: the first batch of casings that Atlantis-Pak produced burst during application due to inadequate transport conditions. Over time, Atlantis-Pak learned from this and other mistakes and gradually evolved into an industry expert. Innovation in the casings industry is a combination of advanced chemistry and leading-edge manufacturing technology. It is by combining these two skills that Atlantis-Pak managed to move forward. The company's first big success took place in 1997 when Atlantis-Pak introduced the world's first-ever plastic casing for frankfurters and wieners, and within just a year acquired 22% of that massive product category in Russia. The following years brought more breakthroughs in innovation, most notable of which was the introduction of permeable casings.

Nowadays the company has more than a dozen inventions and utility models patented in Russia and other countries. Its R&D department includes, among others, six employees with a scientific degree. At present, 15% of the company's turnover consists of products developed in the past 3 years. Besides the development of innovative products, no less critical is Atlantis-Pak's ability to launch new products since meat and dairy producers tend to be highly conservative and, on average, it takes 9–10 months to persuade a client to adopt a new product.

The company sees its sources of growth in promoting its innovative plastic casings so that they substitute other casing categories mainly viscose and cellulose types—as well as in introducing a new product category—shrink films—which are used not only in meat but also in dairy products packaging.

Along with innovation, Atlantis-Pak has been keen to expand beyond its home market. Ex-Soviet republics in the CIS were the intuitive first step, due to economic and cultural ties. During the 2000s, the company also approached European markets. Germany was particularly important for the young company. Gaining a foothold on this mature market with its strong sausage culture and advanced casings industry helped Atlantis-Pak to build a reputation in Europe.

However, it was not until 2011 that a comprehensive international expansion took place. The expansion was triggered by falling margins and exhausted growth opportunities in the Russian market. The acquisition of Atlantis-Pak by Agrocom Group in 2011 provided much-needed capital to support its global strategy. The company worked hard to obtain important international certifications, such as the British Retail Consortium Global Standard certification in 2013 and the international halal certification in 2014, followed by the Sedex Member Ethical Audit in 2017, all of which have eased access to markets worldwide.

Atlantis-Pak also re-adjusted its international distribution system. Rather than relying solely on independent distributors, the company has established its own representative offices in key countries, usually by identifying preferred distributors and bringing them in-house. This new approach not only increased distributors' loyalty but also improved customer service by maintaining close ties with meat-processing companies and promptly responding to clients' feedback and requests.

Speed and flexibility in production at Atlantis-Pak are made possible by its original manufacturing lines. Unlike the fixed equipment lines used by competitors, production lines at Atlantis-Pak were developed by an in-house team of skilled engineers and allow for more adjustability, sometimes doubling the output of a line compared to the industry standard. Atlantis-Pak's production facility is located in the Rostov area in Russia. As mentioned already, in 2015, the company also opened a production and logistics center in the Czech Republic and is examining opportunities to localize production in other parts of the world. Atlantis-Pak actively penetrates the markets of North Africa and South-East Asia. In fact, it is these regions where the company experiences most of its growth, with the European markets largely stagnating, and Russia suffering a decline due to end-consumers' lower purchasing power and changing consumption habits. Nevertheless, the economic downturn in Russia seems to have played to the company's advantage. With a weak rubble, the company is working at full capacity to satisfy the growing international demand.

The challenge ahead is to sustain the company's positive dynamics. Today the overall industry of casings is highly competitive and becomes increasingly concentrated. As a result, Atlantis-Pak competes face-to-face with large international conglomerates, which have the benefit of big budgets and wide international reach. True to its core principles proved over time, Atlantis-Pak intends to withstand rivalry by maintaining a narrow focus and nurturing relationships with its clients.

2.2 BWT Barrier

Overview
Address: 6/16, Proectirooyemiy proezd, Moscow, 115432, Russia

Tel: +7 495 661 21 21
Fax: +7 495 529 42 97
Email: info@bwf.ru
Web: www.barrier.ru

Company Information
Industry: Manufacturing
Year of establishment: 1993
Sales revenues in 2017: 40 million euros
Sales revenues in 2007: n/a
Average number of employees in 2017: 800
Brain(s) behind the company: Five founders

Nature of Market Leadership

The company was the first producer of pitcher water filters in Russia in the segment of the business-to-business market and still is the leading manufacturer of pitcher water filters in Russia and CIS with a market share of about 40%. The company holds the second or third position in the world's pitcher water filters market. Export revenues were about 8% of the revenues in 2017 and the strategic aim is to increase foreign sales to 30–50% in 2025.

Nature of the Competitive Advantage

1. Quality. The quality control process is a core value of the company. Barrier's products are recognized for combining the latest advances in science, engineering, and technology, and for meeting the most stringent local and international water quality standards.
2. Technology. The company has its own state-of-the-art R&D department to research innovative solutions and strive for continuous product development. The company has dozens of patents. Barrier is constantly looking for the best technology in the industry of water filtration. Some of the R&D projects are developed with foreign partners. For example, the company has a collaborative patent with a Japanese partner.
3. Strong brand. The company has a strong reputation in the domestic market and in the CIS region and operates as the "Barrier" brand. Five times in a row, customers named Barrier the number-one brand in the water filter category, and the company was awarded three golden prizes at the Brand of the Year competitions. At the moment, the company is expanding its global presence on the consumer market with two brands: Barrier and BWT.

Core Lessons Learned on the Path to Success

A competitor can assist the company. For instance, the Russian water pitcher filters market was developed by Brita, the main competitor of Barrier. It was that company that promoted the culture of pure water.

Retailers can create big opportunities for growth in the business-to-customer segment. The negotiation process with big retailers is hard. The terms of the agreement are constraining the agility of the business. For instance, the company had losses during the ruble volatility crisis because of the condition of fixing the prices for the duration of its 1-year agreement.

Management and Leadership Development Needs

The top managers have MBA degrees and a lot of experience in the industry. The holding company provides examples of best management practices. The staff development strategy is oriented toward technical personnel. Business schools are expected to provide knowledge, skills, and competences that are not one-size-fits-all solutions but are relevant specifically to medium-sized business.

Financing and Regulatory Environment Development Needs

The company has no financing needs. It uses internal financial sources, such as financing from the holding company. There is a negative effect of the customs policy in Russia that stimulates producers to relocate production outside the country. For instance, the tax on Brita's imported finished goods is lower than the customs duty on Barrier's imported raw materials.

The Vital Need for Clean Water

BWT Barrier was formed when the Austrian holding company BWT (a manufacturer of water treatment systems for the business-to-business segment) acquired a controlling stake of shares in Mettham-Technology in 2015. The latter owned all assets, trademarks, R&Ds, and the Barrier brand. The transaction was more like a merger than an acquisition, due to the need for BWT to buy the company that has competencies in the segment of the business-to-customer market. The partnership with BWT was the opportunity for Barrier to get access to the international markets, in particular to the European market. The decision-making process and company strategy are still controlled by Russian management.

The history of the company starts with the R&D that a group of Soviet scientists conducted during the war in Afghanistan. Enemy troops poisoned water storages to disorganize the Soviet army. Toxic water killed soldiers. The scientists invented portable water purification devices that formed the basis of a commercial product for civil usage. In 1993, the scientists set up the Mettham-Technology company, later renamed Barrier. The company started mass production of pitcher water filters on the space-rocket Energy complex of S.P. Korolev, in Korolyev city near Moscow, in 1995.

In the 1990s, Russian citizens were unaware of the degree of pollution of the urban water supply system. The market for pitcher water filters was small and undeveloped. The market expanded when a foreign competitor, Brita, came to the Russian market and started to invest in consumer awareness. That was a good opportunity for Barrier because it had a price advantage and a better-designed product.

In the following years, Barrier increased its market share and successfully competed with its main rivals: Akvafor, Geizer, and Brita. The key to success was the effectively lined-up business processes of the company, the client-oriented vision, good relationships with suppliers, continuous R&Ds, and persistent innovations.

2.3 Grishko

Overview
Address: Moscow, 3rd Krutitsy per., 11, Russia
Tel: (495) 287-45-77 dob.106; 107
Email: org@grishko.ru
Web: www.grishko-world.com

Company Information
Industry: Manufacture of wearing apparel and accessories: shoes and accessories for ballet and dance
Year of establishment: 1989
Sales revenues in 2017: 6.0 million euros
Sales revenues in 2007: 7.4 million euros
Average number of employees in 2017: 560
Brain(s) behind the company: Nikolai Grishko

Nature of Market Leadership

The company is number three on the global pointe shoes market. Originally, it produced ballet shoes. Later, it also offered costumes for training and performance, dance-wear, and leisure-wear. In the pointe shoes market, there are four main competitors: Bloch, Capezio, Freed of London, and Gaynor Minden. Most of them have been in the market for several decades. The Grishko brand is well known by all professional dancers and dance-lovers in Russia and all over the world.

Grishko is younger than most of its competitors. Its market leadership has been based on its high quality and the natural materials that the company uses, as well as on special technologies for ballet shoes production. The company's leadership is maintained by talent management and contacts with the best theater companies and top performers. Grishko products are sold in more than 70 countries, including Russia, the USA, Canada, Great Britain, Germany, France, Japan, Italy, South Korea, Brazil, Peru, and Uruguay.

Nature of the Competitive Advantage

Grishko's competitive advantage is based on quality: production technology developed through extensive research, combined with the use of exclusively natural materials, and hand-made poducts. This results in excellent quality and product customization.

Another important element of the company's competitive advantage is the maintenance of close relationships with leading theaters and dancers across the world. Most famous ballerinas have their pointe shoes made to measure by Grishko. The company produces a whole collection of costumes and clothes for rehearsals named after famous Russian ballet dancers. Russian prima ballerinas promote the company's new lines of fashion leisure wear.

Grishko supports young talented ballet dancers and develops the professional community through donations of a 1-year supply of pointe shoes to students of leading ballet schools. Thus, the company creates loyal customers from their first steps in ballet and dancing.

Responsible entrepreneurship, including green production, employment of disabled people and talent management, contributes to a better brand perception.

Core Lessons Learned on the Path to Success

1. Understanding the difference between the domestic and foreign markets. Adapting the pricing policy to different markets.
2. A reasonable approach to the selection of distributors, and selection of the most efficient intermediaries.
3. A necessity to build a strong relationship with the ballet community, and support ballet schools and talented young dancers so as to create brand awareness and loyalty. Attracting famous ballerinas to company products presentation and promotion.
4. Deep understanding of all business processes of production, distribution, finding potential suppliers, and production facilities.

5. Early internationalization, export to markets with a big potential: countries where ballet was not only a professional occupation, but also a hobby or a fitness exercise.

Management and Leadership Development Needs

The company has always relied on extensive research and new product development, so the necessary managerial skills related to the company's diversification strategy include deep understanding of the nature of each activity for which footwear and apparel are being produced and the ability to relate those to the company's core business—dancewear.

Financing and Regulatory Environment Development Needs

The company enjoys support from the Moscow government but, as all SMEs, it experiences difficulties accessing financial resources and would like an extension of government guarantees.

From Russia with Love for Ballet

Country perceptions are usually dominated by stereotypes stemming from the image of products, industries, or activities. Concerning Russia, these stereotypes include the vast territory, the cold climate, the long history of communist rule, space exploration pioneers, and ballet. The latter is well known by both art-lovers and theater-goers, as well as tourists coming to Moscow for the first time and wishing to visit Russian churches and the Bolshoi Theater.

There are several large companies in the world producing ballet shoes and theater costumes. One of these is Bloch, an Australian company, set in 1931. Another one is Capezio Pointe Shoes, founded in 1887. Freed of London is a British company, known for its custom-made pointes shoes for the Royal Ballet stars. The list of modern brands of pointe shoes is quite long. It can be found on the website of a popular blog about pointe shoes.[8] The most well-known brands have a long history. Capezio had celebrated its 100th anniversary when Russian entrepreneur Nikolai Grishko was still filling out registration papers for his company. Nowadays, many ballet dancers are loyal customers of Grishko branded products.

In the nineteenth century, special theater workshops made shoes for Russia's famous ballerinas Anna Pavlova and Olga Spessivtseva. The secrets of pointes making were passed by word of mouth as a real secret knowledge and each master added something new to the technology. That is why the pointes made by the

---

[8]https://pointeshoebrands.wordpress.com.

Russian masters were appreciated as much as Russian ballet all over the world. These theater workshops were closed in 1917. However, the secrets of this complicated fine art were maintained.

The Grishko company started the production of pointes as a small cooperative in 1989. The idea to produce pointes shoes for ballet dancers was born when Nikolai Grishko saw that foreign dancers visiting Moscow were buying rather cheap Russian pointes shoes to take home where they then cost at least 50 US dollars. Nikolai Grishko graduated from the Moscow Institute of Foreign Affairs in 1975, and started his professional career as a diplomat. Later, he had some academic experience working as an associate professor at the Plekhanov Institute of National economy. He met a PhD student at the University of Light Industry working on a dissertation about the design of ballet shoes. This is still the only dissertation in the world on that topic. Together, they worked out the idea of ballet shoes production, which started in 1989 as a cooperative, the first private business model allowed in the Soviet Union during the Perestroika (Purg et al. 2016). Further research of suppliers, building distribution channels, and production took another 2 years. Thus, the first sales started in 1991.

A pointe shoe consists of 50 different elements put together in about 40 operations. In traditional ballet shoes, the toe box is made from tightly packed layers of paper, cardboard, burlap, or fabric, held together by glue. The material is compressed into an enclosure (toe box) that surrounds the dancers' toes so that her weight rests on the platform. The shank is generally made of cardboard, leather, or a combination of the two. The outer material is a soft cloth called corset satin. The materials and methods of production have not changed much in the last 100 years (Ballet focus blog by Kent G. Becker Retrieved from: http://balletfocus.com/pointe-shoes-part/).

The average life span of a pair of pointe shoes is estimated at 4–12 h of work, depending on the type of classes and the degree of tear and wear. Experts recommend changing shoes after 45–60 min of work and letting them dry out for a minimum of 24 h before using them again. Given that life span of ballet shoes, major ballet companies go through a lot of shoes. Pointe shoe expenses are a major cost of ballet companies. A professional ballerina goes through 150–170 pairs of pointe shoes a year. Most major companies have a shoe master or manager to manage the process of recording dancer specifications, ordering the shoes, and coloring them if necessary.

Now Grishko exports shoes to more than 60 countries. The US is its first and largest market, with sales of up to 100,000 pointe shoes per year. Over 300 US stores carry Grishko products, which include other dance footwear and active clothing, in addition to the ballet shoes. Grishko factories make 40,000 pointe shoes per month, but even that is not enough to satisfy demand. Convincing the market that these new Russian shoes were worth having was not as easy as one might think (interview with Grishko company representative in 2018). Ballerinas typically use one brand of pointe shoe throughout their careers. Convincing them to switch to Russian brands took more than 10 years. Freed of London, for instance, is still the most popular brand for British dancers and is the official shoemaker for many British dance companies. But things are changing now that Western dancers are more familiar with Russian labels.

Nikolay Grishko runs the company he founded in the late 1980s. Grishko resolved to exploit this market by organizing the Russian workshops to make ballet shoes for export, and in doing so gave employment to many craftsmen during the difficult economic transition of the 1990s. But Grishko was finally convinced to start his own business when a Soviet trade organization responsible for sales to the USA approached him with a request to find pointe shoes for an American dancer. The request sent him searching. But finding the shoes was not easy (interview with N. Grishko in 2011). At first, the company copied older shoe models but Grishko realized that new dance techniques and movements required a new design even for classical dance. The old models were too rigid for modern dance. The company developed and used new technologies and design, yet continued to produce its shoes by hand.

In the early 1990-s, the company produced 500 pairs of shoes per month. Now, it makes 1400 pairs a day.

Production of pointes shoes is a very complicated process. It takes 3 months for the master to study the theory of pointes shoes production and then 6–7 months of practice. It takes a year for a person to become a qualified master. Grishko tried to automate the production but then rejected this idea, as hand-made shoes proved to result in better quality. Some shoes are produced individually to fit the measures of the most prominent dancers in Russia and abroad, catering for the specific needs of individuals as well as different national ballet schools.

The leadership position of the company created several challenges, one of which is increasing production to meet the increasing demand. The company now is taking orders 3 months in advance, because it trains its personnel on its own, using the experience of their most qualified staff, and this takes time. The main characteristics of Grisko's pointes shoes are their quality—their design minimizes dancers' feet deformation, which is a major problem of professional ballerinas.

Being successful abroad, the company managed to win over the Russian ballet dancers, first those of the Mariinsky Theatre in St Petersburg, and then, by offering a 30% discount, those of the Bolshoi. These theaters had their own workshops producing ballet shoes and costumes, so Grishko had to prove his company products were much better.

Since that time, the firm has become one of the most renowned makers of ballet products in the world. Now the Grishko brand is very popular in more than 70 countries of the world. The company's pricing is different in Russia and abroad. After conquering the Russian market of pointes shoes, the company started to diversify and included in its portfolio shoes for classical, jazz, sport, step, and folk dance, shoes for flamenco, and rehearsal, training, and dance footwear. All different dance accessories are manufactured from top quality ecologically pure materials, and some kinds of products are unique and have a license. Ecological and natural materials are very important for dance shoes. Professional ballet dancers never use pointes produced of artificial materials, as this damages their feet.

The Grishko company and its owner won several state and private awards. In particular, in 2008, Nikolay Grishko got the special award "Leader of Russia's Economy." The Grishko company is active in charity, and not only within its realm of ballet and dances. The company employs 76 people with hearing disabilities and participates in two Moscow programs to develop and modernize jobs for disabled people. Grishko thinks that the core of his company's success is "that we believed that we can be the best and we managed to compete even against the Chinese with their low prices. We put a 'made in Russia' stamp on our pointes shoes, and this creates a different image for our country, without weapons and backfires, and we are proud of this."

2.4 Monocrystal

Overview
Address: 4/1 Kulakov pr., Stavropol, 355035, Russia
Tel/Fax: +7 (8652) 56-30-17
Email: pr@monocrystal.com
Web: http://www.monocrystal.com/

Company Information
Industry: Manufacturing of sapphires for the industry of light-emitting diodes and consumer electronics, as well as metallization pastes for solar energy
Year of establishment: 1999
Sales revenues in 2017: 76 million euros
Sales revenues in 2007: 10 million euros
Average number of employees in 2017: 1500
Brain(s) behind the company: CEO Vladimir Polyakov

Nature of Market Leadership

Monocrystal is the number-one producer on the global market of components of synthetic sapphires for electronics and optics. Monocrystal has three factories in Russia and China, an in-house R&D institute of electronic materials, and five sales offices worldwide. The company has a unique production system with continuous development and improvements in all spheres of business. Monocrystal has customers in 25 countries across the globe, including Germany, the USA, China, Japan, France, Spain, Singapore, Malaysia, India, and South Korea, and holds 40–50% of the global market, whereas its closest competitor has about 20%. The market potential has grown almost 20 times. The number of market participants first grew seven times and then shrank. Prices decreased more than 10 times. The company was third or fourth on the global marketplace, and then in 2016 became an absolute leader, producing 33% of all synthetic sapphire.

Nature of the Competitive Advantage

The company has five competitors on the world market, none in Europe. Monocrystal is operating in a high-tech market, where the speed of technology development is one of the key success factors to secure a gap between competitors. The stable high speed of the improvement is achieved through the constant development of a production system that enhances all spheres of the business. The core competitive advantage of Monocrystal is its unique holistic production system, targeting constant improvement and support for high-level technologies and cost-cutting. As a result, the company has achieved a leading position in terms of product quality. The main innovation factor is the production system, including the whole technological process: the sapphires' growth, cutting, and polishing. The company stands out from the competition thanks to its flexibility and speed.

Since 2016, Monocrystal has mastered the mass production of 300 kg sapphire crystals. In February 2017, Monocrystal produced the world's largest sapphire crystal, weighing 350 kg. In 2018, Monocrystal announced, that it had become the first company in the world to produce 6, 8, and 10-in. sapphire wafers for LED and 12-in. optical windows. The mass production of extra-large crystals will make sapphire an affordable material for a variety of new applications in medicine, consumer electronics, equipment engineering, the automobile industry, and gas and oil extraction. Monocrystal produces sapphire with its own development and production equipment. Growth units are produced by the plant in Stavropol, and components for this equipment are supplied by the Energomera concern.

Two of Monocrystal's clients—Osram (a leading light bulbs producer in Germany) and Apple—consume 20% of all the artificial sapphires that it produces. They are used in Apple's built-in camera lenses, fingerprint readers, and watch screens. The demand for sapphire could have grown dramatically if it had been used to make screens for smartphones in large numbers, but now only some luxury models have such screens. The CEO of Monocristal says that precious glass can appear in budget smartphones, only if sapphire plates become much cheaper.

Core Lessons Learned on the Path to Success

1. In the high-tech market, the key success factor is the speed of technology development. Only significant distance from the competitors can provide a leadership position.
2. To ensure a consistently high development rate, you must constantly build a production system focused on continuous improvement in all areas of the company's activities.

Management and Leadership Development Needs

Monocrystal recruits its management talents mainly from the Stavropol region and the nearby North-Caucasian Federal District of the Russian Federation. The company has close relationships with engineering schools and develops its own management talents. The company trains its executives at the Monocrystal in-house educational and training center, which has a learning portal: an internal virtual platform. This center trains engineers, technologists, and operators of synthetic sapphire growth devices.

Financing and Regulatory Environment Development Needs

Monocrystal is part of the Energomera JSC concern.[9] As the company is unique in terms of technological developments, production, and processes, Monocrystal's management has a very independent position in decision-making. Other sources of financing include re-investment of the company's revenues, borrowing from banks and, recently, allocated loans from the Industrial Development Fund, a Russian federal agency established in 2014 to support the development of new high-tech products, and the modernization and creation of competitive production processes.

Concerning the regulatory environment, the company's main challenges are the high custom duties imposed on its products due to their Russian origin. The production of solar panel metallic pastes moved smoothly to China, but the main products—sapphires—are still produced in Russia. And since the logistics costs of pastes have reached 15% of the cost of goods, there was only one option: to open a plant in China.

A Unique High-Tech Russian Leader with an International Vision

Monocrystal was established in the Russian city of Stavropol in 1999 by Vladimir Polyakov, a graduate from Tomsk State University of Control Systems and Radioelectronics. Polyakov started his career in 1977. In 1994, he established his own company Energomera. At that time, three viable business entities were created, and each of them became a leader in its market.

Monocrystal produced electronic materials and components. It became the world's leading supplier of sapphire products for LED.

---

[9]The Energomera concern is a very diversified industrial, fast-growing company, which stably occupies leading positions in different sectors in Russia and the world market. The concern includes seven high-tech factories in Russia, Belarus, and Ukraine, and two corporate institutes. The company is successfully integrated in the global economy. In 2005, 2006, 2008, and 2009, the Ministry of Economic Development and Trade and the Ministry of Industry and Trade of the Russian Federation declared the concern the "best exporter of the industry."

Electrotechnical Factory Energomera produced an electric instrument and became a leader in the Russian electricity meters market.

Agroholding Energomera is an agricultural enterprise with a land bank of over 85,000 ha.

Since then, more than 5000 jobs have been created and maintained. The company has four high-tech factories in Russia and three in Ukraine, Belarus, and China. It has set up two design institutes, as well as foreign representative offices in Taiwan, South Korea, the Netherlands, and the USA. Today, 98% of Monocrystal's production is exported, because of the lack of similar consumer electronics and solar panel production on the territory of the Russian Federation.

Some of Monocrystal's main values are a combination of advanced leading technologies with lean principles of production (technology and reliability) and protection of the environment. The company is planning to reduce the environmental impact of 25 items by 2020, including plastic waste, fluorescent lamps, and carbon-dioxide emission, at least by half. Monocrystal also focuses on human capital development and social obligations for the employees.

As a global leader of sapphire manufacturing, Monocrystal has reason to be optimistic. It is looking forward to market growth thanks to the increasing popularity of the new product in the LED industry—micro-LEDs used to illuminate the screens of mobile devices and television equipment. According to Monocrystal CEO Oleg Kachalov,[10] Samsung and LG had introduced them into the production of TV sets in 2018: "The whole TV set will be a matrix of LEDs. Today, when LEDs are used to illuminate the screen, one TV needs hundreds of pieces. Now, it will take millions. The new technology will radically improve the light transmission and contrast of the picture while reducing power consumption." Analysts predict that the mass use of micro-LEDs will begin in 2022.

2.5 NT-MTD Spectrum Instruments

Overview
Address: Proezd 4922, 4/3 Zelenograd, Moscow 124460, Russia
Tel: +74991102050
Fax: +74991102070

---

[10]Oleg Kachalov—CEO (general director) Monocrystal Joint Stock Company. Education: Materials and Components of Solid-State Electronics, Stavropol State Technical University, 1995, candidate of technical sciences (PhD). He conducted dozens of scientific and applied studies in the field of modern materials and components of solid-state electronics. Over the period of his work in Monocrystal as deputy director for marketing and sales, he made a huge personal contribution to the development of international economic relations of the Stavropol Territory and Monocrystal in the markets of the USA, Europe, Australia, China, and Japan.

Email: info@ntmdt-si.ru
Web: www.ntmdt-si.ru

Company Information

Industry: Manufacture of instruments and appliances for measuring, testing, and navigation (optical instruments, research instrumentation)
Year of establishment: 1989
Sales revenues in 2017: 11 million euros
Sales revenues in 2007: 10 million euros
Average number of employees in 2017: 100
Brain(s) behind the company: Viktor Bykov, founder and current president of the company

Nature of Market Leadership

The company is number two in the world's scanning probe microscopes market. The company's main areas of activity are research, development, and production of the scanning probe microscopes (SPM) and systems combining the AFM methods and optical spectroscopy (AFM-RAMAN, AFM-nanoIR), as well as the development of the software for them. Five products of the company were among the 100 best products of the year.

Market leadership has been based on a fast research and development process and on the availability of adequate IT support. The company's global market share is 15%, while the market share of the main competitor is 25%. This market share has not changed since 2011 due to the market cycles in this industry, caused by the fact that most products become obsolete in 4–5 years. Fast product development and customer support are important to attract and retain customers. The nature of the company's leadership has not changed. It focuses on R&D, a good network of clients and partners, development of a professional community, talent management, and working with the leading technical universities in the country.

Nature of Competitive Advantage

The company's competitive advantage is based on product characteristics, a short product development cycle, customized decisions in product development, and customer support, including reliable IT support. The short product development cycle is maintained through staff involvement and motivation to generate ideas and develop products, as well as effective contacts with research institutions and leading technical universities. Leadership is maintained by talent management. The company considers its employees its main asset and invests in the best talent recruitment and talent development.

Core Lessons Learned on the Path to Success

When a company's target market and core competences are well-defined, it is possible to compete even with bigger multifunctional companies. Access to financial resources has become more expensive, and bigger companies that are affiliates of multinational organizations have a better position in that respect.

Early internationalization helped the company find adequate demand and become profitable. However, the share of the Russian market in the company's portfolio has grown compared to that in 2011, due to increased government financing of Russian research centers and universities, which now order more research equipment. In the last 8 years, the company has developed local design competences and is no longer acquiring these services abroad.

Management and Leadership Development Needs

To be competitive, the company needs state-of-the-art research competences. The discovery of new opportunities for the application of the company products in different spheres and the development of new products takes extensive industrial contacts and networking.

Sales management and exhibition skills are important to present the company's products to customers and stakeholders. However, all sales and marketing personnel should have good knowledge of the product's characteristics and profound understanding of its performance, which means they usually must have an education in engineering and technology.

Financing and Regulatory Environment Development Needs

Research instrument development and production is a research-and-technology-intensive industry where government support and guarantees are needed to improve access to financial resources. For example, signed agreements with customers should be accepted as guarantees for bank loans.

Accelerating Innovation

JCG Nanotechnology NT-MDT Spectrum Instruments is a research intensive hi-tech Russian hidden champion. It started as a research project in 1990 by a group of scientists lead by Viktor Bykov, a 1973 graduate of Russia's leading technical university—Moscow Institute of Physics and Technology. It was thanks to Bykov's entrepreneurial talent that this research group did not quit the scientific research field, unlike many researchers in physics in Russia in the early 1990s, after the closure of research institutions and the very low salaries of those who still did some research.

Nor did they leave the country to take attractive positions in the research centers of the USA and Europe. They started their own hi-tech business, accelerating innovation into a range of products for advanced nanotechnology research.

The principles of STM devices were first developed in their modern form in 1981 by Gerd Binning and Heinrich Rohrer, who shared the 1986 Nobel Prize in physics with Ernst Ruska, who first designed an electron microscope. Since then, scanning tunnel microscopes (STM) and scanning probe microscopes (SPM) have been developed to fit specific research and engineering purposes.

NT-MTD Spectrum Instruments' first device concepts were drawn on a piece of paper torn from a diary, showing the date when this success story started. A group of research enthusiasts, led by Viktor Bykov, did what many talented researchers failed to do—commercialize their research results. It would probably not be right to say that V. Bykov from the very start visualized a successful business unit, but market reforms launched in Russia in the early 1990s combined with Bykov's entrepreneurial and leadership skills in the nearly 30 years that followed. This made it possible to produce and successfully install more than 2000 devices in major scientific research and production centers of Europe, Asia, and North America, offering expert service and applications development through five representative offices and more than 40 distributors around the globe.

Today, NT-MDT Spectrum Instruments is the leader in the Russian STM market and number two in the world. The company has 16% of the world market, with its closest competitor, the Bruker Corporation, with over 3000 employees in 90 locations across the world, holding 25% of the STM and SPM market.

The microscopes market is dominated by global companies offering a wide range of products across a variety of platforms, including the FEI Company, Hitachi High-Technologies, JEOL, Carl Zeiss, and Oxford Instruments Plasma Technology Ltd. NT-MTD Spectrum Instruments represents an important segment of the market: medium-sized and small private companies offering mainly complex solutions for special purposes. NT-MTD Spectrum Instruments' competitive advantage is its customized production of complex scanning solutions working under a variety of conditions—in vacuum, at extra-high or super-low temperatures, in liquids, and more.

The world market for SPM and STM is mainly concentrated in countries developing science and nano technologies. Most of the potential consumers of SPM and STM products are located at industrial and university-based research centers. Each research is special, and nanotechnology instrumentation should be easily geared to meet those specific needs. The products' functionality, ergonomic design, and innovative technologies meet the needs of both students, cutting-edge researchers, and industrial users at R&D centers. The most attractive markets for NT-MTD Spectrum Instruments are those in the USA, Europe, and the Asia-Pacific region. NT-MDT has a very strong market position in Europe. The company's share in the EU market is 25%. The Asia-Pacific region is the fastest-growing region, and NT-MDT Spectrum Instruments showed significant progress there. The sales volume of the company is high in Japan, South Korea, and India. Key end-user groups of NT-MTD Spectrum Instruments include aerospace, biomedical and life sciences, electronics, nanotechnology, and nano-materials producers, as well as manufacturers of semiconductors, electronics, and telecommunication devices.

NT-MTD Spectrum Instruments thinks that one of the ways to guarantee stable sales is to penetrate university classrooms, teach research students to use its products, and in the future get research centers' decision-makers to become loyal clients. One of the popular product lines of NT-MDT Spectrum Instruments is educational devices. Nano-educator student-oriented devices, developed for use by first-time microscope users, can navigate through a step-by-step operation. These devices are designed to capture the student's interest in science and train future nanotechnologists. *R&D Magazine* has included the SPM, based on the Nano-Educator II scientific training laboratory, on the list of the top-100 most technologically significant products in the marketplace. The company's new updated software runs under the operating systems Windows XP; and Mac OS. Data sharing via iPhone™ and iPad™ is also possible.

NT-MTD Spectrum Instruments' success is to a large extent based on the company's corporate policy, encouraging initiative and creativity, and promoting young talent, as well as the company's culture based on cooperation and support, team spirit, and high achievement. The company founder and now honorary president, Viktor Bykov, is a doctor of sciences and professor at a leading Russian research university—PhysTech. He gives lectures to students of his Alma Mater—Moscow Institute of Physics and Technology—and sees his teaching as a way not only to develop future research scientists, but also select the most promising of them to work for NT-MTD Spectrum Instruments. He said that the company employs only graduates with degrees in physics and technology, as "they can learn marketing and strategy if they understand the principles of our products. Without this understanding, they are useless to our business."

NT-MTD Spectrum Instruments participates in all major international conferences and exhibitions, presenting its products and services, and discussing new areas of research and instrumentation needs. The company's mission is clearly demonstrated by the slogan "Built by scientists for scientists."

3 Conclusions and Recommendations

In this research, we have attempted to understand the nature and success factors of Russian hidden champions. Being small, these companies have to be very smart in their competition with other firms, and especially large corporations. Hidden champions do this by focusing on specific product niches. According to the study of Russian mid-sized business (Molchanova et al. 2017), narrow specialization has benefited smaller companies in a number of ways. "First of all, it has allowed them to concentrate time, money, and effort on their core product, avoiding unnecessary dilution of limited resources. Secondly, by aligning their processes and practices around a given product or product range, companies have achieved better operational performance. Finally, working in a niche segment has helped companies to develop a high level of expertise in a particular product and thereby build customer intimacy and lasting relationships" (Molchanova et al. 2017).

This is exactly what we observe in Russian hidden champions. Their focused R&D efforts explain why they manage to stay ahead of the competition in terms of innovation, despite limited resources. Their innovation capacity has been proven by patents and international awards. However, while technological breakthroughs are notable, it is incremental innovation that best describes Russian hidden champions. Just like in the case of the German *mittelstand* firms described by Herman Simon (2009), the key quality of Russian hidden champions is not an ability to come up with something completely new, but rather a capacity for innovation on a continuous basis in order to meet customers' ever-changing needs and requirements. This by no means implies that hidden champions are trend-followers. In fact, being experts in their product category, hidden champions are often more aware of the latest developments and educate their customers about new products, features, and applications.

Another important characteristic of Russian hidden champions is their client-orientation. All of them acknowledge that building and nurturing long-term relationships with their customers is critical to their competitive advantage. This requires trust, loyalty, and co-innovation, specifically in business-to-business sectors, where many hidden champions can be found. Client-orientation also explains why hidden champions prefer to go for customized solutions rather than mass-market offerings. Flexibility and speed in serving their customers would not be possible without well-organized operations. Many hidden champions report that their original production systems contribute to the overall innovativeness of the company no less than their products. So, besides investing in product innovation, Russian hidden champions continually work on the improvement of their internal processes and operations.

The competitiveness of the studied hidden champions is evidenced by their wide international presence. Hidden champions continue to use internationalization and new market development as important growth strategies, strengthening their positions in the markets that they entered in the early stages of their development. However, geopolitical factors did not allow some companies, identified as potential hidden champions during the first wave of research, to become international and evolve into true market leaders. Some of them worked for the special needs of certain industries and ceased to be independent. They joined state-owned corporations. For example, the Chelyabinsk Zink Plant, a producer of special zinc-based alloys, was bought by the Ural Mining and Metallurgical Company in 2016. JSC Isotope is now a subsidiary of the Rosatom state corporation. Russian Helicopters, which produced special-purpose helicopters, is now a subsidiary of Oboronprom United Industrial Corporation.[11]

Hidden champions need government support, but not in the way mentioned above. It is recommended that the government support their export activities with

---

[11]Information about companies received from their web-sites: Chelyabinsk Zink Plant—http://www.zinc.ru/en/; JSC Izotop—http://www.isotop.ru/en/; Russian Helicopters—https://www.russianhelicopters.aero/en/.

financial and non-financial tools, such as searching for foreign partners, insurance and credit programs for Russian and foreign banks, federal guarantee support, and special customs duties.

Financial institutions might play a vital role in the hidden champions' development, as they are all innovative companies. They constantly need loans for their projects. Banks' guarantees for export operations are also considered a support tool.

Studying hidden champions is highly beneficial for business education. It so happens that the curriculum of business schools is usually centered on the experience of large international companies, leaving smaller firms outside of the attention zone. However, in our opinion, the hidden champions provide the most vibrant and compelling examples of how a firm can become globally competitive with limited resources. This is particularly true of companies in emerging markets, which need to overcome and work around many institutional, legal, and financial barriers on their route to international success. Business education can aid such companies in their pursuits by tailoring its educational offerings to SMEs. Instead of offering broad, long, and expensive MBA programs, business schools could provide short-term, practice-oriented modules, focused on the special needs of smaller companies.

References

Chelyabinsk Zink Plant: http://www.zinc.ru/en/
Federal Law No. 116-FZ "On Special Economic Zones in Russian Federation" (2005). http://www.russez.ru/management_company/normative/. Accessed 30 Sept 2019
Gaidar Y (2007) The Soviet collapse: grain and oil. American Enterprise Institute for Public Policy Research. https://web.archive.org/web/20090725114959/http://www.aei.org/docLib/20070419_Gaidar.pdf. Accessed 30 Sept 2019
Golubkin I, Bukharova M, Danilov L (2018) Russian special economic zones: business navigator 2017. Association of Clusters and Technology Parks, Moscow. http://economy.gov.ru/wps/wcm/connect/84d379c6-fcea-45c2-8e52-ed579d20c85b/nb2017.pdf?MOD=AJPERES&CACHEID=84d379c6-fcea-45c2-8e52-ed579d20c85b. Accessed 30 Sept 2019
Golubkin I., Bukharova M., Danilov L. (2019). Russian special economic zones: business navigator 2018. Association of Clusters and Technology Parks. Moscow. http://akitrf.ru/upload/Russian%20Special%20Economic%20Zones%20Business%20Navigator%202018.pdf. Accessed 30 Sept 2019
JSC Izotop.: http://www.isotop.ru/en/
Kotov I, Boutin N, Tuschen S, Yakovlev N, Pogorelskaya E, Ivanova A, Bakhtin M (2018) Russian consumers in new economic reality. [electronic resourse]. https://www.bcg.com/ru-ru/publications/2018/russian-consumers-new-economic-reality
Lo B, Hill F (2016) Putin's Pivot: why Russia is looking east. https://www.brookings.edu/opinions/putins-pivot-why-russia-is-looking-east/. Accessed 30 Sept 2019
McKiernan P, Purg D (2013) Hidden champions in cee and Turkey carving out a global niche. Springer, Berlin, Heidelberg. https://doi.org/10.1007/978-3-642-40504-4
Molchanova E, Remyga O, Di Vito MC, Sokolova K (2017) Russian and chinese mid-sized business: internationalization strategies. Moscow School of Management SKOLKOVO, Moscow. https://iems.skolkovo.ru/downloads/documents/SKOLKOVO_IEMS/Research_Reports/SKOLKOVO_IEMS_Research_2017-03-13_en.pdf. Accessed 30 Sept 2019

National Summary Data Page (NSDP) (2018) Ministry of Finance of the Russian Federation. https://www.minfin.ru/en/key/macroeconomics/national_summary/. Accessed 30 Sept 2019

Popov A (2010) Life cycle of the centrally planned economy: why soviet growth rates peaked in the 1950s. Centre for economic and financial research at new economic school. https://www.nes.ru/files/Preprints-resh/WP152.pdf. Accessed 30 Sept 2019

Purg D, Saginova O, Skorobogatykh I, Musatova Z (2016) Family owned Hidden champions in Russia: Innovations, human capital and internationalization. Indian J Sci Technol 9:12

Russian Helicopters: https://www.russianhelicopters.aero/en/

Simon H (2009) Hidden champions of the twenty-first century: success strategies of unknown world market leaders. Springer, Dordrecht. https://doi.org/10.1007/978-0-387-98147-5

The Consolidated Budget of the Russian Federation (2018) Ministry of Finance of the Russian Federation. https://www.minfin.ru/en/statistics/conbud/. Accessed 30 Sept 2019

The Exchange Rate of Euro (n.d.). https://ratestats.com/euro/2017/. Accessed 30 Sept 2019

The National Champions Project for the Support of Private High-tech Companies-leaders (n.d.). https://www.rvc.ru/en/eco/support_and_acceleration/national_champions/. Accessed 30 Sept 2019

The Population of the Russian Federation by Municipal Entities (2019) The Federal State Statistics Service of the Russian Federation. https://www.gks.ru/folder/11110/document/13282?print=1. Accessed 30 Sept 2019

World Bank Data (2019) Russian Federation. https://data.worldbank.org/country/russian-federation. Accessed 30 Sept 2019

Hidden Champions of Serbia

Goran Pitić, Nebojša Savić, Miloš Erić, Jelisaveta Lazarević, Zoja Kukić, and Ema Marinković

Overview
Official name: Republic of Serbia
Type of government: Republic
Population in 2017: 7,020,858
Land area: 88,360 sq. km

History

Twelfth and thirteenth century	First Serbian state and constitution recorded. Formation of the Kingdom of Serbia.
Fourteenth century	Ottoman conquest of the Balkans. By 1521, Serbia is completely occupied.
Nineteenth century	Following two uprisings, Serbia is once again an independent nation. The new kingdom's first constitution was adopted in 1835.
1912–1918	After the two Balkan wars and the First World War, Serbia becomes a part of the Kingdom of Serbs, Croats, and Slovenes, later renamed the Kingdom of Yugoslavia.
1941–1945	Breaking up Yugoslavia, Nazi Germany occupies Serbia.
1945	Under Josip Broz Tito, a new Socialist Federal Republic of Yugoslavia is formed together with five other constituent republics.
1948	Tito and Stalin end their alliance. Yugoslavia disassociates itself from the communist bloc.
1980	Josip Broz Tito dies. Onset of the political crisis, leading to the breakup of the country.

G. Pitić · N. Savić · M. Erić · J. Lazarević (✉) · Z. Kukić · E. Marinković
FEFA Faculty, Belgrade Metropolitan University, Belgrade, Serbia
e-mail: jlazarevic@fefa.edu.rs

1991–1992	Slovenia, Croatia, Macedonia, and Bosnia declare their independence.
1992	The remaining two constituent republics, Serbia and Montenegro, form the new Federal Republic of Yugoslavia.
1992–1994	UN embargo. Hyperinflation reaches one of the highest levels in the history of the world's economy.
1995	Dayton Agreement brings an end to UN sanctions and the civil war.
1999	NATO bombing of Yugoslavia, ending Serbian sovereignty over its southern province of Kosovo.
2000	Milošević ousted from power in peaceful mass demonstrations.
2003	Serbia and Montenegro decide to abolish the name Yugoslavia and form a loose confederation. Serbian Prime Minister Zoran Djindjić assassinated.
2006	Serbia becomes independent, as Montenegro secedes from the confederation.
2012	Serbia becomes an EU candidate country.
2014	EU opens accession negotiations with Serbia.

1 Introduction: Context and History

Serbia is a landlocked country in Southeastern Europe, with a population of seven million people. The capital city, Belgrade, has 1.7 million inhabitants and acts as an administrative, economic, traffic, and cultural hub of the country. The country is rich in natural resources and arable land. It has plenty of access to freshwater, including two major navigable rivers, the Danube and the Sava. Serbia produces enough electricity for its own needs and exports the surplus. Although it has its own limited resources, it relies on imports of crude oil and natural gas.

The EU accession process started in 2012 and accession negotiations began in 2014. In its strategy for the Western Balkans, in February 2018 the European Commission set 2025 as the earliest possible accession date for Serbia, provided that all conditions are met. Thus far, Serbia has opened 18 out of 35 negotiation chapters and closed only two.

Serbia is an upper-middle-income country. GDP per capita has doubled since 2000,[1] with very high rates of growth recorded until 2008—5.24% annually, on average. Growth was interrupted during the global crisis of 2009–2012 and as a consequence of the devastating 2014 floods. The crisis has also exposed weaknesses in the growth model based on domestic consumption, ever-increasing foreign investment, and loans. Since then, the government has implemented a fiscal consolidation program, resulting in a balanced budget and a drop in the public debt-to-GDP

---

[1] In constant international USD.

ratio from a historical maximum of 71.2–54.5% in 2018. However, growth rates and living standards have been lagging behind those of other CEE countries. The GDP is dominated by the services sector (63%), while industry and agriculture contribute 23% and 13%, respectively.

The road network—totaling over 40,000 km of public roads—includes 876 km of motorways and an additional 290 km of motorways planned or under construction. Railroads transport primarily goods. Some parts of the network either have closed for restructuring or are suffering from the lack of investment in past decades. Serbia has three airports that handle scheduled international passenger traffic,[2] serving six million travellers in 2018. The country's national airline, AirSerbia, serves 59 international destinations, mainly from its Belgrade hub.[3]

The unemployment rate has been dropping since 2012, reaching its lowest value of 10.3% in the second quarter of 2019. The main drivers of employment growth have been manufacturing, construction, and private sector services. Exports have doubled since 2009.[4] The primary trade partners are Italy (14.4%) and Germany (13.7%). The EU member states are followed by other CEFTA countries, which receive 20% of Serbian exports.

The transition of Serbia's economy started at the beginning of this century. It has resulted in an economy that is no longer dominated by large state enterprises. The private sector is becoming the backbone of its transformation and development. The hidden champions presented in this chapter are in the different industry sectors. They produce furniture and equipment, bulbs, software and hardware tools, and plastic packing. The success stories and case studies of Serbia's four hidden champions are told in this chapter. However, three of the analyzed companies lost their hidden champion status after 2011. Three remain on the list after being first identified in 2011, while seven companies gained hidden champion status for the first time in 2019.

Technology in general, and IT, in particular, seem to be a common denominator of the hidden champions as companies that have lost their status are traditional manufacturing firms. Their products, while innovative at times, do not require cutting-edge technology or customized IT solutions. On the other hand, two new hidden champions are IT companies, while almost all others have strong IT departments and base their products on novel IT solutions. Also, two out of the three old hidden champions are IT companies. This is not unexpected—the Serbian government has identified information and communication technologies as one of the pillars of the future economic development of the country, and the fourth industrial revolution as an opportunity to get ahead of other developing nations (Savić et al. 2019).

---

[2]Belgrade Nikola Tesla International Airport (IATA code: BEG), Niš Constantine the Great Airport (INI), and Kraljevo - Morava (KVO).

[3]Vinci Airports has been granted a 25-year concession in 2018 for a 501 million EUR fee.

[4]A steady growth has been registered in both services and goods sectors.

Exhibit 1 Core economic indicators for Serbia

	2011	2012	2013	2014	2015	2016	2017	2018
GDP per capita (current US$)	6809.16	6015.95	6755.07	6600.06	5585.12	5756.38	6284.19	7234.00
GDP per capita growth (annual %)	2.85	−0.20	3.40	−1.13	2.28	3.88	2.59	4.88
Long-term unemployment (% of total unemployment)[a]	N/A	N/A	N/A	63.9	59.7	59.1	52.6	50.5
Foreign direct investment, net inflows (% of GDP)	10.01	2.95	4.23	4.25	5.91	5.80	6.56	8.13
GDP (current US$, mio)	49,258	43,309	48,394	47,062	39,656	40,693	44,179	50,641
Exports of goods and services (current US$, mio)	16,256	15,524	19,286	19,803	17,916	19,743	22,298	25,540
Exports of goods and services (% of GDP)	33.00	35.85	39.85	42.08	45.27	48.62	50.54	50.91
Merchandise exports (current US$, mio)	11,779	11,229	14,614	14,845	13,376	14,883	16,996	19,227
Merchandise exports to high-income economies (% of total merchandise exports)	53.93	53.47	60.30	60.75	62.08	60.46	63.81	65.40
Merchandise exports to developing economies in Europe & Central Asia (% of total merchandise exports)	43.66	43.97	37.54	37.05	35.27	35.64	33.67	32.02
Ores and metals exports (% of merchandise exports)	N/A	N/A	N/A	N/A	N/A	N/A	N/A	N/A
Agricultural raw materials exports (% of merchandise exports)	N/A	N/A	N/A	N/A	N/A	N/A	N/A	N/A
Food exports (% of merchandise exports)	N/A	N/A	N/A	N/A	N/A	N/A	N/A	N/A
Fuel exports (% of merchandise exports)	N/A	N/A	N/A	N/A	N/A	N/A	N/A	N/A
Manufactures exports (% of merchandise exports)	N/A	N/A	N/A	N/A	N/A	N/A	N/A	N/A
High-technology exports (% of manufactured exports)	N/A	N/A	N/A	N/A	N/A	N/A	N/A	N/A

Source: World Bank (2019)
[a]Eurostat (2019)

2 Case Studies of Selected Hidden Champions

2.1 Case Study 1

BG Reklam

Overview
Address: 29. novembra 1M, Barajevo, Serbia
Tel: + 381 11 785 64 64
Fax: N/A
Email: info@bgreklam.rs
Web: www.bgreklam.rs

Company Information
Industry: Printing
Year of establishment: 2001
Sales Revenues in 2017: 4.5 milllion euros
Sales Revenues in 2007: 1.2 million euros
Average number of employees in 2017: 125
Brain(s) behind the company: Luka Stanić and Nikola Trifunović

Nature of Market Leadership

A successful idea, developed by an entrepreneur in a garage, has produced a company with professional management. It is one of the leaders in the Western Balkans in customized POS production by size and export. It is also a regional market leader and globally significant in the design, construction, and production of permanent POS materials and solutions. The company cooperates with more than 50 international clients, including Google and Philips, in more than 20 markets. The company is focused on export in three market groups: Austria, Germany, and Switzerland, followed by the UK and Benelux.

Nature of the Competitive Advantage

The company's strategy is focused on its relationships with clients, and creating and providing customized products and solutions. The competitive advantage is based on knowledge and technology usage in a wide range of material processing. The integrated production process allows quality control from idea development and production to product packaging. The company is a pioneer in using new technologies in point-of-sales production.

Core Lessons Learned on the Path to Success

1. The company's main driver of success is its 10-year vision and its mission.
2. Continuous improvement in production, staff, and team are important success factors.

Management and Leadership Development Needs

- Since the niche is particular, the company's management has difficulty attracting skilled and talented young people. This is because engineers are in short supply in Serbia, and young people prefer to work for multinational and well-known companies (Savić et al. 2020).
- Serbia has a competitive disadvantage in retaining talents. Like many other companies, BG Reklam is facing challenges in this regard, primarily due to the opportunities that employees see in foreign markets.

Financing and Regulatory Environment Development Needs

- When it comes to financing, it is essential to acquire funds for new production capacities and technologies. To stay up-to-date and respond to changes in the global markets, the company has to consider replacing all equipment and technology in the next two years. This is true even though the company is doing well for the moment.
- In the context of the regulatory environment and requirements, Serbia's accession to the EU is of vital importance. EU membership would eliminate the customs and shipping restrictions that the company is facing now in the common market (Erić and Babin 2014) . The fact that Serbia is not part of the EU affects the existence and duration of customs procedures, which often presents challenges to the business as they take up to several days.

BG Reklam, the Hidden Champion

Founded in 2001, BG Reklam was created through the realization of an entrepreneurial idea in a garage. The company's story earned the Ernst & Young Award for Entrepreneur of the Year in 2015 in Serbia. The company designs, constructs, and manufactures permanent point-of-sales materials and solutions—a specialized form of sales promotion that is found near, on, or next to a checkout counter—using the latest technologies. The company works with over 50 international clients, including Google and Philips, which enables it to be present in about 20 markets around the globe.

After expanding its production capacity and operations fourfold in 2006, the company has acquired one of the sources of its leadership. This source is primarily related to the control quality process. Through the integration of processes from idea development and implementation to production and packaging, all under one roof, the company manages to be consistent in delivering quality and technologically advanced products to its customers. By expanding its capacity, the company has been able to increase the variety of materials that it offers in different solutions and products. Eventually, BG Reklam hired professional management with experience from multinational companies. This, as well as the high quality and the unique product, contributed to the expansion of sales in the Western market.

The company's market changed considerably, primarily because of the intensity of investments in the various industries where its new customers operate. In line with the changing strategies of clients from different sectors, its appearance at the points of sale has changed. The company is a pioneer that uses new technologies in point-of-sales manufacturing and strives to innovate and offer customers innovative solutions to their ideas. The most crucial factor in innovation is engaging, activating, and encouraging consumers to interact with products through the use of the most advanced technology that educates consumers about the justification of their purchase.

Regarding the clients' strategy, the clients' structure has changed and extended from brewing and tobacco industries to companies that are part of the electronics and telecommunications sector. The company's clients are exclusively multinational companies. Successful cooperation with these companies in the domestic market has contributed to the expansion of businesses to foreign markets. In this way, for example, the company entered the global supplier list for tobacco industry customers but also became the exclusive Philips supplier in Germany. The company's strategic commitment focused on creating a direct relationship with customers to whom it provides customized solutions and products.

The source of competitive advantage is the knowledge and technology to process a wide range of materials. As a result of its skills, BG Reklam sometimes even manages to set standards in the niche. Also, quality control, through an integrated manufacturing process, contributes to a strong leadership position, ensuring long-term productivity. The team of the company consists of professional sales experts hired specifically to focus on a particular foreign market. Industrial designers offer design solutions to clients, while the engineering team creates 3D models and preparation for the production. Ultimately, the entire production team creates the final product. In addition to manufacturing customized products for its customers, the company produces packaging for those products, ensuring their secure and safe delivery. In its operations, the company applies the 5S workspace organization method and the Lean and Kaizen approach to constant process improvement and waste reduction.

The main driver of the company's success, according to the interviewee, is the ambition and vision of the founder and the entire team about "what the company should look like in 10 years." This ambition leads to the continuous improvement of the production process, people, and organization.

3 Case Study 2

3.1 Buck

Overview
Address: Milorada Jovanovića 9, Belgrade, Serbia
Tel: + 381 11 205 2402
Fax: N/A
Email: export@buck.lighting
Web: buck.lighting

Company Information
Industry: Manufacture of electric lighting equipment
Year of Establishment: 1992
Sales Revenues in 2017: 6.07 million euros
Sales revenues in 2007: 3.4 million euros
Average number of employees in 2017: 80
Brain(s) behind the company: Darko Budeč

Nature of Market Leadership

Unique and customized lighting solutions in architecture and design, medicine, and infrastructure. Buck is one of two leading companies in Europe regarding design, quality, new technology, and technical solutions in the field of medicine lighting and pharmaceutical industry lighting. The company's biggest export markets are Switzerland, Germany, and Ireland.

Nature of the Competitive Advantage

The company operates in a traditional, strategically important industry. By innovating and using new technologies, the company satisfies consumer lighting needs and is building a competitive advantage. However, Buck satisfies other broad needs related to life and work in a well-lighted environment in different places and in different conditions. Buck is among the pioneers that applied human-centric lighting technology with power-over-ethernet technology, which monitors the movement of the sun and the spectrum of light emitted inside the room, and adapts the light to one's natural biorhythm.

Core Lessons Learned on the Path to Success

1. The key success factor is specialization and people excellence in product and solution creation.
2. If your company is a small company in a big market, the key to success lies in an innovative approach and the use of new technology in an effective way.
3. The most important leadership factor is team work, and the most important innovation factor is the team's knowledge.

Management and Leadership Development Needs

- Professional management from the start of business development. The company's future management and development needs refer to the knowledge they need to attain to be leaders in implementing new technologies in their products. Buck strives to have a technology and knowledge advantage, instead of an advantage based on machines, because the company wants to make an innovation and knowledge-driven globally recognizable brand.
- The company needs to prepare its structure and governance for the shift to the second generation.

Financing and Regulatory Environment Development Needs

- High-quality staff creation and staff retention are key success factors for the country and its economy. Consequently, early educational investment is an important factor. In an innovative environment, a competent workforce is a critical success factor (Savić et al. 2018).
- Buck uses short-term bank loans. The company boasts a very high credit rating and reinvests its profits in further development.

The company has no other development needs in terms of financing and regulatory environment.

Buck, the Hidden Champion

According to the CEO and founder of the company, the winner of the 2012 Ernst&Young Entrepreneur of the Year Award in Serbia, the company deals with lighting, which is a strategically important business because it affects people's health, mood, and productivity. Twenty-seven years of the company's presence in the market through investment in product development, human development, and specialized solutions have contributed to creating a unique value proposition and a competitive advantage in the region, Europe, and in some niches, even in the whole world. Buck creates state-of-the-art solutions in lighting. Based on 2–5 years of operational and strategic planning, the company is moving toward implementing cutting-edge technologies, such as the Internet of Things and big data.

The company produces unique lighting solutions in architecture and design, medicine, and infrastructure, and it sends its products to 50 markets worldwide. The company develops and sells its products to various sectors: hospitals and medical centers, ports, stadiums, and ICT companies.

During the 27 years of its history, the company has won many awards. In 2011, for example, the company was awarded by the Chicago Athenaeum Museum of Architecture and Design for the good design of three products (Buck 2019). Two years earlier, Buck's Medico system won the Red Dot product design award, one of the world's most prestigious design awards (Buck 2019). The German Design Council distinguished Buck two times with its awards: for a product catalog, and for the concept of connecting diverse disciplines (Buck 2019).

The company president explains, in a picturesque way, the company's development: "We have started with candles, bulbs, LED bulbs, and the application of the most innovative technologies in order to develop the most valuable products in such a traditional sector."

Gathering knowledge through work for specific sectors of the industry, Buck is now developing hardware and lighting software for other sectors of the industry. The company is highly diversified, developing many specialized, well designed, and top-quality products for entirely different sectors of the economy.

The experience gained and the organizational structure of the company have made it possible to professionalize specific internal sectors that are critical to the quality of lighting. Thanks to highly qualified and trained staff at all levels of the organizational structure, and investment in research and development, the company develops unique ideas. The demand is anticipated 2–3 years in advance and is connected with R&D activities, collaboration with most innovative institutes, and intern development. One such activity contributed to the creation of a leadership position in the medical illumination manufacturing niche in Europe, in terms of innovation and product quality.

Buck bases its development on analyses of consumers' needs in the lighting fixtures market segment and upgrades their needs with the component of healthy living and working conditions. By applying research findings from other scientific disciplines, Buck develops highly innovative, high-value-added products, based on cutting-edge materials and technologies at its development center, as well as in cooperation with research and development institutes and educational institutions.

The company is among the pioneers that applied human-centric lighting technology together with power-over-ethernet technology enabling people to improve their motivation, productivity, and well-being indoors. This lighting technology monitors the movement of the sun and the spectrum of light emitted inside the room, and adjusts the lighting to the natural biorhythm of the people. Even today, the strategy is aimed at developing unique software and hardware that create the necessary indoor lighting conditions. Possibilities of creating unique solutions include different types of products for different kinds of clients and sectors. In addition to knowledge and innovation, the company's main competitive advantage in this sector is the design of products for which it has received 15 international awards.

The lighting market is still dynamic, which is why there is a need for constant innovation. The turning point in the market came when conventional lighting was replaced by LED. The rapid development of LED light technology has prevented many companies from following this trend. However, a drastic change in the market has also enabled the development of new products and solutions. By blending new technologies, such as big data and the Internet of Things, with experience in strategic conventional lighting manufacturing, the company manages to create a competitive edge.

Buck strives to enhance and grow its brand. This goal is achieved through the production of specialized products for different uses, superior design, and quality. Also, a contribution is made through an approach that involves investing in human resources and fostering a team spirit.

Although Buck operates in a traditional industry, the company proves that the application of new technologies is not only a support for the value chain but also an integral part of it (Savić et al. 2019). This has enabled the creation of a unique position in the market. The main lessons learned from the experience of the company's founders relate to the need to innovate instead of embracing innovation, to originality, and to the application of new technologies. People's excellence and specialization is a crucial factor in the success and creation of competitive products.

4 Case Study 3

4.1 *Mikroelektronika*

Overview
Address: Batajnički drum 23, Belgrade, Serbia
Tel: + 381 11 78 57 600
Fax: N/A
Email: office@mikroe.com
Web: www.mikroe.com

Company Information
Industry: Manufacture of computers and peripheral equipment
Year of establishment: 2001
Sales revenues in 2017: 3.8 million euros
Sales revenues in 2007: 1.1 million euros
Average number of employees in 2017: 88
Brain(s) behind the company: Nebojša Matić

Nature of Market Leadership

The company is a globally unique producer of hardware and software tools: compilers and development systems. Mikroelektronika sets the standards in its niche and is the first in the world in the niche of customized hardware and software tools. The CEO also states that the company is often first in doing things in the field of hardware and software tools. Additionally, it is one of the global market leaders as it produces one new product a day in combination with strong logistics and integrated production. The company exports to 130 different countries. It sends 30% of all exports to the USA, and 40% to the EU, mainly Germany, the UK, and France.

Nature of the Competitive Advantage

Mikroelektronika is a global pioneer in its field. The company's primary competitive advantage is innovation. It produces unique solutions, having its own production and development, which creates flexibility and a fast response to market needs. Mikroelektronika was the first company in the world to develop a wifi debugger, a very complex solution that allows a redefinition of technical support.

Core Lessons Learned on the Path to Success

1. A unique and competitive market position requires hard work and investment in retaining and upgrading knowledge accumulated in the firm.
2. Internal transparency and visible progress are important leadership factors.
3. A strong market position implies time, skilled middle management, and a strong team.

Management and Leadership Development Needs

- The success of the company depends on employee skills and opportunities for the team to innovate and produce high-quality solutions.
- The company needs a reliable marketing and sales team to educate the market about product performances and opportunities.

Financing and Regulatory Environment Development Needs

- The company has no issues with financing through bank loans, as it has a good credit rating.
- According to the company's CEO, the domestic regulatory framework does not represent any burden for its operations. Mikroelektronika is an export-oriented

company that distributes almost 100% of its products on foreign markets and was one of the first that started using online sales worldwide.
- If there is a challenge regarding the regulatory framework, the company strives to solve it efficiently, and if the problem recurs, the company implements the solution in its internal procedures.

The company recognizes no other development needs in terms of financing and regulatory environment.

Mikroelektoronika, the Hidden Champion

According to the company's website, Mikroelektronika started as an idea of its CEO, Nebojša Matić. It has since grown by acquiring great talents, making smart moves within the industry, and finally occupying a unique place on the market.

Mikroelektronika is a unique manufacturer of software and hardware tools—compilers and development systems, on a global scale. Besides, product development and production are done with an emphasis on quality. The company is also a leader in product design, functionality, and reliability. The CEO explains that he is only part of the group of people who are developing the company, founded by himself. Mr. Matić founded the company while he was a student in 1995. He also publishes a magazine where he authored many articles (Mikoelektronika 2019).

The company reached its first breakthrough in 2003 when it became the first on the global market to have developed a USB PIC program, and became a Microchip registered consultant (Mikoelektronika 2019). In 2016, with the introduction of the Hexiwear product, founded through the crowdfunding platform Kickstarter, the company won five awards, three of them at ARM TechCon 2016 *Innovation Challenge* (Mikoelektronika 2019).

Today, the company is a globally relevant producer that sets the standards in its niche. The tools are now exported to some 130 countries and enable engineers at various companies to test electronic products and the solutions that they are developing. The company's CEO explains that they are selling time since their tools allow engineers to do the most with the time that they have. The company develops solutions dedicated to its clients, and the main goal is to save time for engineers who are working on product creation in different businesses.

The company is a global market pioneer, and its product innovation is its primary competitive advantage. Based on a thorough reflection on the challenges that engineers encounter in their work, the company still produces unique solutions. Having its production and development enables flexibility and fast response to market needs. Integrated production in the value chain has enabled quality control, as well. Besides, the creation of one new product a day, combined with reliable logistics, has enabled the company to create a unique leadership position globally. The production of microcontroller tools allows engineers to develop an end-user product at various electronic companies. In this way, the company contributes to the broader concept by directly facilitating the development of new products and end-user solutions.

According to Mr. Matić, in the last 10 years the market has transformed itself beyond recognition. Many of the companies that used to exist are no longer around. As the market changed, so did Mikroelektronika. The organizational structure of the company allowed for growth without disruption and enabled adaptation to market changes. The company has integrated the management of key business processes, ERP, which provides dynamism, pragmatism, and agility in meeting market demands every day. Besides the company's agility, the source of a long-term competitive advantage is the anticipation of the needs of electronic companies and their future production.

The main driver of the company's business success is hard work focused on developing and achieving specific goals. As an essential point, the company's CEO states the importance of retaining, upgrading, and developing accumulated knowledge within the company. Additional factors of leadership are internal transparency and the visible progress of the company in terms of increasing its assets and staff.

The company maintains its strong market position thanks to innovation in production and organizational processes. Mr. Matić compares the company to a scientific institute because all employees, regardless of their status, are involved in product development.

The company's wifi debugger solves specific problems with the operation of machines from a distance. As time is a very scarce resource, the company made it possible to reduce costs by addressing certain operating problems of different machines stationed in different countries.

The company strives to develop its brand further in such a way that engineers across different businesses, who are developing its product and appreciating its time, think of Mikroelektronika as their best option.

5 Case Study 4

5.1 Uniplast

Overview
Address: Stara pruga, Preljina, Serbia
Tel: + 381 32 225 054
Fax: 381 32 380 286
Email: officc@uniplast.rs
Web: www.uniplast.rs

Company Information
Industry: Manufacture of plastic packing goods
Year of establishment: 1991
Sales revenues in 2017: 700,000 euros

Sales revenues in 2007: 100,000 euros
Average number of employees in 2017: 10
Brain(s) behind the company: Đorđe Jovanović

Nature of Market Leadership

The company is second in the Balkan region in the manufacture and distribution of pharmaceutical (galenic laboratories and pharmaceutical manufacturers), medical, and cosmetic packaging. Uniplast is a family firm with corporate management and 27 years of market experience. The company develops unique and high-quality products, which contribute to the creation and maintenance of the leadership position. It exports to the countries of former Yugoslavia, Albania, and Bulgaria.

Nature of Competitive Advantage

The company is ahead of market changes thanks to long-term partner relationships with clients and investments in new and innovative product development. Internal development capacities enable Uniplast to produce high-value-added products. Currently, the company is developing antimicrobial pharmaceutical and cosmetic packaging through the Innovation Fund project.

Core Lessons Learned on the Path to Success

1. Create a unique product whose quality justifies its price.
2. The net profit should be reinvested in new product development.
3. The key to a leadership market position is one's long-term partnerships with customers.
4. The corporate management establishment is important in family firms.

Management and Leadership Development Needs

- The transformation toward corporate governance was crucial in achieving a higher level of professional management since Uniplast is a family-owned company.
- However, the company is facing a challenge in the development of organizational culture because its employees need to take responsibility in their daily activities.
- Moreover, the company strives to develop a corporate culture that is more agile and flexible regarding change.

Financing and Regulatory Environment Development Needs

- The changes regarding the regulative requirements in the production domain are at first occurring at the global level. The company is striving to prepare for these changes even before they have become part of the national legislation.
- Also, the company actively seeks support from business associations concerning trade fairs, where it expects to sign new clients and exhibit its product line.

Uniplast, the Hidden Champion

The company is a regional leader in the production and distribution of pharmaceutical, medical, and cosmetic packaging. Uniplast became part of the Innovation Fund's innovation co-financing program in 2018. The company is contributing to this program through an industry of new materials and nano-technologies by developing active antimicrobial pharmaceutical and cosmetic packaging based on polyethylene and silver-zeolite.

Uniplast is a family-owned company with 27 years of market experience, focused on the development of unique and high-quality products for its customers. The development of innovative products, combined with the implementation of global standards necessary for production in this sector, enables the company to solve the challenges that its customers face.

Investments in the development of new and innovative products has enabled the company to be ahead of market changes, which are frequent and dynamic in this sector. These investments allow the company to provide more value-added products to its customers.

In addition to financial resources, the company also invests a significant amount of time in developing new products. The company's sales team enables research regarding customer needs. By discovering the challenges and demands that customers have, the development team builds a basis on which new products are developed. In addition to having employees engaged in the development, the company cooperates with universities and other companies. Commitment to development, according to the interviewee, is the key to market survival and success.

Although family-owned, the company has an established corporate governance system. The management structure of the company does not depend on the ownership structure. However, for family-owned companies in Serbia, it is not typical to establish a corporate governance structure. It is important to mention that this company has already faced this challenge and is successfully operating under the second generation of family entrepreneurs.

The main driver of the company's success is the creation of a unique product whose quality justifies the price. Business-generated earnings are primarily invested in the further development of the quality of existing and new products with more added value. The company invests in creating a long-term partnership by producing quality packaging, and the interviewee explained that the company allows customers to focus on their core business rather than packaging.

The company is currently developing active antimicrobial pharmaceutical and cosmetic packaging. Innovative packaging helps control microbial contamination and extends product life (Innovation Fund 2018). It is especially useful in protecting substances that require intensive transport and have a long storage period (Innovation Fund 2018). The project aims to make products safe for consumers and increase shelf life. This innovative packaging will be used in pharmaceutics, food, cosmetics, and other industries.

6 Conclusions and Recommendations

Although the orientation toward a market-based economy in Serbia is relatively recent, there is an increasing number of private sector companies, whose knowledge and products are competitive on a global scale. The hidden champions presented in this chapter operate in different industry sectors, and all of them are strong knowledge and innovation-driven companies. They are also very young because the Serbian economy consisted of mostly large-scale state enterprises until the beginning of this century.

The application of knowledge gained through education, the monitoring of global trends, and the application of the most innovative technology in production have contributed to the production of high-value-added products.

One of the main strengths of all hidden champions is a high-quality staff that continuously improves internally, but also possesses knowledge gained from traditionally strong hard science colleges that exist throughout the country. However, the country is facing the issue of talents retention, and so do the companies as well. They are also struggling to retain the talents that they have already trained (Savić et al. 2020).

A common characteristic of all presented hidden champions is the use of cutting edge technologies in the development of innovative products. The hidden champions are very flexible and have an agile approach to developing new, customized products for companies from different industries.

Generally, employee well-being and happiness are rated high on the companies' priority lists as workers with such specific skill sets are rare, despite the relatively high unemployment rates in the country. Highly-qualified employees are lost not only to competition but to emigration as well.

Being a hidden champion means that the company is not particularly well known, and, therefore, at times has to provide customized services that are not in its portfolio, to essential clients.

Also, these companies have to have a strong export record to become a hidden champion. However, it is worth noting that most of them have been founded with foreign markets in mind. Some make it a rule not to offer their products and services in the Serbian market, which they consider to be too small or not wealthy enough.

The companies did not emphasize any particular regulatory obstacle, nor did they demonstrate concern about any laws or regulations that could be adopted in the future. However, almost all of them stated that the unhindered EU accession process is a significant factor in the business environment in general, but also in their businesses in particular. This concern is the issues that they face with customs regulations and the time needed for their products to reach EU markets due to the checks involved. Also, they expect financing costs to go down once Serbia joins the EU. Finally, the stability that the EU accession process projects are also essential, as their foreign partners see the candidate status and accession negotiations as a sign of stability of the market and regulatory framework. This is closely intertwined with improving transparency, predictability, and ease of use in public administration services (Pitić et al. 2019).

Some companies even implement stricter regulatory requirements than necessary, as they expect them to become more stringent in the accession process. They all follow changes in the acquis, as well in the national legislation, even though the EU regulations still do not apply directly to Serbia.

References

Buck (2019) Company awards. http://buck.lighting/awards/. Accessed 15 Sept 2019

Chang S-J, Shim J (2015) When does transitioning from family to professional management improve firm performance? Transition from family to professional management. Strateg Manag J 36:1297–1316. https://doi.org/10.1002/smj.2289

Delgado M, Ketels C, Porter M, Stern S (2012) The determinants of national competitiveness. National Bureau of Economic Research, Cambridge, MA

Erić M, Babin M (2014) Extending the single market – investment and trade. In: Balázs P (ed) A European Union with 36 members? perspectives and risks. Center for EU Enlargement Studies, Central European University Press, Budapest, pp 27–46

Eurostat (2019) Eurostat data base. https://ec.europa.eu/eurostat/data/database. Accessed 15 Sept 2019

Galindo-Martín M-Á, Castaño-Martínez M-S, Méndez-Picazo M-T (2019) Digital transformation, digital dividends and entrepreneurship: a quantitative analysis. J Bus Res 101:522–527. https://doi.org/10.1016/j.jbusres.2018.12.014

Hofer CW, Charan R (1984) The transition to professional management: mission impossible? Am J Small Bus 9:1–11. https://doi.org/10.1177/104225878400900101

Innovation Fund (2018) Funded Projects. http://www.inovacionifond.rs/projects/kategorija/psi-cetvrti-ciklus. Accessed 15 Sept 2019

Kurt R (2019) Industry 4.0 in terms of industrial relations and its impacts on labour life. Procedia Comput Sci 158:590–601. https://doi.org/10.1016/j.procs.2019.09.093

Mergel I, Edelmann N, Haug N (2019) Defining digital transformation: results from expert interviews. Gov Inf Q 36:101385. https://doi.org/10.1016/j.giq.2019.06.002

Mikroelektronika (2019) History. https://www.mikroe.com/history. Accessed 15 Sept 2019

Nicholls R (2010) New directions for customer-to-customer interaction research. J Serv Mark 24:87–97. https://doi.org/10.1108/08876041011017916

Pitić G, Radosavljević G, Babin M, Erić M (2019) Digitalization of the tax administration in Serbia. Ekonomika preduzeća 67:131–145. https://doi.org/10.5937/EkoPre1808131P

Savić N, Pitić G, Lazarević J (2018) Innovation-driven economy and Serbia. Ekonomika preduzeća 66:139–150. https://doi.org/10.5937/EKOPRE1802139S

Savić N, Lazarević J, Kukić Z, Marinković E (2019) Digital transformation: challenges for companies in Serbia. Ekonomika preduzeća 67:101–114. https://doi.org/10.5937/EkoPre1808101S

Savić N, Drašković B, Lazarević J, Marinković E (2020) Nurturing and retaining talents in Serbia. Ekonomika preduzeća 68:75–89. https://doi.org/10.5937/EKOPRE2002075S

Sousa MJ, Rocha Á (2019) Skills for disruptive digital business. J Bus Res 94:257–263. https://doi.org/10.1016/j.jbusres.2017.12.051

World Bank (2019) Data; countries and economies. http://data.worldbank.org/country. Accessed 15 Sept 2019

Hidden Champions in Dynamically Changing Societies: The Case of Slovakia

Janka Táborecká-Petrovičová, Jaroslav Ďaďo, and Michal Budinský

Overview

Official name: Slovak Republic (Slovakia)
Type of government: parliamentary democratic republic
Population in 2017: 5,439,232
Land area: 48,080.0 km^2

History

Until 1918	Slovakia is a part of Austria-Hungary.
October 28, 1918	After the end of World War I and the dissolution of the Austro-Hungarian Empire, the Slovaks form an independent republic with the Czechs—Czechoslovak Republic (ČSR).
1939–1945	The Slovak Republic became an independent state in Central Europe under Nazi German control.
1945	The victorious powers after World War II restored Czechoslovakia in 1945.
Elections in 1946	The Czechoslovak Communist Party winning 38% of the total vote in Czechoslovakia seized power in February 1948.

J. Táborecká-Petrovičová (✉) · J. Ďaďo · M. Budinský
Matej Bel University, Banská Bystrica, Slovakia
e-mail: janka.taborecka@umb.sk

1968	Strict Communist control characterized the next four decades, was interrupted only briefly in the so-called Prague Spring of 1968.
November, 17, 1989	Velvet revolution brings democracy. Downfall of Communist Party rule in Czechoslovakia. The first free elections in Czechoslovakia since 1948 took place in June 1990.
January 1, 1993	Declaration of the independence of Slovak Republic simultaneously and peacefully with the Czech Republic. Both states attained immediate recognition from the USA and from their European neighbors.
January 1, 1993	In connection to the split of Czechoslovakia both countries acquired succession in the IMF since January 1, 1993. (Former Czechoslovak Republic was one of the founding members of the IMF.)
2000	Slovakia is invited to join the OECD and is invited by the European Union to begin the accession process.
March, 29, 2004	Slovakia admitted to NATO.
May, 1, 2004	Slovakia joint EU.
December, 21, 2007–March, 2008	Slovakia became a member of the Schengen area
January 1, 2009	Slovakia adopts the single European currency, the euro.

1 Introduction: Context and History

When searching for information or examples regarding the most successful companies in history, we can very easily find companies like Hewlett-Packard, Honda, or Dell with its story how to make it big. Our common picture of the admired company is a huge international corporation. However, economists realized that instead of huge corporations, there are small and medium-sized companies, with high number of innovation and a great export, serving as an engine of economic growth for many nations. Simon found out that SMEs play very important and long-term role in the export in Germany (McKiernan and Purg 2014, p. 2). Germany was the world's largest exporter in 1986, 1987, 1988, and 1990. This rather small country exported 6.8% more than the Americans and 47.2% more than the Japanese (Simon 1992, p. 115). According to the results from the year, 2017 Germany still belongs to the top three exporting countries in the world, occupying the second place (Atlas of economic complexity 2020). It has also several corporations listed in the Fortune Global

500 list, but these companies are not participating on national export to such a large extend. Surprisingly Germany's small and midsize companies, known as the Mittelstand are creating this trade surplus (Simon 1992, p. 115). At the same time, he found out that these companies are very often leaders on the market with the world market share around 80%. At the end of the 1980s, Simon as the founder, decided to name these special companies with similar characteristics as "Hidden Champions."

This, at first sight, strange combination of words, helped to the mystique (Simon 2009). As Venohr and Meyer (2007, p. 4) explain, the word "hidden" is used because "these companies are typically unknown outside their niches, mostly because they are private and relish their obscurity." The use of the second word "champions" is clearer. They are champions thanks to their contribution to the national export. To be classified as HC company should: (1) occupy the number one or two positions in the world market and the number one position in the European market as measured by market share or, if the latter is unknown, an HC must be a leader relative to its strongest competitor; (2) be small or medium-sized and, normally, its sales revenue would not exceed US$1 billion and (3) have a low visibility profile in the public domain. There are also some other criteria and specific characteristics that can help to identify HC. Generally, HC deal with essential goods in niche markets, usually B2B, and are mainly family-run, single product entities. HC usually specialize just in one product and operate only on one market.

Considering "hidden" criterion in the identification stage of our research, we were struggling and discussing how to understand and adjust the meaning of the word "hidden" in the era of the internet and social media. One of the characteristics of HC defined in the theory is the importance of human capital. These companies search for the best talents, they promote themselves through employer branding. Some of them communicate their best achievements or provide interviews in the media. Hence, they do not promote themselves through ads and commercials towards their customers. They are rather hidden from the viewpoint of traditional media and traditional channels. However, certain public awareness can be obvious thanks to the internet and social media for people who are interested in this field or in case that the company's representatives support various public initiatives. Moreover, typical B2B industrial manufacturing companies are more hidden in comparison with the IT industry (operating "on the internet") from which we have the majority of HC. We dare to say that the visibility should be interpreted more specifically with the respect to current trends.

Since Herman Simon introduced his concept of HC relevant for Germany, during the time also other authors followed, developed, and applied this approach in other cultural contexts (Sweden, China, Korea, Spain) from various broader or narrower perspectives (e.g., Din et al. 2013; Lee and Chung 2018; Kamp 2018; Rant and Cerne 2017; Muñoz et al. 2017; Voudouris et al. 2000). One of the most complex research was conducted in Central and Eastern Europe and Turkey with the aim to find, study, and compare identified HC with the original concept (McKiernan and Purg 2014). Slovakia participated in this research in 2011 represented by Taborecka-Petrovicova, Dado, and Bobakova. To study and understand the concept of hidden champions originally developed for Germany within Slovak conditions and provide updated information, it is necessary to understand the context and history of this country.

Slovakia is a small country situated in the heart of Central Europe with Bratislava's capital city, subdivided into eight regions, each named after its principal city. Actually, more than 5.4 million inhabitants live on 48,080.0 km^2 surrounded by Hungary, Ukraine, Poland, Czech Republic an Austria. Previous year, GDP per capita reached 34,329 euros (World Bank 2019, GDP per capita). Slovakia is an open economy, with strong linkage to international partners. According to the Atlas of economic complexity (2020) Slovakia is a high-income country, ranking as the 34th richest economy per capita out of 133 studied. It is also the 39th largest export economy in the world and the 16th most complex economy according to the Economic Complexity Index (ECI) (The Observatory of Economic Complexity 2017). Within recent years (2010–2015) Slovakia belonged to countries with the fastest growing economy in European Union (Slovakia among fastest growing economies in Europe 2016). Slovakia is characteristic by long tradition in industry sectors such as machinery, chemical, electrotechnical, wood processing and food industry. The most important sectors of Slovakia's economy in 2018 were industry (26.2%), wholesale and retail trade, transport, accommodation and food services (20.2%), and public administration, defense, education, human health and social work activities (14.8%). Intra-EU trade accounts for 86% of Slovakia's exports (Germany 22%, Czechia 12%, and Poland 8%), while outside the EU 3% go to the USA and 2% to both Russia and China (europa.eu). Under the influence of time and changes in the market, the automotive industry became a crucial element of the Slovak economy, which now represents 44% of total industrial production (Slovak Investment and Trade Development Agency 2017).

Looking at its history, Slovakia has undergone several changes that influenced economic as well as social-political situation. To focus on the most important milestones it is necessary to mention the twentieth century. In 1918 Czechoslovak Republic was one of the most industrially developed countries from a former Austria-Hungary monarchy. However, it suffered from a lack of purchasing power therefore the majority of production was exported abroad. About 75% of all production was tied to the Czech part. This situation resulted in restriction of building businesses in the Slovak part because the production of Czech businesses was preferred. Later, in pre-crisis period, between 1921 and 1929 Czechoslovak Republic closed about 160 businesses in the Slovak part, especially from metallurgy and leather industry. This fact caused the decline in the standard of living and created hungry valleys. Fortunately, since 1933 economy started to recover, due to the development of an armament industry in a pre-war period (Teich et al. 2011).

Rivet (1949, p. 86) in the publication "World Trade Developments in 1948 in Selected Countries" characterized Czechoslovakia as the most industrialized nation of Eastern Europe and described its post-war foreign trade directions. The large increase in trade with the Soviet Union started and replaced Germany as principal supplier and customer. Czechoslovakia exported machinery and metal products and some consumer goods. Russia in 1948 (and Germany before the war) accounted for about 16% of exports and of imports. Post-war years after 1945 were also characterized by massive nationalization of banks, industry businesses, and mines in the Czechoslovak Republic by government decrees. Nationalization of property peaked in 1948 when communists came to a power. Almost all remaining huge and small businesses in Czechoslovakia were nationalized in this year. Consequence of this was a dramatic drop of private businesses to only 3.5% from the whole industry. This situation was different in comparison with some other countries from former Eastern block like Poland or Hungary where small entrepreneurs existed. Thus, at a beginning of the 1960s private sector nearly did not exist. Initial owners of the nationalized property could gain it back partially after 1989 within the restitution period (Entrepreneurship disappeared in Czechoslovakia after 1945, 2005). Nationalization of foreign trade was represented and carried on by state-owned monopoly firms, dealing only with foreign trade and only in specific commodities (Rivet 1949, pp. 88–90). On the other hand, in 1945 Slovak part contributed to whole industry production only by 8.2%. However, as the government gradually built over 300 industry businesses, in 1985 performance of Slovakia represented up to 30%. Within these decades, the structure of industry started to change. One of the most important became the mining industry, which was recovered from the past. Machinery, electronic, metallurgy, and rubber industry accelerated significantly in these years. These industry sectors took a majority part on overall production on the country and Socialist industrialization improved overall living standard and developed urbanization of several places (Kirschbaum 2005).

The period after the year 1989 represented a new era characterized by the beginning of restitution, the release of communist's power, and privatization. The Velvet Revolution in November 1989 found Czechoslovakia, just like the other states emerging from the era of communist dictatorships, with a centralized economy, no political pluralism, and a civil society limited to a few dissident initiatives. The new political elite faced the tremendous task of creating the institutions of liberal democracy; a market economy, the rule of law, and a civil society. Decrease of communist's influence resulted in orientation on the market economy, linked with the changes in business size, structure, and competitiveness. Several ownership reforms created a competitive environment and conditions for a free business. Privatization of businesses affected this time period significantly. Firstly, so-called "huge privatization" was performed between 1991 and 1993 and in the second wave "coupon privatization" was experienced from 1995 to 1998. Coupon privatization had a huge extent, was fast, and solved a problem with raising a free capital. On the other hand, it was connected with several issues such as questionable privatization methods, negative impact on employment, or lack of transparency. Among the biggest businesses Slovnaft, Duslo Šaľa, Istrochem, or VSŽ have been privatized (Pehe 2014).

Since January the 1st 1993 Slovakia became an independent country after the peaceful division of Czechoslovakia into two separate countries, Slovak Republic and the Czech Republic. In this year economy structure of Slovakia was represented by industry (33.1%), agriculture (13.9%), construction (9.3%), transport (6.3%), and other not production activities (37.4%). Important period in economic as well as social-political history of Slovakia is since May 2004, when we became a part of the European Union. Membership of Slovakia in the EU released inflow of international capital, which boosts its economy. Directly in 2004, FDI net inflow of GDP shot up to 7.094 from the previous 2.074 in 2003 (World Bank 2019, Foreign direct investment, net inflows % of GDP). At this time, many established, successful, or fast-growing Slovak businesses were purchased or joint with investors from abroad. We assume that this situation contributed to the fact why we struggled in the identification of more hidden champions. A lot of successful companies in Slovakia we were considering at the first stages of our research did not qualify as hidden champions due to their ownership structure. The popularity of FDI inflow into Slovakia is represented also nowadays by the fact, that very "promising" businesses we intended to involve in our research as potential HC was recently acquired by international companies before they could became hidden champions.

The end of a first decade of twenty-first century is accompanied by economy decline which culminated in the market collapse as a result of the crisis. As well as Slovakia as open country, with strong connection to international trade was strongly affected. Within the following years unemployment rate gradually increased up to 14.2% in 2013, from pre-crisis to 9.6%. Similarly, GDP experienced a negative impact by year-on-year growth from 5.6% in 2008 to only 1.5% in 2013 (National Bank of Slovakia 2019). Since 2013, the Slovak economy started to recover from global financial crisis and until today it is still on a continual rise. At the end of 2018 unemployment rate reached its minimum at 6.6% and year-to-year growth of GDP was 4.1%. Huge impact on this improvement had an automotive industry. However, not solely assembly of automobiles, but also its linkage on chemical and machinery industry boost Slovak economy. Thus, in 2018 46.8% of total industrial production was covered by the automotive industry, which represented about 35% of the total industrial export of Slovakia (Statistical Office of Slovakia 2019a, b). The economy of Slovakia should gain some speed next year, despite the challenging external backdrop, propelled by strengthening domestic demand. A healthy labor market will underpin consumer spending, while investment activity is set to pick up thanks to rising EU funds inflows and growing car production capacity. Focus Economics panelists see the growth of 2.6% in 2020, down 0.3 percentage points from last month's forecast, and 2.7% in 2021 (Slovakia Economic Outlook 2019). To conclude turbulent socio-economic, political, and historical background of Slovakia formed conditions for the development of the first HC's in Slovakia that can be dated after 1989 when market liberalization started.

We identified eight hidden champions companies in the first research in 2011 that were classified as strong and regional/young ones (Taborecka-Petrovicova et al. 2014). In 2018 we added only two new real ones and one potential HC. One reason is that Slovakia is very small country. We used to have more rural character in comparison with Czech Republic in the past. Despite the situation before 1989 we used to have internationally successful companies not only in B2B sector. But we experienced a huge wave of foreign direct investments what means it is more difficult to find an established international leader fully in "Slovak hands." Ten "best" companies in Slovakia according to Forbes 50 are foreign ones: Volkswagen, Eustream, Kia, Slovnaft, US Steel, or banks (https://www.forbes.sk/top-firmy/). We strongly believe that in Slovakia there are definitely more HC companies that could be considered at least as potential ones and are not mentioned in this chapter. But the result is based on the willingness of the company's representatives to participate and provide data and availability of sufficient secondary data and we did not succeed as we intended.

Moreover, we have seen turbulent changes in ownership structure and recognized interesting phenomenon. We identified several companies that we had in the category of "potential HC" but during the research, they were acquired by big global players and we had to exclude them from our pool. There was a company in the augmented reality field belonging among ten fastest growing technological companies according to Deloitte Technology Fast 50 in CEE but by the meantime, it was acquired by global IT company from abroad. Another potential HC, no. 1 in Slovakia, a major Central European provider of web hosting and web services to over 100,000 customers in Slovakia and Hungary was also acquired by the investment company. Or highly innovative company from the scientific and research field focusing on developing mass spectrometry was also sold, recently to the private investor. We may assume that when the company starts to be exceptionally successful and visible, it will attract the attention of bigger international players. This was confirmed during the interviews with some companies that are trying to resist for now and do not consider such acquisition. Other companies with very specific markets like flying cars or plasma technology well drilling and milling were without a track of history since they still develop their technologies or finalize prototypes but it can be expected that in the future they may become HC.

After the identification stage, we managed in-depth interviews with the CEOs and other relevant companies' representatives that were conducted by the researchers to create profiles of each of them. Interviews provided fiches covering the same areas: identification data (company's address and contact, industry, basic financial data, nature of market leadership, nature of competition advantage, and core lessons learned on the path to success). Majority companies emerged from IT sector or machinery both in 2011 and 2018. In 2018 we followed the similar methodology to track the progress of the companies identified in 2011 and to identify new ones. We also added other perspectives we were interested in like "management and leadership development needs" (in terms of knowledge, competences, and skills) and "financing and regulatory environment development needs."

We revealed various paths throughout the last years of previously identified HC. Majority of them confirmed their position of a strong HC, expanding, winning new international markets and segments even via acquisitions, and bringing innovations. One of the strongest hidden champions became a corporation and global brand present in 202 countries. According to the statistics, it is the most successful company within its field established in EU, a leader and top supplier in CEE region and their aim is to belong to the first three market leaders worldwide until 2020.

Another one is mentioned among top key players in relevant field statistics, belonging to the top two solutions in the respected category worldwide, present across all continents, and continuously pioneering in further innovations. Another HC representative from the machinery field belongs to the top 5 biggest global producers in the sector, exporting 99% of its products all over the world, ranked number 2 in CEE, number 3 in Western Europe, and number four in North America. Also, this company aims to become the world number 3 by 2020. They are all competing with global players with much broader scope but they focus and win within their specific niches.

Tracking the journey of hidden champions since 2011 they still ensure a strong focus and inevitably close connections to their customers and seek continuously on their feedback that is reflected in on-going product improvements. The customers tend to trust the product, which in turn supports the establishment of a long-lasting relationship with them. They have great abilities to find a gap on the market and develop specific and customized solutions differentiating them from competitors. The possession of patents for their innovative design, combined with investment in further research and development creates a powerful product that keeps them ahead of the market. These companies are very strong in quality that imparts a distinct competitive advantage.

For all of them employees are their greatest asset and the best ad for the others. All companies thanks to their reputation take advantage of the skilled workforce Slovakia provides and according to various rankings they belong to the most preferred employers not only in Slovakia but also abroad (Czech Republic). Some also monitor feedback from employees, their satisfaction, and happiness on regular basis—they understand that the happiness of their people has large and positive causal effects on productivity, effectiveness, and higher performance. In some cases, we have seen changes in the position of founders where new successors as CEOs continue with the great leadership of the founders. These new leaders are also as their predecessors winning various competitions and they became the most respected CEOs of the years, like PricewaterhouseCoopers (PwC) competition among 147 CEOs in Slovakia, IT personality of the year, or European Inventor of the year. Their background and technically oriented education fully fits the company's focus and before promotion, they significantly contributed to the global success of the company. They show a drive and passion for work, follow the open and transparent vision and company priorities, fully engaged, and believing in the product.

In this group of strong HC, we found out during the research that one of the companies lost its position as it was acquired by the other global company—their biggest global customer what prevents it to be qualified as HC. If we would not consider this fact and focus on other aspects of the progress they made since 2011, we would see that despite turbulent changes the company came through because of unfair treatment of the partner in public tender resulting in financial problems, they preserved their original, motivational, and very inspiring business culture with continuing strong focus on innovations, revealing and exploiting new opportunities on emerging international markets and orientation on employees and their satisfaction. Other regional/young/potential HC identified in 2011 decided to focus more on the Slovak market and competition for the nearest future with only some minor exporting activities intending to confirm their domestic position. Although the majority has better results than in 2011, demonstrating development plans, expansion activities, investments, changes in business model and some of them are undoubtful Slovak, resp. "Czechoslovakian" leaders with more than 60% exporting activities in 130 countries or holding market share 20%, we have to summarize that none of them became a real HC and for now we even cannot consider them as potential HC. There was only one exception in this group where the company is strongly export-oriented exporting into 60 countries worldwide, they invest into further R&D and exhibiting growing sales but their business was significantly influenced by embargo to the Russian market. One newly identified potential HC is one of two companies in the Slovak market, holding 35–40% of the market share each. In some East European countries, the company has a leading position in the supply for special photo optics used in the aerospace and cosmic industry with ambitions to grow further what qualified them as potential HC.

Newly identified real hidden champions come from two industries: IT and machinery. We will present more detailed information about the representatives from both fields: Innovatrics (IT—biometric technologies) and Microstep (machinery—plasma cutting systems). Data are based on personal interviews and secondary data available on the webpages of companies and various reports (Exhibit 1).

2 CASE Studies of Selected Hidden Champions

2.1 Case Study 1

MicroStep, s.r.o.

Overview
Address: Vajnorská 158, 831 04 Bratislava, Slovakia
Tel: +421 2 3227 7200
Fax: +421 2 3227 7001
Email: marketing@microstep.sk
Web: www.microstep.sk

Company Information
Industry: CNC cutting machines, NACE: C28—Manufacture of machinery and equipment n.e.c.
Year of Establishment: 1991
Sales Revenues in 2017: 30.4 mio euros
Sales Revenues in 2009: 12.6 mio euros (r. 2009)

Exhibit 1 Core economic indicators for Slovakia

	2011	2012	2013	2014	2015	2016	2017	2018
GDP per capita (current US$)	18,187.16	17,274.64	18,191.61	18,629.78	16,182.30	16,544.22	17,579.26	19,546.90
GDP per capita growth (annual %)	2.69	1.48	1.38	2.65	4.08	2.99	3.03	3.96
Unemployment, total (% of total labor force, national estimate)	13.62	13.96	14.22	13.18	11.48	9.67	8.13	6.54
Foreign direct investment, net inflows (% of GDP)	5.53	1.90	1.02	−0.36	1.73	5.28	6.19	2.40
GDP (current US$, billion)	98.18	93.41	98.48	100.95	87.77	89.85	95.62	106.47
Exports of goods and services (current US$, billion)	83.50	85.41	92.39	92.72	81.02	84.01	92.64	103.55
Exports of goods and services (% of GDP)	85.05	91.43	93.82	91.853	92.31	93.50	96.89	97.25
Merchandise exports (current US$, billion)	79.83	80.61	85.75	86.45	75.23	77.57	84.47	94.22
Merchandise exports to high-income economies (% of total merchandise exports)	86.68	86.68	85.92	87.53	88.85	89.12	89.24	N/A
Merchandise exports to developing economies in Europe & Central Asia (% of total merchandise exports)	9.62	9.80	10.20	8.86	7.82	7.60	7.76	N/A
Ores and metals exports (% of merchandise exports)	2.99	3.12	2.23	2.26	2.08	1.74	2.06	2.04
Agricultural raw materials exports (% of merchandise exports)	1.02	1.05	0.97	0.93	0.89	0.83	0.81	0.87
Food exports (% of merchandise exports)	4.84	5.61	4.85	4.06	3.95	3.88	3.63	3.37
Fuel exports (% of merchandise exports)	6.32	5.81	5.49	4.61	3.57	3.21	4.45	3.73
Manufactures exports (% of merchandise exports)	84.70	84.27	86.33	87.92	89.20	90.09	88.85	89.77
High-technology exports (% of manufactured exports)	7.41	9.59	11.02	11.14	11.16	10.73	11.80	10.58

Source: World Bank, September, 2019

Average number of employees in 2017: 460
Brainer(s) behind the company: Founders and CEO Eva Stejskalová, Alexander Varga, Juraj Buša, Alexej Makuch

Nature of Market Leadership

In the field of high-end plasma cutting systems, the company belongs among the world's largest producers. Through a network of authorized dealers and subsidiaries, the company is present in 54 countries across all continents. So far, they have sold more than 2200 cutting systems whereby over 95% of production is destined for export. Apart from Slovakia and almost all European countries, MicroStep cutting machines operate also in the USA, Canada, China, South Africa, the Middle East, India, Vietnam, South Korea, Israel, and China.

Nature of Competitive Advantage

The company customizes every system to fit the customer's needs. They combine marking, drilling, tapping, countersinking, 3D laser scanning, material handling with cutting methods (gas/waterjet/plasma/laser) and they produce complete solutions including CAM systems and production management. They have their own R&D and closely cooperate on these projects with universities. They substituted the heavy robust constructions with dynamic solutions with the modern control system.

Core Lessons Learned on the Path to Success

1. Provide specific innovative solutions and adjust them according to the needs of customers. References are crucial in this business, hence build close relationships with your customers, try to understand their processes, gain deep insight, and co-create value with them. Provide complex solutions.
2. Invest into research and development (55 people work in R&D of Microstep). All competitors are trying to improve: they learn, attend exhibitions, and monitor trends. Without constant investments into research, you cannot succeed. There are also very short product life cycles. Microstep cooperates with their customers on the development of new prototypes (they share R&D with them). Contribute to, form, and use also the newest trends (Industry 4.0, Smart Industry, 3D solutions, automation, digitalization, and robotics) in all fields of your business.
3. Microstep founders are all "researchers by soul." They share and pass on this passion to all people working in the company. Employees can see they contribute to change, their opinions are accepted. A creative environment is important. The highest-skilled employees are offered to become co-owners of the company.

Management and Leadership Development Needs

Company feels a huge lack of skilled employees with the required technical knowledge. They expect that the government support more practically oriented education (especially technical or economic). Their industry (production of CNC machines) is very sensitive to external influences (like the crisis in 2008), causing a huge decrease but they are able to balance it and clearly and more rationally settle priorities of investments.

Financing and Regulatory Environment Development Needs

The company has been experiencing a huge technological development towards more demanding machines or automatization of processes. From 2010 to 2018 they received funding from the Ministry of Education, SR in the stimuli grant scheme for research and development, which amounted to approximately 2.5 million euros. It helped them to innovate significantly and create new job opportunities in R&D. Another supported R&D project started in 2019. So regarding financing, company uses their own resources but they do not have a big problem with external ones (commercial banks with long-term cooperation). The trend of applied research is increasing; the European Commission is going to double investments but they feel like "new countries" do not benefit so much from these initiatives. They would also welcome more cooperation in joint projects and grants with technically oriented universities (they already have some, e.g., APVV projects).

"Success Story of Microstep: The Global Leader in the Field of Plasma Cutting"

When in the year 1991 ten scientists from the Slovak University of Technologies were founding company called Microstep, the first orders received from their former students. Very soon, they started to export to Europe and became one of the top European companies in their field in more than 50 countries of the world. They represent one third of the European market in high-end production. It is unbelievable that they are able to compete with such global competitors like Messer Cutting Systems (Germany) with experiences of more than 120 years with whom they belong to the two leaders in the production of high-end cutting machines in Europe. Worldwide they compete with another historically established companies from highly developed countries: ESAB (Sweden; established in 1904) and Koike (Japan; established in 1918). This success is supported by the unique combination of their strengths, competitive advantages, and ability to define their gap on the market. Microstep is able to customize every system. Their solutions are based on close cooperation and mutual research in developing prototypes with its customers. They focus on permanent innovations that fit current and future trends. Thanks to their background and education, founders are all "researchers by soul" with a huge passion and they are in the company since the beginning pursuing their dreams.

2.2 Case Study 2

Innovatrics, s.r.o.

Overview
Address: Jarošova 1, 831 03 Bratislava, Slovakia
Tel: +421 220714056
Email: info@innovatrics.com
Web: www.innovatrics.com

Company Information
Industry: Biometric technologies, NACE: J62.0—Computer programming, consultancy and related activities
Year of Establishment: 2004
Sales Revenues in 2017: 7.5 mio euros
Sales Revenues in 2007: 1.7 mio euros (v r. 2012)
Average number of employees in 2017: 100
Brainer(s) behind the company: CEO and founder Jan Lunter

Nature of Market Leadership

Innovatrics is an independent and trusted partner for biometric identity management technology—a global top performer in fingerprint and face biometrics. The company develops the fastest fingerprint matching algorithm in the world, which works with a 99.98% accuracy, and also the top facial recognition algorithm according to NIST FRVT Ongoing results (New Europe 100—changemakers in central and eastern Europe 2016). To date, they have successfully completed over 500 projects in more than 80 countries and over a billion people have been biometrically processed using Innovatrics software. Innovatrics was recognized as a leading technology company in Central Europe (Technology Fast 50 Powerful connections 2014). They are present in Africa, Asia, and Pacific, Europe, the Middle East, North America, and South America. Since 2016 new offices in the US (Atlanta) and Singapore have been opened in order to serve American and APAC customers better. According to the assessment, Innovatrics is estimated to be the number 1 at least in the CEE region. This estimation is based on the above-provided information as well as several studies (Global Biometrics Market Research Report 2019; Global Biometrics Market 2018). First report studies the Global Biometrics Market, especially in North America,

Europe, China, Japan, Korea, and Taiwan, focuses on top manufacturers in the global market, with capacity, production, price, revenue, and market share for each manufacturer. The studies explain that the other top key players in the Global Biometrics Market are: NEC, Matrix System, Fujitsu, Nuance, Kaba Group, SMUFS Bio, and Secugen. These competitors are from Japan (NEC, Fujitsu), India (Matrix System), the USA (Nuance), and Switzerland and Germany (Kaba group), while Innovatrics is from the CEE region. Data also shows that many of the competitors have a much broader scope of their business than just "biometric technologies," while Innovatrics focuses specifically on biometric technologies and in some cases covers more countries (100 versus 70 or 80). These facts lead to an assumption that Innovatrics is a leader at least in the CEE region.

Nature of Competitive Advantage

Innovatrics's fingerprint matching algorithm is one of the fastest in the world with a matching speed of 1.04 billion per second on a standard server. Continuous innovation has helped the company achieve blazing performance, consistently ranking among top performers in benchmark tests conducted by NIST (National Institute of Standards and Technology). To ensure it stays ahead of its competitors, its unique algorithm continues to underpin the most advanced ABIS solution available on the market. Innovatrics was recognized internationally in 2008 when it received two prestigious awards in 1 year: The Innovative Entrepreneur of the Year (Ernst & Young) and Global Fingerprint Technology Innovation of the Year. It has reaped numerous accolades since then from prestigious institutions including earning a spot on CIOReview's 20 Most Promising Banking Technology Solution Providers of 2018 and being named by APAC Business Headlines as one of the 10 Fastest Growing Digital Transformation Solution Providers to Watch this year (Innovatrics Awards: https://www.innovatrics.com/awards/).

Core Lessons Learned on the Path to Success

1. Innovations: "We believe in quality. We guarantee and maintain the technological advantage in our products and services through continual improvement and by hiring talented professionals. From the performance of our products to the way we develop and support them, we focus on being the fastest and most flexible partner on the market. We love a good challenge and that is why we approach each project with enthusiasm, skill and innovation. We focus on high added value."
2. Close relationships (not only) with customers: "We remain open to our customers, partners and each other by sharing knowledge and information every step of the way. Having the freedom to choose our own direction, we always recommend what is best for our partners. We work with our partners, not just for

them, with a positive approach and a dialogue-driven attitude to meet the respective goals of our partners as well as of our colleagues."
3. Strong and unique personality of the leader and his passion. The "keywords" he uses are inspiration, future, effort, and innovation. In 2016, Jan Lunter was named Technological leader and received a special price for the most impressive business story.

Management and Leadership Development Needs

A good leadership is a key success factor leading to satisfied employees and following successful company. Company constantly reviews how it rewards people. Salary, bonuses, personal development, the working environment they offer is always up for review. Their aim is to make their people feel great about coming to work (https://careers.innovatrics.com/employees-important-customers/). Practically whole company uses the Kanban method that arises from Japanese kaizen. This agile method is focused on quality and elimination of imperfections with the emphasis to prioritization. During their work, they naturally follow the company's values. E.g., collaborative tools that they use (Confluence, Jira, Ryver, Bitbucket) reflect teamwork. Quality is expressed in the development underpinned by unit tests or systematic measurement of the speed and accuracy of our solutions. What they have in common is the passion for technologies and the effort to intellectually grow. This is for them maybe even more important than experiences. They are interested in graduates interested in their study, having fun from pure studying. People that have passion for solving technological problems are ideal for them. They expect self-educating and gaining knowledge from actual online courses (Beszédeš 2017).

Financing and Regulatory Environment Development Needs

In the 2013 interview, Jan Lunter claimed that he never had any investors. He built it and adjusted the suitable models step by step during his studies. He still rather prefers to grow organically and slowly than to have an investor who would force them to take decisions they may not like. He reflects on his history and thinks that the business would start even more successfully if they had somebody with real entrepreneurial experience in the team. They were "learning by doing," and Jan (as IT developer) had to deal with managerial and leadership challenges. The company was profitable since the very beginning. Innovatrics is proud being independent company financing activities from their own resources, without the presence of any investors. They want to make decisions and choose issue they are interested in (Piko 2013).

"Success Story of Innovatrics: Global Leader in Biometric Technologies"

Since his childhood, Jan Lunter was exceptional in mathematics and physics and studied IT in France. Jan worked on a new fingerprint algorithm during his studies of Image Processing in France in 2003. In 2004 the matching algorithm performed with high accuracy and one of the lowest error rates in the industry. This technological leadership was demonstrated at the worldwide fingerprint algorithm competition FVC2004. This innovative approach to fingerprint recognition led to accuracy results that clearly distinguished them from other competitors. Availing of university support, Jan founded the company in France together with his French professor and friend. In 2006 they moved it to Slovakia. The name Innovatrics is a combination of Innovation & Biometrics. Their success is ensured by more factors. Innovatrics are developing a great product. They are not just leading innovators in the area of fingerprint biometrics; their facial recognition technology is also a top performer. Combining the constant improvement of their algorithm and innovations such as the newly introduced GPU acceleration support means their facial technology is now capable of performing thousands of facial template extractions per second. Innovatrics technology played a significant role in, e.g., increasing the transparency and efficiency of the 2016 general elections in Uganda with tailored biometric voter verification solution. They have a specific approach towards their customers. They cooperate intensively, educate them and build network. As they claim: we simply provide better solutions, being completely independent gives us greater flexibility, our award-winning algorithms translate to better value for money, our customer support is top-notch and it is not just our speed, but accuracy that highly matters (https://www.innovatrics.com/biometric-technology/).

3 Conclusions and Recommendations

Despite the fact recently presented by OECD (OECD Economic Surveys, Slovak Republic 2019, p. 7) that "spending on research in Slovakia is weak, and the share of innovative companies is low, hampering the conditions for improving Slovakia's position in global value chains," we were able to detect unique highly innovating companies showing the path to global success and sharing their best practices. Not all of them are described in this chapter since not all companies wanted to participate in research and disclose their data. Moreover, Slovakia is a small country, with specific history (before 1989 Slovakia was without privately owned companies, family businesses were taken over by government or forbidden), with a lot of FDI inflow and ongoing acquisition of currently successful companies with potential, especially in IT sector. This fact was mentioned also in the paper of Beblavy and Kurekova (2014) stating that during the process of relative global market consolidation, a number of regional companies in CEE were acquired by a larger competitor.

Common features of hidden champions can be evident in various areas. All these businesses were established in the period of 30 years after 1989 what is obviously connected with the change of political establishment. Some of these companies started very soon in 90ties but we could see the ones that set up their business after 2004 proving that also relatively young, but well-established company can become the hidden champion, even without very long tradition and decades of experience. Turnovers of Slovak HC identified in our research are much lower than the obligatory criterion 3 billion euros so we can say that they all fulfill this condition of the size. Measurement based on number of employees would provide three companies exceeding 250 employees what brings them in the category of large companies. All identified strong HC are from IT or machinery sector. Only one new potential HC is from the field of steel casting. In majority of Slovak HC, we would not find the usual character of family business as it is common in German-speaking countries identified by Herman Simon. As it was mentioned, during the history of Slovakia ownership reforms, mainly nationalization, ruled out this business model. It is difficult also due to the short time period of HC's existence to become family-owned business that persisted until today. We revealed that some of them were set up rather by the community of friends, schoolmates, or colleagues. Another difference of Slovak HC compared to German ones is their geographic location. While in Germany they are spread almost around the whole country, in Slovakia majority of them is located in Bratislava region (capital city). This fact may be explained probably by notable differences in geographic regions, such as GDP per capita in Bratislava was about 35,790 euros in 2016, compared to 10,000–13,000 euros in other regions, and better business and networking opportunities (Statistical Office SR 2019a, b).

When it comes to the best practices or lessons learned from HC identified in both our researches (2011 and 2018), we divided them into six areas: market/customer orientation, human resources, company culture and values, systematic approach and strategy, development and innovations and quality and uniqueness.

3.1 Market/Customer Orientation

This group covers the highest number of core lessons mentioned by identified HC. Lessons such as customer approach, customization, image, and credibility are closely interconnected. They are all oriented on customers and their needs and requirements. Customization as core lesson learned by Slovak HC stands for customization of products, following market, and accomplishing special requirements of customers even in the form of value co-creation and joint R&D. Customer relations were included also in Simon's lessons, specifically in Lesson 8, Closeness to Customer. Companies should follow this customer approach typical for HCs in order to be successful. Customization, providing complex solutions, and high performance for the customer can lead to competitive advantage.

3.2 Human Resources

The second lesson of Slovak HC is identical with Simon's Lesson 2 called High-performance Employees. Both of them highlight the importance of the right employee selection. Employing people can be considered as some kind of investment and they represent one of the most precious intangible assets for HC. The best ones may even become a part of the ownership structure. All of them seek for the best talents and rely on their high qualification, motivation, and loyalty. Our HC belong to the best employers on the market and there is an interesting discrepancy in their effort—they build awareness and develop employer branding on one side but on the other side they want to keep their "hidden" status.

3.3 Company Culture and Values

Corporate culture represents values, principles, and believes which are common for members of company. Companies can take advantage of strong company culture and become successful. Partnership, fair approach, informal approach, maintaining long-term partnership, sharing same visions and values, and liking your business are lectures of HC affecting company culture and values shared by employees. These values are frequently explicitly visible and communicated by the company emphasizing courage, making the difference, honesty, fairness, ethical approach, reliability, determination, or passion.

3.4 Systematic Approach and Strategy

It is not enough to have a good idea. Having vision, goals the company wants to achieve and strategy it intends to use is the right way how to succeed. Founders of companies identified as HC exactly know what they want to achieve. They usually prepare business plan. It is important to be prepared, to have a vision, to know key customers and their needs in order to produce the right product. Business plan is important for every entrepreneur also from the financial point of view. It is summary of estimated costs, so entrepreneur can prepare for every possible solution. In case of having partner in the business, it is necessary to share the vision and plans of the company. It also helps to define new business challenges, reveal opportunities and be prepared to face threats. We revealed that in case of business challenges there is a shift in the main focus from western European countries, especially Germany, towards Asian countries (China, India) where our companies perceive a great business opportunities but on the other side they face a strong competition from this growing region.

3.5 Development and Innovations

It is not surprising, that innovation is one of the lessons learned by HC. As we know, it is important characteristic and also the additional criterion for HCs. Companies willing to become successful should invest into the research and development in order to gain leading position on the market. Innovations, in the form of new technologies or patents, are involved in Simon's 8 revised specific lessons, too. It is important to be faster than competitors and to bring new products. It can be considered also as competitive advantage. Our HC is continuously working on R&D in order to keep competitive advantage and technological leadership. Changes in technology, production, or materials can increase efficiency, improve the quality or decrease the price of production. It can be difficult to find finances for R&D, especially for young companies, or invest into patents. Our HC are able to succeed also in this field and contribute to, form, and use also the newest trends (Industry 4.0, Smart Industry, 3D solutions, automation, digitalization, robotics, IoT, augmented, or virtual reality) in all fields of their business.

3.6 Quality and Uniqueness

HCs very often build their leadership and competitive advantage on the quality of their products as well as on the uniqueness and high added value of their production. It has been very important also for Slovak HC on their way to business success. Exceptional quality of products, solutions, and technologies of studied HC were proved by a lot of achievements and awards these companies gained since the beginning of their existence, appearing in various rankings, winning prizes, or receiving patents. And they are able to keep on in this success. It is better to find your own solutions that will distinguish you from your competitors—like a better technological level or increased service quality in comparison with cheaper solutions. From the early days, these companies are focused on producing high-quality technologies and solutions. Due to increasing competition from Asian countries companies realized they cannot compete with them in the case of simpler solutions therefore they are focusing on more demanding solutions, too. They say that what matters is customized high-end quality, not the price.

To summarize, in order to have successful business that might become hidden champion one day, the company can learn from very useful inspirations, and by the reality-approved strategies and steps towards future success. Company should be oriented on the market and listen to the customer's needs. Equally important is to seek for the best employees, invest in human resources, and to motivate them. Successful company should also create company culture and share common values while developing business plan, vision, and planning how to meet the goals of the company. Afterwards it is important to invest into the research and development and to innovate in order to ensure the highest quality and unique production.

3.7 Implications for Government, Financial Institutions and Higher Educational Institutions

Since some of the implications overlap, we decided to join and interpret them mutually. We found out that the same as in case of the research realized recently in Slovakia, also HC companies nowadays experience a huge lack of qualified and skilled people from the labor market that is unprepared for their current needs, with insufficient qualification structure and regional differences (Dado et al. 2018). Typically, companies are "stealing" skilled employees by providing a better wage. Some companies solve it by searching people especially within their existing structure motivating them by creative environments and training them according to their requirements; some of them look for new employees also from abroad or they are trying to motivate experienced Slovak employees from abroad to return. They miss especially highly qualified technically oriented employees (what is natural since our HC emerged from IT and machinery sector) like engineers, CNC programmers and operators, constructors, or developers. They are aware that to train superior CNC operator months and employee for R&D takes years, that is why they are trying to continuously increase productivity and use available people. The required trainings were present in various fields: managerial education for middle-level production managers, English language courses, sales techniques, strategic knowledge on market and customer, systems of quality management, kaizen, lean manufacturing, or project management. Many of them emphasized more general abilities, that education institution should cultivate such as critical, logical, and analytical thinking. HC with strong employer brand presence, belonging to the most preferred employers are in more favorable situation.

HC representatives emphasized more intensive collaboration with universities and other educational institutions not only for gaining relevantly educated employees but also in joint research activities. Some of them already established such co-operations (especially with technical universities or secondary technical engineering schools) but they expect more initiatives and joint research projects. Some companies take this situation into their own hands and create own schools providing relevant knowledge for their purposes. Some of them established centers for education in industrial automatization and IT, they contribute to design requalification courses or they participate in the system of dual education. They provide feedback on curricula to ensure graduates with relevant knowledge. Another point is the willingness to share their knowledge and teach people around them. Some HC organize seminars, presentations, trainings pro bono, because they see it as a good source of candidates and potential employees in the future; to be helpful and connect school knowledge with job practise for students. The founders and CEOs criticize that government should invest more in financing educational institutions, research, and support especially technically oriented schools (to produce skilled computer programmers or software engineers). Besides more relevant and practically oriented technical knowledge HC mentioned also recommendations for business educational institutions. They would expect graduates with the updated knowledge in product management, marketing, able to realize surveys, prepare, manage, and evaluate online campaigns, skilled in new technologies connected with augmented or virtual reality that would be ready for the era of Industry 4.0.

In the case of financing, hidden champions have shown diverse approaches. Some of them want to remain independent and finance everything from own resources or via traditional loans from banks with which they established long-term relationships. Some HC have own investors, used euro funds or were supported from the government by investment add used for the purchase of new technologies or construction of new factory resulting in fostered innovation, increased competitiveness and employment in the region. From the regulatory environment, companies would welcome "usual" measures: less byrocracy, more predictable business environment and legislation, more transparent distribution and assignation of finances from grants with fair rules for competition and solving corruption. They would eliminate useless and redundant regulations (not only in Slovakia but also on EU level) influencing the increase of price. Some of the hidden champions mentioned negative experiences with government institutions but some were satisfied with previous cooperation. Some HC feel the power of big transnational corporations, they try to communicate with them, co-exist but they perceive that sometimes their steps are not correct and they invite measures coming from antimonopoly bodies.

Slovakia has very unbalanced industrial structure strongly oriented in the automotive sector that might cause problems in the future and harm the economy in case of global crisis. Therefore the government should re-consider its focus and support the economy WITH investments in research and development of highly innovative Slovak companies. This is in line with one of the key OCED recommendations that address both problems, stating: "Slovakia must invest in skills and adaptability to labor market developments, as the risk of automation is more acute than elsewhere. It also needs to develop its own capacity to innovate and adopt new technologies and include research collaboration with innovative companies in the assessment of universities and public research institutions" (OECD Economic Surveys, Slovak Republic, February 2019, p. 5). Companies like hidden champions could positively contribute to this effort and inspire other ones to joint them on the path to global success.

References

Atlas of economic complexity by the Harvard Growth Lab's (2020, Jan). http://atlas.cid.harvard.edu/countries/206

Beblavý M, Kureková LM (2014) Into the first league: the competitive advantage of the antivirus industry in the Czech Republic and Slovakia. Compet Chang 18(5):421–437. https://doi.org/10.1179/1024529414Z.00000000069

Beszédeš M (2017) Spája nás nadšenie pre technológie a snaha odborne rásť. https://careers.innovatrics.com/sk/marian-beszedes-spaja-nas-nadsenie-pre-technologie-snaha-odborne-rast/. Accessed Jan 2020

Ďaďo J, Kormancová G, Táborecká-Petrovičová J, Theodoulides L (2018) Management and leadership development needs: the case of Slovakia. Business and society: making management education relevant for the 21st century, pp 177–202. https://doi.org/10.1007/978-3-319-78855-5_10.; www.scopus.com

Deloitte Central Europe (2014) Technology Fast 50 Powerful connections. https://www.ruptela.lt/wp-content/uploads/2015/01/CE_FAST50_2014-FINAL.pdf

Din F, Dolles H, Middel R (2013) Strategies for small and medium-sized enterprises to compete successfully on the world market: cases of Swedish hidden champions. Asian Bus Manag 12(5):591–612. https://doi.org/10.1057/abm.2013.19

Entrepreneurship disappeared in Czechoslovakia after 1945 (2005, Oct) Hospodárske noviny. https://finweb.hnonline.sk/ekonomika/189726-v-ceskoslovensku-po-roku-1945-zmizlo-podnikanie

European Union (2019) Slovakia. https://europa.eu/european-union/about-eu/countries/member-countries/slovakia_en. Accessed Dec 2018

Innovatrics Awards. https://www.innovatrics.com/awards/. Accessed Oct 2019

Kamp B (2018) Expanding international business via smart services: insights from 'hidden champions' in the machine tool industry. https://doi.org/10.1108/S1745-886220180000013012.; www.scopus.com

Kirschbaum SJ (2005) A history of Slovakia. Palgrave Macmillan, New York

Lee SS, Chung YK (2018) A study on development strategy of Korean hidden champion firm: focus on SWOT/AHP technique utilizing the competitiveness index. J Int Entrep 16(4):547–575. https://doi.org/10.1007/s10843-018-0234-7

McKiernan P, Purg D (2014) Hidden champions in CEE and Turkey: carving out a global niche, pp 1–437. https://doi.org/10.1007/978-3-642-40504-4.; www.scopus.com

Muñoz EP, Ripoll-i-Alcon J, Silvente VB (2017) Hidden champions in Spain: the path to successful business decisions. Rev Metod Cuantit Para Econ Empres 24:109–208. www.scopus.com

National Bank of Slovakia (2019) Selected economic and monetary indicators SR [Data file]. https://www.nbs.sk/_img/Documents/_Publikacie/OstatnePublik/ukazovatele.pdf

New Europe 100—changemakers in Central and Eastern Europe (2016) Financial Times. https://www.ft.com/content/ece06f66-90a7-11e6-a72e-b428cb934b78

OECD (2019, Feb) Economic surveys, Slovak Republic. http://www.oecd.org/economy/surveys/Slovak-Republic-2019-OECD-economic-survey-overview.pdf

Pehe J (2014) Czech Republic and Slovakia 25 years after the velvet revolution: democracies without democrats. Heinrich Böll Stiftung. https://eu.boell.org/en/2014/09/15/democracies-without-democrats. Accessed Sept 2014

Piko M (2013) 59 inšpiratívnych podnikateľských príbehov. Ako vybudovať úspešnú firmu na Slovensku (e-book). Inventic. isbn:978-80-971172-1-4

Rant MB, Cerne SK (2017) Becoming a hidden champion: from selective use of customer intimacy and product leadership to business attractiveness. South East Eur J Econ Bus 12(1):89–103. https://doi.org/10.1515/jeb-2017-0008

Report Consultant (2019) Global biometrics market research report 2019. https://www.openpr.com/news/1498951/Global-Biometrics-Market-to-Register-a-CAGR-of-Approx-15-NEC-Matrix-System-Fujitsu-Nuance-Kaba-Group-Innovatrics-SMUFS-Bio-Secugen.html

Rivet KB (1949) Czechoslovakia's foreign trade focus shifts sharply. World trade developments in 1948 in selected countries; a series of seventeen articles on postwar foreign trade of the United States and other leading trading countries of the world, vol 1. U.S. Government Printing Office, pp 86–91

SAC Insight (2018) Global biometrics market report. https://www.sacinsight.com/report/global-biometrics-market-1

See https://www.innovatrics.com/awards/deloitte/ for further information

Simon H (1992) Lessons from Germany's midsize giants. Harv Bus Rev 70(2):115–123. https://hbsp.harvard.edu/product/92208-PDF-ENG?itemFindingMethod=Search

Simon H (2009) Hidden champions of the twenty-first century: success strategies of unknown world market leaders, pp. 1–402. https://doi.org/10.1007/978-0-387-98147-5. www.scopus.com

Slovak Investment and Trade Development Agency—SARIO (2017, Dec). https://www.sario.sk/sites/default/files/data/sario-automotive-sector-in-slovakia-2018-02-01.pdf

Slovakia among fastest growing economies in Europe (2016, Mar). https://spectator.sme.sk/c/20113647/slovakia-among-fastest-growing-economies-in-europe.html

Slovakia Economic Outlook (2019, Oct) Focus economics, economic forecasts from the world's leading economists. https://www.focus-economics.com/countries/slovakia

Statistical Office SR (2019a) Re-registered GDP data—regional data (1995–2011) [Data file]. https://slovak.statistics.sk/

Statistical Office SR (2019b). https://slovak.statistics.sk/

Taborecka-Petrovicova J, Dado J, Bobakova T (2014) Hidden champions of Slovakia. Hidden champions in CEE and turkey: carving out a global niche, pp 331–355. https://doi.org/10.1007/978-3-642-40504-4_20. www.scopus.com

Technology Fast 50 Powerful connections (2014) Deloitte. https://www.ruptela.lt/wp-content/uploads/2015/01/CE_FAST50_2014-FINAL.pdf

Teich M, Kováč D, Brown MD (2011) Slovakia in history. Cambridge University Press, Cambridge

The Observatory of Economic Complexity (2017). https://oec.world/en/profile/country/svk/

Top Ten Slovak Companies (2018). https://www.forbes.sk/top-firmy/ Accessed Dec 2019

Venohr B, Meyer KE (2007) The German miracle keeps running: how Germany's hidden champions stay ahead in the global economy (March 2007). Available at SSRN: https://ssrn.com/abstract=991964 or https://doi.org/10.2139/ssrn.991964

Voudouris I, Lioukas S, Makridakis S, Spanos Y (2000) Greek hidden champions: lessons from small, little-known firms in Greece. Eur Manag J 18(6):663–674. https://doi.org/10.1016/S0263-2373(00)00057-8

World Bank, International Comparison Program database (2019) GDP per capita [Data file]. https://europa.eu/european-union/about-eu/countries/member-countries/slovakia_en

World Bank, International Monetary Fund (2019) Foreign direct investment, net inflows (% of GDP) [Data file]. https://data.worldbank.org/indicator/BX.KLT.DINV.WD.GD.ZS

www.innovatrics.com

www.microstep.com

Hidden Champions of Slovenia

Katja Babič

Overview
Official name: Republic of Slovenia
Type of government: Parliamentary Democratic Republic
Population in 2017: 2,065,890
Land area: 20,273 km^2

History

1918	After the collapse of the Austro-Hungarian Empire, Slovenia joins the Kingdom of Serbs, Croats, and Slovenes.
1929	The kingdom becomes known as Yugoslavia.
1941	Slovenia is occupied by Nazi Germany and Italy during World War II.
1945	At the end of the war, Slovenia becomes a constituent republic of Socialist Federative Republic of Yugoslavia.
1989	The Slovene parliament confirms the right of the country to secede from the Yugoslav Federation.
1991	Slovenia, along with Croatia, declares its independence. The Yugoslav federal army intervenes. Slovene forces defend the country.[1] After the Ten-Day War, the Yugoslav army withdraws.
1992	The EU recognizes Slovenia's independence, followed by the US and many other countries around the world. Slovenia joins the United Nations. First parliamentary

---

[1]McKiernan and Purg (2013).

K. Babič (✉)
IEDC-Bled School of Management, Bled, Slovenia

	and presidential elections in the newly independent country.
1993	Slovenia joins the International Monetary Fund.
1998	Slovenia official started the accession process to join the European Union.
2004	Slovenia admitted to NATO.
2004	Slovenia is one of 10 new states to join the EU.
2007	Slovenia adopts the single European currency, the euro.
2008	Slovenia takes over the EU presidency.
2008	Slovenia is hit by a major economic crisis, and later on successfully resolves it.
2009	Slovenia starts the presidency of the Council of Europe.
2010	Slovenia becomes a member of the OECD.
2011	Slovenia celebrates 20 years of independence.
Between 1991 and 2015	Slovenia's GDP is increased in real times by 75.2%.
2015	GDP per capita increased by 70%, exceeding 18,000 €.
2017	United Nations declared Slovenia as the world's most sustainable country.
2018	Economic growth in Slovenia is the highest in the European Union (4.1%).
2019	GDP per capita is 22,500 €.

1 Introduction: Context and History

Economy

Slovenia is a developed country that enjoys a high level of prosperity and stability as well as above-average GDP per capita by purchase power parity: 83% of the EU28 average in 2015. This was the same figure as in 2014 and two percentage points higher than in 2013 (SURS). Nominal GDP in 2018 was 42.534 million EUR. Nominal GDP per capita (GDP/pc) in 2018 was 21,267 EUR. The capital city Ljubljana has the highest GDP/pc. It is part of the Western Slovenia statistical region, which has a higher GDP/pc than eastern Slovenia (SURS).

Slovenia has a highly educated workforce and a well-developed infrastructure. It is situated at a major transport crossroad. Slovenia's economy was hurt by the European economic crisis in 2008. However, after 2013 GDP per capita has been rising again. Moreover, the level of foreign direct investment has also been steadily rising in the last few years.

Socio-Political Facts

Slovenia is characterized by a large number of small settlements: over 6.000. Ninety percent of all settlements have fewer than 500 inhabitants. Ljubljana is the largest city, with 287,000 inhabitants. Urban centers consist of larger and medium-sized towns. Most of Slovenia's municipalities are situated in sparsely populated areas. Remote hilly and mountainous areas are for the most part unpopulated. Slovenia has over two million inhabitants. Western Slovenia has a population of around 969,000 inhabitants whereas Eastern Slovenia has approximately 1,083,000. With 102.4 people per square kilometer, Slovenia is among the least densely populated states of the European Union. In 2016, around 15,600 people emigrated from Slovenia and around 16,600 immigrated to the country. In 2015, 27% of the Slovenian population had tertiary education.

History
During the Yugoslav era, Slovenia had a well-developed industry. It had a well-educated and highly productive workforce and systematic, centrally planned investments in heavy and light industries. Slovenia's good geographic position contributed a great deal to the international competitiveness of many Slovenian companies. Already in that time, Slovenia produced some hidden champions, some of which are still around, and it is producing new ones (Purg 2010; McKiernan and Purg 2013). Slovenia exports mainly to the countries of the European Union. Its main export partners are Germany (20.3%), Italy (12.4%), Croatia (8.1%), Austria (7.6%), and France (5.6%) (SURS 2018).

Business Environment
Slovenia is a great place to invest in and work, thanks to its favorable business environment. The country's geostrategic position at the crossroads of transport routes, well-developed ICT and physical infrastructure, technological networks and platforms, and centers of excellence and clusters that are evidence of high-level innovation activity, make Slovenia an excellent base for business development and growth (SPIRIT 2019). Slovenia also has a high-performance education system, which allows the inclusion of graduating students in advanced research, and international business projects. Slovenia has a very clear legislation and an entrepreneurial culture. Support networks facilitate the establishment and growth of companies. Like other European countries, Slovenia has many small-and-medium-sized enterprises (SMEs). These are often family-run operations that make up most of Europe's business (SPIRIT 2019).

In Slovenia, most of the identified hidden champions operate in manufacturing, information and communication, and administrative and support services. Being small and medium-sized companies, they are flexible when they need to adapt quickly to market changes. However, those companies are also very sensitive to changes in the industry and the environment in which they operate. The World Bank business survey measuring regulatory conditions for doing business ranks Slovenia 51st out of 189 nations. Moreover, Slovenia is among the top ten countries that have the smallest number of procedures required to start a new business. Another advantage that Slovenia enjoys is high security for investors. Slovenia has a very stimulating business environment where many very successful, internationally-oriented companies have grown. Slovenian companies are in general very successful, wealthy, and competitive (SPIRIT 2019).

We found 10 hidden champions in Slovenia: two potential ones, and five that are no longer hidden champions. Slovenia's hidden champions have become more careful after the economic crisis of 2008. However, companies nowadays invest more in R&D, innovation, and in obtaining new knowledge.

The year 2011 was difficult for the Slovenian economy. The reasons for the decrease in domestic consumption were multiple: fiscal austerity, the freeze on budget expenditure in the final months of 2011, a lack of economic reform, inappropriate financing, and the decrease in export. The construction industry was severely hit in 2010 and 2011. Fortunately, since 2014 Slovenia's GDP has been rising again. The growth is driven by exports, as well as by domestic consumption, which started to revive after the economic crisis. GDP growth in 2015 was 2.3%, followed by 2.7% the next year. All those economic and political changes hit Slovenia's hidden champions. Some of them survived and became stronger, whereas others went bankrupt. In general, they all have learned something from the global economic crisis. Companies have become more careful. Nowadays, the hidden champions' development needs are related to their workforce. Companies need to hire employees with the necessary knowledge, skills, and abilities. Therefore, the education system needs to adapt its programs so as to provide more practical knowledge, which will be used later at work.

Our company selection criteria were based on Simon (2009) definition of hidden champions. We found ten companies that qualify for inclusion in this book. These are small or medium-sized businesses. They are very successful leaders in their niches and quite unknown to the public. All of them have very strong market positions. They enjoy very strong international leadership and operate in unique niches. They all have their own story, explaining their success (Exhibit 1).

2 Case Studies of Selected Hidden Champions

2.1 Cosylab

Overview
Address: Gerbičeva ulica 64, 1000 Ljubljana, Slovenia
Tel: +386 5 375 6301
Fax: +386 5 375 6470
Email: info@cosylab.com
Web: www.cosylab.com

Company Information
Industry: Custom computer programming services
Year of establishment: 2001
Sales revenues in 2017: 15.5 million euros
Sales revenues in 2007: 2.01 million euros
Average number of employees in 2017: 147
Brains behind the company: CEO Mark Pleško

Exhibit 1 Core economic indicators

	2011	2012	2013	2014	2015	2016	2017	2018
GDP per capita (current US$)	24,985.2	22,532.4	23,357.9	24,194.9	20,887.5	21,617.6	23,449.6	26,234.0
GDP per capita growth (annual %)	0.4	−2.8	−1.3	2.8	2.2	3.0	4.8	4.4
Long-term unemployment (% of total unemployment)	44.2	47.9	51.0	54.5	52.3	53.3	47.5	42.9
Foreign direct investment, net inflows (% of GDP)	1.71	0.07	0.22	2.04	4.02	3.24	2.47	2.80
GDP (current US$, mio)	51,291	46,353	48,116	4989	43,102	44,641	48,456	54,235
Exports of goods and services (current US$, mio)	36,095	33,895	35,855	37,835	33,161	34,716	40,158	46,213
Exports of goods and services (% of GDP)	70.4	73.1	74.5	75.8	76.9	77.8	82.9	85.2
Merchandise exports (current US$)	34,682	32,163	34,019	35,956	3193	32,917	38,443	4421
Merchandise exports to high-income economies (% of total merchandise exports)	79.60	77.91	78.14	78.88	80.01	79.53	79.99	n/a
Merchandise exports to developing economies in Europe & Central Asia (% of total merchandise exports)	16.61	17.46	17.38	16.72	15.61	15.49	15.17	n/a
Ores and metals exports (% of merchandise exports)	4.70	4.54	4.37	4.18	4.20	3.87	3.82	4.00
Agricultural raw materials exports (% of merchandise exports)	1.76	1.93	2.08	2.17	2.12	2.12	1.97	1.94
Food exports (% of merchandise exports)	4.11	3.82	4.03	4.11	4.31	4.44	4.37	4.39
Fuel exports (% of merchandise exports)	5.79	6.50	6.70	6.19	5.36	4.57	4.92	5.26
Manufactures exports (% of merchandise exports)	83.48	83.06	82.52	83.03	83.68	84.87	84.76	84.22
High-technology exports (% of manufactured exports)	6.21	6.65	6.73	6.41	7.00	7.14	6.50	6.81

Source: World Bank, August, 2019

Nature of Market Leadership

Cosylab is a global leader in control systems for particle accelerators in big physics development and proton therapy for treating cancer (system integration). The company holds a global market share of approximately 50%. Cosylab has held its leadership position for the last 10 years. It benefitted from the changes that happened during these years (e.g. increase in competition and off-the-shelf solutions) due to its competitive advantage. The main countries the company exports to are the USA, China, Japan, Korea, and the European Union states. Cosylab's particles for treating cancer are used in some of the main hospitals in the USA and elsewhere (Cosylab 2019).

Nature of the Competitive Advantage

Cosylab was one of the first companies to enter the market of control systems for particle accelerators. It also entered the market of proton therapy providers very early. This not only gives the company the advantage of accumulated knowledge and experience in its domain, but also means that its competitors have adopted its products. Cosylab is focused on project execution. The company's human resources selection process is rigorous, making sure that besides knowledge and skills, employees are compatible with one another and capable of giving their best to the company.

Core Lessons Learned on the Path to Success

1. Developing one's value proposition is essential. Where can the company add the most value to what it is selling, and has the team internalized this knowledge?
2. Constant innovation proved essential since the processes that resulted from it enabled Cosylab to attract buyers that needed partners who were able to develop software and equipment according to strict processes and standards, as required in the medical domain.

Management and Leadership Development Needs

Cosylab wants to find the right developers and salespeople. These are the company's current needs in terms of business development and expansion, as well as introducing a more stabilized internal structure (reinforcing middle to senior management).

Financing and Regulatory Environment Development Needs

The regulatory environment makes it difficult for Cosylab to hire foreign nationals, especially non-EU citizens. The company would welcome slight changes in the legislation in that regard. As for financial support, Cosylab does not identify any needs.

How to Become a Global Leader in Control Systems for Particle Accelerators in Big Physics Development and Proton Therapy for Treating Cancer

Before Cosylab was founded in 2001, seven young students of physics had worked together on different projects under the wings of the Jožef Štefan Institute. They had come together in 1996 when Mark, a professor of particle physics, started forming a group to develop a control system for a particle accelerator. Therefore, before Cosylab was established, there was a group of enthusiasts called Kontrollgruppe fur Beschleuniger (KGB). The name comes from the first control system for the accelerator that they created for a German client and it was a symbol of overall control. After they successfully finished their first project in 2000, the group faced the first dilemma. What should they do after finishing this successful project? Should they continue their studies or continue to do similar work? It was at that point that they decided to set up their own company and Cosylab—Control System Laboratory starting writing a successful business story.

Nowadays Cosylab provides system integration and customer adapted products and solutions, covering the complete area of control system and instrumentation. Cosylab is specialized in accelerators for particle therapy and scientific research, as well as tokamaks and radio telescopes. Cosylab services are used by project directors, group leaders, and engineers, who have tough deadlines and user requirements to achieve better performance while significantly reducing commissioning time, manpower, and cost. Cosylab employs over 180 employees, mostly engineers, and physicists. They are expert developers and integrators of state-of-the-art software and electronics.[2]

Cosylab has 20 experts in each of its core technologies. The company's services range from writing specifications, to design, implementation, and installation. With this, Cosylab provides cost-effective, low-risk delivery of a control system or any of its components at a fixed price. Cosylab offers deep inside knowledge. It was one of the first companies to provide control systems for particle accelerators and proton therapy. This gives Cosylab the advantage of accumulated knowledge and experience in the domain. For that reason, the company's competitors have adopted its products. Cosylab's activities include particle therapy, physics, new energy, space, and astronomy.

---

[2]https://www.cosylab.com/

Markets are becoming more competitive, because companies find new solutions and gain technological advantages. Cosylab invests in increasingly big projects. On its path to business success, the company has learned where it could add value. It has learned a lot from its experience in all those years.. In the chief executive officer's opinion, the company's strengths are its culture, the small turnover, and its employees. They like to work together, writing this amazing story. Therefore, Cosylab carefully selects its recruits.

Cosylab's leaders have been with the company since its inception. They are coming from academia and know how to work with students. The teams select their leaders. According to the chief executive officer, a leader is a person who makes a success of the company's projects. Constant evaluations and positive feedback are very useful. With growth, they are adopting a standard company hierarchy while trying to preserve the non-conventional spirit of the early days. Anybody can talk to anybody else. Cosylab invests a lot in its culture and employees.

Innovation is crucial for Cosylab. The company has its origin in the scientific community. Everything that it started was an open source. The company leaders wanted Cosylab to be innovative and have a more general innovative system. This was quite complicated. In the beginning, they invested a lot of time and energy in innovation to build the company's product for the medical market. Cosylab is innovative in processes and products. Initially, it was more innovative in its processes. On the path to its business success, Cosylab learned that it needed to be flexible, innovative, and unique.

Cosylab is constantly innovating and improving its products, aiming to grow further. Developing the right product is also a key concern as the main challenge for the company is to maintain its leadership position in its niche. Cosylab considers knowledge important as it is one of the company's main success factors. Cosylab suggests that academic institutions change their knowledge-sharing methodology. In the company's view, students need to work more in groups. They should talk more to each other, share ideas, going out, and play together.

2.2 Domel

Overview
Address: Otoki 21, 4228 Železniki, Slovenia
Tel: +386 4 51 17 100
Fax: +386 4 51 17 106
Email: info@domel.com
Web: https://www.domel.com

Company Information
Industry: Manufacture of electric motors, generators and transformers
Year of establishment: 1946
Sales revenues in 2017: 133.52 million euros; 2018: 143,57 million euros;

Sales revenues in 2007: 84.30 million euros
Average number of employees in 2017: 946; 2018: 1030;
Brains behind the company: Matjaž Čemažar

Nature of Market Leadership

Domel is one of the world's leading developmental suppliers of electric vacuum motors, DC motors, EC motors, and components. It holds an estimated 40% global market share in the niche of vacuum cleaner motors, and is a global leader in the commercial segment of the vacuum cleaner motors, holding an estimated 20% global market share. Domel strives to be diversified in the heating, ventilation, air conditioning, and cooling (HVAC) niche. Based on energy efficiency, the company is number one in Europe with its ventilation products. Domel is also number one in Europe in the niche of commercial universal motors for gardening equipment. Domel's share of revenues derived from exports is 92%. Its ventilation products are used in data centers of big companies such as Google and Facebook. The company exports mostly to North America, Argentina, the EU (especially Croatia), and Asia. In 2006 a subsidiary production company was established in China.

Nature of the Competitive Advantage

The company's main competitive advantages are the following:

1. Competence, knowledge, and innovation.
2. Satisfied customers, who contribute to the successful marketing and branding of the company.
3. Knowing how to make a good compact and efficient product.
4. Vertical integration of the company and an integrated approach to the final product, which ensures great quality.
5. Technology, and own tool production.
6. Innovation as an important differentiating factor. Domel continuously engages in research, looks for new solutions for customers, and improves its products.
7. Careful attention and knowledge of the competitors.

Core Lessons Learned on the Path to Success

1. Raise awareness of the company's values, be responsible for your local environment, and maintain a strong brand.
2. Financial results provide self-confidence and proof that you are working in the right direction.
3. Invest in your employees and grant scholarships to young people. This improves your brand.

Management and Leadership Development Needs

Domel extended the production capabilities in the field of core technologies for electric motors components with investment in new equipment and establishing a new location in Škofja Loka in the year 2018. Since 2007 Domel has production facility in the Chinese market. Domel entered into the Serbian market with the production of electric motors in the year 2019. In response to structural and demographical challenges, Domel plans to extend the production facility for less automated processes in the Balkan region and create more jobs in Slovenia for high tech products for highly educated people (Domel 2019).

Financing and Regulatory Environment Development Needs

Even though Domel has thoughtful investment plans, it will implement those plans without recapitalization.

The Story of a Leading Producer of Electrical Motors

Domel was established in 1946 in Železniki. The company has a very interesting history. By now, it is a leader in sustainable innovative solutions and from 2009 onwards owned by employees, former employees, and those in retirement. Domel is one of the leading developmental suppliers of electric vacuum motors, DC motors, EC motors, and components. Furthermore, Domel has become a leading developmental supplier across the world. With innovative and market-attractive products, Domel enables the development and growth of the company and ensures work in the broader environment, thereby satisfying the interest of the owners. The company's activities and processes are based on values divided into five sets: creativity and ambitiousness, responsibility and economy, respect and cooperation, care for customers, employees, and belonging. The first place is held by creativity, with functions as the basis for all the other values. This enriches products and relations, clients and buyers, owners, and employees.

Domel's vision is to remain a global development supplier of EC systems and components and maintain a leading position as a developer in the vacuum units market. Domel is a socially responsible company. As a global developer and supplier of advanced solutions in the field of electronic motors and components based on innovative technologies, Domel enables the growth and sustainable development of the entire Domel group. In this way, it provides quality jobs in the broader environment. Domel draws its creative energy from its rich industrial tradition and is one of the largest global producers of electronic motors and suction units, where it has a 60% share of the European market.

Through the Domel network of representative offices, the company is present in all of the world's leading markets. Domel is a development supplier with a clear vision and in-house development, through which the company creates trends and technical solutions at all levels of individual products and devices. Domel has received numerous awards from independent technical and consumer organizations. Its laboratories are part of the national and international development network. Furthermore, Domel invests a great deal into social responsibility and enjoys a long-standing collaboration with manufacturers in numerous branches of industry.[3]

Domel is guided by its values, based on the company's sustainable development and social responsibility. Domel focuses on creativity and ambitiousness. The company invests in its employees in order to achieve individual learning and development, including greater creativity. Domel stimulates design thinking and innovative approaches. It encourages its employees to provide new ideas by rewarding their innovativeness. The company constantly improves its methods and results of its work. Domel sets itself high, yet always attainable, goals. Domel dares to accept obstacles and errors, knowing that it will learn from them. The company encourages healthy competition and aspirations for education and promotion at the workplace. At the same time, Domel strives to maintain a balance between work and family life.

The company's motto is "I do what I say." Therefore, Domel always fulfills its obligations and promises. The company is result-oriented. It develops optimal products so as to achieve optimal conditions in the market, constantly reducing costs, and searching for business opportunities and profit. Domel behaves toward others as it would wish others to behave toward it. The company invests a lot in employees' well-being and a good climate and in positive environment in the company. It encourages teamwork, idea-sharing, and a common way of thinking, stressing the importance of individual contribution to common results.

Domel is aware that the customer is king, and tries to satisfy customers' needs, which is the company's competitive advantage. Domel provides high quality and genuineness to its clients at a competitive price. The company is easily approachable and has a pleasant atmosphere. It is friendly, reliable, and flexible in its dealings with clients.

Domel ensures the personal and professional development of its employees, hiring only people with appropriate skills. Their jobs enable creativity, which creates satisfaction. Domel's employees are proud to work for their company. Domel has built strong employee loyalty, which is the foundation of the company's existence and development, merging career dreams, and company goals. Domel is striving to create a comprehensive system for managing human resources. All employees are aware that it is important to identify with the harmonized goals, values, mission, and vision of the company.

Moreover, Domel focuses on social responsibility, including sustainable development. The company's concern for social and environmental issues is reflected in its operations. Social responsibility is founded on achieving high levels of competitiveness in the local and global markets, on efforts for excellence, and the

---

[3] https://www.domel.com/

sustainable and balanced development of associated companies in the Domel group. The business practices inherent in social responsibilities involve prudent investment in the business environment, which ensures intellectual capital, the health, and safety of employees, easier harmonization of family and work, equal opportunities for all regardless of gender and religion, and cooperation with the local community in all aspects of Domel's business that affects the quality of life.

Finally, Domel's top managers closely resemble those of other hidden champions in terms of knowledge, innovation orientation, and strong values.

What particular lessons can Domel teach us? One strategic way to success is a strong company culture, constant striving for innovation, own tool production, investing in employees, responsibility for the local environment, the loyalty of employees and customers, and a strong focus on innovation and technology.

2.3 EK Water Blocks d.o.o.

Overview
Address: Pod lipami 18, 1218 Komenda, Slovenia
Tel: +386 59 096 622/+386 59 096 615
Fax: n/a
Email: info@ekwb.com
Web: https://www.ekwb.com

Company Information
Industry: Manufacture of computers and peripheral equipment
Year of establishment: 2006
Sales revenues in 2017: 20 million
Sales Revenues in 2007: 0.7 million
Average number of employees in 2017: 44
Brains behind the company: CEO Edvard König

Nature of Market Leadership

EK Water Blocks considers itself to be operating in a "niche within a niche market:" do-it-yourself liquid cooling systems in Europe and North America. Market share is rather difficult to determine as all competitors are privately owned companies, but it is estimated at above 60%. The company has been experiencing considerable growth in the past 10 years, even during the 2008 economic crisis when it grew 25%. At least 80% of the company's customers are in North America and Europe. Other export markets include Australia, China, and Southeast Asia. The company has eight major competitors on the global level. In recent years, transnational companies entering the market have made it more difficult for EK Water Blocks to retain its leading position.

Nature of the Competitive Advantage

1. Supply chain. Unlike many of its competitors, who outsource the majority of their operations to China and similar countries, EK Water Blocks does everything, except the manufacturing, in house. The company's products are manufactured mostly by local suppliers in Slovenia. This not only allows EKWB to overlook closely the maintenance of the high quality of their products, but also enables the company to speed up the entire process so that the final product reaches the consumers faster.
2. Connections with market drivers. EK Water Blocks utilizes its well-established connections with computer-producing companies to speed up the designing new products even further.
3. Customer relationship. The company's approach to managing mistakes and damaged customer relationships stand out as being very transparent and honest. On the occasions that it was needed, it had a positive effect on sales.

Core Lessons Learned on the Path to Success

1. Having the right team is essential. At the core of every success story lies a group of people that trust you and believe in the company. These criteria are essential for being able to motivate them continuously.
2. Leadership is relative. It includes not only leading and knowing how to lead, but also knowing when to take a step back and letting someone else take the reins. One should be careful not to step too far away, however, to keep the integrity of the company intact.
3. Being innovative at all times is essential. Otherwise, you are not considered a market leader anymore.

Management and Leadership Development Needs

EK Water Blocks needs more training, which is required for heads of departments to improve their communication skills. It is hard to find skilled sales people.

Financing and Regulatory Environment Development Needs

EK Water Blocks currently does not have any financial needs. However, the company believes that there is room for expansion. The leaders own 100% of the company and do not wish to change the ownership structure. They have an unfavorable view of Slovenian tax policies. They lamented the fact that Slovenia is losing a lot of money because of its VAT policies. The recruitment of foreign professionals was mentioned as a challenge and an area where changes are needed.

EK Water Blocks: A Hidden Champion Operating in a Niche-Within-a-Niche

EK Water Blocks was the first company that developed computer-cooling techniques professionally. It has rapidly grown in the last 5 years. It was very focused, especially in the beginning, on the needs and wishes of its customers. When the company made mistakes it would apologize. This ensured an open and honest relationship with customers, facilitating the building of a great company and a leading global position. The company has some of the best customer-support services, which is a competitive advantage. Clients get great and well-designed highly-performing products. Another competitive advantage is a personalized approach and fair relationships. EK Water Blocks does everything on its own, except for manufacturing, which is outsourced. Based on that approach the company has been able to focus more on the high quality of its products. The supply chain has been designed in such a way as to speed up the whole process. EK Water Blocks also has a good relationship with other companies in the market, such as producers of computers, which allows them to be fast. Some of their competitors have their products made in China, which takes a lot of time. In contrast, EK Water Blocks does everything by itself. This speeds up the company's processes and represents a competitive advantage as well as a good experience for clients (EKWB 2019).

EK Water Blocks knows that it is important to have the right team in the company. It is essential to build trust with the employees and clients. When the company started, a chief executive officer was the person who contributed technical knowledge as an engineer, whereas owner Matjaž provided business knowledge. The company grew by analyzing its own mistakes. This makes it unique. EK Water Blocks uses professional leadership skills in its operations and instills company values into its culture. Innovation and continuous learning moves the business forward.

EK Water Blocksfocuses on the process and product innovation. It has been the most innovative company in the field for many years. There have been difficulties, but the company has overcome them. When customers buy hardware, they are told what cooling solutions are compatible. In this way, the company educates its customers. This is the best example of how EK Water Blocks thinks one-step ahead and responds to customers' needs.

The current business challenges are in marketing. EK Water Blocks sees a bottleneck there. In previous years, the company did not need much marketing. At that time, the biggest challenge was to manage the company's fast growth. EK Water Blocks found a way to finance the growth, but now it has more customers and needs to find the right way to support them. Because the market is changing continuously, EK Water Blocks has to change even more if it wants to be at the top. Therefore, the company needs to prepare mentally for the changes in the market. It needs to respond to changes rapidly and responsibly, and make decisions fact. Nowadays, a responsible leader is essential. The chief executive officer is responsible for the company's success. He needs to pay attention to every single detail. Furthermore, the chief executive officer and the other company leaders need to be able to ensure good communication across departments.

Because of its knowledge and constant innovations, EK Water Blocks has many opportunities for future growth. It invests in new processes and new products, as well as in its employees and in keeping customers educated and satisfied. Is this not a good example of great leadership?

2.4 Polycom Škofja Loka, d. o. o.

Overview
Address: Dobje 10, 4223 Poljane nad Škofjo Loko, Slovenia
Tel: +386 4 50 70 600
Fax: +386 4 50 70 631
Email: info@polycom.si
Web: http://www.polycom.si

Company Information
Industry: Manufacture of plastic products
Year of establishment: 1985
Sales revenues in 2019: 35.8 million
Sales revenues in 2007: 9.6 million
Average number of employees in 2019: 277
Brains behind the company: CEO Iztok Stanonik, Iztok Novak

Nature of Market Leadership

Polycom is a world leader in the automotive industry in the niche market of gas springs, with 25% of the global market share. Polycom is also number one in Central and Eastern Europe in the niche of hybrid products of thermoplastics and metal parts. Additionally, the company operates in another niche—substitution of metal materials with products manufactured from technical plastics. Each product has at least one or two more functions apart from its basic ones. Year-on-year company growth has been stable. In the last 8 years, annual turnover growth was approximately 10%. Polycom's share of revenues derived from exports is 83%. The main countries that the company exports to are Germany, Austria, Italy, Spain, China, the US, Mexico, South Korea, and the United Kingdom.

Nature of the Competitive Advantage

1. Innovation, focus on research and development, continuous improvement, leading with goals, and good customer segmentation
2. Polycom has its own tool construction and tool production department

3. Flexibility and adaptability, knowledge, tradition and experience, employees' commitment
4. Clear vision, setting the strategy and following the results, as well as a coaching system for managers
5. Human knowledge, good development strategy, following the global trends and adapting the strategy to the new trends

Polycom's biggest advantage in comparison to its competitors is that Polycom has its r own tool construction and tool production department. The company's main success drivers are flexibility and adaptability, knowledge, tradition and experience, and the employees' endeavors. The main leadership success factors that have contributed to the company's success are a clear vision, setting the strategy, and following the results. The company also has a coaching system for managers. The main success factors that have contributed to Polycom's success are knowledge, prediction, knowledge of methodologies, and systematic work.

Core Lessons Learned on the Path to Success

1. Set company goals and follow key performance indicators.
2. Search for new opportunities.
3. Have a quick reaction to changes and innovation, and focus on research and development, as well as human resource development.
4. Observe and follow the trends of your company's industry.
5. Set your company strategy, which includes good cooperation with the research and development department with the aim to help customers with knowledge about the products, including information about new innovative products.

The core lessons learned on the path to the business success of Polycom is the importance of setting goals, searching for opportunities, quick reactions to changes, innovations, research and development, human resources development, and observing and following the trends in the automotive and other industries. Polycom's strategy also includes cooperation with customers' research and development departments so that the company can help its customers with appropriate knowledge about plastic processing. Nowadays, the biggest driving factor of business success is human knowledge, a good development strategy, following global trends, and adapting the strategy to new trends.

Management and Leadership Development Needs

The most underdeveloped skills at Polycom is knowledge of tools and methodology for the assessment of economic factors, based on which it is possible to predict or react to changes. Due to the constant implementation of changes and new customers' requirements, production workers and managers at all levels need to be well educated. Specially, managers need to motivate, coach, and educate productive workers.

Polycom's recommendation for educational institutions is to modernize obsolete programs, to add new concepts and new knowledge, and to implement innovation in the educational system.

Financing and Regulatory Environment Development Needs

Polycom recommends that financial institutions provide more resources for the development and implementation of new products and services into the market.

A World Leader in the Automotive Industry in the Niche Market of Gas Springs

Polycom was established in 1985 in Škofja Loka. It is an innovative quality provider of integrated development solutions for the automotive and other industries. Polycom is a reliable partner for its customers and business partners and is a stable employer.

As the director states, the unspoken rule of today's business world seems to be an uncompromising competitive battle that takes into account not only financial issues but also social and ecological business aspects. The winners are those companies that can incorporate creative work methods into their business operations, all the while offering customers innovation, diversity, uniqueness, and integrated solutions that are designed to allow the user to see further. In developing new advantages and ensuring a sustainable market position, a company must strive for innovation in all its diverse forms: technological, business, organizational, social, and service-related. Quality management, environmental responsibility, and occupational health and safety are combined in an integrated system that commits company leaders and staff to one common goal. Based on common company values, this system shapes their operating principles and leads them to function as a successful and responsible enterprise.

The main reason for the company's market leadership is its innovation. Polycom focuses on research and development, continuous improvement, and good customer segmentation. It invests in its employees and in new knowledge, which brings high added value to the company. In recent years, Polycom has participated in numerous national and international development projects. The company is also involved in the development of green materials for applications in the automotive industry, such as NatureTruck, where it contributes to the production of biopolymers made from renewable sources.

Polycom specializes in the production of demanding technical products made from technical thermoplastics. The company develops its business in two segments. The first one focuses on the substitution of metal material with products manufactured from technical plastics. The second segment, which shows increasing demand, are hybrid products, where the metal part is covered with thermoplastics. Each product has at least one or two more functions apart from its basic function. In these two segments, Polycom has higher value-added, since they require a considerable amount of knowledge and experience from employees (Polycom 2019).

However, the market has changed over the last 10 years. The customers' requirements have changed as has the products' portfolio, and there is a change in prices. Polycom recognizes that it is increasingly difficult to find human resources and the delivery time is currently longer. In the last 10 years, the demands and the environmental standards have been higher. Moreover, there are now electric and hybrid cars on the market. There are also stricter rules in terms of passenger safety.

Polycom's operations are socially and environmentally responsible. The company is getting involved in numerous socially responsible projects supported by the local community. It actively supports various academic, sporting, cultural, and charitable events and organizations. As a stable employer, Polycom takes care of the long-term human resource potential of its community by providing scholarships. Polycom has adopted a code of ethics that sets out all key ethical perspectives of its business and operations.

Polycom faces two main business challenges. Polycom has 82% of the market share in the automotive industry. Its goal is to lower this percentage. The future challenges are to remain connected to the automotive industry and specifically to the production of parts for electronic and hybrid vehicles. Another business challenge is the robotization of production.

3 Conclusions and Recommendations

Although Slovenia is a small country, it has companies that are global leaders in their niches. Slovenian hidden champions are very similar and have the characteristics of Simon (2009) hidden champions. In terms of similarities, they are characterized by the high quality of their products and services, constant innovation, improvement, development, their own production, know-how, flexibility, a focus on customers and employees, and a good working climate. Those are their main competitive advantages.

Slovenian hidden champions invest a lot in innovation, development, research, and new knowledge. They are striving to be sustainable and environmentally friendly enterprises. They want to excel in their processes and with their products, therefore they invest in either of them. All companies state that they strive to recognize their customers' wishes and needs. They are successful also because of their passionate leaders, who motivate their employees and strive for success. The Slovenian leaders of hidden champions are good experts, knowing their niche well, and having superior entrepreneurial skills. They approach their business very carefully, step by step. Slovenia's hidden champions continuously look for new ideas. They try to guess what customers will need so as to create new products or services. Moreover, Slovenian hidden champions do not have any financial development needs. They see a lot of opportunities in the education system. The Slovenian education system needs to adapt its programs to satisfy the needs of business.

The prevalent mindsets in these companies and their leadership distinguishes them from the competition. For example, EK Water Blocks realizes that it must know how to manage mistakes and build transparent relationships with customers. This has a positive effect on sales.

Hidden champions keep their market leader positions and expand their niche through diversification and internationalization. Most of these companies are business-to-business oriented. Most have some unique knowledge. Slovenian leaders are very motivated, hard-working, enthusiastic, flexible, fast, willing to take risks, and persistent. They are driven by their passion, wish, and desire. This is a very common characteristic of successful leaders. They learn a lot on the path to their business success. They obtain significant knowledge, especially from making their own mistakes and analyzing ways to prevent them. Their leadership, good ideas, knowledge, technology, constant learning and commitment to the business, and keeping employees and customers satisfied, guarantees their success.

References

Cosylab (2019) About Cosylab. cosylab.com. Retrieved 15 August 2019
Domel (2019) About company Domel. domel.com/company. Retrieved 20 August 2019
EKWB (2019) About EK Water Blocks. ekwb.com. Retrieved 7 August 2019
McKiernan P, Purg D (2013) Hidden champions in CEE and Turkey, vol 10. Springer, Berlin, pp 978–973
Polycom (2019) About company Polycom. polycom.si. Retrieved 5 August 2019
Purg D (2010) Skriti zmagovalci v Sloveniji. Planet GV, Ljubljana
Simon H (2009) Hidden champions of the twenty-first century. Springer, Berlin
SPIRIT Slovenia, Public agency (2019) Business environment. sloveniaparetner.eu/business-environemnet/. Retrieved 26 August 2019
Statistical Office of the Republic of Slovenia (2019) GDP and National Accounts. www.stat.si. Retrieved 22 August 2019
World Bank (2019) Data; countries and economies. http://data.worldbank.org/country

Hidden Champions of Turkey

Dincer Atli and Nebiye Yasar

Overview
Official name: Republic of Turkey
Type of government: Presidential Republic
Population in 2017: 80.3 million (World Bank report 2018)
Land area: 769,630 km^2

History

1920	After the First World War, the Ottoman Empire lost the war, and the Treaty of Sèvres was signed between the Ottoman Empire and the Allies in 1920. Through this Treaty, the Ottoman Empire is gradually divided by the Allies and was left a minor territory.
1923	Turkey won the War of Independence. Mustafa Kemal Ataturk founded the modern Republic of Turkey. The Treaty of Lausanne provided for new borders, which have been preserved to this day.
1950	Turkey sent troops to the Korean War. Turkey was the second country to respond to the UN call after the United States.
1952	Turkey's membership to NATO was signed.
1960	First military coup in Turkey's history. The Democrat leaders are imprisoned and Prime Minister Menderes is executed.
1971	Military coup by memorandum.
1974	Cyprus peace operation.
1980	Clashes between left and right-wing groups lead to another army coup.
1995	The EU and Turkey signed the Customs Union agreement.

D. Atli (✉) · N. Yasar
Uskudar University, Üsküdar, Istanbul, Turkey
e-mail: dincer.atli@uskudar.edu.tr; nebiye.yasar@uskudar.edu.tr

© Springer Nature Switzerland AG 2021
A. Braček Lalić, D. Purg (eds.), *Hidden Champions in Dynamically Changing Societies*, https://doi.org/10.1007/978-3-030-65451-1_27

1991-	Economic crisis in Turkey
1994-	
1999-	
2001	
2008	Global mortgage crisis
2016	July 15 coup attempt

1 Introduction: Context and History

The Ottoman Empire lost the First World War, and the Treaty of Sèvres was signed in 1920 between the Ottoman Empire and the Allies. The Ottoman Empire was gradually divided by the Allies. In 1923, Turkey won its War of Independence under the leadership of Ataturk. Thereafter, the Turks established a secular and nation-state-based new republic called the Republic of Turkey. The devastation and death that followed wars had severe and enduring economic consequences (Yosun and Çetindamar 2013). Besides, the Republic of Turkey had the distinction of being the first modern, secular state in a predominantly Islamic Middle East (Ahmad 1993).

The Treaty of Lausanne determined new borders, preserved to the present day. Turkey has been influenced both politically and economically by the Lausanne Treaty. Although the significant economic impact of the country's capitulation was mitigated, the Republic of Turkey took over a significant portion of the Ottoman Empire's debts (Boratav 2005). In this period of liberal economic policies envisaged by the Treaty of Lausanne, agriculture and animal husbandry were developed, excessive taxes were abolished, and farmers were given credit through Ziraat Bank, a Turkish state-owned bank. In 1924, Türkiye İş Bankası was established as a semi-official commercial bank to develop the private sector through credit financing and by means of direct bank participation. The Industry and Mining Bank (Sanayi ve Maden Bankası) was founded in 1925 to manage public industrial establishments and to support the private sector. These decisions, taken in 1923 at the Izmir Economic Congress, continued in 1929 until the economic depression, which affected the whole world. Due to this crisis, liberal economic policies became abandoned, and statist economic policies were adopted (Yosun and Çetindamar 2013; Güney 2019; Finefrock 1981).

In the 1920s, approximately 77% of the 13 million population lived in villages. At that time, 82% of the working population was engaged in agriculture, 6% in industry, 5% in trade, and 7% in the service sector. Industry's share of the national income was only 10%, whereas the share of agriculture was 67%. Agricultural production was much unsophisticated and involved very few technological modernizations (Gormez and Yigit 2009).

During this period, industrial development became a priority. Sümerbank—a Turkish bank and industrial holding company owned by the Turkish state—was established in 1933 to increase the state's efficient participation in the economy, and 5 years of industrial plans were implemented after that year. The first five-year industrial plan was successfully implemented, but the second one was not successful due to the start of the Second World War. In that period, the economy shrank and focused on the defense sector (Güney 2019).

Turkey became a member of NATO in 1952. In that period, economic development was the fastest, while the state's effect on the economy was reduced. Infrastructure and transportation were given great importance, and investments in agriculture increased. After the war, the internal economic policies were loosened, and the real income level of all social groups increased. Opening to foreign capital and transition to a free market economy began in 1950–1954. In 1951, the budget was out of balance, and this continued until 1963. The Korean War of 1959 pushed raw material prices in the world market sky-high. Import with credit application was introduced. As a result of this, commercial debts could not be paid. The external debt burden and public deficit increased. The 10-year Democratic Party rule came to an end with a military coup on May, 27, 1960 (Okyar 1979).

Five-year development plans were pursued also in the 1960–1980 period and the State Planning Organization (SPO) was set up. During this period, Turkey's foreign trade deficit increased. The SPO played a vital role in the decisions taken by the private sector. In this period, GNP grew by an average of 6.8% and the output of the manufacturing industry increased by 10%.

A slight crisis shook Turkey in 1969 and the IMF program was implemented. In 1970, the Turkish currency became devalued. In 1971, a military coup was carried out. The explosive rise of oil prices in 1974 had a negative impact on Turkey's economy. In the same year, the Cyprus Peace Operation and an implicit economic embargo on Western countries began. On January, 24, 1980, as a result of the so-called "24 January Decisions," the devaluation of the Turkish lira was reduced (Aydın and Taşkın 2014).

The 1990s can be best described as the "lost decade" in terms of banking and financial stability. The period ended in a huge financial crisis in 2001.

The economic crisis of 1991 triggered the Gulf crisis. Turkey lost capital and the economy was stunned. Turkey's external debt increased in 1994 and the country ended up taking loans from the International Monetary Fund (IMF). In 1994, the Customs Union became an important milestone in this sense. Following the crisis in 1994, a package of measures was adopted.. The 1994 and 2001 crises were characteristically different. Disasters hit the banking sector, and many banks' activities became halted (Gormez and Yigit 2009).

The National Security Council (NSC) meeting held on February 19, 2001 led to an intense economic crisis. In 2002, significant steps were taken to exit the crisis and Turkey's economy entered a period of substantial growth (Koch et al. 2001).

As a result of the economic measures after 2001, high growth rates were achieved, especially in 2002–2007. The global crisis, which started in the middle of 2007, also affected the country, and economic growth fell significantly. This situation affected the real sector negatively.

In 2008, the world economy entered a crisis, followed by a rapid recovery after 2010. However, the average growth rate after 2010 was below the average of 2002–2006.

On July 15, 2016, a coup attempt was carried out by a faction of the military. This was not only the bloodiest coup attempt in Turkish history but also the most organized terrorist attack that Turkey had ever been subjected to.

In 2018, the annual depreciation of the Turkish lira against the US dollar reached 20%.

While the financial system has been developing, with new regulations and agencies, the country lacks institutions for providing small firms with access to capital. The adequacy and efficiency of incentive systems regarding R&D are questionable, and firms typically lack the capital for a scale-up period after their innovations (Turkey, State Planning Organization, 8–9 Development Plans 2001–2005–2007–2013) (Exhibits 1 and 2).

2 Five Case Studies

2.1 Case Study 1

Aksa Akrilik Kimya Sanayi A.Ş

Overview
Address: Head Office/Factory Merkez Mahallesi Yalova-Kocaeli Yolu Caddesi No:
  34 Taşköprü Çiftlikköy-Yalova/Turkey
Tel: +90 (226) 353 25 45 Fax: +90 (226) 353 33 07
Email: aksa@aksa.com
Web: www.aksa.com/en

Company Information
Industry: Preparation and spinning of textile fibers. Manufacturing of chemicals and
  chemical products, and acrylic fiber
Year of establishment: 1968
Sales revenues in 2017: 671.2 million euros
Revenues in 2007:506.5 million euros
ROA/ROE in 2018: ROA: 5.4; ROE: 15.5
Average ROA/ROE in the past 10 years:
  ROA: 6.8; ROE: 13.4
Latest debt-to-equity ratio: 73
Average number of employees in 2017: 1296
Brain(s) behind the company: GM Cengiz Taş, CEO Mehmet Ali Berkman, and
  Founder: Raif Dinçkök

Nature of Market Leadership

Aksa Akrilik became the world's largest acrylic fabric producer through constant growth and by developing its technology. With Aksa, Turkey is the second-largest

Exhibit 1 Core economic indicators for Turkey

	2011	2012	2013	2014	2015	2016	2017	2018
GDP per capita (current US$)	11,335.5	11,707.3	12,519.4	12,095.9	10,948.7	10,820.6	10,499.7	9311.4
GDP per capita growth (annual %)	9.4	3.1	6.7	3.4	4.3	1.5	5.7	1.0
Long-term unemployment (% of total unemployment)	8.8	8.1	8.7	9.9	10.2	10.8	10.8	10.9
Foreign direct investment, net inflows (% of GDP)	1.9	1.6	1.4	1.4	2.2	1.6	1.4	1.7
GDP (current US$, mio)	832,523,680,908.1	873,982,246,612.0	950,579,413,122.6	934,185,915,386.1	859,796,872,677.6	863,721,648,068.8	851,549,231,502.6	766,509,088,837.6
Exports of goods and services (current US$, mio)	185,339,817,496.6	206,848,575,372.9	211,715,472,706.6	222,003,067,915.6	200,727,578,909.6	189,717,174,309.8	211,220,249,990.7	226,981,860,164.6
Exports of goods and services (% of GDP)	22.3	23.7	22.3	23.8	23.3	22.0	24.8	29.6
Merchandise exports (current US$)	134,907,000,000.0	152,462,000,000.0	151,803,000,000.0	157,610,000,000.0	143,839,000,000.0	142,530,000,000.0	156,993,000,000.0	167,967,000,000.0
Merchandise exports to high-income economies (% of total merchandise exports)	58.4	54.4	54.1	57.0	61.4	63.1	63.8	
Merchandise exports to developing economies in Europe and Central Asia (% of total merchandise exports)	15.2	14.4	16.0	15.2	12.4	11.1	11.7	

(continued)

Exhibit 1 (continued)

	2011	2012	2013	2014	2015	2016	2017	2018
Ores and metals exports (% of merchandise exports)	4.2	4.3	4.5	4.1	4.0	3.9	4.3	4.3
Agricultural raw materials exports (% of merchandise exports)	0.6	0.5	0.4	0.4	0.4	0.5	0.5	0.5
Food exports (% of merchandise exports)	10.6	10.8	11.2	11.4	12.1	11.9	11.0	10.5
Fuel exports (% of merchandise exports)	4.7	5.3	4.3	3.8	3.1	2.2	2.6	2.4
Manufactures exports (% of merchandise exports)	78.3	77.7	78.1	78.5	78.8	80.1	80.2	80.9
High-technology exports (% of manufactured exports)	2.1	2.2	2.3	2.3	2.6	2.5	2.9	2.3

Source: The World Bank Data, 24th of November, 2019

Exhibit 2 Hidden champions from Turkey

Name	Market leadership description	Revenue 2017 (€)	Employees 2017
Aksa Akrilik Kimya Sanayii A.Ş.	World's largest acrylic fabric producer	671.2 million	1296
Eko. Tekstil San ve Tic Ltd Şti	Number one in Europe in lingerie and underwear production.	NA	2000
Kanca El Aletleri Dövme Çelik ve Makina Sanayi A.Ş	Number one in Europe in vise production	70 million	650
Kordsa Teknik Tekstil A.Ş	Number one provider of nylon tire cord fabric, number three provider of polyester tire cord fabric globally	604 million	3874
Yünsa Yünlü Sanayi ve Ticaret A.Ş.	Number one in CEE, Middle East and Central Asia, number two in Europe, and number three in the world in glassware production	37.5 million	1000

Source: Authors of the Chapter

acrylic fiber market in the world after China. Aksa Akrilik was responsible for one-sixth of the world's acrylic fiber production in 2017. As of the end of 2018, the company held 18% of the global market and 68% of the domestic market. The company exports an average of 40% of its total production. Aksa exports to more than 300 customers in more than 50 countries on five continents. In 2018, 54% of its sales were in the domestic market, and 46% were in foreign markets.

Nature of the Competitive Advantage

Akkök Group, one of the most well-established and trustworthy industrial groups in Turkey, laid the foundations of Aksa Acrylic in 1968 with 100% Turkish capital. The company sees its uniqueness in recognition as an efficient, innovative, environmentally-friendly partner with a customer-focused business model. Aksa Acrylic implements, reviews, and continuously improves the quality, environmental, occupational health, and safety and energy management systems in all its activities. Aksa Acrylic obtained an R&D Center Certification from the Ministry of Science, Industry, and Technology of Turkey. The company strives to develop new usage areas and new products for acrylic fibers. There are currently 27 innovative and qualified R&D projects at the center, administered with operational perfection and in line with the company's vision of sustainability.

In 2017, the company received the highest award at the ninth Corporate Governance Awards from the Corporate Governance Association of Turkey. This award highlighted Aksa Acrylic's fair, transparent, accountable, and responsible practices. Also, Aksa Acrylic's global and local market knowledge and management skills are critical assets.

Core Lessons Learned on the Path to Success

1. R&D programs are an important means for achieving growth and maintaining a relevant product in the market. One can create a competitive advantage by focusing on quality, cost, sophisticated products, innovation, and customer experience. With its R&D certificate, the company's R&D center was registered as the 432nd active R&D center. A total of 27 R&D projects are being carried out at the R&D center.
2. An effective brand strategy creates a unique identity that distinguishes one from the competition. In 2013, Aksa was accepted into the "Turquality Program," carried out by Turkey's Ministry of Economy. Turquality is the world's first and only state-sponsored brand development program. Designed with the vision of "Creating 10 global brands in 10 years," this support program aims to enhance Turkey's competitive power in global markets by creating global companies out of the country's domestic brands.
3. Understanding customer needs via pre- and after-sales services increases customer commitment and maximizes extra value for the company and its customers.
4. Talented and motivated employees with a robust, high-performance culture can be vital factors leading to successful results.
5. Even in the case of increasing competition and decreasing market demand, a company's know-how, and a leadership position in the industry, can help it maintain and even increase market share.

Management and Leadership Development Needs

Aksa, the world's largest and Turkey's only acrylic fiber producer, continues to direct the sector, create value for its shareholders, and carry forward the values that it creates sustainably. The company has participative management, being open to change, lean thinking, experience, and knowledge accumulation, solution-producing, talented motivated, and engaged employees, compliance with ethical values, openness to cooperation, and customer orientation.

The Global Turkish Acrylic Fiber Giant

Aksa Akrilik is an affiliate of Akkök Holding, which is one of Turkey's most reputable industrial groups. The company was founded in Yalova in 1968 to meet the acrylic fiber need of Turkey and started production in 1971. As already stated, in 2018, the company had an 18% share of the global market and 68% of the domestic market.

With the investments that it has made, its innovations, and the 50 years of experience and a customer-focused approach, the company is becoming the world's leading producer of acrylic fiber. Focusing on active marketing activities in the domestic market throughout the year, Aksa Akrilik managed to maintain its market share and sales volume, owing to its 82% capacity utilization rate.

In 2012, Aksa founded DowAksa as a 50% Joint Undertaking with Dow Europe Holdings B.V., a Dow Chemical Company subsidiary. Today, its annual capacity is 3500 tons. The company embraces sustainability as a guarantee of tomorrow in the rapidly changing and developing world. Aksa focuses on creating sustainable positive value through its strong values from 50 years of experience at the center of its market.

The company views its uniqueness as a model business partner that is efficient, innovative, eco-friendly, and customer-oriented. Aksa Acrylic has successfully introduced, updated, and continuously strengthened its products, facilities, and operations in the areas of performance, climate, occupational health, and energy management systems.

According to Aksa, understanding customers' needs through pre- and after-sales services increases customer engagement, maximizing added value for both business and customer.

The company will continue to work with strong ethical values, social responsibility principles, and full transparency. With assets amounting to 4.2 billion Turkish liras, AKSA will continue to be an exemplary brand that provides the best quality products and services to existing customers, while reaching new clients with new products. With its further increasing investment plans, new projects, new products, and growing business volume, Aksa aims to continue to maintain its position as the world leader for years.

2.2 Case Study 2

Eko Tekstil tic. San. A.Ş

Overview
Address: Namık Kemal Mah. Billur Sok. No 32 Ümraniye, 34,762, Istanbul, Turkey
Tel: +902164431958
Fax: +902164431957
Email: info@ekotex.com
Web: www.ekotex.com

Company Information
Industry: Manufacture of underwear
Year of establishment: 1994
Sales revenues in 2017: N/A
Revenues in 2007: 17 million euros
ROA/ROE in 2017: N/A
Average ROA/ROE in the past 10 years:
   N/A

Latest Debt to Equity ratio: N/A
Average number of employees in 2017: 2000
Brain(s) behind the company: Founder Özcan Sumer

Nature of Market Leadership

Eko Tekstil operates as a contract manufacturer and a manufacturer of its brands in the lingerie and underwear market. Eko Tekstil has become Europe's biggest producer in its field. The company produces and exports to the most critical chain stores in Europe and the USA, Eko Tekstil is also a leader in estimating trends and developing new products. The company has focused strongly on design and creativity and has produced collections with new trends and techniques at its center in Istanbul, with big design, research, and development teams. The company exports to over 50 countries, mostly in the EU, such as Germany and Italy.

Nature of the Competitive Advantage

Eko Tekstil distinguishes itself from its competitors with its high quality, trendy design speed, and continuous investments in research and development. Having acquired the necessary quality certificates, the company keeps the standards with quality and process control teams in its production units as well as a quality department at the center, which provides technical support as a backup service. The company gives prominence to design and creativity and produces collections with new trends and techniques. Eko Tekstil complies fast with changing market needs, and ensures investments in textiles by going beyond customer expectations.

Collaborating with suppliers and customers creates an invaluable strategic impact and an advantage in the competition in today's fast-moving global marketplace. Through collaboration, the company easily procures fashionable materials, and the product design team accomplishes the production of fashionable and superior products by carrying out critical tasks, such as bringing products to the market faster and leveraging the suppliers' expertise in sourcing and cost management. Eko Tekstil has a distinct advantage as it operates in convenient and strategic districts, and sells to all markets where a possibility to sell exists. On the other hand, the founder's mindset, awareness, entrepreneurship capabilities, and dedication create extra value for the company.

Core Lessons Learned on the Path to Success

1. Establish a trustworthy relationship with suppliers and ensure quality and fast material supply.
2. React rapidly to trends and produce fashionable and different products.
3. Adopt a working system focused on customer satisfaction.

4. Become the best in production and design by supporting young, experienced employees, and investing in employees' personal development. In addition to that, the company ensures that all employees share a common purpose and target and create teamwork consciousness
5. Continuously improve the quality of your products.

Management and Leadership Development Needs

Eko Tekstil's vision is to produce and export globally to the most crucial chain stores in Europe and the USA. Hence management and leadership development needs include contemporary and global managing skills, such as agility, global-mindedness, going beyond customer expectations, and managing new-generation employees.

Design and Quality in the Lingerie and Underwear Industry

Eko Tekstil was found in 1994 in Germany and, in the same year, began its production and export operations at its facilities that were established in Turkey. Today, the company manages its organization at its headquarters in Istanbul, Turkey.

Eko Tekstil operates in the lingerie and underwear industry as a contract manufacturer and distributor of its brands. The company has become the biggest producer in its sector in Europe. It manufactures and designs goods in its sector for the most important chain stores in Europe and the US. Eko Tekstil is a pioneer in trend prediction and the development of new goods. It has placed great emphasis on design and creativity and has a large design, research, and development team at its center in Istanbul to produce collections with new trends and techniques. The company also manufactures Marks&Spencer, Victoria's Secret, and H&M based on sub-contracting. With its high quality, trending speed, and continuous investments in research and development, Eko Tekstil distinguishes itself from competitors. The company also advocates "fast fashion". Having obtained the necessary quality certificates, the company maintains high standards with quality and process control staff in manufacturing units as well as a department for quality at its center, which offers technical support as a backup service.

According to the company, one of its success factors is its ability to choose its clients. Besides, design and creativity are crucial, and collections are produced with new trends and techniques. Eko Tekstil rapidly meets the changing market requirements and customer expectations.

Operating together with suppliers and consumers provides an invaluable competitive advantage in engaging in today's rapidly changing global market. The company procures trendy materials with ease, and the product design team manages to produce fashionable and superior products by bringing products to the market fast and using the suppliers' expertise in sourcing and cost management.

The company is aware of the importance of social responsibility. It follows national and international codes of conduct (FLA, ETI, ILO, etc.) to ensure employees' rights, working conditions, and health, and safety conditions. For many years, an internal inspection team has upheld and improved quality standards.

Eko Tekstil Protects biodiversity across the world. It prevents needless creation of waste by making the most effective use of goods, and the most productive and sustainable use of natural resources. Eko Tekstil monitors all its energy sources, minimizes noise pollution, and eliminates the harmful effects of our actions on the health of the environment.

2.3 Case Study 3

Kanca El Aletleri Dövme Çelik A.Ş

Overview
Address: Taysad Organize Sanayi Bölgesi 41,480, Şekerpınar-Çayirova/Kocaeli - Turkey
Tel: +902626788600
Fax: +902626788601
Email: info@kanca.com.tr
Web: www.kanca.com.tr

Company Information
Industry: Mining of iron ores, manufacture of metal products
Year of establishment: 1966
Sales revenues in 2017: 70 million euros
Revenues in 2007: 37 million euros
ROA/ROE in 2017: N/A
Average ROA/ROE in the past 10 years: N/A
Latest debt-to-equity ratio: N/A
Average number of employees in 2017: 650
Brain(s) behind the company: CEO and owner Alper Kanca

Nature of Market Leadership

Kanca's products are hand tools and forged parts. The company produces nearly 30,000 tons of forged products annually and exports more than half of its turnover to the EU. Its primary product line consists of forged bench vices. The company is a market leader in Europe in terms of sales volume and revenue. It has a 36% market share in Europe, compared to the 25% share of its closest competitor.

Nature of the Competitive Advantage

High customer satisfaction is the most critical competitive advantage of Kanca. The company makes frequent customer visits, and quickly introduces new products that align with the needs of the customers. The company produces high-quality products at the right price and just in time. Other aspects of the competitive advantage include innovation, the company's increasing market share, and following the idea of continuous improvement. The company also considers employee satisfaction very important.

Core Lessons Learned on the Path to Success

1. R&D allowed the introduction of new or updated products to the market.
2. The customer-focused design team understands customer needs and reacts quickly to the movements of the market.

Management and Leadership Development Needs

The company's management and leadership development needs stem from the vision, mission, and quality policy. According to the company's mission, shareholders, staff, and customers are its core values. It is crucial to maintain their satisfaction and long-term commitment to the company. Other vital factors are innovation, business ethics, environmental protection, and investing in technology.

Producer and Exporter of Forged Parts for the World's Most Prestigious Automobiles

The products of Kanca consist of hand tools and forged components. Today, Kanca exports over half of its turnover to the EU. It is a market leader in Europe in terms of sales volume and revenue. The company has a market share of 36% in Europe compared to its closest competitor's 25% share.

Kanca started producing hand tools as a family-owned company in 1966. It expanded and modernized its forging lines in 1974. This enabled it to supply other industries with high-quality forged parts. At the beginning of the 1980s, it started supplying high-quality parts to local OEMs, Fiat, Mercedes, Iveco, Ford, and Renault. During the 1990s, Kanca became a reliable partner and an important source of supply for thousands of personal, industrial, and farm vehicles, as well as security and building industries.

Having all the necessary facilities, Kanca has proved to be a single supply point for customers such as VW Group, BMW, Toyota, TRW, Delphi, Bosch, ZF, Scania, and many more. In partnership with global automotive giants, Kanca is involved not only in the supply of forging parts, but also in engineering and design. After audits by Fiat, Renault, Ford, Toyota, and Volkswagen, Kanca was given the title of Group Manufacturer. Kanca's products were copied by some Chinese and Indian vice manufacturers in order to get a foothold in the European market. A fully automated forging plant and laboratories allow the company to conduct all necessary mechanical and metallurgical testing in order to ensure quality.

Kanca's most critical competitive advantage is high customer satisfaction. The company visits consumers regularly and rapidly introduces new items that match customer needs. The competitive advantage includes the principle of continuous improvement.

In 2010, it was time to bring the engineering skills in metal shaping, machining, metallurgy, and design under the same roof. Kanca set up the first warm-forging R&D center in Turkey. This enabled the company to introduce new or updated products. Besides, the company's customer-focused design team understands customer needs and reacts quickly to the movements of the market.

Kanca increases its production capacity by investing in automation and a modern laboratory, and through equipment inspection. By using modern QA techniques and IATF 16949 and ISO 14001 certification, Kanca has become one of the leading forging companies in Turkey, not only in terms of volume of parts supplied to its customers, but also in terms of long-term reliability, customer satisfaction, and financial background. The company aims to increase its market share in the European forged automotive parts market in the next years and to maintain its leadership in Europe.

2.4 Case Study 4

Kordsa Teknik Tekstil A.Ş

Overview
Address: Alikahya Fatih Mah. Sanayici Cad. No 90 İzmit/Kocaeli /TR Post Code: 41310.
Tel: +90 262 316 70 00
Fax: +90 262 316 70 70
Email: info@kordsa.com
Web: www.kordsa.com

Company Information
Industry: Nylon cord fabric, polyester cord fabric, honeycomb core, carbon, aramid, glass, ceramic fabrics, and prepregs
Year of establishment: 1973
Sales revenues in 2017: 604 million euros
Sales revenues in 2007: 677 million euros
ROA/ROE in 2017: N/A
Average ROA/ROE in the past 10 years: N/A

Latest debt-to-equity ratio: N/A
Average number of employees in 2017: 3874
Brain(s) behind the company: Chairman Cenk Alper, CEO Ali Çalışkan

Nature of Market Leadership

Kordsa is a global producer of reinforcement technologies, serving the EMEA, LATAM, North American, and APAC markets with its operations in the USA, Brazil, Thailand, Indonesia, and Turkey. Kordsa is the leading manufacturer of nylon and polyester cord fabric producer for tire reinforcement. The company owns a Composite Technologies Center of Excellence, an exemplary model for industry-university collaboration in Turkey. With an investment of 281 million US dollars, Kordsa has acquired four firms—Fabric Development, Textile Products, Advanced Honeycomb Technologies, and Axiom Materials—which were the strategic suppliers serving leading world brands in the commercial aviation industry.

Nature of the Competitive Advantage

Kordsa believes that an open innovation approach has enabled it to offer innovative products and features. As a global brand, Kordsa sets the quality standards of its sector, breaking new grounds in the sector's production models through Industry 4.0 practices. Kordsa provides high-quality service, high price-performance ratio, and solutions with a high level of technical competency. In addition, the company maintains relationships with customers, both before and after sales. The provision of service facilities close to the customers and cooperation with suppliers are additional advantages. R&D activities and excellence are core components of Kordsa's corporate culture. The company creates sustainable value for customers, employees, and shareholders, as well as for the community, by deploying innovative value-added technologies.

Core Lessons Learned on the Path to Success

1. Kordsa's open innovation approach, superior materials, and know-how, provide customized and customer-focused new services.
2. Kordsa's team of about 100 people in its two R&D centers explores and develops the future's reinforcement technologies.
3. The global functions of Kordsa create global synergies and develop a technical ability to satisfy customer needs.
4. The company aligns production capacity with market demands and is establishing a global supply chain with flexible products.

Management and Leadership Development Needs

Kordsa recognizes that its global talents on four continents are an essential component of its ability to attain its strategic objectives. Thus, the company adheres to a global human resource management strategy. The company has a Global Human Resources unit with the task of developing and implementing this strategy. The unit conducts strategic operations associated with the company's human resource policy. According to this policy, a positive organizational climate, empowerment of employees and employee development, as well as implementation of programs that ensure stakeholder satisfaction are vital. The company also needs competences in intercultural business communication, sustainability, open innovation, digital transformation, occupational health and safety, and environmental protection.

The World's Reinforcement Brand

Kordsa's success story begins in 1973 with Sabancı Holding's investment in Izmit to manufacture tire cord fabric for tire manufacturers. Until 2014 Kordsa produced mainly tire reinforcement technologies. Then, it expanded its business lines to include construction reinforcement and composite technologies. Initially positioned as a market leader in Turkey, Kordsa has achieved global market leadership over the years thanks to its deep expertise in reinforcement materials and processes, advanced R&D, open innovation culture, and a strategic approach to the tire reinforcement sector. Today, Kordsa reinforces one out of every three automobile tires and two out of every three aircraft tires in the world.

In 2017, Kordsa had eight production facilities in five countries with about 4000 employees. In 2019, Kordsa operated in five countries—Turkey, Brazil, Indonesia, Thailand, and the USA—with 12 production facilities and about 4500 employees. This makes Kordsa a global company in the field of tire and construction reinforcement and composite technology. After the opening of its Center of Excellence Composite Technologies, Kordsa acquired three companies—Fabric Development Inc., Textile Products Inc., Advanced Honeycomb and Axiom Materials—, which are among the most strategic suppliers serving the world's leading brands of the commercial aviation industry.

R&D and innovation are part of the corporate culture of Kordsa. Kordsa's first R&D center, established in Izmit in 2007, serves Turkey and the global market as an innovation kitchen for tire and construction technologies. The second R&D center of Kordsa is the Center of Excellence for Composite Technologies, which brings together R&D, innovation, and manufacturing under one roof. It is one of the very few test centers globally. It does basic and applied research, technology, and product development, entrepreneurship, and production processes. It employs researchers, designers, engineers, production process managers, workers, PhD students, post-doctoral fellows, faculty members, and incubation center entrepreneurs. With an open innovation approach, Kordsa cooperates with many universities and institutions, thus extending its R&D and innovation efforts in order to develop technologies that create a difference and value.

Kordsa believes that its open approach to innovation has resulted in important new products. As a global brand, Kordsa sets its sector's quality standards, breaking new ground in the manufacturing models of the sector by developing Industry 4.0 practices. Kordsa offers a high standard of service, high cost-effectiveness, and a high level of technological competence. Moreover, both before and after-sales, the company maintains relations with clients. Additional benefits include the provision of customer-related support centers, collaboration with distributors, and the advantage of distribution channels. Core components of Kordsa's corporate culture include R&D activities and excellence. Through deploying creative value-added solutions, the company creates sustainable value for consumers, employees, investors, and the environment. Besides, the company aims at "zero work-related accidents," "zero quality defects," and "zero breakdowns." In addition to this, Kordsa has attached particular importance to digital transformation practices in recent years. Digital transformation has developed as a result of Kordsa's open innovation and sustainability approaches.

Kordsa's international reputation is evidenced by its innovative technologies, human resources policies, and work ethics. The company has received several prestigious awards. Besides the prizes in Turkey, Kordsa was recognized as one of the most popular employers in Bahia, Brazil, by the Great Place to Work Institute for 4 years. Kordsa has also been named by *Info Bank*, Indonesia's weekly economic publication, one of the "top-100 fastest-growing companies." Kordsa was "Champion of Indonesian Exports," and its project manager was honored with the "Best Employee" award for 3 years for the "Safety Experience Center" project in Indonesia. Through adding value and creative strengthening approaches, Kordsa aims to create sustainable value to its clients, employees, stakeholders, and the society to which it belongs.

2.5 Case Study 5

Yünsa Yünlü Sanayi ve Ticaret A.Ş.

Overview
Address: Sabancı Center Kat 19 4. Levent, 34330 İstanbul, Türkiye
Tel: +90 (212) 385 87 00
Fax: +90 (212) 282 50 67/270 06 65
Email: iletisim@yunsa.com
Web: www.yunsa.com

Company Information

Industry: Manufacture of textiles. Manufacturing of integrated high-segment worsted wool fabric
Year of establishment: 1973
Sales revenues in 2017: 37.5 million euros
Revenues in 2007: N/A
ROA/ROE in 2017: N/A
Average ROA/ROE in the past 10 years: N/A
Latest Debt to Equity ratio: N/A
Average number employees in 2017: 1000
Brain(s) behind the company: CEO Nuri Refik Düzgören

Nature of Market Leadership

Yünsa is the largest integrated high-segment worsted wool fabric manufacturer in Europe and one of the five biggest in the world. It was founded in 1973 and went public in 1990. Sabancı Holding (HOSH) owns 57.88% of the common stock, with the remaining shares publicly traded on the Istanbul stock exchange. Yünsa has customers in more than 50 countries.. Germany is the company's biggest market. Yünsa is the leading fabric supplier to some of the world's major brands. The company has offices in the UK, Germany, and Italy, and agents in Spain, Italy, France, Sweden, Japan, Korea, the USA, Serbia, Finland, Russia, Slovakia, and the Czech Republic.

Nature of the Competitive Advantage

Professional marketing abilities, market expertise, excellent customer relations, positive corporate culture, talented workers, flexible production, small-scale special orders, delivery on time, the ability to satisfy specific design needs for the customer, an excellent price-efficiency ratio, and continuous innovations.

Lessons Learned on the Path to Success

1. Satisfy specific design needs for the customer at a lower price and higher efficiency ratio.
2. Establish strong partnerships with customers all over the world.
3. The company's global success stems from a long-term merged strategy, emphasizing a customer-oriented approach, extraordinary design abilities, an ability to understand market needs and trends, delivery on time, high product quality and flexibility in production, and R&D activities.
4. The corporate culture and the highly talented and dynamic workforce makes a vital difference.

Management and Leadership Development Needs

Yünsa is striving for global leadership in its business in addition to its commercial objectives. Planning all operations and management and leadership development needs in line with this vision, the company will continue to grow by effectively managing its business capital and taking advantage of digital opportunities, and by offering innovative products and services.

Understanding What the Market and Customers Want Is Paramount in Building a Better Customer Experience

Yünsa began producing men's worsted fabrics in 1973, adding women's fabrics to its portfolio in 1998. It became a public company in 1990. Yünsa is Europe's largest and one of the world's five largest integrated high segment wool manufacturers. It accounts for 70% of the exports in its sector.

Yünsa primarily manufactures 100% worsted fabric, as well as worsted fabric mixed with cashmere, lycra, viscose, cotton, and linen. Yarn-dyed, piece-dyed, and top-dyed fabrics are available in a variety of finishing applications, such as washable, water repellent, UV-protected self-cleaning, and natural stretching.. Yünsa has design studios in Biella, Italy, and Çerkezköy, Turkey. Yünsa exhibits its collections of fabrics each season at the world's most influential textile fairs: Première Vision Paris, New York, Munich Fabric Start, and the London Textile Fair.

The company strives to develop professional marketing skills, market expertise, excellent customer relationships, and a positive corporate culture. Paramount factors in the creation of a competitive advantage are the company's talented employees, flexible production, small-scale special orders, timely delivery, and ability to meet specific customer design needs, the excellent price-efficiency ratio, and continuous innovation.

Yünsa has adopted the ISO 9001, ISO 14001, and ISO 50001 quality standards. Also, the Hohenstein Institute in Germany has licensed the Eko-Tax 100 operation, which certifies that the products of Yünsa are not hazardous to the environment or health.

According to the results of the "Top 1000 Export Companies" survey conducted by the Turkish Exporters Assembly (TIM) in 2017, Yünsa broke its own record in 2017 by increasing its exports by 199 million Turkish liras, which is a 19% increase.. Yünsa now aims at global leadership in its industry, as well as business targets. Planning all operations in line with this vision, the company will continue to grow by effectively managing its business capital, taking advantage of digital opportunities, and offering innovative products and services.

Today, Yünsa is one of Turkey's most valuable brands supported by the Sabancı Holding. In line with its export goals, Yünsa aims to continue contributing to Turkey's economic growth and industrial development.

3 Conclusions and Recommendations

Turkey has achieved a stellar economic and social development performance since 2000, leading to more jobs and higher average incomes for Turkey. However, these successes can be compromised by the current economic challenges and the uncertain external environment. Turkey was dramatically urbanized, maintaining strong macroeconomic and fiscal policies, opening up foreign trade and finance, harmonizing a variety of laws and regulations with the standards of the European Union, and expanding access to public services. The effects of the recession in 2008–2009 have also been successfully dealt with. In view of the rising inflation and unemployment, higher corporate and financial vulnerabilities, and the erratic implementation of corrective policies and reforms, the economic outlook is more uncertain than usual.

Hidden champions are characterized by their innovativeness and R&D. They integrate the market, which is rare among large companies. The other characteristics of the hidden champions are a global focus, a strong emphasis on consumers, talented and engaged employees, global and local market knowledge, participative management, being open to change, lean thinking, compliance with ethical values, sustainability practices, quality standards, outstanding design skills, and propensity for digital transformation. As many things in the market can change, from the appearance of new competitors and innovations to a general slowdown in the economy, the hidden champions of Turkey must respond very fast to new customer needs and preferences in Turkey and abroad. All hidden champions in Turkey have strong manufacturing capabilities and use licenses or contract manufacturing. The hidden champions try to be close to the customers, who themselves are manufacturers, to benefit from customers' innovative ideas.

Moreover, these companies emphasize the willingness of their clients to develop products through tailored design and to work closely with them. The benefit of this policy is that if the business is in trouble, the company can use information about its market and existing or potential customers. Some of the Turkish hidden champions grow by sub-contracting for major global brands and exporting their brands to different markets. Some of them are solely exporting their innovative products and brands to a niche market. The hidden champions challenge much of the knowledge created by studying big companies that are part of the business school curriculum since big companies' success stories are not the same as those of the hidden champions. Business schools and hidden champions of Turkey should cooperate in order to shed light on the secrets of these successful companies. Turkish companies have a trend-setter approach to raising their profit margins rather than adjusting to market dynamics. Hence, hidden champions offer high quality and differentiated products and services with a high performance-price ratio.

References

Ahmad F (1993) The making of modern Turkey. Routledge, London
Aydın S, Taşkın Y (2014) 1960'tan Günümüze Türkiye Tarihi. İstanbul, İletişim Yayınları
Boratav K (2005) Where is the New World order heading to? Image Publications, Ankara
Finefrock MM (1981) Laissez-faire, the 1923 Izmir economic congress and early Turkish developmental policy in political perspective. Middle East Stud 17(3):375–392. https://doi.org/10.1080/00263208108700478
Gormez Y, Yigit S (2009) The economic and financial stability in Turkey: a historical perspective. National Bank of Serbia, SEEMHN paper
Güney C (2019) Turkish economy. https://www.cag.edu.tr/tr/akademik-kadro/22/dosyalar?f=91fe68e6-0751-4324-b7a1-4793f6d00d52
Koch L, Chaudhary MA, Bilquees F (2001) February 2001 crisis in Turkey: causes and consequences. Pak Dev Rev 40:467–486
Okyar O (1979) Development background of the Turkish economy, 1923-1973. Int J Middle East Stud 10(3):325–344. Retrieved from www.jstor.org/stable/162142
Yosun T, Çetindamar D (2013). Hidden champions of Turkey. In: McKiernan P, Purg D (eds) Hidden champions in CEE and Turkey: carving out a global niche. Springer, Berlin, pp 383–406. ISBN 978-3-642-40503-7 (Print) 978-3-642-40504-4 (Online)

Hidden Champions of Ukraine

Iryna Tykhomyrova and Vadym Saveliev

Overview
Official name: Ukraine
Type of government: Unitary parliamentary-presidential republic
Population in 2017[1]: 44,800,000
Land area (in sq. km) in 2016: 603,628

History

1917–1919	After the collapse of the Russian and Austro-Hungarian empires, there were several attempts of establishing independent Ukrainian state (Ukrainian National Republic, West Ukrainian National Republic, and Ukrainian State, etc.).
1919	The Ukrainian Soviet Socialist Republic was formally established.
1922	The Ukrainian Soviet Socialist Republic became one of the founding republics of the Soviet Union.
1939	After the division of Poland, west parts of modern Ukraine were annexed by the Ukrainian Soviet Socialist Republic. The last part of modern Ukraine—the Crimea—was transferred to Ukraine at 1954.
1941	Ukrainian Soviet Socialist Republic was occupied by Nazi Germany.
1945	The Ukrainian SSR became one of the founding members of the United Nations.
1990	The Declaration of Independence was passed.

---

[1] The World Factbook (2019). Available at https://www.cia.gov/index.html [Accessed 29 September 2019].

I. Tykhomyrova (✉) · V. Saveliev
MIM Business School, Kyiv, Ukraine
e-mail: irina@mim.kiev.ua; vs@mim.kiev.ua

© Springer Nature Switzerland AG 2021
A. Braček Lalić, D. Purg (eds.), *Hidden Champions in Dynamically Changing Societies*, https://doi.org/10.1007/978-3-030-65451-1_28

1991	After the breakup of the Soviet Union, Ukraine became an independent country. It was adjusted by the results of the national referendum. First presidential elections took place. Ukraine, Belarus, and Russia formed the Commonwealth of Independent States (CIS).
1992	Ukraine joined the Organization for Security and Cooperation in Europe (OSCE).
1996	A new currency, the hryvnia, was introduced and a new Constitution of Ukraine was adopted.
1998	The European Union's Partnership and Cooperation Agreement (PCA) with Ukraine came into operation.
2004	The peaceful Democratic Orange Revolution took place.
2008	Ukraine joined the World Trade Organization.
2011–2013	Ukraine's oligarch-dominated economy grew slowly, but remained behind peers in the region and among Europe's poorest.
2014	The Revolution of Dignity took place. Ukraine's economy fell into crisis because of Russia's annexation of Crimea, military conflict in the East of the country, and a resulting trade war with Russia, leading to a 17% decline in GDP, inflation at nearly 60%, and dwindling foreign currency reserves.
2015	With the loss of a major portion of Ukraine's heavy industry in Donbas and ongoing violence there, the economy contracted by 6.6% in 2014 and by 9.8% in 2015.
2016	Ukraine redirected trade activity towards the EU following the implementation of a bilateral Deep and Comprehensive Free Trade Agreement with EU, displacing Russia as its largest trading partner. Economy returned to slow growth in 2016 and 2017, reaching 2.3% and 2.0%, respectively, as key reforms took hold.
2017	Ukraine implemented reforms, including the creation of a national anti-corruption agency.
2018	Ukraine made attempts to attract foreign investment, privatize state-owned enterprises, and make land reform.
2019	Volodymyr Zelenskyy is elected president of Ukraine.

1 Introduction: Context and History

During its 28 years of independence, Ukraine has faced numerous economic, political, and social problems. However, the last 5 years were the most difficult. In November 2013, the Revolution of Dignity happened, followed by the armed conflict in the East of Ukraine. The political and economic situation worsened, requiring focused action by the government.

Since 2014, a number of reforms have been implemented, concerning energy tariffs, social service, the governmental procurement system, business deregulation, fiscal consolidation, currency exchange rates, and currency regulation, as well as the banking sector. Moreover, Ukrainian business is still suffering from outdated governance and over-regulation by government agencies.

Ukraine needs to increase its production efficiency and adjust its corporate finance and labor market in a way that will enable it to improve its political and economic situation. In particular, facilitation of the alignment of national businesses and FMCG goods standards with the EU requirements is pending. The Deep and Comprehensive Free Trade Area came into effect on January, 1, 2016. It is expected to help Ukraine to integrate its economy into the European markets by creating access to them and aligning the country's regulatory framework with that of the EU.

According to the IMD World Competitiveness Ranking 2019, Ukraine holds the 54th position.[2] The country moved up five points compared to its position in 2018. However, economic growth prospects are still rather weak because of the difficult global economic situation, long period of uncertainty caused by the conflict in the East, and difficulties in the reformation processes caused by the political situation.

There are several important factors that affect Ukraine's economic situation:

- Reduction of the purchase power of the urban and rural population and an increase of the prices in most categories of goods.
- The infrastructure of most manufacturing sites is wearing out.
- National producers are switching to European and Middle East markets.
- Unstable political situation and on-going political crisis.
- Lack of medium and long-term forecasts concerning the economic environment.

Thus, currently Ukraine is facing several important tasks:

- Reform of its judicial system to make it transparent, fair, and reliable for investors.
- Renewal of economic growth which would reduce unemployment and improve living conditions.
- Defeating corruption in legislative and regulatory bodies.
- Generate domestic and international investments that will promote economic growth.

---

[2]World Competitiveness Ranking (2019) Available at: https://www.imd.org/wcc/world-competitiveness-center-rankings/world-competitiveness-ranking-2019/ [Accessed 29 September 2019].

- Stop the military conflict in the East of Ukraine.

Succeeding in accomplishing those tasks will strengthen the national economy and promote GDP growth. GDP is one of the most important economic indicators. The World Bank ranks Ukraine number 57 in terms of GDP.[3] So far, 45% of the national GDP is generated by the export of goods and services (Exhibit 1).

Historically, the share of metallurgy, chemical industry, manufacturing engineering, and agriculture has been the largest in Ukraine's export structure. However, after the Soviet Union collapsed, the export structure changed because some segments of manufacturing collapsed. According to some experts, it happened because of obsolete technologies and high energy consumption. Therefore, the share of raw material grew dramatically.

The share of wheat, maize, barley, and soybeans in Ukraine's exports is approximately 55%. Sunflower oil holds the largest share in Ukrainian agricultural exports. In 2018 its sales reached 4.1 billion US dollars.[4] Ukraine has held a global leadership position in sunflower oil production and export for several years in a row. Ukraine is also one of the leading wheat exporters. According to the Ministry of Agrarian Policy and Food Safety, in 2019–2020 Ukraine exported more than 13,000,000 tons of grain, which is 4,300,000 tons more than in the previous year.[5]

The share of the metallurgy and chemical industry is 37% in the overall export. Large companies are the main exporters because they have expertise relevant in the industry, mainly in the area of specific technologies application. At the same time, the share of small and medium businesses has reached nearly 30% of the GDP.

Small-and-medium-sized businesses development is relatively unattractive because the regulatory and legal framework benefits large financial and industrial groups oriented. This reduces the competitiveness of smaller companies. This situation accounts for the nation's poor positions in different competitiveness and ease-of-doing business rankings. It also explains why Ukrainian entrepreneurs are not willing to publicize their activities. The unfavorable business environment boosts the demand for different optimization schemes and prevents companies from corporatization and sharing their successes with competitors and regulators. Ukraine's hidden champions prefer to stay hidden rather than blow their horns.

Ukraine has participated in the Hidden Champions research since 2011. It was a roller-coaster period of the Revolution of Dignity, Russia's annexation of Crimea, and military conflict in the East of the country followed by an inevitable economic recession. Regardless of those events, three companies from 2011 research have

---

[3]UCAB (2019) – Ucab Export Available at: http://ucab.ua/ua/doing_agribusiness/zovnishni_rinki/osnovni_pokazniki_zovnishnoi_torgivli_ukraini. [Accessed 2019].

[4]Основні показники зовнішньої торгівлі України/Зовнішні ринки/ВЕДЕННЯ АГРОБІЗНЕСУ В УКРАЇНІ/УКАБ. (n.d.). Retrieved September 29, 2019, from http://ucab.ua/ua/doing_agribusiness/zovnishni_rinki/osnovni_pokazniki_zovnishnoi_torgivli_ukraini

[5]Minagro.gov.ua (2019) – Minavgo Export. Available at: https://minagro.gov.ua/ua/news/z-pochatku-201920-mr-z-ukrayini-eksportovano-ponad-13-mln-tonn-zerna [Accessed 27 September 2019].

Exhibit 1 Core economic indicators for Ukraine

	2011	2012	2013	2014	2015	2016	2017	2018
GDP per capita (current US$)	3570	3855	4030	3105	2125	2188	2641	3095
GDP per capita growth (annual %)	5.845	0.487	0.201	−1.145	−9.444	2.855	2.917	3.863
Foreign direct investment, net inflows (% of GDP)	4.417	4.651	2.460	0.634	3.351	3.686	2.520	1.892
GDP (current US$, mio)	163,159	175,781	183,310	133,503	91,031	93,356	112,190	130,832
Exports of goods and services (current US$, mio)	81,280	83,884	78,744	64,873	47,880	46,023	53,867	59,149
Exports of goods and services (% of GDP)	49.816	47.721	42.957	48.593	52.598	49.299	48.014	45.210
Merchandise exports (current US$, mio)	68,460	68,530	64,338	54,199	38,127	36,360	43,265	47,348
Merchandise exports to high-income economies (% of total merchandise exports)	30.062	30.130	31.931	37.026	39.66	41.805	46.016	–
Merchandise exports to developing economies in Europe and Central Asia (% of total merchandise exports)	47.877	44.866	43.802	37.588	31.795	27.081	26.478	–
Ores and metals exports (% of merchandise exports)	8.047	6.839	8.147	8.989	8.435	7.076	8.433	8.313
Agricultural raw materials exports (% of merchandise exports)	1.068	0.982	1.252	1.749	2.109	2.052	1.689	1.961
Food exports (% of merchandise exports)	18.641	25.884	26.785	30.725	37.968	41.877	40.806	39.141
Fuel exports (% of merchandise exports)	8.112	5.049	4.200	3.390	1.070	0.966	1.526	1.458
Manufactures exports (% of merchandise exports)	63.548	60.647	58.707	54.877	50.122	47.514	46.721	48.787
High-technology exports (% of manufactured exports)	4.995	6.914	6.711	7.53	8.524	7.218	6.252	5.406

Source: World Bank, September 2019

lived through all the turmoil to appear even more prosperous thus setting the trend for many Ukrainian businesses. Naturally, other Ukrainian companies followed the trend and joined those researched within the current Hidden Champions in Ukraine project.

Three Ukrainian hidden champions are reviewed in this chapter.

1. Aisberg LTD—A leading producer of customized refrigerated equipment for retail in the Caucasus region (Georgia, Armenia), exporting to 30 other countries globally.
2. JSC Weidmann Malyn Paper Mill—a leading company in the CIS in the production of pulp-insulating materials for the electrical industry.
3. Ukrainian Beer Company (UBC Group)—a world leader in beer coolers manufacturing, a CIS leader among the producers of beer promotion products.

2 2 Case Studies of Selected Hidden Champions

2.1 Case Study 1

Aisberg LTD

Overview
Address: Ovidiopolskaya doroga 3, Odessa, 65036, Ukraine
Tel: +38 (0482) 32-35-28
Fax: +38 (0482) 32-35-29
Email: aisberg@aisberg.od.ua
Web: www.aisberg.com

Company Information[6]
Industry: Manufacture of non-domestic cooling and ventilation equipment
Year of establishment: 1989
Sales Revenues in 2017: N/A*
Sales Revenues in 2007: N/A*
Average number of employees in 2017: 145
Brainer(s) behind the company: CEO Oleg Antonenko

Nature of Market Leadership

Aisberg has up-to-date manufacturing facilities, which allow it to design and implement tailor-made solutions for each client. The company's R&D portfolio contains 23 patents for the most innovative solutions in refrigerating equipment.

---

[6]Aisberg.com (2019). Available at: https://www.aisberg.com/ [Accessed 29 September 2019]

Because of the new ideas and technologies, which secure the high quality of refrigeration, the company's products are sold in highly competitive markets: Europe, Australia, Gulf countries, and other Middle East countries.

Aisberg's main achievements are energy efficiency and the number of countries where its products are bought. Export orientation leads to an increase in solutions development costs to meet the operation requirements in different markets, advertising literature, marketing, brand development, and international traveling.

Nature of the Competitive Advantage

1. Refrigeration quality. Innovative refrigeration and defrost systems have been developed, tested, and successfully applied to improve the preservation quality of meat and convenience foods in supermarkets.
2. Efficient commerce. Aisberg specialists have worked out a lot of solutions for efficient floor space use and efficient sales in deli and convenience food departments.
3. Design and manufacture of refrigerated displays. Customized with maximum regard for the requirements of each client concerning the design and quality of cooling.
4. Energy saving. Aisberg applies a number of energy-saving technologies and innovations while manufacturing refrigeration cabinets and fitting up supermarkets. Among these innovations are special refrigeration and defrost systems, condensation heat recovery, and more.

Core Lessons Learned on the Path to Success

1. High-quality components. Aisberg's refrigeration equipment is manufactured exclusively from high-quality materials and components of well-known European brands.
2. Customization of equipment for the specific client needs.
3. Wide export network, cooperation with international retail chains. Over 80% of the production is exported.

Management, Leadership, Financing, and Regulatory Development Needs

Management accounting system optimization in the manufacturing of customized refrigeration equipment. The company plans to launch an additional production site, which will require investment.

Aisberg Is a Leading Producer of Customized Refrigerated Equipment for Retail

Aisberg exports refrigeration cabinets and installations of its own production to 30 countries.

Aisberg is one of the leaders in the niche of customized refrigerated equipment for retail in the Caucasus region (Georgia, Armenia). The company exports to Iceland, Australia, Kenya, Germany, the United Arab Emirates, Italy, Hungary, and Romania.

Aisberg was founded in 1989 and for more than 30 years has successfully worked on the market of commercial refrigeration. Its activity is the production of a vast range of refrigerated equipment for supermarkets and hypermarkets. Among Aisberg's customers are world retail trade leaders: Spar, Metro, Carrefour, and Bill.

For the first decade of its existence, Aisberg mostly imported equipment from Italy, Spain, Germany, Turkey, and other countries. It bought the refrigerating equipment abroad, imported it to Ukraine, assembled it, and offered maintenance services.

At that time Aisberg was selling 10–15 displays per month, whereas currently the company produces 10–15 complex solutions for supermarkets in the same period. Nearly 15 years ago, Aisberg launched its own manufacturing. It started exporting its products to the CIS countries immediately.

At that time, the company's main markets included Georgia, Belarus, Russia, and Kazakhstan. At the same time, Aisberg's team was collecting intelligence from all over the world. In 2008, it was Aisberg that introduced Ukrainian technologies at the leading retail exhibition EuroShop in Germany. It was a good opportunity to present the company's achievements in refrigeration technologies.

When the Russian market closed, Aisberg re-adjusted its product line to meet all European standards and requirements. Special attention was paid to energy consumption and electricity parameters. Global chains are notorious for their strict requirements for energy efficiency as it helps save a lot of costs.

Nowadays, Aisberg products meet all international certification standards. The company boasts one of the best energy-efficient refrigerating equipment in the world. In fact, the company introduced the standard for global chains.

Aisberg manages to import components without custom duties and thus has open access to markets all over the world because it has made its products globally competitive. Previously, Aisberg paid 11% of custom duties for each item imported from the EU. Not paying custom duties has reduced costs. This became possible as a result of the establishment of the Deep and Comprehensive Free Trade Area. Under any other circumstances, the company would not have been able to break through, especially in terms of quality.

Most of the science-intensive components for sophisticated equipment are produced in EU countries. Aisberg sources 97% of its components internationally.

Aisberg combined a team of designers and the best engineers and technicians, and also created its own scientific testing laboratory and production facilities so as to be able to develop and produce unique solutions and special equipment for each customer: custom-made refrigerated cabinets fulfilling the most difficult requirements for product exposition and refrigeration. Energy-efficient solutions in refrigerated cabinets and store refrigerating systems are provided individually for each project.

2.2 Case Study 2

Ukrainian Beer Company Group (UBC Group)

Overview
Address: 7, Lermontovska St., Kharkiv, 61024, Ukraine
Tel: +38 0577009031
Fax: -
Email: kiev@beer-co.com
Web: www.beer-co.com

Company Information
Industry: Manufacture of non-domestic cooling and ventilation equipment
Year of establishment: 1993
Sales revenues in 2017: 250 million euros
Sales revenues in 2007: 250 million euros
Average number of employees in 2017: 5500
Brain(s) behind the company: President Igor Gumennyy

Nature of Market Leadership

In 2018 UBC Group was number one in the world in the niche of beer coolers, with 20% market share. It also the number-one company in CIS countries in the production of beer promotion products: caps, cafeteria carts, tents, ceramic beer faucets, and more. Almost all world-famous beer producers use the cooling equipment of this Ukrainian company. UBC Group is the certified supplier of beer coolers for InBev, Molson Coors, Anheuser Bush, Heineken, and other companies. In 2011–2018, UBC Group bolstered its position by getting rid of all non-core assets and focusing exclusively on functions that serve the same customer field.

The company's president says that if a business has no leadership potential in a market or a niche, there is no growth capacity for it. Only the areas of possible dominance should be prioritized. Thus, in recent years UBC Group has been advancing in market segments and regions—Latin America, the USA—that offer both growth and leadership opportunities for the company.

Nature of the Competitive Advantage

The nature of the competitive advantage in 2018 had not changed since the 2011 research on HC. The modern technology and strict control over the distribution channels are among the main reasons that this company is a market leader. Distribution channel control means staying closer to the customer and ahead of the competition, quickly responding to customer needs and market shifts.

To achieve this, it is crucial for the company's large team to work in a consolidated and well-orchestrated effort. The corporate university of UBC Group, besides developing specific competencies, devotes much attention to team-building aspects. As the company executives state, "Without understanding each other, it is impossible to swiftly respond to customer needs."

The company's president believes that the teambuilding approach must be inspired by examples where engagement is the key to survival, as in the case of an orchestra conductor or football coach. Another element of the company's competitive edge is the constant increase in operational efficiency and thorough planning of all business processes. When designing new equipment, UBC Group takes into account all the quality standards and equipment requirements of its clients.

Core Lessons Learned on the Path to Success

1. Dominate the home market first, then expand. A company must strive to lead the market or niche and constantly improve its operations.
2. Sales are the most important thing. One of the best approaches to win and retain market leadership is to become highly customer-oriented and practice flexible principles of customer satisfaction. Strict control over the distribution channels is also considered a competitive advantage.
3. Work must be a pleasure.

Management, Leadership, Financing, and Regulatory Development Needs

The company needs skills to understand each other as a team and interact in the most efficient way, as well as deep understanding of various technical matters through hands-on experience. The company's shareholding structure includes EBRD, which allows it to arrange financing for its business development efficiently. It is extremely important to attract credit resources with the higher valuation of mortgage assets. This is a common problem of Ukraine's investment climate. More research of the business cycle of new target markets is needed to maintain the ongoing geographic expansion.

UBC Group Is Number One in the World in the Niche of Beer Coolers

UBC Group is a trade and industrial holding founded in 1993. The company operates in several industries: food manufacturing, HoReCa, and beer distribution.

Moreover, it manufactures beverages cooling equipment, and promotional beer products. Its subdivisions that specialize in promotional products and cooling equipment are typical hidden champions in Central and Eastern Europe and across the world.

UBC Group is a distribution company, operating primarily in the business to business market. The company reaches its objectives through the implementation of an effective direct sales system. The following are the most important achievements of UBC Group:

- The company offers its services in the most convenient format for the customers.
- The company opens its subsidiaries in order to provide the best service to its clients.

The company has the following divisions:

1. UBC Coo" is the division that designs and manufactures refrigerating equipment for foods and drinks. It is:

    - The number-one manufacturer of chilling units globally
    - The number-one manufacturer of cabinet coolers in Ukraine
    - The number-two cabinet cooler manufacturer in Eastern Europe

2. UBC Promo is a division that develops and makes promotional materials. It is:

    - The number-one producer of promotional materials in Eastern Europe.
    - The number-one manufacturer of ceramic bottling towers globally.

3. UBC Engineering is a leading CIS company providing construction, installation, and commissioning in the food and processing industry.
4. UBC Armature is a leading CIS engineering company in the food industry. It designs and installs equipment and launches technological processes. It also distributes fixtures and expendables.
5. UBC Distribution is a division that sells products and services of the UBC Group and similar companies. Its head office is in Kharkiv. It has 26 subsidiaries in all major markets all over the world.
6. UBC Service is the division that offers maintenance services of the professional refrigerators. It is represented in Ukraine, Kazakhstan, Russia, and Belarus. It" is the number-one provider in Ukraine of maintenance of cabinet coolers.
7. Stargorod is a chain of the high-end Czech and German-style beer restaurants operating in CIS and the Baltic countries. It is a National SALT Restaurant award winner as the best beer restaurant. It also won the 2014 Platinum Platter Award as the most popular restaurant in the Baltic countries.

Meeting customers' needs quickly is at the heart of the UBC Group's strategy.

In it underpinned by the ongoing training of its employees in customer needs satisfaction.

The UBC Group's objective is to be number one in its business segments.

The company's mission reflects its main competitive advantages: selling skills, the ability to show the company's goods, service-related advantages, and meeting customers' needs.

Satisfying those needs is the essence of the company's strategy. It believes it is the best in that respect.

Working for the company is like playing an exciting game. The UBC Groups wants its employees to be as excited by their work there as they were excited in their play when they were kids.

2.3 Case Study 3

JSC Weidmann Malyn Paper Mill

Overview
Address: Prykhodko Str. 66, 11602 Malyn, Zhytomyr region, Ukraine
Tel: +380 4133 67222
Fax: +3804133 53343
Email: info.wmpm@weidmann-group.com
Web: www.weidmann-electrical.com

Company Information
Industry: Manufacture of paper and paperboard
Year of establishment:1871
Sales revenues in 2017: 19.1 million euros Sales revenues in 2007:
  5.5 million euros
Average number of employees in 2017: 491
Brain(s) behind the company: Igor Volga

Nature of Market Leadership

Weidmann Malyn Paper Mill continues to hold a leading position in the production of pulp-insulating materials for the electrical industry in the CIS market. The main countries of export are Switzerland, Russia, and Turkey.

Since the 2011 research, the company's profile has not changed. The nature of its competitive advantage is its long-standing expertise in a specific market niche, based on the competencies of its professional team and continuous improvement of production capacities.

Currently there is plenty of demand for the electrical insulating board. Their production is characterized by high capital intensity.

Nature of the Competitive Advantage

A long history of production and traditional market leadership, combined with adequate demand and technological innovations, provide the company with competitive advantages.

Key competitive edge:

- Comparatively lower production costs
- Intellectual potential: generations of papermakers employed in the factory
- Advantageous geographic location of production facilities in terms of logistics

The main drivers of the company's success:

1. Mature distribution system
2. Continuous improvement of production operations
3. High investment
4. Technological barriers for new entrants

Core Lessons Learned on the Path to Success

1. Innovation and distribution continue to be important success factors. Barriers to entry into the market are high because of the highly specialized production processes.
2. It is essential for the enterprise to retain and nurture its brain-power. This is critical as modern production processes require fine adjustment of machinery to yield high-quality products.
3. Follow the principles of accuracy, transparency, and consistency. Study the clients' needs and the expansion of international relations will provide sustainable development for the company.

Management, Leadership, Financing, and Regulatory Development Needs

1. Ongoing improvement of management skills
2. Learning of foreign languages
3. Development of logistics competencies

Weidmann Malyn Paper Mill[7] Is Number One in the Production of Pulp-Insulating Materials for the Electrical Industry in the CIS Market

Joint Stock Company Weidmann Malyn Paper Mill—a member of the international Weidmann Group—is the only mill in Eastern Europe that can supply its customers with almost all grades of electrical insulation paper and board that correspond to local and international standards.

At present, the mill operates five technological lines and produces transformer board, electrical insulation paper for power cables and transformer windings, and paper for various other industrial applications, including packaging, filtration, and wallpaper base.

Weidmann Malyn Paper Mill has a 148-year history, dating back to its foundation in 1871 as a fairly typical European industrial operation, producing paper for "writing and smoking." The enterprise was based in Malyn—a small regional town near Kyiv. At the beginning of the twentieth century, the factory manufactured about 1500 tons of paper per year and its production received several awards at prestigious trade fairs and exhibitions.

In the 1930s of the last century, the mill started manufacturing condenser paper—very thin and clean insulation paper for electrical capacitors. Its thickness is from eight to 20 microns. In the 1960s, large-scale reconstruction took place at the company: new premises were built, and new, more powerful paper machines were installed. This considerably increased production volume. In the next decade, the company became one of the biggest producers of capacitor paper in Europe.

During the last quarter of the twentieth century, because of the installation of two-wire machines and a hot-pressed board machine, the factory started to produce various non-woven materials, hot-pressed board for power transformers, various electrical insulation paper grades, cigarette paper, and paper for food packaging.

In 1994, the enterprise was transformed into the joint stock company Malyn Paper Mill, and in 2000 it became a member of the international Weidmann Group—the world leader in high-voltage insulation for power transformers.

The company is certified in accordance with international standards ISO 9001:2008, ISO 14001:2004, and OHSAS 18001. It is a member of the Zhytomyr Chamber of Commerce and Industry, the European Business Association, and the UkrPapir association.

To maintain its leadership position, the company modernizes its production and increases its capacity. A number of processes and operations are being automated to improve product quality. The company has repeatedly won prestigious competitions and its products are highly rated by consumers.

---

[7]Weidmann-mpm.com (2019). Available at: http://www.weidmann-mpm.com/about-us-uk.html. [Accessed 29 September 2019].

3 Conclusions and Recommendations

It is getting increasingly difficult to find hidden champions in Ukraine. There are several reasons for that.

First of all, niche-oriented companies, which are successful in global markets, are turning from hidden champions into visible ones, and their leadership are more and more often asked for interviews or public comments. They often share their successes with the media.

Secondly, quite a few companies are striving to remain hidden. Their employees avoid participation in studies and reviews, and they do not publicize anything related to their activities or successes.

Thirdly, Ukraine's unfriendly business environment, coupled with the lack of tradition of business transparency, promotes the practice of hiding information from governmental agencies, regulators, and the general public. Unfortunately, hidden champions are not the only category following this tradition.

Although information about the hidden champions is scarce, all of those companies share a number of characteristics, such as international expansion orientation, internal competencies development, and high technological expertise.

Hidden champions pay special attention to team-building and the development of their human resources. They invest in training their people, and in instilling a corporate culture that promotes motivation and low personnel turnover.

Hidden champions' innovation processes depend on staff morale even more than on the market situation. This is so because of genuine, in-company uniqueness rather than external factors. Those companies are often the results of their shareholders' visions. The shareholders usually run those businesses.

A sharp focus on customers' needs is yet another feature of the hidden champions. It is not only their offers that are tailored to the clients' needs, but also the mode of the offers' delivery. This makes Ukraine's hidden champions similar to the German companies described by Hermann Simon.

Setting goals high and achieving them through a well-fitted mechanism of organization and motivated top management is another similar feature of Ukrainian and German companies.

Ukraine's hidden champions are inclined to use financial resources offered by international financial institutions. They raise funds to develop their manufacturing facilities and enter new markets. Those companies are quality and innovation-oriented.

Ukrainian hidden champions make products with high added value. Very often those products are unique and have no substitutes.

Import restriction imposed by the Russian Federation made some hidden champions increase their export to Europe. Because of this situation, they improved their manufacturing processes to meet EU standards and thus gained access to many other markets across the globe.

However, comparing Ukrainian hidden champions to those of Germany is still somewhat pre-mature. The Ukrainian hidden champions' scale of operations and revenues are smaller than those of the German companies studied by H. Simon. The difference is explained by the level of development of the national economy and the lack of economic transparency in Ukraine.

Furthermore, there are a lot of unknowns about Ukraine's hidden champions yet. That is why assessing and comparing is difficult.

So far, Ukraine's economy has been growing. As a result, we may witness new Ukrainian hidden champions in a few years.

The research results allow the following recommendations:

1. Invest seriously in manufacturing energy efficiency.
2. Develop international competencies. If there is a chance of manufacturing goods with high value-added, companies should look beyond the local markets.
3. Maintain a high client orientation and invest most efforts in meeting customers' needs.
4. Promote HR development, and nurture a corporate culture because internal factors shape companies' successes.

References

Aisberg.com (2019) Aisberg.com. [online]. https://www.aisberg.com/. Accessed 29 September 2019

World Competitiveness Ranking (2019). https://www.imd.org/wcc/world-competitiveness-center-rankings/world-competitiveness-ranking-2019/ Accessed 29 September 2019

The World Bank (2019) GDP (current US$). https://data.worldbank.org/indicator/NY.GDP.MKTP.CD?most_recent_value_desc=true&year_high_desc=true. Accessed 29 September 2019

The World Factbook (2019). https://www.cia.gov/index.html. Accessed 29 September 2019

Weidmann-mpm.com (2019) Weidmann-mpm.com. [online] Available at: http://www.weidmann-mpm.com/about-us-uk.html. Accessed 29 September 2019

UCAB (2019) Ucab Export. http://ucab.ua/ua/doing_agribusiness/zovnishni_rinki/osnovni_pokazniki_zovnishnoi_torgivli_ukraini. Accessed 2019

Minagro.gov.ua (2019) Minavgo Export. https://minagro.gov.ua/ua/news/z-pochatku-201920-mr-z-ukrayini-eksportovano-ponad-13-mln-tonn-zerna. Accessed 27 September 2019

Printed in Poland
by Amazon Fulfillment
Poland Sp. z o.o., Wrocław